JOY DAVID'S CHOICE

selected

Self Catering

in

England and Wales

Potted History County by County
Exciting attractions and Places to Visit
Great Venues, Great Food, Great Value

THE PERFECT COMPANION
FOR LOCALS & VISITORS
WHICH YOU CANNOT AFFORD
TO BE WITHOUT

DON'T DELAY

SEND FOR YOUR

JOY DAVID

ADVANTAGE CARD

TODAY

MEMBERSHIP IS ABSOLUTELY

FREE

TO PURCHASERS OF THIS BOOK

THE ADVANTAGE CARD..

..enables members to take advantage of the many special offers; Discounted Accommodation, Entrance Fees, Food and Wines - a more enjoyable time for less outlay.

Save yourselves £££ whenever you visit participating venues featured in this book as well as receiving a chatty newsletter and an up date on special offers three times a year.

Acknowledgments

Joy David would like to thank Lesley Cowie for her assistance in compiling this book and for writing many of the 'Dedicated' Pages, Marie Needham for writing several of the chapters. Their help and enthusiasm has been invaluable. Ian Pethers and Michelle Dunne for their beautiful line drawings and Hilary Kent, Fiona Grafton-Smith, Jayne Jackson for their unstinting assistance and to Karen Vosper whose work in collating the artwork has been beyond the call of duty.

ISBN 1 899311-40-8

British Library Catalogue-In-Publication Data
Catalogue Data is available from the British Library

Typesetting, film and scanning by: Typestyle, Ivybridge, Devon
Printed and bound in Great Britain by : Ebenezer Baylis

Introduction

Joy David's Choice - Self-Catering

Until I started to compile this book I had no notion of the extent of the Self-Catering operation in England and Wales. It is massive and covers an amazing number of totally diverse places but the point that came over to me most strongly was the high standard right across the board. From converted Farm buildings to Castles, Barns to Bungalows, the ones we looked at, or had recommended to us, without exception, were well appointed and we would have been very happy to have stayed in any of them.

This voyage of discovery also introduced us to some new and superb countryside. We also found that all sorts of additional services were offered by landlords. We even found in some places that gourmet meals could be ordered from the main house and delivered to the door! Some owners offered bed linen, towels, the others did not, some allowed pets and some not. Disabled access and viability we also checked and found that almost always for the disabled there would be a welcome on the mat but frequently because of the houses, apartments etc being conversions from old buildings, they were unsuitable. In the Useful Information section of each establishment we have tried to make it clear whether the places are suitable or not.

In this first book, part of the **Joy David's Choice'** series, which we hope to repeat annually after 1998, we have only touched lightly on all that is available. We hope you will find the book useful and in order to improve it I hope you will write to me suggesting new venues and commenting on those you have stayed in as a result of this book.

CONTENTS INCLUDES

Chapter One

CHAPTER 1

THE WEST COUNTRY
Including DEVON, CORNWALL, THE ISLES OF SCILLY, SOMERSET & AVON

INCLUDES

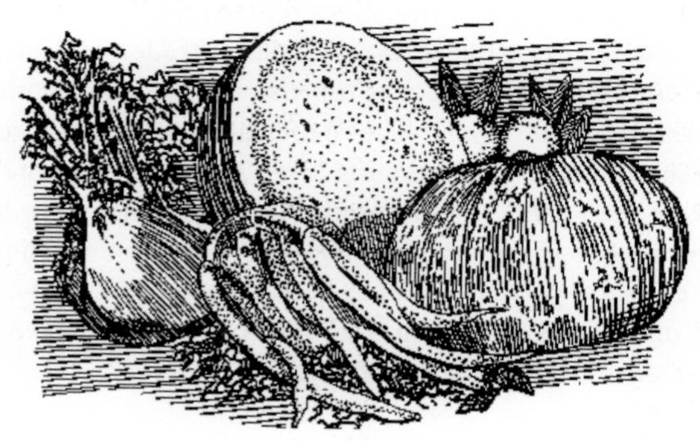

CHAPTER ONE

THE WEST COUNTRY
Devon, Cornwall, the Isles of Scilly, Somerset and Avon

Those of us lucky enough to live in this fabulous part of the world in which everyone of God's ingredients seems to have been made into a perfect cake, sometimes forget to look around us and see the stunning beauty of the coastline, the awesome and sometimes bleak grandeur of the moors -**Dartmoor, Exmoor and Bodmin Moor** -which all come within this Baileywick. The visitor does not make this mistake and as a result sometimes suffers from mental indigestion and the indecision that comes when the choice is great. I hope in this chapter to whet your appetite and encourage you to discover the West Country and all it has to offer.

Because you will inevitably reach **Bristol** first lets take a look at this fascinating city which owes much of its prosperity to navigation, the Avon estuary just before it reaches the sheltered Bristol Channel acting as a harbour, and a wide river to take cargoes inland. Trade was active from the early days of sail when ships left port for many parts of the world, bringing back exotic and unusual goods. The medieval woollen trade to Portugal, Spain and Ireland was at the beginning of a long period of importance for fine woollens in the region. More recent industries which have been at the centre of Bristol's success are papermaking, printing, flour milling, tobacco, engineering, chemical processing, and aircraft production. The city's wealth reached out into the surrounding area and can be seen in the status of buildings in many of the towns and villages..

One of the most impressive sights in Bristol is the **Clifton Suspension Bridge** built by Isambard Kingdom Brunel and completed in 1864, which crosses the Avon Gorge at a staggering 245 feet above the high water level. Brunel's work is much in evidence in this area, often associated with the Great Western Railway which was a feat of elegant engineering. His ship 'Great Britain', the world's first ocean-going, propellor-driven iron ship was built at Bristol in 1843 and following restoration after being marooned in the Falklands, is now on display here at the **Great Western Dock**.

Bristol has its own Cathedral and some of the oldest churches in the country. It also has a fabulous shopping centre which, in addition to the nationally known shops and department stores, are a wealth of small shops of all kinds selling antiques, designer clothes, books and many others.If you have some serious shopping to do the **Broadmead** shopping centre is the place to visit. There was an element of resistence to this project initially. Many believed that some of the buildings planned for demolition should be spared, however there comes a time when new and innovative schemes have to be introduced to prevent a place stagnating. Broadmead is a success, it contains virtually every major department store and literally hundreds of smaller shops many of which are housed undercover in the **Galleries**. It is mainly pedestrianised which makes shopping so much safer and easier especially for families with young children and the less able-bodied. Bristol is blessed with two good theatres, a thriving university and dozens of important art galleries and the exhibitions range from Old Masters to contemporary artists, ceramics, jewellery, sculpture, the list is infinite. So too is the variety of music which can be enjoyed throughout the city. **Colston Hall** offers performances which cannot fail to appeal to the most catholic of tastes. Where else could one expect to find The Bristol Bach Choir and Cambridge Baroque Camerata one week and ShirleyBassey the next?

You will find Bristol full of interesting old pubs, good eateries which in the case of the latter, cover virtually every ethnic variety one can think of. The hotels range from five star to the more modest Guest House but always with a good standard. Bristol makes a wonderful base from which to explore the countryside around Bristol which has been carefully preserved and nurtured and it is still possible to find places where wild flowers grow undisturbed and the best of these is the **Avon Gorge Nature Reserve**. This haven stretches along the West side of the Avon and it is one of the most important lowland limestone reserves in the country. Archeologists among you can see the Iron Age hill fort of Stockleigh camp which lies within the boundary.

There are many other attractions for nature lovers. It is possible to arrange a guided tour around the lovely **Long Ashton Cider Orchards** near **Abbots Leigh** and be reminded of the golden days of apple orchards and farmhouse cider in stone jars. The English Nature Warden will accompany you on seasonal walks through Leigh Woods and you are recommended to wear stout shoes and bring binoculars for an ornithological tour of Blaise.

Bath, a frisson of excitement courses through me whenever I think about this wonderful city. I treat it like an old friend but always with a decorum and an awareness that Beau Nash together with the Master of Ceremonies at the assembly and pump room insisted on the highest degree of civility and manners. Nonetheless it is always with a certain amount of impatience and eager anticipation that I seek out this incomparable city. I prefer to behave in the manner of an ostrich and bury my head in the sand when it comes to the outskirts or the 'new'Bath which arose because of indifferent planning. Thankfully, Georgian Bath still remains. It is not the individual buildings that make this city so wonderful but the whole architectural assembly. Take a walk down through Laura Place looking at the houses in which society used to dwell in its heyday when Bath was a fashionable watering hole, cross Argyle Street and so to Pulteney Bridge which spans the Avon. You could be forgiven for thinking you were in Florence as you cross this enchanting bridge which has small shops on either side of it not unlike the Ponte Vecchio. The Abbey must come high on your list of places to see. It is probably the most beautiful place in the city. There is more glass than stone in the walls which fill it with light. It is sometimes called the Lantern of the West. It is the West front that is its greatest glory. It looks down on the square where all the visitors gather outside the Roman Baths. The West door itself is heavily carved with heraldic shields set in a triple arch, and on each side are wonderful stone canopies covering ancient figures of St Peter and St Paul.

In Broad Street there is **The Bath Postal Museum**. The first known posting of a Penny Black, the world's first stamp took place from this historic building on the 2nd May 1840. The ground floor displays introduce the story of the letter writing and the carriage of mail throughout the ages. There are working machines and a life-size Victorian post office as well as children's activities room. The Museum opens every day from 11-5pm throughout the year and on Sundays from April to October 2-5pm. **The Victoria Art Gallery** in Bridge Street is a major venue for touring exhibitions of national importance. It also has a fine permanent display of European Masters, 18-20th century British paintings and drawings together with decorative art.

The Bath Boating Station in Forester Road, is a unique surviving Victorian boating station with tea gardens and licensed restaurant, a living museum with traditional wooden skiffs, punts and canoes for hire by hour or by day. A pleasant way for a family to spend a summers day on the river Avon. Abundant wildlife, kingfishers, heron, wild geese, moorhens, cormorants etc excites and delights birdwatchers. Punting is a speciality and you need have no fear if this demandingscience is foreign to you; there is tuition! You can find bed and breakfast here and somewhere to park your car - no easy matter in Bath.

If you have ever thought of viewing Bath from the air, may I suggest **Heritage Balloons**. The magic is inescapable and I promise that a trip in a hot-air balloon offers the adventure of a lifetime. From the air, the city of Bath and the surrounding countryside takes on an entirely new dimension. Only from the air can you truly appreciate the beauty of the designs of John Wood, the architect and his son, whose vision came to life in the shape of the **Royal Crescent** and **The Circus**. Flights take place early in the morning and early evening and the whole exercise lasts about three hours. In the oldest tradition of ballooning, each flight is celebrated with a glass or two of chilled champagne. The take off site is Victoria Park and to book your flight which must be between March and October please ring 01225 318747.

The list is endless of exciting things to see and do. There is **The Roman Bath Museum** in the Pump Room, Abbey Churchyard. **Beckford's Tower and Museum** stands on the summit of Lansdown, with extensive views from its Belevedere, reached by 156 easy steps. **The Museum of Costume and Assembly Rooms** in Bennett Street tells the story of fashion over the last 400 years and is brought alive with one of the finest collections of its kind in the world. The displays include 200 dressed figures and up to a thousand other items of costume, accessories and jewellery to illustrate the changing styles in fashionable men's women's and children's clothes from the late 16th century to the present day. **Royal Crescent** which is popularly regarded as the climax of the **Palladian** achievement in this most classical of English cities is epitomised in **No 1 Royal Crescent** which provides one with an opportunity to see how a house in this wonderful crescent might have appeared when it was first built. **The American Museum** at **Claverton** has 18 period furnished rooms from the 17-19th centuries. The building of **Bath Museum** in the Countess of Huntingdon Chapel, The Vineyards, The Paragon is somewhere in which you will discover how one of the architectural masterpieces of Europe was created. At the same address is **The Museum of English Naive Art (1750-1900)**. This is the first museum of English folk painting, by travelling artists of the 18th and 19th century.

Without doubt one of the best ways of seeing Bath is on the splendid **Kennet and Avon Canal**. Run by the Bath and Dundas Canal Company you can join a boat at Brass Knocker Bottom, opposite the Viaduct Inn in Warminster Road, Monkton Combe. From this historic base near the famous Dundas Aqueduct in the beautiful Limpley Stoke Valley, five miles from Bath, attractive self-drive electric boats are available for the hour, day or evening hire. Picnicking becomes a delight or you can visit the canalside pubs and tea gardens along the delightful stretch between Bath and Bradford-on-Avon. You will find a number of these pubs also have bed and breakfast accommodation. The normal availability is from Easter until the end of September from 9am-5.30pm.

Advance booking is advisable. At Sydney Wharf you can join the **John Rennie**, named after the architect and engineer who designed the 87 mile long canal which joins the River Avon at Bath with the River Thames at Reading. This really is a magical cruise with the opportunity of dining on board. If you become addicted to travelling on the canal as many do you will see that there are stretches where it is obvious that work still needs to be done and more time and money spent, especially on the width and dredging but one has to remember that in the 1950s and 60s parts of the 'cut' were merely wet ditches and but for the totally voluntary work of the Kennet and Avon Canal Trust, would still remain un-navigable.

If you have time or the inclination to leave Bath for the surrounding countryside do go a little way up the A4 to **Bathford**, a pretty village, where The Old School House will look after you excellently.

There are various places that I enjoy visiting within easy reach of Bristol. **Badminton** is one of them. It is here on the Duke of Beaufort's estate that one of the great equestrian occasions of the years, the horse trials are held. People come from all around the world to spectate and to take part. It is also one of the rare times in the year when the great house is open to the public and the opportunity to see it should not be missed. It has always been a jealously guarded house by the Dukes of Beaufort and is hardly visible from the village. The trials are always held in April and frequently attended by members of the Royal Family. Indeed the Princess Royal was a winner here one year.

Chipping Sodbury was a 12th century property speculation! It lies on the edge of Old Sodbury parish and was primarily a market centre. The property developers laid out the plots in a regular pattern on each side of the road and so it has remained. It has some wonderful street names - Hatters Lane, Horse Street, Rouncival Street, Hounds Lane and Shoutinge Lane. It really is an attractive place in which to wander and while the population has grown, little has been built to its detriment.

The M4 with its unceasing traffic crosses the county a little to the south of Chipping Sodbury and just below that is **Marshfield**, surrounded by cornfields and at one time a place that supplied malt to Bristol and Bath. Those days have long gone but not so the attractive malthouses. The town thrived on the wool trade and many of the fine 17th and 18th century houses reflect the wealth of the citizens in that era. Its ancient traditions are carried on by the Marshfield Mummers, whose play is performed on Boxing Day each year. The play never varies in its presentation of the traditional conflict between Good and Evil.

Radstock will not please everybody but it is of great interest to the industrial archaeologist and to railway historians. Both of these industries were for many years the main providers of work and money in the town. The last coal mine closed in 1973 but well before that, great thought had been given to grassing and planting the batches - spoil tips for those who have not heard this word used in this context before - I always associate it with cooking and baking! Here **The Radstock,Midsomer Norton & District Museum** at Barton Meade House, Haydon, is an 18th century converted barn and outbuildings standing in beautiful countryside in the former North Somerset Coalfield. You can see how a Victorian miner lived and worked with a re-constructed coalface and cottage. You can see where the colliery children went to school and where the family shopped at the co-op. There are displays covering 200 years of farming and railways, complete with a model layout. Everywhere there are reminders of the past including an early Methodist meeting room, blacksmith shop, and Saxon artefacts. Temporary exhibitions relating to local themes are held throughout the year. The tea room produces an excellent cup of tea but on a fine day you may prefer the picnic area. There is a souvenir shop and free car parking. It is only open at weekends on Saturdays from 10-4pm and Sundays and Bank Holidays from 2-5pm.

Going westwards you come to the **Chew Valley Lake**, a place of infinite beauty. It is a great place for anglers and for those who just want to stroll along its banks. Chew Valley has two villages worthy of note. **Chew Magna** and **Chew Stoke**. At Chew Magna you enter it by traversing one medieval bridge and leaving it by another.

Back on the main A368 you will come to **Blagdon** which also has a beautiful lake attracting tourists from afar for its trout fishing. It is also lucky enough to have a cosy and typically English village inn, **The Seymour Arms**.

You will either love or hate **Weston-Super-Mare**. There seem to be very few people who feel indifferently about it. There is no doubt that it has much to offer the visitor in every conceivable way. The question is where to start. I read one of the promotional brochures put out by the local Tourist Board and it describes the town as 'Miles of Smiles'. It is true that as a good family resort it has something to put a smile on every face whether young or not so young, with its attractive setting and choice of things to do and places to visit. The two miles of clean, golden sandy beach and the Grand Pier, with its large amusement centre and Blizzard white knuckle ride, certainly delight people. For those who enjoy leisure complexes you will not find a better one than **Tropicana Pleasure Beach** with its heated swimming pool, wave machine, water chutes and children's adventure equipment, based on a tropical fruit theme.

The Marine Lake should not be forgotten, here there is always shallow water for children to bathe and splash around in complete safety. I am not sure who is responsible for the flower displays in Weston but whoever it is does the town proud. The spacious beach lawns add a touch of charm to the seafront and the attractive parks and gardens around the resort have superb colourful displays. Just sitting and looking at them is joyous and therapeutic. You can ride in style along the Marine Parade daily during the season in a horse drawn Landau. It makes you feel very important and is quite delightful. If you have small children with you it will take them some time to be lured away from the land train which services the whole length of the promenade from April to September, weather permitting.

For those who want to walk with a purpose I would suggest collecting a series of leaflets published by the Civic Society which will help you follow trails around the town at your own pace. You will find them on sale at both the Tourist Information Centre and the Heritage Centre.

Three interesting museums should not be missed. **The International Helicopter Museum** at Weston Airport holds the world's largest collection of helicopters and autogyros, unique to Britain. You can see restoration work in progress and nobody seems to mind your asking questions in this friendly place. It is open from March-October daily from 10am-6pm and from November to March 10am-4pm. It is closed on Christmas Day, Boxing Day and New Years Day. **Woodspring Museum** is right in the town centre and is a re-creation of everyday life at the turn of the century. Having recently been to the dentist and suffered hardly at all, thank heavens, for I am a miserable coward, I was more than appreciative of the techniques used today when I saw a replica of an Edwardian dentist's surgery complete with the most horrendous implements. There are many displays and if you ever wondered what our Victorian ancestors did when they went to the seaside you can soon find out by examining one area of the museum which is devoted to this very subject. The Museum is open all the year round.

Clara's Cottage is another museum in its own way. This time it is a restored Weston seaside landlady's lodging of the 1890's which also includes the Peggy Nesbitt doll collection. It is open daily except Sundays from 10am-5pm and admission is free.

There are a host of delightful villages to be discovered and with the advent of the motorways which in many ways has been a blessing you can travel more easily from one place to another and they do not prevent you from slipping off at various junctions to explore. **Winterbourne** is one such place, although really it has become part of Bristol today. Its oldest part has managed to stay untouched. In the quiet area around the church are a few cottages, and the adjoining Winterbourne Court Farm. I like to think of Winterbourne when hat-making was a cottage industry and between 1770 and 1870 the whole place flourished with the trade brought to them because fashion dictated the wearing of beaver hats. The church too has a romantic story surrounding a knight whose effigy lies by the north wall. The knight is thought to be Hugo de Struden who eloped with a fair lady but was a bit of a rogue. He made a pact with the devil in return for certain favours. He agreed that when he died he would not be carried into the church, buried in the churchyard, feet or head forward. He managed to cheat even on that and gave instructions that his coffin be carried in sideways and be buried in the wall. On one wall is a brass which I found fascinating. It is about 1370 and one of the Bardestone ladies whose family were lords of the manor. Her dress has pocket holes which show part of the girdle beneath. It is thought to be the oldest brass in the county.

And now for Somerset. The geology of Somerset is very noticeable: the low-lying and flat **Somerset Levels** in the centre of the county dotted with small round hills, through the middle of it running the Polden Hills, to the north the flat-topped Mendip Hills, to the south west the Blackdown Hills and to the west the Quantocks beyond which is Exmoor.

The miles of wet willow-lined Levels are some of the last surviving water meadows in Britain to be left undisturbed by modern farming. Once under the sea, the silt has provided rich soil and peat. Although much has been cut and used in garden composts, where it remains it provides a rare sight of endangered species of flora. Peat is a great preservative and many important finds of Neolithic, Bronze and Iron Age man have been made in the area. Many of the roads that cross this water-logged landscape are on timber Bronze Age causeway and medieval embankments, the suddenly rising hills in the flat landscape once islands in the water. **The Willows and Wetland Visitors Centre** which is at **Stoke Gregory** in the Sedgemoor area tells the story of the district and of traditional Somerset basket making from withies.

On the Levels, the fenland isle of **Athelney** is where King Alfred took refuge from the Vikings in the 9th century. Living as an outlaw he was hiding out in the hut of a herdsman's family when the cakes on the open hearth were burned. The wife, not knowing who he was blamed the King for not keeping an eye on the cooking! Thus came into being the story of Alfred burning the cakes.

Another story relating to food is that of 'Little Jack Horner'. The Abbot of Glastonbury, wishing to placate Henry VIII, sent him a pie containing the deeds of the manor house at **Mells**. The emissary was one Thomas Horner who opened the pie, put in his thumb and pulled out a plum.

Driving south west down the M5 from the Mendips towards Devon, every junction will lead you to attractive and interesting places.**Brent Knoll** can clearly be seen rising from the Levels. Likewise out of the levels, **Cadbury Hill**, with its Iron Age hill fort considered by some to be Arthur's Camelot. Not far from Brent Knoll is the pleasant town of **Burnham-on-Sea**, these days lived in by many commuters to Bristol. It has a laid back feel about it, no one seems to be in a hurry. You can walk for miles along the beach, enjoy the shops and find one or two very good hostelries. Its only drawback is its nearness to the less than pleasant site of **Hinckley Point**.

Bridgwater, now an industrial centre, was a busy port until Bristol overshadowed it. The town grew up around what was the best crossing point of a river which could not be forded. At the Norman Conquest it was held by a Saxon, Merleswain who lost it to Walter de la Douai. At that time it was known as Brugie but became the Bridge of Walter, hence its name today. By the 26thJune 1200, King John granted a Royal Charter giving borough status and permission to build a castle to protect the flourishing river port. The River Parrett has been used for commercial shipping since pre-Roman times and a relic of Phoenician ring money was discovered near the site of the old town bridge. In the 13th century the port was used as a victualling base for forays into Wales and Ireland, and by the 15th century had become a major port ranking 12th in the whole country. Woollen cloth was the principal export, the wool trade forming the basis of West Country wealth, and the main import was French wine.

It became the main point of entry and outlet for much of central and western Somerset, Taunton, Langport, Ilchester and even Yeovil sent, and received, goods through the estuary of the River Parrett and by the canal to Taunton and beyond.

The high ground of **Exmoor** to the west (part Somerset and part Devon) has a great variety of birds, rare plants and flowers, shaggy ponies and large herds of deer. This was at one time a royal hunting forest and still today the deer are hunted, but given refuge on land owned by Paul and Linda McCartney for that purpose as well as the sanctuary land owned by the League Against Cruel Sports. The moorland plateau rises to around 1,700 feet at Dunkery Beacon and terminates with the tallest cliffs in England, overlooking the Bristol Channel, designated as 'Heritage Coast'.

The subterranean rivers of the **Mendips**, have resulted in wonderful caves, potholes and gorges. At first sight the spectacular **Cheddar Gorge** and **Wookey Hole** with the many caves full of magnificent stalactites and stalagmites, must have been a wonderful experience for visitors. Now sadly it is marred by the sheer volume of people who come here - some 1.5million a year - which has resulted in overcrowding and too many tacky tourist trappings. However, the surrounding scenery of the Gorge is wondrous. It can be seen at its best from the vantage point on the **West Mendip Way**, a walk that starts at Wells Cathedral and concludes after 30 breathtaking miles at the Bristol Channel.

If you are a keen walker you will enjoy the 28 miles of the **Leland Trail** following in the footsteps of the 16th century John Leland, starting on the National Trust's Stourhead estate and crossing the quiet, southern Somerset countryside to another National Trust Property , Montacute House, and on to the high viewpoint of Ham Hill. The Gardens at **Stourhead** (just into Wiltshire) are best visited in the early summer, but at any time of the year the lake surrounded by classical temples and monuments are serenely beautiful. One of the loveliest evenings I have ever spent was at Stourhead on a summer's evening, listening to a concert whilst sitting by the lake enjoying a champagne picnic.These concerts are held quite regularly and are almost always with a theme. For example this year it was Chinese and one was expected to dress suitably for the occasion. **Montacute House**, not far from **Yeovil** is another of my favourite places. It is a fine example of Tudor domestic architecture which, although huge, is on a comfortable scale, set within early Jacobean gardens.

Montacute lies on the route of the Roman Fosse Way, one of the four Royal Roads, running from the south west to Lincolnshire. From this point you can follow the Fosse Way to another of the many fine houses in the region at **Cricket St Thomas Wildlife Park** now more associated with Noel Edmunds and Mr Blobby than the television programme with Penelope Keith, Peter Bowles and Angela Thorne, To the Manor Born. It is home to many rare and exotic species of animal and bird and recently also to a Heavy Horse Centre as well as being a place of enormous fun for children with an adventure park etc. At **Rode** is a 17 acre **Tropical Bird Garden.**

Who could resist turning off for Glastonbury and Wells with their wealth of history and beauty.**Glastonbury** is thought of as the cradle of English Christianity, but for me it is a place of legend, history, mystery and an overworked imagination. It may well have been the earliest Christian shrine but it is certainly the site of the richest monastery, and to this day still a place of pilgrimage. The Glastonbury legends are told again and again, and over the centuries have no doubt been embellished, but I never fail to feel excited by the thought of a visit here.

Towering over the town is **Glastonbury Tor**,possibly Arthur's Isle of Avalon, some 521 feet above sea level, and a landmark visible for miles around. St Michael's Tower on the summit is the remains of a 15th century church, the effort of climbing to which is rewarded by stunning views. First the home of primitive man, then a place of Christian pilgrimage, the Tor is still visited by thousands every year. I would advise you to walk up the Tor if it is possible because of the restricted availability of car parking nearby.

One of the legends told is of Christ coming here as a child with his merchant uncle, Joseph of Arimathea. Another is of Joseph coming here with the Holy Grail and yet another of the Apostle Philip sending missionaries from Gaul to establish a church, and one of those missionaries finding a church already here, dedicated by Christ himself. The undoubted Irish influence here is traced back to St Patrick who came first as an Abbot and to whom the lower church in Glastonbury is dedicated. Then there is the story of St Bridget from Kildare, Ireland, who left her bell and wallet behind at **Beckery** just one mile south west.

Glastonbury is so full of history. It was St Dunstan who laid the foundation of its spiritual and economic power. By the time of Domesday, Glastonbury owned an eighth of the county of Somerset covering much of the Somerset Levels, large parts of which were almost immediately drained to bring gain to the Abbot. It was Henry of Blois, Bishop of Winchester who built himself lodgings on such a grand scale that they would have made Buckingham Palace look small, who invited William of Malmesbury to write the history which has helped us develop the legends of Glastonbury over the centuries.

In 1189 when Royal support dried up and monks were thrown back on their own resources, they felt the Lord was smiling upon them when, as legend says, they were digging a grave for a monk, they found between the shafts of two ancient crosses, 16ft down in a wooden sarcophagus, the bones of a large man and a woman who must have been very beautiful; she certainly had long tresses - the story said these locks were totally preserved until one monk with straying hands touched them and they fell to dust. The monks were in no doubt that here were the remains of King Arthur and Queen Guinevere. Strangely however, William of Malmesbury had never mentioned Arthur in his 'History of Glastonbury' but the monks were adamant, and for them their acute need for money was immediately alleviated by this lovely, romantic idea. They never looked back!

Places to visit should include **The Somerset Rural Life Museum** with its relics from Somerset's past.**The Chalice Well** at the foot of the Tor. Set in attractive gardens, the waters of the well are claimed to have curative powers, and legend has it that Joseph of Arimathea hid the Chalice of the Holy Grail here. **The Lake Village Museum**, in the High Street, which displays many of the artefacts from an Iron Age settlement near Glastonbury. At **Westhay** is the **Peat Moors Visitor Centre**, where you can learn about the extraordinary history and natural history of the Somerset Levels. At the nearby village of **Meare** you can see the **Abbot's Fish House** dating back to the 14th century. This is where fish caught in the former Meare pool was dried, salted and stored by the monks of Glastonbury Abbey.

To the east of Glastonbury lies the village of **Boltonsborough**, the birthplace of St Dunstan. It was said that it was he who diverted the River Brue, sending it along the course of the little southward stream so that the village might have more power for its mill. Slightly to the north east of Glastonbury is **Shepton Mallet**, known almost entirely now for its permanenet showground which is the home of the Bath and West show and many others. The town is a wonderful mixture of old and new; a combination of ancient market town and modern industrial community nestling in a fold towards the western edge of the Mendip escarpment. Historically Shepton Mallet has always been strategically well placed; the Roman Fosse Way passes close by; the town's position on the River Sheppey led to its growth during the Midlle Ages as a centre for the wool trade, and enabling the brewing industry to be established. The town is not proud of one episode in its history. It happened in 1685 when the Market Cross was the scene for serveral executions of the unfortunate men of the Duke of Monmouth's 'Pitchfork Army' who were sentenced to death by that dreadful man, Judge Jeffreys.

Godney to the north west of Glastonbury is somewhere the monks used to call the Island of God; one of their seals has been found among the ruins of Glastonbury Abbey. It is older than any monk, older than christianity and in a field is Lake Village dating back to 250BC.

Wells is outstandingly beautiful and very special. A place that delights the eye and makes the heart beat faster. It is the smallest city in England with a population of just 9,400 but it is its Cathedral which gives it city standing. It is in fact Somerset's only city. It lies sheltered beneath the southern slopes of the Mendip Hills, and combines a wealth of historic interest and beautiful architecture with its role as a thriving market centre.

The swans at the **Bishop's Palace** have learnt to ring a bell when they are ready for lunch. The Palace is within the inner walls of the city which also enclose the Chapter House and Deanery as well as the **Cathedral.** What an enchanting place the city is with its narrow streets and lovely buildings. A place in which to spend many happy hours.

Amongst the many places to see around here are the two little villages of **Dulcote** on the Shepton Mallet road and **Coxley** on the A39

To me the little town of **Bruton** is one of the loveliest in Somerset.It has two parts, divided by the River Brue which meanders gently over stones and under a packhorse bridge. The part to the south which runs beneath and beyond the church is the oldest in Bruton, a Saxon religious centre which once had two churches, one founded by St Aldhelm. There was a mint here in the 10th century which opened up the way for the growth of a small town by the 11th century growing beyond the river around a market place near the present Patwell and Quaperlake streets. What attracts me most about this pretty place is the way in which the red roofed houses cling to each other in the winding and narrow streets. Standing on the little pack horse bridge sights of the past evoke all sorts of memories and the bonus is the entrancing peep across the valleys. The architecture of the town shows a rare continuity, through six centuries, of styles and techniques used where stone meets timber in Wessex. The regular form of the High Street is medieval town planning at its best. It includes the former Abbey Court House of the mid-15th century and Sexey's Hospital. Believe it or not this was established by a local stable lad who made his name and fortune and returned to Bruton to found this fine school. The school stands in a suburb called Lusty! Education is now the biggest business in Bruton.

When I have stayed in Bruton I have used it as a base for taking a look at some of the delightful places within easy reach. **Castle Cary** for example which is a charming, bustling place. Everything seems to be on a small scale. It has friendly shops, welcoming people, although you would be hard put to find much in the way of outstanding architecture It once had a castle with a motte and bailey structure but that has virtually gone, and its market hall was rebuilt in 1855 although there are some 17th century pillars. The church was largely rebuilt in 1855 also. There are some nice houses including the 18th century post office in Bailey Hill overlooking an intriguing lock-up of 1779. I am told it is frequently used as a threat of punishment to recalcitrant children!

Whenever I think about **Wincanton** to the east of Castle Cary, I think about horse racing. I have spent many happy hours on the course at various meetings. It is not a fashionable racecourse and is far less formal than its grander cousins but it is great fun. The town is frequently referred to as the 'Queen of the Vale' referring of course, to the Blackmore Vale. It is an interesting old town abounding in hotels and inns to suit all tastes, many of them survivors of the coaching era, when about seventeen coaches day stopped here on their journey from London to the cities of the west.

Going westwards there are two small towns that I have become attached to over the years.**Langport**, a town of narrow streets and full of antique shops, lies on the River Parrett. The old warehouses standing by the riverside bear witness to the time when the town was busy with waterborne trade coming from Wales via Bridgwater. It was once a walled town but all that remains of the wall is **The Hanging Chapel** -built over what was the East Gate. I used to think it had something to do with Judge Jeffreys but for once he is not responsible. Langport did play a decisive part in the Civil War though, in 1645 an important battle was fought on its outskirts, the site of which can still be seen if you follow the B3155 to Somerton. You will find a side road leading to **Wagg** and **Huish Episcopi** with the small waterway of the Wagg Rhyne alongside. The Royalists were well positioned on the Langport side where there was a very narrow ford across the rhyne. Only four horsemen could cross it abreast, but Fairfax ordered his cavalry to charge and after a fierce battle the day was won. The Royalists were defeated, their morale broken and the end of the Civil War was in sight. **Somerton** is the other small town which claims to be the capital of ancient Wessex, and justifiably boasts much to entrance one for hours. The Church of St Michael has a roof that was created by the monks of Mulcheney from 7,000 fetter pieces. These monks obviously had a sense of humour: incorported in the roof is a beer barrel playing on the name of Abbot Bere! If you wander down the leafy lane beside the church you will come into a delightful square of Georgian buildings, which has the misnomer of 'Cow Square' leading you into Broad Stret which was once called Pig Lane. There has to be a reason for these names, but I have found none.

One of England's smallest churches lies hidden in a wooded combe overlooking the Bristol Channel at **Culbone**, away from roads and cars. Nearby in a farmhouse Coleridge wrote 'Kubla Khan'.

Coleridge lived at **Nether Stowey** on the Quantocks at the end of the 18th century and his home is now open to the public. Here he wrote 'The Ancient Mariner'. The 'Rock of Ages'immortalised by Augustus Toplady in his hymn, was written at **Burrington Combe** on the Mendips. The village of Nether Stowey has a lovely old manor house begun in the time of Henry VII and left unfinished until Elizabeth's time, because somebody had carelessly executed the builder on Tower Hill for joining the Cornish men who marched to London protesting against taxation. **Coleridge Cottage** is open to the public from April to September, Tuesday to Thursday and Sunday from 2-5pm. It was here he was visited regularly by his friends William and Dorothy Wordsworth.

Close to Nether Stowey is the village of **Holford** where, according to Dorothy Wordsworth 'there is everything here, sea and woods wild as fancy are painted'. That is not the only pretty village within easy reach. **Combe Florey**, must come high on the list. It is stunningly beautiful and once was the home of the Reverend Sydney Smith and later the home of Evelyn Waugh.

Field Marshall Viscount Montgomery grew up in the village of **Halse**. I wonder if his child's eyes ever appreciated the beauty of the abundance of thatched cottages. Probably not, they would have been commonplace in his childhood. **Milverton** is a village that dates back to the Domesday study and boasts some glorious Georgian houses and a superb church. It was also the home of Thomas Young, whose work enabled the translation of Egyptian Hieroglyphics.

From here you are close to **Wiveliscombe**, not one of my favourite places but the church of St Andrew is outstandingly beautiful and has some fascinating catacombs. It was here that a safe haven was provided for many of the nation's treasures during World War II; a plaque inside the church records this.

Near to **Dulverton** on Exmoor the river Barle is crossed at**Tarr Steps** with huge, closely fitting stone slabs each weighing up to five tons. The age of the bridge is unknown but it was certainly used by packhorses during the height of the successful cloth trade. Wherever my travels take me I am always dumbfounded by the skill and ingenuity shown by the builders of our cathedrals and places like Tarr Steps, all without the assistance of any kind of machinery. Nearly always there is a story to tell and here we have the case of Tarr Steps supposedly being built by the Devil. He brought stones in his apron and dropped them in a sequence so he could cross the river. All this was done in just one night! It was for his exclusive use and he announced that he would destroy the first creature crossing it. A unfortunate cat attempted it and was torn to pieces. The animal's untimely death seems to have broken the spell, for a Parson then crossed in safety, exchanging niceties with the Devil en route! The Devil called the Parson a black crow to which the Parson replied that he was not blacker than the Devil. The woods and hills of Exmoor close around Dulverton on three sides, the Barle flows past its front doorsteps. It is a place steeped in history and one of tranquillity. In the church are two memorials to the Sydenhams who lived from 1540 to 1874 at Combe, a beautiful Tudor House. The life of the moor has made great literature and Dulverton is a name often found in books. Here Jan Ridd met Lorna Doone. Richard Jefferies watched the red deer. If you come to Dulverton in the spring take a walk in Burridge Woods which becomes totally carpeted with bluebells.

Winsford is arguably the prettiest village on Exmoor and it certainly has one of the most charming inns, **The Royal Oak Inn**, with an immaculately thatched roof, soft cream washed walls and a profusion of colourful hanging baskets on the outside. The pub dates from the 12th century and its open fireplaces and oak beams have been subtly combined with the modern facilities we all expect today. Winsford itself was described by W.H. Hudson in 1909 as 'fragrant, cool, grey green - immemorial peace - second to no English village in beauty, running waters, stone thatched cottages, hoary church tower.' Little has changed over the centuries. I believe there is still one lady in the village who has seen aeroplanes and cars but never a ship or a train because she has never left the village.

Simonsbath a few miles west of Winsford is an ideal stepping stone on your way to discover the wild, stark beauty of Exmoor. The quiet village is a wonderful foil for the exquisite scenery which surrounds it on every side.

I would never miss an opportunity to stay in **Dunster** which is charming with its impressive 17th century octagonal market hall by a wide main street, originally used for the sale of locally woven cloth. Here the **Gallox Bridge** which again used to carry pack-horses, has two ribbed arches, spanning the old mill stream in a picture-book setting. The medieval **Butter Cross** once stood in the high street but is now some way from the centre. **Dunster Castle** rises dramatically above the village and the sea. It dates from the 13th century and for over 600 years it has been the home of the Luttrell family. It now belongs to the National Trust and we are privileged to be able to visit it. The gardens and grounds are wonderful especially the terraces where rare shrubs grow. Dunster has a quiet unspoilt beach which is totally safe for children and has the great advantage of being the only beach on to which you can drive in Somerset. It also has one of the most valuable places for tourists, **The Exmoor National Park's Visitor Centre.**

The Visitor's Centre in Dunster is a must for any visitor. The town thrived in medieval times on the woollen industry. An eye-catching feature here draws attention to it. There are 30 metres of wool woven, exactly to the style of medieval cloth, from almost 30 miles of yarn, supplied by Craftsman's mark of Wellington, the proprietor of which, Morfudd Roberts, also supervised the production of the cloth. The yard was woven at **Coldharbour Mill** at **Uffculme**, itself a museum of wool production and well worth visiting. Setting up the loom took several days and involved tying many hundreds of knots by hand before weaving could start.

One length of cloth has been left in its natural, slightly grubby looking state. This would be virtually identical to the woollen cloth worn by the monks of nearby **Cleeve Abbey** in the 13th century. Further lengths of the unique reproduction medieval materials have been dyed by Gill Dalby, a local specialist in the use of vegetable dyes. Indigo was used to create the blue, madder, the red, and weld, the yellow. The invitation to the visitor very definitely is PLEASE TOUCH.

In 1500, many of the homes in Dunster would have had a spinning wheel where the housewife and the unmarried daughters would have toiled ceaselessly for all the daylight hours. Their efforts would have earned them little more than a penny a day. An independent weaver would have kept a team of about five or six women fully employed spinning yarn to meet his needs. This woven cloth was washed and taken out to the Castle Tor to be dried in the open air at the Tenteryarde. It was stretched on tenterframes by means of tenterhooks. Now you know where the expression ' to be on tenterhooks' comes from. I certainly did not know this before. Another term came into being as well. When using a spinning wheel, women (never men) drew fibres from the distaff. This women's work has resulted in the 'distaff side' to indicate the female side of a family.

Yeovil does not draw the visitor in the normal way but it should not be ignored. It has an excellent shopping centre, some good hostelries and is a good base from which to strike out into Dorset if one wishes - it is right on the boundary. One might say much the same of **Street** which was home to Clark's Shoes but now it has **The Shoe Museum** showing the history of shoes from Roman times to the present day. Housed in the oldest part of the original Clark's factory, the exhibits include documents and photographs, shoe buckles, fashion plates, hand tools and shoe machinery, as well of course, as shoes. There are also shoe-making demonstrations and 20 factory shops set within this small town made handsome by the Quaker Clark family who landscaped the factory buildings and built a school, a Quaker meeting house and even a temperance inn.

Not so far from Yeovil **Crewkerne** is a town whose streets converge in the market square. It has many old stone houses and four groups of almhouses but the church is the magnet. It is a grand cruciform church with glorious windows. The west front is almost cathedral like. Inside it is alittle disappointing but the width of the windows brings light to the lovely panelled roofs. Thirteen great stone angels stand holding up the enchanting nave roof. At Crewkerne is one of Somerset's most interesting and beautiful gardens, **Clapton Court**. It has ten acres with formal terraces, spacious lawns, rockery and water gardens. Recently designed is the gorgeous rose garden with arbors.Open March to October, Mondays to Fridays 10.30-5pm and Sundays from 2-5pm.

Another small town close to Chard and Crewkerne is **Ilminster**. Now bypassed it has been able to revert to its sleepy ways and is a nice place to visit. It has the immaculate **Shrubbery Hotel** for those wanting to be pampered. The superb crossing tower of the minster is reminiscent of the central tower at Wells Cathedral, with battlements and pinnacles. It is truly splendid.

Taunton is the county town of Somerset and a very busy place with so much to recommend it. Cricket lovers will know that it is Somerset's ground. There is horse-racing at regular intervals, It is a town of wide streets, a sprinking of medieval buildings even in the centre of the town, notably the timber-framed and gabled houses in Fore Street. It has super shops in well laid out areas, much of it pedestrianised. Several old churches to visit including St Mary's which is a sure reflection of the town's prosperity, and many hostelries and restaurants. It is a place in which to mooch. At least three times in its history Taunton has supported the dissenter; in 1497 it proclaimed Perkin Warbeck king, and in the Civil War, Taunton backed Parliament and many of its population were killed or wounded in the Battle of Sedgemoor fighting for the Duke of Monmouth in 1685. The small team of professionals who run **The Brewhouse Theatre** will tell you that the theatre exists to present a wide range of arts and activities of the highest standard. The range is varied, drama, dance, opera, jazz and films make up the repertoire. It is recognised as one of the country's leading theatres and art centres. It provides hundreds of people with the opportunity to participate in the arts; either through workshops and courses or by joining forces with the hundreds of volunteers who help out.

If I am staying in Taunton I treat myself to a visit to **Poundisford Park**, three and a half miles souht of the town on the by-road between **Trull** and **Pitminster**. The Saxon deer park formed part of the estate granted to the Bishops of Winchester by King Ethelheard, around 730AD. It is still surrounded by the original bank or pale, hunted over by King John, and is the setting for this charming example of Tudor domestic architecture. It was built at the end of Henry VIII's reign by a merchant adventurer, and almost unaltered since. The cream walls, stone mullions and early glass give the house a comfortable and welcoming atmosphere. James I visited the house and his wife, Anne, stayed here. It was ransacked by the Royalists in the Civil War but otherwise it has been a peaceful family home, escaping implication in Monmouth's rebellion. It is open from the beginning of May until the middle of September. Ring for opening times 01823 421244.

A short distance from Taunton along the M5 is **Wellington** which has never quite got over the surprise at the honour bestowed upon it when the hero of the Battle of Waterloo decided to name this rural town for his Dukedom. The Duke of Wellington is believed only once to have visited the town but they have never forgotten. In his honour they built the monument standing high on the spur of the Blackdown Hills. This 175ft high construction looks not unlike Cleopatra's Needle when you see it, especially when it is floodlit at night. This compliment to the town brought them instant fame. The monument was meant to be crowned with a figure of the great man, and to be the centre of a group of cottages for Waterloo pensioners. Sadly, it was too expensive a scheme for the town which for years found the upkeep of the column, with its hundreds of steps, a big drain on the budget. There was great relief when it was taken over by the National Trust. Recently it had a face lift and looks beautiful in the glow of the floodlighting. I must warn you though that the climb up to it is daunting and not for the feeble.

The beautiful and timeless parish church in Wellington is descended mostly from the 13th and 14th centuries and the east window is about 700 years old. Sir John Popham lies here surrounded by his family. He was the man who sentenced Sir Walter Raleight to death. I am amazed he had the temerity when his own character was not without stain. He was reputed to have acquired the manor of Littlecote in Wiltshire as payment for acquitting the owner, William Darell after a sensational murder trial.

The Somerset coast is a must for anyone visiting the county. There is one corner of **Minehead** where a steep flight of steps takes you to the church of St Michael. It is quite charming and reminds me so much of **Clovelly**. Until you have been to Minehead you cannot appreciate what a delightful place it is. Protected by the hills which rise behind it, the houses have flowers climbing over their doors and walls. It is still a little old-fashioned which is part of its charm. It is the home of the **West Somerset Railway** where steam trains will take you on 20 miles of scenic delights. From the vale of Taunton Deane through the rolling Quantock Hills. Past the beaches of Blue Anchor Bay to Minehead or the reverse journey. There are nine restored stations at which you may break your journey, museums, displays and steam locos.

From Minehead there is so much to see and do. Few people can resist the beaches and the golden sands of **Blue Anchor.** Inland the tiny hamlet of **Alcombe** is the prettiest place and just down the road from Dunster is another delightful place, **Timberscombe**.

The little port of **Watchet** is somewhere that has a harbour so small that you wonder how any ship could safely manoeuvre in and out. The 15th century church stands above this miniature seaside town and has a 600 year old cross beside it. A family called Wyndham lived at Kentisford Farm near the church and a square 17th century pew bears their arms. One brass honours Florence Wyndham, an Elizabethan about whom a strange story is told. Whilst she was lying in her coffin in the church awaiting burial, a greedy sexton saw her rings and coveted them. He broke open her coffin and did it so roughly that she woke from her trance, went home and soon after gave birth to a child. History does not relate what happened to the sexton, was he a life saver or hung for being a thief?

Finally in this brief tour of Somerset we come to **Monksilver**, the home of that wonderful house **Combe Sydenham** with its fine Country Park. You must make sure you allow time to spend a day here. It was at Combe Sydenham that Francis Drake courted the beautiful daughter of the house, Elizabeth Sydenham, who finally agreed to marry him. The dashing Sir Francis then sailed away to fight more battles and chase the Spaniards. His voyages were so long and arduous that the lovely Elizabeth became despondent believing that he would never return. Encouraged by her father she finally agreed to wed another suitor. The day of her wedding arrived and she was driven to **Stogumber** church for her marriage. As she alighted from her carriage a cannon ball fell at her feet. Her heart leapt in excitement. It had to be a sign that Drake was back in harbour.

She abandoned her unfortunate bridegroom and went home to await Drake. Drake came and they were married probably in this church. The cannon ball can be seen even today at Combe Sydenham, which experts believe to be a meteorite, in fact. It has become a symbol of good fortune for all those who touch it. It was this marriage that brought Buckland Abbey at Yelverton in Devon into Drake's possession. Their marriage lasted until Drake's death ten years later. Soon after shemarried Sir William Courtenay and became mistress of Powderham Castle in Devon. Her happiness lasted only a few months, until she too died.

Devon is a county of extremes. It has more roads than any other county in England which will lead you through highways and byways, sometimes amid leafy hedgerows teeming with plant and wildlife, sometimes along a coastline that is breathtaking or on the busy A38 which traverses the county to the borders of Cornwall and beyond. The roads will take you to the romantic and stark beauty of Dartmoor and Exmoor, the lush glory of the South Hams, the attractive resorts in Torbay, the spectacular coastline of North Devon, countless pretty villages tucked away and to the two cities of Exeter and Plymouth whose history goes back hundreds of years. It is a county that begs to be explored and will reward anyone who takes the time. It offers an abundance of stately homes, wildlife parks, museums, glorious sandy beaches, safe bathing, water sports and enough golf courses to inspire even the most ardent golfer. Fishing has always been part of Devonian life whether it be along the banks of flowing rivers or from a boat that will take you out from a sheltered harbour to spend hours of pleasure surrounded by the sparkling blue sea with the backdrop of the coast - it almost makes the catch unimportant!

Plymouth tucked away and separated from Cornwall by the River Tamar is a super centre for anyone wanting to tour the county and maybe pop over the border into Cornwall. It is a city which rose from the ashes after the German bombing in World War II. The bombing, horrific as it was, made way for a new city centre to grow, dispensing with the colourful old narrow streets that would have crucified modern commerce.There is no finer vantage point than Plymouth Hoe to take in the brilliance of Plymouth Sound on a sunlit day, its waters dotted with the white and often brightly coloured sails of the innumerable boating enthusiasts who flock to the Marinas and the Yacht Clubs here. Plymouth has been host to many people over the centuries. Catherine of Aragon first stepped ashore in Plymouth when she came to marry the unfortunate Prince Arthur and later Henry VIII. She would have seen a very different city from the one we know today. The narrow winding streets of the Barbican would have been unpaved. I doubt if any of the buildings now exist. Southside Street, now the main thoroughfare of the busy Barbican is first recorded in 1591. What an exciting place this city must have been in the time of Drake and Hawkins. It was from Plymouth that Drake sailed on the 19th July 1588 to defeat the Spanish Armada, and it was on Plymouth Hoe that he played his famous game of bowls. The construction of the Breakwater by Rennie (1812-1840) gave Plymouth one of the largest and safest harbours in Britain.

Plymouth is blessed with many attractions. **The Theatre Royal** is one of the finest in the country and provides theatrical entertainment from drama to comedy, ballet to opera. **The Pavilions**, a complex which offers ice skating, a swimming pool and a venue for concerts of all kinds from Shirley Bassey to the Bournemouth Symphony Orchestra is comparatively new. **Plymouth Dome** on **The Hoe** should be high on any visitors list and then there is the National Trust's **Saltram House** and across the river **Mount Edgcumbe**, given by the family to the city of Plymouth for the benefit of its people. A superb house and wonderful grounds stretching right round the coast to **Cawsand, Rame Head and Whitsand Bay**. Once across the river you are in fact in Cornwall but Cawsand, Rame and Whitsand Bay are favourite day visit places of Plymothians as well as the many visitors who discover the areas untold beauty. Cawsand and Kingsand are two villages separated by only a fluer de lys set in a wall. Delightful places, they have several good pubs including **The Halfway House** renowned for its food.

In the last twenty years Plymouth has grown almost out of recognition and taken under its wing several places which were at one time quiet villages.**Ivybridge** is a prime example. Here a rather sleepy community has found itself woken to life in the 20th century and the influx of massive new housing developments. Oddly this has not destroyed the village but allowed it to develop a community spirit that has found expression in the main street, now pedestrianised, where everyone seems to congregate from time to time either to shop or enjoy the various hostelries and restaurants. This main street now has major food stores and a big branch of Boots for example.

Several small places just outside Plymouth like to be thought of as part of the South Hams. **Noss Mayo** for one nestling on the opposite side of the River Yealm from **Newton Ferrers.** It is a different kettle of fish here because the river and the hinterland prevent either village from growing too large. Both are charming places offering pretty walks along the river, plenty of boating and yachting opportunities and a very pleasant way of life. Then there is quiet, sleepy, **Holbeton** in pretty countryside with a splendid pub,**The Mildmay Colours. Ugborough** has great charm and a busy village square whilst **South Brent** just outside Ivybridge has become almost another commuter village for Plymouth.

Plymouth not only has its magnificent Plymouth Sound but in the hinterland lies **Dartmoor National Park**. Only a short drive from the city and you are up on the moor adapting your eyes from the blue of the sea to the haze and wondrous purple, green and brown colouring of the moor which seems to stretch endlessly with great beauty but at the same time is awesome. **Clearbrook**, on the edge of the moor might be your first stop outside Plymouth; a small hamlet in a nice setting complete with a good pub. **Yelverton** would certainly be your second.. A small community, with a nice church and tucked away at **Leg O'Mutton Corner, The Paperweight Centre** which has given me hours of pleasure over the years. No charge for going in there and certainly worth a visit.

There are many counties who envy Devon's good fortune in having **Exeter** as its county town. It has everything. The River Exe wends its gracious way through the heart of the city, stopping every now and again to prepare itself for the opening of the swing bridge which lets small coasters upstream for unloading. The jewel in the crown is the magnificent cathedral which dominates the city centre and dictates much of the lifestyle immediately around it. Exeter is Roman, Saxon and Norman; it has walls and a tower built by Athelstan, the first King of England, but most of all it is medieval. There are still miles of quaint streets and passageways, rambling walls, a plethora of churches and of course the cathedral bequeathed to us by many generations of the finest builders, apart from its Norman walls and towers. Of course the 20th century has crept in and much has had to be changed, but on the whole it has been done with the greatest care and dedication to the preservation of all that is good. Shopping is a pleasure, with the big stores living comfortably alongside medieval buildings. As in most county towns there are innumerable small shops which entice - most of them hidden away in enchanting alleyways. All the time you are wandering in and out of these alleyways you are probably getting closer and closer to the cathedral. Such is the dimension of its beauty that I find it hard to do it justice on paper. Gazing at the outside will give you hours of pleasure and probably an aching neck!

I love walking along the little Cathedral Close and Southernhay with its beautiful buildings, almost entirely occupied by professional people rather than residents. Perhaps I will walk in the garden of the 14th century Bishop's Palace, with its fine trees taking shade from the great walls of the cathedral. Certainly I will look at the Deanery where Catherine of Aragon stayed. Once inside the cathedral I am always mesmerised by the beauty around me. It is almost like being in a heaven in which modern man is allowed to go about in a peaceful, ordered existence which in no way lacks purpose. There is no strife, no threat of war, no anger, just a great sense of the presence of God in the most wonderful surroundings. If there is any cry for help at all it comes from the need to keep this treasure safe. The years are telling on it and constant war is waged against decay. It takes an immense amount of money which is mainly raised by the public. It is not only money that is needed, craftsmen are continually at work and some of them are getting very old. Finding replacements becomes quite a battle in itself.

Exeter is blessed with many fine churches, some of which are never used but most have stories attached to them. One entrance into the Close is by the tiny church of St Martin with its porch looking across to the Cathedral. It is quite easy to disregard this little gem because of the stunning beauty of the Elizabethan structure alongside, which was known as Moll's Coffee House. The tiers of windows lean out and are crowned by a little gallery. Its front reminds one of an old ship - not surprising because it was here that Drake used to meet his captains. Nothing much has changed since his time. The panelling is oak, almost black with age, and there is an intriguing gallery painted with 46 different coats of arms. The most fascinating sight though is the whole front of the low room, which is glass. I am told that there are no less than 230 panes and no two the same size.

Apart from the Cathedral, nothing can compare to the **Guildhall**, whose walls have stood for 650 years. It makes sure you will not miss it for it thrusts itself out into the busy main street, in amongst all the 20th century buildings. I can almost hear it saying 'I bet I will be here still when you are long gone.' Quite right too. Can you imagine C & A or Marks and Spencers still being there in 600 odd years? Inside it is quite lovely. The hall has a superb roof with gilded beams, from which hang dazzling candelabra. Displayed elsewhere are royal and other gifts that have been collected over the years, including a sword used by Nelson and some of the rarest seals in the land. One dates back to 1175 and is believed to be the oldest in the country.

From Exeter one can take a drive of about ten miles to **Exmouth**, the oldest seaside town in Devon. It is a cheerful resort with a good beach. Not the most attractive place architecturally, apart from the rather distinguished houses on the Beacon, where Lady Nelson lived at No.6 and Lady Byron at No 19. **Ottery St Mary** has an annual carnival. Nothing strange about that except here the young men rush through the main street rolling barrels of flaming tar, a sight worth beholding. **Otterton** has in its midst the **Domesday Mill**, somewhere every visitor should go. It is a collection of old buildings with a flour mill still working. There are a lot of craft shops there and a very good wholefood restaurant.

Budleigh Salterton always makes me think of retired colonels! It is one of Devon's most charming and unspoilt places. There is a gentle brook running right through the street that houses the shops. The brook starts its run at Squabmoor, a drab name for such a beautiful spot adjoining Woodbury Common where Nigel Mansell owns the Woodbury Park Golf and Country Club. Enter the foyer there and you will see his famous Williams Renault Car as well as a McClaren. I had the pleasure of meeting and talking with Nigel Mansell very recently. The subject was not Formula One or Indycar racing but Woodbury Park which is a project in which he is totally involved and financially committed. He has done a wonderful job there. The golf course is a championship one and the clubhouse and its other buildings are unlike any other you will see. Superbly built and furnished, it is open to non-members who may come for the day if they wish, eat in the attractive conservatory restaurant, walk in the woods or on a summer's day sit on the terrace simply absorbing the stunning views. His advent to this area has been beneficial in every direction. Go and take a look you will not be disappointed and if you happen to be a golfer you will be stunned by what is on offer.

Like many beaches along this part of the coast, Budleigh Salterton is not blessed with golden sand but with pebbles that do not entice you to walk barefooted - but it is of no importance, the scenery makes up for any minor inconvenience.

Further along the coast you will come to one of my favourite parts of the Devon coast. Seemingly not quite of the 20th century,**Seaton, Sidmouth** and **Beer** have altered little since coming to prominence in Victorian times. Sheltered in Lyme Bay, all sharing shingle and pebble beaches and the dignity of yesteryears. These are not places to visit if you want a sophisticated life. Sidmouth springs to life for the annual Folk Festival which has become the Mecca for entrants from all over the world. The first time I saw it I could not believe that there were so many variations of Morris Dancing and Folk Singing, let alone the clacking Clog Dancer's. Seaton has that rare item today, a tramway. It is even more of a rarity to find a tramway working on an old railway line. Once run along the promenade at Eastbourne, and doomed when the promenade's extension was planned, the tram was rescued by the enthusiasts who care for it today - a considerable benefit for Devon. The hour's journey travelling the three miles aboard the double-decked tram, through the Axe and Coly valleys along the route of the old railway, will take you to **Colyton** one of the prettiest small towns in Devon. **Beer** is little more than a fishing village which attracts an influx of visitors in the summer, but unlike many similar seaside haunts, it does not die in winter. The community get together and a hundred and one activities spring up to occupy the winter months.

Axminster has a curiously shaped town centre dominated by the parish church of St Mary's. Inside the church you will be astounded by the magnificent carpeting. The pews are set well back so that one can admire this unexpected beauty. Then you realise that it is really quite natural as Axminster is the home of the carpet industry. One of the earliest Axminsters made in 1775, can ben seen in the Guildhall in which is also housed the original market charter dated 1210. Thomas Witty pioneered the carpet industry in Axminster having discovered the techniques from the Turks. His first carpets were produced in a little building alongside the church, and so important was the completion of each carpet that the church bells were rung in celebration.

Honiton is sometimes forgotten today. At one time it used to be a nightmare trying to drive through it when it was on the main road going to London. Now it is bypassed it is still busy but in the nicer way which allows the residents to enjoy their lives. Famed for lace of course, it also has one of the widest main streets in Britain. Two small places always please me close to Honiton. One is **Gittisham**, with its wide street, pale stone cottages, lovely old cob-and-thatch cottages, and its 500 year old church enshrining 500 years of the community's history. It also has a wonderful country house hotel, **Combe House**. The second is the tiny hamlet of **Buckerell** with another charming establishment **Splatthayes.**

Wandering about Devon is one of the pleasures of my life and I find myself equally enchanted with every corner. For those who like a resort atmosphere **Torbay** has to be the answer. It always gives one the feel of being on the French Riviera. The sea is a brilliant Mediterrannean blue coming ashore to sandy beaches and row upon row of sparkling white buildings which range from high class hotels to the many small guest houses. Torbay is made up of Torquay, Paignton and the old fishing port of Brixham. It welcomes visitors all the year round and most people who come out of season seem to prefer it when it is quieter.

Torquay has many admirers from all over the world who come to it for many different reasons.Many people decide to retire here because of the clement weather and the almost Riviera like atmosphere. There are those who come for conferences and seminars whose arrangers are delighted at the amenities the town and its hotels offer. Then there are the holiday makers who fill the resort at the height of the season and who come for the beaches, the sun and all the fun of the fair. Finally there is the group of people who enjoy short breaks and perhaps come here two or sometimes three times during the year to enjoy the beauty and peace of the bay. For all of them there is much to do and not least, if they have any sense, to enjoy the charm of the little theatre at **Babbacombe** which runs a popular, true summer show which manages to keep running almost until Christmas.

Paignton is renowned for having one of the best Zoos in the country. The town and sea front are gentle places generally. Flowers and rockeries along the promenade and a wonderful park, man-made out of marsh this century, are the outstanding features. Paignton is the sort of place that people of my age enjoy in the spring, autumn and even winter but who will probably avoid it like the plague in the height of the season.

Brixham has always been the home of fishermen, whose houses perch on the side of the hills leading to Higher Brixham. Some are close to the harbour or open onto little streets or steps bringing their occupants to the seafront. Whilst tourism is not ignored it has always had to take a second place to the fishing industry and so the character of the town has changed little over the centuries. For me Brixham will always stay in my mind whenever I hear Henry Francis Lyte's wonderful hymn 'Abide with Me'. He was the vicar for over a quarter a century of the 19th century All Saints Church.

It is a hymn that has been sung throughout the Christian world by people in times of great emotion. My father told me that in World War I it was sung by the men in the trenches and when they had finished the Germans would take it up from their dugouts. It has brought peace to thousands. Henry Lyte wrote it in the dusk after evening service. He did not know he had taken his last service in the church. He died not long afterwards. If you listen you will hear the bells of All Saints ring out his hymn every night.

No one comes to Torquay without seeing **Cockington**. If you want to see it at its best go early in the morning, soon after sunrise, when it is still. Later it will be swamped with visitors and all you will remember will be the crowds and perhaps the thatched cottages. Seen early it is as if you were back in the 16th-17th century when Cockington was first built.

Newton Abbot thankfully is by-passed today which makes it pleasanter to look at the town and much easier to reach other places such as **Ipplepen**, a village as old as time. Conan Doyle spent many a happy visit here with his friend Bertie Robinson who lived at Parkhill House. Exploring Dartmoor was one of his great pleasures and he used to be driven in a horse and carriage by the Robinson groom, one Harry Baskerville. Did you ever wonder where the title 'Hound of the Baskervilles' originated ? Now you know. No one ever denies the beauty of **Broadhempston** reached through a network of small lanes. Its church is 15th century with graceful arcades, old carved beams and bosses in the porch and roofs.

If you take the coastal road out of Torquay you will come to **Teignmouth** and **Dawlish** two unashamedly Victorian resorts of great charm. On the approach road to Teignmouth a turning off at **Shaldon** just before the bridge will take you to **Stoke-in-Teignhead**. It lies in one of Devon's combes by the mouth of the Teign. Full of pretty cottages and an old church which must have been here in Norman times. When you look at the mosaics in the sanctuary, you will wonder how so many years ago, such work was done by Italian craftsmen. Where did they stay, how did they cope with the language barrier and how long did their journey take?

Had you approached Teignmouth from Newton Abbot you would have passed by **Kingsteignton**, an ever growing place which has become almost a dormitory for Newton Abbot However one should always remember that this ancient village was thriving at the time of the Domesday Book..

Dawlish is close to **Powderham Castle**, one of the quiet glories of Devon, built between 1390 and 1420. It has been the home of the Courtenay family ever since. Sir Philip Courtenay was the first occupant, the sixth son of the second Earl of Devon, from whom the present Earl is directly descended. If you look at the castle you will see that every generation has made some form of alteration in order to keep up with the changes of their time. None of this has detracted from its beauty. A visit to Powderham will always remain in your mind as a red letter day.

Nearby Powderham is the little estuary village of **Starcross** on the west bank of the Exe. Essentially a residential community with the river as its key attraction it offers great sailing and at one time the oyster beds were a real source of income for the village, and today a shell industry is once more established.

The South Hams is one of the prettiest areas in the whole of Devon.**Modbury** built on the slopes of a valley with four main streets intersecting at right angles is full of nice buildings and many enchanting shops plus a sprinkling of good hostelries and the bonus of a free car park. The road from Modbury towards the sea winds its way towards **Kingsbridge** which rises sharply from the Salcombe estuary but before you get there you will find a turn to the right will take you to **Bigbury-on-Sea** with its enormous beach and the famous **Burgh Island**, which lies off the coast and is accessible by foot across the sand at low tide and by sea tractor from the car park at high tide. A small, magical place which was first inhabited in 900AD. By the 14th century it had a thriving fishing community. There is only one cottage left today and that is now **The Pilchard Inn,**a delightful port of call after a walk across the sands. The island also has a spectacular hotel which is world famous and has a visitor's book with such illustrious names as Edward Prince of Wales, Mountbatten, Noel Coward etc. It went into decline after this era and was closed in 1955 and then brought to life by two exciting people, the Porters, who have restored it in the 1920's Art Deco style. Their love affair with the island and the hotel became almost a cult story with magazines and newspapers, so when they re-opened in March 1988, the word had spread across the world. People came from London, New York, Los Angeles and Europe, and loved every minute of their stay.

Kingsbridge is a charming place in its own right with a church that stands on massive 13th century arches. Apart from the excellent shopping facilities in the main street take a look at the **Cookworthy Museum of Rural Life**. Halfway between Kingsbridge and Totnes is the small village of **East Allington**, a quiet sort of place and most people coming here for the first time are amazed that it was one of the six villages evacuated during the Second World War to enable the Allied Forces to practise for a final invasion of Europe. Luckily, being on the outskirts of the D-Day rehearsal area, most of the houses remained undamaged and the residents were able to return home before the year was out. Another nice village close to Kingsbridge is **Churchstow** two miles to the north-west whose church of St Mary is a prominent landmark between the Avon valley and the sea inlet from Salcombe to Kingsbridge.

Ringmore is another very attractive village west of Kingsbridge. It has some interesting 16th to18th century buildings and the church of All Saints was built around 1300, although parts of it are Norman. The focal point of the village is the well-named hostelry **The Journey's End**.

The A381 takes you from Kingsbridge to **Dartmouth**, the undoubted 'show-stopper' of the South Hams. You approach the town from the top of a steep hill and if traffic permits I suggest you stop for a moment or two to catch the stunning panoramic view of the town and the river. The dramatic scenery is heightened by the tiers of houses which cling for dear life to the hillside overlooking the River Dart. It is always a busy and delightful place to be. You will see constant passenger and car ferries crossing the busy river to **Kingswear** on the other side.

Along the quayside at Dartmouth you will see notices advertising river trips up to **Totnes** and elsewhere. If you have time take to the water, for the trip covers some of the most beautiful scenery in the county. On a sunny day the brilliant blue of the water finds it hard to compete with the endless variation of greens to be seen in the trees and fields. You will see **Dittisham**, a village of thatched stone cottages winding through plum orchards and daffodil fields down to the river. From the quay by an old inn, a passenger ferry plies its trade, signalling its approach by ringing a large brass bell. It is the epitome of a peaceful English scene, but remember this river arguably the most beautiful in England, has been the means of bringing wealth to many places throughout our history.

If you were to continue up the river you would come to **Stoke Gabriel** tucked in the fold of the hills by the river. The village is a mixture of old and new but the essential character remains with the cobbled walk to the much loved church of St Mary and St Gabriel, the old cottages and the ancient yew. For centuries Stoke Gabriel has been the centre of the Dart salmon fishing industry. It is no longer a full time occupation but the netting rights are carefully guarded by those who own them. Visitors flock to the quay which is now a popular beauty spot. Rowing boats, sailing dinghies lie in a sheltered corner of the creek whilst there are many moorings for larger craft in the main river.

Salcombe delights every one who goes there with its colourful streets, vibrant river estuary and lively life style. It is full of good places to stay, places to eat, ferries to take you across the estuary to **East Portlemouth** where there are wonderful beaches. It is a paradise for anyone who enjoys being waterborne.

Totnes, first mentioned in the reign of Edgar about 959AD, was probably a small settlement. Today it is a busy, attractive town which is not much more than one beautiful street climbing up a hill by the River Dart. From choice I would always come to Totnes by river from Dartmouth but in a more mundane fashion this time I have taken the A3122 which is a pretty road and will take me to the village of **Harbertonford**, a village I never forget for several reasons. The first is the awkward bend as you approach it which puts some people off, but don't be. It is an interesting place with the restored **Crowdie Mill**, **The Malsters Arms** and the exciting **Hungry Horse.**

Every Tuesday morning in the summer **Totnes Elizabethan Society** members and local traders dress in Tudor costume to raise thousands of pounds for charity. It has become a world famous spectacle and celebrate's the town's 16th century heritage. There is much to see including **Bowden House**, the home of the British Photographic Museum with its large collection of vintage cameras, as well as antique weaponry, furniture and pictures. **The Devonshire Collection of Period Costume** in the High Street has a beautiful collection which is changed each season and is housed in one of the town's loveliest Tudor merchant houses. **Totnes Castle** was built by theNormans over 900 years ago on an old Saxon stockade. It has spectacular views over Totnes and the Dart Valley. The courtyard is the biggest Norman courtyard in England - wonderful place for picnics. For me exploring the South Hams is a never ending treasure hunt with constantly different and unexpected clues to its beauty.

Changing route entirely, it is time to take a look at some of the places on **Dartmoor** which, when you are in Devon, is never far away. **Tavistock** one of the Stannary towns is a favourite haunt of mine. I love the sense of pride and stability. It has so much history which started a hundred years before the Conqueror, and was originally controlled by its Abbey.

You can seek out a great deal of the past in the fine medieval parish church, with its pinnacled tower, its wide nave, and countless gables that dominate the streets. It may well have been here that Francis Drake was taken to worship as a child for Tavistock was his home town, something one is never allowed to forget.

Many small villages surround Tavistock, all of which are worth seeing. On the Okehampton road there are two **Tavys, Mary and Peter**, the twins grew out of the settlement on either side of the River Tavy. Each has a church linked together by a bridle path and a little bridge over the river known as 'The Clam', an old name for a bridge. In **Mary Tavy** there is an excellent Vegetarian Restaurant,**The Stannary,** probably one of the best in the country. No one should miss seeing **Lydford Gorge**. Water pours off the moor onto the boulders of the gorge with a ferocity which would overshadow a witches cauldron. A mile or so away is **Lewtrenchard Manor**, the composer of great hymns, Sabine Baring-Gould's old home which is now a stunning country house hotel.

To the north of the moor is **Okehampton** with its romantic Castle, Okehampton seldom gets the recognition it deserves and is well worth taking a look at. **Chagford** is a sleepy market town that should also be on your list. It has grown up around the village square. Do visit **James Bowden & Sons**. It is an experience. Founded in 1862 it can only be called an emporium. This is a Stannary Town where tinners would come from miles around to have their precious metal weighed and given the King's Stamp before it was sold. Farmers too would come to sell their cattle and sheep and, in particular, their fleeces, for wool was an important industry. All this activity was watched over by the most distinctive of the town's many historic buildings: the old market house in the middle of the square.

Drewsteignton in addition to having a remarkable hostelry and charming thatched cottages, is home to the amazing **Castle Drogo**, the last castle to be built in this country. Julius Drewe was responsible for it and he got Sir Edward Lutyens to design it. The enchanted world of **Fingle Bridge** is just below Drewsteignton. You do not just simply arrive here, you have to seek it out. It is hidden away at the end of a long winding leafy lane that seems to descend forever, until suddenly there it is; a low pack horse bridge which dates back to Elizabethan times, if not earlier, straddling a river dancing and cavorting as it plays with the boulders strewn in the path. The paths leading away from the bridge were probably the way that merchants came with their laden pack-horses and the terrain was too difficult to develop further. We can count ourselves lucky that this was so, otherwise Fingle Bridge might not have survived the wear and tear of men and vehicles over the years. There are three Iron Age hill forts around Fingle Gorge. **Prestonbury** you can see clearly from the bridge. **Wooston** is down river and if you see it on a spring morning with the sun behind you, it is breathtaking. The third,**Cranbrook**, is higher up. At **Shilston** to the west is the best known of the cromlech or dolmens in Devon, with the odd name of **Spinster's Rock**. Legend has it that three spinsters put it in place, but fact says it is the remains of a Bronze Age megalithic tomb.

Moretonhampstead holds the key to so much that is beautiful. Within my lifetime it has changed considerably. Forty years ago it was a shopping centre for farmers and people living in outlying hamlets. It had everything a community needed. Today the butcher is still here and the chemist but the general store is no more and it is only recently that the baker has returned. It gets its livelihood mainly from tourists. The 'hampstead' part of its name has been added in the last century or so and most local people ignore it, calling the little town Moreton, derived from the Saxon Mor Tun. The 15th century church of St Andrew standing on high ground has tombstones in the porch in memory of two French officers who lived at Moreton during the Napoleonic Wars when they were on parole from their prison at Princetown. Four other villages in the vicinity should be looked at.**Doccombe, Dunsford, Bridford** and **Christow**, each has its own merits and all are part of the Dartmoor scene.

Close to Moreton is **Becky Falls.** High up in the solitude of Dartmoor you approach it through glorious woods. On one side of the road there is a car park, where, if you have any sense, you will don stout shoes or wellies, before making the descent alongside Becka brook, where the water cascades over and between massive boulders until with a roar it reaches its peak, and falls in sparkling torrents on its way to the sea. This enchanted world is at its best in November after the mid-winter rains.

Moments up the road is the isolated village of **Manaton**, with its green nestling beside the church. Mentioned in the Domesday book it seems to have been there for ever. Away to the south the great rocks known as **Bowerman's Nose** look like a petrified sentinel guarding the rugged hills, or a man with a sense of humour wearing a cardinal's hat playing God.

Whilst Manaton remains essentially Dartmoor, **Lustleigh** to the east has changed completely in the last two decades. There was a time when this rural community lived simply in the beautiful valley of the Wrey. They gained their livelihood from small holdings and cultivating productive vegetable gardens, seldom venturing away. A journey to Exeter was a once in a lifetime experience. Nowadays the 13th century church still stands. Look out for the mischievous carving of the small heads on top of the screen which was erected in Tudor times. The craftsman obviously had likes and dislikes; all the heads facing the chancel have a secret grin on their faces and those towards the nave, a scowl. There is a good pub, an excellent tearoom and village cricket still flourishes. At weekends you can sit and watch on a field, fringed with alders, and make believe that the noise and trauma of the 20th century does not exist. You must also explore all the little lanes and byways that surround Lustleigh and hide away some delightful places in which to stay. You will see more details about these hidden places in the dedicated pages at the back of this chapter.

Bovey Tracey is one of the Gateways to Dartmoor and has been important since the days of the Normans. It has charming, narrow streets and sits sedately overlooking the River Bovey. Perhaps not as peaceful as it once was it is still a delightful place to visit.

To describe the routes that one can take on the moor to get the greatest pleasure out of walking takes more space than I am permitted in this book. The Dartmoor Visitors Centre at **Princetown** will provide you with a comprehensive choice of books and pamphlets on the subject. The sort of things I look for are the old guide posts which are no more than pieces of granite standing onend. Each is marked with a letter. From Two Bridges one would be marked 'P' showing the direction of Princetown or 'M' for Moretonhampstead. It is primitive but effective. Frequently you will come across the remains of Bronze Age dwellings, just circles of stones which once were a hut. Sometimes you will see the remains of beehive huts. Not that they ever housed bees! They were used by medieval tinners for hiding their unsold tin, and other bits and pieces.

The clapper bridges are to be seen quite regularly over the streams that run through Dartmoor. **Postbridge** has one of the best examples. It is a tribute to the skill of the 14th century builders. You will see that all the bridges are made of huge slabs of granite balanced one upon the other. Built so well that they have withstood the onslaught of human feet, the insistent hammering of the river and the Dartmoor climate, for centuries.

Then there are the Dartmoor 'Letter Boxes'. If you know nothing about them; it is purely a fun thing that has developed over the years into quite a serious hobby. You seek out the position of the boxes, usually tucked away in a crag somewhere, quite well hidden. You then post your own cards and take out any that are already there, which then become your duty to post on. Inside the hiding place you will find a visitor's book for you to sign, a rubber stamp, and an indelible pad, and you have to stamp your cards with the Dartmoor Letter Boxes' own crest. One for instance, is to be found at Cranmere Pool, south west of Okehampton, another at Crow Tor.

Princetown is always an attraction albeit a macabre one because of the infamous Dartmoor Prison, built by French Prisoners of War. It is a threatening place and dominates this small village. Even on the sunniest of days it still looks formidable and extremely depressing. There is nothing depressing however about the lively **Plume of Feathers** where mine host is James Langton. This is a favourite watering hole for people from miles around and is equally popular with visitors who find the informality and fun infectious.

I am addicted to the road that runs from Two Bridges to Ashburton which has endless places of enchantment that run off it. Past **Dartmeet** and on to **Poundsgate, Widecombe-in-the-Moor** can be seen from miles away with its tall church tower built 400 years ago, by tin miners in thanksgiving for the thriving industry. It is dedicated to St Pancras and known as 'The Cathedral; on the Moor'. For centuries the village remained almost unknown and it was not until 1850, when the vicar decided to hold an annual fair and Sabine Baring-Gould popularised an old folk tune that made Widecombe become world famous. There will be few who do not know the old song 'As I was going to Widecombe Fair wi' Bill Brewer, Jan Stewer, Peter Davy, Uncle Tom Cobleigh an all.' If you are one of the few you may rest assured that someone in Widecombe will tell you the story of Uncle Tom Cobleigh and his grey mare. Whether he was fact or fiction is strenuously argued. What is a fact is that a Thomas Cobleigh was born in the nearby village of **Spreyton** in 1762 and died there in 1884. It could be that he brought his grey mare and his motley crew to Widecombe for the fair.

Buckland-in-the-Moor is enchanting with some of the loveliest thatched cottages I have ever seen. On a hill stands the 15th century church with carved bosses in the porch and old tiles under the tower. When you look up at the clock you will note that it does not have numerals. In their places are the words 'My Dear Mother' and its bells chime out 'All things bright and beautiful'. There is no official explanation for this curiosity but legend has it that it was placed there by a man in memory of his mother. This remarkable lady, when told the news that her son had drowned at sea, refused to believe it. Every night she placed a candle in her window to guide him home. Her faith was rewarded. When she died this is how he repaid her constancy.

Holne is a little village of no more than 300 people. A busy community who have great links with **Ashburton**, a town of contrasts and beauty. In 1305 it was designated a Stannary Town. Tin mining and the wool industry brought it great wealth and with it the building of some fine houses. **Buckfast Abbey** must be one of your ports of call. Not during the day although it is beautiful then, but at night. Buckfast Abbey during Compline is magical. The monks come silently down the aisle, the only sound the swish of their long robes as they pass by, the only light, the bidding one high over the altar. As they reach their stalls, they push back the cowls from their heads and the service begins. Its simple message is chanted and reaches out to every corner of this great building. One cannot doubt that God is present.

In Mid-Devon I would include **Cullompton** and recommend you take a look at this old town with its interesting main street and fine parish church. Close by is the small village of **Kentisbeare** where you will be made very welcome at **Knowles House. Tiverton** is a place that grows on you. The prettiest way to approach this very old town is by the Exe valley road. It goes back to Saxon days when it had fords across the Exe and the Loman, and it is where these two meet that the town looks down from its high ground between the rivers. Right by the medieval gateway of Tiverton Castle is the 15th-century St Peter's Church. Its spacious windows glisten in the afternoon sunlight highlighting its pinnacles and battlemented parapets. The centuries have not destroyed the wonder of the carving on the outside walls. Look for a bear that creeps along a hollowed wall, a monkey holding fast to its baby and the proud lions which crouch on the buttresses. **Tiverton Castle** built by the Normans is still important to the town but it was the wool merchants who provided Tiverton with many of its finest buildings.

The rivers are not the only waterways in Tiverton. The reach of the **Grand Western Canal** has been lovingly and carefully restored and is now open to the public who can enjoy the gentle trip by horse drawn boat along this beautiful canal as far as **East Manley**.

The road that takes you from the very old town of **Crediton** with its ancient and very beautiful cathedral like church, to Tiverton takes you close to **Cadbury**, a small village amongst the hills, with wonderful views over the

Exe valley. The tall church tower which has stood for over 500 years dominates all around it at first sight, until you realise that it, in turn, is overshadowed by the mighty **Cadbury Castle**. Standing 700ft up, it is a fort of the ancient Britons. Nothing much left there now other than two ramparts enclosing a great space. It was here that General Fairfax pitched his camp in the Civil War.

So much beauty and history is crammed into the scenic village of **Bickleigh**. It has everything; a castle, a river flowing under a superb bridge, thatched cottages, an award-winning mill and two very good hostelries. Two other villages should not escape your attention.**Bampton** about 8 miles north of Tiverton should be visited if only to discover its ducks! **Holcombe Rogus** south of Bampton is the other. It is mentioned in the Domesday Book and has Holcombe Court where the lords of the manor from Tudor times were the Bluetts.Supposedly haunted it is said that tough American servicemen during World War II were frightened out of their wits by the persistent presence of an unknown ghost. Worth a nosey, I think.

North Devon is different again, wonderful countryside and a spectacular coast. Starting inland, the quiet market town of **Holsworthy** has two striking viaducts and a good pub. **Black Torrington** got its name because the stones in the nearby river turn black with iron oxide in the water.**Sheepwash** is a great base for anyone wanting to walk along the Torridge valley. Game fishing attracts keen anglers with salmon, sea trout and brown trout all providing excellent sportat different times of the season. Pony trekking and riding are available nearby. There are good golf courses and it is heaven for eager ornithologists. From here it is easy to visit **Rosemoor Garden** only a short journey from Sheepwash and one mile south of **Great Torrington.** Before moving on one should take a look at the sleepy village of **Hatherleigh** with the excellent **George Hotel** which is Heritage at its best.

In a sort of rectangle that has its base between Launceston in Cornwall, and Okehampton and its top end, in Holsworthy and Hatherleigh there are endless beautiful places and some stunning scenery. One of my favourites is **Ashwater** just off the Holsworthy-Launceston road which has one of the loveliest old manor houses, now a hotel**, Blagdon Manor** owned and run by two people who have restored the house, serve wonderful food and have a delightful sense of humour and a smaller but welcoming establishment, **Ransom Mill**.

Clawton a little further down the same main road is a small village with the River Claw running through it and is crossed by two small bridges. The village is very proud of two things, its Norman church and the exquisite **Court Barn Country House Hotel** which is one of the most peaceful places I have ever visited. Another is **Bratton Clovelly** which is rightly proud of its late 14th century church which is one of the few remaining churches to possess wall paintings dating back to the 17th century. Don't be confused, as many visitors are, who arrive here looking for Clovelly with its steep cobbled hill leading down to the sea. One must say that most people are totally happy with what they find in Bratton Clovelly which has a great charm of its own. It used to be the home of the famous politician Alan Clarke, when he was MP for Plymouth. Then between Holsworthy and Hatherleigh is **North Tawton** which can be traced back to Roman times at least and in 1086 it was recorded in the Domesday Book as Tawland. It is a pleasant place which one would not associate with disaster but legend tells us De-Bathe Pool overflows (even in dry weather) immediately prior to some national disaster or bereavment. The inhabitants will confirm this by pointing out that the overflow happened just before the deaths of Nelson, Pitt, Wellington and King Edward VII, and when the First World War broke out! The legend has its roots in 1630 when it was spoken of by one Thomas Westcote.

Close to Holsworthy is **Bradworthy** where people born and bred in the village are known as'Horniwinks'! Why? Because it is the local name for a species of plover, the pee-wit, which used to be found in large numbers on Bradworthy Moors. It was probably founded about AD700 and originally mentioned in the Domesday Book as the manor of 'Braurdina'. It has a splendid village green and at the centre of the village is the Square, the largest village square in the West Country.

In Great Torrington I am always reminded of its past. It was literally blown into history by the great explosion of eighty barrels of gunpowder. It happened in the Civil War, when General Fairfax marching from the east, took the Royalists by surprise, and captured the town. The prisoners were shut off for safety in the tower of the church. They were held in complete darkness and had no idea that they were scrambling about in what had been the arsenal of the Royalists. Somehow the powder was set alight and the ensuing explosion shattered the church, killed 200 men and nearly killed the General as well. Today Great Torrington is the home of the world famous **Dartington Glass**.

North west of Torrington is **South Molton**. This ancient sheep and cattle market town is on the edge of Exmoor. It dates back to the 12th century and until the middle of the 19th-century thrived as a centre of the wool trade.

Now for the coast. **Lynton** and **Lynmouth** are linked together by a remarkable Cliff Railway which opened in 1890. It climbs 500ft above sea level along a 900ft track and allows you to enjoy both villages without having the severe climb from one to the other. Both are attractive places and especially Lynmouth. The Napoleonic Wars were responsible for the rising popularity of the two villages. Restrictions on travelling abroad made people look for alternatives and here they found comfort and beauty. Shelley and Coleridge were regular visitors. The River Lyn runs through Lynton and tumbles over moss strewn rocks and boulders, through thickly wooded hills as it falls to the sea at Lynmouth.

The main road from Lynton will take you to **Combe Martin**, but there are some spectacular walks in between which should not be missed, nor should you leave out the little village of **Parracombe** which lies between steep hills and must have been one of the first places in Devon to have a Christian church, for 1450 years ago, St Petrock came here and built a little chapel of cob and wattles, with a roof of straw.

Combe Martin has one of the longest village streets in the whole of the country. It became part of history over 750 years ago when its silver mines produced the wherewithal to pay for the Hundred Years War. Just inland is the pretty village of **Berrynarbor** which lives a quiet life all of its own and has a first class hostelry. **Ilfracombe** is the next stop and as you drive from Combe Martin you will be bewitched by the panoramic and stunning views glimpsed only occasionally over the cliff to the sea. Wonderful scenery, a good beach and friendly pubs are good reasons for coming here.

The winding coast road takes you to the seaside villages of **Mortehoe,Woolacombe** and **Croyde** with their magnificent beaches beloved by surfers and families. They are all just big enough to have a life style of their own but small enough to remain intimate. From Woolacombe you can just see, far out to sea, **Lundy Island,** the granite haunt of pirates long ago and now chiefly the haunt of sea birds; the island stands out 400ft above the sea.

Baggy Point offers some outstanding walks and this may attract you to **Croyde** which is tucked away on the southern flank of the peninsula. **Saunton** three miles away is renowned for its Championship Golf Course.

A busy main road will lead you from here through **Braunton** and into **Barnstaple** which claims to be the oldest borough in England. Whilst it remains an interesting town, much of the old has given way to the new to allow it to develop as the business centre of North Devon. It has an excellent theatre. From Barnstaple to Bideford you have the choice of two roads. The main A339 or the small B3233. The latter allows you to take a look at the villages of **Fremlingham** and **Instow** on the banks of the River Taw as it comes out of the sea at **Bideford Bay**. From Instow a ferry trip across the river to **Appledore** is rewarding. It is here that the two great estuaries of the

Taw and the Torridge meet. Appledore is charming and picturesque. The little street running up from the quay is nothing short of beautiful.

Bideford is an excellent base for anyone who wants to explore the coast and villages between itself and **Hartland Point**. It is a friendly town looking over the river. Nothing ever changes in **Clovelly**. It is an artist's paradise. Cars are taboo. You leave your vehicle in the car park at the top of the village and descend down the cobbled street which tumbles for half a mile to the sea. On either side are old cottages with flowers and creepers climbing up their walls. The scenery is unforgettable. High above you trees reach for the skies whilst way below the sea sparkles in the sunshine. It is divorced from this world.

Hartland is a place that goes nowhere and makes a good place in which to end this rather hotch potch tour of Devon. Here we have **Hartland Abbey** which stirs the heart and soul of everyone who visits. It dates from the 12th century, is situated near the wild, desolate coastline, has monastic origins and has been lived in by the same family, although frequently inherited through the female line, since the Dissolution, when Henry VIII gave it to William Abbot, the Sergeant of his royal wine cellars. There are many lovely rooms and the grounds are outstanding. The Valley is still as beautiful as it must have been in the days of the Abbots. It is open to the public from May-September on Wednesdays, Bank Holiday Sundays and Mondays from 2-5.30pm. Dogs on leads are allowed in the grounds.

I have an unashamed love for **Cornwall** from whence my family stemmed. It is an incredible mixture of glorious coastline running up either side of the peninsula until it joins Devon across the Tamar, the Atlantic and the English Channel. In the middle of this sandwich are the mining villages which frankly would not be out of place in a sci-fi film and have frequently been used for this purpose. Mineral wealth below ground, shaped the destiny of Cornwall and the Cornish for hundreds of years, changing the landscape and creating these unique villages, harbours and quays. The National Trust now owns a third of the coastline of Cornwall, more than 100 miles of magnificent walking country including many spectacular stretches and popular holiday resorts.

The coastal villages have always been among the most picturesque and sought after for film makers and artists, some liking the softer south side and others the incredible, harsh beauty of North Cornwall. Whichever way you go you are never far from the sea and for this part of the chapter I am going to take you across the North Devon border into Cornwall at **Bude**.John Betjeman described this place of endless golden sands, 'the least rowdy resort in the county'.People come here to enjoy family holidays in the traditional manner, revelling in the sun, sea and sand. Surfers flock here because the Atlantic rollers rise to great heights and provide them with some superb rides. It is only in recent years that Bude has come to prominence. At the end of the last century it was not even on the map. Next door **Stratton** was the established market town where the famous Battle of Stamford Hill took place in 1643 when Sir Bevil Grenville defeated the Parliamentary forces led by the Earl of Stamford. Every year in May this battle is re-enacted by members of the Sealed Knot Society.

Drive down the A38 and turn off towards the coast on a signposted B road and you will come to **Boscastle** which must have been known to sailors since men first sailed the English seas. If you have a choice of roads, then to see Boscastle at its most spectacular, approach from **Camelford** on the B3266 where the road rises until you suddenly see the most glorious prospect over the Valency Valley and the Atlantic Ocean before you drive down the twisting road into the village.

There is no doubt that the little harbour is one of the oddest in the country. It has a medieval breakwater, a long greasy slipwater and a huge dog leg opening into the ocean. For those who pass the stone jetty and clamber over the slippery rocks, the sea opens out in front of them to a sight that is unforgettable. If the tide is right you will not be able to miss the famous blow-hole working and rumbling. It is a natural curiosity throwing out a cloud of spray with a deep rumble like a tiny volcano. I have heard it called the Devil's Bellows.

Thomas Hardy came here as a young architect to help in the restoration of the church where he met his wife, Emma Gifford. This was not a marriage made in heaven although it lasted over 30 years. Oddly enough after her death in 1912 Hardy returned to Cornwall and the memory of their early romance at Boscastle inspired him to write some of the greatest love poems ever.

There are some magical walks around here. You can walk inland or take the coastal path from the harbour to **Penally** and on to **Pentargen** or climb the lane linking Boscastle with **Lesnewth** and nearby **Minster** with its church in an almost theatrical setting with not a house in sight and tall trees forming a backdrop. In spring the whole of the floor of this imaginary stage is covered with a carpet of bluebells and daffodils. The walk along the coast from **Boscastle** to **Tintagel** is nothing short of stunning. When the sun is shining, the sea is unbelievably blue and laps the rocks with such gentleness that it is hard to visualise the fury that is whipped up on a stormy day when the wind drives the sea in. So powerful is the wind that is difficult to stand upright but the sight is awesome.

I lived in the village of **Tintagel** for a while in 1950 and I used to walk up the long hill to the 14th century church which is the oldest in Cornwall. It is set high on the Clebe Cliff exposed to the ravages of the Atlantic storms. Take a look at the gravestones and you will see that the force of the wind has bent them all in the same direction and some have had to be supported by little buttresses. One really does not know whether King Arthur ever set foot here but there is no doubt that Tintagel's most famous attraction is his castle. It is a romantic place identifiable as a settlement from AD400 in the time of the Celts. In the 12th century it became a royal castle but by the 1500s the central portion had been washed away by the erosion of the sea. Edward, the Black Prince is supposed to have stayed here and if you climb down the path that leads to the shingle beach you will find Merlin's cave where it is alleged King Arthur spent his childhood.

Soft golden sand is to be found at **Bosinney Cove** and **Benoath Cove** - havens for the bather and sun-worshipper.**Trebarwith Strand** with its sandy beach is a popular place for surfers. One needs to take care, the tide roars in here and it is not always safe.

Another castle that is worth seeing is **Launceston Castle** which dominates the market town of **Launceston**, and is an easy drive from either Tintagel or Boscastle. It is a small, busy town with friendly people and a wonderful parish church. Market day here is so busy, people come in from miles around including places like **North Petherwin** on the Bude road and **Lifton** just the other side of the Devon border going along the A30 towards Okehampton. Another place no distance away from Launceston is **Virginstowe** which you must seek out for its newly opened, superb restaurant with rooms, **Percy's.** An off shoot of one of the same in London it is a welcome advent to anyone who loves good food. **Camelford** closer to the coast and **Wadebridge** should both be on your visiting list. Between them they form the base of the triangle that takes in so many pretty places. I always enjoy the small village of **Port Isaac** with its charming, irregular steep streets with cottages that lead down to the harbour. It is a village that is the essence of a Cornish fishing port. The estuary of the River Camel divides **Rock** from **Padstow**. Each side of the estuary has its afficionados. One of the strange things about Rock is that it lost its church in the sand! Sand dunes on the banks of **Padstow Harbour** engulfed an ancient chapel and it was out of use for ages until the middle of the 19th century when it was restored. You can see it now as it stands on the sand with a fine view across to Padstow. **Padstow** has a charm of its own. It is a little town that has clung to its own ways and traditions for centuries.For most people Padstow will be synonymous with its curious May Day custom of welcoming summer with songs and dancing in the streets while a man in a mask dances in front of a **Hobby Horse.**

The National Trust own **Bedruthan Steps**. The climb down the steps is definitely demanding and worse on the way back but the reward far and away outweighs the puffing and panting of those of us more used to driving than walking.

Its not that I dislike **Newquay** that I am bypassing it this time. Purely a lack of space and this busy resort is known by everyone. It is an excellent place to stay with some of the best of Cornwall's many good beaches. Beloved by surfers and by those who like to take long walks acorss the cliffs and the beaches. A great place for a family holiday. I like some of the places nearby like**Trerice,** one of the few Elizabethan manor houses in Cornwall which have escaped extensive alterations. For 400 years the home of the Cornish Royalist Arundell family, this glorious house still retains most of its 16th century glass in the great hall window of twenty four lights, comprising 576 panes. It was acquired by the National Trust in 1953. **Perranporth** to the south with its sand dunes and vast beaches is always popular in the summer for family holidays and for day visitors especially at weekends.

St Ives provides a different vista and a different feel from the towns and villages we have just covered. It is the home of so many artists that it does not need me to paint in words how very attractive it is. It was much frequented by Whistler and Sickert who delighted in the light which has a high ultra violet content. The whole reach of **St Ives Bay** from **Navax Point** to **St Ives** is glorious. The sea always seems to be bluer here than anywhere else in Cornwall. The streets are narrow and it is the worst possible scenario for drivers. You are well advised to leave your car at **Lelant** and use the excellent Park and Ride service which operates with stops all along the bay. As you wander round the centre of St Ives you will find pretty aspects at every turn. Little houses jut out at funny angles and lead to other houses, until you have climbed steadily to **St Ives Head** under which the town snuggles, safely sheltered.

Hayle lies at the very beginning of St Ives Bay and for a long time has tried to shed its 'poor relation' image. Peter De Savery promised great reclamations for this little port but he withdrew in the main and now, less speedily than the people of Hayle would like, they are giving the whole place a great facelift themselves. It is a friendly spot and not a bad place to make your base for a holiday at this end of Cornwall.

Now we are approaching **Lands End** and the coast and hinterland change again. There are small villages like **Zennor** clinging to the cliff and further down **St Just** next, not to be confused with St Just in Roseland to which we will come shortly. Spring comes early here with the beauty of the hedgerows ablaze with wild flowers - autumn lingers and in winter, frost and snow are rare visitors. But the exhiliration of facing up to the Atlantic gales is an experience you are unlikely to forget!

Sennen is America's nearest neighbour! It stands high above the sea with a deep cove into which the sun hardly ever shines in winter. There is an odd story about the little medieval church. A great stone stands outside and round it seven Saxon Kings dined and wined, so the story goes, and then continues to say that when another seven kings dine here the end of the world will come!

Once I used to be filled with an enormous excitement when I stood at **Land's End**, the very end of Britain. There was nothing there then except the land and the sea beyond. Now it has a smart hotel, endless attractions and restaurants - not the same at all.

If you take to the lanes from Penzance and drive to the coast a few miles away you will reach **Porthcurno, St Levan** and **Lamorna** right by the sea and so beautiful. Take a look at **Paul**, the last village in Cornwall to speak the Cornish language back in the early 1700's. Winding roads lead to the fishing village of **Newlyn**, beloved by artists and then to **Penzance**. This is a nice old town with a busy port and wide promenade. **The Scillonian** sails daily for the **Scilly Isles**, twenty eight miles south west of Lands End. Directly in front of the fishing village of **Marazion** is **St Michaels Mount** rising out of the sea in **Mounts Bay**. Originally the site of a Benedictine Chapel established by Edward the Confessor, this spectacular castle dates from the 14th-century. To get there you can walk across from Marazion when the tide is out, or during the summer months take the ferry at high tide. It is a wonderful experience and the gardens which seem to grow out of the rock, are unique. Because of the narrow passages within the castle, it is necessary to limit the number of visitors at any one time.

The Lizard will be our next port of call but en route one should take a look at **Helston**, famous for the annual Floral Dance which is performed through the town rather like the Hobby Horse in Padstow on the north coast. The Royal Navy have a presence at Helston. The air station at **Culdrose** is home to several squadrons of helicopters and it is a rare day when you do not see these ungainly creatures of the air, landing and taking off. The skill of the pilots is unmatched. Many a sailor and visitor has been saved from certain death by the efficiency of their rescue skills and their bravery.

It would be sad not to visit the remote and wildly beautiful villages of **Manaccan, St Keverne,** and **Coverack.** Manaccan hides itelf in its hilly slopes. No matter which way you approach it you have to come down or climb up hills. Indeed the whole coastline of The Lizard is on the descent. One incline goes to St Keverne, another down the pretty valley to **Gillian Creek** and yet another to the **Helford River.**

The sea has never been kind to St Keverne and if you wander in the churchyard you will see graves of 400 people who have drowned off this shore in ships brought to their doom on the dreaded **Manacles.** On a calm summer's day when the sea is a brilliant blue and the little church surrounded by palms and hydrangeas, it is hard to conjure up the harshness of this piece of the coast in the height of a storm. But be there when a storm is raging and you will never again doubt the power of the ocean. **Coverack** is more sheltered and is charming. From there you need to go inland a bit to pick up the lanes that will lead you down to **Ruan Minor** and **Cadgwith**, two delightful spots. I almost forgot **Mullion** which has graves of some Ancient Britons on the downs above the cove. The cove itself is enchanting and has an impressive cavern and the striking **Lion Rock**.

Falmouth and **Truro** have not always seen eye to eye. In 1663 Truro was punished for its role in the Civil War and the whole river from **Tregothan Boathouse** was given to the new Co-operative of Falmouth. It was hard on Truro and it took from then until 1709 to assert its rights over Falmouth harbour, a claim strongly contested by Falmouth, which was by then a port of some consequence and saw no reason for Truro to have any say in the matter. It took the courts to settle the matter. Each today is a delightful place in its own right. **Truro** is the county town of Cornwall and with its fine cathedral attracts many a visitor. The cathedral is not all that old, it celebrated its centenary only in the last decade. It gives the appearance of having been there for ever and certainly creates a focal point for the city. If you can take a short while to sit within its walls, taking stock of life, you will find it rewarding. You may be lucky enough to have chosen a time when evensong is being sung by the splendid choir. The music soars into the rafters and the whole church is uplifted.

Almost up the road from Truro on the west coast is **St Agnes**, a quiet place with a delightful cove unusual in shape and ideal for a family picnic. From Truro, the rivers leading to the great **Carrick Roads** wander through some of the most beautiful scenery in the world. There are pleasure boats that will take you on a voyage of discovery that is a never ending delight, right the way down to **Falmouth** and **St Mawes**.

Inland the road from Truro to St Mawes is almost like trying to find the pot of gold at the end of a rainbow. You seem to drive forever, sometimes through sumptuous scenery. And at others indifferent, in the way that Cornwall has of teasing those who seek to know all about her. Finally, less than twelve miles from Truro you are rewarded by sought for treasure, **St Mawes**. Everything is beautiful here, the glory of the sea, the majesty of **St Mawes Castle**, and it is surrounded by the villages of **The Roseland**. No nothing to do with roses. In this instance Roseland means promontory or commonland.

St Just in Roseland is a famous beauty spot with its pretty church nestling against the banks of the river. It has curious stones inscribed with slightly mawkish sentiments lining the steep path through the churchyard down to the church. I heard it described once as 'the sort of churchyard one would be happy to be buried in'. The church is open daily and I would list it as a must for visitors.

On the other side of the Fal, **Pendennis Castle** guards the entrance to the Carrick Roads as it has done, together with **St Mawes Castle**, for hundreds of years. Both castles can be visited. The easy way to get across the river to **Falmouth** is to take the little passenger ferry or go further up the river and take your car across on the King Harry Ferry. The road from there will take you via **Perranorworthal** to Falmouth. From here you are within easy reach of the enchanting inlets of **Feock, Mylor,** and **Restronguet.** Wonderful places in which to wander and spend the most contented of days.

En route for Falmouth you will come to **Penryn**, now by-passed but it does not like being missed out. It always seems to me that it is resentful of Falmouth and puts on a sombre forbidding air. It is far older than Falmouth whom it considers a modern upstart but the problem really lies in the fact that Falmouth became the chosen port and they would not be far wrong, a fact only denied by the seafarers who have used the haven of the Carrick Roads for centuries. Tourism is clearly very important to **Falmouth** but for all that the town is a very busy port with ship repairing facilities and a dry dock which is capable of taking vessels up to 90,000 tons. It is a pleasant town with lovely gardens, beautiful beaches and a climate which permits palm trees to grow.

Before we go inland and take a look at **Camborne** and **Redruth**, lets take the A30 a little north of Redruth and seek the turning for **Chacewater**. It lies in the heart of the Cornish mines - most no longer working - and had the richest vein of copper in the world. It can boast the first steam pumping engine in a Cornish mine, made by James Watt. Today Chacewater is a pleasant rural village with some nice houses and a fine old pub **The Rambling Miner** in Fore Street. From the village it is simple to visit the famous **Wheal Jane** mine and the entrancing **Blissoe Valley.**

Camborne is famous world wide for its School of Mines but apart from that it is a busy market town. The fine medieval church is well worth visiting with a churchyard crammed full of interesting gravestones many with entertaining epitaphs. Near Camborne is **Magor Farm** where in this century, ruins of a Roman villa were found.

Redruth is almost joined to Camborne these days but it still has its separate existence. William Murdoch lived in one of the plain little houses here. It was he who gave us gas light and invented the locomotive. A Scot by birth he married a Redruth girl and it was their house which had the very first gaslight in the whole of the country.

If you find the tin-mining industry interesting, you will not want to miss **Cornish Engines** at **East Pool.** Here there are impressive relics of these great beam engines which were used for pumping water from over 2,000ft deep, and for winding men and ore. The engines exemplify the use of high pressure steam patented by the Cornish engineer, Richard Trevithick of Camborne in 1802. It is open Good Friday to the end of October, daily from 11-6pm or sunset if earlier.

High above Redruth stands **Carn Brea Castle,** silhouetted against the sky, and near it is a great column in memory of Francis Basset who did so much for Cornish miners. It is worthwhile making the effort to climb up the inside stairway of this monument which stands 90ft high. From the top you get the most amazing view of the whole of this mining area and the sight of more coastline than anywhere in the county.

Where did miners go if they had free time? **Gwennap Pit**. This was the place where they would listen to the stirring oratory of John Wesley preaching in this naturally tiered open-aired ampitheatre. In my imagination I can hear the great sound of the Wesley hymns resounding around the place from the glorious Cornish voices. John Wesley converted the Cornish to Methodism in their thousands.

St Austell is one of the busiest towns in Cornwall. It does not have a great deal to offer the visitor other than its fine church which stands among palm trees, rising from a beautifully manicured lawn, right in the heart of the town opposite the premier hostelry **The White Hart**. It has a tower well over five centuries old but the church's rarest possession is its massive Norman font with a bowl carved with extraordinary creatures and resting on columns ending in human faces.

As a base for a holiday St Austell is excellent because there are so many stunning places within easy reach.**Mevagissey** in **St Austell Bay**, is the largest fishing port in the bay and probably one of the most photographed harbours in Cornwall. Colourful fishing boats still sail out from here and nothing can take away the charm of the whitewashed cottages as they cling to the steep sides of the roads to Fore Street, where attractive shops flank the inner harbour. **Gorran Churchtown** should not be missed. Just one and a half miles from Mevagissey. It has a pub,**The Barleysheaf**, built in 1837 by a Mr Kendall who, hearsay states, had it erected for his own use because he was barred from every other hostelry in the area! You are close here to the wild headland that sailors call **The Dodman** with its 550 years old tower, a massive structure rising 110ft; a famous landmark from the sea.

Fowey with its spectacular harbour is a place of discovery; narrow winding streets where flower decked houses and cottages jostle side by side with quaint little shops and pubs on the hillside that slopes down to the glory of the Fowey river. From the days of pirates and smugglers with their barges and brigantines brazenly at moorings, to the hundreds of colourful craft that now fill what is undoubtedly one of the most enchanting harbours in this country, time has changed very little.

Rising in Bodmin Moor, the River Fowey has always been the life-blood of those towns and villages through which it flows on its way to the open sea at St Austell Bay. Directly oppositeFowey and reached by a ferry is **Bodinnick** and at its heart is **The Old Ferry Inn** which has one of the world's most picturesque views from its lounge right over the estuary, past Fowey and Polruan to the sea. It is a great place to stay and full of the atmosphere built up over the four hundred years of its existence.

I am always drawn to the small, and so far unspoilt, harbour village of **Charlestown** where the tiny entrance to the harbour defies belief that any vessel of size, let alone the big clay carrying ships can enter its sheltering arms, but they do and demonstrate this every day. It is the home of the **Shipwreck Museum** which is Britain's biggest exhibition of shipwreck artefacts.

Lostwithiel may not appeal to you because of its rather uninteresting main street but do not judge it by this. Explore this little town on foot and you will find much to please you. The majesty of the ruins of **Restormel Castle** watch over the town. The Castle is a delightful place to be, the ruins enhanced by magnificent rhododendrons, trees and shrubs. Built in the 13th century it was a ruin by the 16th. Lostwithiel was strongly Royalist **in** the Civil War and legend has it that Charles II was hidden in an oak at **Boconnoc**, hence the name of the excellent pub in Duke Street, **The Royal Oak**. Lostwithiel was once the capital of Cornwall. It is an ancient borough with a working community who will tell you that they do not put on a special face for holiday makers for a few weeks in the year, but aim to give the same friendly welcome all year round. It is an excellent centre for fishing, walking or just relaxing and enjoying the Cornish countryside. The 13th century church of St Bartholomew is worth a visit.

From Lostwithiel the river continues meandering past the lovely little church of **St Winnow** on the east bank, which dates mainly from the 15th century, although there are some remains of Norman and 13th century architecture. A little further on is the creek that leads up to the pretty waterside village of **Lerryn**, where once sailing ships came to discharge their cargoes of road-stone from the quarries at **St Germans**. Now it is so silted up that you must keep a watchful eye on the tide if you are water-borne. It might be worth being stranded if it gave you the opportunity to visit **The Ship Inn**, a delightful hostelry with good food, good beer and good company.

On the west bank is an even smaller village, **Golant**, much beloved by small boat owners. They come to enjoy the sailing but also to visit **The Fisherman's Arms** which you will find at the end of a road marked 'Road liable to flooding at high tide'. The pub overlooks the water but it is out of harm's way - even the pavement is 2ft high!

Almost in the centre of Cornwall is the old county town of **Bodmin** and if you take the road from St Austell to the town you will go through English China Clay country. Go via **Nanpean** and **Carthew** and you will come to **Wheal Martyn Museum**. This will give you an unforgettable insight into Cornwall's single largest industry. Great white, eerie mountains appear on all sides, evidence of the industry that has provided so much of Cornwall's employment. In Bodmin, the handsome church of **St Petrock** delights all who see it. It is the biggest in the county, 151ft long and 65ft wide. Mainly 15th century it has been much restored. On **Beacon Hill**, looking down on the town, is a column of granite rising 144ft high. It is in memory of Sir Walter Raleigh Gilbert, a brave soldier, and belonging to the family of Sir Humphrey Gilbert who was the step-brother of Sir Walter Raleigh. Bodmin has a lot to offer including **The Bodmin and Wenford Railway** which allows you to explore some of Cornwall's finest countryside from a steam-hauled Branch Line train. **The Light Infantry Museum** is opposite the station and **Bodmin Town Museum** is a short walk away from the town centre. **The Camel Trail** paths to Wadebridge and Padstow start near the historic Bodmin Goal.

Just outside Bodmin is **Washaway** where you will find **Pencarrow House**, the home of the Molesworth family and has been so since it was completed by Sir John Molesworth, the 5th baronet about 1770. Essentially a family home, it is a delight to explore. For Gilbert and Sullivan fans it is interesting to know that Sir Arthur Sullivan composed the music for Iolanthe here. The Pencarrow Gardens cover some 50acres. Huge rhododendrons and camellias provide a wonderful display every Spring. There are several gardens within striking distance from here which should not be missed. At **Prideaux Place,Padstow**, there is a deer park and a newly restored garden overlooking the Camel estuary. **Lanhydrock** has rare trees and shrubs, the unique circular herbaceous garden and exceptional magnolias. **Lancarffe** at Bodmin has four and a half acres of sheer beauty and then there is the fabulous **Longcross Victorian Gardens** at**Trelights**, near Port Isaac, which is open all the year round from 10.30am until dusk. It has fascinating maze type walkways and one of the best cream teas anywhere.

One should always take a look at the many small villages virtually encircling Bodmin, **St Tudy** off the main Launceston road for one and on the other side **Lanlivery** which one used to pass on the main road and today it has reverted to a quiet backwater - an ideal spot in which to stay.

Had we started this tour of Cornwall from **Plymouth** crossing by the **Torpoint Ferry** we would have had a pleasant run through the small town of **Torpoint** and then on to **Anthony**, a small hamlet really which has a pub, **The Ring of Bells** in which the Duke of Edinburgh used to play skittles before his marriage. It also has one of the nicest, small stately homes, **Anthony House**, now belonging to the National Trust but also the family home of the Pole-Carews. Open to the public it is a pleasure to spend time there both in the house and the gardens which reach down to the River Tamar The ferry route takes you through leafy roads with offshoots to all sorts of villages including **Deviock** where there are two interesting places to stay. Reach the coast road and it will lead you to the small seaside villages of **Downderry** and **Seaton**..

The traffic from the ferry and from the **Tamar Bridge** which has made entering Cornwall so much easier, meet at **Trerulefoot**, having by-passed **Saltash** en route and passed the turn to the right which would have led you past the championship Golf course at **St Mellion** and thence to **Callington**, a small town at the cross roads between Dartmoor and the west coast. At Trerulefoot maybe you would have decided to carry on deeper into the county but for our journey we are cutting off to the east and through the pretty **Hessenford Valley** until you reach the quaint fishing villages of **East** and **West Looe**. Here the river meets the sea, picturesque houses climb the steep hills, fishermen set sail every day in their colourful boats and visitors set out with some of them to go shark fishing. For the less adventurous Looe itself is fascinating, full of good pubs, sandy beaches and a plethora of hotels from which to choose if you should decide to stay. If you drove out of Looe towards **Liskeard** you would have a short, but delightful drive arriving in another small town which has benefitted enormously from being by-passed. It has a big square, a market, lots of odd, wandering streets and some good hostelries. From Liskeard you might well go out towards **Sibleyback Lake,** the haunt of anglers or perhaps to one of the small villages like **St Neots** where **The London Inn** is where locals meet for good ale and visitors come to enjoy the banter and the good pub food.. The great thing about Liskeard is its central position allowing one to take off for almost anywhere in Cornwall.

Across the old bridge which divides East and West Looe you will find the road that will lead you to **Talland Bay**, surely the most beautiful stretch of smuggling coast in Cornwall! And from there on to the little fishing village of **Polperro** which is a visitor's dream come true. So small are thestreets that you have to leave your car at the top but the reward is a journey that will take you between houses that almost touch each other. They are quaint as are the shops and the pubs. Every road leads to the harbour and if one had to talk about somewhere that paints the picture of what the visitor imagines Cornwall is all about then **Polperro** has to be that place.

CLIFT HOUSE,
Beside the Lynher Estuary,
Cornwall.

Contact : ***HELPFUL HOLIDAYS***
COOMBE, CHAGFORD,
DEVON TQ13 8DF.
TEL : 01647 433593
FAX : 01647 433694

Clift House is a beautiful ancient farmhouse on the edge of the stunning Lynher Estuary, with breathtaking vistas over the surrounding countryside, and perfect peace and tranquillity! It is furnished with antique and reproduction furniture throughout, and is a house of enormous character and warmth. There are low beamed ceilings, eccentric staircases, marvellous granite fireplaces, lovely studded ancient wooden doors, and huge rooms. Everything you could wish for is here! Along with all this antiquity is the modern conveniences that make this a pleasure to live in - three lovely bathrooms, shower, sauna and jacuzzi are there for your comfort. The kitchen facilities are just as luxurious with a four-oven Aga, microwave, dishwasher and almost every necessity you could think of. The lounge is charming with a flagstone floor covered in scatter rugs, a huge stone fireplace with woodburner, piano, TV, video, CD player....the list goes on and on! A games room with table tennis, a half size snooker table and various other games are here too! If you actually decide you ever want to leave this wonderful house, there is a boat for use on the river, and a terraced lawn with a barbecue for those balmy summer evenings. Stroll through the orchard and exalt in the beauty and serenity that surrounds you without even leaving the grounds.

USEFUL INFORMATION

OPEN : *All year*
CHILDREN : *Welcome*
PETS : *Welcome*
CREDIT CARDS : *All major*

SELF CATERING
DISABLED ACCESS : *No*
GARDEN : *Extensive*
ACCOMMODATION : *5 bedrooms*

DOVECOT COTTAGE,
Ashwater,
Devon EX21 5DF.
Tel : 01409 211224

Dovecot Cottage is a small converted 17th century stable set in the grounds of Blagdon Manor Country Hotel. The accommodation suits up to four guests and is beautifully furnished and decorated. There is a double bedroom featuring stone walls, beams and pastel colours, a twin bedroom, bathroom with shower and bath, lounge, and a brightly coloured kitchen furnished in pine. The cottage is fully centrally heated, and has all essential facilities. Pets are welcome, and children can be easily entertained with a theme park being close by.

The hotel grounds offer 20 acres of beautiful gardens, where croquet and practice golf are both available. There are beautiful views of the Devonshire countryside, and in addition the grounds hold a trout lake and an orchard. The cottage is approximately 30 metres from the hotel and guests of the cottage can enjoy the lawn and orchard to its rear. A takeaway menu is available from the hotel, with food being ordered by phone and delivered to the cottage. This is the ideal spot to relax, with easy access to many National Trust properties, beautiful beaches and many quaint fishing villages to explore.

USEFUL INFORMATION

OPEN : *All year*
CHILDREN : *Welcome*
PETS : *Welcome*
ACCOMMODATION : *Up to 4 guests.*
SELF CATERING : *Takeaway service*
DISABLED ACCESS : *No*
CREDIT CARDS : *All major*

HUMES FARM COTTAGES
Bradiford Cottage, Barnstaple,
Devon EX31 4DP
Tel: 01271 45039

A selection of tastefully furnished and decorated cottages, each individually marked with its own English Tourist Board award, 3 or 4 Keys Commended or Highly Commended, makes a wonderful base to explore the countryside and coastline of North Devon, renowned for its impressive and inspiring scenery. Bright and airy and equipped to an exacting standard, the cottages cater for between 2 to 12 persons. Kitchens are afforded gas hobs/electric cookers, fridge/freezer and microwave, most with washer/tumble dryers. Each has its own lawned garden complete with picnic table and garden furniture. Humes Farm dates back to the 17th century and stands amid 8 acres, with an old millstream running through the grounds. Peace, tranquillity and relaxation are assured in this delightful setting.

USEFUL INFORMATION

OPEN; *All year*
CHILDREN; *Yes*
CREDIT CARDS; *None taken*
ACCOMMODATION; *A range of self-catering cottages, sleeping between 2 and 12 persons*
DISABLED ACCESS; *No*
GARDEN; *Yes, all properties have lawned area with picnic table and chairs*
PETS; *Yes by prior arrangement*

GARLANDS
Stovar Long Lane, Beer,
Devon EX12 3EA

Tel: 01297 20958
Fax: 01279 23869

Garlands is an excellent Edwardian house just outside the village of Beer. With views over the sea and Devonshire countryside, this is really an idyllic spot. Adjoining the main house is a self-catering cottage which has one double ensuite bedroom and there are bunk beds available for children if required. There is a lovely fitted kitchen equipped with all you will need. A lounge with colour TV. All bed linen, towels, heating and lighting are included. You are more than welcome to use the Garlands facilities such as payphone and dining, for this you will be charged separately. You are within walking distance of the beach and there are many local pursuits available. This is quite a spectacular stretch of coastline and with the standard of accommodation, well worth a visit.

USEFUL INFORMATION

OPEN: *All year*
CHILDREN: *Welcome*
CREDIT CARDS: *All major taken*
LICENSED: *Residents*
ACCOMMODATION: *Self-contained cottage*

DINING ROOM: *Good choice, 3 course evening meal*
VEGETARIAN: *By arrangement*
DISABLED ACCESS: *No*
GARDEN: *Complete access*
PETS: *Dogs by arrangement*

HELMAN TOR COTTAGES
Lanlivery,
Bodmin,
Cornwall PL30 5HT

Tel: 01208 872372

The five holiday cottages on this wonderful farm have been carefully converted from a range of old granite farm buildings which date back to the 1860s. The cottages are separated from the rest of the farm by a low wall and have their own car park and entrance lawn. Although there is easy access to both North and South coasts and to many of Cornwall's attractions, I believe you will not want to leave the 200 acres of this farm. There is an archeological site dating back to Neolithic times and a Bronze Age Hut Circle; there are Exmoor ponies, there are goats, there are ewes, there are wild flowers managed in conjunction with the Countryside Commission. Gill and Des Girdler are to be highly commended on this idyllic location which they have nurtured.

USEFUL INFORMATION

OPEN; *All year*
CHILDREN; *Welcome*
CREDIT CARDS; *None taken*
LICENSED; *No*
ACCOMMODATION; *Self-catering cottages*

RESTAURANT; *Not applicable*
VEGETARIAN; *Not applicable*
DISABLED ACCESS; *Some, with restrictions*
GARDEN; *Not applicable*

WEBBERY GARDEN COTTAGES,
Webbery, Alverdiscott,
Bideford, Devon EX39 4PU
Tel: 01271 858430
Fax: 01271 858314

For the artist, the writer or just simply those who long for peace, there can be no more delightful place in North Devon than Webbery Garden Cottages. Whatever the season it is a magical spot. Webbery is a place that time has passed by. Recorded in the Domesday Book as being given to Nicholas the Crossbowman, Webbery has developed a unique tranquility over the centuries which is apparent to everyone who comes here. There are nearly five acres of woodland and garden with the Victorian walled garden as the centre piece of the grounds. Within these walls, no artificial fertilisers have ever been used and guests can see superb produce (available for sale in season) together with rare varieties of fruit trees, and even a small vineyard.

Situated just three miles from the old picturesque port of Bideford and within easy reach of the unsurpassed beaches at Saunton and Croyde, close to Instow, one of the best sailing centres in the South West and with many exciting other places to visit, Webbery Garden Cottages offer everything for those wanting to enjoy an idyllic self-catering holiday. There are woodland walks, coastal trails, Exmoor's wildness, championship golf, cycling and walking on the Tarka Trail, all close at hand. On the lawn in front of the arbour you can play croquet, or badminton by the walled garden or perhaps just settle down with a glass of wine and a good book. The summer is perfect but the other seasons bring their own delights.

There are three cottages. The Apple Cottage was once an apple loft and cider house which has now been converted into a self-contained cottage, ideal for a family and sleeping six. It overlooks the walled garden and paddock to Webbery Wood and beyond. Crossbow and Longbow cottages have been created from the old Coach House of Webbery Manor and overlook the gardens with views towards Lundy Island in the distance. These two cottages offer stylish accommodation for the smaller family or group, each sleeping four people in two bedrooms, one double bedded room and one with bunk beds. All three cottages are beautifully furnished to a high standard, and are all equipped with fitted carpets, electric cooker, refrigerator, microwave cooker, colour television, toaster, clock radio etc. The Apple Cottage has full central heating whilst the other two keep beautifully warm in winter with electric fires and heaters in all main rooms. Laundry facilities are provided (small charge), and a deep freeze is available for guests' own food. A cot and high chair are available. You will probably prefer to bring your own towels and bed linen, but sheets, pillow cases and duvet covers can be hired from the owner, Mrs Wilson. This helpful lady also supplies an information board and brochures about local attractions.

USEFUL INFORMATION

OPEN:*All year*
CREDIT CARDS;*None taken*
ACCOMMODATION; *Three cottages sleeping 6, 4 & 4*
CHILDREN; *Welcome*
DISABLED ACCESS;*Not suitable*
GARDEN; *Beautiful with croquet*
PETS; *By arrangement*
LOW SEASON; *Short breaks at special terms. 'Couples only' tariff*

2 BELOW CHAPEL,
Blackawton,
Totnes, TQ9 7BN.

Tel : 01803 712409

Sue and Chris Wills are the proprietors of this fine, self catering cottage situated on a country road on the edge of Blackawton village. The cottage is an old semi detached (1700 circa) property with Sue and Chris living next door on hand if needed. It is very picturesque, with colourful hanging baskets in season and a lovely garden with views down the valley to the sea.

A barbecue is there for your use, and is an excellent way to spend those balmy summer evenings, after a day's exploring. The cottage has two double bedrooms with an additional single bed on the landing, partitioned by a curtain, giving plenty of privacy.

There is a sitting room with a multi burner - splendid if you visit in the winter when the weather is cooler- and a dining room next to a well equipped kitchen which caters to all necessities. The house is centrally heated throughout and is fully carpeted. All rooms are very tastefully furnished and ensure a high degree of comfort. Sue and Chris offer an unusual service in that if you wish, they will drive you to and from the local pub.

This is an excellent idea and shows the depth of hospitality of the Devon people. They also offer a babysitting service if perhaps you want that quiet evening away from the children. There are some good restaurants locally which Sue and Chris are only too happy to recommend, and they can also be a good source of information on local activities.

Further afield you have Dartmoor, Torbay and the towns and beaches of the beautiful South Hams. This is a great location with plenty of activities if you wish, but also with the peace and tranquillity of a small Devon village in a beautiful part of the country.

***To find us** :From Totnes, follow the Kingsbridge to Dartmouth road until you reach the village of Halwell, turn **left** at the village church following the sign for Dartmouth. After about 3 miles you will see the Forces Tavern on your left, you turn **right** and continue to a T-junction turn **right** again and after approx. 150m yards on will be the Normandy Arms, turn **left** where after a short distance (100 yards) is the Methodist Chapel. The cottage is beside it.*

USEFUL INFORMATION

***OPEN** : All year*
***CHILDREN** : Welcome*
***PETS** : Welcome under control*
***CREDIT CARDS** : None taken*
SELF CATERING
***DISABLED ACCESS** : No*
***GARDEN** : With BBQ*
***ACCOMMODATION** : 2 dble, 1 sgl.*
OFF ROAD PARKING

MENNABROOM COTTAGES
Warleggan, Bodmin,
Cornwall PL30 4HE

Tel: 01208 821272

Bodmin Moor is a wide open expanse of land, scattered with granite tors shaped by the weather, where time has stood still for generations. This beautiful rugged countryside is a popular tourist area; with the main A30 running through the centre it is easily accessible. If you head south along this road, shortly after passing Jamaica Inn, where Daphne du Maurier wrote her books, turn left signposted Colliford Lake Park, take the first right turn signposted Warleggan, and turn first left for Mennabroom Farm Cottages. Mennabroom is a medieval farmhouse, whose listed barns have been sympathetically converted to provide superior self-catering accommodation. The 3 cottages, which sleep between 2 and 6 persons, offer very comfortable living with all modern day conveniences of microwave oven, washing machine, colour television, tumble-dryer, etc. Cots and high chairs are available on request. All linen is provided but you are asked to bring your own cot bedding. Jenny and David Lucas have certainly made a delightful haven where one can relax and enjoy the peaceful seclusion; the English Tourist Board agree and have awarded Mennabroom with '3 Keys Commended'. Jenny is an excellent baker; she makes bread, cakes, jams and chutneys all available to guests. There are also seasonal salad vegetables from the farm and delicious free range eggs. You will find it very hard to pack at the end of your stay.

USEFUL INFORMATION

OPEN; *All year*
CHILDREN; *Welcome*
CREDIT CARDS; *None taken*
LICENSED; *Not applicable*
ACCOMMODATION; *3 Self-catering cottages*

DINING ROOM; *Not applicable*
DISABLED ACCESS; *No but welcome*
GARDEN; *Yes*
PETS; *Dogs welcome*

SKISDON,
St. Kew, Bodmin,
Cornwall PL30 3HB.
Tel : 01208 841372

This Grade II listed country house is divided into six self-contained apartments which provided excellent holiday accommodation all year round. It is in a quiet rural setting, only four miles form the coast, and is surrounded by beautiful gardens. Two streams meet within the very large gardens, and along with magnificent trees and shrubs, there are 10 acres of surrounding pasture and woodland.

The apartments are of varying sizes, and can cater for up to seven guests. All are well furnished and equipped, and some even allow access between apartments for the larger family. They have been very well thought out, and any further information required can be obtained from the owners, Tom and Sandy Chadwick.

USEFUL INFORMATION

OPEN : *All year*
CHILDREN : *Welcome*
CREDIT CARDS : *None taken*
ACCOMMODATION : *6 apartments; various sizes*
DISABLED ACCESS : *No, but each case considered, please phone for more details.*
GARDEN : *Yes*
PETS : *no*

HIGH PARK
Bradworthy,
Devon EX22 7SH
Tel: 01409 241492

Five acres of garden and grounds surround this elegant and refined Victorian house, home to Marilyn and Michael Cook, who it is obvious has ensured that all their guests are truly spoilt and pampered. The pristine bedrooms are bright and airy and very welcoming. Furnishings are modern with king size beds, colour TV and tea and coffee making facilities. Each room has a private bathroom and the added bliss of fluffy white bathrobes. Stunning views of the Devonshire countryside can be enjoyed from all rooms, and throughout vases full of fresh flowers and bowls of fruit are an absolute delight. Delicious breakfasts are a wonderful start to the day and these are beautifully presented, home cooked and plenty of it. Evening meals are optional but highly recommended. The English Nature Moorland area adjacent to High Park is teeming with wildlife including, badgers, fox, rabbits and many more. This haven is home to numerous species of birds who share this habitat with sheep, cows and ponies. Being situated close to the North Devon coast outdoor activities are plentiful, long stretches of golden beaches offer surfing, swimming, fishing and spectacular coastal walks. Golf courses are close by.

USEFUL INFORMATION

OPEN; *All year*
CHILDREN; *Welcome*
CREDIT CARDS; *None taken*
LICENSED; *No*
ACCOMMODATION; *3 ensuite rooms, 1 double, 1 twin, 1 single*
DINING ROOM; *Excellent home-cooked fare, Optional evening meal*
VEGETARIAN; *Catered for*
DISABLED ACCESS; *No, but welcome*
GARDEN; *Yes, large lawns*
PETS; *Dogs but not indoors, kennels available*

TREMORLE FARM,
St.Juliot, Boscastle,
Cornwall, PL35 0BU.
Tel : 01840 250233

There are four properties at Tremorle Farm, all English Tourist Board approved and fully equipped to either three or four Keys category. The setting for these properties is one of quiet, rural beauty with the advantage of the sea and countryside on your doorstep. The village of Boscastle is protected by the National Trust, and enjoys 14th century cottages and also the site of Bottreaux Castle. It is protected from the weather by the steep hillside behind it and the famous harbour is shielded by the spectacular cliffs. This is an area of stunning and dramatic beauty, and is an ideal haven for relaxation and leisure. There are many areas of interest to be found with fishing and birdwatching, walking, or just admiring the views, and as this is where much of Thomas Hardy's earlier works were based, it is interesting to see how little it has changed since his time. Originally an architect, the church at St.Juliot is where he met his wife, when he was awarded the job of restoring the little church, and it was 'love at first sight' upon meeting Emma Gifford. Together they wandered and explored the nearby countryside, and Hardy always considered this part of Cornwall as having a special magic. You can still feel this 'magic' and the vistas will have you reaching for your camera or even perhaps stringing a verse or two together yourself!

***East and West Wideacres** are two of the properties for letting, and are quietly situated in a country lane with charming sea and countryside views. The accommodation is for four or five persons, and each have a comfortable lounge/ diner with seaviews, a modern fitted kitchen, and with all the necessary fittings to make this a 'home from home'. There is plenty of parking space, a lawned garden at the front, and a further 'suntrap' area with picnic tables, shrubs and lawn at the other side.*

***The Old Dairy** is as the name states, a converted old dairy adjoining the farmhouse, and has views over the large front garden, and a patio. This accommodates two people (plus a cot if required), and offers superb furnishings and equipment. Beamed ceilings and exposed stone accentuate the character of this house and this is complimented by the pretty floral fabrics in curtains and cushions. Again, there are sea views from the end of the garden, and the tranquillity of the countryside is all around you.*

***Tresquare** is a large dormer bungalow about 200 yards from the village centre, and offers accommodation for eight people (again with cot). It is situated in a delightful lawned garden with views over the valley and is a peaceful refuge from the outside world. There is a large lounge with a Cornish stone open fireplace; ideal for those cooler evenings, and a pretty sun lounge where you can enjoy perhaps the winter sun on those late breaks. The kitchen/diner is a large room and has all the necessities included. There is an en suite double room on the ground floor, with a further double and a family room on the first floor. All are beautifully furnished and are perfectly equipped for guests.*

USEFUL INFORMATION

***OPEN :** All year*
***CHILDREN :** Welcome*
***PETS :** On application*
***ACCOMMODATION :** From 2 to 8 persons plus cot.*

SELF CATERING
***DISABLED ACCESS :** No*
***CREDIT CARDS :** None taken*

BRIGHTLAND HOLIDAY APARTMENTS

Maer Lane,
Crooklets,
Bude,
Cornwall EX23 9EE

Tel: 01288 352738

Brightland Apartments are set in beautiful countryside, a short distance from the beach and picturesque town of Bude. This part of Cornwall is close to the Devon border and has much to offer; from rugged cliffs and coastal walks to quaint villages and the haunting beauty of the moors. The people of Cornwall are as special as their views, with their friendly, open ways and helpfulness to visitors. Bude itself is a water sport haven and many a surfing competition can be seen here. The beaches are good and provide an ideal playground for all the family, with plenty of good shops, restaurants and pubs in the town. There are numerous things to do in this area, all the water sports you can imagine, historical houses, gardens, deep sea fishing, golf and who could go to Cornwall without taking a stroll along a coastal path on a warm Summer's evening? The Brightland apartments are self-catering and are Cornish Registered Accommodation, they are modern and of a very high standard, and all have large south facing windows giving spectacular views over National Trust countryside and the Maer Lake Nature Reserve. Twelve apartments are available, depending on your needs, and are equipped with all necessary appliances. A really wonderful place for all the family and definitely a good base from which to visit the rest of Cornwall.

USEFUL INFORMATION

OPEN; *All year*
CHILDREN; *Welcome*
CREDIT CARDS; *None taken*
LICENSED; *No*
ACCOMMODATION; *12 Self-catering apartments,*
BBQ facilities
PETS; *Welcome*

DINING ROOM; *Not applicable*
VEGETARIAN; *Not applicable*
DISABLED ACCESS; *By arrangement*
GARDEN; *Spacious and secluded, play area for the children overlooked by apartments*

FORDA HOLIDAY LODGES
Kilkhampton, Bude,
Cornwall EX23 9RZ
Tel/Fax: 01288 321413

Whatever you are looking for in a self-catering holiday in superb surroundings, Forda is the place at anytime of the year. The lodges are built on Scandinavian lines and are located to ensure maximum privacy. Delightful to look at, they have steeply pitched roofs, verandah and the cosy warm feeling of a decorative wood interior. Everything about Forda spells out peace and tranquillity and yet you are close to the frenetic excitement of the North Cornwall coast at Bude with its sandy beaches.

Forda is set in 17 acres of unspoilt countryside with an abundance of wild flowers, woods and meadowland, together with three lakes, which add to the beauty of the setting and provide excellent fishing. The Lodges are spacious, with an open plan living and dining area, fully equipped kitchen with fitted cupboards and work surfaces. Additional features include a prominent pine staircase and exposed beams which contribute to their warmth and quality. The lodges are heated by night storage heaters in the lounge and panel heaters in the bedrooms. Hair dryers are provided and there are no hidden extras, as electricity and linen are inclusive. For added convenience there is a separate launderette, with washing and drying facilities, together with electric iron, ironing board, and pay telephone. What more can you wish for?

USEFUL INFORMATION

OPEN: *All year*
CREDIT CARDS;*None taken*
ACCOMMODATION;*10 lodges*
CHILDREN;*Welcome*
DISABLED ACCESS;*No special facilities*
PETS;*Yes*

VENTERDON HOUSE
Venterdon, Callington,
Cornwall PL17 8PD
Tel: 01579 370179

Self-catering accommodation here in a newly converted three bedroomed Grade II Listed Barn on three levels. The Barn sleeps six comfortably in 2 double rooms and a twin bedded room, a cot is also available. Fully furnished in an antique cottage style in 1996. It has been done with great style and taste and much thought has gone into equipping the accommodation with everything needed to make a self-catering holiday a success, including a TV and video for wet days. The Listed attached main house dates from 1684 and is full of interest, as is the barn. The attractive garden with a well and fishponds is a sun trap, children are very welcome but dogs and other pets, regretfully, not. The barn is not suitable for disabled persons. The area surrounding Venterdon has the moors in one direction and the coast on the other, you can fish, walk on the moors, ride and take advantage of the specialist guided tours.

USEFUL INFORMATION

OPEN: *All year*
CHILDREN: *Welcome*
CREDIT CARDS: *None taken*
ACCOMMODATION: *Self-catering barn*
DISABLED ACCESS: *No*
GARDEN: *Yes*
PETS: *No*
NO SMOKING

HOUNDAPITT FARM COTTAGES
Sandymouth, Bude,
Cornwall EX23 9HW

Tel: 01288 355455

Houndapitt Farm Cottages are delightful, the 9 cottages which sleep 2-6, and one farmhouse which sleeps 9, have been converted from 200 year old Cornish stone barns, arranged around a central courtyard full of hanging baskets and pots which form a riot of colour. The cottages are beautifully decorated and furnished and are equipped to a very high standard with everything you should need, microwave, fridge with freezer compartment, toaster and coffee maker, some even have a dishwasher. The sitting areas have colour T.V. and video. The bedrooms all have matching linens and are made up before your arrival. The bathrooms have a shower, bath or both depending on the cottage, towels are not supplied.

There is a complimentary welcome tray with eggs, tea, coffee and milk. A fully equipped laundry is also available. The children are well catered for with their own safe play area which consists of a large trampoline, Wendy house, see-saw, swings and a giant slide. There is also a Pets Corner with several small animals and supervised pony rides. Fisherman will be in their element as nearby is a well stocked lake with carp, golden tench and golden rudd. Each week there is supervised clay pigeon shooting. Within 10 minutes of the farm is Sandymouth Beach with little rock pools and lovely golden sands. Houndapitt is a working 154 acre farm rearing cattle and sheep and is worked by the Heard family. It is situated in a lovely part of Cornwall with glorious scenery and lots of things to do play golf, go fishing, riding, walking, just right for a superb holiday.

USEFUL INFORMATION

OPEN: *All year*
CHILDREN: *Welcome*
CREDIT CARDS: *None taken*
ACCOMMODATION: *9 cottages, 1 farmhouse*

DISABLED ACCESS: *No*
PETS: *No*
GARDEN: *Yes*
PARKING: *One for each cottage Three for the farmhouse*

LANGFIELD MANOR
Bude,
Cornwall EX23 8DP

Tel: 01288 352415

Langfield Manor run by Ann and Trevor Farbrother, is a fine Edwardian house siting in about an acre of delightful, sheltered, south facing gardens.

The house has been carefully turned into seven individual, self catering apartments which cater for between two and six persons. Each apartment has it's own lounge/dining area and a fully equipped kitchen. There is a bar, for residents use, which is open most evenings, and a recreation room which includes a full size snooker table. Outside, the solar heated swimming pool is a great gathering place and the patio and gardens are a real suntrap, ideal for sunbathing or watching the great variety of bird life. This is a very informal place and has a great family atmosphere. With various pleasant fun evenings planned you cannot but make friends amongst the other guests (or perhaps renew accquaintances from the previous year!) There is a BBQ most summer Friday nights and this is just like a house party.

Bude has some of the finest beaches in Cornwall and the coastal walks are superb. For those who would rather be in the sea there is every watersport imaginable, from surfing, water skiing, sailing to fishing. There is a tropical leisure pool in the town for those who like it a little warmer! Golf, horse riding, bowling and much more is on your doorstep.

Bude is a thriving seaside town with much to offer the visitor. The shops keep late hours and the variety is excellent. There are numerous restaurants to suit any pocket and pubs where you can choose to be entertained or just have a quiet drink.

People always talk about the quality of light in Cornwall. It is something to do with the lower sun shining through the clean air from the Atlantic. Spring seems to come earlier, and autumn later, so this is the perfect place to take a late or early break. The climate is mild and the way of life unhurried. The friendly locals will always be happy to 'yarn' and you can enjoy a drink in front of a roaring open fire. Many attractions are still open and Langfield Manor caters for it's guests all year round.

USEFUL INFORMATION

OPEN: *All year*
CHILDREN : *Welcome*
PETS : *Welcome*
ACCOMMODATION : *Self catering.*

DISABLED ACCESS *: No*
CREDIT CARDS : *None taken*
GARDEN : *Spacious with heated pool*

MINESHOP HOLIDAY COTTAGES
Crackington Haven, Nr Bude,
Cornwall EX23 0NR

Tel: 01840 230338

The area between Bude and Boscastle is one of first-class sandy beaches, where the Atlantic rollers give superb conditions for surfing, and the children can play safely in rock pools and build those all important sand castles. This stretch of coast line is an area designated as outstanding natural beauty, and certainly one of the best places to have a holiday. It is along this coast that Mr. & Mrs. Cummins and Mr. & Mrs. Tippet have their self-catering cottages. There are several to choose from, all are exceptionally well appointed, comfortable and warm.

***Mineshop Bungalows** are 6 detached bungalows a mile from the beach at Crackington Haven and 9 miles from Bude with its shops, pubs and restaurants, and stand in approximately 14 acres of the peaceful wooded valley. Each bungalow is double glazed and has a patio or balcony with garden furniture. The interiors have been well thought out, with an open plan living room, colour television, night storage heaters, fully fitted kitchen, one double bedroom, and one bedroom with bunk beds which can be converted into single beds, bathroom and WC. For your convenience there is an iron and ironing board and vacuum cleaner. Three of the bungalows sleep 4, and the other three sleep 6 using a double stand-*

*easy bed. A shared laundry room serves all the **Mineshop Cottages**. You are sure to feel very relaxed in **The Old Smithy**, an idyllic one-storey cottage standing on the banks of a stream, with its own parking space, lawn and private paved area for sitting out. The same goes for **The Old Shippon**, another one-storey cottage, with a door from the sitting room leading onto a paved area and lawn beyond. Both cottages are very well equipped to cater for your needs, peaceful and cosy.*

***Millook House** and **Little Millook Cottages,** 100 yards from a pebble beach, are superb, very tastefully decorated and furnished including multi-fuel wood burners, night heaters, colour television, comfy seating, and kitchens equipped with washer/dryers and microwave, sleeping 6 and 8 persons. **Strawberry Cottage,** so named as it stands in old strawberry fields at Mineshop, is a delightful modern one-storey cottage, sleeping 8 in comfort. Cancleave, also sleeps 8, stands in half an acre of rough lawned garden surrounded by fields and cliff land, with stunning views across Bude Bay. A footpath, definitely for the young and fit, leads down to the pebble beach. The interiors of both these cottages are excellent, with everything to make your stay comfortable and pleasant.*

Whichever cottage you choose, you will be staying in superior accommodation, in the most idyllic surroundings. Once you have stayed here, you will definitely want to return.

USEFUL INFORMATION

OPEN; *Mid Feb-end Dec*
CHILDREN; *Welcome*
CREDIT CARDS; *None taken*
PETS; *At extra cost. Well behaved dogs must be kept under control*

ACCOMMODATION; *Superior self-catering cottages sleeping between 4 to 8 persons. Bed linen is supplied in all cottages except Millook House, Little Millook and Cancleave. Electricity is by meter using £1 coins*

THE BULLERS ARMS HOTEL
Marhamchurch, Bude,
Cornwall EX23 0HB

Tel: 01288 361277
Fax: 01288 361541

Guests at the Bullers Arms Hotel at Marhamchurch have the choice of opting for self-catering suites or a serviced bedroom with ensuite facilities. In either case you will be delighted at the attention given to detail in ensuring your stay will be one to remember. Rooms are spacious and comfortable, with quality furnishings and a decor pleasing to the eye. 'The Bullers' as it is called by the locals, is renowned for its fine cuisine, which is reflected in the busy day to day life of the Hunters Bar and Restaurant offering an A La Carte menu at reasonable cost. Bar meals are available and a traditional Sunday roast is served every Sunday at noon. Also on offer is an extensive range of vegetarian dishes. The 'Redvers' function room is a banqueting suite catering for weddings, parties, dances or conferences and no need to drive home afterwards. The magnificent beaches of Widemouth Bay and Bude are 2 miles from the Bullers and boast some of the safest bathing and surfing in the area. There are wonderful coastal and country walks, one of which leads from the Hotel, via the canal towpath, through a nature reserve to the sea at Bude. Horse riding, fishing, cycling and golf at Bude, Holsworthy and Launceston are also favourite pastimes in this area.

USEFUL INFORMATION

OPEN; *All year. Summer-all day. Winter-closed between 3 & 6pm*
CHILDREN; *Welcome*
CREDIT CARDS; *All major - except Amex*
LICENSED; *Full*
ACCOMMODATION; *2 rooms B&B 5 self-catering units. All ensuite*

RESTAURANT; *High quality home-cooked fare Varied A La Carte menu*

BAR FOOD; *Wide choice*
VEGETARIAN; *Extensive range, excellent*
DISABLED ACCESS; *Pub and Restaurant*
GARDEN; *Small beer garden*
PETS; *By prior arrangement*

GIB HOUSE,
Nr Drewstiegnton,
Dartmoor.

Contact : ***HELPFUL HOLIDAYS***
COOMBE, CHAGFORD,
DEVON TQ13 8DF.

TEL : 01647 433593
FAX : 01647 433694

This is a stunning thatched cottage set in secluded grounds in the heart of the moor, close to Castle Drogo, and is the most idyllic location for relaxation and peaceful tranquillity. It is furnished simply in stripped pine with plush settees and chairs, and offers the ultimate comfort in holiday accommodation. On the ground floor there is a bathroom en suite specially equipped for the disabled, whilst upstairs is another superb bathroom adjacent to the bedroom. The kitchen is fully fitted with all 'mod cons' including dishwasher and microwave and is designed to make everything as simple as possible. Outside is a delightful garden with pond and waterfalls, and this really is the epitome of a Dartmoor cottage. Nature is all around you here with foxes, deer and badgers part of everyday life, and there are plenty of country sports to keep you busy, if that is what you desire. Why not just enjoy the peace and quiet of the countryside, (something we all miss living in the busy cities) and recharge your batteries as never before!

USEFUL INFORMATION

OPEN : *All year*
CHILDREN : *Over 12 years welcome*
PETS : *No*
CREDIT CARDS : *All major*

SELF CATERING
DISABLED ACCESS : *Yes*
GARDEN : *Exceptional*
ACCOMMODATION : *2 rooms ensuite; 1 dbl,1Twin.*

SUNGATE HOLIDAY APARTMENTS,
c/o Market Cross Hotel,
Church street, Cheddar,
Somerset BS27 3RA.
Tel : 01934 742264

These lovely apartments have been constructed to a very high standard within a elegant listed Georgian house adjacent to the family run hotel. They are equipped for between 2 and 4 guests, and consist of one twin or double bedded room, a charming lounge, fully fitted kitchen and bathroom. There is a studio couch in the lounge which converts to a comfortable double bed. Meals are available at the hotel dining room if required and are excellent, and in addition there is a cosy lounge where guests gather, especially in the winter when the roaring log fire acts as a magnet.

Cheddar is an excellent centre for visiting the many attractions of the area. Wells with its beautiful cathedral is only a drive away, as is historic Glastonbury, where you can have a great day out. Cheddar, in addition to its wonderful caves at Cheddar Gorge, is famous for its strawberries and cheese, and has many attractions of its own. The hotel and apartments are within walking distance of the shops, and there are many restaurants and inns to choose from.

USEFUL INFORMATION

OPEN : *All year* ***SELF CATERING***
CHILDREN : *Welcome* ***DISABLED ACCESS :*** *No*
PETS : *No* ***CREDIT CARDS :*** *None taken*
ACCOMMODATION : *Apartments for 2 -4 guests.*

COPPER OAK COTTAGE
East Village
Crediton EX17 4DW
Tel: 01363 772530

If your idea of a holiday is to forget it all, to relax and unwind in idyllic surroundings of fields, trees and wildflowers then look no further than Copper Oak Cottage, set in a peaceful hamlet this lovely old property built around 250 years ago has roses, honeysuckle and vines covering the front. The cottage has 3 bedrooms, and will sleep 5 comfortably, a camp bed and a cot are available. The cottage has been tastefully decorated throughout, and your needs catered for with a washing machine and dryer, microwave, ceramic hob and built-under electric oven, there is also an oil fired Rayburn for you to cook on as well as supplying the hot water. There is a modern bathroom with bath but no shower. All bed linen is provided but towels are not. In the lovely garden is a pond, if you ask Mrs. Georgina Edwards the owner, she will have it fenced off for your stay if you have small children. The location is ideal for painting, birdwatching, walking and riding. If you want to bring your horse there is a loose box. There is plenty of parking in the drive.

USEFUL INFORMATION

OPEN; *May-Sept* ***DISABLED ACCESS;*** *No*
CHILDREN; *Welcome* ***GARDEN;*** *Yes, beautiful with pond and stream*
CREDIT CARDS; *None taken* ***PETS;*** *Horses and dogs*
ACCOMMODATION; *3 bedroomed cottage* ***PARKING;*** *Yes*

TRELAY FARM COTTAGES

Trelay, St Gennys,
Bude, Cornwall EX23 0NJ

Tel:01840 230378

Oliver and Andrea Tippett have converted the traditional Cornish farmstead of stone-built barns with slate roofs into six cottages. It has been done with care and imagination and the end result are cottages that will delight any visitor both visually and because they are as beautifully appointed inside as they are full of character in the exterior. So often self-catering accommodation lacks so much in the way of home comforts but this is not so here. Each lounge has colour TV and fitted carpets. The kitchens have modern fitted units, toasters, coffee makers, ovenware and pretty china apart from the more mundane necessities like cookers!

The garden of each cottage has something different to offer. For example The Old Stable has a French door leading from the lounge onto the sheltered, sunny lawn which is fenced for children or pets. There is a patio of local slate slabs with a picnic table and a barbecue. Little Trelay has an enclosed courtyard with tables and chairs and you are more than likely to be welcomed by large families of house martins which return each year to nest under the eaves.

Trelay is a small working farm with sheep and some beef cattle. The setting is idyllic at the head of a wooded valley looking out over rolling countryside. From the fields, where visitors are welcome to walk, the views are superb across Bude Bay, along the coast of this unspoilt part of Cornwall. On a clear day Lundy Island can be seen. Trelay is 100 yards off the road, along the tarmac drive. The A39 at Wainhouse Corner is three quarters of a mile away, where there is a general store, petrol station and country pub which serves food. Bude , with its splendid beaches is only 8 miles away . Crackington Haven which has a lovely sandy beach is just two miles away.It is ideal for surfing or swimming or simply exploring the rock pools.

USEFUL INFORMATION

OPEN;*All year* ***CHILDREN;****Welcome. Baby sitting by arrangement*
CREDIT CARDS;*None taken* ***DISABLED ACCESS;****No special facilities*
PETS;*Welcome but some breeds not accepted*

ORCHARD FARM
Cockhill, Castle Cary,
Somerset BA7 7NY

Tel: 01963 350418

This is a very special place to stay not only because the farmhouse and the two cottages are delightful but because of its history. For example the story is told of a Wedding Party at the farm who fell out and a number of guests disappeared! Is this the explanation for the 16ft thickness of the party wall between this and the adjoining 14th century farm? Then you may well be surprised to find Giants and Fairy Tales passing before your eyes because it is here on the farm that the floats are built and kept for the local Carnival.

The area is wonderful for a holiday with superb scenery, great walks, golf at Wheathill Golf Course where you 'Pay and Play', the glorious Montacute House to explore plus many superb gardens and other National Trust properties. The Royal Naval Air Museum at Yeovilton is only 6 miles off. There is the 17th century Grade II Listed farmhouse and two well-renovated, semi-detached cottages, The Owls and The Birds Nest. Whichever one you choose you will find most comfortably furnished and decorated throughout, retaining charm and character and all three located on a working farm amidst the open countryside only 30 miles from the coast. Cockhill Farm is a spacious farmhouse standing in its own attractive lawned gardens in the midst of open countryside. It provides excellent family accommodation with a lounge, dining room, kitchen, 3 bedrooms, ground floor bathroom and toilet, first floor shower rooms and toilet. Electricity is included in the price and you will find there is an open fire, electric cooking, fridge, dishwasher, microwave, electric fires, night storage heaters, colour TV, cot, highchair, duvets and linen. A deep freeze and washing machine is available at Orchard Farm. The garden is enclosed and has furniture and barbecue. You are welcome to bring two well-behaved pets. At Christmas and New Year short breaks are available. The Owls has an open plan lounge/kitchen/diner, 2 bedrooms (1 double, 1 bunk) single bed settee, bathroom with separate toilet, suitable for the partially disabled. The Birds Nest is similar except that in addition to the two double bedrooms there is a double bed settee. It is suitable for anyone in a wheelchair. Both cottages are all electric with is included in the price and has the same equipment as Cockhill Farm as well as a shared lawned garden with furniture and barbecue. One well-behaved pet is welcome in both. Your hostess Olive Boyer, is a friendly lady who will do everything in her power to make your stay a happy one.

USEFUL INFORMATION

OPEN: *All year*
DISABLED ACCESS: *Yes to The Owls and The Birds Nest*
CHILDREN: *Welcome*
GARDEN: *Yes + barbecue*
PETS: *Well-behaved welcome, see above*
ACCOMMODATION: *Farmhouse + 2 semi-detached cottages*

COMPTON POOL FARM COTTAGES

Compton, Nr Torquay,
South Devon TQ3 1TA

Tel: 01803 872241
Fax: 01803 874012

There will be few more attractive places and more conveniently situated than Compton Pool Farm Cottages. Set in 13 acres of beautiful countryside, surrounded by red Devon hills, Compton Pool was once a prominent farm probably dating back to 1140 and certainly to Tudor times. From the fresh springs at the farm the villagers drew their drinking water. Now the old stone barns, which are grouped around a central fishpond in a pretty courtyard planted with seasonal flowers, have been sympathetically converted into extremely comfortable cottages. It is a wonderful place for a relaxed country holiday in which you can do as much or as little as you wish. The farm fields invite you to wander, meet the farmyard animals, discover the wildlife on the lake, walk through the unspoilt wilderness area, or try your hand at fishing in one of the lakes. For the energetic there is an indoor heated pool, tennis or the facilities of the Games Barn. Torbay is only three miles away with its stunning beaches and many attractions for the visitor, Dartmoor with all its majesty and mystery is within easy distance, Compton Castle belonging to the National Trust is nearby and a host of other places.Golf and Riding are ready available. John and Margaret Phipps will arrange a babysitter for you if you wish to go out at night. There are takeaway meals available from a local restaurant, the village shop is about a mile away and both groceries and newspapers can be delivered.

There are nine cottages and one caravan, all with charming names: ***Old Farm Cottage, The Cider House, The Stable Cottage, Owl Loft, The Coach House, The Old Barn, The Garden Cottage, The Hayloft, Rose Cottage, The Orchard Caravan.*** *They sleep anything up to eight people and each one is furnished traditionally to a very high standard. They are centrally heated, fully equipped including microwaves, electric blankets - everything for your comfort in fact. Bed linen with duvets is supplied and laundry is included in the cost. Individual barbecues are supplied.*

Open all year round the accommodation is as cosy in winter as it is cool in summer.

USEFUL INFORMATION

OPEN; *All year*
CHILDREN; *Welcome*
PETS; *Not permitted*
DISABLED ACCESS; *No special facilities*
CREDIT CARDS; *None taken*
GARDEN; *Yes, 13 acres*
ACCOMMODATION: *9 cottages & 1 caravan, Sleeping from 4-8 people*

CHESTNUT COTTAGE,
Croyde, North Devon

Tel:01271 813777
Fax: 01271 813664

Chestnut Cottage which sleeps 8 + Cot + Highchair, is a detached dormer style bungalow offering spacious accommodation. Having recently been completely refurbished throughout, it has every modern comfort and convenience and is ideally situated in the heart of Croyde village. Lounge with separate dining recess, remote colour TV. This is a very attractive room with stone fireplace, a pine clad floor, built-in-desk and beamed ceiling. Newly fitted oak kitchen with electric double oven, microwave, fridge/freezer and dishwasher. Utility room housing extra sink with washing machine and tumble dryer. Downstairs bathroom with bath, wc, wash hand basin and over bath shower. Four bedrooms, two downstairs 1) double with built-in-wardrobe, 2) twins with built-in-wardrobe.

Upstairs to two further bedrooms: 3) 5' pine double bed with matching pine furniture together with en-suite bathroom, wc and wash hand basin; 4) Twins with en-suite bathroom with bath, wc and wash hand basin. Both upstairs bedrooms and bathrooms have sloping ceilings. Very good use has been made on the first floor with a play area, together with chintz suite and additional TV. Very small children's seats and bench is provided together with toys and games. Linen and towels are free. Payphone. Electric is inclusive, full central heating is available on request at twenty five pounds per week. Parking on site for 3 cars. Garden is flat and mostly lawned and garden furniture is supplied. The owners have gone to considerable lengths at Chestnut Cottage to ensure the comfort of guests, and the cottage is well appointed throughout with attractive paintings and homely touches.

USEFUL INFORMATION

OPEN; *All year*
CREDIT CARDS; *Yes*
PETS; *No*
GARDEN; *Yes with furniture*

CHILDREN; *Welcome. Play area*
DISABLED ACCESS; *No special facilities*
PARKING; *For 3 cars*
ACCOMMODATION; *Sleeps 8 + Cot*

OUTER BIAS,
Croyde, North Devon

Tel: 01272 813777
Fax: 01271 813664

This uniquely located detached home with direct access to the beach, sleeps 9 + cot and offers an idyllic setting with panoramic views of Croyde Bay with Baggy Point beyond. Croyde village, with its local store and Post Office, is within a few minutes walk. Situated in an acre of lawned level garden, there is a pathway which leads directly onto the sandy beach. The property has now been refurbished throughout and offers very substantial accommodation for family groups. Stable door into newly fitted modern kitchen with electric cooker, microwave, fridge/freezer, dishwasher, washer/dryer, a light airy double aspect room.

Lounge with gas fire, colour TV/radio and doors through to summer room with additional seating. Dining Room. These rooms benefit from having magnificent panoramic sea views across the bay to Baggy Point and seaward to Lundy Island. Four bedrooms, two being downstairs 1) Double with wash basin 2)Twins. Ground floor bathroom with bath and over bath shower and wash basin. Separate w.c. Both are very convenient being accessible directly from the garden and beach as well as internally. Upstairs to two further bedrooms with 3) Master bedroom with 5' double, wash basin, sea view. 4) Three singles. Upstairs bathroom with bath, wc and wash basin.

All duvets. Linen hire available. Sorry no pets. Electricity and gas inclusive with full gas central heating and radiators in all rooms. Large level garden with direct access to the beach. Picnic table and garden furniture. Ample car parking on site and private driveway. Payphone. Having undergone considerable refurbishment, new kitchen and redecoration, Outer Bias offers a unique opportunity to stay at this outstanding beachside location.

USEFUL INFORMATION

OPEN; *All year*
CREDIT CARDS; *Yes*
GARDEN; *Yes. Large flat lawns*
ACCOMMODATION; *Sleeps 9 + cot*

CHILDREN; *Welcome*
PETS; *No*
DISABLED ACCESS; *Yes*

HIGHERCOMBE FARM
Dulverton,
Somerset TA22 9PT

Tel: 01398 323616

Idyllically located adjacent to the moor and set within 450 acres including 100 acres of woodland stands Highercombe Farm. This is a working farm rearing beef and lamb. The modern and luxurious farmhouse offers a self-contained wing with its own entrance, sleeping 4 to 6 people, in two double bedrooms. One has a large double bed and 2 bunk beds, the other a double bed only. A cot is available. Beautifully furnished and equipped this really is the perfect retreat. The lounge/dining room has glorious countryside views and offers a woodburning stove, colour TV and video, and a CD player. The kitchen is very modern and includes electric cooker, fridge, microwave and cooking utensils etc. A washing machine and tumble drier are available. Full central heating, bed linen and towels are included in the tariff.

A £1 coin meter is provided for electricity. Hosts Abigail Humphrey and Tom Flanagan, will be only to pleased to escort you on farm walks and to answer any questions you may have, or a farm drive can be arranged to observe the many wild animals that frequent the fields and woods, including deer. For those wishing to explore further afield there are castles, stately homes, museums, galleries and various mills. Should you wish to partake in any of the country sports including horse riding, various forms of shooting, lake or sea fishing, then your hosts will be only to pleased to point you in the right direction.

USEFUL INFORMATION

OPEN; *All year*
CHILDREN; *Welcome*
CREDIT CARDS; *None taken*
GARDEN; *Extensive lawns and 450 acre farm, and woodlands*

DISABLED ACCESS; *No*
ACCOMMODATION; *Self-contained wing of farmhouse, sleeping 2-6 persons*
PETS; *Welcome including grazing and barn for horses*

FURSDON
Cadbury, Exeter,
Devon EX5 5JS

Tel: 01392 860860
Internet:http://www.eclipse.co.uk/fursdon/

Fursdon is a small country estate with an elegant manor house, charming cottages and 700 acres of tranquil and glorious Devon countryside. The family-owned property offers well furnished holiday apartments within the manor and cosy, peaceful cottages in the grounds, all of which are well-equipped. Bed linen is charged per person and guests need to bring their own towels (and baby linen if necessary). Electricity is metered and coin operated laundry facilities are available for apartments, each cottage having its own washing machine. Fursdon has been the family's home for over 700 years and guided tours of the house and museum with its family costume collection are available from Easter to the end of September. In addition to woodland walks and spectacular views the estate has a grass tennis court, badminton and croquet facilities, table tennis and board games. Only thirty minutes from historic Exeter, Fursdon is an ideal holiday location centred in the heart of Devon between Dartmoor and Exmoor and north and south coasts and close to several National Trust properties.

USEFUL INFORMATION

OPEN; *All year*
CHILDREN; *Welcome*
CREDIT CARDS; *None taken*
ACCOMMODATION; *3 self-catering apartments in manor house and 3 cottages in the grounds. Sleep 1-8 persons*

DISABLED ACCESS; *Downstairs bedroom, shower and toilet in a cottage*
GARDEN; *Interesting garden and grounds*
PETS; *Dogs are welcome*

'GARDEN COTTAGE',
c/o Hatches, Lower Calstock Road,
Hatches Green, Gunnislake,
Cornwall, PL18 9BX.
Tel : 01822 833948

This pretty stone cottage provides excellent self catering accommodation and has beautiful views along the picturesque Tamar Valley. Converted some twenty years ago from a stone barn, there is on the ground floor, a spacious, well equipped kitchen, a lounge cum double bedroom, and a shower room. On the first floor there is a double bedroom with door to the garden, a single room with bunk beds and a second shower room. All is beautifully decorated and furnished with pine floors and stairs, and pretty cottage fabrics. The atmosphere is warm and welcoming, and there is a pot bellied stove in the lounge for those chillier nights. It is fully central heated and your hosts, David and Anne Chapman, try to operate a non smoking policy. The bedrooms and lounge all have roof windows with blinds which takes advantage of the sunshine. The charming terraced garden has views across the valley and there is a barbecue area for lazy summer evenings. You are just half a mile from Gunnislake and just 200 yards from 'The Rising Sun', a fabulous 16th century pub with quality food and ales. This is an idyllic spot, and one to which you will be drawn again and again.

USEFUL INFORMATION

OPEN : *All year*
CHILDREN : *Welcome - cot available*
PETS : *Dogs by arrangement*
CREDIT CARDS : *None taken*

SELF CATERING : *Up to six persons*
DISABLED ACCESS : *No*
GARDEN : *Excellent*

BARKHAM COUNTRY COTTAGES,
Sandy Way, Exmoor,
North Devon.

Tel: 01271 813777
Fax: 01271 813664

Barkham Country Cottages are named after old fields from the original site and offer one of the best locations from which to explore and visit North Devon. Situated within the Exmoor National Park on the Devon/Somerset border, the cottages are just 10 minutes from the North Devon link road and South Molton is a mere seven miles. Picturesque Landacre with its 13th century bridge spanning the River Barle and the Two Moors Way are only minutes away. Northwards you can travel to Porlock with its dramatic rugged coastline, and to the West, visit North Devon's famous sandy beaches all within easy motoring distance. North Devon is rich in places to visit from local attractions, to Dunster Castle or Arlington Court, both National Trust houses. The owners reside in the original farmhouse, and the adjacent barns have recently been converted around an attractive courtyard. Surrounded by lovely Exmoor countryside, the three delightful cottages stand at the head of their own valley with a mixture of woodland, pasture and a small stream. From the farmhouse, the owners are able to offer a three course evening meal or light supper.

***Dobbins Close** which sleeps 6 + Z bed or cot, has superb views down the valley with its ponds and small stream. Attractively furnished it has a beamed lounge/dining area, an open plan style very comfortably furnished throughout with colour TV and video. Kitchen with gas cooker, washing machine, fridge/freezer. There are three bedrooms, two of which are on the ground floor. Ground floor bathroom with shower attachment. A cottage full of character.*

***The Old Copse** sleeping 5 + Z bed or cot, is a very attractive cottage approached by a few steps and with the benefit of a completely private secluded patio area.Quarry tiled hallway. Sitting/dining room with colour TV, video and lovely valley views. Fully equipped modern kitchen with gas cooker, fridge, washing machine. Ground floor bathroom with and bath and shower over, wc and wash basin.There are three bedrooms, charmingly furnished and very cosy, homely and welcoming. **Turnips Close** sleeps four + cot and is situated off the main courtyard area with principle rooms on the first floor to take full advantage of the glorious views across a patio area and croquet lawn. 1 double and 1 twin bedroom on the ground floor. Ground floor bathroom with bath and shower over. Stairs to sitting room with fine views, colour TV and video.Kitchen/Breakfast Room with Gas Cooker, Washng Machine and Fridge. Totally charming throughout.Linen is provided, a barbecue is available and a croquet lawn with equipment provided. Babysitting by arrangement. Use of owners extensive video library, tumble dryer and freezer. French and German spoken.*

USEFUL INFORMATION

***OPEN:** All year. Shortbreaks welcome* ***CHILDREN;** Welcome*
***CREDIT CARDS;** Yes* ***DISABLED ACCESS;** No special facilities*
***ACCOMMODATION;** 3 cottages**PETS;** By arrangement*

BURNTREE COTTAGE
Trenoweth Farm,
Gunwalloe, Helston,
Cornwall TR12 7QD

Tel: 01326 241202

Burntree Cottage is approximately one mile from the beach and golf course. The countryside around it is delightful and provides some splendid coastal walks and having acquired a thirst you will find the local Pub is within five minutes walk of the cottage. The nearest town is Helston just three miles away, an interesting place to visit and shop. The Royal Navy has a presence here with the Air Station at Culdrose from which helicopter squadrons fly. The cottage is interesting. It is a reverse level house well furnished and equipped. There is a kitchen/diner, with an electric cooker, microwave oven, fridge/freezer, washing machine etc. The lounge has an open fire, comfortable chairs from which to watch the colour television or take in the superb sea views.Also upstairs is a separate toilet and handbasin, and downstairs a double, a twin and a bunk bedroom plus a cot. The main bathroom is also downstairs. Centrally heated throughout, the heating and the hot water are oil fired. All the bedding is provided and electricity is included in the price.

USEFUL INFORMATION

OPEN; *All year* ***CHILDREN;*** *Welcome*
PETS; *Yes* ***DISABLED ACCESS;*** *No*
ACCOMMODATION; *Double, twin & bunk + cot.*

PHEASANTRY
Combe Raleigh, Honiton,
Devon EX14 0TG

Tel: 01404 42130

Pleasantly situated in the hamlet of Combe Raleigh, this self-contained accommodation is perfect for 'getting away from it all'. It is attached to the main house where Dorothy Retter, the owner, caters for bed and breakfast, and is situated in a quiet road off the main track. The accommodation consists of one double bedroom, and there is a sofa bed in the lounge that is suitable for small children. The kitchen is fully fitted with cooker, fridge, washer, microwave, toaster etc., and the bathroom has a bath with a shower over. This is a pleasing property, and is sure to fulfil all your requirements.

Local facilities are good. The town of Honiton is only about 1 mile away and you will find plenty of shops and market stalls selling local produce. Honiton is famous for both it's lace and pottery, and on market day you are sure to find something to your liking. There is a good golf course here, and for those who enjoy walking there are plenty of river walks on the Otter. This is a lovely part of Devon and you will enjoy the scenery and hospitality afforded you by these friendly people.

USEFUL INFORMATION

OPEN: *All year* ***ACCOMMODATION:*** *Self-contained one bed-roomed property attached to main house*
CHILDREN: *Welcome*
CREDIT CARDS: *None taken* ***DISABLED ACCESS:*** *No*
GARDEN: *Yes* ***PETS:*** *No*

CHARTWOOD HOLIDAY FLATS
Torrs Park,
Ilfracombe,
North Devon EX34 8AZ

Tel: 01271 864590

Since 1975 Chartwood Holiday Flats have provided very comfortable and happy housing for visitors. Within this Victorian residence each flat is self-contained with separate entrances from the gardens. The house is set on a hillside surrounded by gardens facing south with delightful views. It backs onto National Trust land and Clifftop walks. The house is also within walking distance of the town, beaches, harbour and local amenities. There are six flats sleeping any number from 2-6 people. Each flat has a comfortable lounge with colour TV, a modern bathrooms, and a fully equipped kitchen. Car parking for one car per flat is available at owner's risk. In addition to all the other facilities there is a Games Room with Pool table, Darts, Table football, Bar skittles, books and games for the very young. The Laundry Room has an auto washing machine and a tumbler dryer. Baby Listening is available by arrangement.

USEFUL INFORMATION

OPEN;*All year* ***CHILDREN;****Welcome*
CREDIT CARDS;*None taken* ***DISABLED ACCESS;*** *No*
GARDEN;*Yes* ***PETS;*** *By prior arrangement*
ACCOMMODATION;*6 flats well equipped*

THE FIRS,
37A Station Road,
Ilminster, Somerset
TA19 9BG

Tel: 01460 57383

The Firs is a pleasant modern house within 5 minutes walk from the centre of the old market town of Ilminster. Much thought has gone into the equipment and furnishing of the complete first floor of the house in order to provide those wanting to enjoy a relaxed and stress free self-catering holiday with everything they need. In addition to the modern day necessity, a television, the kitchen diner is well appointed complete with a microwave and a very useful warm dish unit. The two bedrooms are warm and comfortable and the lounge is a charming, relaxed room. There is parking space within the property. It would be a good place to stay at anytime of the year but special rates can be discussed for retired people out of season. From Ilminster there is so much to visit, stately homes, gardens, interesting villages and a wealth of good places to eat and drink. Alan Spuffard who owns the property is always willing to tell you about places and provide information on walks etc.

USEFUL INFORMATION

OPEN; *All year* ***CHILDREN;*** *Over 5 years*
DISABLED ACCESS; *No special facilities* ***GARDEN;*** *Yes*

BAY BUNGALOWS
Challaborough Bay,
Kingsbridge,
Devon TQ7 4JB

Tel: 01548 810425

The glorious South Hams in the County of Devon is where Val and Steve Chapman's holiday homes are situated. Bay Bungalows offer the visitor very modern and delightful accommodation adjacent to the secluded and award winning beach of Challaborough, where safe bathing is assured. Within their own garden the detached fully furnished bungalows boast fully equipped up to date kitchens, fridge/freezer, microwave ovens, washer dryer, cooker, iron and ironing board. Furnishings are of a high quality and includes a bed/settee in the living area. All the bungalows are fully electric and include dimplex heaters in bedrooms and coal effect or fan heaters in the main reception area. The electric meter accepts £1 coins only. A play ground for the children is close by. For the golf enthusiast there are several excellent golf courses and for those wishing to enjoy a more relaxed pursuit the angler is well catered for both river and sea fishing are available. Swimming and surfing or for those desirous of a lazy day on the beach this is a superb location, and don't forget to wander the wonderful coastal path with spectacular views of the sea. Challaborough has a well stocked general store and there is an excellent 'Fryers Tuck' take away the only one in this vicinity and very convenient if no-one is in a cooking mood, or enjoy good wholesome home-cooking in one of the local public houses.

USEFUL INFORMATION

OPEN; *All year*
CHILDREN; *Welcome*
CREDIT CARDS; *None taken*
ACCOMMODATION; *3 self-contained*
PARKING; *Own space next to bungalow*
bungalows, 1 x sleeps 4, 1 x sleeps 6, 1 x sleeps 7

DISABLED ACCESS; *Not really, ask when booking*
GARDEN; *Yes*
PETS; *Yes, dogs must be kept on a lead*

FERN LODGE,
Hope Cove, Near Kingsbridge,
South Devon, TQ7 3HF.
Tel : 01548 561326

Picture this - an idyllic location with commanding views over the countryside, cliffs and out to sea, three minutes walk from the glorious beaches, a beautiful garden where a vast array of birds visit, quiet evenings when a badger family come to call. A stunning part of the country with quaint fishing villages, secluded beaches, acres of National Trust country and a vast amount of water sports just waiting for you to try. Walks through countryside and along cliff tops that will have you reaching for your camera time and time again! All this and excellent accommodation too!

Gerald and Molly Lonsdale are the proprietors of this charming house, which has three modern flats available for self catering. The flats have two or three bedrooms, with a large lounge/diner, bathroom, toilet, car parking, and garden. Each is equipped fully with all the necessities and really are of a very high standard. All linen is supplied and there is a laundry service available. Disabled access is limited in that there is no access for wheelchairs, but do contact Gerald or Molly and if it is possible, they will accommodate you.

Hope Cove is in an ideal location for visiting many of the attractions of the West Country. The towns of Salcombe, Kingsbridge and Totnes are all within easy reach, and the distinctly haunting heaths of Dartmoor are only a car journey away. Spend some time in this 'paradise' and you will never want to leave!

USEFUL INFORMATION

OPEN : *All year*
CHILDREN : *Welcome*
PETS : *Welcome*
CREDIT CARDS : *None taken*
SELF CATERING
DISABLED ACCESS : *Please ring*
GARDEN : *Charming*
ACCOMMODATION : *3 units/ 2 or 3 bed roomed.*

SEAMARK HOLIDAY APARTMENTS
Thurlestone Sand,
Kingsbridge,
South Devon TQ7 3JY
Tel: 01548 561300

Seamark stands on the point of the cliff-tops at Thurlestone and has unrivalled views over the seas; in the west to Bigbury and Plymouth and in the east to Hope Cove and Bolt Tail. It is worth coming here just for the magnificent sunsets. Thurlestone Sands, a large sandy beach, is below and you actually overlook the famous Thurlestone Rock. This is an ideal centre for bird watching, walking, fishing and many water sports. Seamark also has a wonderful recreational building complete with indoor heated swimming pool, sauna and well equipped games room. John and Trish Gange have equipped these apartments to a high standard and they are tastefully furnished and comfortable. You can either be self-contained or have bed and breakfast and if you are too tired after a hectic day on the beach then you can collect a meal for the evening from the main house which can be heated at your convenience. A superb idea!. There are gardens where children can play in safety and also a games room with a wide range of games, toys and books for all. John and Trish live on site and are always happy to help with further games or equipment.

USEFUL INFORMATION

OPEN; *All year*
CHILDREN; *Most welcome*
CREDIT CARDS; *None taken*
LICENSED; *Not applicable*
ACCOMMODATION; *5 cottages with 2 or 3 bedrooms*
DINING ROOM; *Not applicable*
VEGETARIAN; *Not applicable*
DISABLED ACCESS; *Poor*
GARDEN; *Large and level*
PETS; *Welcome*

TROUTS
South Hallsands,
Nr. Kingsbridge,
South Devon TQ7 2EY
Tel: 01548 511296

Perched high above the sea, situated on the southwest coastal path and commanding spectacular views of countryside and coastline, stands the superb holiday apartments and cottages of 'Trouts'. Sleeping from 2 to 8 people, the accommodation is fully equipped, tastefully decorated and furnished. All linen is supplied except beach towels and cot linen. The amenities are excellent with a luxury outdoor heated swimming pool, all weather tennis court, putting green and a wonderful adventure play ground. The Games room offers table tennis and pool table, and a variety of toys, books and games for all the family. Laundrette and ironing facilities are available. Golden sandy beaches are a short distance away. Trouts Tea Room is relaxed with very friendly service, it is licensed, and boasts one of the finest Cream Teas in the area. This is positively a wonderful holiday venue for all the family.

USEFUL INFORMATION

OPEN; *All year*
CHILDREN; *Welcome*
CREDIT CARDS; *All major cards*
LICENSED; *Residential*
ACCOMMODATION; *7 apartments and 1 cottage sleeping 2-8 people*

DISABLED ACCESS; *Yes, the cottage and 2 apartments suitable, special equipment is available*
GARDEN; *Yes*
PETS; *Yes*
RESTAURANT; *Tea Room open to non-residents*

CHELSFIELD FARM
Nr. Week St Mary, Launceston,
Cornwall Pl15 8NU
Tel: 01566 785285

Bob and Pam Jones make you feel instantly welcome upon arrival at these attractive log cabins, set in the beautiful rolling countryside of the West Country. You are greeted by a welcome tray of tea and coffee with biscuits, and some fresh eggs and milk. The eggs are from the farm itself as Chelsfield is a registered organic farm, specialising in vegetables, fruit and free range eggs. The cabins themselves are set in 10 acres of conservation land surrounded by woodland, streams, ponds and wildlife habitat. Each cabin is tastefully furnished in cane and pine, and have all that is necessary for full comfort (including central heating).

Cornwall has everything for the visitor and these cabins are only a short drive from many attractions. Enjoy the beaches and coves and coastal walks. Visit the historic town of Launceston with it's castle and steam railway. Try your hand at the many water sports available such as sailing, surfing or even microlites! There is an otter and deer sanctuary close by and golf courses a short drive away. What more could you ask? If you are a nature lover then you will be enchanted by this idyllic location.

USEFUL INFORMATION

OPEN : *All year*
CHILDREN : *Welcome*
PETS : *By arrangement*
CREDIT CARDS : *None taken*
LICENSED : *No*
ACCOMMODATION : *2 cabins; 3 bedrooms comprising 1 dbl, 1 twin & 1 bunkbed room (adult size).*

RESTAURANT : *Not applicable*
BAR FOOD : *Not applicable*
VEGETARIAN : *Not applicable*
DISABLED ACCESS : *Yes, assisted*
GARDEN : *Yes, with patio and BBQ areas farmland walks. Garden furniture & BBQ supplied*

COURTYARD FARM COTTAGES
Lesnewth,
Nr. Boscastle,
Cornwall PL35 OHR
Tel: 01840 261256

Courtyard Farm and cottages is set in a small hamlet, two and a half miles from the picturesque harbour of Boscastle. The self-catering cottages are converted from the original 17th century mill and farm buildings and retain character and atmosphere, many of the cottages overlook the Valency Valley and the sea. The cottages are equipped to a high standard and are key rated 2-4 by the English Tourist Board with a quality rating of Commended. The gardens have been lovingly cared for and there is a barbeque/picnic area. The lane to Boscastle is steep and winding and covered in wild flowers, bluebells in the Spring, cool and leafy in the Summer. As you descend down the valley you are followed by a babbling stream that meets the river at the bottom. Close to the cottages is St. Juliot's church where Thomas Hardy was married. There are 3 Shetland ponies, Toffee the oldest, is trained for driving and enjoys giving rides to the visiting children. A provisions pack can be ordered, complete with fresh home produced free range eggs. There is a good range of home-cooked foods and a beer and wine list. Clay pigeon shooting is on offer also creative workshops, with a crafts showroom, opening in 1997.

USEFUL INFORMATION

OPEN; *All year*
CHILDREN; *Welcome*
CREDIT CARDS; *Access & Visa*
LICENSED; *Part, wines and beers*
FOOD; *Home-cooked food*
DISABLED ACCESS; *No*
GARDEN; *Delightful, with barbecue*
PETS; *No*
ACCOMMODATION; *7 self-catering cottages sleeping 2-8 persons*

MILFORD FARM COTTAGES,
Lifton,
Devon PL16 0AT.
Tel : 01566 783425

Located at Dingles Steam Village are two lovely self catering cottages; The Pound House and Gingerbread Cottage. Each cottage is unique with The Pound House (a converted cider house) adjacent to the main farmhouse, and having spectacular views over the surrounding countryside from the first floor living accommodation. Gingerbread Cottage sits in it's own private garden just off the main driveway and is surrounded by mature trees and shrubs. Both are beautifully furnished and decorated and have full facilities. Each will accommodate up to six guests.

Dingles Steam Village is a most interesting place with working traction engines, steam rollers and many more exhibits. Mrs Dingle's Kitchen is available during the season for coffee, light snacks and cream teas. There is a play area for children, a gift shop and scenic walks and picnic spots along the banks of the rivers. If you are staying in accommodation then this is all free, apart from a discounted entrance fee to the museum and adventure playground.

USEFUL INFORMATION

OPEN : *All year* ***MRS. DINGLE'S KITCHEN :*** *Snacks etc in season*
DINGLES STEAM VILLAGE : *Easter to end Oct.*
10am to 6pm - closed Fridays
CHILDREN : *Welcome*
DISABLED ACCESS : *No*
PETS : *Gingerbread Cottage only*
PARKING : *Each cottage up to 3 cars*
CREDIT CARDS : *None taken*
GARDEN: *Yes*
ACCOMMODATION : *2 cottages : each sleep 6.*

ROSECRADDOC LODGE
Liskeard,
Cornwall PL14 5BU
Tel: 01579 346768
Fax: 01579 346768

Roscraddoc Holiday Bungalows are set in an idyllic valley at the foot of Caradon Hill. The setting is wonderful in that the gardens and woodland are never dull with the different seasons of flowers and shrubs and also with the abundant wildlife, not including the ornamental ducks which may have occasion to visit you! The bungalows are all individually decorated to a high standard and there is everything a visitor could possibly need. Within a 2 minute walk is a bar and clubhouse, it is actually on a neighbouring property but welcomes visitors from Roscraddoc, serving bar meals and Sunday roasts. Because you are in such a central area there is more than ample to do if you wish. Both the south and the north coasts are easily accessible and also the moors of Bodmin and Dartmoor. For a day's shopping Plymouth is easily reached and the owners Louise and Richard are only too happy to give any further information you require.

USEFUL INFORMATION

OPEN; *Mar-Dec inc.* ***DISABLED ACCESS:*** *2specially adapted*
CHILDREN; *Welcome bungalows, carefully thought out and well fitted*
CREDIT CARDS; *None takenfitted. Have been inspected and recommended*
LICENSED; *Nofor the disabled.*
ACCOMMODATION; *25 self-catering bungalows* ***PETS:*** *Welcome*
GARDEN: *Attractive and level*

TREDINNICK FARM
Duloe,
Liskeard,
Cornwall PL14 4PJ
Tel: 01503 262997
Fax: 01503 265554

This Duchy farm accommodation is run by Angela Barrett who maintains very high standards and welcomes her guests warmly. The accommodation is self-catering, sleeping up to 10, and is attached to the farmhouse. This is actually a working farm and guests are most welcome to view the likes of cow milking. The nearest village is Duloe with a post office and shop, but even so you are never far from other major attractions such as Looe or Polperro. A lovely rural setting if you want to get away from it all, but not too far away. Ye Old Plough House Inn in Duloe serves very good food on those occasions you don't want to cater for yourself.

USEFUL INFORMATION

OPEN; *Mar-Dec*
CHILDREN; *Welcome*
CREDIT CARDS; *None taken*
LICENSED; *No* ***GARDEN;*** *Very nice, safe play area for children*
ACCOMMODATION; *Self-catering*
RESTAURANT; *Not applicable*
VEGETARIAN; *Not applicable*
DISABLED ACCESS; *No*

TREWORGEY MANOR
Liskeard,
Cornwall PL14 6RN

Tel: 01579 347755
Fax: 01579 345441
- Coach House Cottages

The ancient manor of Treworgey has been in the same family for 400 years. The present members of the family, Jeremy and Jane Hall have completely renovated and converted their 16th century Coaching Yard into 4 luxuriously appointed, self-contained cottages, sleeping between 4 and 8 people, with open fires and full central heating. Each cottage is designed to be self-catering and is comprehensively equipped and presented. It is an enchanting place with the Manor House lying adjacent to the Coaching Yard with its formal gardens and clock tower. Everything about Treworgey which nestles in 110 acres of beautiful pasture and woodland, is peaceful and ideal for a relaxing holiday. Guests are invited to take advantage of all the amenities including walks around the estate and through the woodland, and to make use of the all weather tennis court, heated swimming pool (seasonal), boule pit and games room.

Attractions and places for guests to visit are plentiful. Plymouth with its Barbican from which the Mayflower sailed, historic towns and the castles of Launceston, Lostwithiel and Tintagel, and quaint fishing villages such as Fowey and Polperro are close at hand. There is fishing, horse riding, golfing, sailing and windsurfing available locally as well as shark fishing at Looe and excellent surfing on the north coast at Polzeath or Constantine Bay. Fabulous walks along coastal footpaths and cliff tops plus a wealth of beautiful Cornish gardens that are open to the public at certain times of the year just add to the pleasure of staying at Treworgey. There are so many local attractions that Jeremy and Jane have prepared an information pack for each cottage.

USEFUL INFORMATION

OPEN; *All year* ***CHILDREN;****Welcome*
PETS; *Limited to one cottage only* ***DISABLED ACCESS;*** *No facilities*
ACCOMMODATION; *4 cottages sleeping maximum 24*

PEREGRINE HALL

Lostwithiel,
Cornwall PL22 0HT

Tel/Fax: 01208 873461

Built in 1864 in Gothic style by George Edmund Street, architect of the Law Courts in London, its purpose was a nunnery and a home for wayward women - history does not relate what success rate the nuns had! Today Peregrine Hall has a vastly different role. The Chapel and the West Wing, together with the Stables, have been converted into charming and very individual holiday cottages. The Chapel cottages, called 'Rose', 'Fountain', 'Cloisters' and 'Gable End' are especially designed for couples, look out over the long broad, south facing terrace and the gardens; and have galleried bedrooms with canopied or fourposter beds. 'Harry's Cottage' also sleeping just two people, is tucked away in its own little corner, and its garden looks south and west over the meadow which is part of the ten acres surrounding Peregrine Hall. The remaining three cottages 'Wing', 'Little Peregrine' and 'Stable' are two or three bedroomed, and so are suitable for families or a larger group of friends. Almost all are fully centrally heated, and three cottages have attractive log burning stoves, which are not only easy to use and highly efficient, but enhance the warm cosy atmosphere, whatever the weather! Though some cottages have their own gardens or patios, all are welcome to use the terrace, house, gardens and the solar-heated swimming pool.

If for no other reason you should come to Peregrine Hall for the stunning views from many of the rooms and the terrace. From April to October given that the soft Cornish rain holds off, the hills and valleys are an arresting sight. The cool bright light of early morning sparks and flashes through the trees; because the house is south facing, the sun warms the old flags throughout the day and in the evening it is time to sit out and watch the scene before you gradually soften in golden light - the sheep and lambs turn almost a pinkish colour reflecting the peachy pink clouds; the sense of peace is timeless and disturbed only by rooks and smaller birds hurrying late to their nests, and occasionally an early owl. As the sun finally goes down over the western aspect and the majesty of Restormel Castle, the lights of the small town of Lostwithiel far below are a friendly reminder that 'civilisation' is not far away. Turn away from looking west and look across the valley in front of you, lift up your eyes to the glorious beauty of the night sky - it is breathtaking.

Lostwithiel is an excellent centre for anyone wanting to explore the magic of this part of Cornwall. Within six miles is Lanhydrock House and Gardens, Bodmin Steam Railway, Restormel Castle, Fowey and the South Coast. Many other National Trust properties, Padstow and Newquay and family attractions are within easy reach.

USEFUL INFORMATION

OPEN; *All year*
CHILDREN; *Welcome*
CREDIT CARDS; *None taken*
ACCOMMODATION: *8 self-catering cottages. B & B available - Long weekends/short breaks*
DISABLED ACCESS: *No facilities*
PETS: *Welcome by prior arrangement in cottages*
GARDEN: *10 acres gardens*

TREDETHICK FARM COTTAGES
The Guildhouse,
Tredethick,
Lostwithiel,
Cornwall PL22 0LE

Tel: 01208 873618

Cornwall has some of the most beautiful rugged coastline and safe sandy beaches in the country, that is why it is a popular holiday location. There are so many places to stay you will be spoilt for choice, however, there is superb self-catering accommodation one mile from the historic town of Lostwithiel and once here you will not want to leave. These multi award winning Farm Cottages are graded '4 Keys Highly Commended' by the English Tourist Board and it is no wonder, the accommodation is second to none. Tredethick is a 200 acre farm lying in the heart of rolling countryside in an area of outstanding natural beauty.

On arrival at these lovely cottages you are greeted with a delicious Cornish Cream Tea, there is no better way to start your holiday. The 6 cottages, sleeping between 2 and 6 persons plus cot, have been lovingly converted from an attractive range of traditional farm buildings encasing a delightfully landscaped courtyard, where each cottage has its own garden and picnic table. The high quality fittings include dishwasher, washer/dryer, microwave, fan oven and hob and fridge. There are comfy sofas and armchairs, together with television and all are warm and cosy. Three of the cottages have woodburners, the logs are free. Linen is included in the price, although you do have to provide your own cot sheets and blankets, towels are also available. Cots, high chairs, and stair gates are provided free. Electricity is by a £1 coin meter. There is ample parking and you may even bring your own horse by prior arrangement.

The children will love the adventure play area, there are supervised rides on the farm pony and a pets corner with chickens, lambs and goats. The conservation minded farm trail joins onto a footpath leading to the delightful creekside village of Lerryn, the inspiration behind Kenneth Graeme's classic 'Wind in the Willows'. Also available is a games room with table tennis, snooker and darts. A wonderful base for touring, the area offers so much golf, fishing, riding, delightful walks and cycling, surfing, sailing and windsurfing the activities are endless and then at the end of the day you return to the peace, quiet and luxury living of Tredethick farm cottages.

USEFUL INFORMATION

OPEN; *All year*
CHILDREN; *Welcome*
CREDIT CARDS; *None taken*
LICENSED; *Not applicable*
DINING ROOM; *Not applicable*
DISABLED ACCESS; *2 cottages are suitable*
GARDEN; *Individual gardens and washing lines*
PETS; *By prior arrangement*
ACCOMMODATION; *6 Self-contained cottages sleeping 2 to 6 persons*

DURCOMBE WATER
Furzehill,
Barbrook, Lynton,
Devon EX35 6LN

Tel: 01598 753658

Richard and Mary Luckett have two excellent self-catering units in a secluded spot just two miles from Barbrook, along a beautiful winding country lane. The first is a delightful cottage with one double and one single bedroom. The second is a Studio Flat with one double bed and kitchen/Living Room. Both of them have fantastic views over gardens, fields and High Exmoor with access a short walk from the farm onto the Moor. The furnishings in either one of the places is good quality with fitted kitchens and equipped with everything you could possibly need for the enjoyment of your holiday. They both have a patio with furniture and the extensive gardens complete with a stream are shared. The only strict rule is -No smoking!

From Durcombe Water you can set out to enjoy so much of the glories of North Devon. Walking is a splendid experience along the coastal path. The Cliff Railway will take you down to Lynmouth with its pretty harbour and quaint houses. Golf course are closeby, fishing either at sea or on trout lakes locally. You can ride, cycle, birdwatch, play watersports or seek out the Nature Trails. Whatever you do you will never be bored at anytime of the year.

USEFUL INFORMATION

OPEN; *All year*
CREDIT CARDS;*None taken*
PETS;*No*
CHILDREN;*Welcome*
DISABLED ACCESS: *No*
ACCOMMODATION; *2 self-catering units*

HIGHER RODHUISH FARM
Rodhuish,
Nr Minehead,
Somerset
TA24 6QL

Tel: 01984 640253

Higher Rodhuish Farm is situated in the hamlet of Rodhuish, one and a half miles off the A39, surrounded by unspoilt countryside, on the edge of the Exmoor National Park and close to Dunster and Minehead. The Farmhouse itself provides excellent Bed and Breakfast but it also has two cottages for those who prefer a self-catering holiday. 1 Crown Cottage is semi-detached with good views of unspoilt countryside with private garden. It sleeps 5/6 people comfortably, has three bedrooms, a well equipped kitchen with electric cooker, fridge, washing machine and microwave. There is a Lounge with a woodburner, a Dining Room and Children's playroom. Colour TV and Night Storage Heaters are there as well. Payment is inclusive of electric. Duvets and bed linen supplied. Short breaks available with a minimum of 3 nights. Crown Cottage is open all year.

Tacker Street Cottage, Roadwater is also semi-detached and sleeps six. This comfortable cottage is set in a delightful wooded valley with large garden, one edge of which is bordered by woods and very close to a stream with small wooden bridge, which must be crossed to reach the cottage from the lane. It has a modernised kitchen with woodburner, electric cooker, refrigerator and microwave. There is a Lounge, bathroom and three bedrooms. Heating is by electricity or open fire. 50p meter, immersion heater, colour TV. There is a car parking space nearby.

This is an ideal centre for touring coast and moors, there is superb walking, horse riding, mountain biking, birding watching. An ideal place for a relaxed, healthy holiday.

USEFUL INFORMATION

OPEN; *All year*
CHILDREN; *Welcome*
DISABLED ACCESS; *No facilities*
PETS; *Accepted*

WESTERMILL FARM,
Exford, Minehead,
Somerset TA24 7NJ

Tel: 01643 831238
Fax: 01643 831660

In a unique setting on the 500 acre Westermill Farm are six outstandingly attractive Scandanavian Pine Log Cottages in three sheltered paddocks plus a cottage adjoining the farmhouse for those who enjoy the luxury of peace and quiet and the informality of a self-catering holiday. Each cottage has been lovingly created and well furnished with delightful, cheerful colour schemes. Television is available in all of them and there are laundry facilities. Natural water comes direct from the farm and outside each cottage is a raised verandah where you can sit and enjoy the views, sometimes of wild red deer, foxes and birds.

Children can safely play on the surrounding grass lawns. Dogs may run free in the adjacent dog exercising field by a small stream. The cottages are named, Bracken, Molinia, Whortleberry, Ling, Holly and Gorse. Molinia is being replaced and built from scratch ready for the summer of 1997. It is equipped with a disabled bedroom and a disabled shower & loo room and the whole will be of a very high standard.

The farm is family run with cattle and sheep on the upper reaches of the River Exe. Four waymarked walks allow you to explore the glorious scenery and observe the changing seasons of farm life. Lambs are in the cottage paddocks in April and calves are born on the farm in August. Mallard ducks fly around and swim on the river and lake. It is quite idyllic. Situated in the centre of Exmoor it could not be better for walking, pony trekking or exploring by car. The number of places to visit are endless and the golden beaches of North Devon are within easy reach. Trout fishing is available along the 2 ½ miles of the river. Children love paddling in the shallow clearwater or bathing in the river pools (more so if you bring a small rubber boat). A small campsite for tents is completely separate beyond the farmhouse.

USEFUL INFORMATION

OPEN; *Log Cottages open April-Dec inc Farmhouse Cottage available all year*

CREDIT CARDS; *None taken*

ACCOMMODATION; *6 Log Cottages + Farmhouse cottage. Small campsite*

CHILDREN; *Welcome*

DISABLED ACCESS; *Special log cabin*

GARDEN; *Yes 500 acre farm*

PETS; *Yes*

CHIPLEY MILL COTTAGES,
Bickington, Newton Abbot,
South Devon, TQ12 6JW.

Tel : 01626 821681

The two cottages here, **River View** *and* **Mill Wheel,** *have been converted from a grade II listed mill building, complete with water wheel and over-shot leat. The situation is glorious as is the accommodation provided. Set in approximately 12 acres of land, there is plenty to see and do without even leaving the property! The beautiful gardens lead down to the River Lemon where Christine and Mike Swift the owners, have fishing rights and where herons can frequently be seen fishing for brown trout. There is a lovely wooded walk beside the river which opens on to a large field, and Christine and Mike are only too happy for you to explore their marvellous grounds. The gardens include a picnic table, children's swings, and a tree house, and there is a gas barbecue available for those balmy summer evening outdoor meals.*

Each property is charmingly appointed, and are both warm and comfortable to ensure that 'home from home' atmosphere. The ground floors are open plan with timber beams creating lots of character. The main bedroom boasts a four poster bed, whilst the other bedrooms are twin bedded. All are very appealing with pine furniture and pretty floral fabrics complementing. Each bathroom has bath, shower, washbasin and toilet, and there is an additional separate toilet with washbasin. The kitchen is superbly equipped with cooker, dishwasher, fridge, microwave, and all other necessities, even down to tea towels. There is a communal laundry room with washer and tumble dryer. **River View** *is as it states - the large arched window gives wonderful views across the garden and down to the river, while* **Mill Wheel** *has a window at the rear which looks out on to the wheel itself, making it a fascinating feature of the property. This is charming accommodation with charming hosts who are anxious that your stay is a memorable one - which it is sure to be!*

This is an excellent location for exploring what Devon has to offer. Dartmoor and its haunting beauty is only 4 miles away and there are lots of local attractions to visit, including the English Riviera, which is only a short drive away. The River Dart Country Park has much to offer all ages with its beautiful walks and facilities for children, while a day at Paignton Zoo is always an event to be enjoyed. Steam railways, castles, beaches and golf are all available and there is something for every member of the family. A unique location with superb accommodation and the most congenial hosts to ensure you will return time and time again!

USEFUL INFORMATION

OPEN : *All year*
CHILDREN : *Most welcome (cot,highchair av.)*
PETS : *No*
CREDIT CARDS : *None taken*
SELF CATERING : *2 cottages each with 3 double beds*
DISABLED ACCESS : *Not really*
GARDEN : *Wonderful*
NON SMOKING

WARMHILL FARM,
Henock, Newton Abbot,
South Devon TQ13 9QH.
Tel : 01626 833229

Warmhill Farm is a 100 acre dairy farm situated on the slopes of the glorious Teign Valley, on the south eastern side of the Dartmoor National Park, ideal for moor and sea. It is situated on the edge of the farmyard and children are encouraged to help with the animals and milking. Visitors are welcome to explore the farm, which has an abundance of wildlife and beautiful views over the valley.

The farmhouse is a large traditional beamed and thatched barn conversion, adjacent to the owners cottage. The original barn was built in the 16th century and many of the old features remain. It has lovely spacious rooms, and is furnished in keeping with the character of the property.

USEFUL INFORMATION

OPEN : *All year*
CHILDREN : *Welcome*
PETS : *Up to 2 dogs*
ACCOMMODATION :
Suitable for up to 12 guests

SELF CATERING
CREDIT CARDS : *None taken*
GARDEN : *South facing with BBQ & garden furniture*

FAIR HAVENS HOLIDAY FLATS
89-91 Tower Road,
Newquay,
Cornwall TR7 1LX
Tel: 01637 874005

What could be better than spending a holiday at Fair Havens Holiday Flats, these self-contained units sleep from 2-6 and are specially for young people. They are equipped with everything you need electric cooker, fridge, heaters, colour television, all crockery, cutlery, cooking utensils, vacuum cleaner and ironing board. All the electricity is metered, in the small flats the shower is also metered. All bed linen is supplied, but you are asked to bring your own towels. The units are ideally placed close to the town centre, where there are shops, banks and entertainment. There is a general grocers next door to the flats that is open everyday. Parking is in the street. Newquay is Cornwall's surfing capital, Fistral Beach being the main beach for competitions, with competitors from all over the world. Being near the coast water sports are very popular not just surfing, but also windsurfing, swimming, sailing and fishing. The beaches along this part of the coast are wonderful with plenty of room for everybody. If you fancy a game of golf you only have to go next door, not far from the flats you are able to go horse riding. What more could you want, an excellent location for an excellent holiday.

USEFUL INFORMATION

OPEN; *All year*
CHILDREN; *No*
CREDIT CARDS; *No*
LICENSED; *Not applicable*
ACCOMMODATION; *10 Self-contained flats, Electricity by meter*

DINING ROOM; *Not applicable*
VEGETARIAN; *Not applicable*
DISABLED ACCESS; *No*
GARDEN; *No, but line drying available*
PETS; *Yes, certain types*
PARKING; *On street*

EASTERBROOK FARM COTTAGES
Exbourne, Okehampton,
Devon EX20 3QY.

Tel : 01837 851674 or 0831 855183

This is the ideal retreat if you wish either a farm holiday, or if you wish to explore the charming South West. Situated about 5 miles from Dartmoor and the town of Okehampton, these self contained cottages are the perfect haven for an idyllic holiday. They date back to 1580 and although having all the luxuries of modern living, manage to maintain the charm and appeal of a bygone age. The main farmhouse is partially thatched, and the cottages have stone and cob walls, making this a very picturesque scene. The farm consists of 70 acres which is half hay and grazing land, and half woodland. There are many animals here, and as such is ideal for children. You are most welcome to wander round, and even join in the activities such as hay making or apple picking! This is one of those places that can only give you fond memories, and have you wishing to return time and time again.

USEFUL INFORMATION

OPEN : *All year*
CHILDREN : *Welcome*
CREDIT CARDS : *None taken*
ACCOMMODATION : *3 cottages*

EVENING MEAL : *By request*
VEGETARIAN : *Catered for*
DISABLED ACCESS : *no*
PETS : *Horses by arrangement*

HOLLYHOCKS
4-5 High Lanes Cottage,
Nr Padstow,
Cornwall PL27 7RZ

Tel: 01208 812183

This pretty Georgian cottage is less than two miles from the charming fishing port of Padstow. The superb property, which was once two houses, has been tastefully converted to provide very comfortable accommodation. It is owned and lovingly cared for by Christopher and Thelma Riddle, who ensure that their guests have the best of everything. The cottage has many original features; slate flagged floors, beamed ceilings a 'Cornish Range' and an open fireplace. The soft furnishings are excellent, you feel totally relaxed and at home the moment you walk in the front door. Hollyhocks is well appointed with colour television and video, washing machine, tumble dryer, freezer, ironing board with iron, an enviable fitted kitchen including a Rayburn and all the cutlery and crockery you will require. The 3 bedrooms are delightful with ample wardrobe space. The bathroom has a sunken bath and a separate shower area. All bed linen and towels are provided and a cot and high chair are available. Cot linen however is not provided. To the front of the house is a good sized patio area and to the rear a small lawn and flower beds with access to the parking area. Garden furniture and a barbecue are there for your use. This is an area which offers endless leisure activities and with the beautiful countryside and coastline offers an ideal relaxing holiday or break.

USEFUL INFORMATION

OPEN; *All year*
CHILDREN; *Welcome*
CREDIT CARDS; *None taken*
ACCOMMODATION; *3 bedroomed self-catering cottage*

DISABLED ACCESS; *No*
GARDEN; *Yes with patio area, garden furniture and barbecue*
PARKING; *Yes*
PETS; *Dogs welcome*

PEAR ASH FARM
Pen Selwood, Nr. Wincanton,
Somerset BA9 8LX
Tel: 01747 840377

This delightful recently completed barn conversion, has resulted in an attractive and intimate two bedroomed cottage attached to Pear Ash Farm, a 200 acre homestead set in the heart of glorious Somerset. The accommodation is light, airy, well furnished and equipped with all basic requirements. There is one twin bedded room on the first floor, on ground floor level is a second twin bedded room, bathroom, WC and shower. The lounge/diner is furnished in a classic style with woodburning stove and colour television. A recessed kitchen area offers cooker and refrigerator. A washing machine is available at the farm. Bed linen can be hired at a reasonable rate. Electricity is by a 50p meter. On arrival you are greeted with a welcome pack containing fresh farm eggs, flapjacks and a tea tray. This is a working farm with cattle, sheep, horses, donkeys, ducks and chickens, where guests are very welcome to experience what life is like 'down on the farm'.

USEFUL INFORMATION

OPEN; *All year*
CHILDREN; *Very welcome*
CREDIT CARDS; *None taken*
ACCOMMODATION; *2 bedroomed self-catering cottage attached to farmhouse*
DISABLED ACCESS; *No wheelchairs*
GARDEN; *Share lawned garden beside farmhouse*
PETS; *Prior notice required. Must be under control on the farm*

'THE HARBOUR HOUSE'
Self Catering Holiday Apartments
& Bed & Breakfast,
1, Trevelyan Road,
Seaton, Devon EX12 2NL
Tel: 01297-21797

The first thing that strikes you as you arrive in Trevelyan Road alongside Axmouth Harbour, is the extraordinary sense of peace , almost as if you are shutting out the rest of the world. Strange in many ways because there is a lot of activity amongst the boats lying at anchor, some just returning and others setting sail. The pretty apartments which are available are delightfully appointed and are also suitable for out of season holidays and short breaks (minimum - 3 nights). Bed linen is included in the price but please bring your own towels and tea towels. The Harbour House also offers Bed and Breakfast in the three first floor bedrooms which all have colour TV, H & C and refreshment trays. A full English Breakfast is provided and Vegetarians can be catered for. The Harbour House is just 100 yards from the beach and a short level walk along the Esplanade to the town centre.

USEFUL INFORMATION

OPEN; *February-November*
CHILDREN;*Welcome*
CREDIT CARDS;*None taken*
ACCOMMODATION;*B&B 3 rooms Self-catering 3 apartments*
PETS;*No*
DINING ROOM;*Full English Breakfast*
VEGETARIAN;*Catered for*
DISABLED ACCESS; *1 Ground floor S/C*

'ADANAC',
Maria's Lane,
Sennen Cove,
Penzance,
Cornwall,
TR19 7BZ.

Tel : 01736 871348

The views out over Sennen Cove across the 'blue flag' beaches of Whitesands and Gwynver to Cape Cornwall are some of the finest in the country. Seals play in the bay and even dolphins can be seen at times. A path leads from the house to the cove, and National Trust land is nearby, leading to Land's End. St. Just is only 4 miles away and the drive to St. Ives can only be described as beautiful. A more idyllic location is difficult to imagine, and the views and scenery around you are bound to have you reaching for that camera or paint easel. Water sports are part of nature here, and walks are available for all abilities: a romantic evening stroll along Whitesands Bay, or a day hike over cliff tops where the breakers crash on the rocks below. The famous open air Minack Theatre is only 4 miles away, and a round of golf can be played at Cape Cornwall, 5 miles away. This location has everything, including the quiet balance of sea and countryside in charming and relaxing surroundings.

Adanac is a self contained apartment in an old fisherman's cottage, situated at the end of a quiet private lane on the headland. The lounge is on the first floor, and when you see the stunning view through the large picture windows, you will understand why. Even on a dull day the spectacular vista of sea and countryside will give you endless pleasure and sitting here in the evening after a day's exploring, must be a very satisfying and peaceful end to the day. The lounge is open plan with a dining and kitchen area, and all necessities are included. There is a shower, bath, shaver point, radio alarm, colour TV, autowasher and tumble dryer for your use, and parking is outside the house (no passing traffic - imagine the peace!). Accommodation is for three or four persons, with one twin bedroom on the first floor, and a single or small twin bedroom on the ground. The house is beautifully decorated throughout and comfort is obviously a high priority. Outside there are enchanting gardens and a patio (again with stunning views) where you can enjoy the balmy summer evenings. Your hosts, Mr & Mrs Scotts, are anxious their guests enjoy their stay, and offer that famous Cornish hospitality and friendliness that ensures you will relax in this informal atmosphere.

USEFUL INFORMATION

OPEN : *Easter to Oct inc.*
CHILDREN : *Welcome (not suitable for toddlers)*
PETS : *No*
CREDIT CARDS : *None taken*
SELF CATERING
DISABLED ACCESS : *No*
GARDEN : *With patio*
ACCOMMODATION : *3 or 4 persons*

FRENCH & GERMAN SPOKEN

THE OLD FARMHOUSE,
Rosehill, Alverton,
Penzance,
Cornwall
TR20 8TF

Tel: 01736 364199

It is almost imposible to imagine when you arrive at The Old Farmhouse that you are only just a mile out of the busy town centre of Penzance. Rosehill is known as the place where the birds never stop singing and one can understand why; it is so tranquil and peaceful with not much more than the sounds of the countryside to disturb your thoughts. A wonderful place for anyone to stay who wants to recharge their batteries in such a pleasant house with a wild and beautiful garden, on a working farm where widlife is in abundance, and at the same time know that the bright lights are not far off as well as some wonderful beaches, breathtaking scenery and some superb walks. You can fish, if you wish, play golf and go exploring the mysteries of St Michael's Mount or the exquisite cathedral at Truro not too far away. Take a leisurely stroll across the fields to the famous National Trust property of Trengwainton with its beautiful woodland gardens at their best in spring.

People have been coming to stay in the Old Farmhouse which sleeps six comfortably, for a long time and they would all tell you that the accommodation is spotlessly clean and very comfortably furnished. Upstairs there are two bedrooms, one with a double and one with twin beds, as well as bathroom with shower and heated towel rail. Downstairs there is a further double bedroom, living room with open fireplace, and kitchen with oil-fired cooker providing hot water and heat from three radiators. There is an automatic washing machine, fridge freezer and electric cooker. There is parking space and an outside toilet and, of course, the beautiful garden.

You will find Margaret Jewell, your landlady, to be a kindly and very helpful lady who will help you find just the right places to eat locally, tell you where you can shop and do anything within her power to make sure you have a thoroughly enjoyable and memorable stay.

USEFUL INFORMATION

OPEN; *Easter to November*
Other times by arrangement
CHILDREN; *Welcome*
CREDIT CARDS; *None taken*
ACCOMMODATION; *2dbl 1tw*
DISABLED ACCESS; *No special facilities*
PETS; *By arrangement*
GARDEN; *Yes. Wild & beautiful*

OLD SOWTONTOWN,
Peter Tavy, Tavistock,
Devon, PL19 9JR.

Tel : 01822 810687

Just a ten minute walk from the open moorland of Dartmoor is the ancient farm of Sowtontown. Owned by Chris and Ruth Boswell who made the farmhouse their home in 1994, this now provides a desirable and comfortable dwelling, with many advantages for those wishing to explore the attractive surrounding area. There are two properties for letting: **The Shippen** *sleeps up to four persons in the galleried bedroom, and has a wonderful open plan interior (loung/dining/kitchen) with lots of natural stone and wood.*

It has all modern services including central heating from an oil based Rayburn in the kitchen. There is a secluded cobbled courtyard with picnic table and parking for two cars. **The Barn** *is again open plan but the kitchen/ dining/living area are on the first floor to take advantage of the breathtaking views surrounding you. It sleeps up to six persons, and again is equipped with all modern facilities including tumble dryer, washer, colour TV, central heating and woodburning stove for those cooler evenings. There is parking for two cars along with a patio area and garden.*

Babysitting facilities can be arranged and well behaved pets are welcomed. Riding is a great sport here and stabling can be arranged for those visitors wishing to bring their own horses. There are plenty of activities in the area with wonderful landscapes, local history, golf and fishing. The north and south coasts are both within reach, and Peter Tavy is close by with it's 15th century inn where good food is general. The ancient market town of Tavistock is just three miles away and here you have excellent facilities for shopping, eating and enjoying the local hospitality.

USEFUL INFORMATION

OPEN : *All year*
CHILDREN : *Welcome (cots available)*
PETS : *Well behaved*
CREDIT CARDS : *None taken*

SELF CATERING
DISABLED ACCESS : *Please ring*
GARDEN : *With BBQ*
PARKING : *Yes*

TOLRAGGOT FARM,
St Endellion, Port Isaac,
Cornwall PL29 3TP

Tel: 01208 880927

Jill and Robert Harris own Tolraggot Farm and it is they who have converted Dinham Farm Courtyard into three attractive Courtyard Cottages approximately 3 miles away from the farm at St Minver. They also have Barton Cottage which adjoins the farmhouse at Tolraggot. All four properties will delight those who like self-catering holidays especially when the accommodation is of such high standard.

The Courtyard Cottages set in the countryside off the B3314 road from Wadebridge to the coastline have splendid views of the Estuary and some of the most beautiful beaches in Cornwall are within a few minutes drive by car. They have been beautifully converted from a traditionally Cornish barn to provide quality accommodation, tastefully furnished and spacious, fully double glazed and insulated with Economy 7 heating and electric fires - ideal for all year round holidays. The ***Round House*** *has 1 double, 2 twin bedrooms, large round open plan room with lounge, kitchen and dining areas, bathroom. 2 bedrooms have vanity basins, open fire if required and a dishwasher is also installed.* ***Barn End*** *has 1 double, 1 twin and 1 bunk bedroom, kitchen with dining area, separate lounge with open fire, vanity basin in double room, bathroom. The third is* ***Barnsdale Cottage*** *with 1 double, 1 twin bedroom, open plan kitchen diner lounge. Bathroom with separate toilet, vanity basin in double room. All the properties have fitted kitchens and bedlinen is included in the price. The Garden areas have garden furniture and barbecue. You may also use the outdoor heated swimming pool in the summer months. One dog only by arrangement is permitted.*

Barton Cottage *is such a pretty cottage and furnished delightfully with plain carpets and pretty curtains and matching bed linen. There are 4 bedrooms, 2 doubles, one twin, and one bunk. One of the double rooms has a shower and vanity unit. The bathroom has a heated towel rail and radiator and an airing cupboard. There is a downstairs toilet. The lounge has an original fireplace with cloam oven plus a woodburner. The pine fitted dining room also has an original fireplace, a large well-fitted pine kitchen completes the accommodation. There is a large garden area with picnic bench and barbecue. From the cottage you have immediate access to Port Isaac, Port Quin and Port Gaverne plus inland villages of St Kew, Chapel Amble, St Teath and a host of country lanes to explore. The Victorian Gardens at Longcross are within a few minutes as too are the beaches between Tolraggot Farm and Dinham Courtyard.*

USEFUL INFORMATION

OPEN; *All year*
CREDIT CARDS; *None taken*
PETS; *By arrangement*
ACCOMMODATION; *4 cottages*

CHILDREN; *Welcome*
DISABLED ACCESS; *Partial*
GARDEN; *Yes with furniture & Barbecue*
Outdoor heated swimming pool in summer months

COAST & COUNTRY COTTAGES,
Church Street, Salcombe,
South Devon, TQ8 8DH.

Tel : 01548 843773
Fax : 01548 843330

Picture the scenic South Hams with its myriad of rolling valleys and haunting moors, sandy beaches and craggy cliffs, quaint fishing villages and historic towns, and you are sure to find something which will interest you. Whether you are a walker who enjoys striding across the open moorland, or a sailor who likes the challenge of the open sea (or even a dinghy bobbing in the harbour), or the artistic type who sees the landscape in palette colours, then this is definitely the place to be. Coast & Country Cottages is a letting agency for a variety of cottages in South Hams. This can be anything from a studio apartment to a much larger cottage and they are all of a very high standard. A typical property is that at ***9 Victoria Quay, Salcombe.*** *This is an attractive waterfront cottage with superb views over the harbour and main anchorage towards South Pool creek. The accommodation is for four persons, consisting of two bedrooms; one double and one bunk bedded, an attractive lounge with stone fireplace, colour TV, a well equipped kitchen/diner, and a cosy bathroom. In addition each bedroom has a handbasin with hot and cold water. Outside is a paved patio area overlooking the harbour, perfect for those lazy summer evenings. Salcombe is a popular place to stay due to it's fishing and sailing connections, and also due to the appealing character of it's streets and shops, but there are many more locations depending on what you want from your holiday. Malborough, Thurlestone, and Hope Cove are just a few of the places on offer, and you are bound to find something to suit your taste and interests. With names like Smugglers End, Peep-O-Day, and Poets Cottage, the romanticism and charm of these very individual properties will have you eagerly reserving your accommodation! The South Hams is very engaging and within easy reach of the cities of Plymouth and Exeter. The moors are on your doorstep and there are many walks of various degrees for your pleasure. The vistas are stunning and you are advised not to travel without a camera! Those with a historic leaning will find plenty of interest, such as Compton Castle, a 14th century fortified Manor House, and many museums covering anything from China Clay to Motor Vehicles. The Dart Valley Steam Railway is there for the enthusiasts, and is also a great way to see much of the fascinating countryside. There are nature trails and wildlife parks, golf courses and many other outdoor sports. Water sports are obviously in great demand, and you can do anything from sea fishing to scuba diving on wrecks. Dartmouth is another beautiful town with 800 years of history and is still home to the Royal Navy Officer Training College, as attended by most of the Royal Family. Take a boat from here up the River Dart to Totnes and by ferry from here to Kingswear. Enchanting! Whether you want a busy schedule with full days entertainment, or just to relax in the peace and tranquillity, then these cottages cater for your requirements. Book today, and ensure a great time in a great place!*

USEFUL INFORMATION

OPEN: *All year*
CHILDREN: *Welcome*
CREDIT CARDS: *None taken*
PETS: *No*
GARDEN: *Depending on property*
ACCOMMODATION: *Selection of self-cateringproperties*

WEST RIDGE
Harepath Hill, Seaton,
Devon EX12 2TA

Tel/Fax: 01297 22398

This excellent, spacious self catering accommodation is situated just outside Seaton, and stands in 1.5 acres of its own grounds with beautiful views over the Axe Valley and Estuary, and the sea itself. It is ideally suited for two or three persons but can cater for up to five and has all the modern facilities required. The garden has a barbecue area and there is a summer house which can be available by arrangement for all to enjoy on those balmy evenings. The area of Seaton is excellent for walking and most water sports are available. Golf and fishing are amongst some of the other pastimes and day trips can be taken to Exeter, Dartmoor, Exmoor and the Hardy country of West Dorset. The English Tourist Board has awarded West Ridge '3 Keys Commended'

USEFUL INFORMATION

OPEN: *March-October*
CHILDREN: *Welcome*
CREDIT CARDS: *None taken*
ACCOMMODATION: *Self-catering up to 5*
DISABLED ACCESS: *Some*
PETS: *Welcome*
GARDEN: *Very good*

WATERSIDE
24, Mill Street,
Sidmouth, Devon
Tel:01404 850355

This charming holiday cottage is within a short, level walk of the sea and shops. Sidmouth itself is almost a backwater in holiday resorts. It still has a delightful Victorian air about it and attracts people who enjoy a true seaside holiday with plenty to do away from the sea. Waterside is double fronted and has a sitting room with colour television and a modern, well equipped kitchen. There is a utility room complete with washing machine and ceiling drying rack. A ground floor loo with hand basin and a smaller, second Sitting Room with a 4ft sofa bed which makes it a fourth bedroom if required. There is one double bedroom with a cot and 2 twin bedrooms.The spacious bathroom also has a large airing cupboard. The cottage will sleep six comfortably. You are asked to bring your own bed linen; blankets are required for the cot. The cottage is centrally heated which makes it ideal for early or late season lettings. Between the house and the river wall is a small path and sitting area with picnic table and benches and a drying line. There is a numbered reserved parking space. Please ring Mrs Jan Steele-Perkins for further information or write to Glebe Farmhouse, Buckerell, Honiton, Devon EX14 0EP. Tel: 01404 850355.

USEFUL INFORMATION

OPEN; *All year*
CREDIT CARDS;*None taken*
PETS;*By prior arrangement*
CHILDREN;*Welcome*
DISABLED ACCESS;*No. Narrow passages*
GARDEN;*Patio on riverside*

DRUPE FARM
Colaton Raleigh,
Sidmouth,
Devon
EX10 0LE

Tel: 01395 568838

Fourteen cottages are available at the ancient Drupe Farm whose history goes back some 400 years and is part of the Clinton Devon Estate. Set in beautiful gardens these cottages are exceptionally well maintained and presented. The high quality cottage style furnishing, beautiful decoration and linens as well as thoughtfully equipped kitchens makes staying in any one of them a pleasure at anytime of the year. In addition to the gardens there are orchards and farmland on which you may walk or potter. The surrounding countryside and coast will provide you with walks along the Heritage Coast, with Birdwatching, Cycling, Riding, Sailing, Water Sports - you will find maps and guides in all the cottages to help you choose where to go and what to do. The village of Colaton Raleigh is pretty in its own right and within easy reach are many more Devon villages as well as the county town of Exeter, the seaside resort of Exmouth with its golden sands. Drupe Farm itself provides its residents with a Skittle Alley, Badminton and indoor Basket Ball as well as excellent facilities for children and a Barbecue.

Grouped round a courtyard the cottages sleep anything from seven plus a cot to four people plus a cot. The choice is yours. Warren Cottage for example sleeps four plus a cot and has accommodation all on the ground floor. Also on one floor is similar accommodation in Thorntree Cottage. Both of these are ideal for older or less active people. Wheathill Cottage sleeps seven plus a cot and has downstairs rooms including a bathroom designed for wheelchair use.Over the last few years all the cottages have been refurbished to a very high standard. Gill Elliott is your contact and she will be only too happy to tell you more and send you a booklet which will help you assimilate how splendid a holiday would be in any one of the cottages.

USEFUL INFORMATION

OPEN; *All year*
CREDIT CARDS;*Yes. Visa*
PETS; *Yes*

CHILDREN;*Welcome*
DISABLED ACCESS;*One cottage adapted*
GARDEN;*Yes. Skittle Alley, Badminton, Basket Ball (indoor) BBQ*

WINTERSHEAD
Wintershead Farm,
Simonsbath,
Exmoor,
Somerset
TA24 7LF

Tel: 01643 831222
Fax: 01643 831628

No more idyllic spot for self catering holidays than Wintershead can be found. It stands 1300ft above sea level, right in the heart of Exmoor amidst breathtaking scenery. Here you are far away from the stresses of modern life, in a tame wilderness covering 265sq miles of spectacular countryside and home to the famous red deer, Exmoor ponies and gracious, soaring buzzards. . For those who appreciate walking, riding, fishing or touring it is a paradise. Unpoilt spaces, pretty villages, quiet lanes, the stunning North Devon coastline and sandy beaches are all within reach.

No Hidden Extras could be said to be the motto of this outstandingly good self-catering accommodation. Whether you choose to stay in the 3 bed-roomed detached Well Cottage, or the 2 bed-roomed Spring Cottage and Beech Cottage or the most recent conversion Fern Cottage with its one bedroom or indeed the self-contained flat, you will find everything is done to the highest standard and complete with everything you need. The owners Jane and Barry Styles drew on their own holiday experiences when they were designing these holiday homes. Electricity, fuel, bed linen, cooking utensils are all included. Full central heating is provided and Wintershead has its own private water and electricity supply. On arrival you will find the beds made and everything spotless plus a warm welcome and personal attention.

USEFUL INFORMATION

OPEN;*All year* ***CHILDREN;****Welcome*
CREDIT CARDS;*No* ***DISABLED ACCESS;****No special facilities*
GARDEN;*Extensive lawns, stunning views* ***PETS;****Welcome*
ACCOMMODATION;*4 cottages 1 flat*
Stabling available. 5 acre paddock. 5 loose boxes. Laundry room

CHERITON HOUSE
Market Place, St Ives,
Cornwall TR26 1RZ

Tel: 01736 795083

St Ives is one of those places that is attractive all year round. In the summer season with the hustle and bustle of the visitors it is a hive of activity, but in the winter it is a wonderful place to explore with it's quaint shops and exquisite galleries. Eating is a distinct pleasure and need not be expensive with the numerous restaurants, cafes and hostelries in the town. Alec and Ann Luke run these good quality and well appointed apartments in the centre and are at hand if needed. There are also 2 fully equipped cottages for up to 5 persons near the harbour. Special attention should be paid to the paintings on the walls of the apartments as they are all originals. Short breaks off season which includes a garage, price from £30 per unit per night.

USEFUL INFORMATION

OPEN; *All year*
CHILDREN; *Most welcome*
CREDIT CARDS; *None taken*
LICENSED; *Not applicable*
ACCOMMODATION; *9 apartments accommodating between 2 and 5 persons, plus 2 cottages for up to 5 persons*

DINING ROOM; *Not applicable*
VEGETARIAN; *Not applicable*
DISABLED ACCESS; *No*
GARDEN; *No*
PETS; *Not really*

BUCKLAWREN FARM COTTAGES,
St.Martin-by-Looe, Looe,
Cornwall, PL13 1NZ.
Tel : 01503 240738

These superb cottages have been converted from a former stable block to provide excellent self-catering accommodation, with all the comforts of modern life but retaining the character and charm of a time gone by. There are three cottages; two of which cater for four people, and one which caters for up to six. Each is individually and tastefully decorated, light and spacious, and with pretty floral fabrics in a country style. The kitchens and bedrooms are all fully fitted and the bathrooms include shower, bathroom suite and heated towel rails. Everything to make you comfortable has been thought of, and your hosts, Robert and Jean Henly, offer a warm friendly welcome to all their guests. The farmhouse caters for bed and breakfast plus an optional evening meal, and an arrangement can be made for the self catering guests to order an evening meal. This is wonderful location, deep in the quiet rural countryside, yet only one mile from the beach and three miles from the lovely harbour town of Looe.

USEFUL INFORMATION

OPEN : *All year except February*
CHILDREN : *Welcome*
PETS : *Welcome*
CREDIT CARDS : *All major*
GARDEN : *Extensive lawns with magnificent views.*

SELF CATERING:*3 cotts: 2 for 4 persons, 1 for 6 persons.*
DISABLED ACCESS : *Yes, all ground level cottages*

HIGHER AYR COTTAGE,
Ayr, St.Ives,
Cornwall,
TR26 1EN.

Tel : 01736 795394

This charming semi detached Cornish cottage is owned by Ray and Brenda Drew, who moved to Cornwall just six months ago. Having moved to a very interesting and scenic part of Cornwall, Ray and Brenda set about providing the ideal holiday home for their guests, and to my mind have succeeded! This property is typically Cornish with it's lintels and granite walls all adding to the authenticity, but with the warmth and comfort of modern conveniences such as central heating, fully fitted kitchen, and cosy furnishings. There are three double bedrooms, one with additional single divans, a separate bathroom with shower and wash basin, and toilet with washbasin. On the ground floor is a lovely kitchen/diner, and a lounge with colour TV. This is an extremely charming and welcoming property, in a quiet area, but within easy reach of all of St.Ives' facilities. An additional bonus is the car parking for two vehicles, which is of prime importance in this popular harbour town!

The history of this cottage is quite enchanting, and Ray and Brenda have kindly provided some details. It was bought in the 1940s by an 'artistic' couple and at this time was almost derelict. (It is described in the article as 'unloved' and was noticeably abandoned with its 'sad smell of neglect') With a lot of attention (and obviously some money) it was restored to it's 'former glory' with a few modern conveniences. The work was done by a traditional Cornish mason who had great enthusiasm and love for his work. Many of the old beams were taken from the ship breakers, and he spent a great deal of time ensuring that the wood used was seasoned and weathered correctly. Apparently he was a great aid and could lay his hands on almost anything required. (I wonder if any of his ancestors are still in business - we could use his skills!) The couple who bought this cottage and restored it put a great deal of their artistic qualities into it, and with Ray and Brenda adding their traits, it has become a very desirable and comfortable dwelling.

St.Ives is a great location for any break, whether it is a long weekend in the winter months or a summer holiday in the height of the season. There is something for every member of the family from children to grandma, and you will not be disappointed by the sights and scenes of this very special part of the country. St.Ives is awash with artists and galleries, and at any time you may see someone with a palette and brush capturing a moment in this wonderful vista. Shops are delightful with the utmost variety, and the harbour is always a fascinating place to spend a few moments just 'people watching'. The sandy beaches are great for the children, while walking along the cliffs gives wonderful views out to sea. There are plenty of restaurants, and inns where you can spend a quiet (or loud) evening, and the tea shops with their Cornish ice creams and selections of delicious pastries provide escapes from shopping or sight seeing.

USEFUL INFORMATION

OPEN : *All year*	***SELF CATERING***
CHILDREN : *Welcome*	***DISABLED ACCESS :*** *No*
PETS : *No*	***GARDEN :*** *With picnic & BBQ area*
CREDIT CARDS : *None taken*	***PARKING :*** *2 vehicles*

ROSEMORRAN HOLIDAY APARTMENTS,
The Belyars,
St.Ives,
Cornwall,
TR26 2AD.

Tel : 01736 796359

Rosemorran is a splendid building sitting in 3 acres of its own grounds. It is in one of the best residential areas of the picturesque St.Ives and most flats enjoy charming views of St.Ives Bay. The grounds offer a play area for children and there is free parking in the grounds. (A very important factor when visiting St.Ives!) This is a haven of peace and tranquillity amidst a very busy holiday destination. Rosemorran is within an easy stroll of the town centre and is excellent for Porthminster Beach. The flats and cottage each have either one, two or three bedrooms and all are decorated very tastefully to a high standard. Each has its own entrance, hallway and lounge/dining room with full facilities of central heating, fridge/freezer, washer/dryer, and all other necessities including a colour TV. There is a large communal patio overlooking the garden at the front of the property, and also overlooking the Bay. There is a very informal, relaxed atmosphere here, and with Brian Buckley, your host, on hand you are sure of a wealth of information and background to this charming part of the world. The Cornish welcome is known for its warmth, and Rosemorran is no exception. Here you will find yourself relaxing in the comfort provided, and enjoying a high standard of accommodation.

Brian is a prolific walker, and can provide much in the way of information on coastal walking and the surrounding area. He is also a great scholar on the history of St.Ives and can relate much of interest regarding the town. It is really a beautiful place with its shops and tea rooms, and with the artists who flock to this area, you will see much in the way of painting and sculpture. The Tate Gallery here has some wonderful exhibitions, and the Dame Barbara Hepworth Museum which is encompassed by the gallery is renowned as the best place in England for sculpturing. The site of this astounding gallery is overlooking Porthmeor Beach and the four storey building is a welcome modern addition to the town. The busy little harbour with its colourful boats can provide hours of interest, and the views from the cliff tops will have you gasping at their beauty. Cornwall has much in the way of history with its smuggling activities and mining, and you will hear many a good story on the activities of these profound, independent people. This is a really interesting part of the world and you are sure to enjoy your stay with Brian at Rosemorran, and return again and again to sample the hospitality and warmth of the Cornish people.

USEFUL INFORMATION

OPEN : *All year*
CHILDREN : *Welcome*
PETS : *No*

SELF CATERING ACCOMMODATION
PARKING : *Available*
DISABLED ACCESS : *No*

CUMBRAE COTTAGE

Trebarwith Strand,
Tintagel,
Cornwall PL34 0HB

Tel: 01840 770585

Nestling in the delightful hamlet of Trebarwith Strand with its splendid surfing bay and beach are 4 individually furnished and equipped cottages. Superbly renovated and overlooking the sea. The accommodation is heated by electric panels in all rooms with £1 coin operated meters, also included, colour TV, electric cooker, refrigerator and microwave. All bed linen is supplied, except for cots. High chair and cot available on request. Parking is limited to one space, but access to further parking is within walking distance. Swimming, surfing, fishing, golf and spectacular cliff top walks are some of the many leisure facilities to be enjoyed.

USEFUL INFORMATION

OPEN; *All year*
CHILDREN; *Welcome*
CREDIT CARDS; *None taken*
ACCOMMODATION; *4 cotts*
DISABLED ACCESS; *Limited*
GARDEN; *Yes*
PETS; *No*
ARKING; *Limited, with access to more*

MERRIFIELD HAYES FARM COTTAGE

Cruwys Morchard,
Tiverton, Devon EX16 8PG

Tel: 01884 860378

This warm, friendly farmhouse cottage is ideal for anyone wanting a holiday in very peaceful and beautiful countryside. Merrifield Hayes is a working farm so you will be staying where cattle roam the fields and the farm horse is a friendly creature. Your meals cooked in the excellently equipped kitchen/living room will be made more pleasureable with fresh vegetables straight from the farm. The double bedroom is comfortable and attractive and the other bedroom has full width pine bunk beds. Everywhere is simply but immaculately furnished. Linen is supplied but not towels and there is no extra charge for electricity or fuel. Riding, walking, golf, wonderful country walks on Dartmoor and Exmoor make Merrifield Hayes an ideal place to stay.

USEFUL INFORMATION

OPEN;*All year*
CREDIT CARDS;*No*
DISABLED ACCESS;*No*
CHILDREN;*Welcome*
GARDEN;*Yes, with furniture & BBQ*
PETS;*Well behaved dogs welcome*

HALGABRON HOUSE & HOLIDAY COTTAGES

Halgabron,
Tintagel,
Cornwall
PL34 0BD

Tel: 01840 770667

Just off the Tintagel to Boscastle road snook away is the small peaceful hamlet of Halgabron, which only consists of a working farm and two cottages, here you will also come across Halgabron House and Holiday Cottages. These delightful self-contained properties are full of charm and character and have been sympathetically converted from the original stone farm buildings retaining many of the features from the past. This lovely little community stands in about 3 acres of beautiful countryside with woods and open fields, the views are stunning. There are 6 cottages altogether offering one, two, three and four bedroomed accommodation sleeping up to ten people comfortably, cots and highchairs are available at no extra cost. They are fully equipped with all conveniences of modern day living, colour television, electric fires, cooker, fridge/freezer and microwave ovens, electricity is by meter. All bed linen is provided except for cots, towels can be hired, but you are asked to bring your own beach towels. Full laundry facilities are available for your use. The largest cottage 'The Coach House' has its own washing machine and dishwasher. There are home-baked cakes and quiches available from Christine Alexander, the owner, and as a special touch you are welcomed with one of her cakes and the table set for tea on your arrival, there is also delicious fresh clotted cream from the neighbouring farm. The open garden is shared by all the cottages and has tables and barbecues. There is a super childrens play area with a timber climbing frame and swings, including a scramble net, monkey bars and baby swing. Although not a working farm there are a few sheep, friendly ducks, rabbits and cats. The beaches are safe and sandy especially Trebarwith Strand which is only two and a half miles away. With so much to do in this area, including fishing, golfing, riding, birdwatching and some wonderful walks, this will far exceed your wildest dreams as the perfect holiday.

USEFUL INFORMATION

OPEN; *All year*
CHILDREN; *Welcome*
CREDIT CARDS; *None taken*
ACCOMMODATION; *6 cottages,*
2 x 1 bedroom, 1 x 2 bedroom, 2 x 3 bedroom, 1 x 4 bedroom (sleeps 10)

DISABLED ACCESS; *No*
GARDEN; *Open shared gardens*
PARKING; *Central area with lighting*
PETS; *Yes, by prior arrangement*

WEST PITT FARM HOLIDAYS
Uplowman, Tiverton,
Devon EX16 7DU

Tel: 01884 820296

One could not wish to spend a self-catering holiday in a more delightful or peaceful setting than the small exclusive group of cottages belonging to West Pitt Farm at Uplowman nestling in the rolling Devon hills.It is quite unique and designed to give one tranquillity, peace of mind in a non-regimental and relaxed manner. The owner Rod Crocker has converted part of the original 16th century farmhouse and the stables to produce the three cottages. In addition to them there is a traditional farm pond complete with ducks and a rowing boat, lawns, garden furniture and barbeque; grass tennis court; croquet lawn and ample space for children to play. There is a luxury Indoor Heated Swimming Pool open all the year round with adjoining Sauna and Solarium - also a small games room with snooker, table tennis and darts. On the farm there are four large fishing lake, well stocked with mirror and common carp, bream, roach and rudd. One contains chub, tench, perch and crucian carp. Numerous rivers and other private lakes in the area also offer fishing but even if you do not fish -the area is perfect for quiet walks and the enjoyment of the Mid-Devon countryside. The Golf Course at Tiverton welcomes visitors and 'Pay as you Play' golf is available on other nearby courses. Horse riding at various local riding schools will offer you Pony trekking on Dartmoor if you wish.. Exeter and Taunton as well as Exmoor and Dartmoor National Parks are about a half an hour's drive. Uplowman is an attractive village in its own right with a centuries old church and a good village pub which serves excellent food. Sampford Peverell about one and a half miles away has its own stocked grocery store which opens 7 days a week and has its own bakery attached producing super bread, pies, croissants and cakes.

Lake View Cottage *sleeps 6/9 people and is a fascinating building dating back in part to 1450 and some of the exposed cruck beams are over 500 years old. It has a cosy living room with an open fire inglenook fireplace with bread oven. The kitchen/diner is heavily oak beamed. On the first floor there is double and a twin en suite room, one family room with a double bed a single and bunks again en suite. Oil central heating is included if required as it is in the other cottages.* ***Two Stable Lodges*** *each have a comfortable first floor living room with bed settee and a fully equipped kitchen and dining area, commanding superb views of the Culm Valley. Downstairs there is an en suite twin-bedded room.* ***The Loft*** *which sleeps 2 is a unique conversion into a fully equipped open-plan flat (en suite bathroom/WC) of great character and charm. Very comfortable and cosy. All accommodation has coin meters for electricity, toaster, colour TV, microwave oven, duvets with full linen and towels. There is a laundry room which is centrally located and has coin operated washing machines, tumble drier, iron and public telephone.*

USEFUL INFORMATION

OPEN; *All year*
CREDIT CARDS; *None taken*
PETS; *By prior arrangement*
ACCOMMODATION; *4 cottages*
CHILDREN; *Well behaved welcome*
DISABLED ACCESS; *Not suitable*
GARDEN; *Yes. 8 lakes. Indoor heated Swimming pool, sauna and solarium. Tennis Court & croquet lawn*

TORVIEW FLATS AND FLATLETS
Rousdown Road,
Chelston, Torquay TQ2 6PB

Tel: 01803 606060

This elegant detached grade 2 Victorian villa of charm and character which stands in its own grounds, has fine views over Torbay and harbour and has been converted into 8 flats plus the one belonging to the resident owners, Vic and Maureen Leighton. Whether it is a flat or the smaller flatlet, the decor and the furnishing is to the standards demanded by the Torbay Self Catering Association and English Tourist Board. Comfort and cleanliness are the main aims of the Leightons, You have your own key and come and go as you please. Each flat is completely different so there is something to please all tastes. The whole atmosphere is friendly and happy and conducive to ensuring you have a great holiday. Torview is close to local shops, pub and station, a bus passes the door. Torview offers Short Breaks out of season with Christmas and New Year weekly from any day.

USEFUL INFORMATION

OPEN;*All year*
CREDIT CARDS; *None taken*
PETS;*Please enquire when booking*
GARDEN;*Yes. Secluded overlooking Torbay.*
CHILDREN; *Welcome*
DISABLED ACCESS;*No*
No special facilities

CANT COVE COTTAGES,
Cant Farm,
Rock, Nr. Wadebridge,
Cornwall PL27 6RL.

Tel : 01208 862841

Overlooking the Camel Estuary, in 70 acres of beautifully landscaped gardens and countryside are the self catering cottages of Cant Cove. Constructed partly from the original stone and partly from carefully selected local stone, these cottages blend into the landscape as if they have been there for centuries. Retaining the original charm and character but adding triple glazing, central heating, log fires, fully equipped kitchens and either whirlpool bath or sauna, has enhanced these properties to the highest degree. Awarded the highest accolade of '5 keys de luxe' by the English Tourist Board confirms the luxurious standards of these delightful cottages. There are six in total, all with private garden and BBQ area. One, The Orchard, is suitable for those of limited mobility as it is situated on ground level. Accommodation at the cottages ranges from five to eight guests, and all are very spacious and immaculately cleaned and maintained. Cant Cove Cottages have a lot to offer, whether it is a short weekend break or a longer holiday to rest and revitalise a busy life!

USEFUL INFORMATION

OPEN : *All year*
CHILDREN : *Welcome*
CREDIT CARDS : *Visa/Mastercard*
ACCOMMODATION : *6 cottages.*
SELF CATERING
DISABLED ACCESS : *Some*
GARDEN : *70 acres*

TRINITY MEWS HOLIDAY FLATS
Trinity Hill, Torquay,
Devon TQ1 2AS

Tel: 01803 296969
Fax: 01803 212123

The mild climate of Torquay is 'reminiscent of the Mediterranean' and the same can be said of the sunny and flower filled courtyard which is the centrepiece of Trinity Mews. This heavenly retreat is located close to the harbour and town centre, and offers tastefully furnished and up to date accommodation to suit from 2 to 6 persons. There is wall to wall carpeting, comfortable modern effects and fully equipped kitchens. Bedrooms are complete with all linen. High chairs and cots are available and must be booked in advance. Cot bedding to be provided by guests. Separate laundry facilities comprising washing machines, driers and irons are available. For those cool summer evenings or colder winter months the flats are warmed by electric heaters, the cost of which is included. Each lounge has a colour television. Should you require bread or milk on arrival then the owner will be only to pleased to oblige. General groceries are available locally including the weekend. Parking is unrestricted adjoining the flats. Should you require to garage your car then a lock up type is available. Pets are very welcome by prior arrangement. Torquay and the surrounding area offers visitors a wonderful choice of attractions and a host of activities to satisfy all tastes. Within a short distance is the marina and the promenade, a variety of shops and excellent restaurants. Glorious beaches for which Devon is renowned are within easy reach, as are swimming, fishing, boating, cycling and riding. Babbacombe is the home to a fascinating Model Village, it also offers stunning coastal walks. Shaldon Wild Life Trust offers an insight into the lives of small mammals and exotic birds. Dartmoor National Park has some of the most panoramic views in this area. An abundance of wild life abound including deer, fox, badger and the famous Dartmoor ponies. Olde Worlde pubs and hostelries offer refreshment and hospitality, sample the local delicacy, a Devon Cream Tea, or a tasty pasty noted for its unique manner of contrivance. There is a sanctuary for otters at Buckfastleigh as well as a Butterfly Farm, or a trip of nostalgia on the Dart Valley Steam Railway which runs alongside the River Dart to the Tudor town of Totnes. A visit to the 70 and growing acres of Paignton Zoological Gardens, is an excellent opportunity to observe normally wild animals in an environment as close as possible to their normal habitat.

USEFUL INFORMATION

OPEN; *All year*
CHILDREN; *Welcome*
CREDIT CARDS; *None taken*
LICENSED; *Not applicable*
ACCOMMODATION; *12 self-contained flats, 6 x 2 bed flats (sleeps 2-6), 6 x 1 bed flats*

DISABLED ACCESS; *No*
GARDEN; *No, a courtyare*
PETS; *Yes, by prior arrangement*
PARKING; *Unrestricted close to flats. available*

CHUCKLE TOO COTTAGE,
Blackawton,
Totnes,
South Devon,
TQ9 7BG.

Tel: 01803-712455

A quote taken from the visitor's book says it all about this delightful cottage in the charming village of Blackawton in South Hams. 'Came to unwind - totally unravelled!' A very satisfied customer! This is a quiet and relaxing location, attached to Jilly Hanlon's (the owner) cottage in the middle of the village. There are three good pubs on the village street who serve excellent food, and there are two village shops who sell everything from milk to 'elastic'.

The cottage itself is fully fitted and very comfortably furnished, with a superb kitchen which has cooker, microwave, fridge and washing machine. The pine bathroom has shower and bath with constant hot water supplied from Jilly's Aga, and the large lounge is a delightful room with a sofa bed and easy chairs, colour TV, dining table and chairs. The bedroom is pretty, with a very comfortable bed and all the necessities supplied! Everything here is of excellent quality and you will be charmed by the intimacy of this cosy cottage. The central heating also comes from the Aga, and this cottage is never cold! Outside you have a wonderful garden with a patio which is furnished with table and chairs, and portable barbecue. There is a bridge from the garden out on to the nearby fields and this really is an idyllic setting. You can just imagine sitting here on a warm summer's evening with a nice glass of red, taking in the luxury of the stillness and solitude which is so often missing in our busy lives.

The area has plenty of activities (if you wish) with lots of scenic walks, a golf course, and the town of Dartmouth, or the wild rugged beauty of Dartmoor within easy distance. Exeter and Plymouth cities are only about an hour away, so if you long for the 'hub' of the city then it too is within reach! I think you will find yourself 'totally unravelling' here too, and enjoying the experience!

USEFUL INFORMATION

OPEN : *All year*
SELF CATERING : *Caters for two or three*
CHILDREN : *Yes, not suitable for toddlers*
GARDEN : *With patio & BBQ*
PETS : *Dog by arrangement*
CREDIT CARDS : *None taken*

OLD HAZARD
Higher Plymouth Road,
Harberton,
Totnes, Devon
TQ9 7LN

Tel: 01803 862495

Do you yearn to escape the hustle and bustle of modern day living? Then Old Hazard offers just this welcome opportunity. A delightful haven with the very best accommodation, run by Mike and Janet Griffiths, Old Hazard is a former farm and the site is mentioned in the Domesday Book. Two holiday units are offered, both furnished and equipped to a high standard and as clean as a new pin for every visitor. Sleeping 4/5 persons is the well proportioned Farmhouse Flat, situated on the 1st floor with access on this level, comprising large lounge/dining room, bathroom, kitchen/breakfast room and 2 bedrooms, 1 double and 1 twin with wash hand basin.

The second option, The Linhay, an attractive and cosy cottage converted from an original barn sleeps 3 people in 2 pretty bedrooms, one double and one single, with convenient bathroom. An open plan lounge/kitchen leads from a small entrance hall with a stable door from parking area. Old Hazard is conveniently located just three miles from Totnes and within easy reach of the spectacular Dartmoor National Park where walking, horse riding and fishing are readily available. It is an easy drive to the South Devon coastline with it's abundance of activities, surfing, swimming and wonderful walks. Discover secluded coves and fascinating villages with many attractive inns and restaurants then retire to the peace and seclusion of Old Hazard. What could be better?

USEFUL INFORMATION

OPEN; *All year*
CHILDREN; *Welcomed*
CREDIT CARDS; *None taken*
LICENSED; *Not applicable*
ACCOMMODATION; *2 self-contained properties*
PETS; *Yes, welcomed*

DINING ROOM; *Not applicable*
VEGETARIAN; *Not applicable*
DISABLED ACCESS; *No, although level*
GARDEN; *Linhay has secluded private walled patio. Flat has lawned garden adjacent to open farmland and car parking*

HIGHER TREWITHEN

Stithians,
Truro,
Cornwall,
TR3 7DR.

Tel : 01209 860863

This part of Cornwall is really an ideal spot for visiting both the North and South Coasts with their beautiful beaches, rugged coastlines, and peaceful bays. Although situated in a quiet location these cottages and apartments offer the visitor unlimited attractions, but at the same time allow for that privacy and 'getting away from it all' we sometimes require. The stunning scenery that surrounds you will have you reaching for your camera, whilst walking along the country lanes or coastal paths, will have the artist in you etching the memory in your head. Whatever your sport interests you will be able to indulge it here. Bowls, tennis, cricket, fishing windsurfing, sailing, and many more sports are available nearby, and many National Trust properties are also at hand.

Higher Trewithen has a range of cottages and apartments catering for various sized families. Anything from 2 to 8 persons can be accommodated in this charmingly elegant complex, and children are most welcome, with cots being provided for the little ones. Cot linen is not available so remember to bring baby's sheets and blankets! The farm is a converted old Cornish Farmstead made from traditional granite under slate roofs, and although all have double glazing and the modern 'trappings' necessary, they still retain the charm and character that suits the surrounding countryside. They are all very tastefully decorated, and the resident proprietors, Peter and Avril Stokes, ensure a high standard of care and attention. The cottages and apartments all have fitted carpeting, colour TV, and all beds are made with all linen provided. The kitchens are all electric with full size cookers and refrigerators, and electric fires are provided in each lounge for those cooler evenings. There is a laundry room for guests equipped with two automatic washing machines and tumble dryer. Outside are lawns with swings and 'things' where children can play and there is a barbecue area with tables and picnic benches.

The village of Stithians is about 1 mile by car or 15 minutes walk through the fields. Here you have everything from butchers shop to fish & chip shop, and there are two good local pubs. Everything is at your fingertips, and whether you wish an active or a relaxing break, come here and enjoy the friendliness and hospitality of the Cornish, and leave with memories of a wonderful holiday in a charming locality.

USEFUL INFORMATION

OPEN : *All year* ***SELF CATERING***
CHILDREN : *Welcome* ***DISABLED ACCESS :*** *No*
GARDEN : *Spacious with BBQ* ***CREDIT CARDS :*** *None taken*
ACCOMMODATION : *Various catering from 2 to 8 persons.*

MEAD BARN COTTAGES
Welcombe, Nr. Bideford,
North Devon EX39 6HQ
Tel: 01288 331721

The beauty of this area is hard to beat with its nearness to the coast and cliffs, and the lovely countryside.Mead Barns nestle in a hollow overlooking the sea, close to the Cornish border. It is reached by driving down a typical Devon lane with its high banks covered in wild flowers, and is peaceful and serene. There are plenty of activities in the area such as fishing, surfing and especially walking. The multitudes of coastal paths offer walks for all abilities. Hartland Forest is near by offering its golf and leisure facilities. As an area of outstanding beauty it is definitely worth a visit. The cottages are built of slate and stone dating back to the 1850's. The theme is pine throughout but each cottage has a different colour scheme which enhances its individuality. All modern facilities are present with fridges, freezers and microwaves amongst others. A laundry room is available to everyone and also a games room housing billiards, pool, table tennis and darts. The childrens' play area is excellent with swings and tennis courts. There is a B.B.Q. area with garden furniture for those balmy summer evenings.

USEFUL INFORMATION

OPEN: *All Year*
CHILDREN: *Welcome*
PETS: *Welcome*
ACCOMMODATION: *Self Catering Cottages*
DISABLED ACCESS: *No*
CREDIT CARDS: *None Taken*
GARDEN: *Spacious and Individual*

COVE COTTAGE
Sharp Rock,
Mortehoe, Woolacombe,
North Devon EX34 7EA
Tel: 01271 870403

Cove Cottage has an amazing position on the cliffs over Mortehoe and looking over Woolacombe Bay. One could literally get hours of pleasure just looking out of the windows of this self-catering flat which has been built into the roof of the house. It is so comfortable, light and airy and furnished in a simple but attractive manner. The bathroom is luxurious and the kitchen equipped with everything one could wish for including a microwave and tumble dryer. In the sitting room there is a TV and a Video and also a portable TV in the kitchen. The terrace garden is delightful and once again you have stunning views. Open all the year, except at Christmas, the flat is centrally heated and double glazed throughout so that you can enjoy the bracing air of the North Devon coast out of season knowing you are going home to warmth and comfort. Ideal for anytime of the year. Mrs Lawrence will happily baby sit for guests.

USEFUL INFORMATION

OPEN; *All year except Xmas*
DISABLED ACCESS; *No*
ACCOMMODATION; *One flat*
CHILDREN; *Welcome. Baby sitting*
GARDEN; *Terraced. Stunning views*
PETS; *Yes*

SHALOM
32, Jocelyn Drive,
Wells,
Somerset
BA5 2ER

Tel: 01204 418576

Wells is the smallest city in England, and has a medieval feel about it. The Cathedral is one of Britain's finest, the west front was built around 1230 and it shows some wonderful figures. Wells also has one of England's oldest houses which is still lived in today. The Bishop's Palace and Moat has swans that ring a bell when they want food. Just 10 minutes walk away from all this is 'Shalom' a 3 bedroomed bungalow owned by Mrs. R. Rees. It has the usual accommodation 1 double and 2 single bedrooms, lounge/dining, kitchen and bathroom. The furnishings are modern and includes colour television, radio, microwave oven, cooker, fridge and washing machine. It has ample crockery and cutlery. To the side of the bungalow is a conservatory/sun lounge complete with patio chairs and a table. Shalom also has a lovely garden full of trees, shrubs and lawns to the front and side. Sheets, pillowcases, towels and tea towels are not provided, however, blankets and eiderdowns are there for your use. The disabled have not been forgotten in this property, apart from the entry into the bungalow which is by means of a step at the front and back doors, a hand rail has been fixed to the wall alongside the bath, and of course everything is on one level. A few minutes walk away you will find a newsagent and food shops, these are generally open early in the morning until early evening. There are several places of interest for you to explore Wookey Hole and its limestone caves, Cheddar Caves and Gorge to name but a few. For beach lovers a short drive away is Weston-Super-Mare and Burnham-on-Sea. An excellent location for a wonderful holiday.

USEFUL INFORMATION

OPEN; *All year*
CHILDREN; *Welcome*
CREDIT CARDS; *None taken*
LICENSED; *No* ***PETS;*** *Yes*
ACCOMMODATION; *Self-contained 3 bedroomed bungalow*

DISABLED ACCESS; *Apart from the one step at hand rail in bathroom, all on one level outside doors,*
GARDEN; *Yes, with garden furniture*
PARKING; *Cul-de-sac 30 metres from property*

WORZELS
Wheddon Cross,
Nr Minehead,
Somerset

Contact: *Helpful Holidays*
Coombe Farm, Chagford,
Devon TQ13 8DF

Tel: 01647 433593

Worzels is a charming single storey converted coachhouse approached via a long drive with wonderful views down across the valley. Situated in the little high village of Wheddon Cross - the gateway to Exmoor's most beautiful part, it has a shop and is bustling with farmers on auction days. The large comfortable sitting room has a stone fireplace housing a woodburner for chilly nights, a music centre and superb floor to ceiling windows which take in those beautiful views; the French doors lead to a patio and the garden beyond. The kitchen/diner is exceptionally well equipped with microwave, hob, oven, fridge/freezer and dishwasher, from here French windows lead out to a cobbled yard which is a real suntrap. There is a utility room complete with washing machine and tumble drier. Also on this floor is a WC with wash basin. Upstairs you will find 4 bedrooms, the master has ensuite facilities with the luxury of a jacuzzi, corner bath and hand-shower, another double and two twin. Each room is well furnished, attractively decorated, light and airy. A second bathroom has a shower. Worzels is set in three acres and has direct access onto the open moor, there is even a paddock and stabling for horses or ponies, so if you cannot bear to be away from your horse bring it with you! Table tennis, mini-snooker and darts can be played in the Games Room. For walkers and hikers this has to be the place to come, the area has a variety of spectacular walks and views to match. For those who just want peace and tranquillity Worzels is the ideal choice.

USEFUL INFORMATION

OPEN: *All year*
CHILDREN: *Welcome*
CREDIT CARDS: *None taken*
ACCOMMODATION: *Superb ETB '5 Key Highly Commended' coachhouse sleeping 8 persons*

DISABLED ACCESS: *Suitable for partially disabled*
GARDEN: *Yes + paddock and stabling*
PETS: *Horses/ponies*

CLIFTON COURT
FLAT 1
Putsborough Sands,
Woolacombe,
North Devon

Tel: 01271 813777
Fax: 01271 813664

The apartments in the prestigious Clifton Court development offer a wide range of facilities. The panoramic views stretch from Baggy Point to Morte Point with three miles of golden sands immediately below. Accessed by a short stroll, Putsborough Sands is a safe place for children sheltered by cliffs with ideal surfing conditions, with access onto the National Trust Coastal path. Each apartment has private parking. Electricity is included. There are Storage/ convector heaters in all rooms. You are offered the free use of the indoor heated pool and there are lockable cupboards available for bikes and surfboards.

Flat 1 which sleeps 4/5 + cot + high chair, is an exceptionally well maintained apartment with high quality fixtures and fittings. Approached by steps, with landings, the apartment is at ground floor level. Porch leading to Lounge/Dining Area, colour TV and video, a sofa bed offering an additional space for an extra person. Fully fitted modern Kitchen. Electric cooker, fridge, washer/dryer and microwave. Double patio doors open onto a large paved terrace with table and chairs provided to relax and enjoy the breathtaking views. Two bedrooms: (1) double with built-in wardrobe (2) twins with built-in-wardrobe. All duvets. Free linen and towels. Bathroom with bath,wc and wash basin. Additional separate shower room with electric shower and wash basin. All electric included. Storage/convector heaters throughout. Non-smokers preferred. This offers first class accommodation and benefits from an additional rear shared courtyard with bench style seating and suntrap patio. Being double aspect at the end of the building, all rooms are light and airy and offer a comfortable, well appointed apartment.

USEFUL INFORMATION

OPEN; *All year* ***CHILDREN;*** *Welcome*
CREDIT CARDS; *Yes* ***DISABLED ACCESS;*** *No special facilities*
GARDEN;*Paved terrace, table & chairs. Shared* ***PETS;*** *No*
Rear courtyard with bench seating & suntrap patio
Indoor, heated swimming pool

WESTERINGS
Forrabury, Boscastle,
Cornwall PL35 0DT

Tel: 01840 250389

This 200 year old Georgian house was once a rectory, and has now been tastefully converted into luxury, spacious apartments. The house is in a conservation area above the harbour of Boscastle which is a National Trust property. Situated on the grounds are three self-contained bungalows and the old coach house has also been converted to accommodate guests. All apartments are fully furnished in a modern style, have central heating and are fully equipped for self-catering. A short walk takes you up on to the headland where the sea views are magnificent and there are many walks along the coast. A room book in your accommodation gives you plenty of ideas of the local facilities including fishing, golf and pony trekking. Boscastle itself is a most attractive village, with its 14th century cottages and the friendly Cornish people. It is perfect for touring and one can visit any part of the peninsula and return within the day. Relax and unwind in these congenial surroundings in splendid, rural Cornwall.

USEFUL INFORMATION

OPEN: *All year*
CHILDREN: *Welcome*
CREDIT CARDS: *None taken*
LICENSED: *No*
ACCOMMODATION: *3 apartments, Coach House and 3 bungalows*

DINING ROOM: *Not applicable*
VEGETARIAN: *Not applicable*
DISABLED ACCESS: *Not really*
GARDEN: *Very pleasant*
PETS: *Welcome*

CHAPTER 2

SOUTHERN ENGLAND
Including
DORSET, WILTSHIRE, HAMPSHIRE & ISLE OF WIGHT

INCLUDES

Chapter 2

SOUTHERN ENGLAND
Dorset, Wiltshire, Hampshire

Southern England covers many counties and each has its own characteristics and charm. If you asked me to name my favourite I would be hard put to choose and in fact I find that wherever I happen to be at the time means the most to me. My journey through these counties must be fleeting and you will have to forgive me if I leave out some of your favourite places. Each county would make a book in itself.

The whole of the region is crammed with history, from the abundant fossils on the Dorset coastline, to the hundreds of stone circles and monuments of early man. The Bronze Age settlements and Iron Age forts, and later sites of events so momentous that they have marked the course of history itself.

Dorset has that lovely sleepy feeling about it. It is both comforting and timeless with its smoothly-rounded hills and convexities which have a passive and ancient solidity that soothes and reassures. 'Here I stand and here I be' might well be the motto of a landscape that has sustained Man since his earliest days, from the cliffs, coves and shingle of the coast, the whin-clad heaths, the hills and dales and woodlands of the hinterland. The configuration is so attractive and so varied that it might almost be taken as an epitome of the scenery of Southern England.

It is an intensely rural county, averaging rather more than one acre per inhabitant and is not disturbed by motorways or major road works. There is only one major conurbation, that of **Poole** and **Bournemouth** with the remainder of the population residing mainly in the numerous small market towns and countless villages and hamlets whose names have a resounding ring out of all proportion to their size and present day standing: Rime Intrinsica, Melbury Osmond, Toller Porcorum, Chaldon Herring and Tarrant Gunville. The names, the people and the scenery have inspired writers and artists over the centuries.

In common with many other such rural areas, early settlements seem to have proliferated along the banks of streams and rivers, hence the numerous Winterbournes, Piddles, Puddles, Tarrants, Cernes, Chars and Weys. The great expanse of enclosed water that is Poole Harbour provided the county's earliest sheltered part, and one that remains of great economic importance to this day.

My journey this time started in the extreme south-west in the delightful little town of **Lyme Regis** close to the boundary with Devonshire. Once an important harbour and protected from prevailing south-westerly winds by the massive breakwater known as the Cobb, Lyme Regis was granted its royal status by Edward I in 1284 during his wars against the French.

The town is enchanting, set on the shore surrounded by a backcloth of high steep hills and withhouses and shops set around narrow winding streets. It is a deservedly popular seaside resort, a role that replaced smuggling as a local, and profitable, pastime in the late 18th century. Jane Austen gives a vivid portrayal of the town in her novel 'Persuasion' written in 1815:

'..as there is nothing to admire in the buildings themselves, the remarkable situation of the town, the principal street almost hurrying into the water, the wall to the Cobb, skirting round the pleasant little bay, which in the season is animated with bathing machines and company, the Cobb itself, its old wonders and new improvements, with the very beautiful line of cliffs stretching out to the east of the town, are what the stranger's eye will seek; and a very strange stranger it must be, who does not see charms in the immediate environs of Lyme, to make him wish to know it better.'

I disagree with the eminent novelist's opinion of the local architecture, but wholeheartedly endorse the rest.

The wide main road through the village of **Charmouth** was first laid by the Romans on the foundations of an ancient pack-horse trail and after their departure it was favoured by the Saxons. The ancient highway became of increasing importance, linking the county towns of Exeter and Dorchester and the handsome Georgian and Regency buildings bear witness both to the popularity of the village as a coaching stop, and to the attractions of the area as a resort. Some of this history can be seen reflected in the displays at the **Charmouth Heritage Coast Centre**, together with exhibitions of fossils, geology and wildlife.

The lovely coast and inland scenery, combined with these small seaside communities, offers the holidaymaker a glimpse of more certain and simple pleasures and it is hardly surprising that families return year after year. Neighbouring **Chideock** has much the same atmosphere, albeit on a small scale; the houses here also line the hillside but the thatched cottage, rather than the grander Georgian and Victorian buildings of Charmouth, predominates. The happily named Duck Street leads to the tiny sea-side hamlet of **Seatown,** where the small River Winniford flows into the sea. The little beach is dominated by the highest cliff of the South Coast, **Golden Cap**,

618 feet above sea level. Now under the stewardship of the National Trust, the gorse clad cliff was the look-out post for an 18th century smuggling gang based in Chideock.

Apart from the obvious enjoyment to be had beside the sea, this western-most area of Dorset has a multitude of attractions inland; historic sites, lovely walks, pretty villages, friendly pubs and stately homes. **Whitchurch Canonicorum**, two miles inland from Charmouth has a link with those Viking raiders of long ago; the 13th century Church of St Candida and the Holy Cross contains the tomb of the saint, also known as St Wita, and who is thought to have been a Saxon woman slain in a raid.

Pilsdon Pen also bears evidence of an earlier culture with Iron Age earthworks to be found on the bare top of the highest hill in Dorset, at 909 feet a landmark for half the county and one that offers the most wonderful views.

Further north,**Thorncombe** clings to a steep hillside close to the border with Devon and Somerset, and between the village and the Somerset town of **Chard,** lie the lovely buildings of **Forde Abbey.** Started at the beginning of the 12th century, the Cistercian monastery was not fully completed for another 300 years. To avoid destruction at the Dissolution, the Abbot handed the Abbey over to the King. It has been a family home since the 17th century when Sir EdmundPrideaux, Attorney General to Cromwell, commissioned Inigo Jones to convert it into a private house. Set beside the River Axe in some 30 acres of beautiful gardens, the house and monastic buildings contain remarkable tapestries and furniture and pictures.

To the east, across the high rolling hills, lies the rambling village of **Broadwindsor**, reputedly the highest in Dorset, and close to the lovely wooded crest of **Lewesdon Hill**. Charles II stayed the night here after his failure to set sail from Charmouth; once again he had a narrow escape as the Parliamentarian soldiers were diverted by the site of one of their own camp-followers giving birth.

The principal market town for the area is **Beaminster**, a pleasant place which has had more than its share of bad luck, having been virtually destroyed by fire in 1644, 1684 and 1781; nevertheless it is a cheerful place where the little River Brit runs beside the main street with its handsome 18th century buildings.

Parnham House is world renowned as the home of John Makepeace furniture workshops, where innovative use of wood and the highest standards of woodworking skill reign supreme. The house dates from the Middle Ages, was rebuilt in Tudor times and further altered by the great Regency architect, John Nash. For 500 years it was the home of the Strode family, who are remembered in the church at Beaminster and within the park there is the grave of Lieutenant Rhodes-Moorhouse, the first airman to be awarded the Victoria Cross. The Makepeace family have restored both house and gardens and the result is superb.

Not far away is another house with lovely grounds, **Mapperton House** is perhaps the most beautiful manor house in Dorset and is set beside terraced gardens through which water gently flows. It is serene and timeless; qualities to be found throughout the county, but particularly in this region where the hills seemingly enfold and enclose minute communities guarding themselves against the intrusion of the modern world.

Now that **Bridport** has been by-passed it is much easier to enjoy this nice town with its very wide and handsome main street where no two buildings are quite alike, and the brick and stone Town Hall, complete with stately cupola, presides over all. To the east **Burton Bradstock**, a pretty village tucked away from the sea by a low ridge, lies close to the beginnings of the extraordinary **Chesil Beach.** One of the great wonders of England's coastline, the Beach is some 15 miles of blue-clay reef covered with an immense coating of shingle, more than 40 feet high in parts. No expert has yet produced a convincing theory as to why the pebbles get progressively smaller the further west along the Beach one goes. Behind Chesil Beach is The Fleet, a brackish and reed-filled lagoon.

North-east of Bridport, the narrow roads lead over the hills to **Powerstock**, a delightful village nestling beneath the 800foot high **Eggardon Hill**, where, from the massive earthen ramparts of an Iron Age fort on the top, excellent views are to be had of the surrounding countryside.

Returning southwards towards the fascination of Chesil Beach, the hilly country bounded by the A35 to the north and the Beach to the south has much to offer. **Kingston Russell** was the birthplace of Admiral Sir Thomas Masterman Hardy, Nelson's flag-captain at Trafalgar, and in whose arms Nelson died. A great seaman in his own right and passionately fond of his native county, particularly the village of **Portesham** where he spent much of his early life. The Hardy monument on neighbouring **Blackdown**, should not be confused with any memorial to Dorset'sgreatest author. The solid chimney like structure was erected to the memory of a great sailor and is still a notable landmark for those ships of the Royal Navy going about their lawful occasions in the Channel waters far below.

The gorse-laden heights overlooking the Beach are studded with reminders of far earlier civilisations; barrows, standing stones and circles mark the last resting places of forgotten tribal chieftains. **Abbotsbury** has a reminder of those pagan times in the survival of the ancient custom, Garland Day, held on May 13th. Thought to be a survival of sea-god worship, two garlands are carried through the village and one cast into the sea.

The village is one of the loveliest in the county, its narrow streets lined with mellow stone cottages, many of them thatched. Abbotsbury has had but three owners in its long history. First there was Orc, a steward of King Canute, and it was he and his wife Thola who established the Abbey. After the Dissolution, the village passed from the Church to the Strangways, Earls of Ilchester. The village suffered grievously during the Civil War; cottages were set alight, the Royalist Strangways' mansion was burnt to the ground and the pulpit of the parish church still bears bullet-holes received during a short but bloody battle, described by the Parliamentarian commander as being a 'hot bickering'. A masterful understatement

The Abbotsbury Sub Tropical Gardens have a wonderful display of rare and tender plants laid out around a walled garden with the added protection of a shelter-belt of trees. They were first laid out in 1760 and provide a stunning display of exotic blooms. **The Abbotsbury Swannery** dates back to the days when the monks reared swans for meat. Now the swanherd cares for around 1,000 mute swans, plus innumerable wildfowl, and his concern is that of a naturalist rather than that of an epicure.

Chesil Beach has long had a deserved reputation as a graveyard of ships and, together with the Fleet, as a haven for smugglers. This reputation was enhanced by the classic story of 'Moonfleet', which was written at the turn of the century by Meade Faulkner. It featured Fleet House, of Tudor origin and which is now the splendid **Moonfleet Manor Hotel.**

The eastern end of Chesil Beach runs into the massive rocky outcrop of **Portland**, the **'Gibraltar of Dorset',** with its great harbour until recently one of the main bases for the Royal Navy, and narrow isthmus connecting to the ancient town and port of **Weymouth**. A seaport since Roman times, the small harbour is still busy with fishing boats, yachts and cross-channel ferries, It is also a cheerful seaside resort, with a beautifully protected sandy beach and a fine esplanade, where the variety and irregularity of the buildings make for a view that is both comforting and good looking.

Portland has been a fortress since Roman times but it is perhaps best known for the high quality of the stone that has been quarried there since the 1700's. From this rocky hump, some four miles long and less than two miles wide, came stone for buildings as diverse as St Paul's Cathedral, London University and the United Nations Building.

The southern tip of Portland is known as **The Bill,** and is marked by a lighthouse which warns shipping not only of rocks but also the presence of a dangerous tidal race, where currents up to seven knots flow.

Economically, Portland's future is questionable. Stone is no longer a principal building materialand the naval presence has gone. There are many plans for its future and one hopes that the final outcome will be a happy and prosperous future for its friendly people.

Just north of Weymouth, to the west of the road to Dorchester lies the immense Stone Age hill fort of **Maiden Castle**, one of the largest in Europe. Dating back to 2000BC, the earthworks are truly impressive, covering some 47 acres, and stand as a still, silent tribute to the energies of the simple military engineers of long ago. **Dorchester,** the county town is fascinating. It has a colourful and sometimes violent past and its Roman origins are indicated by the layout of its main street, the square outlines of the town wall which ran where there are now tree-lined walks, and the remains of a magnificent villa behind County Hall, which reveals some of the original mosaics and the hypocaust, or central heating system. Just south of the town, at **Maumbury Rings**, an ancient 'henge' type monument of the stone circle variety was adapted by the Romans as an amphitheatre; it is a gruesome fact that the public gallows stood here until well into the 18th century. Judge Jeffreys opened his Bloody Assizes here trying those who were involved in the disastrous Monmouth Rebellion in 1685. The victims were involved frequently for no greater crime than being absent from their habitations from and at the time of the Rebellion. Those executed were hung, drawn and quartered, and their butchered bodies exhibited throughout the county as a grim warning.

Nearly 250 years later, the town was the scene of another famous 'trial' when six farm labourers from **Tolpuddle** were sentenced to seven years transportation for attempting to form a trade union.

It has to be said that today's town is far more just and friendly and wears its status as the county's capital far more lightly than many of its contemporaries. I feel this is partly to do with the character of Dorset and the fact that Dorchester is not a cathedral city; there is a light-hearted market town atmosphere with little of the dignity of the diocese. There is plenty to do and see including the excellent **Dorset County Museum** in West Street which has a section devoted to Dorset's most famous literary son, Thomas Hardy. Hardy was to Dorset as Wordsworth was to the Lakes, with much of their writing inextricably bound to their place of birth. Wessex was a long forgotten Saxon Kingdom until Hardy revived the title for use in his novel 'Far from the Madding Crowd' and many of the fictitious names in his writings refer to actual places. For instance, Dorchester is 'Casterbridge', Weymouth is 'Budmouth' and Sherborne 'Sherton Abbas.

Part of the charm of Dorchester is the fact that it is totally surrounded by the lovely rolling countryside. Nearby **Charminster** provides a link with the enterprising Spanish-speaking farmer, Squire Russell, for it was at **Wolferton House** that the future King of Castile stayed after his ship was driven into Weymouth by foul weather.

The modern traveller heads north along the A352, passing through the old and delightful village of **Cerne Abbas**. Lying in a chalk-lined valley and once more of a town than a village, the community's wealth was originally derived from the Benedictine Abbey, first established by the Saxon Ethelmaer, Earl of Cornwall, in 987 AD. The Dissolution brought the usual destruction and the only obvious remains are the handsome gatehouse, guest-house and tithe barns. The lovely 15th century church has a buttressed tower, a later Norman chancel and some early heraldic glass.

Cerne Abbas is probably best known for the enormous pagan figure of a priapic giant carved into the turf on the chalk hillside. His origins are unknown; local legend has a David and Goliath account of a local shepherd boy killing the giant while he slept on the hill, whereupon the villagersimmediately rushed up and marked the outline of the massive corpse, some 180feet from head to toe. He may be Neolithic or he may be the god, Hercules, carved by Roman Soldiers; no-one seems quite certain, although there is a strong belief that fertility is assured by spending the night on the giant phallus! Whatever the truth, the giant's outline still lies on the hillside, surrounded for miles around, by the stone pillars and earthen mounds of earlier and more superstitious times. In this rounded and hilly landscape, a turn away from the main road brings the traveller, by way of narrow twisting lanes, to tiny settlements and hamlets and one has the feeling that even in the 20th century, the ancient ways are given more than passing acknowledgment.

Mintern Gardens, at **Minterne Magna**, are a series of beautifully landscaped gardens which utilises lakes, cascades, streams and pools to show off a wonderful array of trees, shrubs and plants. Before reaching Sherborne, the road runs down to what Hardy called 'The Vale of Little Dairies' Blackmoor Vale. In comparison with the chalk downland grazing, this is rich, lush countryside and many dairies still survive, albeit somewhat larger than in Hardy's day.

Who could not be enchanted by **Sherborne** which is rightly claimed as Dorset's loveliest town. It has charm, character, it abounds with fine buildings set beside curving little streets. The learned St Aldhelm founded the Abbey and School in the 8th century, and to our good fortune both have survived to this day, the school being re-founded by Royal Charter after the Dissolution. Sherborne Abbey as seen today dates principally from the 15th century although evidence of its Saxon and Norman Predecessors clearly remain. The delicate stone fan-vaulting is beautiful and intricate and the local yellow stone from which the building is constructed lends to a feeling of warmth and mellowness to the magnificent interior. The people of Sherborne showed great far sightedness when they bought 'the Abbey, the grounds about it, the lead, the bells and other fittings' for the sum of three hundred pounds. Many of the abbey's old monastic buildings have been incorporated into the school, which rambles around much of the southern half of the town with its numerous halls, houses and playing fields.

The town and the surroundings are full of the most marvellous treasures and attractions. **Sherborne Museum**, in the old Abbey gatehouse holds items of local interest, including Roman remains, a splendid 15th century wall-painting and a model of the town's original Norman castle. The actual castle was built between 1107 and 1135 by Roger, Bishop of Salisbury, and if the construction of a fortress seems a somewhat un-ecclesiastical act, it should be remembered that Bishops in those days were not 'all gas and gaiters'. Between 871 and 933AD three Bishops of Sherborne fell in battle against the Danes.

The castle passed into the ownership of Sir Walter Raleigh in 1597, but he was not to enjoy ownership for long, being indicted for treason in 1603. Nevertheless, he left his mark; evidently deciding that the massively-built stone castle offered little in the way of home comforts, he therefore initiated the building of a more suitable abode almost immediately adjacent to the grim fortress. Thus Sherborne has not one, but two 'castles'. **Sherborne Old Castle** and later **Sherborne Castle**. The old castle remained as a defensive position until the Civil War, when it was stormed by Parliamentarians under General Fairfax and destroyed. The new castle, originally known as The Lodge, is owned by the Digby family who have been there since Sir John Digby was awarded the estate by James I in recognition for his services as Ambassador to Spain - another Spanish-speaker made good! The Digbys utilised much of the ruins of the old castle to enlarge and enhance the house, and later employed Capability Brown to landscape the area around the two castles. The lake, waterfall and lovely gardens are the result, while the interior of the house is in restrained elegance, with notable collections of furniture and porcelain.

To the west of the town, close to the border with Somerset, lies another lovely home,**Compton House.** This 16th-century building is at the heart of an unique enterprise; for thirty years it has been the home of **Worldwide Butterflies**, where a variety of habitats provide the settings for butterflies and moths from all over the world. In conjunction with this amazing programme of conservation and breeding is **Lullingstone Silk Farm**, which has provided the silk used on many Royal occasions.

Just to the south is the intriguingly-named village of **Purse Caundle**. Amazingly this delightful community was described at the beginning of the century as a 'poor village... where most thatched roofs of the cottages have been replaced by corrugated iron, the churchyard of a ruinous condition...' All is now well, with the lovely 15th-century church possessed of an unusual panelled chancel arch, and the beautiful Elizabethan **Purse Caundle Manor** lying close beside the 'clear stream' that goes on to feed Sherborne lake. The manor has a most attractive garden, a great hall with minstrel's gallery, and an interior well, dug in case of siege!

Between Sherborne and Blandford Forum is **Sturminster Newton**, a truly lovely Minster town, cut in two by the gently flowing River Stour. It is full of picturesque cottages and has an ancient bridge which still bears a notice threatening to deport you if you cause damage! It really is a corner of rural England that seems to have remained unchanged. The little shops still have 19th century facades, the narrow roads cause a nightmare on market days but it is all taken in good part by the residents who would not change their delightful town for the world.

Continuing eastwards, the road leads on to Shaftesbury, but the unhurried traveller will find it well worth turning off and exploring the area around **Gillingham**, the county's most northerly town. Centuries ago there was a forest around these parts and at the time of Elizabeth I, it was recorded as being 'Her Majesty's Park and Forest of Gillingham, and Sir Walter Raleigh once held the honorary post of Forest Ranger.

South east of Gillingham, the land rises steeply to a 700foot plateau where stands the Saxon town of **Shaftesbury**. It is claimed that this ancient town contains more history in one square mile than any other settlement in ancient Wessex; a claim the visitor can well believe. For all that, it is far from being a fusty old museum of a town, being bright, lively and cheerful. Today as it has ever been it is an important market centre and has expanded to take advantage of its position and the talents of its population. Nevertheless, from both the physical and historical viewpoint it is extremely attractive and, in places like the steep cobbled Gold Hill with its wonderful views and varied architecture, quite enchanting. It has to be said though that particular view is oddly familiar to many since it is a favourite with art directors and has been used in television drama as well as numerous advertising campaigns.

The handsome Georgian appearance of **Blandford** owes everything to a great fire and two Bastards; the town was almost completely destroyed in 1731 and restored by two talented architects with that unfortunate name.

Stourpaine nestles at the foot of the great chalk hills, guarding what was once an important crossing of the River Stour. The country lanes meander to the south-west, climbing along the side of the steep chalk downs. Tucked into the lee, small villages and hamlets huddle against the hillside, which rises to its peak at **Bulbarrow Hill**, at 902 feet, the second highest in Dorset. It is alleged that both the Bristol Channel and the Isle of Wight are visible from this point.

Some three miles to the south-east, along a large tree-clad ridge, the road runs down into a steep narrow combe containing what must be the most unique village in Dorset**, Milton Abbas**. Essentially it is little more than a grass-lined street flanked on either side by twenty identical thatched cottages. There is a lake, a school and a pub,**The Hambro Arms**. The story behind this extraordinarily neat litle community begins with the founding of the Abbey in 932AD by King Athelstan. Later it became a Benedictine Monastery and was surrounded by a small market town that contained a famous brewery, a grammar school and numerous pubs. This was the state of affairs until 1786 when one, Joseph Damer, acquired the Abbey and its estates from the descendants of Henry VIII's lawyer who was awarded the Abbey (for a small consideration) at the time of the Dissolution for his servces in securing the said Monarch's divorce from Catherine of Aragon. Damer, afterwards Earl of Dorchester, proposed to build a great house on the site and objected to the rowdy presence of the small town. His solution was to buy up the entire town, lock, stock and barrel . This he accomplished over a period of twenty years demolishing each property as it fell vacant. Those who wished to stay in his employ were removed to the new village, built to a plan by the ever industrious Capability Brown. The house that Lord Dorchester built from the monastic buildings is now a school, but the Abbey Church remains and is a superb Gothic building dating from the 12th and 14th centuries.

The adjacent villages such as **Melcombe Bingham**, are every bit as attractive but rather more conventional; the 'toy town' effect of Milton Abbas takes a little time to get used to, but there is no denying its charm and fascination.

The River Piddle lends its name to the villages east of Dorchester known collectively as the Piddles and Puddles. **Tolpuddle** is celebrated for its association with the ill-treated farm workers of 1831. Public outcry forced the Government to pardon six men, but it took time for the message to reach Australia and one of the Martyrs only found out by sheer luck; four years later on a remote sheep station, he read of his pardon in an old and discarded newspaper!

Piddlehinton has a good Perpendicular church and two fine houses in **Glebe Court** and **Marston Manor**, while **Piddletrenthide's** church is of Norman origin with the village school sporting gates that once graced Westminster Abbey; the gift of a local man who became a famous London jeweller. **Puddletown** has a superb medieval church with box pews, a musician's gallery and tombs and memorials of the Martyn family.

Bovington Heath has been the site of an army camp since the First World War, and the **Tank Museum** must be the most complete collection of armoured fighting vehicles in existence, containing over 260 such vehicles from 23 countries. The narrow chalk ridge that divides the sea from heath has many notable beauty spots, the best known being the nearly circular **Lulworth Cove**. The coastline here has been carved into fantastic shapes by the ceaseless motion of the sea, and just to the west, a great natural arch of limestone projects out into the water at **Durdle Door.**

Corfe Castle was begun in the 1080's and expanded over the centuries. King John made much of the place, which is understandable given his undoubted unpopularity, any large, remote and easily defended castle must have been immensely appealing. He kept his crown, his ill-gotten treasure and his unfortunate prisoners at **Corfe**, few of whom were ever seen again.

The great white cliffs of **Durlston** guard the attractive little resort of **Swanage**, once the principal port for the shipping of Purbeck stone and marble. The sandy beach and sheltered waters of the Bay and that of neighbouring **Studland** make the area ideal for family holidays. Swanage is justlypopular and the town is attractive and welcoming; apart from water-sports of every variety and the obvious attractions of the area, there is a fine parish church, built in the 13th century and sited next to the Millpond, the steam engines of **The Swanage Railway**, the **Tithe Barn Museum** and numerous pubs, hotels and restaurants.

The northern side of **Purbeck** is bounded by the huge natural expanse of **Poole Harbour**, whose perimeter, laid in a straight line , would stretch for some 95 miles.! The oldest community on the shores of this great lake-like harbour is **Wareham**, at the western end. The town suffered a terminal decline due to the silting up of the River Frome, attacks by pirates, plague and a succession of fires, the worst destroying over 140 buildings in 1762. The town fared no better in the Monmouth Rebellion with some of the citizens being brutally despatched by the dreadful Judge Jeffreys. It is hard to see what this most attractive and friendly little town ever did to encourage such a catalogue of disasters. It has two fine churches, plenty of interesting buildings, wonderful surroundings and in spite of the past, a remarkably cheerful atmosphere.

Poole has become almost as one with its neighbour to the east, **Bournemouth,** but still retains a strong streak of individuality; besides being a port it is a major residential centre, a light industrial centre and a recreational centre. There are two excellent museums, **The Waterfront Museum** and the **Guildhall Museum** and the delightfully restored **Scaplen's Court**, a medieval merchant's house. On the Quay, **Poole Pottery** has an international reputation, while the revamped and pedestrianised High Street has a modern indoor shopping centre and a wide variety of shops, pubs and restaurants. Within the harbour, boat trips are available to such attractions as **Brownsea Island**, a nature reserve and bird sanctuary where Baden Powell held his first scout camp. If the weather is unkind then the **Tower Park** is a vast indoor complex housing such diverse activities as bowling and ice-skating, together with water-slides, cinema, shops and restaurants.

Bournemouth is a town full of hotels and places to stay which concentrates on caring for tourists and business people. It is many things to many people depending on what you are looking for. Wonderful place for a quiet holiday with excellent beaches, pleasant walks along the cliffs and good entertainment in the theatre and concert hall. It has several attractive places around it including **Southbourne** and of course, the dignified **Christchurch** to the west - a wonderfully central position for anyone who wants to stay on the borders of Dorset and Hampshire.

Wimborne Minster is where the great twin towers of St Cuthberga stand on the site of an 8th century monastery. The church is a splendid amalgamation of ecclesiastical styles, from Norman to late Gothic, and contains many treasures, including an 800 year old font, a chained library, an Orrery or astronomical clock, and many interesting tombs and memorials. The town is an attraction in itself with an award winning local museum to tell its story in **The Priest's House Museum**. Other places of interest are the lovely **Knoll Gardens**, a six acre site of rare and exotic plants, and, to the south of the town, the Georgian **Merley House,** with its fascinating model toy collection, and **Merley Bird Gardens**, with avians ranging from parrots to penguins.

Kingston Lacy, a National Trust property has wonderful pictures and grounds and should be visited. Some half a dozen miles north of Wimborne lies **Wimborne St Giles**, on the edge of the old royal hunting grounds of **Cranborne Chase**. The Ashleys, Earls of Shaftesbury, have their seat here and the pleasant but ornate little church is full of their memorials. Many of the family were noted political reformers and philanthropists and the welcoming **Bull Inn** was built forworkers on the estate. Another great political family are the Cecils, Marquesses of Salisbury, who's home has been at neighouring **Cranborne** since 1603. The fact that there was once a great Saxon Abbey on the site of the 13th century church and that William Conqueror gave the manor to his Queen, Matilda, shows the esteem that this attractive little village was once held in; perhaps because from 908AD to 1120, it was the seat of the Chase Court, which administered the hunting rights.

The deer that were once so prized by Saxon and Norman nobility still graze among the woods and coverts in this lovely part of the county. In the neat village which delights in the enchanting name of **Sixpenny Handley**, the cheerful **Roebuck Inn** is a reminder that the descendants of those noble animals are around; as too are the descendants of those who hunted them so long ago. Somehow, this seems only right in an ancient county possessed of timeless charm.

WILTSHIRE

The true inhabitants of South Wiltshire are unhurried rather than slow, thoughtful rather than thick. Their character has been shaped by the countryman's compromising attitude to the seasons and the weather, yet they don't lack for native wit. True Wiltshiremen are known as 'Moonrakers' after two of their number were challenged one moonlit night, raking the surface of a village pond with hay-rakes. Their explanation for this strange activity was that they were trying to retrieve 'they gurt yaller cheese' pointing to the reflection of the moon in the water. The interrogators rode away laughing and tapping their heads: but the last laugh was on them, for they were excisemen and unknown to them, the pond contained smuggled casks of brandy! There 'bain't no flies' on a Moonraker, as the over confident outsider can find to his cost. The story has echoes in other counties associated with the free-traders, but in Wiltshire it rings the truest.

My journey in Dorset ended on the edge of **Cranbourne Chase** which runs into the south-west of Wiltshire towards Salisbury. In medieval times much of this area was heavily afforested but now it is a region of chalkland divided by the valleys of the Ebble and the Nadder. The clearwaters flow by some of the most lovely little villages and hamlets in the county, often settlements of great antiquity that lie tucked into folds of the hills and protected by woodland. This is delightful country and an area that repays the peripatetic wanderer in full.

Ebbesbourne Wake is a rambling village to the south of **White Sheet Hill** (incidentally, there are two hills of this name in the area - this one is south of the Shaftesbury-Salisbury road and the other is near Mere, to the north). Thatched cottages cluster around what was once an important cattle drover's trail. Continuing eastwards via **Fifield Bavant** with its miniature Norman church, the valley floor begins to broaden by the time one reaches the 'capital' of the stream-set villages,**Broadchalke**. The Ebble provides nourishment for watercress beds and is splendid for trout fishing and brewing! On the northern side of White Sheet Hill where the bridleways are still a favourite with local riders, are the neighbouring villages of **Ansty** and **Swallowcliffe** close to which are two castles with the name of Wardour. Strictly speaking neither are true castles; **Old Wardour Castle** was more akin to the fortified chateaux of France and was a tower house of octagonal shape. Its defensive capability was proven in 1634, when the elderly Lady Blanche Arundell, commanding a force of twenty five men and some dozen or so womenfolk, held out against a besieging Parliamentarian force of 1,300. The siege lasted five days and nights and was ended when Lady Blanche negotiated an honourable surrender. The Parliamentarians reneged on the conditions, imprisoned the gallant defenders and looted the castle. When her son Lord Arundell heard the news, he became the besieger but at great cost: in order to force a conclusionto the siege, he was forced to blow up his own inheritance. In 1776, the family built a new house within sight of the romantic ruins of the old. **Wardour Castle** is a rather austere Palladian mansion designed by James Paine for the eighth Lord Arundell, which became a school after the Arundell family's tenure came to an end.

The surrounding countryside and villages are a delight to the curious visitor. **Chilmark**, where the best of the beautiful creamy limestone was quarried, has a wealth of lovely houses built of the same material; the stone being first utilised by the Romans and later in the construction of Salisbury Cathedral and then Wilton House. A stream running through the village is spanned by a delightful little stone bridge and the Early English church has a broad spire. The Teffonts, **Teffont Magna** and **Teffont Evias**, are charming. Many of the cottages in the latter have their own little stone bridges giving access across the stream from front door to street. To the south of the A30, at **Fovant**, there are some moving examples of 20th century graffiti; the huge regimental crests carved into the hillside by soldiers undergoing training during the First World War. Sad to reflect on how few returned to see their handiwork, and how few of those regiments have survived. **East Knoyle's** chief claim to fame is that it was the birthplace of Sir Christopher Wren who was far from being the only talented member of that family; the ornate plaster-work in the chancel of the parish church was designed by his father, the rector of the parish.

Close to the Somerset border, at **Mere**, is one of the finest churches in Wiltshire. St Michael the Archangel is an elegant blend of 13th and 15th century styles with fine decorative work and a 100foot tower which dominates the handsome small town. The undulating downlands to the north contain two of Wiltshire's most famous stately homes. The first is **Stourhead** where the famous gardens contain the source of the meandering River Stour. In 1714 the estate was sold to the Hoare family, goldsmiths and bankers, the old house was demolished and a handome Palladian mansion built in its place. However the chief glory of Stourhead are the grounds; the talented Henry Hoare was inspired by a Grand Tour of Europe and devised a delightful series of romantic gardens surrounding the lake, complete with temples and a grotto sheltering amongst the magnificent specimen trees.

The Hoare family continued to enhance both house and estate until, following the loss of their only son in the First World War, the late Sir Henry Hoare generously donated it to the National Trust. There is a sad but touching postcript to this story when Sir Henry and his wife, having given away their beloved home to which they had devoted most of their lives, died within two hours of each other.

The second great stately home stands just to the north and close to the Somerset border. **Longleat**, a palatial Elizabethan mansion set in wonderful grounds landscaped by the inimitable Capability Brown, is perhaps the best known such house in the country. Until the Dissolution it was the site of a medieval priory; the great house that replaced it was built by Sir John Thynne and has remained in the hands of the same family ever since. During the late 19th century it was redecorated in Italian Renaissance style with elaborately painted ceilings. Some idea of the scale of the house can be gained by the fact that it has seven libraries housing over 40,000 volumes! The late Marquess of Bath, faced with the horrendous problems of maintaining such a huge and elaborate building was the first peer to open his house on a business basis to the public,and as an added attraction, turned much of the surrounding estate into a fine Safari Park. Other entertainments, rallies and events have meant that these radical and pioneering measures have produced one of the country's premier tourist attractions.

Warminster is an appropriate name for the old town that plays host to a number of military establishments who exercise on the great open spaces of **Salisbury Plain**, immediately to the west. It is near the head of the third of the river valleys that run from the western county boundary back towards

Salisbury. The river is the Wylye, one of the loveliest of the gin-clear chalk streams so beloved by trout fisherman and its valley was described in 1824 by William Cobbett as being 'Fine, very fine.'

Roughly halfway between Warminster and Salisbury is **Wylye** itself now thankfully by-passed. The river runs past an old mill and many of the cottages feature the checker-work stone and flint to be found throughout this part of Wiltshire.

Wiltshire takes its name from the West Saxons who settled in the valley at **Wilton**, the 'farmstead beside the banks of the Wylye'. Although now a small well-to-do town, Wilton was once capital of Saxon Wessex: Alfred founded an abbey here and there was also a royal palace. The Dissolution saw the Abbey in the hands of Sir William Herbert, first Earl of Pembroke, and the estates have remained in the possession of that family ever since. Sir William demolished the Abbey and asked his friend Hans Holbein to design him a house utilising much of the remains. It was a wonderful house. Elizabeth I held court here, Shakespeare's company first performed 'As You Like It' before James I, and Charles I declared that he did 'love Wilton above all places, and did come here every summer.' Sadly a great fire destroyed much of the house in 1647, but happily the great Inigo Jones was on hand to rebuild. The result is one of the most magnificent and dignified stately homes in the country.

The Pembrokes have a strong entrepreneurial streak and although Wilton has long been the centre for weaving, it was the eighth earl who established the famous Wilton reputation for carpets. He combined the local assets of plentiful wool from the sheep of Salisbury Plain with the talents and skills of French weavers, then renowned throughout the world for the superb quality of their work. Unfortunately, Louis XIV of France regarded his weavers as a national asset and guarded them accordingly; the earl was forced to adopt some underhand methods and smuggled a number of the coveted craftsmen out of France in a giant barrel of wine! **The Wilton Carpet Company** was established in 1655 and is still going strong. It has an excellent museum and shop.

Some pretty villages surround Wilton including **Barford St Martin** and **Burcombe**. It is well worth spending time seeking out the narrow lanes and B roads which will lead you to these and other delightful spots.

There is a triumvirate of ancient and important dwelling-places close to where the three valleys of the Wylye, Nadder and Ebble meet, and their histories are all intertwined. The oldest recorded site is that of **Old Sarum**, a 56 acre earthwork on a rise to the north of Salisbury. Of Iron Age origin, it was appropriated by the Romans and later became a Saxon fortified town, important enough for King Edgar to hold a Parliament there in 960AD and to have a mint. The Normans, probably by virtue of its raised and protected position, made a great to-do about the place, using it as an administrative headquarters and building a citadel and cathedral. It was here, in 1086, that William held council to establish the feudal system and to initiate the compilation of the Domesday Book. However, by the beginning of the 13th century all was not well within the ancient ramparts; friction between the soldiers and the clergy, coupled with cramped conditions and shortage of water led to Bishop Richard Poore seeking a new site for the cathedral. Naturally, he went first to Wilton, since it was the nearest community of size and importance, but the Abbess objected strongly to the thought of a rival religious foundation. Eventually Bishop Poore selected a site where the Wylye, Nadder and Avon met amongst lush green meadows. Legend has it thatthe spot was chosen by loosing an arrow from the ramparts of Old Sarum. The archer must have been an exceptional man, doubtless aided by a northerly gale, for the new site is some two miles from the old!

Under the direction of one Elias Dereham, rightly described as an 'incomparable artificer', building proceeded apace. The stone which has weathered over the centuries to a lovely greeny-grey was quarried and carted over the rutted lanes from Chilmark to New Sarum, or **Salisbury**, where the master-masons gave it its final shaping before it was hoisted into position. The building was completed in the remarkably short time of 40 years and is consequently an almost perfect example of Early English throughout. Almost certainly, Elias was aware of the problems that beset another cathedral, Winchester, which was also built on marshy ground and whose central tower had collapsed in 1107, for he left the construction of the elegant spire to his successors in the next century. By the time the people of Old Sarum, who appeared to have sided with the Bishop against the uncouth soldiers, had deserted the old hill-fort and settled around the new cathedral. There was nothing haphazard about this settlement; the new town was carefully planned from the start with the streets neatly laid out in a grid system which lasted almost untouched until the present century. There were numerous water-channels which led to the medieval nickname 'The Venice of England' and it may be that the drainage effect of these channels gave Bishop Wyvil and his architect, Richard of Farleigh, the confidence to add the audacious and elegant 404foot spire in 1334. Aware that vibration is the cause of collapse, the master-builder housed the peal of bells in a separate campanile. Over 400 years later, it was left to the 18th century architect James Wyatt to add, or rather subtract, the finishing touches. He was much criticised at the time for his ruthlessness, but it is to him that we owe the parity and beauty of what, externally, is the most beautiful cathedral in the country. Wyatt demolished the campanile, cleared away the jumble of tombstones in the graveyard and laid out the great sward of mown grass that surrounds the building. He removed much of the ornate that was within, including much of the early glass; the result is the austere Gothic nobility of the original craftsmen, who dared in those far off times to construct such a great and lofty edifice on marshy grounds; their decision must have been an act of faith in itself.

The great spire is a landmark from far and wide and every year thousands come to wonder and pay homage to those old master-builders. Glorious as the building is, with its great cloisters, massive Purbeck pillars, lovely choir vaulting, copy of Magna Carta and ancient clock (1386 - and still ticking!), it has to be said that part of its attraction lies in its incomparable setting. The Close is rectangular in shape, surrounded by an intact medieval wall, with a wonderful collection of buildings, houses, some contemporary with the great church, others fine examples of Queen Anne or Georgian. Three of these are not only fine examples of the architecture of their day but also excellent museums. A 13th century house, The Wardrobe, so named because it was once used for storing clothes belonging to the Bishop and his entourage, is now home to **The Museum of the Duke of Edinburgh's Royal Regiment.** It contains a fascinating collection of the historical items relating to 250 years of military history. The King's House is a 14th-century building housing the award-winning **Salisbury and South Wiltshire Museum** with a fine collection of archaeological and historical artefacts. The classic facade of **Mompesson House**, built in 1701, conceals a fine collection of glassware and furniture together with a delightful garden.

Salisbury is altogether a beautiful city and one which rewards the interested visitor with hours of pleasure. A Cathedral city always attracts the arts and Salisbury is no exception; there is a festival in September, music in the Cathedral and the Guildhall, exhibitions in the Arts Centre and live theatre at the excellent Playhouse. There is an attractive and well patronised racecourse whilst virtually all forms of recreation and sport are catered for in and around the city. You may find it easier to stay outside Salisbury and if you wish to I can recommend the hamlet of **Britford**, with the river running alongside and where **Bridge Farm** will open its welcoming arms to you.

The Avon runs south from Salisbury; passing the great estate of **Longford Castle**. The splendid mansion is a testament to one woman's ambition; she was Helena, wife of Sir Thomas Gorges, Governor of Hurst Castle during the reign of Elizabeth I. Hurst is on the Hampshire coast and during the battle of the Spanish Armada, a galleon was driven aground closeby. Lady Gorges prettily asked the Queen if she might have the wreck, omitting to inform her sovereign that the galleon was laden with silver! Consequently Sir Thomas' modest medieval manor-house was transformed into a large and imposing castle. Unusual in that it is triangular in shape with a tower at each corner; the castle is now the home of the Earl of Radnor, whose family have owned it since the 18th century.

The little town of **Amesbury** is always worth visiting for many reasons. It is one of the oldest continually-inhabited sites in the country and has a strong connection with the Arthurian legends. Legend has it that after the death of Arthur, Queen Guinevere became Abbess of Amesbury. Modern Amesbury is a friendly, bustling place, providing shopping facilities and accommodation for many of the modern military establishments that lie around it. The great expanse of Salisbury Plain to the north and west is the principal area where the weaponry and soldiers of today exercise to protect our civilisation - but surrounding Amesbury are the mysterious relics and memorials of civilisations of which we know little. The best known of these, of course is **Stonehenge**. Viewed from the main road, the stones appear insignificant against the sky-line; approach closer and they become massively impressive, the largest weighing some 50 tons. The image is so familiar to us we almost take it for granted until closer contact with its scale and brutal bulk begin to impress on our consciousness together with an almost indefinable sense of wonder and awe. Gazing at the marvellous circle of upright stones with their huge lintels, the question that comes to mind are Who, When, Why and How? The answers range from the wildly fanciful to the reasoned and scientific, but it must be admitted that even the soundest of answers is but theory and there are still great gaps in our knowledge when it comes to a matter of actual fact.

The high ground of the Plain is divided from the richer and lower soil of Northern Wiltshire by the road that runs from **Westbury** to **Upavon**. Protected by the bulk of the downland, numerous villages, hamlets and farmsteads are spread along the road. Solidly prosperous **Westbury** made its money from cloth-weaving, glove-making and later from foundries exploiting a seam of iron-ore that was discovered nearby. It is a nice town with an imposing Town Hall, fine Georgian houses and a nice little market place, but the chief attraction for most visitors lies on the hillside to the east of the town where a great White Horse is carved into the chalk downland. Some 160 feet high, the present shape was cut out of the turf in 1778 and overlies an earlier, somewhat oddly shaped animal of unknown origin. It is claimed that the original was made to commemorate King Alfred's victory over the Danes at the Battle of Ethandun in 878 A.D. This is by no means certain since no-one is sure where Ethandun actually is; no matter, the great horse is undoubtedly impressive and worth a visit. On the heights above is the 23 acre site of **Bratton Castle**, a massive and ancient earthwork hill-fort whose presence gives some credence to theories about that battle so long ago.

Continuing eastwards, **Edington's** past is reflected in it's great church. Edington Priory was built between 1352 and 1361 and is therefore a fine example of the style known as Perpendicular. The Priory was the scene of a brutal and scandalous murder in 1449; at the time, the county was unsettled by the peasant's revolt, known as Jack Cade's Rebellion and the Bishop of Salisbury,one William Ayscough, felt Edington to be safer than his own cathedral. Sadly he was wrong, for the mob sought him out and dragged him from High Mass. At the top of the hill he ws savagely stoned to death. These days the church is widely known for its annual music festival.

Erlstoke has a connection with the legendary Dick Turpin for Tom Boulter, a highwayman whose exploits were often attributed to Turpin, stole a horse - and its name really was Black Bess!

Devizes lies not far to the north and close to the geographical heart of Wiltshire. It is a pleasant small market town. There are two attractive Norman churches and it has a thriving market. The town is an important centre for agriculture and light industry.

In medieval times it was second only to Salisbury in cloth-manufacturing and was one of the principal corn-markets in the West of England. There are a great many interesting and picturesque buildings including **The Bear Hotel**, an old coaching inn where, in the 18th century, the father of Sir Thomas Lawrence, the portrait painter, was once landlord. There is also the excellent **Devizes Museum**, which makes a speciality of displaying many of the Bronze Age finds taken from the county's innumerable sites.

Every year the Devizes to Westminster canoe race takes place using much of the old Kennet and Avon Canal which once linked London to Bristol. The Trust now administers the canal and has an exhibition centre on the wharf and, to the west of the town, at Caen Hill there is an amazing example of early 19th-century civil engineering where the canal is made to 'climb' the steep gradient by means of a flight of 16 locks.

The Vale of Pewsey runs between the high ground of the Plain to the south, and the even higher ground of the Marlborough Downs to the north. The Vale is some twelve miles long by five wide and contains some of the richest farmland in the country. The settlements between the hills are quiet and peaceful, their pasts containing no great historical dramas or events. The ecclesiastical architecture is particularly fine, probably as a result of agricultural wealth, and at **Chirton** there is one of the finest Norman churches in England. Built in 1170, it has a magnificent timber roof and fine decorative work, particularly around the doorway and the font.

The little town which lends its name to the Vale, **Pewsey**, is a friendly and cheerful place with good buildings and a fine statue of King Alfred gazing across the River Avon from the crossroads, a reminder of the time when the community was owned by Saxon Kings. The marketing and milling of corn and an iron foundry contributed to past wealth and every September there is a riotous celebration described as 'the Mother of West County carnivals'.

South of Pewsey, **Upavon** is situated at the foot of downland and overlooked by the extensive earthworks of **Casterley Camp**, a fortification dating from the first century A.D. To the east of the village is another, but more modern reminder of military activity in the area. **RAF Upavon** was one of the earliest purpose-built airfields in the country, constructed in 1912 to house the Central Flying School of the Royal Flying Corps.

The nobility who came to **Ludgershall** for sport would have looked to the preserves of the **Chute Forest** for their entertainment; the great medieval woodland spread from Hampshire through to Wiltshire and would have harboured huge herds of deer. The border between the two counties is hilly and broken and still contains large clumps of woodland. It is beautiful countryside, crossed by the **Chute Causeway**, a Roman road that is far from being perfectly straight and populated by a number of attractive little villages sheltering amongst the trees.

To the north-west, via the Causeway, is the pleasant village of **Burbage**, once totally surrounded by the **Savernake Forest**. Nearby **Wolfhall** was the home of the Seymours, hereditary wardens of another once vast forest, a favourite hunting ground for Norman kings. It was at Wolfhall tht Henry VIII met and courted Jane Seymour, his future queen who later died in childbirth. Half a mile from Burbage Wharf is the **Bruce Tunnel**, which is some 1500 feet long; horses were not used here since the boats were pulled through by hand using chains strung along the tunnel wall..

On the edge of Savernake is another of those ancient burial mounds known as **Barrows**; this particular one is believed to have been the last resting place of Maerla (in local legend, Merlin the Wizard) and the conjunction of names has been taken by the town that lies alongside, **Marlborough**. A handsome and popular town with fine, predominantly Georgian architecture lining the immensely wide main street. Where cars are parked down the middle of this street today, market stalls and livestock were tethered in the past; in fact, life in this cheerful town often seemed to be little short of one great long street party. A visitor in the 19th-century reported that there were '1333 partakers of conviviality seated at one long table from the market house to St Peter's Church, nearly half a mile'. Because of the town's past importance as a staging post on the main London to Bristol road, the modern 'partaker of conviviality' is well provided for at the many coaching inns that have survived.

The road to the west passes through small rural communities in the Downs, containing many a delight so typical of Wiltshire, sites where the historic and pre-historic sit peacefully side by side. **Fyfield** has a 13th-century church with a splendid 15th-century tower, complete with pinnacles and gargoyles. Half a mile away are the strange stones that comprise the **Devil's Den**, actually the remains of the stone-framed burial chamber that was once covered by a barrow, or mound. At first glance, **Avebury** appears little more than a picturesque downland village with an attractive grouping of part-Saxon church, the gabled Elizabethan **Avebury Manor**, thatched cottages and farmsteads - and then one notices the stones. Massive weather wrought lozenges of sandstone, many weighing more than 40 tons, stand upright in groups, around and amongst the village.

Avebury Stone Circle pre-dates Stonehenge by some two centuries and differs particularly in that the great stones are undressed; called sarsens (a local corruption of 'saracen' or foreign) they are found locally on Marlborough Downs. They surround the village, contained within the remains of a large earth ring, some 1200 feet across. Many are missing, having been broken up over the centuries for use in local houses and barns, but expert excavation has revealed their originl placement. The Stone Circle is by no means the only prehistoric site in the area and by no means the most mysterious. A 50 foot wide avenue of megaliths, nearly a mile long, once led to an older site, named the **Sanctuary**, near the village of **West Kennett**. The stones here have long vanished but, once again, patient archaeological detective work has established their positions. On the southern flank of Avebury is perhaps the strangest object of all, the vast conical earthwork of **Silbury Hill**; an earthen pyramid, 130 feet high whose base covers a staggering five and a half acres, large enough to fill Trafalgar Square and reach three quarters of the way up Nelson's Column. Described as ' the largest man-made mound in Europe' its purpose and origins are obscure; since the 18th century, shafts have been driven into its mighty bulk in search of burial chambers or similar but with no success. All that we know is that it was built over 4,000 years ago, that a million cubic yards of chalk were excavated and, given the simple tools of the period, would have taken 500 people ten years to build! Local legend has it that a certain King Sil or Zel, is somewhere beneath the mound buried upright on his horse and clad in a suit of golden armour.

Close by Silbuy Hill is **West Kennett Long Barrow**, a 350 foot long burial mound from around3,500 BC while to the north is **Windmill Hill** a series of concentric earthworks which was the home of a Neolithic race of farmers who were probably responsible for the long barrow. The excellent small **Alexander Keiller Museum** has many exhibits and finds relating to these ancient sites, and is named after the archaeologist who did so much to interpret the extraordinary works of so long ago. Nearby the splendid thatched Great Barn houses **The Museum of Wiltshire Folk Life**, with fascinating displays of rural crafts, skills, tools and equipment.

There is no doubt that it can be extremely breezy up on the downs and it has been suggested that specialised forms of miniature tornadoes or whirlwinds are responsible for a phenomona known as **Corn Circles**, strange geometric shapes that appear in the great cornfields around this area. Ineveitably, fanciful theories have been produced linking the shapes with the ancient stone circles, or even with aliens from outer space. Undoubtedly, some are the work of hoaxers but others are not so easily explained although cosmic doodling seems highly unlikely.

The highest village in the county **Baydon** stands at 750feet and is set in the heart of race-horse training country, close to the famous **Lambourne Downs**. An ancient settlement its name may be derived from Mount Badon, the last of Arthur's twelve great battles against the invading Saxons in the 6th century. St Nicholas church has internal piers of chalk blocks, put in place some 700 years ago, which aptly illustrate the old Wiltshire dictum that chalk was an excellent building medium providing that it has 'a good hat and boots', a sound roof and foundations to keep out the damp.

The M4 motorway effectively chops off the flatter lands of the northern tip of the county and contains the great mass of **Swindon**, the largest industrial town in Wiltshire. It was the railway that brought prosperity to the town, particularly since the town became the centre of Brunel's Great Western Railway, affectionately referred to as 'God's wonderful railway'. By 1867, the town could boast that it was 'neatly and regularly built.... and is lighted by gas. The Mechanics Institute is a noble building, having a library with upward of 3,650 volumes, and is one of the finest institutions in the kingdom; lectures, concerts and dramatic performances are frequently given in it. A free recreation ground, with a permanent pavilion, has been established for the use of cricketers, of whom there are several clubs. At the factory locomotives for the whole line are manufactured. Such is the perfection to which the building of engines has arrived here that one engine per week can be turned out. Also about 330 tons of rails per week are turned out at the rolling mill, The works cover about eighteen acres of ground.....'

Although the great locomotive works have been phased out **Swindon** remains one of the principal termini for goods and passengers and the great days of the GWR are remembered in the **Great Western Railway Museum** in Farringdon Road, which has a comprehensive display of old locomotives and railway memorabilia. Just opposite is **The Railway Village House**, a perfectly restored foreman's house from the turn of the century. Both exhibits are situated within the area known as the Railway Village, a model community built by GWR for their workers.

The River Thames, although little more than a stream, takes a meander into the extreme north of Wiltshire, running under **Cricklade**, an ancient market town, important from Roman days onwards because it sits on the old Roman Road of Ermine Street.

An ecclesiastical establishment of great importance was situated at **Malmesbury**, a handsome small town, built on a rocky outcrop above the waters of the Avon. The abbey and the town flourished trading in wool and exploiting the rich agricultural land that lay around. It reached itsheyday in the 14th century when riches gained from the wool trade led to the Abbey having a spire higher than that of Salisbury. However pride comes before a fall, and at the end of the next century, that is precisely what happened; the spire collapsed and the great gilt ball that adorned its tip ' rolled unceremoniously down the High Street'. With the Dissolution the Abbey fell into the hands of an upwardly mobile clothier, one William Stumpe, who promptly filled the great building with weaving looms and cared nought for the great literary treasure house; manuscripts and parchment torn from books were put to varied uses, including making patterns for gloves, wrapping parcels, making bungs for beer-barrels and scouring guns. Stumpe went on to make a vast fortune, married his daughter off to the aristocracy, and perhaps to make amends for his earlier philistine behaviour, gave the great nave of the Abbey to the town as a parish church. What remains is lovely, with a splendid porch with fine, intricate Norman carving and a simple and elegant interior of the same period.

Malmesbury went on to establish itself as a centre of excellence in the manufacture of silk, gloves and lace and there are some fine Cotswold stone houses from the 17th and 18th century that bear testament to the wealth of those who dealt in these trades.

South of the M4 lies a mecca for tourists to this area of the county. **Castle Combe** is almost impossibly pretty, with its immaculate grouping of houses of golden Cotswold stone, thatch, and tile, trout-laden stream, church, old market cross, and manor house set below wooded hills, where a castle once stood. It looks like a film set, indeed it has been used as one, but its original prosperity came from weaving.

Chippenham was once the site of a Saxon palace, which would appear to have been a comfortable and hospitable establishment since the normally alert King Alfred was caught napping by the Danes, whilst spending Christmas here in 877 AD. Chippenham's greatest attraction to me is **Maude Heath's Causeway**. Maude was a market woman who, in the reign of Henry VII would make her way to **Chippenham** from her home in **Langley Burrell**, carrying heavy baskets full of eggs and butter. The roads in those far off days were generally appalling and the fact that most of the area was low-lying, boggy and riven with streams did not help matters. The good Maude was evidently industrious, far-sighted and charitable for, when she died, in 1474, she left all her savings to build and endow a cobbled footpath between Wick Hill and Chippenham Clift, linking the little villages of the Avon Valley with their principal market. She is commemorated not only by her Causeway, but also by a statue set high on a column on Wick Hill and by an inscription near Chippenham church which reads:

'Hither extended Maude Heath's gift,
For where you stand is Chippenham's Clift'

Going south west towards Bath from Chippenham you would come to the little town of **Corsham**. Nothing very exciting about it but it is a friendly place and a good base for anyone wanting to be close to the incomparable Bath but preferring to stay in the countryside. Just along the A420 from Chippenham and almost at the junction with the A46 is the small village of **Cold Ashton**, also worth a visit although just over the border from Wiltshire.

Due south you will come to another pretty place,**Melksham**. A quiet little town living up to Wiltshire's sleepy image. At one time however it had aspirations to be a Spa but did not succeed.Bath was already firmly established but it did mean that some very attractive Regency houses were built which can be seen today. It is a thriving market town and became prosperousfrom the Cloth Weaving Industry. You can see Weavers' Cottages in Canon Square and two Roundhouses in Lowbourne and Church Street where wool was stove-dried.

To the east of Chippenham is **Calne**. Once again weaving was the original basis of prosperity but when the Industrial Revolution ended that trade, it became famous for bacon-curing and the production of sausages and pies. This came about through the enterprise of a local family of butchers, the Harrises. At the time, the town was on the principal route for livestock being driven from the West to London and among the animals were large quantities of Irish pigs, having been off-loaded at Bristol. The Harris family realised that if they bought the pigs at Calne, before they became weary and lost weight on their long trot to London, then the pork would be of superior quality. From 1770 until the 1980's, their factory dealt with literally millions of those versatile beasts of whom it is said, 'everything can be used except the grunt.' Economic and regulatory factors conspired to close the factory and the only memorial to this once great business that made the name of Calne synonymous with bacon, is a bronze pig by the small shopping precinct.

Two miles to the south-west is the great estate of **Bowood**, home of the Marquesses of Lansdowne since 1754. Robert Adams spent eight years enlarging and improving Bowood House while Capability Brown was at work on the gardens and glorious parkland. The house has fine collections of sculpture, paintings and costumes. There is a Laboratory in which Dr Joseph Priestly discovered oxygen in 1774, a fine library and chapel, but undoubtedly the real glory is the setting, the wonderful park and gardens, over ninety acres of which are open to visitors.

Lacock Abbey was founded in 1232 by Ela, Countess of Salisbury, the grieving widow of William Longspee. An Augustinian order flourished there until the Dissolution, when it fell into the hands of one William Sharington, a man described as 'being of dubious character'. Fortunately, he also had excellent taste and did not go in for the usual large scale demolitions that most of the ecclesiastical property developers of that time seemed to enjoy. Indeed, such additions that he had made were very well-executed and in perfect harmony with the preserved Abbey. The Talbot family were next on the scene, but not without incident; Sir William's niece, Olivia, was being secretly courted by young John Talbot and in a scene reminiscent of Romeo and Juliet, she offered to leap from the battlements of the abbey church to join her suitor below.

The young man not believeing that she would jump told her to go ahead. The young Miss Sharrington, however was no simpering ninny and happily leapt into her lover's arms, flattening him to the ground. The story goes that 'she cried out for help, and he was with difficulty brought to life again. Her father told her that since she had made such a leap she should e'en marry him.' The Talbots were fine stewards of both Abbey and the village of **Lacock** and in 1944 Miss Matilda Talbot presented both, together with 284 acres of land to the National Trust. There is no building later than the 18th-century in the winding streets of grey stone and half-timbered cottages. The perpendicular church, dedicated to St Cyriac, has an elegant interior and beautiful east window. **The George** is one of the oldest continuously licensed pubs in England while **The Sign of the Angel** dates back to the 14th century. A stone barn contains a museum dedicated to William Fox-Talbot, pioneer of photography. One cannot help but wonder what he would think of his invention now as yet another coach-load of tourists arrive with motor-driven self-focussing cameras at the ready.

Another lovely house lies some six miles to the south-west at **Great Chalfield. Great Chalfield Manor** was built about 1480 by a prosperous wool-merchant, one Thomas Tropenell. Now under the care of the National Trust, the Manor is one of the loveliest houses of its era, lying in rich meadowlands on the edge of a moat.

Tropenell's wealth came from the same source as that of the neighbouring town of **Bradford-on-Avon** - wool. It is hard in these days of man-made fibres and multi-national fashion corporations to appreciate just how important fleece was to medieval life; suffice it to say that there were no other fibres that were so adaptable or so economical to produce and that the best wool came from the backs of English sheep raised on the chalk downlands. Until the early Middle Ages, wool was the country's principal export; later, with the development of the weaving trade, finished cloth, took that position. An indication of the little town's one time importance in this vital trade is the fact that the Yorkshire wool and textile town of Bradford was named after it.

It is a charming, picturesque town today with some wonderful buildings. The medieval Shambles is now a charming shopping area, full of antique shops and tea-rooms, light-years removed from its original purpose as the place where the town's slaughter-men worked. Wherever you go through the twisting winding streets there is always something to interest and delight.

To understand the history of **Trowbridge**, now the administrative centre of Wiltshire, a position gained by virtue of its old rail links, make a visit to **Trowbridge Museum** in the Civic Hall where the life and times of the community is well recorded.

Heading south and within sight of the White Horse at **Westbury**, the gentle countryside seems so peaceful and idyllic, the villages so friendly and welcoming that it is hard to imagine what life must have been like when that ancient Anglo-Saxon chronicler set down his despairing account of anarchy and misrule. Yet many of the small communities one drives through existed then and it is a tribute to the spirit and purpose of their habitants that they survived.

At **Hawkeridge**, there is a fine example of those characteristics that brought the countrymen and women of Wiltshire through the worst of times to the best of times. It is not the saga of a wealthy wool-merchant or rich clothier who became landed gentry, but a rather more modest account: in 1851, Mr Ephraim Dole and his wife Sarah invested their savings into converting three labourer's cottages into an ale-house. Nearly one hundred and fifty years later **The Royal Oak** is still going strong, complete with skittle-alley and dining room. Just goes to show that 'there ain't no flies on Wiltshire volk...'

HAMPSHIRE

Michael Drayton, a Warwickshire contemporary of Shakespeare, intended nothing derogatory in his description of one of England's finest counties. In ancient times, the thickly wooded downland of the northern part of the county must have been something of a procine paradise for the hirsute and thick-set wild boar, rootling amongst the myriad oaks in a never ending quest for acorns and other such delicacies. No true son of the county has ever objected to the sobriquet of Hampshire Hog, for the long vanished beast represented those qualities of independence, nimbleness and strength that has enabled the area to cope amd come to terms with both invasion and innovation.

Romans, Danes, Saxons and Normans found the rolling countryside much to their liking, whilst in recent times, industry and urban development have stamped their mark on the landscape. Nevertheless, adjacent to the roar of the motorway and the bustle of the conurbations, there exists a seemingly timeless world rich in history and bucolic charm. The Wild Boar of Hampshire, had he been somewhat less tasty and rather more intelligent, would still find much to please him.

An apt example of this happy balance is to be found in and around the county town of **Winchester.** The M3 noisily snakes it's way past to the east of the town, cutting a giant's furrowthrough the chalk downs. Motorways may not be the most attractive of man's creations, but they are far from being the worst; merely the 20th century equivalent of the railway bringing life and prosperity, even in these difficult times.

Winchester was once the capital of England until it was supplanted by Westminster (London). It is the county town of Hampshire and rich in historic associations and remains with a wealth of fine old architecture but it is not somewhere in which one feels trapped in a time-warp or historical 'experience'. The city bustles and flourishes; there is room for both tourist, citizen and trader. Much of the city centre has been set aside for pedestrians and it is a real pleasure to meander amongst the thoroughfares and narrow medieval streets, enjoying the wealth of shops and buildings, yet never being far from greenery or running water, for the River Itchen, one of the finest trout rivers, flows rapidly through the city towards the water-meadows to the south.

The great grey Cathedral dominates; at 556 feet, it is the longest medieval churh in Europe. Magnificent and awe-inspiring, it was founded in 1079 and consecrated in 1093. Over the centuries it has beome a graceful melange of styles, reflecting the energy, determination and skill of those who built 'to the greater glory of God'. The broad lawns and fine buildings of the Close set off the ancient Cathedral to perfection. To my mind, one of the greatest glories of English cathedral liturgy is to be found in it's music and Winchester's choristers are trained at the Pilgrim School, with its fine Pilgrim's Hall, worth visiting for its magnificent hammer-beamed roof that dates back to the early 14th century. I can remember reading that Sir Andrew Lloyd-Webber used to visit the Cathedral regularly when he lived nearby and found much inspiration for his own work from the music that poured out.

Education has long been an integral part of ecclesiastical life. In 1382, Bishop William of Wykeham founded **Winchester College** which is to be found south of the Close. 600 years later, the school is still going strong and using many of the same buildings. You will find a profusion of interesting museums to visit, good restaurants, old inns and shops. Although Winchester places a strong emphasis on preservation and heritage, its real charm comes from the fact that it possesses a past that is truly alive; clerics still tread the cloisters, scholars are still in the school-room and quadrangle, soldiers stamp the parade-ground, and traders hawk their wares in the market place.

Sport and recreation are strong in Hampshire traditions, the ethos of 'work hard, play hard' obviously appealing to the county character, yet even in play it is hard to escape a sense of the past. For example in the village of **Littleton**, to the north-east of Winchester has a recreation area which seems to accommodate an amazing range of sport including Cricket, Tennis, Bowls, Football and Croquet and closeby are some grassy mounds which are Bronze Age burial chambers dating from perhaps 1000 BC. As I watched children play, it was strange to reflect that those earthworks were created at about the same time King David ruled from Jerusalem.

Skirting the north of Winchester and heading east, I crossed the M3 and almost immediately found myself in fine countryside. Woods and coverts speckled the broad acres of rich plough and pasture through which ran the gin-clear waters of the Itchen. My first stop was at **Alresford** (pronounced Allsford), a delightful, predominantly Georgian town, whose fortunes were founded on the 14th-century wooltrade In more recent time, the inhabitants turned to the cultivation of watercress and because of the importance of the industry, the Mid-Hants Railway became known as **The Watercress Line**. A victim of Dr Beeching's now infamous cuts, the railway has been happily restored by dedicated individuals and is now one of Hampshire's most popular - and most useful - attractions. The steam railway runs via **Ropley, Medstead and Four Marks**, to the market townof **Alton**.

South of Alresford I came across another example of 'living history'. At **Tichborne**, the Tichborne Dole, in the form of a gallon of flour, bread or money has been handed out yearly to each deserving adult since the 12th century. It is said that the custom originated with the dying Lady Isabella who begged her husband Sir Roger Tichborne, to grant her enough land to care for the sick and the needy. In reply, Sir Roger, a chauvinist if ever there was one, took a flaming brand from the fire and told his sick wife that 'she could have as much land as she could crawl round before the flame was extinguished'.

Astonishingly she managed to cover some 23 acres before the flame burnt out, and the land thus enclosed is known to this day as The Crawles. Tradition has it that tragedy will befall the family if Lady Isabella's request for the Dole is ever ignored, and, astonishingly, on the few rare occasions that this has happened, the consequences have been singularly unpleasant.

Close by lie the small and attractive villages of **Hinton Ampner** and **Kilmeston**. The wonderful countryside provides a fitting setting for the handsome facade and beautiful gardens of **Hinton Ampner House**. The house, its origins going back to the Middle Ages, has been re-built several times - the last time as recently as 1960. Now in the care of the National Trust, the house is a tribute to the dedicated persistence of one man, Ralph Dutton, the last Lord Sherborne. In 1936 he lovingly restored the house and its contents. In 1940, he relinguished the house to a girl's school, and in 1960 he saw the house destroyed by fire. Undeterred, he started again to rebuild and refurbish and the house is now immaculately maintained and has fine displays of Regency furniture, pictures and paintings.

It is difficult when writing a guide to this part of the world to avoid the over-use of the word 'attractive'. So many of the small villages and hamlets nestling in the chalk downland catch the eye and are worthy of mention; not necessarily because they are linked with historical sites or notable personages, or because they possess a fine church or noble house, but simply because of their charm and character - their very individuality attracts. Six miles east along the A272, I turned south to visit **East Meon**, a village, which to me, represents the epitome of the Hampshire downland village. Old Izaak Walton fished the trout-rich waters of the River Meon, which rises from the chalk not far from the village to run under and beside the main street. The Norman church is one of the finest buildings of its type and set to perfection above the village in what was once a bishop's deer park.

I wandered roughly south-east from here to where the landscape is dominated by the imposing mass of **Butser Hill**. At nearly 900 feet, it is the highest point in the western end of the South Downs and is contained within **Queen Elizabeth Country Park**. Jointly administered by Hampshire County Council and the Forestry Commission, it is an admirable example of how an area can be successfully managed to incorporate a multitude of quite different interests. Recreation, forestry, conservation and education all take place within the 1,400 acres which is liberally strewn with nature trails, bridle ways and woodland walks I was fascinated by a modern reconstruction of an Iron Age farm of around 300BC, partly based on information gathered from local excavations. Crops of the period are grown here and it was intriguing to learn that the prehistoric varieties of wheat produce have nearly twice the protein content of today's. Not only that, but experiments have shown that yield per acres would have been not far off our modern figures - so much for selective breeding and generic engineering!

Petersfield is a handsome market town that has much to offer, but has suffered heavily since theintroduction of the internal combustion engine; too many people pass through and never stop to investigate. In a sense, it was ever thus since the town sits astride the main Portsmouth to London road and was an important coaching stop long before the car was invented. In the square, there is a heroic statue of William III on horseback, dressed for some odd reason as a Roman emperor.

North of the town, there is some of the finest scenery to be found in the South of England. Around **Steep**, and further north at **Selborne**, the remarkable landscape features great beech 'hangers', great clumps of mature trees hanging (hence the name) precipitously over almost sheer chalk inclines that run down to a base of greensand rock. Known as 'Little Switzerland', it is an area of great beauty and contrasts favourably with the more serene charms of the **Meon Valley**.

Selborne is, of course, the mecca for all English naturalists. It was the birthplace and home of Gilbert White (1720-93), four times curate of the church and author of that delightful classic 'The Natural History and Antiquities of Selborne'. Published in 1789, it is based on his forty years of observations of the wildlife, plants and habitat found in the immediate vicinity. The book, in the form of letters to the interested parties, has a singular freshness and charm which reflects the enthusiasm and character of the man. His old home, The Wakes, contains much relating to his studies, and also houses collections belonging to a later owner, the explorer Francis Oates, uncle of Captain Oates who perished with Scott on the expedition to the South Pole in 1912. The joint exhibitions are housed together as **Gilbert White's House and Garden and The Oates Exhibition**.

Leaving the Selborne area, where the National Trust has done so much to preserve and maintain the landscape, other literary and botanical connections are to be found a few miles further north. At **Chawton, Jane Austen's House** provides an insight into the life led by the novelist and her family from 1809 to 1817, while she wrote or revised her six great novels. The delightful garden surrounding the house contains many old fashioned varieties of flowers and visitors are welcome to picnic on the lawns.

Nearby **Alton**, a busy and good looking market town, is home to the **Curtis Museum** named after William Curtis, the founder of the Botanical Magazine. As well as exhibits relating specifically to Curtis, the museum possesses excellent displays relating to local industry and crafts and all manner of historical exhibits including the exquisite **Alton Buckle**, a 1500 year old item of Saxon jewellery. There are also exhibitions of children's games, toys, silver and pottery.At **Beech**, just to the south of Alton you will find a quiet hamlet which offers hospitality at **Glen Derry.**

My next destination was amongst the big wooded downland that lies close to the border with Berkshire and to the south of Newbury. Trees fringe wide expanses of chalk soil either under cultivation or down to rich pasture. This is a county of quiet wealth and great estate, with small villages, hamlets and farms scattered across the countryside.

At **Highclere** a steep climb up **Beacon Hill** is worthwhile for the splendid view over the Downs. The summit is crowned by an Iron Age hill-fort and the grave of the fifth Earl of Caernarvon, who, with Howard Carter, led the expedition to find the tomb of Tutankhamun. The Earl's palatial home, **Highclere Castle** lies close to the foot of the hill surrounded by lovely parkland and laid out by the inimitable Capability Brown. The Castle, the largest mansion in the county, was rebuilt in the middle of the last century and is renowned for the richness and variety of its interior decoration.

On the subject of decoration, I recommend a visit to the **Sandham Memorial Chapel** at **Burghclere**, to view the paintings by Stanley Spencer (1891-1959). They are considered to be the most important of English murals. They reflect on the futility and horror of war and were painted between 1926 and 1932 ; the chapel was built in memory of Lieutenant H.W. Sandham who died in the First World War.

The largest of the 'Cleres' is **Kingsclere**, at the foot of **Watership Down** - made famous by the author Richard Adams. His hero was a rabbit, but for many years mine was a horse, the great Derby winner Mill Reef. He was trained at Kingsclere and throughout the area, studs and racing stables breed and train in an endeavour to produce another such equine star.

The most notable of Hampshire's rivers is The Test, and seven miles south of Highclere lies the attractive ancient town of **Whitchurch**. Here the fast running alkaline waters once served both sport and industry, providing power for silk-weaving and at nearby **Laverstock**, for the manufacture of bank-note paper. Both industries have survived and **The Silk Mill** is beautifully preserved and open to the public with a shop well worth visiting; not surprisingly the banknote contract with the Bank of England dates back to 1727 and continues to this day.

The nearby town of **Andover** is representative of much of the change occurring within the County in recent times. The area has been home to man since ancient times; at **Danebury**, together with some fascinating reconstructions and audio-visual displays. Andover was first recorded in 955AD and grew to become a prosperous market town and coaching centre but perhaps the most dramatic changes in the town's history occurred in the early 1960's when it became an overspill area from London. However, it must be said that Andover has not suffered quite so badly at the hands of the planners as have other such communities within Hampshire; the handsome town centre, with its market place, guildhall of 1825, fine Victorian parish church of St Mary's and numerous coaching inns, have survived. The coaches, with post horns blowing and horses snorting, no longer rumble down the high street, but it is nonetheless a cheerful and lively place.

Thatch is common throughout the area and doubtless owes its origins to the readily available supply of reed from along the river banks. The splendidly named Wallops, (the name means, rather disappointingly, 'valley of the stream') also have a wealth of thatched cottages. Strung along the valley of Wallop Brook, the three villages retain a wealth of character and tradition, with **Nether Wallop** being noted for its fine Saxon wall paintings in the church, **Over Wallop** for a magnificent 15th century font, and **Middle Wallop** for its **Museum of Army Flying**. This award winning museum houses a unique collection of flying machines, equipment and displays depicting the history of Army Aviation since the end of the last century, from balloons to kites to the latest in helicopters.

It is a truly lovely part of England with plenty of footpaths for the walker and bridleways for the rider. At **Stockbridge**, the Test flows under the London to Salisbury road and the wide main street reflects its past as a drover's town.

Income, and not an inconsiderable one at that, is unfortunately a necessity to enable one to fish much of the Test, and on the rare occasions that private stretches of river come on the market they change hands for quite astronomical sums. Even if you are not interested in the 'gentle art of the angle', a walk along the accessible sections of the river bank will offer a clue to the extraordinary costs involved. The water is alkaline, crystal clear and the brown trout thrive growingprodigiously within the food rich waters whilst the banks, feeder streams, wiers and sluice-gates are immaculately kept and maintained; skilled work on such a scale does not come cheap. Sadly, the river, like so many of its kind is under threat. The rapidly increasing populations of the new urban developments within the country require water for both domestic and industrial use and increased abstraction by the water companies mean a decrease in flow and greater threat of pollution.

I like the village of **Broughton** close to Stockbridge surrounded as it is by so much history - the hillfort of Woolbury for example from which there are stunning views.

My journey around North Hampshire ended close to where it began, just a few miles to the west of the ancient capital of Wessex. In 1201, a group of followers of St Augustinian established a priory in one of the most idyllic situations imaginable. **Mottisford Abbey** became a private house after the Dissolution and work over the centuries has resulted in the present handsome Georgian south front, perfectly complemented by the wonderful gardens that sweep down to the Test. Green lawns are shaded by great trees and the celebrated rose garden contains the National Trust's collection of old-fashioned roses. It has to be said that this is the most harmonious setting of any house in England - and one can well believe it.

The River Avon, noted for the variety of its fishing (particularly its fine, though sadly declining runs of salmon) runs southward, marking the eastern boundary of the county spur. The A338, from Salisbury to Bournemouth follows the river for much of its course, passing through the attractive towns of **Fordingbridge** and **Ringwood.** Ringwood is a cheerful market town. Tourism plays an important part of the town's economy and angling is a major attraction. Many of the hotels and inns cater especially for those enthusiasts who travel from all over the country to fish the Avon and its tributaries. It is popular too with those who love the diversity of sport to be found in the waters of the Avon. Because of its depth, the river offers unrivalled opportunities to both the game-fisherman after trout, salmon or grayling, and the coarse angler, pursuing the like of the chub, pike, dace and barbel.

The town lies on the western edge of another great area of natural beauty within this county of contrast - **The New Forest.** It is an area of over 90,000 acres of heath and mixed woodland with an abundance of wildlife. Paradoxically, it is the oldest of the forests of England but that is simply because the word 'forest' is of Norman origin; it means an area set aside for hunting and the New Forest was the first of these preserves to be created by William the Conqueror. Savage penalties were exacted on those who broke the forest laws; at one time a person could be blinded for merely disturbing deer, whilst death was the automatic penalty for poaching. The modern day visitor might like to be reassured that the passing of the centuries have seen extensive modification of these draconian measures: apart from occasional necessary culling the deer are left in peace while the tourist can wander freely through much of the beautiful country. There are three distinctive habitats within the forest boundaries. The high heath-lands, covered with heather and gorse together with Scots pine and birch, give a somewhat barren impression - particularly to the motorists travelling along the main east/west route of the A31. However the lower slopes and better-drained land provides true forest in the modern meaning; superb traditional woodland planted with oak, beech, yew and thorn, producing in the summer great sweeping canopies of foliage. Finally there is the marsh land where the white cotton-grass conceals the bogs and where the alder and willow grow.

Amongst this vegetation can be found all manner of wildlife, from grouse on the high heath to the four varities of deer (Red, Roe, Fallow and the tiny Sika) who favour the woodland. Domesticanimals, their numbers strictly controlled by the Verderers, graze amongst the trees and shrubs. These include cattle, pigs, donkeys and the celebrated New Forest ponies. Mention was first made of wild 'horses' at the time of King Canute (1017-35) while some believe them to be descendants of the Jennets, the small Spanish horses which swam ashore from the wrecks of the Spanish Armada in the 16th century. Many of them are employed in the numerous riding stables and schools to be found within the forest.

Leisure is the principal 'industry' of the New Forest and much has been done to encourage its development. Picnic area, camping sites, trails, drives and paths are to be found throughout, and hotels and boarding houses, inns and pubs all do their very best to make the visitor welcome.

'Badger's Wood' is the meaning of **Brockenhurst**, a village that grew in popularity with the arrival of the railway in 1847. It has a fine Norman church with many memorials; one of which is of particular local interest. 'Brusher'Mills, who died in 1905, earned his nickname because he brushed the cricket pitch at Balmer Lawn between innings. Of singular appearane, with a grey beard, long coat and furry hat, he made his living by catching snakes, mainly adders, with his bare hands. It is said he was never bitten because he drank a bottle of rum a day and never washed !! Undoubtedly, he would have approved of his other memorial in the village, a pub named **The Snake Catcher** - although I doubt whether the customers would have enjoyed his company.

A couple of miles to the south of Brockenhurst lies **Boldre**, one of the best looking villages in the New Forest, where the thatched cottages spread out along the numerous country lanes. The church is a happy mixture of Norman and early English but is most celebrated for having been the living, from 1777 to 1804, of William Gilpin. Gilpin was a contemporary of Gilbert White, and like him, a writer and naturalist.

He must have been something of a saint, for he recorded, on first arriving in the parish, that the village was 'utterly neglected by the former pastor, and, exposed to every temptation of pillage and robbery from their proximity to the deer, the game, and the fuel of the forest, for these poor people were little better than a herd of banditti.' Thirty years later, the 'herd of banditti' clubbed together to erect a memorial within the church to Gilpin's memory, a tribute earned by remarkably few vicars in English village history. There is also a memorial to the ship's company of the battle-cruiser HMS Hood, sunk in May 1941; the 1,406 officers and men are remembered in an annual service.

In her eighteen years in commission HMS Hood frequently sailed through the narrow patch of water that guards the western entrance to the Solent. **Hurst Castle**, built at the end of a shingle spit less than a mile from the Isle of Wight, was built by Henry VIII with a formidable armament of 70 guns. It can be reached on foot from **Milford on Sea**, a small but popular resort, or by ferry from the little harbour of **Keyhaven**.

The mud flats and marshes run eastward to **Lymington**, an attractive market town whose popularity attests to its position by the water and close to the southern fringes of the New Forest. Now a popular yachting centre, its elegant streets lined with nautical boutiques and smart hostelries while every inch of shore-line appears dedicated to the parking of cars or the mooring of boats, it is hard to visualise this chic little town as being the great trading port that it once was. Its origins are ancient; it has to be one of the oldest charters in England, dating back to 1150.

Although the present facade of Lymington would appear smart and leisurely, its trading past has far from disappeared; the international reputation of its yacht designers, boat builders, sail makers and marine electronic manufacturers contribute significantly to the national export market, albeitin a less obvious manner than when the quays and warehouses bustled with rude life.

The only commercial shipping that survives comes from the operation of the Lymington-Yarmouth ferry and a handfulof fishing boats.

Some five miles to the north-east, set in the Forest and at the head of a lovely stretch of river, lies **Beaulieu** (the beautiful place), founded by the Cistercian monks more than 750 years ago. Now a ruin its remains are still singularly beautiful and well-kept. The second Lord Montagu did much to preserve and his successors have carried on the tradition in like manner. The present Lord Montagu took over the Abbey and retained only the Great Gate House (now known as Palace House), the porter's lodge, the cloisters, the lay brother's dormitory and the refectory, which has long served as the parish church.

Beaulieu apart from its attraction as the site of a great religious house, lovely situation and immaculate small village is also home to the splendid **National Motor Museum**, which was founded by the present Lord Montagu in memory of his father, a pioneer motorist. Downstream from Beaulieu lies the neat little community of **Bucklers Hard**, a single wide street of Queen Anne cottages that runs down to the river. Originally created by a Montagu for the importation and refining of sugar, political events in the West Indies made the development obsolete. Instead the site became one of the most famous naval shipyards in Britain, building many of the Royal Navy's most famous ships, including Nelson's favourite command, the Agamemnon. Today, yachts moor where the ships grew upon their slipways and **The Maritime Museum** at the top of the village recounts its past glories.

Exbury Gardens, on the opposite bank of the river, are made up of 200 acres of the most stunning displays of shrubs, trees and flowers. Particularly beautiful are the spring-time displays of the noted Rothschild collection of rhododendrons, azaleas, magnolias and camellias.

A meandering cross-country drive brings one back to the heart of the New Forest, to it's capital **Lyndhurst.** This pleasant little town is the administrative headquarters of the Forest; the Verderer's Court meets six times a year at the Queen's House which is also the headquarters of the Forestry Commission. At **The New Forest Museum and Visitor Centre**, an excellent introduction to the history, customs, traditions, flowers and fauna of the area is provided through the medium of displays and audio-visual presentations.

To my mind **Minstead** is the perfect New Forest village and it is here that Arthur Conan Doyle is buried. Although best known for his Sherlock Holmes stories, he also wrote many fine historical novels. His principal character in 'The White Company' becomes the spelndidly-titled Socman of Minstead, and Doyle obviously had much affection for the place for he and his wife spent several years there.

Heading eastwards, after the peace and tranquillity of the forest glades, the heavy traffic rumbling towards **Southampton** comes as an unpleasant shock. The city, much of it modern , appears initially as an industrial sprawl, with pylons marching along the low marshy ground towards the tall cranes that indicate the presence of the docks. Further investigation of this unprepossessing facade is richly rewarding; Southampton is a city that rewards the inquisitive - its history is ancient and its treasures many.

Although the M27 and its associated developments are essential to the livelihood of this area ofthe country, there is no doubt that the great swathe of countryside that it occupies is lost to us forever; nevertheless charming pockets of rural calm are to be found with little trouble and often lie remarkably close to the motorway.

Equally, if you have small children in tow who are not enamoured of churches and museums, then there are plenty of suitable entertainments. Both forms of attractions can be found in close proximity to each other, just off Junction 2 of the M27. **Paultons Park** is 140 acres of gardens and woodland that was once part of a large estate and has now been transformed into a family leisure park with fairground rides, boating lake, aviary, pet's corner and numerous other features that appeal particularly to the young.

Of the many villages that put Southampton at the end of their address, I found **Droxford** on the A32 close to **Bishops Waltham**, a pleasant place, much of it Georgian. Here Izaak Walton, whose daughter married the rector of the village, spent many happy hours. The old hostelry **The White Horse**, has an extraordinary history going back some five hundred years. It is seldom that ladies are invited to visit the men's loos but here I was shown a huge forty foot well! It was used by Churchill and his staff when he was planning and making preparations for the D-Day landings of World War II. Apparently he approved of the food and that reputation has continued until today.

The River Test flows south through the town of **Romsey**, where it once provided the power for milling and water for the many breweries. The town grew around the building of **Romsey Abbey**, founded in 907AD by Edward the Elder for his daughter, Ethelflaeda. Sixty years later, it was re-founded as a Benedictine nunnery by King Edgar. The abbey church was begun in the early part of the 12th century and construction continued over the next hundred years; it is second only to Durham cathedral as the finest Norman building in England.

The North Aisle acted as the townspeople's church and they must have been more than fond of the building and its wonderful proportions because, at the Dissolution, they raised the sum of one hundred pounds to save it. The conventual buildings were destroyed but the church was saved; a wonderful bargain which is recorded by the Bill of Sale being displayed inside.

The peaceful tranquillity of the abbey is a cheerful contrast to the bustling little market town surrounding it. Some idea of the town's history can be gained in the **King John's House**, a 13th century stone upper-hall house containing a small museum. Tudor, Georgian and Victorian domestic architecture are to be found throughout the town centre and the local Preservation Trust has done an excellent job.

Broadlands, to the south of the town, once belonged to the Abbey. The Palladian style mansion was remodelled for the Palmerston family (a statue of the third Viscount who became Prime Minister stands in Romsey market place) by Capability Brown, who also laid out the surrounding parkland. It was later the home of Earl Mountbatten until his tragic death, and the stables have been converted to an exhibition of his life and career.

From Romsey it is easy to visit the **Hillier Arboretum** at **Ampfield**, where a world renowned display of rare and beautiful plants is set in 160 acres together with a magnificent collection of trees and shrubs.

The reformer William Cobbett (1763-1835) farmed at **Botley** to the east of Southampton and described it as 'the most beautiful village in the world.' Much has changed since he penned those words but the large village still retains a rural atmosphere. An important market was held here for many years and at one time there were fourteen inns catering to the coach and carriage trade. Two of them still survive, **The Bugle** and **The Dolphin**, as does the mill, the only one in Hampshireto be listed in the Domesday Book and still working. Until the 1930's small trading vessels would come up the River Hamble to Botley to load timber and corn.

I think Cobbett would have approved of the **Upper Hamble Country Park** to the south of Botley. This is a clever blend of working farm and preserved wood and marshland: bridle paths and walkways allow almost unlimited access and the traditional farm buildings house livestock as well as displays of old farm machinery.

The lower reaches of the Hamble River must contain more yachts than any other waterway in the world. A forest of masts bristle upwards from the marinas and moorings that run the entire length of the river, from Swanwick Bridge to the rivermouth. At first sight it hardly seems possible for any of them to move, but on closer inspection a reasonably wide channel is revealed, running up the middle of the rows of moored pleasure craft.

Like Lymington, the industry on and alongside the water is yachting and from the boatyards have come many notable vessels, including America's Cup yachts and record-breaking power boats. Two pubs, **The Jolly Sailors** at **Burlesden**, and **The Bugle** at **Hamble**, are ideally situated for eating and drinking and watching life on the river go by.

Both villages were once renowned for ship-building and The Elephant, Nelson's ship at the Battle of Copenhagen was built next to the Jolly Sailors; the boatyard still exists there and proudly carries the same name.

Of course, the name of Nelson will always be associated with one ship in particular, that of HMS Victory, both she and many other links with the Royal Navy are to be found less than ten miles to the east, at **Portsmouth**. 'Pompey', as it is affectionately known to both servicemen and natives alike, is situated on a peninsula that projects southwards between the two natural harbours of Portsmouth on the western side and Langstone to the east.

Like its civilian counterpart, Southampton, Portsmouth enjoys certain natural advantages: there is deep water throughout a large part of the harbour, the Isle of Wight offers shelter from much of the Channel weather and the narrow entrance is easily defended. These assets were first recognised by the Romans who ignored the site of present day Portsmouth and sailed right up to the top of the harbour, landing at what is now **Porchester**. Here they built **Porchester Castle**, the best preserved Roman fortress in northern Europe.

Undoubtedly the best place to start a tour of the city and its heritage is at **The Royal Dockyard** which houses three of the world's major maritime attractions as well as an excellent museum. Indisputably the most famous of the three is ,**HMS Victory**, Nelson's flagship at Trafalgar. Beautifully restored and maintained she still serves as Flagship to the Commander-in-Chief, Portsmouth. Once on board, it is not hard to imagine the appalling conditions in which officers and men lived and worked, fought and died. Close by are the impressive remains of the **Mary Rose**, complete with exhibits of thousands of artefacts salvaged from the ship. The third historical ship is **HMS Warrior**, who saw no battle action, but was the world's first steam-powered iron-hulled warship and was launched in 1860.

No visitor to the Dockyard should leave without viewing the excellent **Royal Naval Museum**, which contains much of interest relating to the Navy over the centuries. Other aspects of Naval and Military life are displayed in **Fort Nelson** near **Fareham**, the splendid **Royal Marines Museum** in Eastney Barracks on the Southsea front, **The D-Day Museum** which is adjacent to**Southsea Castle**, and **The Royal Naval Submarine Museum** across the water at **Gosport** (a good excuse to get afloat and see something of the harbour itself).

For those with young children, **Southsea,** the southern tip of the peninsula, has much to offer with its promenade, beach and common, which includes a boating lake and attractive gardens. Pleasure cruises around the Solent depart from **South Parade Pier** which, true to its Edwardian beginnings, offers entertainment seven nights a week. Alongside **Clarence Pier** the only hover-craft passenger service in the country runs to the Isle of Wight.

One tends to forget the virtues of **Hayling Island** especially for the holiday maker. It is a residential area as well as being the home of hotels, holiday parks and all the fun of the fair, especially for families.

North of Portsmouth one rapidly finds oneself back in the quiet charm of rural Hampshire. One moment it is all hustle and bustle with lorries, coaches and cars shooting past, while the next moment the scenery changes to narrow lanes, rolling green fields and small rural communities. A pleasant meandering drive westwards brings one to **Hambledon**, an isolated red-brick village celebrated as the early home of cricket,and in recent times for the fine vineyards planted on the chalk slopes behind the village. Cricket actually began some two miles to the north-east, on **Broadhalfpenny Down**, where Hambledon Cricket Club was the parent of the celebrated Marylebone Cricket Club. Hambledon's finest moment came in 1777; they played All-England and beat them by an innings and 168 runs. It is interesting to note that they played for the huge sum of one thousand pounds.

To the south of **Hambledon** is **East Meon** which to me represents the epitome of a Hampshire downland village. Izaak Walton fished the trout rich waters of the River Meon which rises from the chalk not far from the village to run under and beside the main street. A good and God-fearing man, he doubtless worshipped at East Meon Church, one of the finest Norman buildings of its type and set to perfection, built above the village which once was a bishop's deer park. The beautiful mellow stonework contains a Tournai marble font, wondefully carved and an unusual stained glass window depicting the patron saints of all the Allied Countries that took part in the First World War. The Court House, south east of the church is said to have been built about 1400 but the origins of the village are obviously far earlier, and reputedly it was the first community to be mentioned in the Domesday Book. Like all good villages it has an excellent hstelry, **Ye Olde George Inn.** It has charm, character and comfort complementing the warm welcome and excellent cuisine. Old Izaak may have been a Puritan but he was no kill joy and I have no doubt he would have enjoyed this inn. The furthest point east in Hampshire is **Emsworth** once upon a time noted for its oysters. Unfortunately in the beginning of the 19th century it was dealt a body blow, when oysters supplied for a banquet in Winchester were found to carry typhoid, resulting in a lot of deaths. Those days are long gone and this busy little place has become a yachting centre with excellent facilities for boat building.

It seems only fitting in this area of England so riddled with contrast to finish with ;'something completely different'. A little to the west is an area of gentle downland, once the site of a great estate belonging to the brother of Henry VIII's third wife, Jane Seymour. In this quintessentially English landscape, the visitor can come face to face with one of the world's rarest animals. Such exotica as Przewalski's horse, the snow leopard, or a scimitar-horned ibex are all to be foundwithin the confines of **Marwell Park**. The park is a charitable foundation that exists to promote breeding and conservation of rare animals that are threatened with extinction. It is both a zoo, as well as a scientific and educational trust with the administration housed in the Tudor facade of Marwell House. For the young and young-at-heart, it is a splendid place to visit and a fine example of the many and diverse attractions that South Hampshire has to offer.

LEWESDON FARM HOLIDAYS
Stoke Abbott,
Beaminster,
Dorset
DT8 3JZ

Tel: 01308 868270

Stable and Barn Cottage is a barn conversion using local stone and designed with the disabled in mind. Level access to both plus extra width doors etc for wheelchairs and adapted bathrooms. In fact Jack and Jackie Spooncer the owners have been awarded Holiday Care Services Accessible Award Categories 1 & 2 as well as the ETB 4 Keys Commended. The conversion is delightful and is enhanced by the outstanding natural beauty with breathtaking views in all directions. You will find it is peacefully situated well back from the B3162 Broadwindsor to Bridport road, in open countryside. With excellent walks, an abundance of wildlife and the closeness of the Heritage coast as well as many marvellous National Trust properties and 8 beautiful gardens to visit, it makes the perfect place for a holiday. The farm is actually bounded by National Trust woodland.

Both properties are capable of sleeping 4-6 adults and both are fitted out with everything you could wish for; open plan sitting room/kitchen dining rooms with feature window seat, cooker, refrigerator, dishwasher, and microwave oven. One double bedroom with bathroom and toilet ensuite, one twin bedded-room with toilet and shower ensuite. Electric blankets are fitted in the double and single beds when required. Heating is Night Storage Heaters and an open log/coal fire. Both logs and coal can be supplied at a small charge. Stable Cottage is also fitted with a washer dryer whilst Barn Cottage double room also has adult size stacking bunk beds. Cots, high chair and playpen are available. Dogs are welcome subject to prior agreement. For the children there is a play area with swings, slides and sandpit and other outdoor games. For the adults, a shared barbecue area with a brick built barbecue. It is the ideal place for a truly peaceful holiday. Non-smokers only please.

USEFUL INFORMATION

OPEN; *All year*
DISABLED ACCESS; *Purpose built*
CHILDREN; *Welcome*
PETS; *By prior arrangement*
GARDEN; *Terracing to front + 20 acres*
ACCOMMODATION; *2 units each sleeping 4-6. Strictly non-smoking*

THE OLD GRANARY,
Luccombe,
Milton Abbas,
Blandford Forum,
Dorset
DT11 0BE.

Tel : 01258 880558
Fax : 01258 881384

The self catering accommodation at this working farm is of a very high standard. Surrounded by peaceful and tranquil scenery, the setting for this wonderful experience can only leave you refreshed and relaxed. The farm itself extends to about 650 acres, and you are very welcome to wander round and enjoy the views. There is also a riding school which is suitable for all abilities, including the disabled. The Old Granary is some 200 years old, and is unique. It stands on twelve saddle stones, with the weight being distributed between large oak timbers, so you are literally above ground! It is built of irregularly fired bricks with a tiled roof. Inside is to a very high standard, and is full of character and charm. It is suitable for two adults with some room for children's cots or Z-beds, and there is a fully fitted kitchen, and many accessories which will make your stay both welcome and enjoyable.

The Sty and Cakehouse are two further cottages which have accommodation for up to four adults, with Z-beds being available for extra bed space. Both have been designed with the disabled in mind and offer various facilities. There is also a laundry, cleaning and babysitting service available and this can be arranged in advance through Murray and Amanda Kayll, the owners.

Luccombe is perfectly situated for visiting various attractions in the area. The ancient Abbey of Middleton is close by, and in the historic village of Milton Abbas, Capability Brown created a beautiful lake. Dorset has many areas of interest, and Murray and Amanda are happy to advise you on places to visit and things to do.

USEFUL INFORMATION

OPEN : *All year*
CHILDREN : *Welcome*
PETS : *By arrangement*
ACCOMMODATION : *3 self catering cottages*

SELF CATERING
DISABLED ACCESS : *Yes*
CREDIT CARDS : *All major*

MORN LODGE COTTAGE
Chickerell,
Nr Weymouth,
Dorset DT3 4DL

Tel: 01305 784967

Morn Lodge Cottage stands in a pretty garden in the small village of Chickerell close to the popular seaside town of Weymouth with its lovely sandy beach and beautiful harbour. Recently the cottage has been totally renovated but has not lost any of its original features. It is part of a Georgian Farmhouse and set in 8 acres of garden and paddocks. Within the cottage which sleeps 4/5 plus a cot has two bedrooms and ample parking. The lounge diner has colour television, a video and a music centre. The kitchen will please anyone with its modern fittings, electric cooker, microwave, washer-dryer and fridge freezer. The open staircase leads to the first bedroom which has 3ft pine twin beds and a wash hand basin. There is ample space for an additional bed. The other bedroom has a pine double bed. All beds have continental quilts and they are ready made up for your arrival. The large bathroom has a spacious airing cupboard, a bath, wash hand basin, toilet and a shower. There is also a toilet and was hand-basin downstairs. The walled garden is secluded and has garden furniture and a Patio with built in BBQ.

With so many exciting places to visit within easy reach and some excellent eateries closeby., Morn Lodge Cottage will provide you with a super base for a memorable holiday.

USEFUL INFORMATION

OPEN; *All year* ***CHILDREN;*** *Welcome*
CREDIT CARDS; *None taken* ***DISABLED ACCESS;*** *No special facilities*
PETS; *By arrangement only* ***GARDEN;*** *Walled with furniture. BBQ. Patio*
ACCOMMODATION; *1 dbl 1 tw +cot & fold down*

COOMBE HOUSE
41 Coombe Street,
Lyme Regis,
Dorset
DT7 3PY

Tel: 01297 443849

Lyme Regis is a charming place which delights visitors both for its history, its cobbled streets and of course, The Cobb, made famous by Jeremy Irons and Meryl Streep in the film 'The French Lieutenant's Woman'. Coombe Street is in the oldest part of the town and in its midst is Coombe House, 150 metres from the sea, south facing, on level ground and quite delightful. Dympna Duncan the owner, not only looks after her guests in her delightful house, but cares for those who use her charming self-catering flat. This unusual flat, reached via external steps from the courtyard, has been sensitively converted from an old working loft. The spacious accommodation will more than happily sleep 6 people.

The sitting room has comfy sofas and a colour television, the French windows open on to a wooden balcony, this is child-proof but a watchful eye is required. The fitted kitchen has every modern convenience to make your holiday easy including a gas cooker, fridge, washing machine and tumble drier. The three bedrooms, one with twin beds, one with bunk beds and a gallery bedroom with a double bed with views across the old roofs of Lyme. The family sized bathroom has a powerful shower over the bath. This light and airy flat is centrally heated and carpeted throughout. Linen and towels are included in the tariff, but electricity is by meter reading at the beginning and end of your stay. The flat is excellently placed being only two minutes walk from the main beach and shopping street. If you don't feel like cooking in the evening then there are numerous restaurants to suit all tastes within walking distance. Dympna will be more than happy to assist with anything you need. An excellent choice in a lovely location.

USEFUL INFORMATION

OPEN; *All year*
CHILDREN; *Welcome*

DISABLED ACCESS; *No*
PETS; *No*

CREDIT CARDS; *No*
ACCOMMODATION; *Spacious 3 bedroomed flat*
GARDEN: *Courtyard garden*

EASTCOTT
Lower Woodford,
Salisbury,
Wiltshire
SP4NQ

Tel:01722 782393

Self catering accommodation at Eastcott, the family home of Heather Yelland, consists of a cosy lounge with dining area, well equipped kitchen and 2 bedrooms, one of which is a double and the other a twin and both are ensuite. It is attractively furnished and decorated through out. It really is a good option for people who enjoy the freedom of self catering. As it is a bungalow it means there is ground floor access for the disabled although there are no specific facilities for wheelchairs. It is available all the year round, children are very welcome and pets by arrangement. The nice, private, lawned garden is a pleasant place to be on a summer's day and in winter the apartment is beautifully warm and snug. There is ample parking space.

Eastcott, in Lower Woodford, is set in a very peaceful valley with much wildlife to see. It not only provides a totally peaceful retreat but is an excellent base for all sorts of activities, some strenuous and others less demanding. For those who enjoy walking the valley is a popular haunt, Eastcott is on the cycle way, one can fish nearby and within easy distance there is more than one golf course, good enough to tempt the keenest player. Salisbury will provide any visitor with hours of enjoyment whether it is within the majesty of the cathedral, the beautiful Close, exploring all the streets and architectural gems in this remarkable city, or visiting the Salisbury Playhouse and Cinema. Stonehenge is a mere five miles away and the coast is not too far at Bournemouth and Poole. The gourmet will find good restaurants within easy distance, nice country inns are in abundance and in Salisbury itself there are eateries to satisfy anyone's taste whether ethnic or vegetarian and other diets.

USEFUL INFORMATION

OPEN; *All year* ***CHILDREN;*** *Welcome*
CREDIT CARDS; *None taken* ***PETS;*** *By arrangement*
ACCOMMODATION; *Self-contained* ***GARDEN;*** *Private lawned garden*
With 1 dbl & 1 twin (both ensuite)

HIDEAWAYS
Chapel House,
Luke Street,
Berwick St John,
Shaftesbury,
Dorset SP7 0HQ

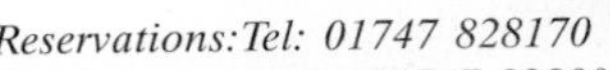

Reservations:Tel: 01747 828170
Brochure request+ 01747 828000
Fax: 01747 829090

What do you do if you decide to take a holiday in a country or coastal cottage? Unless you have previously done so, or have been given a recommendation by friends, you may well spend a lot of time looking in newspapers, books and other places and never be quite sure about what is on offer. All that anxiety can be removed by using Hideaways, an impressive medium-sized agency based near Shaftesbury, Dorset who have a wonderful selection of picture-book cottages covering an area from Kent to Cornwall, right across the South of England and northwards to the Cotswolds and the Forest of Dean . If you are interested they will send you a colourful brochure showing the many enchanting cottages available and within the brochure you will find a lot more detail of how to set about renting a cottage, and everything else one needs to know. Hideaways has a great reputation which is reinforced by the many letters they have from satisfied clients.

Let's look at one or two of them. ***Cobwebs*** *at Downton, nr Salisbury - the one we have chosen for the line drawing at the top of this feature - has so much character from its thatched roof to its interior beams and inglenook. It is a listed property dating back to Cromwellian times and has been beautifully restored. This is a cottage for non-smokers and will sleep 5/6 + a baby.****Bartley Manor Stables*** *at Bartley, nr Lyndhurst, the traditional capital of the New Forest, is set in the grounds of a manor house, within easy walking distance of the open Forest and sleeps 4/6 + baby.* ***Rose Cottage*** *at Lymington, a delightful yachting village, is an old fisherman's cottage dating back to 1835, now extensively restored by an interior designer and decorative artist of repute who has used her talents to provide accommodation of quite outstanding quality. Rose Cottage sleeps 3/5 + baby. These three cottages may give you some idea of what a superb, happy and very comfortable holiday you could have in any one of the properties marketed by Hideaways. We have found their service to be excellent, full of integrity and with a great desire to please both their clients and the increasing number of people who are using the agency.*

USEFUL INFORMATION

OPEN; *For enquiries all year* ***ACCOMMODATION;*** *Delightful cottage Fully equipped.*

BOURNEMOUTH HOLIDAY BUREAU
Henbury View,
Dullar Lane,
Sturminster Marshall,
Wimborne,
Dorset BH21 4AD

Tel: 01258 858580

Dorset really is one of the most charming counties with it's chocolate box thatched roof cottages, with their pretty well tended gardens. It has the best of both worlds, beautiful countryside and stunning coastline. The area is teeming with castles, country houses and gardens, museums, nature reserves and sporting activities for everyone to take part in. Which makes it an ideal location for Bournemouth Holiday Homes to have it's office. They have been in existence for over twenty five years, offering an efficient, friendly and reliable service. Situated in Sturminster Marshall near Wimborne, they specialise in self-catering accommodation in and around the Bournemouth, Poole, Christchurch and Ringwood areas.

There are 3 sections in their comprehensive colour brochure: Flats, Flatlets and Maisonettes, Houses, Bungalows and Cottages and finally Caravans and Chalets. Each entry explains the property, how many it sleeps, what is included in the tariff eg. linen, gas, electricity and whether pets and children are welcome. Great care has been taken with the selection of properties, the standard of accommodation ranges from superior to the more modest, some are in the countryside and some are in town situations, so you are sure to find something to suit your taste and your pocket.

USEFUL INFORMATION

OPEN: *Most of the year* ***DISABLED ACCESS:*** *Depending on property*
CHILDREN: *Depending on property* ***GARDEN:*** *Depending on property*
CREDIT CARDS: *None taken* ***PETS:*** *Depending on property*
ACCOMMODATION: *A selection of self-catering holiday homes*

LOWER FIFEHEAD FARM
Fifehead St Quinton,
Sturminster Newton,
Dorset
DT10 2AP

Tel/Fax: 01258 817335

Lower Fifehead farm built of a mellow stone in the early 18th century, is ideally positioned in the glorious county of Dorset where many beauty spots are just waiting to be explored. This listed building offers various forms of accommodation part of which is a two bedroomed cottage, modernly furnished with one double bedroom and a 2nd bedroom with a single bed and bunk beds, it sleeps 5 plus a cot if required. There is a bathroom and toilet upstairs and downstairs a cloakroom, lounge and a fully equipped kitchen. There is also a newly converted one bedroomed flat, with ensuite bathroom, a combined dining and sitting room with one bed chair and a large kitchen. The flat sleeps 2/3 persons. Both kitchens have everything you will need including an electric cooker, microwave, fridge and modern units. Each accommodation is fully carpeted, centrally heated and with a colour television.

And finally bed and breakfast where one is made to feel most welcome. Bedrooms are tastefully furnished, ensuite facilities are available. All rooms have a tea/coffee tray. A resident's lounge with a colour television is available for guests all day. Full English breakfast is served with various choices. Vegetarians are catered for, and where possible fresh locally produced ingredients are used. Farm tours are available around this interesting 400 acre dairy farm, other activities include horse riding and a nearby golf course will satisfy the needs of the enthusiast. As for ramblers and walkers there are many glorious walks. Lower Fifehead Farm has the English Tourist Board '2 Crowns Recommended' award for bed and breakfast and '3 Keys Recommended' award for self-catering.

USEFUL INFORMATION

OPEN; *All year*
CHILDREN; *Welcome*
CREDIT CARDS; *None taken*
ACCOMMODATION; *Self-catering 2 bedroomed cottage. One bedroomed self-contained flat. B&B 2 rooms, 1 dbl, 1 twn*

DINING ROOM; *Breakfast only*
VEGETARIAN; *Catered for*
DISABLED ACCESS; *No but welcome*
GARDEN; *Yes with tables outside*
PETS; *Only in self-catering cottage*

YEW HOUSE COTTAGES
Yew House Farm,
Marnhull,
Sturminster Newton,
Dorset
DT10 1NP

Tel: 01258 820412
Fax: 01258 821044

Yew House Farm is on the edge of the village of Marnhull in the Blackmore Vale. Here within the grounds are three delightful cottages, Foxes, Willows and Dove which stand in a very secluded position with superb views of the vale. Dove cottage has been designed to accommodate the partially disabled. Each cottage has identical accommodation comprising one double bedroom and one twin-bedded room with bunk, a cot is available if required at no extra cost. Linen is supplied except for the cot and personal towels. There is a shower room tiled throughout with wash basin, electrically heated shower, WC and shaver point. The kitchen is compact and fully equipped whilst the living/dining area is spacious and comfortable with fitted carpets throughout. Letting is from Friday to Friday, this helps visitors avoid possible heavy traffic on the journey. The time for arrival is 3pm onwards and you are asked to leave by 10am. Electricity is charged by a pound coin meter. Children are very welcome but regretfully pets are not permitted. During the season generally May to September, the outdoor swimming pool is available. There is ample parking for cars.

Dorset is one of the most beautful counties in England - unspoilt and undiscovered by the crowds. Inland, North Dorset can offer you peace and tranquillity and an unhurried pace of life. Lovely villages to explore especially in the Blackmore Vale area, referred to by Thomas Hardy as the 'vale of little dairies'. Westwards from Shaftesbury with its famous 'Gold Hill' you can travel through unspoilt open countryside to Beaminster, Bridport and on to Lyme Regis. To the south is the lovely Piddle Valley, the historic town of Dorchester and the coast with the resort of Weymouth, or the cliffs of Lulworth. There are castles, stately homes, gardens and safari parks, military and rural life museums and much more to interest all age groups. Fishing is very popular in season and licences can be obtained locally, there are also excellent facilities for golf and other sports nearby.

USEFUL INFORMATION

OPEN; *March to October*
CHILDREN; *Welcome. Cot available*
GARDEN; *Yes. Outdoor swimming pool*
PETS; *Not permitted*
DISABLED ACCESS; *Dove cottage designed for the partially disabled*

THE GARDEN COTTAGES,
Thickwood House,
Thickwood,
Nr Bath
Wiltshire
SN14 8BN

Tel: 01225 744377
Fax:01225 742329

These English Tourist Board 'Four Keys- commended' cottages offer the ultimate in a retreat for couples who want to have time to themselves away from the madding crowd. Thickwood Garden Cottages lie in the grounds of Thickwood House a fine Grade II Listed Jacobean Farm House, which is the home of Sandra and Colin Agombar. A stone byre has been skillfully converted to make two attractive self-contained cottages, each with a double bedroom, bathroom en-suite, kitchen and lounge/dining room. In winter the cottages are warm and have full central heating, the ceilings are vaulted and there are a wealth of exposed beams giving a wonderful atmosphere. There is only one step into each cottage and no internal staircase. Each has its own front patio and lawn, and they have a private rear garden with garden furniture. The cottages are located opposite a small orchard and have a splendid view of a range of very attractive old stone barns which are among the largest in the county. There is ample parking in the grounds and stabling and bicycle storage is available by arrangement.

Everything has been thought of to make your stay a happy one. The cottages are beautifully furnished and the beds are made up ready for your arrival. If you stay for more than a week then fresh linen is provided. You will find the cottages spotless and they are cleaned on a weekly basis during your stay. By arrangement you are very welcome to bring one small, well behaved dog or cat, but it must not be left in the cottage unattended nor allowed to stray. Groceries can be ordered for you in advance and there is a 24 hour laundry service (washing/drying) at an extra charge. You will find the rental charges are fully inclusive of heating, hotwater, towels and linen. Local shops and a Post Office are within one mile. There is a bus service within a few hundred yards but it is infrequent.

Thickwood is only 8 miles from the incomparable city of Bath and 9 miles from the M4 at Junction 18 and 17.

USEFUL INFORMATION

OPEN; *All year*
ACCOMMODATION; *2 cottages For 2 people in each only*
PETS; *By arrangement one small dog or cat*

CHILDREN; *No*
CREDIT CARDS; *None taken*
DISABLED ACCESS; *No stairs but one step at the entrance*

BESSINGTON LODGE
Beach Road,
West Bexington,
Dorset

Tel: 01308 897616

This attractive bungalow is owned by Richard and Jayne Childs who are the proprietors of the excellent Manor Hotel in Bexington where you are welcome to drink in the bar or enjoy the excellent food. It is situated ideally for those who want a carefree self-catering holiday. From here all Dorset stretches out within easy reach. Whether you want sparkling sandy beaches, country walks, stately homes, attractive villages with good hostelries or to visit Lyme Regis, Weymouth, Bridport and many other interesting towns, it is all there for you.

Inside Bessington Lodge which was built in the latter part of this century, you will find there is everything you need to make a holiday pleasureable. The rooms are attractively furnished and it will sleep seven people comfortably. There is plenty of hot water and in the well equipped kitchen you will find all you need including a microwave and good quality utensils and crockery. It does not feel like a holiday let; far more like a home from home. The garden is beautiful and has a barbecue as well as garden furniture. Pets are not permitted and Bessington Lodge is strictly non-smoking.

USEFUL INFORMATION

OPEN; *All year*
CREDIT CARDS;*Visa/Master/Diners/Amex*
PETS; *No*
PARKING; *Yes, double carport*

CHILDREN; *Welcome*
DISABLED ACCESS; *Facilities*
GARDEN; *Yes with BBQ*
ACCOMMODATION; *Sleeps 7*

Strictly non-smoking

Dorset, Wiltshire, Hampshire

CHAPTER 3

THE HOME COUNTIES, THE THAMES VALLEY & GREATER LONDON,
Including
SURREY, SUSSEX, KENT, ESSEX, BUCKINGHAMSHIRE, BEDFORDSHIRE & BERKSHIRE

INCLUDES

CHAPTER 3

THE HOME COUNTIES, THE THAMES VALLEY & GREATER LONDON *Including* SURREY, SUSSEX, KENT, ESSEX, BUCKINGHAMSHIRE, BEDFORDSHIRE and BERKSHIRE

The Chilterns, dividing Oxfordshire and Buckinghamshire, with their centuries old beechwoods were the home at one time of hundreds of 'bodgers', wood turners making chair legs with manual lathes, and whittlers of clothes pegs. The area is one of outstanding beauty, the mainly small buildings a mixture of brick with knapped flints. Where the Chilterns meet the Berkshire Downs and the river has created the **Goring Gap** through the chalk, the ancient **Icknield Way** and **Ridgeway** come together.

The Ridgeway runs along the Berkshire Downs (now in Oxfordshire) heading towards Stonehenge and Avebury although the ancient road pre-dates the great monuments. Being away from modern roads, the Ridgeway provides for peaceful walking or horseriding with extensive open views. Towards the west of its Oxfordshire section the Ridgeway passes by the **White Horse of Uffington**, nearly 40 feet high, cut through the turf into the chalk. If you leave a horse and a coin in the nearby **Wayland Smith's Cave**, rumour has it that by the morning the horse will have been shod. Here too is **Dragon Hill**, said to be where St George slayed the dragon.

Over the Berkshire Downs from Oxfordshire is the Royal County of Berkshire itself, now a small county with, sadly, much of its Iron Age and Roman history obscured by recent development. For all that it is an interesting county and the whole is really overshadowed by the majesty of **Windsor Castle**. This enormous fortress which dominates **Windsor**, is the largest inhabited castle in the world. It has been one of the principal residences of the sovereigns of England since the days of William the Conqueror, who built it. When you come to examine it closely you will see that almost every monarch since William's time has taken a hand in rebuilding. For our present Sovereign Lady, Queen Elizabeth II, the rebuilding has been forced upon her by the devastating fire just five years ago which destroyed much of value, although the works of art, furniture and books were saved by a human chain passing the priceless masterpieces gently down the line, hand to hand - hands that included the Queen, the Duke of York and many local people. The damage has now been restored and the castle is as magnificent and awe inspiring as ever. Three wards or enclosures make up Windsor Castle. The Round Tower in the Middle Ward was built by Henry II to replace the wooden

Norman fortress. George IV added its upper half in 1828-32. The Lower Ward contains St Georges Chapel and the Upper Ward has the State Apartments.

Within the Castle, parts of which are open to the public, you must not miss the 15th and 16th century St Georges Chapel. It boasts some of the finest fan vaulting in the world, the helmets and banners of knights, the tombs of Henry VII and Charles I and a memorial to Prince Albert. The State Apartments also must not be missed. These magnificently furnished rooms on the precipitous north flank of the castle are still used on official occasions. On a quite different scale is the world's most famous **Doll's House** designed by Sir Edwin Lutyens in the 1920's for Queen Mary.

Everywhere in Windsor there are Royal connections. Indeed the town grew up because of the presence of the castle. It is a delightful town with a good theatre, attractive shops, fine museums and a beautiful parish church built in 1820 on the site of an earlier church. The building was supervised by Jeffrey Wyatt who later, as Sir Jeffrey Wyatville, designed the Castle's Waterloo Chamber for George IV.

Eton is always inextricably mixed with Windsor but it is a little town in its own right. It has always had a fascination for people especially because of the world famous school, Eton College.Each year on the 4th June Eton College celebrates its founding by Henry IV in 1440 with a firework display on the river. Also in June is Ascot Week when royalty, the gentry and celebrities as well as other racegoers, many of them in huge flamboyant hats, attend the meetings at **Ascot Racecourse**.

There are some wonderful drives along the River Thames to small towns and villages, **Maidenhead, Taplow**, amongst many. I always enjoy visiting **Cookham**, the home of the artist Sir Stanley Spencer (1891-1959). He loved his birthplace with an intensity that shows in his paintings. Cookham High Street, the parish church, the River Thames, the meadows, are all recognisable in his works. It is fitting that Cookham should be the home of the **Stanley Spencer Gallery**. It stands in the centre of Cookham in the former Wesleyan Chapel to which he was taken as a child by his mother. Pride of place is held by the immense, unfinished Christ Preaching at Cookham Regatta. There are some touching reminders of this talented man; his spectacles, easel, palettes, sunshade, and folding chair, and even a baby's push chair that he used to carry his equipment when he was off on a painting expedition.

Reading is a town that tends to be omitted from Guide Books but this should not be so. It is a busy place and has much to interest the visitor and if you are looking for somewhere comfortable to stay which will provide you with a base in order to discover all that this fascinating area has to offer then **Windy Brow** in Reading is the answer. Two good places to visit within easy distance of Reading are **Swallowfield Park** off the B3349 and just 6 miles south-east of the town. The house was built in 1690 for the 2nd Earl of Clarendon and then considerably altered in the 18th century when the redbrick stables were added. The house has great charm and the beautifully landscaped gardens are a delight. Covering 4 acres they contain a variety of flowering shrubs and roses, as well as many fine specimen trees. You can wander along an ancient yew-tree walk, muse by the small lake and revel in the banks of massed rhododendrons in season. Open May-Sept, Wednesday and Thursday afternoons. The second is the **R.E.M.E Museum** at **Arborfield** off the A327 5 miles south of Reading. Here you can study the history and many-sided work of the Royal Electrical Mechanical Engineers, your understanding helped by the life sized tableaux and large model dioramas.Formed in 1942, the corps came into being to support the rapid growth of military technology from the outset of the Second World War. Today it is still busy repairing army aircraft and seagoing ships, electronic equipment and so on. This is all reflected in this interesting museum, which also contains displays on R.E.M.E activities worldwide. Open all year. Monday to Friday. Free admission.

Over the Thames from Windsor and beyond the town of **Slough**, Berkshire joins the tall narrow county of **Buckinghamshire** on its short southern boundary. At this point Buckinghamshire is low and leafy, rising sharply further north to the Chilterns with its thick beechwoods, then further north still becoming a land of streams and marshes.

A prehistoric boundary known as **Grim's Ditch** runs across the Chilterns near to **Great Hampden** and nearby are two crosses cut through the turf into the chalk. Not as exciting as the White Horse of Uffingham but nonetheless intriguing.

The Chilterns are renowned for the many footpaths and there are walks both short and long, but rarely strenuous, that can take advantage of the scenery, giving just occasional glimpses through the trees of distant views. The **North Bucks Way** starting near **Wendover** on the Chilterns escarpment takes walkers down to **Wolverton** in the Vale of Aylesbury. On the North Bucks Way can be found the **Quainton Railway Centre** with trains in steam on the last Sunday of each month. The ancient trees of **Burnham Beeches** east of **Maidenhead** form a beautiful area which was bought for the people by the City of London in 1879. At one time this area was also home to Romany gypsies, now long gone.

Along the Thames, Buckinghamshire has some attractive towns such as **Marlow** which is particularly beautiful. This was the home of the poet Percy B. Shelley and Mary Shelley of 'Frankenstein' fame. The poet William Cowper spent the second half of his life in **Olney** where the **Cowper Museum** celebrates his works, including 'Amazing Grace' which was written here.

Stoke Poges church is where Thomas Gray wrote his 'Elegy written in a country Churchyard' and at **Beaconsfield** lived G.K. Chesterton and Enid Blyton who it is believed was inspired by the **Bekonscot Model Village** with tiny houses spread over a large garden. Milton lived in**Chalfont St Giles** when he fled from London to escape the plague and in addition to a small museum, his cottage is now open to visitors.

Near Beaconsfield the small town of **Jordans** was home to William Penn, the founder of Pennsylvania and he is buried at the small 17th century **Quaker Meeting House. The Mayflower Barn**, also open to the public, incorporates beams taken from the Mayflower after the Pilgrim Fathers sailed to America in 1620.

Hughenden Manor near **High Wycombe** was the home of Benjamin Disraeli and the house still contains much of his furniture and other belongings. Today's Prime Minister has a country residence southwest of **Wendover**, a Tudor house known as **Chequers**, presented to the nation for just this purpose during World War I.

From pretty, small villages such as **Hambleden** to modern towns like **Milton Keynes,** Buckinghamshire has absorbed a large increase in population in the latter part of this century, yet outside these conurbations retains its character as a rural area.

Bedfordshire to the north east is very much more rural, a green and peaceful county where water meadows flank the River Great Ouse and the rolling downs climb towards the mighty Chilterns. John Bunyan was born in the village of **Elstow** in 1628. Later he was imprisoned for his religious views in the county town of **Bedford**. Both places have much to remind us of this great man. **Elstow Moot Hall** is a beautiful brick and timber building built about 1500. Its purpose to house the goods for the famous May Fair at Elstow. It was also used as a court house and it has been suggested that Bunyan might have had Elstow Fair in mind when he described the worldly 'Vanity Fair' in the Pilgrim's Progress. The Hall belonged to the nuns of Elstow Abbey and after the abbey was dissolved at the Reformation, the Moot Hall continued as a court house. For centuries it was neglected until in 1951 it was restored. The upper floor has been opened up to display the superb medieval roof, with massive beams and graceful uprights.

Two miles south west of **Dunstable** , the rolling hills of **Dunstable Downs** form the northern end of the Chilterns chalk escarpment and from them there are wide views over the Vale of Aylesbury and beyond. Thousands of years ago they were a highway for prehistoric man, who trudged along the Icknield Way (now the B489) at their foot. In a 300 acre area the ground has been left untreated by chemical weedkillers or fertilisers and the result is stunning. Rare plant species flourish,including fairy flax and chalk milkwort. Little muntjac deer browse among the scrub, and whinchats and grasshopper warblers dart over the hillside.

At **Whipsnade Heath** there is a reminder of the First World War. Here is the Tree Cathedral, in a sun dappled grove, laid out to a plan of nave, transepts and chapels. It was planted in the 1930's by Edmund Kell Blyth in memory of his fallen friends. Quite moving and very beautiful.

Nearby on top of the downs, more than 2,000 animals roam over 500 acres of **Whipsnade Park Zoo**, in conditions as nearly as wild as climate and safety will permit.

If you are a narrow gauge railway enthusiast you will want to visit **Leighton Buzzard Narrow Gauge Railway.** An average speed of five and a half miles an hour might not seem much by to-day's standards but it is quite enough for the locomotives of the Leighton Buzzard Railway which was built to carry sand from the quarries north of the town to the main London and North Western Railway. Due to be scrapped at the end of the 1960's, it was saved by a band of enthusiasts who have acquired steam and diesel engines from as far away as India and the Cameroons, constructed rolling stock, and built an engine shed for maintenance.

Market gardening flourishes around the town of **Biggleswade** set amidst highly productive arable land, showing the diversity of one of the smallest counties in England. Near here you can visit **The Swiss Garden**, a beautifully restored 19th century garden with fine trees. An intricate French garden features in a park that was laid out in the 18th century and partly re-landscaped by Capability Brown around **Wrest Park House** at **Silsoe**, modelled on the French chateaux style. The history of gardening through the ages can be seen here in a setting which includes some splendid water features.

Judging by its huge popularity, no visit to Bedfordshire would be complete without a tour around the splendid **Woburn Abbey**, home of the Dukes of Bedford, with its stately parklands, complete with wild animals, boat trips, art galleries and shops.

Hertfordshire, along with the extinct county of Middlesex, made up the Northern Home Counties and it is here that the mix of grand country houses and new towns is in greatest contrast - or greatest harmony depending on your viewpoint. **Letchworth** was the first of the new 'Garden Cities', created as early as 1903 in a bid to bring better housing to ordinary people. Its **First Garden City Museum** tells the story of the somewhat radical social ideas which were held by those who originally created this town as well as those who lived here. **Welwyn Garden City** followed in 1920 and several other new towns, often around old town or village centres, sprung up in the post-war period of the 1950's.

I have to admit that for me Hertfordshire is principally **St Albans** with its fine cathedral in which thousands of years of worship have continued on the site of St Alban's martyrdom. Many centuries ago Alban was the first Christian martyr in this country and his shrine has always attracted pilgrims in search of spiritual and physical healing. It is a beautiful place which emanates strength.

You feel as if the Almighty is reaching out for you and endeavouring to pour into your soul the fortitude shown by St Alban, and at the same time give you hope for the present and peace eternal. The history of the cathedral is well documented and you will do no better than to purchase the beautifully presented, colourful Pitkin Guide to St Albans Cathedral which will cost you about two pounds and be a constant reminder of your visit.

Almost surrounded by motorways, St Albans is easy to reach and having done so you drive into quieter realms and begin to realise that you are going to discover in this one place, which offers the unusual combination of the dignity of a Cathedral City and the intimacy of a rural markettown, the full span of British history. For a moment or two the sense of history is overwhelming. St Albans is full of museums, beautifully laid out and providing easily digested information.

A totally different atmosphere you will find at **The Mosquito Aircraft Museum** in Salisbury Hall, **London Colney**. The historic site of the moated Salisbury Hall, mentioned in the Domesday Book, was chosen by the de Havilland Aircraft Company in 1939 to develop in secret the wooden, high speed, unarmed bomber, the Mosquito; with 41 variants of the type of the most versatile aircraft of the war. This began the museum's long association with Salisbury Hall making it the oldest Aircraft Museum in the country. Visitors to the museum soon discover that it can offer more than a collection of static aircraft. Close inspection of the exhibits provide a unique hands-on experience. Members are always on hand to assist the visitor and demonstrate the working displays. With a varied programme of regular events that include flying displays, vintage car and motor cycle rallies and model exhibitions, there is always something to appeal to all ages.

From the air to the ground. **The Royal National Rose Society** at Chiswell Green, St Albans on the outskirts of the town, invites you to enjoy the world famous 'Gardens of the Rose' at the Society's showground where there is a collection of some 30,000 roses of all types.

The 12 acres of gardens are a marvellous spectacle for the casual visitor and fascinating to the rose enthusiast. The gardens are being continuously developed - in particular by associating roses with a great many other plants - to create greater interest for visitors and to stimulate ideas leading to more adventurous gardening.

The British Rose Festival is a spectacular national event held every year in July. It includes a magificent display of roses organised by the Society and the British Rose Growers Association on an excitingly new and different theme each year. The competition is for the leading national amateur rose exhibitors and floral artists. All the best of British roses can be seen at this unique show.

Of particular interest in this county for vegetarians will be **Shaw's Corner** at **Ayot St Lawrence. Sir George Bernard Shaw,** playwright and critic, vegetarian and humanist, lived here for the second half of his long and active life. His vegetarian ideals were based on both moral and health grounds, proclaiming that 'Animals are our fellow creatures. I feel a strong kinship with them.; The house has been kept exactly as it was at the time of his death in 1950.

The many houses on a truly grand scale include **Hatfield House** originally home to the Bishops of Ely and later to Henry VIII's children and other members of the Royal family, **Brocket Hall** which was the home of Lord Melbourne and Lady Caroline Lamb, **Moor Park,** the historic home of Cardinal Wolsey later transformed into a Palladian mansion and now a golf club. and **Basing House** home of William Penn founder of Pennsylvania.

Sadly others have fared less well, such as the Castle at **Bishop's Stortford** now just a mound, and another earthworks with just a little masonry which was the Castle at Berkhamsted, presented by William the Conqueror to his brother, later visited by Thomas a Becket, Chaucer and three of Henry VIII's wives and involuntarily visited for a long term, by King John of France. Another was Ware Park which originally housed the 'Great Bed of Ware' mentiond by Shakespeare in his plays, now in the Victoria and Albert Museum.

Near **Ware** at **Amwell** is one of the most unexpected of museums in Britain, a **Lamp-Post Museum.**

Similarly bordering on the outer suburbs of London, the county of **Surrey** has a very high population, much of it in large villages or small towns, and all of it spread out in pleasant green surroundings.

The well know geographical feature of the **Hogs Back** is a part of the North Downs and other high points such as **Leith Hill** with its view of 13 counties, and **Box Hill** offer outstanding panoramic views. On the high point of **Chatley Heath** stands a tower which was part of the communication system, sending messages from London to Portsmouth in less than one minute in the days before telegraph.

Box Hill overlooks some of the prettiest of scenery along the River Mole. Despite its rather unpoetic name it is probably the river most written about in poetry, by Spencer, Milton, Pope and others, and the riverside village of **Brockham** is said to have given the name of 'brock' to the badger, many of which used to live here.

The riverside meadows of **Runnymede** are famous as being the site of King John's signing of (actually fixing his seal to) the Magna Carta in 1215. The memorial buildings at Runnymede were designed by Sir Edward Lutyens.

Architecture from the early part of this century can also be seen to great effect at **Whiteley.** Built according to the will of William Whiteley who left one million pounds for the creation of this retirement village for staff of Whiteley's Department Store. Surrey contains other fine recent buildings such as the **Yvonne Arnaud Theatre** at **Guildford**, as well as **Guildford Cathedral**, started in 1936 but not consecrated until 1962 due to the intervening war. With its position high on Stag Hill on the edge of the town it makes a magnificent spectacle. Close to Guildford at **Peaslake,** one of the most out of the way villages in the county, tucked away on the slopes of Hurt Wood, is the **Hurtwood Inn Hotel**, and at **Albury, Stream Cottage,** the most peaceful of places to stay. Both are great bases for anyone wanting to stay in and around Guildford. A mill and a church in Albury were recorded in the Domesday Book. The great architect Pugin influenced much of the style of building and his famous chimneys are still in evidence today.

Surrey has several special gardens, the most important of which is **Wisley Gardens**, for over 80 years the show gardens of the Royal Horticultural Society and a source of inspiration for all kinds of gardeners. There are features at their best at each time of the year; the Alpine Meadow in spring, the rhododendron-clad Battleston Hill in early summer, and for winter the Orchid House with its naturalistic 'rainforest setting'. Wisley is full of fascinating shapes, textures, sounds and smells, and the special garden for disabled people enables all those with a handicap to take full advantage of them all. There are occasional guided walks and the RHS also runs a series of courses, some of them on aspects of gardening, others on flower arranging or botanical painting. The Information Centre is reputed to sell the most extensive range of horticultural and botanical books in the world, and the range of plants for sale, is staggering with something like 8,500 varieties, many of them far from common-or-garden.

Peppermint used to be an important crop in **Banstead**. The watercress beds at **Abinger Hammer,** fed by underground springs are one of the claims to minor fame for the village, and its history as a centre for the iron industry is another. The iron working made use of a hammer mill (hence the name) driven by the stream.

Loseley Park between **Godalming** and **Guildford** is a splendid Elizabethan house, the home of the More-Molyneux family from the 16th century to the present day. The family farms 1,400 acres around the house, and it is here that Loseley ice-cream and yoghurt is made. All Loseley dairy products are free from artificial additives and they also grow organic crops. However the farm tour shows little of the dairy aspect and does incorporate other farm animals.

One of the most interesting of the many towns in Surrey is **Farnham**, an attractive small market town with elegant Georgian housing and with some interesting literary associations including Sir Walter Scott, Swift and William Cobbett (who described the beauty spot of **Hindhead** as 'the most villainouse spot God ever made') There are several historic houses open to the public in and around the town.

Mystery surrounds **Shalford Mill**, an early 18th century water mill which was in full use until 1914 when it fell into some disrepair. It was acquired by the 'Ferguson's Gang some years later and after restoration was given to the National Trust. The 'Gang' members used code names such as 'Bill Stickers' and none of their identities has ever been known.

Surrey has become one of the most popular commuter counties for London. It might well have destroyed its character but it has not and there are some truly charming towns with fine churches, good shops and excellent hotels and eateries. Between **Reigate** and **Dorking** at **Betchworth** is **Gadbrook Old Farm House** where the hospitality on offer highlights the welcoming attitude of the county. Betchworth is a quiet place through which the River

Mole wanders peacefully. It has a good hostelry, **The Dolphin Inn** and some attractive 16th century cottages untouched by any fake restoration. In Reigate itself an equal welcome awaits anyone who stays at **Barn Cottage.**

Anyone who loves horse racing will be familiar with **Epsom** and its famous downs on which The Derby is run. **Leatherhead**, **Woking**, **Walton-on-Thames** and **Esher** all have character. I probably have an unfair liking for **Weybridge** where I lived for a while enjoying the busy little town, its river, its shops and hostelries and finding out about some very good eateries within easy distance like the **Cedar House Restaurant** at **Cobham.**

Ending on a happy and smiling note, **Cranleigh Church** is believed to hold the inspiration for Lewis Carroll's Cheshire Cat, a grinning cat head carved on the transept arch.

London, how can anyone possibly cover the majesty, the excitement and the sprit in this probably the greatest of all capital cities, in one part of a chapter? I am not even going to try because suffice it to say there is so much literature available to the visitor, and totally up to date data, that any in put of mine would be trivial. I know that the years I spent living in London were probably the most exciting of my life. I lived just behind Oxford Street in Montague Square, and so I was in the heart if the West End. Theatreland was only a short distance, and I think I saw every play, musical, opera and ballet that was performed. It was a mental and visual experience that is unrepeatable and for which I will always be grateful that I had sufficient money to do it. The London stage attracts the very best theatre in the world.

Strangely enough when I lived in the great metropolis I seldom visited any of the tourist attractions like the Tower of London unless I had visitors staying with me. It was American friends from Texas who really made me take notice of things and places which I had come to take for granted. Something I will always be grateful for and I would urge you to see as much as you can whether it is from the river, on foot or maybe using one of the splendid sightseeing buses. It is frequently the unexpected vista that enchants or the sun glistening on the waters of the RiverThames, throwing odd lights onto familar buildings. The Houses of Parliament, Lambeth Palace, the great Savoy Hotel all seen from the river look totally different. You can take boat trips the length of the river and it is more than rewarding. It will leave you with indelible memories.

London is crammed with excellent museums, most of them in **South Kensington**, and no visitor should miss the splendid **Victoria and Albert Museum**. On **Butler's Wharf** is Britain's first **Tea and Coffee Museum**, featuring hundreds of different coffee grinders and machines, over 1,000 teapots, teabags, prints, photographs, maps and drawings documenting the history of tea and coffee drinking over the past 350years. There are even tea bushes growing in the museum!

Visitors to **Greenwich's Fan Museum** are introduced to fans and their history through displays which also show their making and the materials used. There are some exquisite examples of 18th and 19th century fans in an elegant Georgian setting, in this, the first and only museum dedicated to the art and craft of fan making.

Just a few of the other exceptional museums around London are the **Bank of England Museum** with the history of the bank, displays of gold and banknotes: **The Design Museum** in the Docklands which has collections of well designed, mass production items along with a series of special exhibitions; **Dickens' House Museum** where the great man lived: **Florence Nightingale Museum** telling the story of her life and work, the **Freud Museum** in Sigmund Freud's last home. **The Guinness World of Records** with lifesize models and electronic displays to show the biggest, fastest etc. **Kew Bridge Steam Museum** with its unique collection of impressive, working steam pumping engines; and the **London Diamond Centre** where you can see the diamonds being cut and polished.

An extraordinary museum, if you can call it a museum, is to be found at **18 Folgate Street** in the heart of what was the Huguenot rag trade district of **Spitalfields**. The house is opened a few times a week by the owner who lives there as the house was when it was built in the 18th century, perfect in every detail of decor and, of course, with only candle and gas power. However those intending to visit are requested to 'telephone' for details!

The underground **Cabinet War Rooms** feature a Transatlantic Telephone Room and another 20 historic rooms which were operational during the 2nd World War. Very closeby in **Horseguard's Parade**, and also underground is **Henry VIII's Wine Cellar** which can only be seen by appointment, on a Saturday afternoon.

At **Wimbledon** is what must surely be the only **Lawn Tennis Museum** in the world. It is open during the Wimbledon Tennis season to ticket holders.

Also at Wimbledon, as part of the **Polka's Children Theatre**, is a toy and puppet exhibition. In Scala Street in central London, **Pollock's Toy Museum** displays not just Pollock's card cut-out theatres but puppets, dolls' houses and teddies of the past. The **London Toy and Model Museum** covers a similar subject, in Craven Hill in **Bayswater.** Somewhat different, but on the theme of puppets, is the **Spitting Image Rubberworks** in **Covent Garden.**

Also in Covent Garden, displays of work on an environmental theme are often held at the **London Ecology Centre**, founded on World Environment Day in 1985. The Centre's focus is the Information Service for the general public, a forum for environmental organisations and a single point of contact for the channelling of enquiries. Its 'London Sustainable Development Network'collects information on examples of good environmental practice which it then publicises to those interested. The offices of the Bat Conservation Trust and the Environmental Film Festival are also within the Centre, as is a Meditation Centre.

Covent Garden is an exciting development of mainly shops, cafes and small museums, several of them quite specialised and unique, mixed with street entertainment and an electric atmosphere, in what was the old fruit and vegetable market. No longer are there flower girls to be found under the portico of St Paul's church, but although the area has changed considerably since those days it has retained its lively spirit.

A short walk from Covent Garden via the Aldwych brings you to **Fleet Street,** another part of London now much changed. For centuries until just recently, Fleet Street was the home of all the important national newspapers, now most have moved, mainly to the **Docklands.** The other association with this area, that of the legal profession, continues. Although different, the charm of the old pubs and alleys persists, with much of its history on view such as the **Pepys Exhibition** within the **Prince Henry's Room**, and the **Wig and Pen** where lawyers and journalists have traditionally met, but Sweeney Todd's Barber Shop and the Pie Shop on the other side of St Dunstan's Church are no longer there. In the Strand, **Twinings** tea shop is said to be the longest established shop on its original site and also claims to be the narrowest. The names of the streets and alleys sum up something of their past history, with Wine Office Court and Old Cheshire Cheese.

An aerial view of London will show that much of it is covered in green. Not only are there large numbers of private gardens, but there are hundreds of public gardens and parks right up to the size of **Richmond Park**, which with deer roaming wild, really does seem to be a bit of the countryside within London. In **Westminster** the pretty **College Garden** with its **Little Cloister** is only occasionally open to the public. It is said to be the oldest garden of its type in England.

London probably has the most varied and best restaurants in the world - the French would not agree with me! It would be invidious to choose any one place in which to eat but because I know **The Portobello Hotel** and discovered that **Julie's Restaurant** was under the same management, it therefore gave me a sound reason for going there. If the standard was anything like that of the Portobello I would not be disappointed - and I was not. What an astonishing place. A labyrinthe fantasy warren made up of five rooms decorated in different styles, housed in three terraced houses and an ex builder's yard. The five rooms are Gothic; with chairs salvaged from nearby St Paul's Church; Forge, decorated in pink with an original forge as a set-piece; Back, with a pulpit and huge oval table that required a wall to be demolished to fit it in (this is the stag party room where the Prince of Wales, Mark Phillips, Mark Knopfler and Sting bade farewell to bachelordom;) The Garden, which has a removable canvas roof, and the Conservatory. Each room can be reserved for parties. The theatrical look evokes the novels of Jules Verne, but makes a congenial atmosphere for stars who want to let their hair down. It is a calm, romantic place and uncrowded. Somewhere to enjoy dinner by downlighters and candles. At Lunch, most customers are on business, usually from the local fashion and record industries. In the evenings, locals and stars alike enjoy the intimate atmosphere and well-known absence of paparazzi. You may see anyone from Joanna Lumley eating Vegetarian to Princess Margaret, Sean Connery, Roger Moore, Kenneth Branagh, Madonna - a never ending list. When booking, regulars specify rooms and then tables. George Michael for example, likes Table F6 in the Forge, somewhere to see and be seen! Sunday Brunch goes on from 12.30-7.30pm, there is a Morning Coffee Menu and delicious, imaginative food throughout. You will find Julie's at 135 Portland Road, W11. Tel:0171 229 8331 and Julie's Bar at 137 Portland Road, W11. Tel: 0171 727 7985.

Where to stay? Well, the list is endless but I have chosen a small selection of places that I can personally recommend having either stayed there or had friends who have. I have already mentioned the excellent **Portobello** at 22 Stanley Gardens. It gets its name from the thriving Notting Hill Portobello Market although Stanley Gardens is a quiet street. **The Goring Hotel** is a distinguished, dignified establishment, privately owned and run immaculately. It is delightful, has beautiful gardens, which provide the view for many of the bedrooms, some balconied. Next the old family hotel in George Street, **Durrants**. It has been owned by the Miller family for over 70 years and provides a service that meets the needs of today's travellers in an atmosphere of yesteryear.

To find a tranquil haven in the heart of London is a godsend. **Number Sixteen, Sumner Place**, in South Kensington is just that. The premises just ooze warmth and a sense of being in your own private dwelling cared for by an efficient and friendly staff. Another such place is **11 Cadogan Gardens, Sloane Square.** Which was the first exclusive Town House Hotel ever. It is set in a tree-lined square in the heart of Chelsea, just a few minutes walk from Sloane Square, close to Harrods and the shopping delights of Knightsbridge and the Kings Road.

If you feel in the mood to pamper yourselves and live a little in the past then go to **The Waldorf Hotel** in Aldwych. Taking tea and dancing the afternoon away in the magical terraced **Palm Court** is a truly unique experience, popular with Londoners and visitors alike. Held every Saturday and Sunday, the tea dance has also become a favourite pre-theatre venue - The Waldorf's location on the Aldwych, in the heart of theatreland, makes most theatres within easy walking distance. Afternoon tea at **The Ritz** in **Piccadilly** is another thrilling experience, quite different but equally memorable. Wonderful service, exquisitely thin sandwiches, delicious cakes and pastries and the lush greenery of St James Park outside the tall elegant windows. Both The Waldorf and The Ritz will long be remembered.

The ancient walled **Chelsea Physic Garden**, just along from the Chelsea Royal Hospital with its red-coated pensioners, was only the second botanical garden to be opened in Britain. It is a serene and beautiful place. It was the seed of a cotton plant taken from here that resulted in America's successful cotton industry.

The most famous London garden is undoubtedly **Kew Gardens**, and indeed it is accepted as being the finest botanic garden and plant research centre in the world, aimed at creating a better future for our planet. It consists of 300 acres of magnificent tranquil gardens alongside the River Thames in West London, with 6 acres under glass from the exquisite Victorian Palm House to the stunning new Princess of Wales Conservatory. There are buildings too, including Kew Palace and **Queen Charlotte's Cottage**. One of the most unusual features is the Pagoda, completed in 1762 as a surprise for Princess Augusta, the Dowager Princess of Wales, who had founded the gardens only a few years earlier. The ten storey octagonal structure reaches a height of 50 metres, and was at the time the most accurate imitation of a Chinese building in Europe, (although to be accurate it should have had an odd number of storeys). Vistas through the garden enable the Pagoda to be seen in superb settings. The 18th century Kew Gardens was just a tiny portion of that seen today, having the Richmond estate added to it early in the 19th century, with some of the areas coming more recently into cultivation.

In addition to the nine exceptional glass houses, the dozen other buildings, the many special garden features and the wonderful parkland of the three arboreta, work goes on behind the scenes to preserve endangered plant species and to conserve habitats. The 44,000 different types of plants at Kew represent one in six of known species (it is believed that there are many plant species still undiscovered and work too continues in this direction), with 13 species extinct in the wild and 1,000 threatened. The botanists at Kew now have some 6 million preserved specimens which through their research could be found to contain important medicines, fuels or food.

Another very important although less well known garden is in **Enfield.** The National Gardening Centre at **Capel Manor** is actually not just a garden but a College for the study of landscape and garden maintenance and management, a Countryside Centre predominantly used by schools, and it incorporates 'Which? Magazine's' demonstration garden. The gardens extend over 25 acres and illustrate many different designs, styles and periods, from formal images to habitats for attracting wildlife.

In the centre of London, next to Lambeth Palace, is the **Museum of Garden History**, run by the Tradescant Trust. The Trust was founded less than 20 years ago to save the historic church of St Mary at Lambeth from demolition. There they establised the Museum of Garden History as a centre for plant displays, lectures and exhibitions. The Tradescants, father and son, were royal gardeners in the 17th century and brought back from their frequent travels many of the plants which we know, making them still today possibly the best known name in plant collecting. The plants were propagated in their famous 60 acres garden in Lambeth. Development of the garden is ongoing, with some exciting plans for the future.

Kent has long been known as the 'Garden of England' and the rich soils continue to provide abundant crops. The view of Kent as a county of hop fields dotted with oast houses is certainly inaccurate in certain parts, although a great many of the oast houses have now been converted into dwellings. The largest collection of oast houses in the world, dating from the Victorian era, are to be found at the **Whitbread Hop Farm** which is near **Paddock Wood**. You won't actually see beer being produced but you can see **The Hop Story Exhibition** as well as the **Whitbread Shire Horse Centre** and many other attractions.

As well as hop gardens, orchards feature frequently in this fertile landscape in the area known as 'The Weald' which actually covers about half of the county's total area in the south west. Further to the north is the North Downs, a high chalk ridge which ends at the White Cliffs of Dover, possibly the best known British landscape, seen from the ship and from air by many thousands of visitors each year. The highest point is known as Shakespeare's Cliff, having featured in King Lear.

Very different landscapes can be found in some coastal districts, such as the pretty meadows of the **Isle of Sheppey** in the north and next to it the **Isle of Grain** with the country's largest heronry, and **Romney Marsh** in the south, where the flat open marshes appear sumptuous in the bright summer light but truly desolate by winter. The Marsh was created by the Romans who constructed the Rhee Wall to claim the land from the sea. Although the sea is retreating, the small town of Old Romney once on the coast now stands well inland and even **New Romney** further out is now dilocated. In the centre of the marsh stands St Thomas Becket Church, with no village or even hamlet nearby. Several other communities have gradually become more distant from the sea such as **Sandwich** once a Cinque Port and now almost two miles from the coast. Although not necessarily as close to the water as they once were, an amazingly large number of castles and other fortified buildings can be seen around the coastal area, built because Kent, being the closestpart of Britain to foreign soil, has been subject to many invasions, and attempted invasions, over thousands of years.

Kent can also show signs of very much earlier occupation with flints found from the Old Stone Age and dwellings from around 6,000BC. **Kit's Coty House** and **Little Kit's Coty House**, taken from the Celtic for 'tomb in the woods' are two Neolithic burial chambers near **Aylesford**. It was in what is now Kent that the Romans first arrived, and later the Angles, the Saxons and the Jutes all came to these shores. **Dover** is now the busiest of the ferry ports with frequent trips to Calais, which can actually be seen on clear days. Increases to the 'friendly' invasion via the long planned Channel Tunnel are now a reality. Dover has always been of historical importance. Apart from being an ancient port linking Britain with the Continent, it was once the walled Roman town of Dubris, and the start of the Roman Road, Watling Street.

One particular rare Roman structure is the lighthouse, or 'pharos' which stands within Dover Castle, overlooking the White Cliffs. The castle reflects much of the county's history in one, being a mixture of many dates with its history in the Iron Age and the current buildings being part Roman, part Saxon and extensively Norman, with some later additions. Actually additions is possibly the wrong word to use for the most recent alterations to Dover Castle: tunnels were excavated within the White Cliffs to counter the threat of invasion by Napoleon, and during the Second World War these became a secret operational centre. It was from here that the evacuation from Dunkirk was masterminded. The expected Napoleonic invasion was also responsible for the construction of artillery towers such as the **Dymchurch Martello Tower** which formed a chain of strongholds around the coast.

The whole of the Kent coastline, many of the castles and several other historic sites are included on the **Saxon Shore Way**, a 143 mile walk, which links in the middle at **Dover** with the **North Downs Way**, following the crest of the North Downs and in places incorporating the **Pilgrims' Way** linking **Canterbury** with Winchester in Hampshire. The Pilgrim's Way is actually far older than the name would imply, and was probably first used by the Neolithic peoples.

If one wanted to choose somewhere that spelt out beauty, history, heritage and national pride then **Canterbury** would probably top the poll. Canterbury was welcoming pilgrims 900 years ago and even then it was an ancient city. Three hundred years later Chaucer brought attention to it with his Canterbury Tales. The Cathedral dominates the city and is the spiritual centre for Christians who belong to the Church of England in many countries but the non-believers in the tenets of the Anglican Church are as much addicted to its beauty as anyone else. Thomas a Becket who was murdered within its walls by four knights who heeded Henry II's plea to rid him of ' this low born priest' has been revered as a martyr ever since that gruesome day. The martyrdom of Thomas a Becket is a well known fact and within days of his murder it turned Canterbury into a place of pilgrimage. He was canonised in 1173 and a year later a remorseful King Henry himself made the pilgrimage in an act of penance. The pilgrims were to help make Canterbury one of the richest and most magnificent churches of medieval times.

You may think Canterbury Cathedral holds the record for the number of steps one climbs up and down during your tour of the building. There are steps up the chancel, steps down to the transept and a flight of steps ascending to the pulpitum. It is a journey of never ending thrills, stunning architecture, glorious glass and always this awareness that the Almighty is gazing upon us.

Canterbury springs to everyone's mind when you talk about Kent but the county has much more to offer. Fifteen minutes to the north you come to **Whitstable** long renowned for its oysters. Here there is good fishing, bathing from a shingle beach and good yachting facilities. A spit of land known as 'The Street' juts out about a mile and a half into the sea and provides a pleasant promenade at lowtide. The Castle dates mainly from the 19th century but has a 15th century brick tower originally used as a look out post. Its parkland is open to the public.

To the east the seaside resorts of **Westgate on Sea** and **Margate** have been popular for generations. The former is less boisterous than the latter but both have their adherents who would not go anywhere else. I cannot say that it is a holiday that would appeal to me but the countryside and the sea are both beautiful and you see a lot of happy, smiling faces, so who am I to judge!

Broadstairs just round the North Foreland is a different kettle of fish. Here is a Regency resort which has not changed much since the society of those times put their stamp on it. It has miles of sheltered and sandy bays and to the north stand the chalk cliffs and lighthouses of the North foreland, with wide views over the Thames Estuary. Bleak House is now a Dickens Museum containing early editions of his books, pictures, photographs and some personal items. Nearby Dickens House which also contains a museum was immortalised as the home of Betsy Trotwood in 'David Copperfield' written while Dickens was living in Broadstairs. In June every year a Dickens Festival is held, when the local people throng the streets in costumes of the period.

Down past the busy ferryport of **Ramsgate**, **Sandwich** and **Deal**, one comes to the beautiful St Margaret's Bay, part of the South Foreland Heritage Coast. Here at **West Cliff** is the stunning **Wallets Court Hotel** with the tiny church of St Peters opposite. It is a fascinating hotel in its own right but add that to the history of the bulding which first gets its mention in the Domesday Book and you cannot help being enthralled.

The garden at Wallet's is open to the rolling fields and the bracing sea air with its regularly swirling mists. It now contains a rather unusual treehouse, an all weather tennis court, and a recently restored granary on Kentish straddle stones. During your wanderings you might visit the tiny church of St Peter where the Gibbon family who restored the house in the early 17th century, are all buried, or take a stroll up Pond Lane to a local vantage point. St Margaret's Bay has provided great inspiration for many writers, poets and artists over the years. The quintessential Englishman Noel Coward and also the man who created James Bond, Ian Fleming who both lived in the Bay at one time. One can lie there in the long grass for hours listening to the skylarks and watching the traffic on the Channel. On a clear day you can even see the French coastline which lies just over twenty miles away.

The next part of my travels takes me to the 'Garden Coast' encompassing **Folkestone, Hythe and Romney Marsh** which offers me endless pleasure both in the beautiful countryside, the sea and the history of the area together with the monaticism of the Romney Marshes. You will see from the list of attractions in the back of this book that there is so much to see and so varied that it must please everyone whatever age.

The M20 will take me to the busy town of **Ashford** and to the small medieval village of **Woodchurch** dating from the 11th century. There is a delightful house here in which you can stay. **Prospect House** overlooks the large village green where cricket and football are played in season.It is a wonderful house built in 1789 but could possibly be older judging from its very oldbeams in places. An old redbrick wall surrounds the house on two sides and the other sides are hedges. On warm summer days guests frequently have breakfast outside or sit in the shade of a large apple tree for tea. The owners Fiona Adams-Cairns and her South African husband are widely travelled, welcoming and excellent hosts. Look at the visitors book and you will find comments such as 'Every night is a dinner party'. An hours drive will take you to Glyndebourne, Canterbury, of course, Dover Castle, the moated Leeds Castle, Churchill's home, Chartwell and some wonderful gardens including Sissinghurst.

Royal Tunbridge Wells is beyond Sissinghurst to the west from Ashford. This is a town that delights the eye. A distinguished spa at one time especially among persons of fashion in the 18th century, though the waters can still be drunk. Samuel Pepys and John Evelyn both visited and Beau Nash left Bath to become the master of Tunbridge Wells ceremonies in 1735. However it was Lord North who had made the waters popular a hundred years earlier. Charles I's wife, Henrietta Maria came here after the birth of their son, the future Charles II in 1630. This was when the building of the town began. The Pantiles, the spa's oldest street was started in 1700. How beautiful this elegant arcade is enhanced by lime trees; its Italianate pillars supporting diverse frontages and a music balcony. The tiles were laid because Princess Anne - later to become Queen - threatened not to return after her son slipped on the original walk. Today flagstones have replaced almost all the tiles.

The town is blessed with many parks and gardens and a fine common with outcrops of weathered sandstone rocks. Such rocks are typical of the area, the source of its mineral waters, and an attraction for climbers: the nearby High Rocks, the Toad Rocks on Rushall Common; Bowles Rocks, Eridge, Harrison's Rocks, Groombridge and the Happy Valley. There are many places to visit including a leisurely cruise around **Bewl Water,** Southern Water's beautiful reservoir at Lamberhurst. This is the largest area of inland water in south east England and set in most attractive countryside. Also at Lamberhurst is **Scotney Castle Garden**, one of England's most romantic gardens, surrounding the ruins of a 14th century moated castle. Rhododendrons, azaleas, waterlilies and wisteria flower in profusion.

Groombridge Place Gardens and **Enchanted Forest** provide another stunning day out. Surrounded by breathtaking parkland this mystical medieval site includes the famous Grade I Listed 17th-century walled gardens set against the backdrop of the classical moated mansion and Enchanted Forest, which have inspired writers, artists and connoisseurs of beauty for hundreds of years.

To the north of Tunbridge Wells is **Tonbridge**, a prosperous market town at the navigable extremity of the River Medway, where it diverges into formidable streams. A settlement that has been strategically important since

Anglo Saxon and probably Roman times. The River Walk along the Medway, through willow-lined meadows gives a fine view of **Tonbridge Castle**. Its Norman to 13th century ruins, on a site defended since 1088, are substantial: the shell of the keep, curtain walls, round-towered gatehouse. Some of Tonbridge's 18th century houses are built of castle stone. It is an exciting place to visit and you are invited to travel back over 700 years to join the Lords of Tonbridge Castle and experience a vivid recreation of the sights, sounds and excitement of 13th century life.

Penshurst Place and Gardens, near Tonbridge must be visited. The beautiful medieval stately home of Viscount de L'Isle, with its magnificent Baron's Hall dates from 1341. The splendid gardens were first laid out in the 16th century. Two of the loveliest castles in Kent and some would say in the world, are **Leeds Castle** 4 miles east of Maidstone and **Hever Castle** near Edenbridge, the childhood home of Anne Boleyn. Both will provide you with hours of delight and will remain in your memory for years to come.

The Medway towns must not be forgotten. They have always been places of great interest. Made up of Strood, Gillingham, Chatham and Rochester, they are steeped in history and none more so than the ancient cathedral city of **Rochester** on the lower reaches of the Medway. It is a major port and an industrial centre and such a busy place but Rochester's older buildings are clustered around the Cathedral and in the High Street where they were confined by medieval walls. The city is closely associated with the novelist Charles Dickens, and features more often in his books than any other place, apart from London, although Portsmouth, where he was born, has The Charles Dickens Birthplace Museum. Many great cities have been built around a river and Rochester is no exception.

Chatham has had a long and distinguished history and until recent years been inextricably involved in the life of Her Majesty's Royal Navy. Those days are gone but a visit to **The Historic Dockyard** will give you at least five hours of absorbing interest. There are no less than 47 Scheduled Ancient Monuments, forming the most completely preserved Georgian dockyard in the world, dry docks, and covered slips, timber mast houses and seasoning sheds, huge storehouses and the quarter mile long working ropery stand beside the elegant Commissioner's house and garden, officers' terrace and dockyard church. Now a living, working museum, this tells of the lives of the dockyard craftsmen whose skills - from carpentry and caulking to rigging and forging - made the British fleet the finest in the world. No one can fail to be fascinated by what they see. With seven main attractions plus skills and crafts in action, it is not surprising visitors stay an average of 5 hours.

Kent has so much beauty to offer in every direction. Its name 'The Garden of England' is fully justified. I constantly promise myself that the next time I come here I will spend more time - however long I stay it is never long enough.

I lived in Suffolk for a while on the Shotley Peninsula looking over the River Stour to**Harwich**. This allowed me to become happily familiar with the corner of Essex that includes the old Roman town of **Colchester**, and the glorious **Dedham Vale** as well as many of the smaller villages including **Wix** between Harwich and Colchester, bypassed by the A120 which is a direct route to London. It is a place surrounded by local beauty spots like **Mistley** where one of Great Britain's largest population of mute swans live and the twin 'Mistley Towers' stand the only remains of Robert Adams ecclesiastical work in England.

New Farm House is very much part of Wix and the owners, Pat and George Mitchell offer comfort, friendliness with good farmhouse cooking. They have a good reputation both in this country and abroad which is confirmed by the number of overseas visitors who return annually. The house is only 10 minutes drive from Parkeston Quay at Harwich from which Car and Passenger ferries depart for the continental ports of the Hook of Holland, Denmark, Germany and Sweden which makes it an ideal and convenient place to stay overnight before embarking for, or returning from, the Continent.

Colchester is Britain's oldest recorded town and has 2,000 years of fascinating history and heritage to discover. It is a history involving the Romans, the Saxons and the Normans which has been interpreted and displayed using the most exciting and up-to-date methods in the town'smuseums. Colchester Oysters were famous inRoman days and are still so today, but as a fishing and trading port, the town is no longer significant. It is significant however for the 1000 acres of public gardens and parks. You should not fail to walk in the glorious park surrounding the Castle which was built by William the Conqueror in 1076 and a visit to its museum is highly recommended.

The Vale of Dedham is somewhere very special and immortalised by John Constable. This north-east corner of Essex is where the River Stour forms the boundary with Suffolk and is an area of outstanding scenic beauty. It is still possible to stroll through the meadows and along the river banks with their abundance of flora and fauna, or explore the delightful villages with their impressive medieval churches and old pubs. It is constantly changing scenery. From **Bures** to **Harwich** the river loses its quiet willow-lined banks enclosing the gently flowing water, home to colourful ducks, elegant swans and moorhens and becomes tidal flats beyond Manningtree and the dominant east coast. Many places in Essex have been entrapped by the ever stretching tentacles of London but there are still delightful places, **Halstead** is one with a delightful establishment in which to stay at **Timbers**. It is a small town built about a hill overlooking the River Colne. The wide High Street has some charming gabled shops and houses.

Sussex now known as two counties **West Sussex** and **East Sussex** is a part of England that is totally delightful. **West Sussex** takes in an area bounded to the west by the Hampshire border, to the north with that of Surrey with an imaginary eastern division runnng south from the new urban mass of Crawley down to meet the coast at **Angmering-on-Sea**. As an introduction to the whole it serves well: there are great estates and houses, high hills where sheep graze and skylarks sing, ancient villages and hamlets nestling in natural folds and large stands of mature woodland, the remnants of mighty tracts of forest which once covered much of the county. Balanced against this rustic idyll are modern developments, new roads and a population that has expanded rapidly over the last few decades. Better communications and an increase in personal wealth has meant an influx of commuters, together with a large amount of light industry attracted to the area since the Second World War; all this is to the good, even if the aesthetics occasionally offend. Employment and prosperity has done much to preserve the rural charm that so attracted the likes of Belloc, even though that charm can often seem synthetic. But consider; the thatched farm-labourer's cottage with roses climbing over the porch would be no more than a weed-ridden mound of rubble if left to purely local concern. Estates, councils, and conservation bodies have but limited budgets and must spend accordingly; a tumbledown cottage of uncertain ancestry has no priority in their scheme of things, and few private landowners have sufficiency of cash to modernise such places to the standards that today's agricultural worker rightly expects. It is the outsider, the commuter, weekender or retiree who has the money and the determination to conserve. There are many students of the countryside and its vernacular architecture who grumble a great deal about the 'chocolate-box' or 'stockbroker-belt' image of many of these small rural communities, but to my mind it is better that it should be thus than down-at-heel and crumbling or worse, abandoned. One may raise an eyebrow at a satellite dish or an ill-advised conservatory - but doubtless our more affected ancestors reacted in like manner when confronted with innovations such as glazed windows or inside sanitation.

The newcomer rarely receives thanks and seldom praise for his efforts. However, those who have chosen Sussex in which to settle and 'improve' have made a wise choice for the natives have long been known for their pragmatic and friendly attitude to the outsider, whether Roman, Saxon,

Norman or modern city worker. It is a county with an almost magical ability to absorb, adapt and change almost seemlessly. Throughout its long history, it has been directly affected by great politcal and economic upheavals, yet, when the dust has settled and the shouting died away, the essential Sussex still remains; quietly welcoming the visitor to its tranquil beauty.

My own tour began in the cathedral city of **Chichester**, just a few miles to the east of the border with Hampshire. Other than the cathedral spire, little of the city's fine heritage can be glimpsed from the outskirts by the passing traveller, who sees a flat countryside bounded to the north by the distant South Downs. This fertile land used for growing a wide variety of crops, is also home to numerous light industrial estates that seem to fringe the northern edge of the by-pass. Chichester is no grand cathedral city. Its scale is domestic and it has the air of a prosperous market town, friendly, unpretentious with nothing to intimidate. Even the lovely cathedral seems to stand at the pavement's edge without benefit of grand close or walled surround. No great avenues or parades, merely a sensible crossroads of four main streets running out in the direction of the cathedral points and the areas in between being filled with a happy warren of lanes, narrow alley-ways and delightful little squares. Modern development has inevitably led to the introduction of pedestrian precincts, shopping arcades and car parks but happily the process has not been over-intrusive and the human scale remains. The cruciform layout owes much to the Romans who found the area of fertile plain to their liking when they arrived in AD43.

The lovely interior of this Norman cathedral contains some startlingly modern decorative art.The most obvious is John Piper's huge representative tapestry hanging behind the high altar, there is also a window by Chagall, a painting by Graham Sutherland and numerous other contemporary works including a pulpit of concrete and steel. George Bell was bishop from 1929 to 1958 and it was he who introduced the concept of modern art into the cathedral. A bold move, but one that added new dimensions of colour and life that had been effectively missing since the Parliamentarians destroyed so much of the decorative work during the Civil War.

The Pallants is a charming area of principally Georgian redbrick and once under the exclusive jurisdiction of the Archbishop of Canterbury. **Pallant House** built in 1713, is the finest of these buildings and has a link with the cathedral as it contains a fine collection of modern art, the bequest of the late Dean, Doctor Walter Hussey. There is also a wonderful collection of porcelain and a beautifully reconstructed small garden in keeping with the period of the house. It is both museum and gallery and succeeds in either sphere.

An old granary houses the excellent **Chichester Museum** while nearby stands **St Marys Hospital**, built as an infirmary and converted in the 1600's into eight small dwellings for old people. It has been little altered since and it is often held up as an example of excellent planning for the needs of the elderly. Further north of this area is **Priory Park**, a large open space named after the Franciscan Priors who established themselves here in the early 13th-century. The choir of their church survives as a museum and within the bounds of the Park is a grassy mound that once was the site of Chichester Castle, dismantled around the time of Henry III.

Chichester is representative of much of the county in that its prosperity comes from the ability to adapt without losing its essential character. As the visitor can see, ancient and modern co-exist happily and one of the principal examples of this is to be found in Oaklands Park to the north of the old city walls. **The Chichester Festival Theatre** was constructed in the 1960's and now has an international reputation, attracting audiences from all over the world to see productions of the highest quality. The city also has a major Arts Festival, inaugurated all but a quarter of a century ago which takes place every July.

To the west is **Fishbourne** where **The Fishbourne Roman Palace and Museum** is one of the most important Roman relics in Britain and contains much of the remains of a magnificent first century villa. For todays visitor, apart from this gem, there is an interesting if slightly eccentric pub, **The Woolpack Inn** where you will be fed at sensible prices.

Just west of Fishbourne lies one of the jewels of the Sussex shore, the small Saxon village of **Bosham** (pronounced 'Bozzum'). Lying at the top of an arm of Chiechester Harbour, this is a delightful little community jumbled around the waters of Bosham Creek. Canute had a palace here and it was on the foreshore that he was reputed to have commanded the tide to retreat. Anyone able to work such a miracle would undoubtedly be in much demand at the **Anchor Bleu**, a cosy pub by the creek, where the unwary motorist is frequently caught out by the rapidly rising tide which can cover the shore road. The Anchor is the sole survivor of several small pubs which once traded in the tiny and attractive High Street.

Northwards to the very border with Hampshire I was off to visit **Stansted Park** near Rowlands Castle. Ancient woodland, once part of the Forest of Bere, sets off this most decorative Wren-style house, which is full of treasures. There is an extraordinary and highly decorative chapel which owes its appearance to a previous owner of the house who spent most of his time trying to convert Jews to Christianity.

From here head across the country to the B2147, a splendid Downland drive where thick woodland alternates with pasture and plough, and the road steadily climbs to the crest of the chalk hills. The Mardens, West, North, Up and East are all worth a diversion to visit the small churches and to admire the way in which the little communities seem to typify the essential SouthDown village. If you feel like stretching your legs, the **Stoughton Down Forest Walk** can be found to the south of East Marden.

Uppark is a National Trust property which was partially destroyed by fire in 1989 and is now restored to its former glory. It has the most handsome facade, the gardens are by Humphrey Repton and the views are breathtaking. Uppark has had a number of owners since it was built at the end of the 17th century and the most colourful of these must have been the splendidly rakish Sir Henry Featherstonhaugh. He was in his early twenties when he inherited the house and in no time at all it housed his mistress, the beautiful Emma Hart. Before long she had left the rackety Sir Harry to marry the diplomat Sir William Hamilton and later achieved further notoriety by becoming Lord Nelson's mistress. Her former lover never forgot her though, and when she fell on hard times after Nelson's death in 1805, Sir Henry helped her out. His own life of debauchery and scandal continued until 1810 when he quarrelled with the Prince Regent and retired from London life to lead the life of a country squire. However, he was far from finished with the world of scandal and gossip, for at the age of seventy, he shocked the fashionabe world by marrying his head dairymaid. He remained happily married until his death at the ripe old age of ninety-two.

The steep hill that runs down into **South Harting** is said to have deterred the Duke of Wellington when the house was offered to him after the Napoleonic Wars; the necessity for constant replenishment of horses was his excuse. The church here is unusual in that the short spire is clad in copper that has oxidised to a brilliant green; inside there are fine timbers in the roof and a sporting reminder of old Sir Harry from Uppark in the form of a grieving woman and a somewhat woebegone spaniel. In his time he would undoubtedy have patronised **The Ship Inn**, a suitably atmospheric establishment in the main street. You may think it odd that an inland pub should have a marine name. It was really because the pub was constructed of ship's timbers, a sort of 'quidpro quo' for the local timber being commandeered to build new ships for His Majesty's Navy. The Ship has been mentioned by the poet Hilaire Belloc and also appears in one of Nevil Shute's novels when the hero took tea in what was then the upstairs tearooms.

The country to the north of Chichester is both varied and well endowed with numerous attractions, both natural and man-made. From West Stoke a delightful walk takes one up to the escarpment of **Kingley Vale**, now under the administraion of the Nature Conservancy Council. The Vale is most notable for its ancient yew-woods, dark, dense and silent.

A cheerful and lively contrast to the mythical, perhaps Druidical, stillness of Kingley Vale can be found in the nearby village of **Lavant**, where the 17th-century pub, **The Earl of March**, dispenses good food and hospitality. The pub's name is the honorary title given to the eldest sons of the Dukes of Richmond, owners of the famous estate of Goodwood. **Goodwood House**, set in lovely parkland, lies a couple of miles to the east.A handsome, porticoed central section is flanked by two wings of flint construction with green-domed towers. As originally designed, this is only part of what would have been a truly palatial building and some idea of the projected scale can be gained by inspecting the enormous stable-block, which was completed before money for the main house ran out. The house contains numerous treasures including Old Master portraits, tapestries, porcelain and furniture, but to me, the real attraction of Goodwood is the magnificent setting and the fact that the 12,000 acre estate is a diverse working entity. Agriculture, forestry and recreation go hand in hand; the small airfield is surrounded by a once famous motor racing track (now used for club events and testing), and there is a golf course and a country park. The first Duke purchased the original Tudor house as a hunting lodge and, above all, it was the passion for all things equine that the Duke and his successors made the estate world famous. Today, international dressage competitions, horse trials and the principal attraction of 'Glorious Goodwood', Goodwood races, bring enthusiasts and competitors from all over the globe.

The Selsey Peninsula the home of everything horticultural and agricultural for centuries has produced grain, vegetables, fruit and flowers for generations, and its rich soil is keenly exploited. Nevertheless it is an attractive area with small villages and reed-fringed rivulets, popular with holiday makers and yachtsmen. On the western side it is bounded by Chichester Harbour and the yachting centres of Dell Quay (once the original port of Chichester), Birdham, and Itchenor, neat and trim beside the water. On the westernmost tip, close to the popular sands of East Head, is the small resort of **West Wittering**. Sounding rather like the title of an old BBC radio comedy, the village is attractive with a most welcoming pub, **The Lamb Inn** and a church that is definitely 'organic'in that it is a happy mixture of period and styles. A walk along the seaward shore reveals some massive chunks of wave-smoothed rock, geological analysis shows they are probably originated in the Channel Islands, detritus from an Ice Age glacier.

At the beginning of the chapter, I made mention of the fact that the great majority of country cottages owe their survival to the wealthy newcomer, at **Singleton** there is an exception to this at the **Weald and Downland Open**

Air Museum. This is a collection of vernacular buildings from all over the county that have been painstakingly re-erected and restored to as near their original condition as possible. Cottages, mills and farm buildings are grouped attractively, and the site is brought alive by the presence of the rural crafts of the period - wheelwrights, potters, sawyers and charcoal burners. To inspect some of these 'idyllic' rural dwellings is to receive a salutary lesson; no sanitation or glazing and the 'central heating' being literally central- merely a fire in the middle of the earth floor!

Some five miles to the north, 20th century comfort is to be found in 16th century surroundings.**The Crown** at **Midhurst** is everything a small country town inn should be - warmly hospitable and full of character. The town is equally charming with a cheerful and prosperous air, good brick and half-timbered buildings from across the centuries line the streets around the centre. Its origins as a market town since the early 13th century are reflected in names such as Sheep Lane, Wood Lane, Duck Lane and Knockhundred Row. A curfew bell is still rung at eight o'clock every evening; a tradition that was begun when a lone traveller was lost in the mist one night and the tolling of the Midhurst bell led him to safety. In gratitude the man bequeathed a piece of land to enable the bell to be rung in perpetuity.

Cowdray is the name given to the large estate that virtually surrounds Midhurst and the great fire-blackened ruins of **Cowdray House** can be seen to the east of the town. It was begun in 1530, at the instigation of Shakespeare's patron, the Earl of Southampton and then passed to Viscount Montague, who had received Battle Abbey from Henry VIII. Legend has it that the last monk to leave the Abbey cursed Montague prophesying that his family would perish by fire and water, It was an effective although somewhat slow-acting curse, the house was burnt down in 1793 and shortly afterwards, the then Viscount was drowned in Switzerland and his two sons at Bognor. The remains of the house have a tragic splendour and a look round gives an indication as to why it was once compared to Hampton Court as an example of courtly Tudor splendour. The estate however, has flourished in the hands of the present owners, the Pearson family, and the great Park with its immense oaks, is internationally known as a venue for polo, From Midhurst, a pleasant drive takes one north towards the gentler hills of the Surrey border, although to the east of the main road lies **Blackdown**, the highest point in Sussex at 919ft. It was a favourite beauty spot of Tennyson's who described the view as 'green Sussex fading into the blue, with one grey glimpse of the sea'. The character of the countryside changes; it becomes more intimate with wood and copse interspersed by streams and small fields. The soil is healthy and acid with huge banks of rhododendrons hanging over some of the small lanes.

The third of Sussex's great estates is centred on **Petworth**, a lovely, if cramped, little town, which has the reputation of being the centre of the antiques trade. It has a number of interesting 16th and 17th century buildings set around winding narrow streets and a small market place with a simple arcaded Town Hall from the 18th century. The town's condensed effect comes from being huddled against the east wall of **Petworth House** which with its 700 acre deer park, dominates both town and surrounding countryside. The house is now looked after by the National Trust.

To the east, the A283 runs close to the pretty village of **Fittleworth**, once the home of Sir Edward Elgar, and where the coach-horses were once changed in the 14th century **Swan Inn**. A little further along the main road passing over the medieval bridge at **Stopham**, is the 'longest village in Sussex' **Pulborough'** settled since Neolithic times and lying beside a flood plain of the river Arun, was once an important Roman encampment guarding Stane Street, which runs from Chichester to London.

In the hamlet of **Hardham**, a mile or so to the south, the little Norman church contains a wonderful set of wall paintings, rendered around 1100, they rank amongst the most important treasures of their kind in England. The South Down Way is some 80 miles of bridle and footpath that runs along the crest, affording riders and walkers views of some of the most lovely scenery in the country. South-west of Hardham, the Way runs close to **The Bignor Roman Villa**, site of an enormous farmstead andhouse, where the wonderful Roman mosaics, discovered in 1811, are displayed in a covered area.

The wealth and importance of Sussex in earlier times are also seen in three other major attractions that lie not far away to the east.**Amberley**, a truly lovely village seated at the foot of downland overlooking grazing marshes, was considered of such strategic importance in the 14th-century that the then Bishop of Chichester built a massive castle, the remains of which surround the ancient manor house. The name Amberley is reputed to mean 'fields yellow with buttercups' and the setting is exquisite.

The nearby **Amberley Chalk Pits Museum** contains fascinating displays of bygone Sussex industries, crafts and skills. Further to the east is **Parham House,** one of the loveliest of Tudor mansions, set in a deer park with a church standing on the lawns, all that is left of a medieval village. Parham was built on the site of an earlier house that belonged to the Abbey of Westminster and was rebuilt around 1580 for Sir Thomas Palmer, a wealthy mercer, or textile merchant. Surrounded by beautiful gardens, the house contains some wonderful treasures, including needlework said to have been done by Mary, Queen of Scots, and her ladies in waiting, while imprisoned.

Arundel is the home of the premier Duke and Earl Marshal of England, the Duke of Norfolk, and it undoubtedly looks the part. Norman streets wind up from the fast flowing River Arun towards the immense turreted mass of **Arundel Castle.** With a great, grey cathedral thrusting alongside,

Trees and hills provide a backdrop to a sight that has the air of a Gothic fairytale. The castle's owners have nearly always been Catholics and the fourth Duke of Norfolk's son, Philip Howard, was canonized in 1970, he kept faith although persecuted and imprisoned during the reign of Elizabeth I. His remains are interred in the Cathedral of Our Lady and St Philip, which was designed in 1879 by A.J. Hansom, of Hansom Cab fame.. It is a large but not particularly distinguished building unlike the Parish Church of St Nicholas, a Perpendicular construction of the 14th century, which is unique in containing the Catholic Fitzalan Chapel, divided from the Protestant main body by a screen. The town itself has a great deal of charm, with some handsome buildings of timber, flint and brick crowding the narrow, steep streets.

The Arun flows into the sea at **Littlehampton**, a cheerful little portion of 'Sussex by the Sea', a popular family resort with all the usual attractions of an Engish sea-side town. Originally a small fishing settlement in Saxon times (mullet being the local delicacy, then as now) the arrival of the railway in 1863 helped develop the small port into resort status. However medieval Littlehampton was a far cry from the cheerful unpretentious town of today; stone from the vast quarries of Caen was landed here and some of Henry VIII's warships were constructed on the banks of the Arun.

Remains of a far more ancient industry are to be found in the downs to the east of **Findon**. A pick made from an antler, has been carbon-dated to 4000BC, and was one of the tools used by Neolithic flint miners of **Cissbury Ring**. Artefacts from these mines have been found all over Western Europe and it is no exaggeration to describe the area as 'the Sheffield of Flint' but Cissbury is better known for its enormous earthworks, built around 280BC during the Iron Age.

Findon today is renowned for its racehorse stables which have produced strings of winners including the famous Aldaniti and it is common to see champion jockey and Classic trainer Josh Gifford in the village. In the High Street **Findon Manor** standing in its own grounds is a charming hotel owned and run by Mike and Jan Parker-Hare whose welcoming presence adds to the pleasure of staying in this comfortable and friendly house. Excellent food, beautiful ensuite bedrooms and ample parking are just additional reasons why one should bide awhile.

Not far to the north lies an even better vantage point which must be the most famous landmark in Sussex. **Chanctonbury Ring** is a great clump of beeches planted around the remains of Neolithic earthworks. Although many of the beeches were blown down in the October 1987 storm, by a freak of nature it was principally the inner trees that suffered and not those on the perimeter. Although it is a stiffish walk, the views over the magnificent rolling hills are wonderful. The site has mystical significance; the Romans built a temple here and witches used to meet her on Midsummer's Eve.

Two very popular resorts lie along this coast. Just south of Chichester is **Bognor Regis**, beloved by King George V. Here the beaches are clean, the bathng safe and the people friendly. **Worthing** is a quiet, dignified resort which is all the more surprising when one knows that the lively 'London by the Sea' Brighton, is only a few miles along the coast. It has long been a place where people wanting a quiet, refreshing break, have found comfort and relaxation. Worthing has theatres, cinemas and first class shops as well as many good hotels, guest houses and restaurants. There is a wide variety of indoor and outdoor sporting activity. The town's location on the south coast provides an ideal base for exploring the beautiful Sussex Downs and the many pretty villages.

Until the River Adur silted up in the 14th-century,**Steyning** was a busy port. It was at the head of the Adur estuary and the task of guarding this strategic site fell to the lot of **Bramber.** Derived from the Saxon 'Brymmburh', meaning a fortified hill, there remains only a fragment of the grim Norman keep that kept watch atop the steep hill. The castle, which was torn down by the Parliamentarian forces after the Civil War, guarded not only the approaches to Steyning but also a great stone bridge that crossed the Adur. Th wardens of this bridge were monks and their home was the wonderful **St Mary's House,** one of the finest timber-framedbuildings in the county. Set in lovely gardens, the house contains finely panelled rooms, including the Painted Room, said to have been decorated for a visit by Elizabeth I. The Virgin Queen was not the only Royal visitor for Charles II hid here on his way to France.

Bramber had a colourful history; pitched battles were fought in the street between tariff-collectors and ships' crews during the 11th and 12th centuries, the Knights Templar owned Chapel House (now part of St Marys) until they were ruthlessly supressed for 'unlawful acts and gross immorality" in 1312, and the Benedictine Order which succeeded them was also accused of much the same charges in 1539. Finally in the era of the 'rotten boroughs' Bramber was described as the 'most rotten' - with eighteen voters returning two MPs! Things are distinctly quieter nowadays; the village has a unique little museum, **The House of Pipes**, devoted to what could best be described as 'Smokiana' and an excellent hotel and restaurant **The Old Tollgate**, which cleverly combines old and new in an attractive setting.

The vagaries of the sea which turned Steyning into a market town were to benefit **Shoreham**, a town that is a thriving port and with a history stretching back to Roman times. The modern part of Shoreham harbour is an enclosed dock, the largest between Southampton and Dover, handling a tonnage nearly as great as the latter. Shoreham itself, a friendly and busy town, is on the western edge of the harbour by the mouth of the Adur, an area popular with small boats and sailing dinghies. Shoreham Harbour is a recent innovation; the old port was on the eastern side of the estuary and was of major importance from Saxon times until around the beginning of the 15thcentury. The little port saw great military expeditions setting out for the French Wars whilst trade with that same country continued. From an historical point of view, this has been an almost continuous process; in 1347, soldiers left from here to capture Calais and throughout the centuries, the campaigns continued, culminating in the D-Day invasion in 1944. Hopefully, this process is now at an end although the trading aspect still continues and it is worth noting that one of the principal imports in the 14th century was wine - a commodity still brought into Shoreham today.

To the south lies the ruins of **Knepp Castle**, built by the Broase family from Bramber in the 11th century. A new, and private castle was built by John Nash in 1809. **West Grinstead** should not be confused with its larger, but far distant relation **East Grinstead**. They lie some 17 miles apart and whereas East Grinstead is a town, West Grinstead is little more than a hamlet. The great house of West Grinstead Park was demolished many years ago, but the battlemented stables, once headquarters of the National Stud can still be seen. The real attraction of the village is the Church of St George, tucked away at the end of a lane overlooking the river. Once again the homely exterior belies the treasures inside. There are several brasses, one to a knight who fought at Agincourt, and a number of classical-style monuments. The pews have the names of local farms carved on them and there is a large scale parish map showing where these lie; the names are redolent of the Wealden countryside, Priors Bine, Thistleworth, Hobshorts, Sunt and Figland.

Lower Beeding is separated, like the Grinsteads, from **Upper Beeding**, by several miles of countryside. Also, for some unaccountable reason, Lower Beeding is well to the north and higher than Upper! However, the real reason to visit has nothing to do with the somewhat eccentric nomenclature, but to see the wonderful gardens at **Leonardslee**. The Loder family have lived here since 1889 and have created magnificent woodland gardens within a deep valley. Streams and ponds lead the visitor past magnificent trees and shrubs, including world famous displays of rhododendrons, azaleas and camellias.

Although springtime is obviously the most spectacular, the gardens are a year-round attraction with deer, and, believe-it-or-believe-it-not, wallabies living semi-wild among the trees and grassy banks.

Leonardslee takes its name from the surrounding forest of St Leonard, where the Saint, a French hermit is reputed to have slain a dragon. The blood from St Leonard's wound dripped on the ground, where lilies-of-the-valley immediately spring up. Later, the hermit, who must have been more than a touch grouchy, banned nightingales from the forest, on the grounds that they disturbed his meditations. Whatever the truth, it is a fact that lilies grow there and the nightingale is never heard.......

Horsham is not unlike Chichester, in that it has a sensible arrangement of streets in the centre based on the cardinal points. The market town stands on the western edge of St Leonard's Forest, and although it has become a commuter town, modernisation has not spoilt the charm tobe found around the Carfax, the old centre (the word means a crossroads), and in particular the Causeway, a delightful tree-lined street of mainly 17th century houses. **Causeway House**, a lovely late Tudor building houses the fascinating **Horsham Museum.** In the Middle Ages, the town was renowned for the manufacture of horseshoes, crossbows and quarrels, and in the early 19th-century it had a bloody reputation as an Assize town. Those who escaped the gallows were sentenced to transportation and it is a sad reflection of the times that so many place names in Australia owe their origin to this harsh penalty.

Just south of the town is **Christ's Hospital School**, and the pupils can often be seen walking around in their distinctive uniform of dark blue coat, white neck-band and yellow stockings. The dress is based on the Tudor uniform worn by those who attend the original school established by Edward IV in 1553. The school moved from London to Horsham in 1902.

The iron works that once were found all over the Weald used water to drive the bellows and trip-hammers, and many of these mill, or hammer ponds still exist. There is one at **Warnham**, a well kept village just off the A24, which was once the home of the poet Shelley, and who was reputed to have sailed model boats on the pond. **The Warnham War Museum**, outside the village on the A24, contains an impressive collection of relics and memorabilia from the two World Wars.

Ignore the bland New Town of **Crawley** and neighbouring **Gatwick Airport**. Noisy and busy places. It is much pleasanter to take the network of minor roads that skirt around the north of Crawley towards the Surrey border. **Charlwood** is only ten minutes away from the busy airport yet retains a pleasant and calm rural air, The Norman church has a fine chancel screen, re-coloured and gilded in 1858, and a number of memorials to the Saunders family, including a good brass of 1553. In Rosemary Lane is the 18th century village prison, a small squat brick building. Of the same period but much nicer and more welcoming, is the attractive white-painted frontage which houses the excellent **Limes Bistro**.

South of Crawley, close to the small community of **Handcross**, are the lovely National Trust Gardens at **Nymans**. There are a whole series of quite different gardens set in 30 acres around the gaunt but romantic shell of a burnt-out house. The gardens are both formal and informal yet not in the least overpowering. Nymans has been described as a domestic garden on a grand scale rather than a grand garden on a domestic scale. Without a doubt, this is a truly Sussex garden.

Place names are often a delight, the Saxon word of 'Cucufelda' meaning a field full of cuckoos, is said to be the origination of **Cuckfield**, a friendly village on the western outskirts of **Haywards Heath**. The two communities have a common link in that their prosperity was based on transport; Cuckfield was a major coaching centre and in 1828 it was recorded that over 50 coaches were passing through every day, on the London to Brighton run. Naturally, this trade employed vast numbers of people such as grooms, wheelwrights, harness makers and smiths, to say nothing of the staff employed by the coaching inns, such as **The Kings Head**, a favourite of George IV then Prince of Wales, and deservedly popular to this day. Although a coach service ran until as late as the first World War, the advent of the railway in the middle of the 19th century effectively killed off this lucrative and colourful trade almost overnight. However by refusing to accommodate this new fangled innovation, Cuckfield lost the financial rewards but retained its rural charm, while nearby the hamlet of Haywards Heath rapidly expanded into the commuting and shopping centre of today.

The other community to refuse the benefits of steam was **Lindfield**, on the opposite side of Haywards Heath. Although the financial penalties must have been severe at the time, the village's loss has been Sussex's gain; this is truly picturesque, situated on a gentle slope with the village pond at the bottom and the church with its tall spire, at the top. The houses are nearly all a delight, ranging from Tudor through to Georgian. There is a wonderful story concerning Church House, which was once a pub called the Tiger Inn; apparently the ale it served to the bellringers in 1588, triumphantly signalling the defeat of the Spanish Armada, was so strong that it caused them to crack a bell and all the ropes.

Hickstead, is internationally famous in the equestrian world as the home of the **All England Show Jumping Ground**, although there is rumour that the owner Douglas Bunn does not want to carry on. It would be a pity because the arena, with its grandstand, and supporting facilities is set in an attractive area just to the west of the A23 and close to the pleasant little village of **Sayers Common**.

The rear escarpment of the South Downs, the last geographical obstacle before breaching the coast is breached by the **Devil's Dyke**, where the devil is said to have tried to dig a giant ditch through the downs in order to let the sea through. His intention was to flood the lower Weald and drown the churches, but he was foiled by a woman holding a candle. The Devil, who could only work in the dark, mistook the light for the rising sun and fled.

It's well worth a diversion to the east, to skirt the hills on their northern side and to visit **Newtimber Place**. Although the busy traffic rushes by within a few hundred yards, the moated house, built in 1681, is close to perfection with mellow brick and flint facade. The steep woodlands of Newtimber Hill, together with the dewponds, are owned and maintained by the National Trust.

The up-and-down route to the east takes one through the village of **Pycombe**, best known as a centre of the crook-maker's craft; an ornately carved shepherd's crook was once both badge of office and indispensable tool of Downland shepherds, The road to **Layton** takes one past some odd chimney-like structures which are just that; ventilators for the steam trains that once ran through the chalk hills.

The tunnel entrance near the village is an imposing Victorian Gothic affair with turrets and battlements, with a small house actually built over the entrance itself. One cannot help feeling inhabitants must be extremely fond of railways! Clayton's other claim to fame is the simple little village church with its marvellous wall paintings that are thought to have been created as early as 1080. They portray scenes such as The Last Judgment and the Fall of Satan, with the centrepiece of Christ in Judgment over the pre-Norman chancel arch.

High above the village stand two well-loved landmarks, a pair of windmills christened Jack and Jill. A mile or so to the east, one of the highest vantage points of the South Downs gives some wonderful views. **Ditchling Beacon** stands at 813 feet above sea-level, towering over the village of **Ditchling** that lies on the lee of the Downs. Artists such as Sir Frank Brangwyn and Eric Gill lived here and the village has some lovely buildings; the best-known being **Wing's Place**, said to have been given by Henry VIII to Anne of Cleves.

South of the Downs is truly 'Sussex by the Sea' and **Brighton**, its capital, the best known and loved town in the country- although there is really nothing of Sussex about the place since the influences that created it are distinctly metropolitan in tone. Invasion, Royal patronage, scandal, outrageous architecture, culture, sport and tragedy have combined in equal parts to create a town with a history both rackety and respectable. Like the favourite aunt of fiction, Brighton is settling into quiet and prosperous middle age although a fondness for eccentric dress and garish make-up hint at a lowly beginning and a picaresque past.

Brighton owes its fame - or notoriety - to its discovery by the Prince Regent, son of George III. An afficionado of the newly invented 'dirty-weekend' (A Brighton speciality in the years to come), and obviously in need of Dr Russell's glandular treatment, he instigated the construction of the **Royal Pavilion**. In this extraordinary Indo-Chinese confection he secretly married his favourite mistress Maria Fitzherbert, a Catholic. Naturally, this was in direct contravention of the Act of Succession and the Royal Marriages Act and was thus doomed to end in politic divorce, nevertheless, His Royal Highness, later George IV, set the tone for the centuries ahead.

If the Royal Pavilion was, not to put too fine a point on it, outrageous, then much of the other contemporary development was in restrained, albeit fashionable form. Great crescents and squares, in classical Regency style, were built to house the cognoscenti and their households, and the town expanded into the neighbouring borough of Hove. The popularity of Brighton grew steadily and with the advent of the railway in the 1840's the town was brought within the reach of almost everybody. Hotels and boarding houses sprang up to cater for this new trade, and the three miles of sea-front were provided with elegant, wide promenades, splendid piers, amusements and fairgrounds. That great British instituition, the Seaside Holiday, was now firmly established, along with that redoubtable figure, the Seaside Landlady.

The visitor is spoilt for choice, where to go and what to see ? -perhaps the best plan is to establish a base-camp, and Brighton is renowned for the quality and range of its accommodation to make it eay for you.

Seaford was the principal port of this area until a series of events caused the mouth of the River Ouse to be diverted to **Newhaven**. Now it is a quiet and prosperous seaside town. From Seaford Head where there was once a Roman cemetery, there is a fine view of the **Seven Sisters**, the dramatic vertical chalk cliffs that mark the end of the South Downs. At their far end stands the towering bulk of **Beachy Head**; on a clear day the seaward view extends over 60 miles from the 536foot cliff.

Between Seaford Head and the first of the Sisters, Haven Brow, lies **Cuckmere Haven** where the meandering River Cuckmere runs into the Channel. This was a favourite haunt of those Sussex gentlemen averse to paying import duty; in particular, of the Alfriston Gang, a notorious bunch of cut-throat smugglers who terrorised the area for years. Almost hidden by the tall cliffs and with the river winding its way inland through marsh and tall reed, the Haven and surrounding area attract a wide range of flora and fauna, and 700 acres of marsh and Downland to the east of the river have been turned into the **Seven Sisters Country Park**. This includes a unique mini zoo, **The Living World**, which displays marine creatures, reptiles and insects.

Close to the river, to the north of the secluded and idyllic village of **Westdean**, is the lovely **Charleston Manor**. The house dates in parts, back to Norman times and is reputed to have been built for William the Conqueror's cup-bearer. Later additions are Tudor and Georgian with medieval dovecote. This splendid mixture is handsomely set off by a remarkable garden, created by the artist Sir Oswald Birley (1880-1952). The rich alluvial soil has been planted in terraces divided by low yew hedges to give an effect that it is a delightful combination of English and European.

Some three miles further up the river valley and set amidst lush water-meadows is **Alfriston**, once the smuggler's headquarters. Stanton Collins, the leader of the gang, lived in the Market Cross Inn, otherwise known as **The Smugglers Inn**. By a trick of fate, he was eventually caught and sentenced to transportation - but for sheep-stealing not smuggling!

The Star Inn dates from the 15th century, when it was probably built to house pilgrims on their way to visit the shrine of St Richard at Chichester. There are some splendid medieval carvings on the timbered facade, including one of a basilisk being slain by St Michael. There is also a small **Heritage Centre** and **Blacksmith's Museum**, housed in the Old Forge in Sloe Lane.

Drusillas Park, to the north of the village, has been a favourite with families for over 60 years;a winning combination of children's zoo, gardens, workshops, amusements and restaurants. Attached to this is the rather more grown up attraction of **The English Wine Centre**, which has its own vineyard and museum.

Wilmington's attraction is obvious; carved into the chalkface of the downs above the village is the outline of a giant, with a staff in either hand. No one knows the origin of **The Long Man of Wilmington**, first recorded as late as 1779; it has been variously suggested that he was a Bronze Age Chieftain, or the Saxon King Harold, or even an advertisement to guide pilgrims to **Wilmington Priory**. The Priory fell on hard times well before the Dissolution and became a farmhouse which now houses a museum specialising in bygone agricultural equipment. The little church next door is overshadowed by a huge and ancient yew, which probably dates back to when the priory was completed.

At **West Firle**, **Firle Place**, a Tudor mansion extensively remodelled in the 18th century, has been the home of the Gage family for 500 years. Set amongst wooded parkland beneath the 700 foot Firle Beacon, the house contains a fine collection of paintings and furniture. The family includes Henry VIII's Comptroller of Calais, a Governor of Massachussetts and the importer of the greengage, and the 13th century village church has a fine family chapel, containing amongst other memorials and brasses, an exquisitely-carved alabaster memorial to Sir John and Lady Phillipa Gage, and a window by John Piper, commemorating the sixth Viscount Gage. The village pub, **The Ram Inn**, dating from 1540 is well worth a visit.

North of the main road lies another handsome house, **Glynde Place**, also a mix of Tudor and Georgian architecture. The house was built for William Morley whose descendants Colonel Herbert Morley was one of the Parliamentarian judges at the trial of Charles I, although he refused to sign the death-warrant. The house contains much of interest, including collections of Bronzes, needlework and a small aviary. The small parish church is in the Wren style, not unlike a miniature version of St Paul's Covent Garden.

Glyndebourne, which was also a Morley home is world renowned for the quality of its opera. For over 50 years, opera lovers have flocked here to listen to the music and to enjoy picnicking in full evening dress during the long interval. Glyndebourne now has a new, purpose built Opera House which is thrilling audiences. There is a solid, respectable charm about **Lewes** with the old houses clustered around the castle on the hill, and its steep narrow streets and alleyways. **Anne of Cleves House**, Southover, once belonged to Henry VIII's 'Flander's Mare' and is an excellent place to begin a tour of the town since it is also a museum containing items of local and country life and history.

That early 'Hooray Henry' the Prince Regent, often stayed at **Southover Grange** in Keere Street and doubtless this was where the coaching wager was laid. A wager in which the Prince Regent drove a coach and four down Keere Street, a street which is narrow and precipitous. Did he win - I imagine so!

Simon de Montfort spent the night before the Battle of Lewes in prayerful vigil at the church of St Mary and St Andrew, **Fletching**. The village's name probably originated with the medieval industry of arrow making; a fletcher is the name given to such craftsmen. Edward Gibbon (1737-94), the historian and author, of 'The Decline and Fall of the Roman Empire' spent the last months of his life staying at **Sheffield Park**. The battlemented lodge and gateway lie just acrossthe road from the church where Gibbon is buried.

The Park, landscaped by both Capability Brown and Humphrey Repton and now administered by the National Trust, was at one time as renowned for its cricket as for its beauty; the Australians used to play their first tour game here before Arundel became the venue and the Lord Sheffield of the day was such an enthusiast that he played on the lakes in the park when they were frozen over, and once aboard his yacht off the coast of Spitzbergen! James Wyatt built the lovely Gothic Revival house in the 1770's and it is perfectly complemented by the superb landscape with rare trees and shrubs arranged around five lakes, set at different levels and linked by cascades.

One of the finest steam railways in the country is **The Bluebell Railway** which has its southern depot, headquarters and museum close to the park entrance. Named after the flowers which grow along the length of the line, this famous railway has operated steam locomotives to **Horsted Keynes** for over thirty years, and it is a sheer delight to chuff gently through the wooded Sussex countryside.

Uckfield grew with the advent of the railway although originally it was a small village at the intersection of the London to Brighton turnpike and the more ancient pilgrim's route from Winchester to Canterbury. **Framfield** has a church that is long and low and built in 1288. An attractive village square with a number of pretty tile-hung houses face the church which seems to have been severely damaged by fire in 1509, while the tower collapsed in 1667, and was not replaced for two centuries. According to one authority, Framfield once fielded a cricket team of 15 men whose combined ages added up to 1,000 years - sadly they could find no suitably aged opponents.

Ashdown Forest is a mere shadow of what it once was when it was a mighty blanket of woodland that filled the valley between the North and South Downs. In the three heather thatched barns of the **Ashdown Forest Centre** at **Wych Cross**, you can learn all about its history and see what is going on in the conservation work alongside the natural process of regeneration.

In the old days the area was favoured by outlaws such as cutthroats, highwaymen and, of course, smugglers. **West Hoathly**, high on the ridge at the westernmost end of the forest, and once a centre of the iron industry, was a great favourite of the unofficial import brigade.

Sensibly **The Cat Inn**, was their headquarters and the church tower, their look out post. The 15th century **Priest's House**, with its roof of massive Horsham stone, is now a museum, and a fine Norman church and manor face each other across the street. With proper Sussex contempt for geographical exactitude, East Hoathly is some 15 miles to the south...

Across the border with Surrey is the attractive Wealden village of **Lingfield** with its 15th century buildings and fine race-course. Eastwards the Sussex border runs with that of Kent, and at **Hammerwood Park** there are strong links with the capital of the United States. Benjamin Latrobe, who also designed the Capitol and the White House in Washington DC, built Hammerwood in 1792. As the name implies, Hammerwood was an iron-working community, as was the nearby village of **Cowden**. Today's visitor will find this hard to believe when gazing at the community of half-timbered houses nestling amongst the hills. Nevertheless, to the west of the village are the 30 reed-fringed acres of Furnace Pond, which gives some indication of the size of the industry in times past.

Returning south towards the forest, the B2026 passes through the River Medway and enters the immaculate and substantial village of **Hartfield** with its weatherboarded stone, brick and tile-hung cottages. The church with a magnificent spire, acting as a landmark for miles around, has a most unusual lych-gate, half under the projecting floor of a fine little timber cottage. There is something cosy and comforting about this part of Sussex, and that feeling is engendered, together with childhood memories, by the sight of a small wooden bridge over a stream; this is the bridge where Winnie-the-Pooh and Christopher Robin first dropped twigs into the water, thus inventing the immortal game of 'Pooh-sticks'. Somehow fiction becomes reality in this timeless part of the Andredsweald.

The easternmost area of Sussex stretches along the coast from Eastbourne to Rye. It is lower lying than the country to the west, a pleasant, welcoming and varied landscape where small winding lanes take the visitor past farms, hamlets and villages which possess an almost timeless air. Deer browse in the shelter of thickets and wood, while fat fleecy sheep graze in gentle rolling pasture and ancient meadows. Well pruned orchards are laid out with military precision and along the Kentish border, the coned towers of oast houses denote hop-growing. Although the vast majority of these buildings seem to have been converted into what an estate agent's love of abbreviation would describe as a 'des-res', the hop is still grown to flavour our ale.

If Brighton is 'London by the Sea' then **Eastbourne** is more akin to 'Bath by the Sea'; refined, elegant and restrained, it has a three mile seafront with its terraced parades and fountained gardens. In contrast to other South coast resorts, one is immediately struck by the absence on the front of shops and the more raucous form of entertainment and amusement emporiums. At night, with gardens and fountains floodlit, the effect can be breathtaking. After having seen the sweeping grandeur of the front, with the sea breaking gently on the shingle and sand beach it no longer seems unusual or incongruous that Claude Debussy should have written his greatest orchestral work 'La Mer' while staying here in 1905.

Martello towers are to be seen from the shore road leading eastwards but at **Pevensey** there are traces of an older and greater fortification. The Saxon Shore Forts were built by the Romans and at Pevensey they constructed the fortress of Adnerida to repel the northern invaders. When the Romans departed, the Romano-British took the fortress over, but after a six month siege in 491AD, the Saxons took the castle and slaughtered every inhabitant. It is said that the Saxons never inhabited Anderida because of the savage deeds done that day and that the village was thus created. They took the name of the fortress and applied it to the vast hinterland of forest - Andreadswald, the Forest of Andred later known as The Weald. For such a small and seemingly insignificant community, Pevensey has had a long, important and violent history. Nearly six hundred years after the Saxon massacre, the long ships of William of Normandy loomed out of the Channel haze and grounded in the creeks and inlets of what was then a swamp natural harbour. This was the beginning of the Norman Conquest; Pevensey was where they landed and where they consolidated their position before moving on to capture Hastings and ultimately, to defeat Harold at Battle. **Pevensey Castle's** Roman curtain walls still stand, along with the 11th and 13th-century gatehouse and keep.

The Pevensey Levels is the name given to the low lying area of marsh inland from the town, once a region of shallow dykes and creeks until silting and storms filled the watery shallows. At the head of this area stands the striking shape of **Herstmonceaux Castle**, built of Flemish brick in 1440. By the time it was finished the introduction of the cannon had made that form of medievalfortress redundant; nevertheless,it is a satisfying, solid structure that could grace any romance involving knights in armour and damsels in distress. When it was finished it had a window for every day of the year and a chimney for every week; it was restored after decades of decay in 1913 and occupied by the Royal Observatory until recently.

Turning southwards towards the shore, **Bexhill** is the next coastal town to the east. Its history is not dissimilar to that of Eastbourne, a small village developed by the major landowner as a resort. The landowner was Lord De la Warr, who in 1885 began by building on his land that lay between the original village and the sea. Perhaps because it was a latecomer to the resort scene, Bexhill never achieved the size and status of its fellows and still retains something of a village atmosphere. However the town has led the way on many occasions. It had the first mixed bathing in the country in 1901 and followed this piece of daring by holding the first Motor Race in 1902. The De La Warr Pavilion is the town's best known building; a grade one listed architectural masterpiece designed in 1933 by the German Erich Mendelsohn. Overlooking the sea, it houses an 1100 seat theatre, restaurants, bars and function rooms. In delightful contrast to the sweeping modern design are the neighbouring Edwardian designs of Marine Arcade and Marina Court Avenue with their passing resemblance to Brighton's Royal Pavilion.

Hastings in common with other towns on this once troubled shore, has had an epic history; a past that is not easy to divine at first sight of this cheerful and easy-going seaside resort. The town was one of the Cinque Ports, a confederation that supplied the medieval monarchs with ships and men in time of war in exchange for certain privileges, such as the right to hold their own courts and to keep the revenue from fines. The other ports were Sandwich, Dover, Romney and Hythe, all in Kent. Until the 12th century, Hastings was a rich and powerful town, but then events both natural and political conspired to drastically reduce its importance.

The first was the loss of Normandy in 1204, which led to a considerable reduction in trade and the partial dismantling of the castle by King John, who feared it might be seized by the French. Great storms during the 13th century led to the loss and silting up of the harbour. In addition during the Hundred Years War (1338-1453) the French attacked and razed the town four times. Although Henry III restored the castle, erosion by the sea and subsequent collapse of the cliff-face led to its collapse and abandonment. West Hill Cliff Railway takes the modern visitor to the top of the hill where the ruins lie. There is an audio-visual presentation called 'The 1066 Story' while nearby St Clements Caves, which honeycomb the hill, contain an entertainment entitled 'the Smuggler's Adventure.'

From the 14th century onwards smuggling, fishing and boat building appear to have been the principal occupation of the inhabitants, who managed these occupations from an unprotected shingle beach. Immediately below the East Cliff is an area known as the Stade, from the Saxon word meaning a landing place. To this day, boats are still drawn up the shingle by winch to lie alongside the extraordinary tall net-sheds. These structures date from Tudor times and were built in this odd manner for two remarkably good reasons. The small base area meant paying less ground rent, and the tall height meant the fishermen could work out of doorways on the mast and rigging as well as the hull. The nearby fishmarket is also of historic interest; by local custom the auctioneer starts with a high price and works down, leaving the bidder just one chance to buy. Along the quaintly named Rock-a-Nore road there is also a Fishermen's Museum, Shipwreck Heritage Centre and an aquarium, the Sea-Life Centre.

To complete the story of Hastings it is important to head north-west to **Battle**, where Harold met William at what is known as the Battle of Hastings, although it actually took place some six miles from the town at Senlac Hill on October 14th 1066. After Harold's defeat, William vowed to build an abbey with the high altar on the spot where Harold fell. The abbey, dedicated to StMartin, was consecrated in 1094 and the town grew up around its walls.

The town is delightful, with a mainly Georgian High Street running up from the Abbey with a number of arched entrances between buildings acting as a reminder of the days when coaches needed to pull into yards of inns. Incidentally I stayed a night or two in the village of **Etchingham** just off the A21 to the north, while I explored this wonderful area. I found Etchingham fascinating and was particularly attracted to its beautiful church built in 1387 which is lovely in its simplicity. Certainly worth a visit.

Returning to the coast east of Hastings, the A259 takes one past the oldest windmill in Sussex, dating from 1670 at **Ickleham**, and on to **Winchelsea**, sometimes described as ;'the smallest town in England'. It is really no more than a small village, although it still boasts a mayor and corporation. Peaceful and utterly charming in the late 20th century, its past is every bit as bloodthirsty and tragic as any of the ancient towns of the Sussex Shore, having been destroyed by storm, razed by French raids and de-populated by the plague.

The original town, part of the Cinque Ports confederation, was set below Igham Hill on a shingle spit, and was the principal Cross-Channel port. The violent storms of 1250 destroyed much of the town, and, under the direction of Edward I, a new community was built on the hill, 'where the only coneys did dwell', the rabbits quickly lost possession of the area, for another storm in 1287 washed away the remainder of the old town, and construction of the new, neatly laid out in grid pattern, continued apace. However, further disasters were to strike; the French attacked Winchelsea seven times in the 14th and 15th centuries, while over the same period, the harbour was gradually silting up to the extent that the coastline today lies nearly two miles to the south of the town.

Roses and wisteria cling to the attractive remains of England's first planned town since Roman times. Although the town was never completed, the existing buildings are a delight. The Church of St Thomas the Martyr was largely destroyed in one of the French raids but what remains is wonderful; the original building was of cathedral-like proportions although all that is left is the chancel and a ruined transept.

Looking eastwards across the flats where the River Brede wanders is arguably one of the most beautiful small towns in Britain, **Rye.** Like its neighbour, it also suffered at the hands of the sea and the French but survived through a combination of good fortune and the tenaciousness of its citizens. Julius Caesar noted that they were 'fierce and hostile' and the citizens of the little town had no compunction about turning to piracy and smuggling when times were hard. The town stands on a hill-top now two miles from its harbour mouth. Its narrow cobbled streets probably have a greater concentration of old houses and more of the atmosphere of a 16th-century town than anywhere else in the country. The waters of three rivers, the Tillingham, the Brede and the Rother combine to scour a channel through the marshy flats to the sea, and small craft can still make their way up on the tide to lie alongside the ancient wharves under the town.

Although the town is a major tourist attraction, it is still very much a working community and there is no feeling of being 'preserved in the Aspic of Time'. Rye is a market town and still retains a fishing fleet. There are boatyards, chandlers and marine engineers alongside the more obvious attractions of antique shops and craft galleries. Rye Harbour lies some two miles south, the road going over bleak and flat countryside. Some measure of the shore's vagaries can be seen by thefact that **Camber Castle**, built in the 1530's to protect the Harbour entrance, is now stranded well inland. Rye Harbour consists of a few houses, a pub and a stark Victorian church with a tragic memorial to the crew of the lifeboat, all drowned in full view of their families earlier this century.

North of the town is **Rye Foreign**. There are two theories as to the origin of this strange name and both equally convincing since they are based on fact. The first is that the Manor of Rye was given by King Canute to the Abbey of Fecamp in Normandy. This was fine until King John lost Normandy in 1204; a legal and political wrangle then began which was not resolved until Henry III negotiated the town's return to crown governance. However, one small area was not returned - hence Rye Foreign. The other theory is that most of the French Protestant refugees, the Hugenots, who settled in Rye during the 17th century, chose to live in their own community on the edge of the town - hence Rye Foreign. Take your pick!

Just north of Rye Foreign is the pretty village of **Peasmarsh** one of many delightful villages around to discover and several interesting historical buildings including **Bateman's** at **Burwash**, an attractive village of little more than one street. Bateman's is best known for being the home of Rudyard Kipling from 1902 until his death in 1936. It contains many of his manuscripts and personal possessions. At the bottom of the lovely garden, a restored watermill grinds flour alongside a water turbine that once provided electricity for the house.

Robertsbridge is a small town on the River Rother with a large number of Wealden Hall houses, built as a result of prosperity in the 14th and early 15th century. In 1794 Horace Walpole when visiting the area, found that one of the inns was full of smugglers and another full of excise men, and a pitched battle at nearby **Silverhill** resulted in victory for the smugglers and the death of a captain of dragoons.

A splendid eccentric, 'Mad Jack' Fuller is buried in the pyrmidal mausoleum in **Brightling** churchyard; he declined to be buried conventionally as he had a fear of being eaten by his relatives -' the worms would eat me, the ducks would eat the worms and my relatives would eat the ducks'. Legend has it that he was buried sitting in an armchair, holding a bottle of claret. Far from mad he was an MP and a great benefactor, a patron of Turner, and a builder of numerous follies, such as the obelisk on Brightling Beacon, most of which were constructed to alleviate unemployment. An exception is the Sugar Loaf at **Dallington**. The story goes that Fuller, over a good dinner, bet a substantial sum of money that he could see the distinctive spire of Dallington church from his home at Brightling. On returning home from the meal, he found to his consternation that he was wrong, he immediately summoned help and had the folly built overnight in a field, so that from a distance it resembled the tip of a spire!

Finally to **Hailsham** where the cattle market once attracted drovers from as far away as Wales, and is still one of the most important in Sussex. A couple of miles to the west, **Michelham Priory** stands in beautiful grounds surrounded by a moat, founded in 1229, the Augustinian Priory had a fairly uneventful history until it was dissolved in 1536. Two thirds of the buildings, including the church, were destroyed and the remainder, together with the estate, became a large working farm belonging to the Pelham and Sackville families. Now the buildings belong to the Sussex Archaeological Society and are run as a fascinating and lively museum with numerous events being held in and around the Priory and its grounds. There are displays of crafts and separate museums related to skills such as that of the wheelwright, blacksmith and rope-maker. The last named is an industry still continued in Hailsham, which also made the special ropes used for executions.

Perhaps one of these gruesome products dispatched the evil Lord Dacre who murdered a gamekeeper at Hellingly in 1541. He was hung at Tyburn after Henry VIII refused his plea for clemency. The evil deed occurred close to the magnificent **Horselunges Manor**, a moated timber-framed manor house built in the late 15th-century. The unusual name is thought to be a corruption of two of the original owners, Herst and Lyngyver.

The pretty little village has a Saxon churchyard, probably dating from the 8th century, although the church was built much later, around 1190. Appropriately for a village whose appearance and history represents much that is best about Sussex, the village inn bears the name of the county's heraldic bird, **The Golden Martlet.**

HUNSTON MILL,
Hunston,
Chichester,
West Sussex,
PO20 6AU

Tel : 01243 783375
Fax : 01243 785179

This beautiful property, less than three miles from Chichester, has three cottages and two flats of excellent standards, for the self catering enthusiast. Situated in approximately an acre of ground with extensive lawns for croquet and putting, a summerhouse, barbecue, and wendy house. The area is a haven for wildlife and there is a great variety of birds both resident and migrating. The property is surrounded by farmland and is a peaceful and tranquil location for any break. The village of Hunston is just about a mile away and here you can buy almost anything you will require for your holiday. There is also a good pub called 'The Spotted Cow' where you can sample some fine ales and the local hospitality.

The history of the Mill makes very interesting reading, and your hosts, Richard and Tricia Beeny, have compiled a leaflet which gives some idea of the history, the environment and what's on offer in the surrounding area. It is a fascinating place to stay, as you are actually housed in one or another part of the old working holding. ***Coach House Cottage*** *and* ***Stable Cottage*** *are as they state, and can accommodate up to five persons.* ***Millstones*** *is the lower flat in the old Mill and will sleep two people or a couple with a small child.* ***Mill Top,*** *which is reached by a charming outside staircase, again will sleep two persons.* ***The Engine House,*** *which housed the old engine to power the mill, has been carefully converted into a studio flat which sleeps two people. All the units have gas central heating, fully equipped kitchens, colour TVs, and plenty of linen including tea towels and a bath towel for each guest. Initial supplies of toilet rolls, soap, fairy liquid, tea bags, coffee, sugar, salt and pepper, add that extra little touch to superb accommodation. Morning papers and milk can be ordered, and there are laundry facilities with an outdoor drying area.*

There is plenty to see and do in this area; Chichester has many attractions including the Cathedral, museums and art galleries, the Downs are only six miles away and here you can walk for miles on the South Downs Way. The new Chichester Golf Course is only 1/4 mile away from Hunston Mill, and there is a host of eating houses and pubs in the surrounding area of Chichester. The Southern Leisure Centre, less than two miles away, has excellent facilities for sailing, wind surfing and swimming, and there are many National Trust properties, all within travelling distance. This is an excellent place to stay with friendly hosts, superb accommodation, and much of interest in the area.

USEFUL INFORMATION

OPEN : *All year*
CHILDREN : *Welcome (cots available)*
PETS : *By arrangement*
CREDIT CARDS : *All major*
SELF CATERING : *Up to 5 persons*
DISABLED ACCESS : *No*
GARDEN : *Excellent*

'THE STUDIO',
High Wray, 73 Lodge Hill Road,
Farnham,
Surrey GU10 3RB.
Tel : 01252 715589

'The Studio' stands in the beautiful grounds of High Wray in a quiet wooded area. The accommodation is of the highest standards and can house up to four adults plus room for a cot. There is a charming living area in which the double sofa bed can serve as a third bed. The bedroom has two single beds which can be linked to form a double, leaving room for a cot. The kitchen is fully equipped and a shower/ toilet leads off the entrance hall. This is an exquisite location with the afternoon sun streaming into the living room and the peace and quiet of the woods making a soft lullaby for those lazy days of rest. You need never leave the three acres of grounds which High Wray stands on but there is a wealth of interests in the area if you do. High Wray caters for bed & breakfast guests with evening meals, so if you wish to partake of this, you are very welcome to join them for dinner and enjoy some of Alexine Crawford's superb cooking. As long as you have given advance notice of this there will be no problem! A charming location for 'getting away from it all'.

USEFUL INFORMATION

***OPEN :** All year* — ***SELF CATERING** Evening meal available at High Wray*
***CHILDREN :** Welcome* — ***DISABLED ACCESS :** No*
***PETS :** Welcome* — ***GARDEN :** 3 acres*
***ACCOMMODATION :** Up to 4 adults/cot available.*

WHITEPOST FARMHOUSE,
Chiddingstone Causeway,
Near Penshurst,
Kent TN11 8JE.
Tel : 01892 870629

Whitepost Farm is a secluded Tudor house situated in a quiet rural area of the Weald in Kent. The self catering accommodation comprises of two cottages carefully converted from a Georgian stable and a beamed Tudor barn. Each is very individual and extremely well furnished. Both accommodate up to three guests, and you will be delighted by the quality and charm of the properties. There is a garden for each cottage and both have ample parking space.

The surrounding area has many attractions, with historic houses and gardens to view, and many country walks from the grounds themselves. The local pub is only 200 yards away and offers bar and restaurant food in addition to ale. This is a wonderful location, and one which you will find yourself returning to time and time again!

USEFUL INFORMATION

OPEN :** All year* — ***SELF CATERING
***CHILDREN :** Welcome* — ***DISABLED ACCESS :** Not really*
***ACCOMMODATION :** 2 cottages* — ***CREDIT CARDS :** none taken*

RISEBRIDGE FARM,
Risebridge Farm House,
Goudhurst,
Kent
TN17 1HN.

Tel : 01580 211775
Fax : 01580 211984

Imagine yourself in the beautiful Kent countryside, surrounded by traditional hop gardens, apple and pear orchards, and pastures and fields of barley and wheat. This is a small farm of 100 acres set in what is called the 'Garden of England', and is designated an area of outstanding beauty. If you are looking to relax and unwind then this is the haven you have been searching for. The beautiful mellow countryside with ancient woodlands and quaint villages and towns, will have you exclaiming in delight, and will ensure that you return to this wonderful part of the world.

The self catering accommodation has been carefully renovated from a range of old brick and slate Cattle Yards, a Dairy and Granary and a wonderful Kentish Oasthouse. All are superb, and great care has been taken to retain the charm and character of each building. There are all modern facilities available, and the high standards makes this an enjoyable home from home.

The farm itself has many amenities, with an adventure playground for the children, and a playroom for the smaller variety. In addition there is a sumptious leisure centre with swimming pool, sauna and Jacuzzi, solarium, extensive fitness studio and much more available.

USEFUL INFORMATION

OPEN : *All year*
CHILDREN : *Welcome*
PETS : *Some*
ACCOMMODATION : *Various sized cottages*

SELF CATERING
DISABLED ACCESS : *Some*
CREDIT CARDS : *All major*

THE HOLIDAY COTTAGE AND FLAT

New Hall,
Small Dole,
Henfield,
West Sussex
BN5 9YJ

Tel: 01273 492546

The delightful name of Small Dole is where you will find New Hall, a rather impressive listed house, it was once the manor house of Henfield. Built around 1620 and then modernised in the early 19th century, it is tucked away at the end of New Hall Lane surrounded by three and a half acres of gardens and fine trees. The house is adjacent to New Hall Farm, a 400 acre working farm, mainly cereals, making it the perfect spot for a peaceful and relaxing break. Mrs. Carreck has converted the north and south wings of the house into modern and comfortable holiday accommodation. They are both completely self-contained having their own front doors which open onto the rear courtyard. Each are exceptionally well appointed with fitted carpets, night storage heaters or radiators and fully equipped kitchens. All electricity, hot water and heating are included in the tariff, you can provide your own towels and linen or hire them. ***The Cottage*** *forms the whole of the north wing, with a large sitting room including a colour television and a folding bed for extra visitors, a dining room with pay phone, upstairs there is a double bedroom with an ensuite bathroom. Outside, The Cottage has its own small terrace complete with table and chairs.* ***The Flat*** *forms the upstairs part of the south wing and comprises a sitting room with colour television and pay phone, one double bedroom, one bedroom with two 3ft beds and a single bedroom, there is also a folding bed if needed, kitchen and bathroom. A south facing terrace with table and chairs is for the sole use of The Flat. Barbecues and charcoal are available if required. Ample parking.*

New Hall is ideally situated for getting out and about, walkers will delight in the abundant footpaths leading to many attractive villages. Worthing is only eight miles away with its excellent beaches, Brighton with all it has to offer is 11 miles. There are stately homes and gardens, wildlife trusts and castles. One of the most peaceful and magical gardens to visit is High Beeches, you can stroll around the acres of woodland and water gardens taking in the glorious colours and beauty of this enchanting landscape.

USEFUL INFORMATION

OPEN: *All year*
CHILDREN: *Welcome. Cot available*
CREDIT CARDS: *None taken*
ACCOMMODATION: *The Cottage sleeps 2/3, The Flat sleeps 5*

DISABLED ACCESS: *Not really*
GARDEN: *Own courtyards with table and chairs & barbecues. Guests have full use of the grounds*
PETS: *Dogs only by special request and additional cleaning charge-£15 per week*

NIGHTINGALES,
The Avenue,
Kingston,
Lewes, Sussex
BN7 3LL

Tel: 01273 475673
E.Mail J. Hudson @ sussex.ac.uk

Nightingales is as charming as its name. This quiet bungalow in the South Downs village of Kingston is set in beautiful gardens which are part of the National Gardens Scheme and bring delight to visitors when they open to the public twice a year. Geoff and Jean Hudson have devoted years to the planning and planting to achieve today's stunning result.

The same loving care has gone into furnishing and equipping the flat and you will receive a very warm welcome at Nightingales, reinforced by Ben, their black labrador.

The flat faces south giving views of the garden and Downs. It has a cottage atmosphere with pine furniture including a Welsh dresser with antique china. It is carpeted throughout and the large bedroom sleeps two with handmade single beds. A sofa-bed is available. The large kitchen contains a washer/drier, dishwasher, microwave and oven. Bed linen and towels are provided. There is a 21" TV with Teletext and a telephone. Above all, apart from being a very special place to stay, it is so peaceful and must make even the most tense person relax.

This area of Sussex is great for those who want to walk on the South Downs or explore the county town of Lewes. If you are feeling energetic, you can play golf or tennis or go horseriding. Fishing is available. If you enjoy opera, Nightingales is ideally situated for a visit to Glyndebourne. Geoff and Jean also have excellent Bed and Breakfast accommodation for those who prefer to be pampered. (AA 4Q Selected)

USEFUL INFORMATION

OPEN; *All year*
CREDIT CARDS; *All major cards*
ACCOMMODATION; *1 bedroom + bed sofa*
TELEPHONE; *Own line*

CHILDREN; *No*
DISABLED ACCESS; *No*
GARDEN; *Yes. Part of National Gardens Scheme*

CHURCH FARM HOLIDAY VILLAGE,
Bourne Leisure Group Ltd.,
Pagham,
Nr.Chichester,
West Sussex,
PO21 4NR.

Tel : 01243 262635

Family fun is what this holiday village offers, with a variety of entertainment to suit toddlers to grandmothers! This is a home from home with all the equipment necessary to cater for yourself, but with the option to 'eat out' if desired. There are selected grades of caravans which cater for different size families, but all are superb in their quality and furnishings. There is hot & cold water, gas & electric, fully fitted bathroom, colour TV, fully fitted kitchens, and luxurious lounges where you can relax at the end of the day! Church Farm is situated on a beautiful coastline where sailing and other water sports are extremely popular......but that is not all! A heated outdoor pool, (and indoor pool) children's play area, cycle hire, amusements and a nature reserve on the headland.... and this is just during the daylight hours! In the evening the whole place comes alive with various entertainment for all the family - live cabarets, discos, bingo, the 17th century pub (for those exhausted adults wishing a quiet drink!), dancing to live bands, (how does anyone ever find enough time!) and that's for those going to bed at nine! For those 'nighthawks' the party goes on! Food is in great demand (especially after using all that energy!), and there is certainly plenty of choice. If you don't want to cook you can enjoy breakfast in the Conservatory Bar, plus lunch and dinner, or just have a snack at the terrace barbecue, or have traditional fish and chips, or something from the bakery in the convenience store! The choice is endless!

Children are well catered for too; tots to 12 year olds can join the Bradley Bear Club and be entertained by Bradley and his team (giving Mum and Dad a bit of free time), or for the teens there are lots of sport events where they can get to know each other and overcome that usual teenager shyness. There are special theme weekends; perhaps you fancy 'country & western', or even a bit of 'rock & roll', well you can dress up and enjoy the event! The list of social events is endless and there must be something you and your family would enjoy!

The surrounding area has a lot on offer too! The historic city of Chichester is nearby with its magnificent cathedral, shops and Festival Theatre. The harbour with its array of colourful boats would surely tempt anyone, and a range of museums and galleries are there to wander round and enjoy at your leisure. The small, gay villages round the coast are worth a visit as are numerous fine house and castles, and many more alluring attractions. There is no doubt this is an attractive holiday with ample entertainment, comfort and downright good fun to be had by all!

USEFUL INFORMATION

OPEN : *March to October*
CHILDREN : *Welcome*
PETS : *By prior arrangement*
CREDIT CARDS : *All major*

SELF CATERING ACCOMMODATION
DISABLED ACCESS : *Yes*
RESTAURANT : *All meals available*
ENTERTAINMENT : *Enormous variety.*
New development of Tennis/Multi Courts adj to reception

CHURCH FARM,
Rowton,
Telford
TF6 6QY.

Tel : 01952 770381

Only a few miles from the M54 is the peaceful hamlet of Rowton and Church Farm. This is a working dairy farm, and guests are welcomed into the farming way of life. Virginia and Robert Evans offer many facilities for guests; bed and breakfast in the lovely old 17th century farmhouse, self catering cottages, caravans, and a small campsite. There is a lovely garden where you can sit and relax under the trees, or enjoy an informal game of football or cricket on the lawn. There is fishing, barbecue and an indoor games room all available too. Breakfast is available for all guest s in the farmhouse dining room - you can even collect your own free range eggs. This is the idyllic location with many attractions on site but also within easy access to the surrounding area and all it has to offer.

The cottages are beautifully furnished and decorated in a country fashion, and have full facilities. They are centrally heated throughout, and cot and high chair are available on request. The cottages are suitable for partially disabled guests. Controlled pets are welcome.

USEFUL INFORMATION

OPEN : *All year*
CHILDREN :*Welcome*
PETS : *Welcome*
ACCOMMODATION ; *Varied*

DINING ROOM : *Country breakfast*
DISABLED ACCESS : *Partially*
CREDIT CARDS : *None taken*

GOLDHILL MILL
WALNUT COTTAGE &
CIDERPRESS COTTAGE

V & S Management Ltd, Golden Green,
Tonbridge, Kent TN11 0BA

Tel: 01732 851626
Fax: 01732 851881

If you require a holiday away from it all, surrounded by peace , tranquillity and luxurious accommodation, then a stay at the Goldhill Mill's magnificent **Walnut Tree Cottage** *or* **Ciderpress Cottage** *is definitely the setting for you. These wonderful retreats are in an idyllic position, situated in the Mill's twenty acre grounds, close to the River Bourne and encompassed by beautiful countryside.* **Walnut Tree Cottage**, *once an old cowshed, offers superior accommodation for six people. The spacious living room has a inglenook style fireplace incorporating an open log burning stove, colour television, video and direct dial telephone. The fully fitted kitchen has every modern day convenience including oven, hob, microwave, dishwasher, and fridge/freezer, from the kitchen a door leads out to a small private garden. A double bedroom with an ensuite bathroom, colour TV and telephone is also on the ground floor. An automatic washing machine and tumble drier are housed in a laundry cupboard. From the living room a spiral staircase leads to the bedrooms on the first floor, one double ensuite, colour TV and telephone, and an ensuite twin room which also has a telephone and a TV point.* **Ciderpress Cottage** *sleeps 4 in total comfort on one level, it acquired it's name from an old ciderpress in what was once the old applestore. Once again the accommodation is exceptional, the generous living room has wonderful old beams, with the furnishings being similar to those in Walnut Tree Cottage. The kitchen also has the same high standard of equipment. There are two double bedrooms, one with an ensuite bathroom plus a second bathroom and a laundry cupboard containing the washing machine and tumble drier. From the kitchen an apple ladder leads to a gallery above, which contains an additional third double bed if required. Both cottages have been beautifully decorated and tastefully furnished. The cost of gas and electricity is included in the tariff from June to September, from October to May a charge is levied. All linen and towels are provided.*

The cottages are in an excellent location for touring the surrounding area, you will be spoilt for choice with many castles, stately homes and gardens, towns and villages to explore, your days will be filled to overflowing. There are several golf courses nearby and swimming in Tonbridge. These lovely cottages have been awarded the English Tourist Board's top '5 Key De Luxe' rating and it is not hard to see why, you will definitely not be disappointed.

USEFUL INFORMATION

OPEN: *All year*
CHILDREN: *Welcome*
CREDIT CARDS: *None taken*
ACCOMMODATION: *Superior cottages*
Parking spaces for two cars at each cottage
Walnut Tree Cottage sleeps 6, Ciderpress Cottage sleeps 4

DISABLED ACCESS: *Not really*
GARDEN: *Yes, small garden areas*
PETS: *No*
NO SMOKING in cottages

THE HOPPER'S HUT &
CARTER'S COTTAGE

New Barn,
Wards Lane,
Wadhurst,
East Sussex
TN5 6HP

Tel: 01892 782042

New Barn must be in one of the most idyllic situations, this 18th century farmhouse built in a traditional Sussex style with lattice-paned windows and adorned with climbing plants sits next to a wonderful blue lake with hills beyond, it oozes peace and tranquillity. Christopher and Pauline Willis, the owners of the superb house, have two charming self-contained holiday cottages. **Carter's Cottage** *is perfect for two people, it is extremely well furnished and very comfortable with a wood burning stove in the sitting room for extra warmth. Cooking and heating are by electricity which is charged weekly.* **The Hopper's Hut** *is aptly named as it used to house Hop Pickers, the cottage has been carefully converted to provide accommodation for 4/5 persons. Once again it is superbly furnished and very spacious. There are two bedrooms one with a 5ft bed and the other with two 3ft beds. Over one end of the large sitting room is a gallery which is suitable for a 5th person. A log burning stove provides extra warmth. Both cottages have colour televisions and radios. They also share the use of a Laundry Room and a Games Room in the Cattle Byre. Bed linen is provided and a pay phone available.*

The cottages are surrounded by the most magnificent scenery, the glorious countryside abounds with wildlife and it is here sheep graze and Shetland ponies roam, not only that but only 50 yards away are the shores of Bewl Water, where you may fish. Horse riding and bike hire are also available. The Willis' are on hand at any time to help or answer any queries you may have. Having stayed here you will want to return again and again.

USEFUL INFORMATION

OPEN: *All year*
CHILDREN: *Welcome*
CREDIT CARDS: *None taken*
ACCOMMODATION: *Carter's Cottage sleeps 2, The Hopper's Hut sleeps 4/5*

DISABLED ACCESS: *Not really*
GARDEN: *Large and well tended. Plus a Games Room*
PETS: *No*

BUTTS HILL FARM

Labour-in-Vain Road,
Wrotham,
Kent
TN15 7PA

Tel/Fax: 01732 822415

The North Downs is an area of 'Outstanding Natural Beauty and 'Great Landscape Value', this beautiful part of the country is where Gerry and Sheila Morel have their superb timber lodges. Set in a small wooded area amidst farmland and countryside these delightful properties are an ideal holiday location. The three bedroomed lodges have one double bedroom, one twin and one room with crossover bunk beds, there is a large bathroom and two WCs. The comfortable sitting room has a gas fire, radio and colour television. In the kitchen you find all you need with fridge, cooker, microwave and dishwasher. The two bedroomed lodges are similarly furnished apart from the dishwasher and extra toilet. All the lodges have a large full length patio doors which look out across a grass glade and patio area where you can sit and relax or plan your day away. The whole setting is very safe for children and there is plenty of off road parking. Gas, electricity, bed linen and towels are all provided and included in the tariff.

Butts Hill Farm is in an ideal location for exploring the area, close by there are golf courses, indoor swimming pools, horse riding and plenty of lovely walks in the countryside where there is an abundance of fauna and flora. Further a field there are many towns and cities with all they have to offer. Superb accommodation in wonderful surroundings with something to keep everyone happy.

USEFUL INFORMATION

OPEN: *All year. Closed mid Jan-mid Feb*

CHILDREN: *Welcome, cots & high chairs available.*

CREDIT CARDS: *Yes*

ACCOMMODATION: *4 superb timber lodges - 2 x 2 bedroom, 2 x 3 bedroom*

DISABLED ACCESS: *Ramp to each lodge*

GARDEN: *Yes. Patio area with garden furniture. Children's play room*

PETS: *No*

Safe off road parking

Laundrette available

CHAPTER 4

CENTRAL ENGLAND
Including
HEREFORDSHIRE, WORCESTERSHIRE, STAFFORDSHIRE, SHROPSHIRE, WEST MIDLANDS & WARWICKSHIRE

INCLUDES

CHAPTER 4

CENTRAL ENGLAND, HEREFORDSHIRE, WORCESTERSHIRE, STAFFORDSHIRE, SHROPSHIRE, WEST MIDLANDS & WARWICKSHIRE

Pulchra Terra Dei Donum' (This fair land is the Gift of God) is the county motto of Hereford and the more I see of this beautiful land, the truer I know that statement to be. Although Hereford is joined to Worcester for administrative purposes, the charactrs of the two counties have little in common. A perfect illustraion of this is gained from the viewpoint atop the Herefordshire Beacon in the Malvern Hills. To the east lie the rich fertile lowlands of Worcestershire through which the Severn and Avon wander, whilst to the west, the undulating wooded scenery of Herefordshire extends to the lowering ridge of the **Black Mountains**, some forty miles away.

The M50 motorway is a western spur of the M5 and runs some five miles into Herefordshire before ending at **Ross-on-Wye**, a delightful market town overlooking the River Wye. Agriculture, light industry and tourism form the basis of the local economy and Ross (from the Welsh ros, meaning a spit of land) is ideally situated for exploring the glorious country of the Wye Valley. Its friendly and welcoming atmosphere owes much to the example set by the town's best loved inhabitant, John Kyrle (1637-1724). Trained as a lawyer, he inherited a small fortune and never practiced, preferring to spend his time and money on good works and acts of great public generosity. He died, a bachelor, at the age of 89, having given all his money away but never incurred a debt. He is remembered as the 'Man of Ross' and among his many philanthropies were the provision of a town water supply, a causeway enabling the bridge to be used when flooding occurred, and a walled public garden, known as Kyrle's Prospect. He built a summer house in the grounds of his home, now known as **Kyrle House**, and paid the poor and unemployed to find horse's teeth from animals killed in a nearby cavalry skirmish during the Civil War; these were set into mortar to create a mosaic in the shape of a swan. A much loved man.

The little town on its steep rocky outcrop has been a favourite with visitors since the early Victorian era when, as now, the attractions of the surrounding countryside and the excellent salmon fishing brought people back year after year. Hotels, pubs and restaurants are plentiful. I was impressed by the enthusiasm and high standards to be found.

The Lost Street Museum is a charming and very well thought out museum in the form of an arcade of Edwardian shops containing all manner of period items including amusement machines, musical boxes, toys, costumes and gramophones. An unusual local industry is candle-making and **Ross-on-Wye Candlemakers** open their workshop to the public in old Gloucester Road. Two gardens are worth visiting. **Hill Court Gardens and Garden Centre** to the east of the town and **How Caple Court Gardens** to the north, are a gardener's delight.

At **Symonds Yat West**, the Jubilee Park offers a wide range offamily entertainment, including a maze, craft shops and a butterfly farm. **The Herefordshire Rural Heritage Museum**, set in an attractive rural location, houses one of the country's largest collections of historic farm machinery and agricultural implements. About three miles downstream in the wooded Doward Hills above the river is **King Arthurs Cave** where excavations have revealed that its occupancy by man dates back nearly 60,000 years! Five miles south of Ross and upstream from Symonds Yat are the romantic and massively impressive ruins of **Goodrich Castle**.

Goodrich is an entertaining though somewhat scattered little village and the 12th century castle is sited on a high, rocky spur overlooking a crossing of the river. Square in shape with a tower at each corner and surrounded by a moat hewn out of the red rock, Goodrich was besieged by Parliamentarians under the command of Colonel Birch, in 1646. Legend has it that Birch's niece, Alice, was inside the castle with her Royalist lover, and that they were both drowned in the Wye whilst trying to escape. Her shrieks of distress can still be heard on stormy nights when the river is in spate.

Heading north-east from Ross on the A449 and lying close to the eastern border of the county, is the attractive village of **Much Marcle**, blessed with a fine church of 13th-century origins, **St Bartholomews** and two historic houses. Just over four miles further along the A440 is the delightful ancient market town of **Ledbury**. Set by the old cross-roads to Tewkesbury, Hereford, Gloucester and Malvern, it has been inhabited since around 1500BC. The church of **St Michael and All Angels**, Herefordshire's premier parish church was built on an earlier Saxon foundation and has a Norman chancel and west door, and a magnificent medieval north chapel. The wide main street, flanked by many half-timbered houses including the Elizabethan **Feathers Inn** was the scene of a desperate charge by Prince Rupert's cavalry during the Civil War, when a Parliamentarian force was routed. Bullets are still embedded in the church door and in the walls of **The Talbot** in New Street. Church Lane, cobbled and narrow, offers a delightful period view of St Michaels and opens out into a small close with some handsome houses surrounding the church.

The south- eastern quarter of Herefordshire is the main hop-growing region, and hopyards, with their trellis work of poles, wires and strings can be seen throughout the area. At **Bishop Frome**, on the Ledbury to Bromyard road, **The Hop Pocket Hop Farm** is open to visitors interested in a form of cultivation that is regrettably in decline. Drying kilns, hop-picking machines and the hopyards are all open to inspection.

Further information on the history and practices of hop-growing can be found at the Bromyard Heritage Centre along with other displays relating to matters of local interest. **Bromyard** sits in a natural bowl, amongst rolling downland and was one of the most important towns in Herefordshire long before the Norman clerks started to compile the Domesday Book. It had a Saxon church in 840AD and the present church of **St Peter** was probably built onthe same site in about 1160. The town's wealth came principally from its market and local agriculture - later came an added bonus in the form of its geographical position halfway between Worcester and Hereford which led to its development as a coaching centre. Notable amongst the inns catering to the trade was **The Falcon** whose postboys wore a smart uniform of white hats, breeches and yellow jackets. Somehow I cannot believe they stayed smart for very long.

The River Teme wriggles through the three counties of Herefordshire, Worcestershire and Shropshire in the area around **Tenbury Wells**. A borough since 1248, Tenbury has remained an attractive small market town surrounded by hopyards and apple orchards. Hopes of fame and fortune came its way in the 19th century with the discovery of saline springs - but the town lacked an entrepreneur of the quality of Doctor Wall at Malvern and the spa never became fasionable. The incongruous Pump Rooms survive known locally as the 'Chinese Temple' because of the style of architecture.

Leominster (pronounced 'Lemster') a thriving market town,lies nine miles to the south-west and is Herefordshire's second largest town, set amongst a gentle landscape of fields, hills and meadows where river, stream and brook wander. The town's fortunes were based on the fine quality of the wool from the local breed of sheep, the Ryeland, an animal that thrives on the poorer grazing to be found on the neighbouring hills and the less fertile outcrops of sandy soil from which the name is derived. The demand for this wool was so great that at one time the fleece was known as 'Lempster Ore'.

Cider orchards along the road heading south to **Hereford** hint at one of the city's major industries. Bulmer's have been making cider in Hereford for well over a century and their premises in Plough Lane are open for tours and samplings. The contrast with modern automated production techniques with those of yesteryear are enormous, and a visit to **The Cider Museum and King Offa distillery**, in Ryelands Street, is a real eye-opener.

Any town or city engaged in the convivial pursuit of brewing or distilling has a rather jolly atmosphere, and Hereford is no exception, although its early history would suggest otherwise. Never free of strife until the end of the Civil War in 1651, the city suffered numerous attacks and sieges over the preceding centuries, yet during that time, managed to become one of the most thriving medieval cities in England, a centre for both trade and scholarship.

Items relating to the turbulent past, as well as to more peaceful interests such as bee-keeping, can be seen in **The Hereford City Museum and Art Gallery**, in Broad Street. The modern military presence in the city is restricted to the **Herefordshire Regimental Museum** at the TA Centre in Harold Street, and to the discreet gentlemen of the SAS, at Bradbury Lines. Hereford is rich in museums; apart from those already mentiond, there are the **Bulmer Railway Centre**, for steam enthusiasts, **The Churchill Gardens Museum**, displaying fine furniture, costumes, andpaintings of the late 18th and 19th centuries, **The St John Medieval Museum** containing armour and other relics relating to the order of St John, and **The Old House**, built in 1621 and beautifully furnished in period.

The medieval visitors to the city-scholars, men-at-arms, and traders - would have had their numbers swelled by large numbers of pilgrims, visiting **The Cathedral of St Mary the Virgin and St Ethelbert the King**. The cathedral was begun in the 7th century - in fact, the appointment of the first Bishop of Hereford dates back to that time. A large proportion of the Norman masonry work survives, particularly inside, but the siege and structural collapse in the 17th and 18th centuries led to extensive rebuilding and renovation. For all this, it is still a wonderfully handsome building, quite small compared to most cathedrals, and full of many unique treasures. Chief amongst these is the Mappa Mundi, a map of the world drawn around 1290 and of great importance because it shows us how the scholars of that time saw their world, both in spiritual, as well as geographical terms. The medieval draughtsmanship is superb with all manner of beasts, both fabulous and familiar. The cathedral also has a notable collection of manuscripts and early printed material in the Chained Library, including the 8th century Anglo-Saxon gospels still used when Hereford bishops are sworn in.

The choral traditions of the cathedral are long and the origins of the magnificent Three Choirs Festival can be traced back to an 18th-century chancellor, Thomas Bisse. To listen to soaring music in such surroundings is surely close to 'the rudiments of Paradise'.

The south-western region of Herefordshire and the Welsh Borders was known as **Archenfield** and stretched from the western back of the Wye to the long ridge of the Black Mountains, twenty miles away. It remained a Welsh enclave in England for around six centuries until well after the Conquest. Many of the laws and customs remained peculiarly Welsh until as recently as the present century. An attractive, yet sparsely populated region, with few large villages but a wealth of churches, which point to the fact that this area had possibly the longest history of continuous Christianity in England.

Welsh Newton is still the scene of a yearly pilgrimage since the graveyard contains the last of Herefordshire's many saints. John Kemble, who was canonised as recently as 1970, was a Jesuit priest who administered to the many catholics in the area, including the wife and daughter of the man who arrested him for complicity in the Popish Plot. An innocent and greatly loved man, he was executed in the most barbaric manner at Hereford, in August 1679. He was eighty years old.

At **Kilpeck**, just off the A465 from Hereford, is the most famous of Archenfield churches, Saint Mary and St David. Saxon work remains in the north-east wall of the nave but the church is principally Norman and the local red sandstone from which it was built has survived the weathers of time remarkably well. The real glory of the little church is its carvings; work of skilled masons who are sometimes referred to as the Herefordshire School,and who flourished during the 12th century. Behind the church can be found the remains, little more than a stump, of Kilbeck Castle, built around the same time that the carvers were indulging their strange fantasies with hammer and chisel. King John visited here a number of times, and it is recorded that a pretty widow, Joan de Kilpeck offered him a bribe of fifty marks and a palfrey (a small horse) if he would allow her to marry whom she pleased.

It was to the men of Archenfield that England looked in time of strife. From this area came the medieval equivalent of the machine-gun; the long bow, made from yew, and in the hands of a master, capable of piercing through the mailed thigh of a horseman and nailing him to the saddle at fifty paces or more. More importantly the next arrow would be on its way within seconds, whereas the cross-bowman would still be tensioning his weapon. Once the major disputes between English and Welsh were settled, it was the bowmen of Archenfield who led the armies in attack and held the rear in retreat.

Men-at-arms of higher rank, but of common experience, are remembered amongst the high, sheep grazing hills of **Garway**. These were the Knights Templar, Soldiers of Christian belief and noble birth who wore a red sign of the cross on simple white surcoats that covered their armour. Formed to protect pilgrims on the long and dangerous journeys to and from Jerusalem, they showed great bravery during the Crusades and later founded numerous religious houses throughout Europe. Garway was one of their estates and the church of **St Michael** is one of only six Templar foundations left in England. It seems strange to think of those grim monastic soldiers, used to the blazing sun and the desert battles with the Saracens, ending their days on these damp hillsides. The place is moving in its simplicity and well worth the meandering drive south.

The Golden Valley gets its name from a justifiable piece of linguistic confusion on the part of the Normans; they muddled the Welsh 'dwyr' meaning water with their own 'd'or' meaning gold - hence Golden Valley and the **River Dore**. Also Abbey Dore, a mile or so from **Ewyas Harold Castle** (pronounced Yewas) on the west side of the valley. This was a great Cistercian monastery until the Dissolution. The remains were carefully restored under the direction of the first Viscount Scudamore, and he and his craftsmen did a most excellent job. The present building possesses a simple grandeur and contains good glass, some interesting glazed tiles, and a knightly effigy of the grandson of the founder of the Abbey, Robert de Clifford.

Michaelchurch Escley sits tight under the lee of the Black Mountains, truly a dark and brooding mass, frequently blue or purple in tint. From these slopes the Celtic warriors of long ago would rush in ambush, only to vanish into the woods and hills when ambush threatened. The trout laden waters of **Escley Brook** run parallel to those of the Monnow, into which it eventually merges, and the area is border country at its best - remote and beautiful.

The road running north alongside the Monnow passes through **Crasswall** with **Hay Bluff**, the source of the river rising high over the hamlet. The Order of the Grandmontines, an offshoot of the Cistercian order and named after their founding house in Limoges had their abbey here. The remote situation must have suited an order which emphasised strict discipline and reliance on alms and agricultural labour.

The road continues northward, climbing to around 1500 feet, before dropping down through the steep, wooded slopes and into Wales at **Hay-on-Wye**. Hay changed hands several times in its turbulent early years, being burnt down five times, which may account for the fact that there are the remains of two castles in the small town. Hay is known worldwide for its bookshops. Second-hand books in their millions line the shelves of the castle, the cinema, a garage and shops that once catered for the more mundane demands of the local populace. Rare first editions and fine leather bindings lie in close proximity to heaps of dog-eared paperbacks and bundles of yellowing magazines. Sleepy little Hay woke up to the fact that it is now a tourist attraction in its own right - thanks to the wonderfully eccentric, but undoubtedly shrewd local entrepreneur, Richard Booth, who started the whole idea.

Turning back from Hay towards Hereford, it is worth taking a detour to view the remains of Clifford Castle, whose ivy-clad ruins tower over a shallow bend in the Wye. It was built by Walter de Clifford in the early 1200's and first saw action not long after when it was captured, not by Celt or fellow Norman Marcher Lord, but by Henry III. This unfortunate episode was as a result of Henry's request that Walter's debts be paid off. Walter's reply was to make the King's Messenger 'eat the King's writ, waxe and all', so the incensed Henry promptly sacked the castle. The 'Fair Rosamund'; an earlier Clifford who was the mistress of Henry II, was probably born here. The King kept her hidden from the jealous Queen Eleanor, but eventually the Queen found Rosamund and forced her to drink poison. The Mortimers succeeded the Cliffords, so the old fortress was held by two of the greatest Marcher families.

Weobley (pronounced Wedbley) is where the first tough Hereford strain of cattle, dark red with white faces, bellies and hocks, were first bred on the Garnstone Estate. The village was evidently one of the more successful Norman settlements. Only the castle's earthworks remain today, but Weobley;s prosperity is indicated by the wealth of half-timbered housing and the large parish church. Weobley is the place where the expression 'pot walloper' was first coined; the term referred to Shropshire tenants of the Marquess of Bath who had the right to vote in local elections - providing they had set up thir cooking fires in the main street the previous night. Needless to say, during the corrupt political era of the 18th century, His Lordship took full advantage of this strange custom to ensure the successful return of his chosen candidates.

The half-timbered black and white theme is continued at **Eardisland** to the north of the A44. A picture postcard village by the banks of the Arrow, the enchanting Mill Stream Cottage was once the village school and was built in the 1700's at a cost of fifty pounds! Close by was the site of an ancient British settlement, now the site of Burton Court, a Georgian house of 14th-century origins which houses a fascinating collection of European and Oriental costumes and curios, together with natural history displays, ship models and a working model fairground.

Almost next door to Earidland is the beautiful and unspoilt village of **Pembridge** with a wealth of 13th and 14th century buildings and none more beautiful than **The New Inn** which is a hostelry of warmth and atmosphere acquired over the centuries. Everything about it reeks of history. It was the Court House before it became an inn and even after that one room was used to administer the majesty of the law. It has two ghosts who refuse to leave!

It does seem extraordinary that in such an area, outstanding in its natural beauty, combining peace and solitude with the scenery of the hills, woods and rivers, should have been the scene of so much strife - yet reminders lie all around. Wigmore Castle has a connection with Brampton Bryan in that it was briefly owned by the Harleys before being dismantled by Parliamentarian troops, but it was first built by William Fitz-Osborn, Earl of Hereford, and then owned by the Mortimer family. The castle is impressively and strongly sited on a ridge in a most commanding position. It was to this great fortress that Prince Edward fled, before rallying his forcs against Simon de Montfort (he had been imprisoned at Hereford and escaped by the simple ruse of challenging his captors to race their horses. When the animals were exhausted, the cunning Prince produced a fresh beast that had been kept hidden by a sympathiser and disappeared in the proverbial cloud of dust.

Of this great family who held the castle, perhaps the most astute and savage of the Marcher Lords, little remains but a tablet in the nearby gatehouse, where once stood an Augustinian Abbey. 'In this Abbey lies the remains of the noble family of Mortimer who founded it in 1179 and ruled the Marches of Wales for 400 years.' Henry VIII took little notice, even though his mother was a Mortimer, and the tombs vanished with the Abbey. Their name is, however, commemorated a little further down the road where the A4110 intersects the B4362. This innocent looking junction in the valley of the River Lugg, was the scene in 1461 of 'an obstinate bloody and decisive battle'. Four thousand men died at what is now known as Mortimer's Cross; the first defeat to be inflicted on the Lancastrians by Edward, Duke of York - himself half a Mortimer, and later to become Edward IV. Before the fight began an extraordinary sight was seen in the sky - three suns appeared. We now know that this phenomenon is caused by the refraction of light through particles in the atmosphere, and is called a parhelion, but to the superstitious medieval warriors it appeared as an omen, a sign from God. The Yorkists took the three suns to represent the triumvirate of Edward, Duke of York, Richard, Duke of Gloucester and George, Duke of Clarence, and the ' sun in splendour' became a favourite heraldic badge with the House of York.

Turn to the east at Mortimer's Cross, and you will come to three large houses lying within a few miles of each other, the firstof which acted as a rendezvous for the Yorkist forces. The Croft family have lived at Croft Castle since the time of Domesday, with the exception of 177 years - due to some unfortunate debts incurred by an 18th century Croft - and still live there, although the house and the estate is administered by the National Trust. In its present guise the castle is a massive but handsome house with turrets at each cornr, and stands in beautiful parkland with an avenue of Spanish chestnut trees - said by some to have been grown from chestnuts carried in a galleon of the Spanish Armada. For all its troubled history, it is a wonderfully peaceful and attractive home. A strong feeling of continuity and service hangs in the air; as exemplified by the memorials in the little church to two more recent members of the family. Both the tenth and eleventh baronets, father and sone, were killed while serving with the Herefordshire Regiment in the First and Second World Wars, nearly eight hundred years after their ancestor, Jasper de Croft, was knighted during the Crusades.

The other two house stand almost side-by-side to the east of the Leominster to Ludlow road. the smallest is **Eye Manor**, a neat restoration house, built for a slave-trader and plantation owner from Barbados, with the exotic name of Sir Ferdinando Georges. Known as the 'King of the Black Market', he spent a good deal of his ill-gotten gains on the interior decoration, particularly the ornate and well-crafted plasterwork.

Berrington Hall has links with Moccas Court and Brampton Bryan, for the estate once belonged to the Cornewells, who sold it to the Harleys in 1775. Thomas Harley, a prosperous banker, employed Henry Holland, later responsible for the original Brighton Pavilion, to design the house, and Holland's father-in-law, Capability Brown, to lay out the grounds. They succeeded splendidly and Berrington is surely one of the most attractive and elegant Georgian houses in the country. Berrington Hall is now run by the National Trust but from 1901, it belonged to Lord Cawley. and there is a moving memorial in the Norman church at Eye to his three sons, all killed in the First World War.

It is tragic, that they, like their neighbours the Crofts and so many other thousands of Herefordshire's sons and daughters, could not have been laid to rest in the soil of their birth, the land that Henry James described as 'The copse-chequered slopes of rolling Hereford, white with the blossom of apples.'

WORCESTERSHIRE

This is an area of richness and contrast in terms of agricultural wealth, historical association and scenic beauty. The dark fertile soils of the Vale of Evesham produce the finest vegetables and fruits while farmers throughout the region happily indulge in the old-fashioned concept of mixed farming with seeming success. Orchards, arable fields and pasture lie happily grouped together while on the ancient western hills, contented sheep graze on both enclosed and common land. Man's presence on this rich, dark earth dates back to paleolithic times and its fertility was appreciated by Celt, Roman, Saxon and Norman as it is by the agricultural industrialists of today. Paradoxically, such pastoral splendour has also been the stage for savage blood-letting and the scene for king making and king-breaking. The power of the Barons was smashed at Evesham in 1265. **Tewkesbury** saw the Lancastrian claim defeated by the Yorkist Edward IV in 1471 and nearly two centuries later, Cromwell's greatest victory over the Royalists was at Worcester in 1651. Such viscious yet decisive battles, seem strangely at odds amongst such a gentle landscape where rivers meander through a countryside of quiet moderation and simple continuity; violence appears ill-suited to rolling hills and broad blossom strewn plains, lacking the bleak heathland or craggy peaks normally associated with such savageries.

The venerable Cathedral City of **Worcester** is capital to the region and reflects much of the contrasts to be found within the region as a whole with historical associations, architectural contrast and industrial, as opposed to agricultural wealth; yet even its industry has a bucolic air to it, for the black smoke and noisome forges of the industrial revolution have little place in the manufacture of gloves, Royal Worcester porcelain, or that secret blend of 'brown vinegar, walnut ketchup, anchovey essence, soy sauce, cayenne, and shallot's' known world-wide as Worcestershire sauce.

I am extremely fond of the city for it has much of interest and has always been a welcoming and friendly face, but it has to be said that the twentieth century has not treated it kindly. William Cobbett (1763-1835) described Worcester as 'One of the cleanest and handsomest towns I ever saw, indeed I do not recollect to have seen any one equal to it'. Sadly his description no longer tallies; ring-roads, multi-story car parks, power stations and other civic developments have changed forever what was once 'the noblest Georgian townscape in the Midlands'. Nevertheless, there remains much that is good and visitors will find their time amply repaid.

The Cathedral of Christ and the Blessed Virgin Mary contains much of interest, particularly if you have a sharp eye. The craftsmen of old were noted not only for their skills but often for their sense of humour, notably when it came to decoration: the 14th century choir stalls have a fine set of misericords (a rather grand name for a hinged support) and these represent a perfect riot of carver's fantasies - biblical characters, mythical beasts, scenes from both court and everyday life and even a wolf saying grace before devouring his victim! Memorials to the famous and the not-so-famous are scattered throughout but the real glory of the building, like so many of its kind, is in the construction and harmony of the interior which was skillfully overhauled in the last century by the famous Victorian architect, Sir George Gilbert Scott. Scott was responsible for many such restorations and was something of a workaholic, indeed he was so busy that he once telegraphed his London office from Manchester, with the perplexed request 'Why am I here?'

The Cathedral stands on a rise overlooking the River Severn and the Worcestershire County Cricket Ground, where traditionally, touring Test teams play their first county matches. Ornamental gardens cluster around the Watergate at the bottom of the rise where a ferry once ran when the city was walled and a tablet onthe gate records the impressive heights gained by the river during floods.

It is a splendidly English backdrop, ideally suited to our summer game but in 1651 the area now dedicated to peaceful recreation would have seen the Royalist forces stumbling in retreat before Cromwell's invincible Model Army. The clash of steel and thunder of guns rang out where leather meets willow today. Relics, displays and mementoes of the Battle Worcester and other aspects of the Civil War are to be found in the Commandery, a fine 15th-century timber-framed building built on the site of an earlier hospital founded by St Wulfstan, and in the baroque 18th century Guildhall with its sumptious assembly rooms. The City Museum and Art Gallery attracts many people and apart from much of general local interest contains the Regimental Museum of the Worcestershire Regiment, who rejoiced in the stomach-turning nickname of the 'Vein-Openers'! Their heroism in battle earned them the approbation of Wellington who called them ;'the best regiment in his army', while the city's loyalty to the Crown was recognised by Charles II, who gave it the motto 'May the faithful city flourish'. Music is an important part of Worcester life and every third year it plays host to the world's oldest musical celebration, the Three Choirs Festival, which was started in 1717. The other cathedral cities involved are Hereford and Gloucester.

There is a great deal to see and do in Worcester not least Spetchley Park which is an early 19th century museum with a deer park and splendid formal gardens that are open to the public. Greyfriars, a splendid half-timbered building (Tudor with later addition) has been fully restored under the aegis of the National Trust and has a delightful walled garden. The five hundred year old Tudor House Museum is close by and has fascinating displays of social history while in Severn Street, the Dyson Perrins Museum contains examples of Royal Worcester porcelain dating back to 1751 and includes the dinner service made for the Prince and Princess of Wales.

The River Avon almost entirely encircles **Evesham**, a town which owes its beginnings to a vision of the Madonna seen by a local swine-herd called Eoves. Egwin, Bishop of Worcester, established a monastery on the site in 704 and became its first abbot. The Abbey rapidly became an important place of pilgrimage and a town grew round the site. The original shrine of Eoves'vision increased in importance with the canonisation of Egwin and then, 560 years after the Abbey's foundation came the battle which would lead to a third shrine within its precincts. The Barons, led by Simon de Montfort, fell out with Henry III over the interpretation of the Magna Carta and a short but bloody war resulted. The Barons held Henry captive after defeating him in battle but had failed to hold on to his son, who later became Edward I.

The Battle of Evesham, which took place on the 4th August 1265, resulted in a crushing defeat for the Barons and was an astonishing feat of arms by the young prince who had left Worcester on the morning of August 2nd, marched to Kenilworth and captured it, then turned to the south to approach Evesham on the morning of the 4th - sixty miles in forty-eight hours, not forgetting the hand-to-hand combat on the way! De Montfort'sbody was dismembered but the trunk was buried before the High Altar of the Abbey where it soon became the shrine of a man the common people considered a folk-hero, and who is remembered today as the 'Father of Parliaments'. The Abbey grew evermore wealthy and two churches were built outside the monastic grounds to cater for the townsfolk and the pilgrims respectively, and these churches, dedicated to St Lawrence and to All Saints, still remain. The Abbey was pulled down during the Dissolution and the principal remains include the magnificent Perpendicular bell-tower, built by the last rightful abbot, Clement Lichfield who is also remembered in both churches.

The Almonry Museum chronicles much of Evesham's history and, although the town is a busy marketing and light industrial centre, its fascinating history is reflected in the ancient buildings and streets. It is also very much a town of, rather than by, the river since the Severn, has acted as a means of both defence and transport in times past and recreation today.

The Vale of Evesham was described by the American writer Henry James, as 'the dark, rich, hedgy flats of Worcestershire'. Since he wrote those world in 1875, the majority of the hedgs have long gone in the pursuit of intensive cultivation of fruit and vegetables. All manner of varieties are grown in the fertile tilth including such exotics as asparagus and peppers, but it is the fruit that gives the area its greatest glory - albeit for only a short time. Generally around late March and early May, depending on the climate, the area becomes almost magical with blossom from cherries, apples, pears and plums. There are well marked Spring Blossom Trails that can be followed by car, bike or on foot and it is one of the most wonderful sights that the English countryside has to offer. It is nothing less than a total transformation and there are many who come back year after year to view the splendour. It is an interesting fact that although local farmers had appreciated the fertility of the vale's soil for centuries, it was left to a foreigner to reveal its true potential. Francesco Bernardi was a Genoese envoy in the 17th century who settled in the Vale after a dispute with his country. He spent the enormous sum of thirty thousand pounds to begin, in effect, the local industry of market gardening.

Pershore is the second town of the Vale and was once the 'third town' of the county after Worcester and Droitwich. A handsome town with a predominance of seemingly Georgian architecture (many are facades built onto older buildings) it lies to the north of Bredon Hill amongst water meadows beside the Avon's meanderings. It too has an Abbey although considerably more survives than that of neighbouring Evesham. Pershore Abbey is still a magnificent building although much reduced in size, it has a splendid pinnacled tower supported on high Norman arches and a wonderful vaulted roof to the choir with much fine carving. The original religious settlement dates back as far as 689 but depradations from Danish pirates and disbelieving Saxons meant that little of import was established until the Benedictines founded a monastery dedicated to King Alfred's grand-daughter, St Eadburgh. Over the centuries the Abbey grew, surviving set-backs like the fire in 1288 which led to the rebuilding of the present tower, until the Dissolution of the Monasteries when thefaithful citizens of Pershore bought the monastic part of the buildings for their own use at a cost of four hundred pounds. Pershore's prosperity, like Evesham, is strongly linked to the surrounding fertile lanmd and to the River Avon which for many years enabled agricultural produce to be sent downstream to Bristol, including the famous Pershore Plums.

The Lower and Upper Avon Navigation Trusts have done tremendous work in restoring the numerous locks and weirs dating back to the 17th century that enable the river to be fully navigable. The advent of the railways meant that many of these riverine structures fell into disrepair and the work done by the Trusts has been extensive and of benefit to all. I recommend a boat trip to appreciate not only the beauty of this unique part of England but also to see and appreciate the work that has been and is being done.

To the south-west lies another small town of considerable appeal whose fortunes have also been linked to a river: **Upton upon Severn.** The Severn is stronger and more direct than the meandering Avon and for many years Upton possessed the only bridge across the river between Gloucester and Worcester and was such an important meeting place for river craft that what became known as the 'Bridge of Parliament' was held there. Obviously the bridge was of major tactical importance during the Civil War and the Royalists, based at Worcester, blew out two of the spans to prevent an outflanking movement - but in vain. Due to the negligence of a sentry, a small party of Roundheads crept across the plank that had been left across the gap and barricaded themselves in the church, resisting all efforts to displace them until relieved by their own cavalry which had crossed at an unguarded ford. Upton fell to the Parliamentarians and the church was partially destroyed. There is a romanitc sequel to this brief but savage skirmish; that evening Cromwell himself arrived to congratulate his men and saw, at an upstairs window, a beautiful girl in obvious distress. He asked her name and was told it was a Miss Morris whereupon he pardoned her brother whom he had just condemned to be shot. It is nice to know that Old Ironsides had the human touch.

Upton-upon-Severn is a charming little town where such a story seems eminently believable. The medieval church tower survives, crowned with a copper covered cupola and is now used as an heritage centre, whilst in the churchyard can be found the well known epitaph:

'Beneath this stone, in hope of Zion,
Doth lie the landlord of the Lion,
his son keeps on the business still,
Resigned unto the heavenly will.

Apt lines for a town that has a greater number of pubs per head of resident population than most - probably as a result of the old river traffic. Incidentally **The White Lion Hotel** is still thriving and is a delightful place to stay. All the pubs do a roaring trade during the many Summer events that take place here, such as The Steam Rally, The Water Festival, and The Jazz and Folk Festivals.

Worcestershire's greatest natural glories are to be found to the west of the Severn. **The Malverns** are perhaps the originators of that well-known phrase 'as old as the hills' for this ridge of pre-Cambrian rock is more than 500 million years old. The name means 'the bare hills' and they rise gently from fertile soils and woodlands to stand guardians against the prevailing winds.Although of no great height (the highest point is only 1394 feet) their appearance is impressive in contrast to the lowlands from which they spring, and the infinite permutations of light and shade sweeping over their bracken-strewn slopes and barren summits have inspired musicians, poets and artists over the centuries. Walking the beautiful hills is one of the great pleasures of staying in The Malverns. The name is not only applied to the hills but to the straggle of six distinct settlements often referred to collectively as Malvern. These are **Little Malvern**, **Malvern Wells, Malvern Link, Great Malvern, North Malvern** and **West Malvern**.

Little Malvern is the smallest and southernmost of the Malverns nestling cosily in the lee of steeper slopes. The church of St Giles is all that remains of a larger priory church and was treated roughly by the Parliamentarians during th Civil War who removed the misericords and damaged some of the beautiful 15th century glass. They also left a sword behind in the graveyard which is now kept in a glass case. Next to the church is **Little Malvern Court**, parts of which date back to the 12th century and which was the refectory of Prior's Hall of the original monastic foundaion. Long a family home, it contains a priest-hole, a magnificent 14th century roof and a number of treasures including a travelling trunk and silk quilt belonging to Catherine of Aragon.

The shifting play of light and shadow on the ancient hills, sometimes dramatic, more often subtle and complex is nowhere better artistically represented than in the wonderful music of Sir Edward Elgar. It seems only right that this man of Worcestershire whose genius was acknowledged worldwide, but who remained a countryman at heart, should be buried, together with his wife and daughter, in the quiet peace of the Malverns at St Wulfstan's Roman Catholic Church.

The strict contemplative life of a monastic order would seem ideally suited to this region and Malvern Priory Church is the sole, but impressive remnant of a large priory which dates back to 1088. Unfortunately the monastic order was not always strict or contemplative for, in 1282, the prior was accused of adultery with twenty two women! Although the conventual buildings (the living quarters) were nearly all pulled down in the Dissolution, the church was retained by the payment of twenty pounds (in two instalments) - a wonderful bargain for a building which externally is a fine example of Perpendicular architecture with a light and airy interior which includes a six-bay Norman nave of the early 1100's. The 15th century stained glass is wonderfully complimented by some beautiful tiles of the same period, together with a fine set of misericords. Once again the humour of the old craftsmen has been given full sway, for example, there are three mice hanging a cat and a drunkard being beaten by his wife, to name but two. The Malvern Museum is housed in the other surviving part of the prior, the Abbey Gateway.

Great Malvern surrounds the church and is essentially 18th and early 19th century in character and is a product of the period's preoccupation with spa waters. There are distinct parallels with life today; our preoccupation with health, diet, fitness and beauty has led to the establishment of fashionable 'health farms' while the Georgian and Victorians had their spas and hydros.

Perhaps the only difference being the emphasis our ancestors placed on ailments affecting digestion - hardly surprising when one considers the amount they ate! Four meals a day, breakfast, lunch, dinner and supper were the norm, even for the lower middle classes and a menu from a local hotel, now defunct, offers the following delights:

Caviare
Soups: Mulligatawny or Julienne
Fish: Brill or Stewed Eels
Entrees: Salmi of Wild Duck or Chicken Cream
Roast: Sirloin of Beef or Haunch of Mutton
Sweets: Orange Fritters, Benedictine Souffle or Ices
Savouries: Angel on Horseback or Cheese Straws

All this was accompanied by copious quantities of the appropriate wines and liquers and eaten in tight restricting clothing; well-laced whalebone corsets being de riguer for the women and the vainer men. Consequently, anyone offering relief from such embarassing disorders as 'Constipation, Flatulence, Diarrhoea and Indigestion or similar ailments arising from Impure Blood or Disordered Stomach' was undoubtedly on to a winner.

The first entrepreneur to exploit the area's water was the founder of the Royal Worcester Porcelain Works, one Doctor John Wall. He had, however, one slight problem in extolling the curative properties of the liquid: it tasted pleasantly fresh and sparkling - quite the reverse of the generally foul-flavoured, mineral rich fluids experienced at other fashionable resorts. Doctor Wall was evidently made of sterner stuff and had a marketing ability that would have made him a target for all major executive recruitment agencies were he still alive today.

'Malvern Water, said Doctor Wall,
is famed for containing nothing at all.'

This was the essence of the campaign and it worked! His premise was quite simply, that since the water was so pure, the cure was effected faster ' as it could pass more rapidly through the vessels of the body.'

The town quickly became fashionable and hotels, pump rooms and lodging houses were built. The Victorians added a further refinement by introducing a form of 'water-cure' that was horrific by anyone's standards. This consisted of being wrapped tightly in cold wet sheets for hours on end, having hundreds of gallons of icy water dropped on you from a great height, cold baths, long walks, a strict diet and naturally nothing but water to drink. Recreation was strictly controlled with even reading being banned as 'too demanding'. It was a wonder that anyone survived; nevertheless, the resort attracted the likes of the Royal Family, Gladstone, Florence Nightingale, Macaulay, Carlyle, Wordsworth and Charles Darwin.

The waters have not been forgotten and are bottled and exported all over the world by Cadbury Schweppes, while the awful Victorian water treatments have been replaced by the delights of a 'water activity centre'. The Splash an indoor complex complete with water-slide, wave-making machine and 'beach'. Above all Malvern are the hills, and to walk their eight mile length and savour the amazing views, is to see England at its very best. The Malvern Hills Conservators were set up by Parliament in 1884 to protect the common land from commercial exploitation and they have done their job wonderfully well. There are more than twenty six miles of footpaths, together with a number of discreet car-parks so that the hills can be enjoyed by all.

To the north, at the end of a lane in meadows bordering the Severn, lies the village of **Grimley**. Apart from some gravel pits and a number of farms, this would seem a quiet prosaic country community. However, in the churchyard lies Sir Samuel Baker (1821-93) an African explorer of renown, discovrer of Lake Nyanza and the Murchison Falls, big-game hunter and colonial administrator, While at neighbouring **Thorngrove** lived an even more exotic character, in the shape of Lucien Bonaparte. He was the younger brother of Napoleon and offended the Emperor by marrying the ex-wife of a planter. Napoleon offered Lucien the Kingdoms of Spain and Naples if he would renounce the woman, but Lucein refused and, in trying to escape to America, was captured by the British. He evntually settled with his wife in this remote corner of Worcestershire, where they happily whiled away the remaining war years by writing turgid epic poetry together.

At **Wichenford** the National Trust has restored a marvellous 17th century half-timbered Dovecote and the nearby **Wichenford Court** is said to play host to two female ghosts, both members of the Washbourne family. One stalks around holding a bloody dagger aloft (she was reputed to have murdered a French prince) and the other plays a harp whilst sitting in a silver boat drawn by white swans. Makes a change from grey ladies and headless horsemen!

The landscape of Worcestershire reveals many gems whether man-made or natural. The glorious blossom, the ancient buildings and the views from the hills - even in the most mundane little corner there is always something to interest and delight.

SHROPSHIRE

Shropshire is such a wonderful mixture of countryside, architecture, agriculture and industry. It has wonderful places to visit, history which is fascinating and at times awe inspiring, stately homes, gardens and all manner of other attractions. I cannot tell you as much about the county as I would wish but I hope it is enough to encourage you to come here.

The temptation when you come to South Shropshire, is to seek out immediately places like Ludlow, a place of historical romance and one of the most beautiful country towns in England. This is what I have always done in the past but this time I was invited to stay with friends in **Telford**, a new town that is light years ahead. My friends had moved there with reluctance when a new posting for the husband made it imperative. To their surprise they have found living in this new town a good experience. Some of their enthusiasm rubbed off on me and I, too, was agreeably surprised at the great effort that has been made to make it a 'green and pleasant land'. For example, over a million trees, plants and shrubs have been planted throughout the town. The park is a mixture of landscaped and natural scenery complete with a lake at the side of which is an amphitheatre and a sports arena. The town offers all sorts of facilities and seems to me to be full of young and enthusiastic people who enjoy what it has to offer.

One of the reasons that made my friends happy with Telford was the unique range of top class sporting facilities, with everything from golf and tennis to skiing provided in a range of superb modern sports centres. In addition to the National Sports Centre at nearby **Lilleshall**, Telford has six fully equipped sports and leisure centres of its own. The Telford Ice Rink is one of the finest in the Midlands, and it is the home of one of the country's top ice hockey teams.

Newport is only eight miles to the north-east of Telford and is as different as chalk from cheese. Here I found a pleasant, unspoilt market town, centred around the broad, elegant High Street, a street just asking to be explored. The town has a large and graceful church, **St Nicholas**, standing on an island site in the middle of the High Street. There is a font from the year of the Restoration, a coffin lid carved quite wonderfully 700 years ago, and a list of rectors going back to the Normans.

The most famous son of Newport was the wise and extraordinary man, Sir Oliver Lodge, who experimented in wireless and sent wireless telegrams long before Marconi. He interested himself in all sorts of things from the mysterious problems of telepathy to the conquering of fog.

Just 3 miles north of Junction 3 on the M54 is **Weston Park** on the A5 at **Weston-under-Lizard**. This classic 17th century stately house is the historic home of the Earls of Bradford. The interior has been superbly restored and holds one of the country's finest collection of paintings, with originals by many of the great masters. There are fine tapestries from the famous 18th-century makers Gobelin and Aubusson, letters from Disraeli which provide a fascinating commentary on Victorian history. It is quite wonderful. It is used all the year round for Conferences, Banquets, Product Launches, Wedding Receptions and for very special 'Dine and Stay' gourmet evenings which are open to the public. These are truly wonderful occasions and will long stay in your memory. If you are interested ring 01952 76207 and askabout dates.

From Weston Park it is only a short distance to **Boscobel House**, in which Charles Stuart sought refuge after his defeat at Worcester. As I drove along the quiet road I wondered if the King had wished he was just a simple Shropshire man, secure in his everyday life rather than a hunted royal. The Giffords of Chillington owned Boscobel and as staunch catholics they had honeycombed the house with hiding places for priests. If you see the house today many of them still exist. One will be pointed out to you as the kings hiding place, reached by a short flight of stairs leading to the cheese room.

William Penderel tenanted Boscobel and he was one of the six brothers who were loyal supporters of the Stuart cause. However it was not Boscobel which hid Charles Stuart but **Whiteladies**, where Humphrey Penderel lived. Here, he left all his retinue but Lord Richard Wilmot and became a countryman wearing a coarse shirt, darned stockings, a leather doublet with pewter buttons, a ragged coat and breeches, a battered old hat and rough boots. He darkened his face and his hands with soot and accompanied only by Richard, he crept out, avoiding troops that he knew to be in the neighbourhood. He was attempting to make his way over the Severn into Wales, stopping at Madeley, the home of Francis Woolf. The journey was fraught with danger and at one stage he and Richard were chased by a miller and a number of soldiers. The journey became so perilous that the only thing they could do was to return to Boscobel. The only way to do this was to swim across the river but Richard could not swim. Charles helped him over but by this time the King's feet were so blistered and torn and his boots so full of grit, that he felt he could not go on. It was Richard who kept him going and at last they reached the safety of Boscobel. Here Charles's feet were doctored, he was given a change of stockings and his boots were dried. Outside the house was a great oak and into this Charles climbed. He slept during the day but woke to the sound of Cromwell's men searching for him in the wood. There was a price of a thousand pounds on the king's head: something all the Penderels knew about but such was their loyalty that not one of them even thought for a moment about betraying him. They would have died in his cause if need be. For two or more days and nights Charles stayed at Boscobel, sleeping in the hole beneath the trapdoor in the cheese room until finally it was thought safe enough for them to set out on the long journey which would eventually end in France.

You must visit **Tong**. It is only a small village but the magnificent 14th-century church of **St Bartholomew** would not be out of place in a city. It is frequently referred to as 'the Cathedral of the West Midlands'. Just north of the village, off the A41, you can see a peculiar pyramid-shaped building set back a few hundred yards from the road. It is called the **Egyptian Aviary**, and it is a bizarre hen-house designed by a celebrated eccentric, George Durant in the early 19th century.

The whole of the **Ironbridge Gorge** is one big real life museum that tells you every chapter of the fascinating story, on the spot, where it happened. There is no place anywhere like it in the world. Make sure you allow yourself plenty of time to enjoyit.

The Severn flows through this deep gorge and the houses cling to the hillsides looking as though a puff of wind would blow them into the swirling river, but they have been there for hundreds of years and are as much a part of this incredible place as the Museums. The chief distinction is, of course, the bridge, believed to be the first iron bridge ever built. It was built by Abraham Darby of Coalbrookdale in 1777. It is 196ft long with one span of 100 feet and two smaller ones, the total weight of iron being 380tons. So much for the statistics, worth knowing but fading almost into insignificance alongside the many things to be seen.

Over 250 years ago the Severn Gorge witnessed momentous events which culminated in the Industrial Revolution and it was the fortunate combination of coal, iron, water power and transport, all concentrated in this Shropshire Valley, which sparked off the series of events which affected all of us. Of the many places to visit perhaps **Rosehill House**, one of the elegant mansions where the Darby family lived in the 18th and 19th centuries, is probably my favourite. It is sheer pleasure to wander through the beautifully restored rooms with original period furniture. The house gives you an understanding of how a wealthy ironmaster would have lived.

In total contrast is **Carpenter's Row**, a terrace of workers' houses built by the company in the late 18th century. There is nothing grand about them. Four cottages have been restored and furnished to recreate a home from different periods between 1780 and 1930. Carpenters' Row is open to small groups by special appointment only. You will find many more places listed under 'Attractions' at the back of the book.

After the strenuous activity in Ironbridge it might be as well to take a look at **Broseley** across the Gorge. This was the great urban centre of the Coalbrookdale coalfield during the Industrial revolution. The ironmaster, John Wilkinson, built his furnace here, and in its heyday it was a rival to Coalbrookdale itself as a centre of the iron industry. John Wilkinson was the man who had the idea of building iron barges. He persevered in spite of being laughed at and he had the last laugh when, on one summer's day in 1787, the first iron barge was launched on the Severn. From this the idea of an iron ship was born and Broseley was its birthplace. John Wilkinson was so dedicated to the use of iron that he asked to be buried in an iron coffin!

Much Wenlock cries out to be visited; it is a lovely old market town full of history. Arthur Mee describes it as somewhere that' sleeps in the hills, dreaming of all that has been, stirring with the memory of warrior kings and the ancient strife of the Border valleys, and inspired by the natural spectacle of Wenlock Edge.

The steep wooded escarpment known as **Wenlock Edge**, runs for 16 miles and provides as series of spectacular viewpoints across to the Stretton Hills and the Long Mynd. It is essentially a geological phenomenon; the rock, Wenlock limestone, was formed more than 400 million years ago in a tropical sea. It developed as a barrier reef built up largely from the skeletons and shells of sea creatures.

Three miles north east of Much Wenlock, on the B4378 you will come to **Buildwas Abbey**. Standing in a beautiful situation on the banks of the River Severn quite close to Ironbridge Gorge, it is a worthwhile place to visit. It must be one of the country's finest ruined abbeys. Dating back over 800years to Norman times it is surprising that so much is still standing today. The imposing walls of the abbey church with 14 wonderful Norman arches remain. It was probably completed in 1200 with Norman and Early English architecture remaining virtually unaltered since the Dissolution in the 1530s.

When you are in Telford, Wellington, Ironbridge or Much Wenlock you should make the effort to reach the summit of **The Wrekin**. It is a curiosity and one of the most distinctive landmarks in the Shropshire Hills. The Wrekin is 1335 foot high, rising sharply from the flatness of the surrounding countryside. It is the site of the ancient Iron Age hill fort and it has been the focus of local legends and superstitions for hundred of years. My favourite is that the hill was formed by a giant who had quarrelled with the people of Shrewsbury. The giant was determined to punish the townsfolk and set off with a huge spadeful of earth to bury the whole town. On the way he met a cobbler by the roadside carrying a sack of shoes to be mended. The cobbler thought the giant was up to no good so he persuaded him that Shrewsbury was too far to walk, showing him the whole bag of shoes he had worn out with walking the enormous distance from the town. The giant decided the cobbler was right: he ditched the spadeful of earth on the spot - and the Wrekin was formed.

Bridgnorth is two towns in one perched dramatically on a steep cliff above the River Severn. It is naturally beautiful and quite unlike anywhere else inEngland. This picturesque market town has High Town and Low town linked by the famous Cliff Railway, which climbs up a hair raising incline. The only other I know like it is the Cliff railway which joins Lynton and Lynmouth in Devon. There is something reminiscent of old italian towns as you climb the Stoneway steps cut sheer through the rocks, or wander about the maze of old half-timbered buildings and elegant 18th-century houses. one of these is the curious 17th century Town Hall. this timber framed building is built on an arched sandstone base partly across the roadway in the middle of the high street. AZt the east end of the street is The North gate, the only remaining one of five gates in the town's fortifications. there is a Museum over the arches.

Bridgnorth castle is famous for its leaning tower which is 17 degrees out of straight. the leaning Tower of Pisa is only 5 degrees! It has survived safely for 850 years. the castle grounds are now a public park where you can admire a splendid view over the river and Low town. Take time out to discover this delightful town and it many interesting buildings which include the **Church of St Mary Magdalene, Bishop Percy's House** and the **Bridgnorth Costume and Childhood Museum**.

Ludlow beckoned and I happily answered the call. Here is a town that has few equals. Its river rings it like a moat and to walkabout its castle and streets is quite thrilling. We are lucky to claim it as part of England because it is almost on the Welsh border. It became a fortress from which Wales's unruly and mutinous tribes were eventually knocked into submission. **The Church of St Laurence** soars upwards and vies with the castle for supremacy. It is an outstandingly beautiful Perpendicular church with an earlier foundation, twice restored in the 19th century. The church is open in summer from 9-5pm and in winter until 4pm.

The most exciting culinary event in Ludlow was the recent arrival of the celebrated international chef, Shaun Hill who opened a superb restaurant, **The Merchants House** in Lower Curve Street. This black and white timbered building invites you to enter its modest front door and inside you will find two rooms, with covers for only twenty people. It is the epitome of charm and stylish simplicity. Shaun produces food to dream about and together with his delightful wife Anja, they have quickly created an atmosphere that will make anyone remember and savour with sheer pleasure a meal here.

There are some beautiful places to visit between Ludlow and Shrewsbury. one of my favourite haunts is **Stokesay Castle**. It stands just off the Ludlow-Shrewsbury road half a mile south of Craven Arms. There is a car park up the signposted lane and past the church, only a few yards from this romantic ruin. The marvellous state of preservation does give a very clear idea of the conditions in which well-to-do medieval families lived. It is one of the earliest fortified manor houses in England with the oldest parts dating from the 12th century and the Great Hall from the 13th. It is an extraordinary structure with massive stone towers topped with a timber-framed house.

The A49 going towards Shrewsbury will take you to **Little Stretton** which must be one of the most beautiful villages in Shropshire complete with a little thatched church and its big neighbour, **Church Stretton** is somewhere else you should visit. Houses dot the valley and climb the slopes. To the west is the great moorland ridge of the Longmynd rising nearly 1700feet, with the beautiful Cardingmill Valley below and the prehistoric Portway running along the top. To the east are the rugged Caradoc Hills with Watling Street at the foot, and the banks and trenches of Caer Caradoc's stronghold 1500ft up.

The strange cross-shaped church goes back 850 years and in the old churchyard is a stone of 1814 to Ann Cook which says:

'On a Thursday she was born
On a Thursday made a bride
On a Thursday broke a leg
And on a Thursday died.'

Thursday was not a lucky day for Ann Cook!

Bishops Castle to the west and surrounded by the beauty of the South Shropshire hills, was plundered by Royalists during the Civil War in 1645 but somehow missed out the inn, **The Boars Head Hotel**, in which Roundheads were slaking their thirst.

Here you are on the edge of the Clun Forest, a delightful place and if you have ever read A.E. Housman's 'A Shropshire Lad' you will know his description of the Cluns, he thought it a quiet area:

'Clunton and Clunbury
Clungunford and Clun.
Are the quietest places
Under the sun.'

And so to **Shrewsbury** where once again A.E. Housman says it all:

'High the vanes of Shrewsbury gleam
Islanded in Severn stream;
The bridges from the steepled crest
Cross the water, east to west.'

It is almost an island with its castle standing in a narrow strait and more than half-a dozen bridges crossing to and fro. It has old black and white houses, half-timbered of the Elizabethan era, fine brick buildings of the 17th century and wonderfully elegant Queen Anne and Georgian town houses, narrow streets and alleyways with strange names - Grope Lane, Shoplatch, Dogpole, Wyle Cop and Pride Hill. Everywhere oozes history and clamours for your attention.

There are people who may tell you that North Shropshire is dull. That is absolutely untrue; it may be flatter than the south but within it you will discover it has miles of gentle green countryside, reed fringed meres, the excitement of the Shropshire Union and Llangollen Canals, red sandstone hills, a wealth of small villages and five historic market towns, **Oswestry, Ellesmere, Whitchurch, Wem** and **Market Drayton**.

Oswestry is on the Shropshire side of the border with Wales and has very strong ties with the Principality. Apart from being a charming market town to explore it is equally splendid to wander the hilly, sparsely populated border country. This is a town that has much to offer ; you could well stay here for a month and still not have seen everything. Market days are full of life with one of the busiest street markets in the county. Over 120 traders set up their stalls with every imaginable kind of product and produce. The Market days are all the year round on Wednesdays with an additional market on Saturdays in the summer. There is ample car parking near the town centre.

Canals are very important to the way of life in this part of Shropshire and provide so much more than just water transport. Following the canal or 'the cut' is a wonderful way of exploring North Shropshire whether you have a boat or not. The towpath is a splendid, traffic free footpath on the level for miles albeit in some places it is distinctly rough going and very muddy. You are rewarded though by the wildlife that abounds on the water, in the bankside vegetation, and along the hedges. You can learn so much from the canal which tells its own story of our industrial and architectural heritage.

At **Whittington** you will meet with the **Llangollen Canal**, which wends its way across the country right up into Cheshire where it joins the main Shropshire Union Canal close to **Nantwich**. Whittington is a very large village in the centre of which is Whittington Castle. All that you can see today of this important border castle is the magnificent gatehouse and the moat. It is a delightful place to visit, with a childrens play area, ducks to feed and a tearoom in which to relax. The village is reputed to have been the birthplace of Dick Whittington, the famous Lord Mayor of London and cat owner!

From here I went north a little until I came to **Chirk** where it is the only way to cruise from England into Wales. This is quite a place with a lot of history, right on the border of Shropshire and Clwyd; it has withstood the slings and arrows of outrageous fortune. **Chirk Castle** which belongs to the National Trust, is a place you must visit and you should make sure you get to **Llanrhaedr Falls**, another of the seven wonders of Wales. They are stunning.

The Shropshire Union Canal, a popular waterway for pleasure craft, has played a great part in the history of **Ellesmere**, and the **Old Wharf** with its warehouse and crane is a reminder of a prosperous period for the development of the town when it was a centre of plans for a link to the River Mersey (at what was to become Ellesmere Port).

This was nearly 200 years ago when some of Britain's leading industrialists first met to discuss the project. Thomas Telford included. Circumstances caused them to build instead a most attractive canal from Llangollen's Horseshoe Falls to Hurleston junction near Nantwich.

Wem is a town that still manages to preserve more of the old market town atmosphere than most others. It is delightful and dates back before the Conquest in 1066. In fact it is the only town mentioned in the Domesday Book which can race descendants from before and after the Conquest. The fire of 1677 destroyed many of the ancient houses and it suffered for its staunch support of the Protestant Cause in the Civil War, being th first town to declare for Parliament and hence became the prime target for the Royalists of Whitchurch and Shrewsbury who laid siege to it for a long period without success. The church dates from the 14th century and has an uncommon doorway of that period, and a Perpendicular style upper tower.

Whitchurch is the most ancient of the market towns dating from 60AD when it was founded as a garrison for the Roman legions marching between Chester and Wroxeter. Many Roman artefacts and buildings have been found in the town centre notably in 1967 and 1977, and Pepper Street, High Street and Bluegates occupy the same situation as the Roman streets.

Market in name and market by nature, ideally you should come to **Market Drayton** on a Wednesday and join in the bustling bargain hunting tradition that has been going on for over 750years. Since the Norman Conquest, this seemingly sleepy and isolated town has been the scene of revolt, riot, murder, adventure and trade; its links have extended worldwide. Clive of India was born here and he will never be forgotten. You will find much to enjoyincluding the celebrated product of local bakers' shops - Gingerbread Men, which come in a range of novelty shapes and packages, all faithful to recipes over 200 years old. A true taste of history.

You must find time to travel 6 miles down the A53 to **Hodnet** where the **Hodnet Hall Gardens** covering 60 acres, are unrivalled for their beauty and natural valley setting. The magnificent trees, lawns and lakes provide a background to an ever changing seasonal colour and interest. Between April and July the rhododendrons are fantastic. The gardens are famous nationally and have been the subject of several TV and radio programmes. This was a visit to remember among the very happy recollections I have of this county.

STAFFORDSHIRE

With limited time to spend in Staffordshire I decided to devote my time to a few places which interest me and in so doing hopefully stir in the reader a desire to see more of this most versatile and handsome county.

Thomas Telford's sixty-six mile canal was built to link the industrial city of Birmingham with the great port of Livrpool and was originally named the Birmingham and Liverpool Junction Canal. Looking at the peaceful waters running straight through the lovely countryside, it is difficult to see them as the 17th and 18th century equivalent of our motorways - yet that is what they were. Quiet tree-fringed stretches where the tranquillity is only disturbed by the quacking of the mallard and the puttering of an occasional leisure boat, were once bustling highways where entire generations of families lived their lives afloat. Goods of every concievable kind were carried by boat, together with passengers and even livestock, and a community such as **Gnosall**, situated beside both canal and major road, would have been important as a distribution centre. The popularity of the canals can be understood when one realises the appalling state of the majority of roads which were virtually impassable except by packhorse. Almost overnight the waterways enabled vast quantities of raw materials and finished goods to be moved quickly and economically - thus contributing enormously to the prosperity of the nation as a whole.

It is easy to forget the logistics involved in such a venture, as our own century place an enormous reliance on powerful and sophisticated machinery to construct the roads and motorways - today's equivalent of the canal systems. Labour in enormous numbers had to be accommodated, fed and paid during the building of such projects; to drive the great waterways through the heart of our country relied chiefly upon the speed and expertise of men aided with little more than picks, shovels and wheelbarrows.The problems were not over once the canal was built, for there was the continuous problem of maintenance - reinforcing banks, clearing weed, surfacing towpaths, breaking ice in winter and all the more skilled work involving locks, their gates and associated machinery.

Failure in any of these departments could lead to blockage of the canal, or worse still, to loss of water, leaving boats and their cargoes stranded for days, even weeks. Gangs ofmen were allocated a length of canal to maintain, and many spent their lives working to keep the waterway running. Close to the aqueduct carrying the 'Shroppy' across the attractive countryside at **Shebdon**, is **The Wharf Inn**, once headquarters for a maintenance gang of 'lengthmen'. These gangs were noted for the prodigious amounts of food and drink they could consume - the Wharf obviously did a good job in these departments and carries on the tradition by catering to today's visitor with the same cheerful generosity.

Shebdon is close to the Shropshire border, a mile or so to the north of the A519 which runs through **Eccleshall**. The beauty of the surrounding undulating and wooded countryside, together with the architecture and charm of this small town make it one of the most attractive communities in Staffordshire. Pronounced 'Eccle-shawl', it has a long history dating back to a Roman settlement and over the centuries became an important strategic, ecclesiastic and market centre. Soldiers, bishops and traders have all gone but their legacy remains in the buildings they left behind. **Eccleshall Castle** was the principal residnce of the Bishops of Lichfield for 600 years. Bishop Muschamp was granted a licence to fortify his house in 1200 and this led to the construction of the castle. Interesting to note that bureaucracy ruled even then, and one wonders whether there is still a department deep in the bowels of Whitehall dealing with requests of this nature. **The Church of the Holy Trinity** has been described as one of the finest 13th-century churches in the country. Restored in 1868, it is a tall, light and lofty building of considerable grace and contains the tombs of five of the Bishops of Lichfield.

Stone is a thriving and good-looking town. Two local stories account for the name; some say it comes from a cairn of stones that marked the graves of two Christian Mercian princes murdered by their pagan father, while others maintain it derives from a mineral-rich local stream that petrifies plant life. Whatever the truth, the area has been inhabited for a long time - as shown by the number of fine stone axe-heads found locally. A market town which did well out of the Canal era (the River Trent and the Trent and Mersey Canal run parallel south of the town), Stone produced two notable figures; Admiral John Jervis, later Earl St Vincent (1735-1823) and the water colourist Peter de Wint (1748-1849). The neat 18th-century Gothic Church of St Michael, with its galleries and box pews contains a memorial to the Admiral who lies with other members of his family in a small palladian-style Mausoleum.

South down the A34 is the county town of **Stafford**, the city constructed on the site of a hermitage built by St Pertelin some 1200 years ago. Commercial development has left the town surprisingly untouched - apart from the jutting intrusion of a few tower blocks. Stafford still wears the bucolic air of a country town, even though it has been an imporant manufacturing centre for centuries; manufacturing internal combustion engines and electrical equipment since the beginning of the present century. Nevertheless its ancient heritage is on proud display for all to admire. Here you have **Stafford Castle** built in 1070, an impressive example of an early Norman fortress. The central building in Stafford is the late Georgian Shire Hall, a most handsome building that fits the part well, while not too far away is a positive triumph of the timber house builders art, **The High House**. Built in 1595 for a wool mnerchant, John Dorrington, it is the largest timber-framed town house in the country. Nor must one forget **Chetwynd House**, a handsome Georgian building that is now the Post Office. Here the ebullient playwright, theatre-manager and MP for Stafford, Richard Brinsley Sheridan, would stay on visits to his constituency.

Due west of Stafford, on the very tip of Cannock Chase, is **Shugborough Estate**, ancestral home of the camera-wielding Earl of Lichfield. A beautiful mansion, dating back to 1693, and set within a magnificent 900 acre estate. Shugborough contains fine collections of 18th-century ceramics, silver, paintings and French furniture. **The Staffordshire County museum** is housed in the old servants quarters and there are splendid recreations of life behind the 'green baize door'. Shugborough Park Farm is a working agricultural museum where rare breeds are kept, horse drawn machinery used and an old mill grinds corn.

Whether you arrive by canal or car, **Cannock Chase** remains the greatest attraction of the region. As its name implies it was once a Royal hunting ground, but Richard I, in need of funds, sold it to the Bishops of Lichfield. In those times it was a much larger area, extending from the River Penk in the west to the Trent in the east, with Stafford to the north and including Wolverhampton and Walsall to the south. Now it is around 26 square miles of forest and heath land that have been declared an 'area of outstanding natural beauty'. Medieval industrial activities meant the loss of much of the native oakwoods while the southern part was given over to coalpits, but these activities have long ceased and the deer and wildlife have returned to their natural habitat. The highest point is at **Castle Ring** with wonderful views over the countryside and the site of an Iron Age hill fort, dating from around 500BC.

Close to the eastern side of Cannock Chase lies the ancient city of **Lichfield** with its unique **Cathedral of St Mary and St Chad**, a magnificent red sandstone structure with three spires, known as 'the Ladies of the Vale'. The Cathedral is considered the Mother-church of the Midlands and is the third building on the site since it was consecrated in 700AD by St Chad. The present structure is a magnificent example of Early-English and Decorated work, a triumph of medieval craftmanship. The surrounds of the cathedral are equally beautiful with attractive houses of the 14th and 15th centuries surrounding the green lawns of **Vicar's Close.**

Uttoxeter is the mecca for Midlands horse racing fans. This cheerful little market town (every Wednesday since 1309) has three different ways of pronouncing its name - 'Uxeter', 'Utcheter' or 'U-tox-eter' - and its name has been spelt in seventy-seven different ways since it was first recorded in the Domesday Book as Wotochesede. The town evidently suffers no neuroses and goes about its quiet business, waking up for market days and race meetings. There is a tendency to think of the **Peak District** as belong exclusively to Derbyshire, but natural physical features have a distressing habit of ignoring man-made boundaries, and there is more than a little truth in the local boast that 'the best parts of Derbyshire are in Staffordshire'. This is fascinating countryside, almost cosy in scale one minute and then possessed of a wild grandeur, the next. North-east of **Oakmoor**, through the hills and dales, lies one of the most beautiful valleys in the region, The Manifold Valley. The village of **Ilam**, standing at the southern end, makes a good starting point for exploring the area, and the old mansion Ilam Hall, is now a Youth hostel. The valley is relatively flat at this point but becomes increasingly deep and narrow as one journeys northwards. The River Manifold has a disconcerting habit of disappearing underground and at Ilam Hall it re-emerges from its subterranean journey from **Darfur Crags**.

Obviously this beautiful area has long been a favourite with those who love what is described in the glossy-brochure trade as 'the great outdoors' even if writers of such hyperbole rarely get nearer to the fresh air than kicking the cat out last thing at night! Over three hundred years ago, two learned gentlemen, close friends and 'Brothers of the Angle' rambled the length and breadth of the glorious river valleys in pursuit of the shy brook trout. Izaak Walton and Charles Cotton could discuss the classical poetry of Homer or the merits of a fishing lure with equal facility and enthusiasm, and had a particular fondness for the river that runs down the border between Staffordshire and Derbyshire, the Dove.

Cotton, who was to contribute a chapter on the art of fly-fishing in Walton's 'Compleat Angler' was a poet and author in his own right who lived at **Beresford Hall** near **Alstonfield**. The Hall was pulled down in the 1800's but the fishing lodge by the river still survives, and the village church still contains the Cotton family pew.

Longnor is a tiny market town in the farthermost corner of north-eastern Staffordshire on the same road the intrepid Greyhound rattled its way across the rutted potholes over the moors. The road may have improved, but Longnor is little altered; good looking 18th-century facades and a square with a small Market Hall dated 1873. Stone lined streets and alleyways with determined little houses of the same material give a sense of dogged continuity.

Wandering westwards one comes across the highest village in England, set close by the high road from Leek to Buxton. The oddly named **Flash** claims the title at 1,158 feet above sea level. A Nepalese would doubtless fall off his mountain laughing, but it is a respectable height for our 'sceptr'd isle' and probably just as cold in winter as the Himalayas.

'The Metropolis of the Moorland' was how one writer described **Leek,** though Doctor Johnson was not so charitable ' An old church but a poor town'. nowadays it is a neat mill town standing in magnificent countryside. Like so many of its kind Leek has a cheerful and generous nature and welcomes visitors; particularly on Wednesdays when the old cobbled market square is thronged with stalls and the air filled with cheerful banter. There are asurprisingly large number of antique shops and many of the mills have their own shops.

The great canal-builder, Brindley, started his working life as a mill-wright and the Brindley Mill in Mill Street, tells the sotry of his life and graphically demonstrates the many facets of this one, important craft. One of his later works was the Caldon Canal which runs with the River Chernet in the valley alongside the hillside of Cheddleton. Cheddleton Flint Mill ground up flints from Kent and Sussex for use in the pottery industry, and the waterwheels and grinding equipment are on display, together with other items associated with the trade, including a restored canal barge. The canal's successor, the railway, is also commemorated at the Cheddleton Railway Centre, with displays, mementoes, engines and other paraphernalia set in and around the attractive Victorian station.

The two different forms of transport were obviously of major importance to the development of the industries of the north-western sector of the county, Newcastle-under-Lyme and Stoke-on-Trent lie side by side, geographically close yet separate in terms of history and character.

Coming from the east, the first is **Stoke-on-Trent**, a combination of the six communities of Tunstall, Burslem, Hanley, Longton, Stoke and Fenton - known the world over as The Potteries. The companies based here, both large and small, have a world-wide market for their products and their heritage dates back many centuries. Wherever fine china-ware is used and appreciated, such as Spode, Copeland, Minton, Coalport, Royal Doulton and Wedgwood are revered and respected.

The Potteries have the flavour of a rural area; a feeling of continuity and a sense of tradition. The same family names crop up time and time again and, even in these difficult times, there is a pride in the past and has made enormous efforts to clean up the detritus of yesteryear and make Stoke an attractive place in which to work and live. Trentham Gardens cover 800 acres of parklands, gardens and lakes with numerous sporting facilities. Festival Park, is an amazing 23 acre complex which includes a sub-tropical aquatic playground with flumes, water slides and rapids.

The architecture is predominantly Victoria red-brick since the city was in a constant state of development, but there are exceptions; the Minton family brought over French artists to decorate their wares and built them ornate Italianate villas - their sense of geography being obviously inferior to their business acumen.

Newcastle-under-Lyme is the oldest of the two cities, dating back to its incorporation as a borough in 1180, at a time when the neighbouring Potteries were hamlets or villages. Although Stoke-on-Trent and Newcastle have grown into each other, they still retain their separate identities; the delicate craft of the Potteries being complemented by the ruder skills of the iron workers and colliers of their older neighbour. Modern Newcastle is an attractive town with much good architecture and is host toKeele University. Markets and a Fair date from medieval times.

Staffordshire is a little-known county of remarkable contrast, interest and beauty that will repay the curious a thousandfold.

WARWICKSHIRE

This other Eden, demi-paradise, This fortress built by Nature for herself....'

These lines from Richard II conjure up images of a rural idyll and doubtless the beautiful countryside around Stratford-upon-Avon did much to inspire Warwickshire's most famous son. More than two centuries later, Shakespeare's affection for his native county was to be echoed in the words of the eminent novelist, Henry James, who described Warwickshire as 'the core and centre of the English world; mid-most England, unmitigated England... the genius of pastoral Britain'. James was an American and his words have done much to encourage his fellow countryman and women to visit this quintessentially English region Although the twentieth century has left its mark with evidence of industrialisation, the construction of motorways and some of the less appealing manifestations of the intensive tourist industry, there is still much of gentle grace and beauty beloved by both men; turn off the coach-laden main roads and one can enjoy pastoral scenery little changed since the Bard's day or, turning away from a modern shopping precinct, one can delight in architectural gems that would have been equally familiar to the great playwright and his contemporaries.

If Warwickshire can be described as the Heartland of England then the Avon must be its principal artery in that its waters have provided the means of irrigation, transport and power. **Stratford-upon-Avon** is without doubt the central tourist attraction of the county - perhaps of the entire country. Shakespeare may be synonymous with Stratford, but the town was of importance long before his birth (reputedly on St George's Day, 23rd April 1564) and had its beginnings as a Roman camp, and a Saxon monastic settlement. The name Stratford simply means 'a ford where the street crosses the river' and a market was first recorded in 1196. King John granted the right to hold a three-day fair in 1214 and in 1553 the town was incorporated as a borough and, regardles of Shakespeareama, Stratford is still an attractive and prosperous market town. the central part of the town which contains its chief attractions is arranged along the north bank of the Avon with three streets running parallel to the river and three at right angles, the names being unchanged since before Shakespeare's time. The predominant style of architecture is Tudor/Jacobean half-timbering, much of it genuine but with more than the occasional false facade; nevertheless the overall effect is pleasing and the town is an attraction in its own right.

Holy Trinity church, lying beside the banks of the Avon, is an excellent place to start exploring the town, for it is a dignified and graceful building that reflects both the early importance and history of the town as well as being the last resting place of England's greatest dramatist. The proportions and spaciousness are almost cathedral-like and the church was granted collegiate status by Henry V in the year of Agincourt (1415) and remained as an important theological centre until the Reformation in the 16th century. Throughout the building there are numerous memorials to many local worthies and associations and the former Lady Chapel is almost entirely given over to the Cloptons who contributed much to the growth and development of Warwickshire and to Stratford-upon-Avon in particular. They, like many of their medieval neighbours, made their fortune from the wool-trade and Sir Hugh Clopton is doubly remembered for having built the multi-arched bridge upstream from Holy Trinity and for being a Lord Mayor of London in 1492.

William Shakespeare died at the age of fifty-two on St George's Day, April 23rd 1616 and is buried, along with his wife Anne and other members of his family, in the chancel, and every year, on the anniversary of his death, the whole area around the tomb is covered with floral tributes from all over the world. We sometimes forget how great a man he was and just how much his works are appreciated throughout the world; he would not be forgotten even if he had been buried in an unmarked grave and perhaps this is best summed up by the epitaph written by his friend and contemporary, Ben Jonson:

'Thou art a monument without a tomb,
And art alive still, while thy book doth live,
And we have wits to read, and praise to give.'

At the age of eighteen Shakespeare married Anne Hathaway and it is believed he earned his living at this time as a schoolmaster although a year or so later after his marriage he left for London. However he was to return to Stratford at regular intervals and, with the prospering of his fortunes, he purchased **New Place** in 1597 and twelve years later settled there permanently with his family. That the house no longer exists is ascribed to the fact that a later owner, the Reverend Francis Gaskell,irritated by the rating assessments and constant pestering by Shakesperean enthusiasts was moved to pull down the entire house! That there is nothing new about the pressures that can be caused by tourism is evidenced by the fact that the demolition took place in 1759. The foundations have been preserved together with a beautifully re-created Elizabethan garden. The entrance is by way of **Nash's House**, once the home of Thomas Nash, who married Shakespeare's grand-daughter, and now containing what is effectively the town museum.

Quite rightly, Stratford-upon-Avon is home to the **Royal Shakespeare Theatre**. Originally known as the Memorial Theatre, it was designed by Miss Elizabeth Scott, a niece of the great Victorian architect Sir Gilbert Scott, and was opened by Edward, Prince of Wales in 1932. Considered controversial and innovative when first built, it stands massively beside the river and is a wonderful place to spend an evening being entertained by one of the greatest companies in the world. In the **Bancroft Gardens**, adjacent to the theatre is the impressive Shakespeare Monument, cast from sixty-five tons of bronze which shows the dramatist seated on a plinth surrounded by four of his principal characters (Hamlet, Lady Macbeth, Falstaff and Prince Hal.) Also in close proximity to the theatre are the **Other Place**, a small intimatetheatre which presents a wide range of drama, and the **Black Swan Inn**, a favourite theatrical haunt that is better known as the Dirty Duck.

On the whole the town copes well with its immense number of visitors and has developed an infrastructure that operates extremely efficiently but it should be appreciated that Stratford-upon-Avon is perhaps the country's premier tourist attraction. A little planning will pay dividends in enabling you to enjoy your visit and the **Tourist Information Centre** at **Bridgefoot**, Stratford-upon-Avon (Tel: 01789293127) can provide considerable help and advice including details of guided tours.

Kenilworth will always haunt me because of the extraordinary and impressive sight of tall windows rising beside a massive fireplace in the ruins of the 14th-century Great Hall of Kenilworth Castle. Looking at it my imagination runs riot and I see the arrival of Queen Elizabeth I and her entourage to attend a lavish banquet in her honour. The whole castle would have been alive and busy. No doubt Her Majesty and her followers would have to be housed and their individual staffs cared for. On one occasion she stayed fifteen days. Quite wonderful. You will see the red-sandstone castle keep standing four-square on a grassy slope, aloof from the bustling market town below, serene in its own world. Though its towers are crumbling and its windows as blank as sightless eyes, it still retains the imposing strength and grandeur that made it one of England's chief strongholds in Norman times.

Approach it on foot across the causeway that leads from the car park on the south side and you will see that much of the castle's outer wall still stands. Beyond it is the Norman Keep standing dignified and alone, separated from the ravages of war, time and weather from the buildings added to it in later centuries. Only the walls remain of th great banqueting hall built by John of Gaunt in the 14th century and little more of the buildings added by Robert Dudley, Earl of Leicester in the 16th century.

The castle has not been lived in since the Restoration and the best preserved parts are Dudley's gatehouse, which was designed to impress distinguished visitors and still impresses with its tall corner towers and battlemented parapets. Then there are the stables built of dressed stone with a timbered upper storey. The Roundheads held the castle during the Civil War and destroyed the keep's north wall after the war.

Shipston-on-Stour dating from Saxon times has the flavour of other days about it. The streets are lined wih houses and inns of the Georgian period built when the woollen industry made Shipston a more prosperous place than now. It is charming with weathered roofs of Cotswold tiles, quaint little dormers and handsome doorways with old brass knockers. I came here to visit the **George Hotel** which dates back to the 15th century and a fireplace in the Front lobby dates to 1508. Queen Victoria stayed here before she became Queen and in more recent times it has been the haunt of famous racing people, actors and writers including George Bernard Shaw.

The Grand Union Canal and the River Avon make their way through **Royal Leamington Spa**, whose tree-lined avenues, riverside walks and wealth of handsomely proportioned architecture are laid out in a grid pattern. Named after the River Leam, a tributary of the Avon, Leamington (or Leamington Priors as it was then known.) was little more than a hamlet until the beginning of the 19th century when the fame of curative powers of the local spring-water became more widely known. Speculators and developers created the town we see today at the most astonishing speed; some idea of the rapid development that took place may be gained from the fact that in 1801 there were 315 inhabitants and yet by 1841 there were 13,000! As the town rapidly expanded, the rich and fashionable flocked in to see and be seen, to promenade, to take the waters and indulge in entertainments. One writer declared the town to be the 'King of Spas' and Queen Victoria, shortly after coming to the throne in 1837, granted the prefix 'Royal'. The locals must have been somewhat bemused since the original use for the salty waters was for seasoning meat and curing rabid dogs! Although the town has expanded further since the 19th century, much of the architectural interest has been retained around the centre and the original source of prosperity, the spring water, can still be sampled at the **Royal Pump Room and Baths**. This elegant building designed in the classical style with a colonnade, was first opened in 1814; the waters are described as being a mild aperient (a polite word for laxative), and 'particularly recommended in cases of gout, chronic and muscular rheumatism, lumbago, sciatica, inactivity of the liver and the digestive system, anaemia, chlorisis and certain skin disorders'.

The town is blessed with many parks and gardens, perhaps the best known being **The Jephson Gardens** whose entrance lodge faces the Pump

Room. Originally planned as an arboretum, these spacious gardens contain mature specimens of many unusual trees together with magnificent floral displays, a lake and two fountains modelled on those at Hampton Court. The gardens were named after Dr Henry Jephson who did much to promote the curative effects of the waters as well as much Charitable work.

Warwickshire is a wonderful county - enjoy it.

THE WEST MIDLANDS

It seems only fitting that the West Midlands,like so many of its products, should be of modern invention, being an amalgamation of the most heavily industrialised areas of Staffordshire, Warwickshire and Worcestershire. created in 1974, the region covers an area of 347 square miles and incorporates the cities of Coventry and Birminghams with a population in the millions.

It is an area preoccupied with production, effectively created by the Industrial Revolution and vastly expanded by the insatiable demands of Empire. It has been touched by the dread hands of War and Recession, yet continues to thrive, producing goods and providing services that are in demand all over the world. Thousands of its acres have disappeared under industrial and suburban sprawl and it is soil scarred and riven by roads, motorways, canals, mines and railways, yet there is still much of beauty and a great deal of value. It can be both depressingand inspiring but if the poet's vision of the 'Heart of England' referred to the rural charm and historical assests of neighbouring Warwickshire then the West Midlands is where the pulse can be felt.

Droitwich in the south west of the region, was probably a Roman centre for the salt and mineral trade which was well developed by the time of the Domesday Book. The town lies on the western side of the M5 and the production of salt continued until quite recently. It was in the 1830's that John Corbett, the Droitwich Salt-King rose to prominence by modernising and developing the salt-mines and workings, particularly around **Stoke Prior** where he achieved the astonishing feat of turning the annual output of salt from 26,000 tons to 200,000 tons. Very much a man of his period, he had started life as the son of a bargee and at the peak of success controlled a vast empire. He built himself an ornate home, now an hotel, the **Chateau Impney**. He was an enlightened employer providing his workers with gardens, schools, a dispensary and cottages.

The many rivers, streams and canals that vein the entire Midland region mean that angling is one of the most popular local past-times and **Redditch** has been providing fish hooks for generations, as well as many other items of fishing tackle. The hooks are a natural adjunct to the town's chief industry and claim to fame, that of being the headquarters of the needle-making industry, indeed **The National Needle Museum** is situated here.

Between **Bromsgrove** and **Kidderminster** lies the pretty village of **Chaddesley Corbett** with its fine timbered houses and church dedicated to St Cassian, a schoolmaster who was condemned to death by his own pupils! The building is a good example of 14th-century architecture on an earlier base and has a handsome 12th-century carved font. Nearby are **Chaddesley Woods** with nature trail and reserve and **Harvington Hall**, a late medieval moated manor house which has a number of ingenious priestholes.

Weaving and carpet-making built up the wealth of **Kidderminster** and the industry continues to this day. I do not know whether this trade is particularly renowned for its friendly spirit but certainly the town's good natured atmosphere is as tangible today as it was over two hundred years ago when one John Brecknall established a charity to provide every child or unmarried person living in Church Street with a plum cake every Midsummer's Eve.

Stourport-on-Severn is unusual in that it is almost entirely a product of the Industrial Revolution, and an attractive one at that. The canal systems of the Midlands were the fore-runners of the Victorian's railway networks and our own motorways, opening up the country's industrial centres to national and international trade and Stourport was created as a 'new town' around the point where the Staffordshire-Worcestershire canal ran into the River Severn. Neat rows of cottages were built tidily around the central basin, which is almost an inland port, and the town still has a pleasant late-Georgian feel to it, although it has grown considerably since the days when the hard-working and often hard-driving bargees would gather to exchange cargoes, swap horses and gossip.

A couple of miles to the north-west lies **Bewdley** which also contains many fine Georgian houses but also architecture of earlier periods. It also rose to prosperity because of water-born traffic but that of the pre-canal era utilising the natural facilities of the River Severn in the 15th and 16th centuries. It was also a centre for weaving, manufacturing saltpeter, brass, horn goods, and cap-making (apparently this trade was so important that at one time the citizens of Bewdley were compelled to wear caps on pain of a fine).

The image of grime, poverty and pollution in the Midlands may be out-moded now but it has a basis in truth and particularly applied to that area known as the Black Country, banded by **Wolverhampton** to the north and **Stourbridge** to the south and so-called because of the region's numerous open-cast coal mines and smoke-belching factories. Thomas Carlyle, visiting in 1824 described it as; '...a frightful scene...a dense cloud of pestilential smoke hangs over it forever.. and at night the whole region burns like a volcano spitting fire from a thousand tubes of brick.

But oh the wretched thousands of mortals who grind out their destiny there!' Paradoxically, from this vision of hell on earth came skills and objects of beauty that were to be admired and coveted the world over and a tough, warm hearted people proud of their heritage. The mining has gone, along with the old style furnaces but many of the skills, trades and industries survive albeit in a cleaner more efficient, and pleasant surroundings. Stourbridge was, and still is, a great centre for the glass-making industry. Familiar names such as Royal Brierley, Stuart and Thomas Webb still produce glassware of the finest quality. To see how glass is made and the incredible standards and varieties that are available, go and visit the **Broadfield House Glass Museum** in **Kingswinford**. The factories themselves welcome visitors and I particularly enjoyed the Stuart Crystal factory with its amazing glass cone; a brick structure like an elongated beehive which housed the furnaces and the glass-makers.

As with so much of the region, canals played a large part in the growth of industry and the **Stourbridge Branch Canal and Wharf** is worth visiting to see the old restored Bonded warehouses and canal company offices and also to take a trip on one of the boats.

Industrial, political and social history all combine at **Dudley** in the heart of the Black Country, together with varied architecture and attractions. The ruined castle, standing on a wooden rise above the busy industrial town, dates back to the 11th century although the basic structure that we can see today is principally 14th century. **Dudley Castle** has had a checkered history and was first destroyed in 1175 when the then owner made the tactical error of backing Prince Henry in the revolt against his father, Henry II. A century later, rebuilding began but proceeded slowly; one of the reasons being the unpopulatiry of the bullying and dishonest John de Somery, whose forcible taxations and reluctance to settle debts led to a natural disinclination on the part of the locals to help with construction.

The Dudley family took over during the reign of Henry VIII, but John Dudley followed in the footsteps of his predecessor by backing Lady Jane Grey for the throne and paid the supreme penalty. The family fortunes, like those of the castle, must have declined somewhat for in 1585 a report was submitted that the castle was unfit for Mary, Queen of Scots to visit - and she was a prisoner at the time! The massive ruins still stand and are well worth a visit especially as they are now part of the well known **Dudley Zoo**.

You should make the effort to visit the **Black Country Museum** at Tipton Road.An open-air site, it is essentially a reconstruction of a 19th century Black Country village complete with canal, mine, houses and factories where all the skills and crafts are demonstrated. Its authenticity can be judged from the fact that special permission had to be sought to contravene the regulations of the Clean Air Act so that cottages could burn coal!

Working museums are always fascinating with their emphasis on ancient skills and crafts and to the north-east of the Black Country can be found at the **Walsall Leather Centre Museum**. Leather working developed alongside the specialist metal trades in stirrups, bits, buckles and spurs with hides being provided by the sheep and cattle of Shropshire anbd Warwickshire and bark for tanning coming from the surrounding oak forests. Saddlery and tack manufacture are still local trades to this day, surviving amongst the more high-tec industries of the 20th century. **Walsall** is proud of its past and possesses a charter dating from the early 13th century and yet has always taken a progressive and enlightened approach to its own affairs, having been one of the first towns in the country to have its own police force, library and cottage hospital.

As I drove south to **Birmingham** I reflected on the facilities offered by **The National Exhibition Centre, The International Convention Centre and The National Indoor Arena**. These impressive and still expanding buildings are equipped to the highest standards and play host to a multitude of events as diverse as opera, international athletics and Cruft's Dog Show as well as numerous conferences and trade shows which attract several million people a year representing some 95 countries! Nevertheless these massive centres are not alone and it is typical of Birmingham's ability to react to market demand that numerous other conference venues are available from five-star hotels to stately homes, together with an impressive infrastructure that covers everything necessary, such as accommodation, travel, leisure facilities and marketing. Perhaps more than any other skill, it is this ability in the market place that has brought Birmingham from being a 'vill of ten adults and value at £1' in 1086 to to-day's priceless 65,000 acre metropolis of one million inhabitants.

The city is constantly changing and intensely alive so it is difficult to know where to start in order to give you some idea of this vibrant place. Perhaps the best place is the **Birmingham Museum of Science and Industry** in Newhall Street which amongst many other fascinating exhibits features the world's oldest working steam engine. For an insight into an early example of mass-production allied to social concern (plus a thoroughly enjoyable time) visit **Cadbury World** at **Bournville** - a must for every chocoholic! Old skills still relevant today can be seenin the **Jewellery Quarter** in **Hockley** whilst the network of canals provide a unique opportunity to explore the many waterways that wander through the city - Brum has more miles of canals than Venice!

The rural area lying between Birmingham and Coventry is well worth exploring containing a number of villages and small towns of interest such as **Knowle**, with its timbered buildings, Guildhall and church with beautifully carved chancel screen. **Temple Balsall** is a unique and historic hamlet which owes its origins to the Knights Templars, a religious order of knights who fought in the Crusades. They are remembered in the lovely 13th-century church which reflects much of the pageantry of those long-past times and in the village's name whilst charity and kindness of a later period is marked by the almshouses that were founded in 1670 by Lady Katherine Leveson. **Hampton-in-Arden**, a mile or so to the north, slopes down to the River Blythe, where there is a fine pack horse bridge built for salt-traders. The village has connections with Shakespeare, being the setting for 'As You Like It' and with the Peel family; Sir Robert Peel (1788-1875) founded the Metropolitan Police Force and was twice prime minister.

The region's second city is **Coventry** and although smaller than Birmingham is much older, originating in the 7th century. It was the centre of the old cloth-weaving industry from the 14th to the 17th century, was the fourth city in England in importance and from its iron-worker's skills developed the engineeering expertise which led it to become the centre of the British motor industry. The city's proud past was very nearly wiped out on November 14th 1940, when German bombers destroyed 40 acres of the city centre, killing or wounding 1500 inhabitants. The fire-gutted ruins of St Michael's Cathedral remains as a moving memorial and a charred cross made from the remains of two oak beams was set up in the ruined church with the words 'Father Forgive' inscribed on the wall behind. Immediately adjacent is the new cathedral designed by Sir Basil Spence and consecrated in 1962. It contains works by Graham Sutherland, John Piper, Jacob Epstein and many others and the whole is a moving testimony to the faith and optimism of the people of Coventry.

Re-building of the city centre began shortly after the war and the occasion was marked by the erection of a statue to one of Coventry's earliest notable citizens, Lady Godiva, who is best remembered for having ridden naked through the streets in order to persuade her husband, Leofric, to reduce the heavy taxes that he had imposed upon the townsfolk. History records that Leofric relented but I doubt that today's inland Revenue would take much notice!

Although the city centre is now a bustling modern development some notable remnants of the city's medieval past escaped the Blitz and are well worth a visit. **The Guildhall** contains some splendid glass, wonderful carvings, the Arras tapestry and a minstrel's gallery with a display of medieval armour. Mary, Queen of Scots was once incarcerated in its tower. **Bond's Hospital** and **Ford's Hospital** are both 16th-century almshouses and are still used as such while **Spon Street** is a rec-constructedmedieval cul-de-sac with ancient houses enjoying a new lease of life as shops and galleries. The 14th-century **Whitefriar's Gate** is a renovated Carmelite friary housing a number of exhibitions including a charming **Toy Museum**. The immediate past has not been forgotten and in Hales Street can be found the **Museum of British Road Transport**, which includes the Land Speed record holder, Thrust II, while at nearby **Baginton** there is the **Midlands Air Museum**.

One of our greatest novelists who made much use of this area of the Midlands in her books was Marian Evans (1819-80), better known under her pen-name of George Eliot. She was born north of Coventry at **Nuneaton** where her father was steward at nearby **Arbury Hall**, a fine example of Gothick Revival built onto an earlier Elizabethan house and with a porch and stables that were designed by Sir Christopher Wren. There are fine landscaped gardens and the stables are now home to **The Pinkerton Collection of Cycles and Motorcycles.**

Tamworth, once capital of the ancient Saxon Kingdom of Mercia is a pleasant town with some attractive architecture but surrounded by modern development; nevertheless the town is well worth visiting, particularly for its splendid castle. The predecessors of **Tamworth Castle** were destroyed by the Danes in 874 and 943AD but the present structure has stood firm since Norman times and, apart from the odd ghost, has an almost homely feel about it! A Jacobean manor house was built within the circular keep and occupation has been continuous until recent times. There is now a museum in the castle and the attractive grounds are open to the public and include a garden for the blind and disabled.

Tamworth is like so much of the region with modern development and ancient heritage happily co-existing; forward-looking yet concerned with the older values of a caring and friendly society. The West Midlands is continually evolving to meet the challenges of tomorrow whilst acknowledging the traditions and achievments of the past.

HIPSLEY FARM COTTAGES

Waste Farm,
Hurley,
Atherstone,
Warwickshire
CV9 2LR

Tel/Fax: 01827 872437

Warwickshire is truly the heart of England, with the country's geographical centre claimed to be the village of Meridian. The countryside is stunning and it is in this beautiful rolling countryside Mrs. Ann Posser has her delightful farm cottages. These carefully converted cottages were once barns and a cowshed, today they offer comfortable and attractive accommodation. There are 6 altogether, the ***Dugdale, Drayton*** *and* ***Wainwright*** *are '3 Key Highly Commended' and the* ***Bramley, Brooke*** *and* ***Eliot*** *are '4 Key Highly Commended'. The* **Dugdale** *and* **Drayton** *cottages have been formed from the 17th century barn and each has an open plan kitchen/sitting room with original oak beams, a spiral staircase leads to a twin bedded room in the Drayton and a double room in the Doughtily. The* ***Bramley*** *is the original farm cottage, and it provides a kitchen, veranda, sitting room with an open fire, a double and a single/double bedroom. The cowshed has been used to create the* ***Brooke*** *on the ground floor and the* ***Eliot*** *on the first floor. The* ***Brooke*** *has a kitchen/diner, a spacious sitting room with lovely views across the countryside, a double bedroom and a twin bedded room. The* ***Eliot*** *is equally comfortable with kitchen, very spacious sitting room again with lovely views, a room with twin beds in and a double bedroom. And finally the* ***Wainwright****, this delightful single storey stone cottage is suitable for a wheelchair, it provides a kitchen/living area and one large bedroom with twin beds. Each cottage is exceptionally well furnished with everything you will need to make your stay a very pleasant one, with full central heating, electric cooker, microwave, and fridge with ice-box. Duvets, bed linen and towels are provided and there is a fully equipped laundry room. Ann also offers a special service, if you have been out sightseeing all day and you would like a cooked meal, she will prepare one for you and deliver it to your cottage, what could be better. Newspapers, milk and groceries can also be arranged.*

There is plenty to do in this part of the country, you will never be bored. You are sure to leave here refreshed and relaxed having had an excellent holiday.

USEFUL INFORMATION

OPEN: *All year*
CHILDREN: *Welcome cot and highchair available*
CREDIT CARDS: *None taken*
ACCOMMODATION: *6 delightful self-catering cottages*

PETS: *By arrangement. Well behaved £10 per week*
GARDEN: *Yes with barbecue and garden furniture. 9 hole putting green*
DISABLED ACCESS: *Wainwright is suitable for a wheelchair*

EUDON BURNELL COTTAGES

Bridgnorth,
Shropshire
WV16 6UD

Tel: 01746 789235
Fax: 01746 789550

Bridgnorth is a charming mixture of attractive half-timbered buildings and red brick terraces which are the character of this delightful town. The town is divided in two, in the valley is Low Town and above on the cliff top is High Town. Just outside the town is a 330 acre working dairy/arable farm owned and run by the Crawford Clarke family. Situated on the farm are three superb self-contained cottages set amidst rolling countryside and with wonderful views of the Clee Hills. Eudon Burnell Cottages provide excellent accommodation, they are all very well furnished with everything to meet your needs, they all offer a very high standard of comfort and cleanliness, and this has been reiterated by the awards of '4 & 5 Key Commended' by the English Tourist Board. ***No1 Eudon Burnell*** *sleeps 5 people and has a fitted kitchen including washing machine, tumble dryer, dishwasher, microwave and an electric cooker. The sitting room has a gas fire, TV, radio, pay phone, dining table and chairs, there is also a bathroom downstairs. Upstairs are 3 bedrooms, 1 double, 1 twin and a single, a separate shower room with WC and washbasin. Attached to No1 is* ***No2,*** *which is slightly smaller, but still offers excellent accommodation. The fitted kitchen has a table and 4 chairs plus all the furnishings of No1 except for the dishwasher. The bathroom has an over bath shower. There is dining area in the sitting room which as an open or electric fire. On the first floor are 2 single bedrooms and one double room. No2 sleeps 4 people. These two cottages share an attractive garden with lawns, shrubs and trees.* ***No3*** *has a kitchen/dining with an Edwardian table and chairs and the same high quality furnishings afforded to the other cottages. The sitting room has an open or electric fire and a pay phone. The bathroom also has a shower over the bath. The bedrooms upstairs consist of a double with ensuite shower, WC and washbasin, 1 twin and a single room with washbasin. The cottage has its own pretty garden front and back. The stairs in No3 are quite steep so a bed settee can be arranged for an elderly or disabled person. As an extra special touch all the cottage bedrooms have patchwork quilts.*

There is something for all the family in and around Bridgnorth with the Costume and Childhood Museum, Daniels Mill, Rays Farm Country Matters plus sports and leisure facilities. Further afield there is Much Wenlock Museum, Wenlock Priory, The Severn Valley Railway and Wyre Forest the list goes on and on. The Crawford Clarke family are waiting to extend a warm and friendly welcome.

USEFUL INFORMATION

OPEN: *All year*
CHILDREN: *Welcome*
CREDIT CARDS: *None taken*
ACCOMMODATION: *Three very comfortable 3 bedroomed self-catering cottages*

DISABLED ACCESS: *A bed settee downstairs in No3*
GARDEN: *Yes with garden furniture. Car parking for 2 to 3 cars*
PETS: *Well behaved dogs. Must be under control*

BRONYDD HOLIDAY COTTAGES

Bronydd,
Hay-on-Wye,
Herefordshire
HR3 5RX

Tel: 01497 820766

The owners of these outstandingly attractive holiday cottages ask you to imagine a beautifuly holiday home ina tranquil setting poised between two cultures. To imagine full modern facilities, remote control TV, full fitted kitchens and gas fired central heating. Imagine a private garden patio overlooking the breathtaking vista of the Wye Valley and the Black Mountains. Your imagination becomes reality if you decide to come to Bronydd Holiday Cottages.

You will find the cottages at the end of a quiet cul-de-sac perched above the hamlet of Bronydd. The cottages are surrounded by gardens and set in 35 acres of farm and woodland where you are very welcome to roam. The six cottages, Elm, Pine, Chestnut, Ivy, Honeysuckle and The Old Dairy have recently been converted from the old farm buildings. Each one is individual with its own character and they are all comfortably furnished and very well equipped. The view from the private patio garden of Honeysuckle Cottage for example must have the best situated pincic tables in the Welsh Marches! You could not wish for more to make a perfect holiday and yet there is more!

To the West are the dramatic mountains of Wales, to the East the tranquillity of a still unspoilt part of England. Here in the Welsh Marches you can explore on foot, by bike, on horseback, by canoe, by car or even by hang glider. The walking here in Kilvert country is excellent; nearby Offa's Dyke path threads its way through the Wye Valley and on across the Black Mountains. Just two miles away is Hay-on-Wye,famous for its secondhand book shops and Spring literary festival.

USEFUL INFORMATION

OPEN; *All year*
CREDIT CARDS; *None taken*

GARDEN; *Each cottage has one*
ACCOMMODATION; *6 cottages*

CHILDREN; *Welcome*
DISABLED ACCESS; *One cottage purpose built*

PETS; *Welcome (not limited)*

BROUGHTON MANOR,
Mill Lane,
Broughton Hackett,
Worcester WR7 4BB
Tel: 01905 381504

In addition to very attractive Bed and Breakfast accommodation, Broughton Manor has one self-catering property converted in 1989 which provides everything one could wish for to make a stay comfortable and enjoyable. The two bed-roomed cottage is spotless, warm and furnished to a high standard with an nice mix of modern and classic pieces. The well appointed kitchen has a Fridge/Freezer, Microwave, Dishwasher and Washing Machine to make life simple. Within a hundred yards there is fishing. Six golf courses are within easy reach or you can have fun Clay Pigeon shooting, riding or even go-karting. For those who like walking the countryside is enticing and the cathedral city of Worcester is nearby. Relaxing in the pretty garden is another option.

USEFUL INFORMATION

OPEN; *All year* | ***CHILDREN;*** *By arrangement*
DISABLED ACCESS; *No* | ***PETS;*** *No*

COPPICE COTTAGE
Church Stretton, Shropshire SY6 6NJ

Tel: 01694 751206
Fax: 01694 751203

Church Stretton is a delightful village and in it, set in the peaceful and unspoilt Shropshire hills is Coppice Cottage standing in its own grounds, surrounded by an area of superb natural beauty. A wonderful place to stay if you feel like getting away from it all in order to enjoy a relaxed, carefree holiday or break. You will find Coppice Cottage superb for this purpose and yet close enough to enjoy the amenities larger towns have to offer. From Coppice Cottage you can set out for wonderful walks in the hills or on kinder teritory, you can fish, ride horses, cycle, swim or play golf. For the more adventurous there are historic market towns, castles and museums within easy striking distance to explore for a day out, passing through some truly beautiful countryside on the way. Coppice Cottage has over half an acre of established gardens with superb views in every direction of the beautiful rolling Shropshire hills. Although the cottage has been modernised it retains much of its olde worlde charm with a wealth of old oak beams. The cottage sleeps six in one double ensuite room and 2 twin rooms with separate bathroom and toilet. The pretty sitting room has colour TV and the dining room has french windows leading to a patio. The fitted kitchen is fully equipped and there is central heating throughout. Bed linen is supplied.

USEFUL INFORMATION

OPEN; *All year* | ***CHILDREN;*** *Welcome*
CREDIT CARDS; *None taken* | ***DISABLED ACCESS;*** *No*
PETS; *No* | ***GARDEN;*** *Mature and extensive*

SWAINSLEY FARM COTTAGES

Swainsley Farm,
Butterton,
Nr Leek,
Staffordshire
ST13 7SS

Tel: 01298 84530

Swainsley Farm is in an enviable setting, surrounded by the most wonderful scenery which only the Peak District National Park can offer, spectacular moorland and beautiful dales. The Farm overlooks the River Manifold and just below it is The Manifold Trail, where you can walk or cycle, wheelchair users can also have access to magnificent countryside.

The cottages have been carefully converted from traditional farm buildings into very comfortable holiday accommodation. There are three cottages and each is centrally heated and double glazed. **The Coach House** *has lots of character with timber beams and a wonderful gallery bedroom with a double bed. The other bedrooms are on the ground floor, one twin and one with bunk beds, because of this it makes it ideal for disabled visitors, indeed the English Tourist Board has designated this cottage 'Category 2 Accessible'.* **The Haybarn** *has lots of exposed woodwork adding to the cottagey feel. There are two bedrooms, one double and one twin with a Z-bed for an extra visitor. The one bedroomed* **Old Byre** *is recently converted and has superb views. All the cottages are fully equipped with all you will require including microwave oven, washer/dryer, colour television, electric cooker, there is even a dishwasher in The Coach House. Bed linen and towels are included in the price. Electricity is by meter reading at cost. Cot and highchairs are available. There is a large courtyard with garden furniture where you can enjoy a barbecue and look at the stunning views of the valley. Chris and Liz Snook, the lucky couple who own Swainsley Farm, are looking forward to welcoming you and making you feel at home.*

USEFUL INFORMATION

OPEN: *All year*
CHILDREN: *Welcome*
CREDIT CARDS: *None taken*
ACCOMMODATION:
The Coach House sleeps 6 - ETB '4 Keys Deluxe',
The Haybarn sleeps 4/5 - ETB '4 Keys Highly Commended',
The Old Byre sleeps 2 - ETB '4 Keys Deluxe'
Ample parking

DISABLED ACCESS: *The Coach House has bedrooms and bathroom on ground floor, ETB Category 2 Accessible*

GARDEN: *Yes. Large courtyard with garden furniture and barbecue*

PETS: *No pets in cottages, kennel and run available free of charge*
NON-SMOKERS preferred

RIVERSIDE COTTAGES,
Mill Cottage,
Canon Frome,
Ledbury,
Herefordshire
HR8 2TD

Tel: 01531 670506
& 0378 591889

Situated in a peaceful spot in the Frome Valley, away from main roads, though within easy reach of Ledbury, Hereford and Malvern with the Malvern Hills, the Wye Valley and the Black Mountains close by, Julian and Lorna Rutherford offer bed and breakfast in the main house. Mill Cottage has two en-suite bedrooms, each with colour TV and tea and coffee making facilities and there is a guest lounge with log fire in a self-contained, spacious wing with views towards the river.

In addition there are two cottages within the grounds. The Swiss Cottage is pleasantly situated on the bank overlooking a waterfall. From the balcony, which overhangs the river, a wide variety of wildlife can be seen, including the resident kingfishers and sometimes otter and leaping salmon if you are lucky. Built in 1838, it has recently been restored and modernised, most of the beams being exposed. It comprises a double bedroom with adjoining bathroom downstairs, and an open-plan living room/kitchen on the first floor. There are windows with lovely views on all sides. French windows lead onto the balcony which runs around three sides of the cottage and has a staircase leading down to the front door. It is fully equipped for two people but may not be suitable or safe for some pets or children.

Lime Cottage is situated in a different part of the garden, overlooking fields at the front and a pool to one side. It is a conversion of an old building once used for storing lime. It has a light high-ceiling living area with exposed beams, leading through an arch to a small bedroom, with double bed, and adjacent shower room. The kitchen facilities include an electric Baby Belling oven with two rings, a microwave and a small fridge. It is equipped for two people. Both cottages are well insulated. Heating is provided by modern night storage units with supplementary day-time electric heating. Electricity is paid for by taking meter readings. Bed linen and towels are provided. Both have colour TV's and are attractively furnished.

USEFUL INFORMATION

OPEN; *All year*
CREDIT CARDS; *None taken*
GARDEN; *Yes. 5 acres of wooded grounds*
ACCOMMODATION; *2 cottages-equipped for 2 people.*
Main house self-contained wing with B&B.

CHILDREN; *By arrangement*
PETS; *By arrangement*

THE ACORN,
Oaklands,
Marshbrook,
Church Stretton,
Shropshire
SY6 6RQ.

Tel : 01694 781448

Little Switzerland is the name this area is known by, and The Acorn fits right in with the description. Built in a detached Swiss Chalet style, standing in 5 acres of grounds at the top of a sweeping drive, this immaculate cottage offers the utmost in tranquillity and peace you could possibly desire. The views are of the open countryside and of the famous Long Mynd and with the many walks and bridle paths near the property, this is heavenly country for walking or riding. There are many places of historical interest also within easy reach which make for a delightful variety of entertainment for all the family.

Stabling and grazing are available for those visitors bringing their own horses - even cat chalets can be procured at prior arrangement, for those cat lovers who wish to bring them along!

The cottage is delightfully furnished and equipped and has one double and one twin bedroom. There is a large comfortable lounge with a tasteful dining area and a superb kitchen. The linen is of excellent quality as is the tableware and other furnishings. There is a fully fitted bathroom, and outside is a charming patio area where you can enjoy the view and 'listen' to the peace on a summer evening! John and Lily Cooper are the owners and are available for any help or advice you may require, and to ensure your holiday is one to remember.

USEFUL INFORMATION

***OPEN :** All year*
***CHILDREN :** Welcome*
***PETS :** By prior arrangement*

SELF CATERING
***DISABLED ACCESS :** No*
***HORSES :** Stables & grazing available*

'THE CRISPEN'
Stone Acton Road,
Wall Bank,
Church Stretton,
Shropshire
SY6 7HL.

Tel : 01694 771319

This beautiful cottage snuggling in one of England's most enchanting areas is both delightful and practical. A semi detached building on a small working farm, it is surrounded by the farmyard sounds of free range hens, ducks, geese, cows and sheep. It was only built six years ago so has all the conveniences of modern living, but being built of local stone with exposed beams and stone fireplace, it lends itself to its environment and the heritage of this area. This does not detract from the central heating, double glazing and full carpeting throughout! The bedroom has twin beds with ample bedding and a variety of storage space, all very tastefully decorated. The en suite bathroom has a bath with electric shower overhead, and there are grab rails for the disabled at various points. Incidentally, all rooms have access for wheelchairs, and there is even a ramp leading up to the front door. The sitting room overlooks the orchard and has lovely views over the renowned Ape Dale. The log fire is a warming edition on those cooler evenings when one feels the need for a little extra luxury! The kitchen is fully fitted with all the modern appliances necessary, but I am afraid that you may have to fill the dishwasher by hand.......but that must be about all!

This is one of Shropshire's Environmentally Sensitive Areas and as such offers a great deal to the nature lover in us all. These hills were meant for rambling, and if you have any artistic tendencies then you will love the vistas before you. Further afield you can visit many historic sites in Shrewsbury and even Ludlow, or perhaps have a day at the Welsh Borders, another lovely area steeped in history. The town of Church Stretton is less than 4 miles away where you have the benefits of shops, supermarket and a railway station......all the modern conveniences you could possibly want to see in this dream landscape!

USEFUL INFORMATION

***OPEN :** All year*
***PETS :** By prior arrangement*

SELF CATERING
***DISABLED ACCESS :** Yes*

LITTLE LIGHTWOOD FARM

Lightwood Lane,
Cotheridge,
Worcester
WR6 5LT

Tel: 01905 333236
Fax: 01905 333468

This working farm owned and run by two very friendly people, Richard and Vee Rodgers caters not only for bed and breakfast but self-catering as well. There is a chalet and two detached bungalows, all very well appointed and set in such peaceful surroundings. This part of Worcestershire is excellent for those planning to explore the beauty of the county including the Malvern Hills only 8 miles a way and the glorious Teme Valley a little further off. Locally there is fishing, golf, walking, swimming and even closer to home cheese making on the farm; a fascinating process which Richard and Vee are happy to show you.

If you would rather not cater for yourselves then one can strongly recommend the Bed and Breakfast accommodation in the farmhouse. The spacious, comfortable bedrooms are all ensuite and have TV as well as tea and coffee making facilities. Breakfast is a true farmhouse meal with eggs from the farm as well as fresh fruit and cheese. Whichever option you choose you will have a very happy stay at Little Lightwood Farm.

USEFUL INFORMATION

OPEN; *All year*
CHILDREN; *Welcome*
PETS; *No*
ACCOMMODATION; *3 rooms ensuite*
1 chalet, 2 detached bungalows

DISABLED ACCESS; *No*
CREDIT CARDS; *None taken*
GARDEN; *Yes. Wonderful views*
NO SMOKING
ESTABLISHMENT

HESTERWORTH HOLIDAYS
Hesterworth,
Hopesay,
Craven Arms,
Shropshire SY7 8EX

Tel: 01588 660487

Shropshire is full of small villages and hamlets in some of England's most beautiful countryside, one of these small villages is Hopesay. It lies in an area of outstanding natural beauty in the Shropshire hills. In this charming place is Hesterworth a very elegant Victorian house built around a 150 years ago, encompassed by trees, fields, stream, pond and garden amounting to 12 acres. This stunning property emanates peace, tranquillity and friendliness as soon as you walk through the front door, to be greeted by your host Sheila Davies. The house is divided into very attractive cottages/flats, and are all named after local hills. Each one has a character all of its own, they are comfortably furnished, fully carpeted and are well appointed with colour television, fridge, cooker, iron, toaster, kettle and ample crockery and cutlery. All the rooms have adequate heating, hot water is via an immersion heater. Electricity is by a 50p meter. 3 of the cottages are in the house, 5 are next to the house situated around a small courtyard, and 3 are beyond the courtyard, each sleeping between 2 and 8 persons. They all have sitting rooms, kitchens, bathrooms and bedrooms. One of the cottages has wide doorways to make wheelchair access easy, and another is on the ground floor. You can hire bed linen, towels, and tea towels as they are not supplied, or you can bring your own. If you require a meal on your arrival, casseroles and desserts can be ordered and delivered to your accommodation, there are at least 7 delicious dishes to choose from, all served with potatoes and vegetables, plus desserts. Breakfast and evening meals can also be taken in the large dining room, at a reasonable price. The Hesterworth is licensed and they have a particularly fine range of wines at competitive prices.

With the flexibility of self-catering you are free to come and go as you please, and you will need to get an early start each day in order to see as much of this beautiful area as possible. If you like castles, country houses and gardens, then Hesterworth is the place for you. This is a wonderful centre for the walker, birdwatcher or those who simply love the countryside. The grounds and gardens are magnificent and guests are more than welcome to wander around, or use the grass badminton court. As you drive up the leafy lane towards the house and catch your first glimpse of it, you will be more that satisfied with your choice. It will be a lot harder driving back the other way to go home.

USEFUL INFORMATION

OPEN; *All year*
CHILDREN; *Very welcome*
CREDIT CARDS; *None taken*
LICENSED; *Yes*
ACCOMMODATION; *11 self-catering cottages/flats. Bed and breakfast also*

DINING ROOM; *Reasonably priced breakfast and 2 course evening meals available. Casseroles available for your arrival book in advance*
DISABLED ACCESS; *One ground floor cottage and one with wide doors for wheelchair*
GARDEN; *Beautiful with grass badminton court available*
PETS; *By arrangement*

RUXTON FARM
Kings Caple,
Hereford
HR1 4TX

Tel: 01432 840493

Set within 20 acres in the tranquil Kings Caple area of Hereford is the well known Equestrian Centre of Ruxton Farm. Here, training for Eventing, Showjumping and Dressage are taught to horses and riders. Although this is the main venture of the owners, Mrs. Milly Slater also has tourist facilities, Bed and Breakfast and self-catering accommodation very high on her list of priorities. Ruxton Farm is very old, some of the more modern features are 17th century, but more recently a conversion of the Cider Mill and Granary to a superb holiday home has been completed. Every detail appertaining to modern day living has been thoughtfully included into what is now called Ruxton Mill. On the mezzanine floor is a very large living area containing at one end a luxury kitchen with a comprehensive range of equipment, dishwasher, microwave oven, washer dryer, fridge/freezer and cooker, this entire area is heated by a multi purpose stove. In addition the whole property benefits from oil fired central heating, the cost of oil and electricity is included as are towels and linen. Bedrooms are situated at ground floor level, the first of which is furnished with a double bed and ensuite shower, bedroom 2 has a double bed with wash hand basin and double patio doors have direct access to the garden , the smallest of the bedrooms has 3ft bunk beds large enough to sleep adults and here again is a wash hand basin. The main bathroom and toilet is on this level. The whole property with the exception of the kitchen is fully carpeted, and with a wealth of exposed beams this is a wonderful holiday home. Close to the Mill is off road parking and within a short distance one will find the local post office and hostelries offering excellent food. The nearest local shop is 3 miles away. Here in this beautiful Wye Valley area, are woods and rivers, charming and olde worlde villages and towns to explore, thatched cottages with displays of flowers to be enjoyed. Close by is Ross-on-Wye, Hampton Bishop and Ludlow reputed to be the loveliest of towns, or a visit to the Cathedral city of Hereford, with its Saxon history and interesting museums. For those who enjoy fishing the farm has its own and for walking, riding and golf, the amenities within this locality are boundless, brochures and pamphlets are readily available for guest. The owners are members of the Association for Promotion of Herefordshire, and are registered with the Heart of England Tourist Board.

USEFUL INFORMATION

OPEN; *All year*
CHILDREN; *Welcome*
CREDIT CARDS; *None taken*
DISABLED ACCESS; *No*
PARKING; *Off road parking*
GARDEN; *Yes, lovely lawns*
ACCOMMODATION; *3 bedroomed self-catering holiday home and Bed and Breakfast facilities in main 17th century Farmhouse*

THE BUZZARDS
Kingsland,
Leominster,
Herefordshire
HR6 9QE

Tel: 01568 708941

The border county of Herefordshire is steeped in history and this is visible by the ruined castles, Iron Age and Roman hillforts, you can imagine the battles that took place here with all the noise, now the countryside is tranquillity itself, with delightful small towns and villages with their pretty gardens. The Buzzards Cottages are 10 miles west of Ludlow and Leominster, and 8 miles from the Welsh border town of Presteigne. They are situated in 16 acres of established woodland, pastureland, orchards and ponds. This peaceful location, where you will not fail to relax, has a variety of wildlife also ponies, goats, ducks, hens and bees.

The 3 self-contained cottages are comfortable, spacious and very well equipped with all you need, washing machine, microwave, cooker, and plenty of crockery and cutlery. The furnishings are attractive and a mixture of antique and modern. To maintain the peace and quiet televisions are not provided, but you may bring your own if you wish. Outside each cottage is a lovely garden with garden furniture. Facilities are available for people with mobility difficulties, 2 of the cottages have access for wheelchair users, and have special features including ramps, ground floor shower room and sleeping accommodation. All bed linen and towels are provided, cots and high chairs are also available. A wonderful holiday is in store when you stay at The Buzzards.

USEFUL INFORMATION

OPEN; *All year*
CHILDREN; *Welcome*
CREDIT CARDS; *None taken*
LICENSED; *Not applicable*
ACCOMMODATION; *3 Self-catering cottages*

DINING ROOM; *Not applicable*
DISABLED ACCESS; *Yes,*
GARDEN; *Yes 16 acres*
PETS; *No*

NO SMOKING

THE OLD HAY BARN APARTMENTS

Corporation Farm,
Watery Lane,
Curborough,
Litchfield,
Staffordshire
WS13 8ER

Tel: 01543 263095
Fax: 01543 414899

Two miles from the beautiful Cathedral City of Lichfield - the birth place of Dr Johnson - you will find the village of Cudborough, it is here Mrs Margaret Lees has her farm. Surrounded by superb open countryside Corporation Farm is the perfect setting for a relaxing holiday. The three luxury holiday apartments have been carefully and beautifully converted from a 300 year old brick and tile barn. Each apartment has been delightfully appointed to an exceptionally high standard. ***Hay Byre*** *is suitable for disabled or elderly visitors being all on one floor, there is a sitting room with kitchenette, a double bedroom and a bathroom with shower.* ***Hay Racks*** *sleeps 7 people in a ground floor apartment, which consists of a large comfortable sitting room plus a 'put you up' double bed, a kitchen and dining area. Of the two bedrooms, one has a double and single bed and the other has 2 bunk beds. There is a bathroom with shower. Above the Hay Racks is the* ***Hay Loft****, very similar in design but without the single bed in the double bedroom. The views from this apartment are stunning. For eating out a paved patio area has been provided. There is also plenty of parking space. Bed linen is provide and all electricity is included in the tariff.*

Guests are more than welcome around the farm and you are sure to enjoy walking across the fields. Corporation Farm has cultivated a small conservation area, here you will find 2 pools well stocked with Carp in which you may fish for a small charge. The area abounds with places of interest with something to keep everyone happy. A very warm welcome awaits at this charming location.

USEFUL INFORMATION

OPEN: *All year*
CHILDREN: *Welcome.*
Cot & highchair available
CREDIT CARDS: *None taken*
ACCOMMODATION: *Hay Byre sleeps 2, Hay Racks sleeps 7, Hay Loft sleeps 6*

DISABLED ACCESS: *Hay Byre is especially suitable*
GARDEN: *Paved patio area*
PETS: *No*
Ample parking available

BRON HEULOG,
Waterfall Road,
Llanrhaeadr YM Mochnant,
Nr.Oswestry,
Powys
SY10 0JX

Tel: 01691 780521

In the grounds of Bron Heulog, a charming Victorian, Welsh stone house which is owned by Karon and Ken Raines and run by them as an exceedingly comfortable and enjoyable guest house, is what was once the gardener's cottage and which they have converted into self-catering accommodation. The same meticulous care and attention has been taken with the conversion as they did with the house. The cottage has an unusual elevated walled garden. The rooms are attractively decorated with one bedroom with a balcony that overlooks the Tanat Valley. The cottage is equipped with everything you could possibly need to make your stay a comfortable and happy one. It is strictly non-smoking.

For anyone who enjoys the sheer beauty and tranquillity of this part of Wales, the village of Llanrhaeadr on the border of two counties marking the division between Mid and North Wales, makes an ideal base. It feels like another world and wonderful for those who just want to potter. For the more energetic it is an ideal location for climbing, cycling, paragliding and many outdoor activities. For those who like walking, Waterfall Road, a four mile road lined with rowan trees, leads to Pistyll Rhaeadr, the highest waterfall in Wales which is one of the traditional 'Seven Wonders of Wales', a truly breathtaking sight.

USEFUL INFORMATION

OPEN; *All year*
CREDIT CARDS; *All except Amex*
GARDEN; *Victorian walled garden*
NO SMOKING
CHILDREN; *Welcome*
DISABLED ACCESS; *No facilities*
PETS; *No*
ACCOMMODATION; *Sleeps 2/4 with sofabed*

LONGVILLE ARMS

Longville-in-the-Dale, Much Wenlock,
Shropshire TF13 6DT

Tel: 01694 771206
Fax: 01694 771742

Much Wenlock is a lovely old market town full of history. The ancient Tudor Guildhall is still in use as a Court House and Council Chamber. There are charming timber-framed buildings in the Bull Ring. You will find picturesque half-timbered cottages, a wealth of graceful Georgian houses and a 15th century house near St Owen's Well, which features an archway made from oak boughs. Much Wenlock Museum brings alive the social history of the area with special displays on local trades and crafts. Wenlock Priory was founded long ago in the 7th century, and is one of the regions most ancient religious foundations founded by the granddaughter of King Penda of Mercia. It was the site of the Olympic Games in 1850 and is the precursor to the Modern Olympics. On the B4371 between Much Wenlock and Church Stretton is an attractive village called Longville-in-the-Dale, situated on the doorstep of Wenlock Edge, where you can follow the paths set out by the National Trust taking in some of the most wonderful scenery. It is in the village that the Longville Arms can be found, an old coaching inn which was built approximately 200 years ago, owned and run by Patrick and Madeline Egan. The public rooms furnished in a country style with exposed oak beams, contribute to the restful atmosphere and natural character of the pub. At the side of the pub is a very tastefully converted Barn which is use for self-catering accommodation. It is exceptionally well appointed with everything you need to make your stay comfortable, it is also centrally heated throughout. On the ground floor there is a twin room and a bunk-bedded room, shower, WC and a fully equipped kitchen/ dining room. On the first floor is another bedroom, a double ensuite, which could be used as a treble. The cosy sitting room is where you can relax, watch some television, read or plan your days outing. With bedrooms on the ground floor it is suitable for the partially disabled. If you don't feel like cooking after a hard days sightseeing, then why not try the food at the Longville Arms it is very good indeed, it is also mentioned in the 'Good Pub Guide'. A comprehensive menu is available at lunch time and in the evening, except Tuesday evenings. It is all home-cooked using fresh local produce whenever possible. Children are well catered for with their own menu and a black board is available with 'Specials of the Day'. You will definitely not go hungry during your stay. Bed & Breakfast is also available. The Longville Arms is very well placed for visiting the many places of interest in the area, and you are assured that you will always be given a warm welcome by Patrick and Madeline.

USEFUL INFORMATION

OPEN; *Pub: 12.00-3pm, 7.00-11.00pm*
B & B: All year except Christmas Day
Self-catering: All year

CHILDREN; *Welcome*
CREDIT CARDS; *None taken*
LICENSED; *Yes*
GARDEN; *Beer garden*

ACCOMMODATION; *Self-catering converted Barn up to 6 persons.*
B & B available
DINING ROOM; *Excellent home-cooked fare*
Comprehensive menu, Daily Specials
VEGETARIAN; *Catered for*
DISABLED ACCESS; *Category C. Limited*
PETS; *By arrangement*

GRANGE COTTAGES

Lower Hayton Grange,
Lower Hayton,
Ludlow,
Shropshire
SY8 2AQ

Tel: 01584 861296
Fax: 01584 861371

Lower Hayton Grange has two roles. It has two charming holiday cottages within the grounds available for those who enjoy the freedom of self-catering and at the same time the benefit of the swimming pool and the tennis court. Pear Tree sleeps 2 adult + 2 children + cot or 3 adults + 1 child + cot. It is comfortably furnished and has everything you could wish for in the way of equipment. Apple Tree sleeps four adults and is the same high standard as Pear Tree. Both cottages are centrally heated. One small pet is allowed in each cottage. Garden furniture is provided for the cottages' own private patios and there is parking for two cars for each cottage. Bed linen is provided but you are asked to bring your own towels. Towels are provided for overseas visitors.

The second role that the 15th century Lower Hayton Grange provides is delightful bed and breakfast accommodation in the main house. The house is quite beautiful and furnished with a combination of antique and traditional furniture combining harmoniously with the drapes and covers. Owned by Malcolm and Margaret Lowe who clearly love their home and equally enjoy sharing it with their guests, you will find yourself offered two attractive en suite bedrooms, one of which has a four poster and the other an adjoining private lounge and separate front door. Breakfast is a memorable meal, freshly cooked to your choice. An evening meal is available by arrangement. Set in glorious grounds it really is a great place to stay and there is so much to do and see in this part of Shropshire. Ludlow is said to be the prettiest town in Britain.

USEFUL INFORMATION

OPEN; *All year*
CHILDREN; *Cottages only*
CREDIT CARDS; *None taken*
PETS: *1 per cottage only*
ACCOMMODATION; *2 cottage + 2 B&B bedrooms*
PARKING; *2 cars per cottage*
GARDEN; *Glorious. Swimming pool. Tennis Court*

BROOKLYN
Leinthall Starkes,
Ludlow, Shropshire SY8 2HP

Contact: *Mrs. V Morgan*
Marlbrook Hall,
Elton,
Ludlow,
Shropshire
SY8 2HR

Tel: 01568 770230

North Herefordshire has to be one of the most prettiest and unspoilt parts of England, and it is here in the small village of Leinthall Starkes that Brooklyn can be found. Owned by Mrs. Valerie Morgan, this large three bedroomed house offers excellent accommodation, it is spacious, extremely well kept and is surrounded by private grounds. Brooklyn is tastefully decorated and has fitted carpets throughout making it comfortable and warm, a real home from home. The sitting room has a sofa, chairs and colour television, the perfect room for relaxing after a strenuous days sightseeing. The kitchen is very well appointed with every modern convenience including an electric cooker, microwave, toaster filter coffee machine and enough crockery and cutlery for six people. The dining room seats six comfortably plus a high chair. Also downstairs is a utility room which is equipped with a washing machine, tumble dryer and fridge and a cloak room with WC. Upstairs there is a large bathroom and three bedrooms, two double and one twin, a cot is also available. You won't have to load your car with bedding, Mrs. Morgan provides duvet covers, linen and towels. The electricity meter is read on arrival and charge accordingly.

About a mile away is the village of Wigmore where you can shop at the local store, there is also a post office, garage and two country pubs. In the village are the ruins of Wigmore Castle which is believed to date back to the Norman Conquest. Come and visit this beautiful area and while you're here stay in comfort. Brooklyn has awarded '4 Keys Commended' by the English Tourist Board and is a member of the Farm Holiday Bureau.

USEFUL INFORMATION

OPEN: *All year*
CHILDREN: *Welcome, cot and high chair available*
CREDIT CARDS: *None taken*
ACCOMMODATION: *Spacious three bedroomed house with garage*
DISABLED ACCESS: *No*
GARDEN: *Large private garden with furniture*
PETS: *No*
Ample parking

HALFORD HOLIDAY HOMES,
Halford Farm,
Craven Arms,
Shropshire
SY7 9JG.

Tel : 01588 672382

Originating from an old Shropshire red brick barn, these holiday homes have been thoughtfully designed and created to ensure the utmost comfort coupled with the original appearance which is in keeping with the surrounding countryside. There are four properties of varying size, and a separate barn conversion which is suitable for up to 16 people. The conversion, Halford Big Barn, has eight bedrooms, four bathrooms, en suite facilities and ample space for a large family party. Some of the bedrooms are suitable for those partially disabled and there are many added facilities to give you that sense of luxury and style. You may think that this is rather a large number of people to be together, but there is honestly 'tons of space!' The beamed lounge is just one room, there is a second sitting room, dining room, entrance hall and sitting area, a large farmhouse kitchen, utility room....... the list just goes on! You could probably lose half the family for a week (if you so choose!) All this and character too! The property loses nothing of its charm and ambience, and really is a delightful relaxing holiday home.

The other four properties consist of two apartments and two cottages. The ground floor apartment is again suitable for the partially disabled and is for two people. It consists of one double bedroom, a lounge with dining area and an immaculately equipped kitchen. The second apartment is for two to four people and again is equipped to a very high standard. This apartment has the addition of an attractive balcony lounge which is ideal for relaxing on those balmy summer evenings. The two cottages are for five and six persons, and the standards are consistent with the other properties. Halford Big Barn is a four key property (highly recommended), and the remaining are three key. This is an idyllic location for a holiday at any time of year, with the scenery all around you and a wealth of activities at your fingertips. Walking is a joy here, with some superb walks direct from the property, and with the historic towns of Ludlow, Shrewsbury and Ironbridge a mere drive away there is not much more you could ask for. Craven Arms is less than a mile away with a host of shops, pubs and restaurants. Fishing, golf, horse riding, even hang gliding.........its all available...... and even if none of these pastimes appeal, there is just the beauty of the country and the clean fresh air.

USEFUL INFORMATION

OPEN : *All year* ***SELF CATERING***
PETS : *By prior arrangement* ***DISABLED ACCESS :*** *Some*
ACCOMMODATION : *Various sized parties from 2 to 16.*

LILLESHALL COTTAGES

Nantmawr,
Oswestry,
Shropshire
SY10 9HL

Tel: 01691 659358

The two cottages consists of two bedrooms (one with a double bed, and with bunk beds, one with double bed and single bed), shower room, living room, kitchen and porch. The kitchen is fully equipped and has a washing machine and tumble dryer. A log burner allows for cosy winter evenings, but central heating is also on for convenience. Both the renovation and the furnishing has been done to a high standard, making it somewhere you will want to come back to again and again. A open-plan garden looks out over fields with swings, a playhouse, and a very sociable pony! Car parking is next to the cottages and off the public road. All the services are included in the price, as is the linen. You need only to bring your food and yourselves.

The Cottages were built at the turn of the century with limestone hewn from the quarry close by. This was the major employer of labour in Nantmawr and the surrounding villages until it closed thirty years ago. Now it provides a home for buzzards, peregrines and kestrels along with foxes and badgers. A freshwater pond is home to newts, frogs and toads. Above the quarry is The Moelydd, a specified prime site for wild flowers and, because it is 1,000 feet above sea level, has spectacular views over Shropshire, Cheshire and Wales.

The Offa's Dyke path passes over The Moelydd providing a well-marked trail through beautiful countryside. Or you can take a gentle stroll through the lanes to the Horseshoe Pub where good food is served in lovely old fashioned surroundings. The village shop and post office, public telephone and the Royal Oak pub are all within a mile. A spectacular Mountain Bike Training Course covering 4,300 metres offers an exciting opportunity for mountain bike enthusiasts. Horse riders can use stabling on site for DIY livery and take advantage of the top quality cross country training course and surrounding countryside. Lilleshall Cottages really are a splendid base for a holiday in this wonderful part of Shropshire.

USEFUL INFORMATION

OPEN; *All year*
CHILDREN: *Welcome*
CREDIT CARDS; *None taken*
DISABLED ACCESS; *No special facilities*
ACCOMMODATION; *1 dbl 1 bunk beds, 1dbl, 1 single bed*

THE ASHE,
Bridstow,
Ross-on-Wye,
Herefordshire,
HR9 6QA.

Tel : 01989 563336

From farm barns to holiday homes of outstanding quality - this is what you will find at The Ashe, a 15th century sandstone farmhouse, set in 200 acres of arable farmland. Original beams and stone exposed walls all add to the character and ambience of these enchanting units, as does the excellent facilities provided in each. ***The Granary*** *and* ***The Mill*** *both have one double and one twin bedded room with bathroom and shower. There is a charming lounge with TV and video. The kitchen is fully fitted with all the necessities including microwave and dishwasher. Laundry facilities, linen towels and advanced grocery requirements can be provided on request. The Mill is on the ground floor with the Granary above, via access from the original stone steps.* ***Stable Cottage*** *is adjoining, and has one double and one single bedroom. This is suitable for the disabled and is as delightfully furnished as the others and has the same facilities.* ***Orchard Cottage*** *is detached and sits in the sunny orchard in a peaceful and tranquil garden. There are three bedrooms, one double, one twin, and a twin loft room. The attractive lounge opens into the garden , and the kitchen is fully and magnificently equipped. There are two bathrooms and a shower room. There is ample parking for all and you will have great delight in exploring the farm grounds themselves. Visitors are welcome to play their hand at the 3 par 18 hole golf course, or try a spot of fishing in the lakes, a game of tennis, or just sit and enjoy the beautiful vistas of the Wye Valley before you. The barbecue area is ideal for those evening get togethers, or perhaps a solitary stroll in the evening air is more to your liking. This place has everything, and you are sure to enjoy any length of stay at any time of year. It is ideal for a walking or touring holiday and is close enough to drive to many other attractions.*

USEFUL INFORMATION

OPEN : *All year*
CHILDREN : *Welcome*
PETS : *In Mill only*
ACCOMMODATION : *From 2 to 18 persons.*

SELF CATERING
DISABLED ACCESS : *Yes*
CREDIT CARDS : *None taken*

HALL FARM COUNTRY HOLIDAYS

Sedgeberrow,
Evesham,
Worcestershire
WR11 6UB

Tel: 01386 881298

Alan and Daphne Stow are busy farmers who 17 years ago took the brave step of buying Hall Farm and rather than demolishing all the buildings which were in a bad state, they opted for the far more difficult but very rewarding course of a restoration scheme. The result is an award from Wychavon for the best conversion in the county, and the holiday accommodation available to visitors is both delightful and comfortable. There are nine cottages and apartments altogether. The large Georgian Farmhouse and cottages overlook the green fields of the surrounding countryside and are set in over an acre of secluded, well-kept gardens with grass tennis court and orchard - marvellous place in which to relax. Daphne and Alan Stow live in the village at Lower Portway Farm and it is here you are invited to swim in the heated outdoor pool which is open every day from June to September except on Sundays when maintenance has to be carried out. The grass tennis court provides hours of fun, bicycles are available free of charge and you may fish from the banks of the riverside fields belonging to the farm. You can imagine how good walking is in this beautiful countryside and there is an abundance of wild life to be seen. For anyone feeling particularly energetic, the Stows are always delighted to have extra help at haymaking time!

Each property is centrally heated and equipped and furnished to a high standard including a number of antiques. The elegant, high ceilinged rooms in the main house, now skilfully converted into four charming apartments, and the cottage atmosphere of the adjoining properties give individuality to these splendid holiday homes. Moat Path & Stable Yard Cottages sleep 6 in 3 bedrooms. Hall Farm Cottage sleeps 4, Russet sleeps four but is not suitable for young children. Bramley sleeps 5 but is also not suitable for young children. Greengage sleeps 2 . Grooms and Carters both sleep 2 and Coopers a superb two-bedroomed cottage has a double and a twin both ensuite. One could go on writing about these extra special holiday homes but if you ring and get a brochure sent to you, you will begin to understand why Hall Farm is so highly recommended.

USEFUL INFORMATION

OPEN; *April-October*
CHILDREN; *Welcome*
CREDIT CARDS; *None taken*
DISABLED ACCESS; *Yes*
GARDEN; *Yes. Swimming Pool. Grass tennis court.*
PETS; *No*

WINTON HOUSE COTTAGE,
Winton House,
The Green,
Upper Quinton,
Stratford-upon-Avon,
Warwickshire
CV37 8SX.

Tel : 01789 720500
Mobile : 0831 485483
Email : lyong@ibm.net
Internet : www.hotelroomsonline.com/BHXWINT.htm

Winton House Cottage is situated in an area of outstanding beauty, in the lovely hamlet of Upper Quinton. It is overlooked by Meon Hill which is steeped in witchcraft and folklore, and is really a romantic setting for two. Set in the grounds of the original Victorian farmhouse this lovely cottage boasts a four poster bed in the charming studio room, which is fully equipped with all facilities including colour TV. The kitchen has a 'Parkray' which supplies all hot water and heating (there are additional electric heaters if required), and is fully fitted with the modern conveniences. The garden is south facing and there is a BBQ area with picnic table. Car parking is available in front of the cottage.

This is an idyllic spot which gives you access to many interesting places in the area. There are lots of walks and cycling paths, and many National Trust properties for you to visit.

USEFUL INFORMATION

OPEN : *All year*
CHILDREN : *Cot available*
CREDIT CARDS : *None taken*
ACCOMMODATION : *Cottage*

SELF CATERING
DISABLED ACCESS : *No*
GARDEN : *yes*

CHAPTER 5

THE MID-SHIRES
Including NOTTINGHAMSHIRE, LEICESTERSHIRE, LINCOLNSHIRE, DERBYSHIRE & NORTHAMPTONSHIRE

INCLUDES

THE MIDSHIRES
including NOTTINGHAMSHIRE, LEICESTERSHIRE, LINCOLNSHIRE DERBYSHIRE & NORTHAMPTONSHIRE

Nottinghamshire brings back memories of childhood stories and games involving the famous Robin Hood. Nowhere is there more evidence of the history and heritage than in the main city of **Nottingham** itself. Nottingham Castle, high above, overlooking the thronging streets, is the home of the annual Robin Hood Pageant which is held each year in October. It is also a museum and art gallery with impressive collections of glass, silver and ceramics. A short walk along Maid Marian Way will take you to the 'Tales of Robin Hood', where you can relive the legend in sight, sound and smell. But Nottingham has much more on offer. Take the underground caves - 400 hand chiselled caves beneath the city that were used for numerous reasons - first as dwellings and later as air raid shelters, tanneries and wine cellars. Famous names are associated with this city; Jessie Boots opened his first chemist shop here on Goosegate in 1864 - I wonder if he could foresee the success 'Boots' would have. The cycle manufacturers Raleigh also began in this city, but the most famous of all her products is probably Nottingham Lace. The story is that this became so popular that country girls were brought from the fields to work indoors, giving rise to the reputation of Nottingham girls having the best complexions in England! The Lace Hall tells the fascinating story of lace, and the Lace Centre offers a floor to ceiling array of the products which you can admire and even buy.

The modern Nottingham is a great shopping centre having been voted the fourth best in the UK. It has two spacious shopping centres and many pedestrianised streets to browse round. Derby Road is for the antique enthusiasts, and there are lots of bistros, cafes and restaurants where you can take a break. The indoor market in the Victoria Centre is a must for bargain hunters, and much good local produce is sold here.

The surrounding countryside is full of things for the active and not so active. Cycling along quiet byways, self guided walks and horse riding for trekking round what they call 'Robin Hood Country'. There are plenty of golf courses, and archery is quite popular here - again probably due to the historic Robin. You can visit the birthplace of author DH Lawrence at **Eastwood**, or visitthe Bramley Apple Exhibition at **Southwell.** At **Winthorpe**, the Newark Air Museum has more than 30 historic aircraft on show, including a Vulcan bomber. Sherwood Forest at **Edwinstowe** is not only famous for being the home of Robin Hood, but for it's natural history and fascinating wildlife. Rangers offer guided walks telling of the impressive stagheaded oaks and silver birch glades. The visitors centre has an excellent range of heritage shops and superb catering facilities. Edwinstowe village and the church of St. Mary is where Robin married Maid Marian, and the painted scenes and carvings in the church would seem to endorse this. For the serious walker the 'Robin Hood Way' is a charming manner in which to link and visit the many sites associated with this hero.

Nottinghamshire also has links with the Pilgrim Fathers as the leaders of the Mayflower Expedition were born at **Scrooby.** Babworth Church is the focus of many ancestral seeking visitors, as this was where the first sermons were preached by Richard Clifton. There are many places of interest in this fine county - **Wellow,** close to Rufford Abbey still has a maypole in the village green, **Scarrington's** blacksmith shop has a collection of over 50,000 horseshoes, and **Hawksworth** has a glorious church and manor house, along with a huge dovecote. Clumber Park at **Worksop** is high on my list as a place to visit. 3,800 acres of forest, countryside and beautifully landscaped gardens with an 80 acre lake at it's centre. This was once home to the Dukes of Newcastle, and includes a fine Gothic Revival Chapel, walled garden and the longest double lime tree avenue in Europe.

Tea is a popular pastime in Nottinghamshire, and in most towns and villages there are ample opportunities to sample many home made recipes in tea shops. The friendly people are only too anxious to make you feel welcome, and are justifiably proud of their Shire and it's background.

Derby is a particularly fine city. With over 2000 acres of parkland and green open spaces, the city has a spacious, roomy feel to it, and with so much parkland it is a simple task to get away from the hustle and bustle for a few hours. Derby is known for it's porcelain, and any visit must include a tour of the Royal Crown Derby Porcelain Company. Shopping is very good too, with modern and traditional blending well together, and with many areas being pedestrianised. The Markeaton Craft Village is where you will find a host of hand-made items, and you can watch many of the artists at work, practising their skills. The museums here are different, an example being Rolls Royce and the Industrial Museum. The Cathedral of All Saints has one of the highest perpendicular towers in the country, and houses the oldest ring of ten bells in the world.

To the north of the city, near **Ashbourne,** is Kedleston Hall. This is a neo-classical palace designed by the great Robert Adams in 1759 for the Curzon family. This beautiful house is set in handsome landscaped gardens, and features include the magnificent Marble Hall and Lord Curzon's Indian Museum.

Sudbury Hall at Ashbourne is another fascinating place to visit, and includes intricate wood carvings by Grinling Gibbons and a magnificent carved staircase by Edward Pierce. Also here is the National Trust Museum of Childhood where you can take a bewitching look at childrens play in Edwardian and Victorian times. This appeals very much to children and there is a wonderful shrinking corridor and chimney climb for the bold (you must be sweep size!).

Outdoors you have the South Peak Estate at **Ilam** where the National Trust have an information centre giving details of the 3,800 acres. The green fields and drystone walls are very characteristic of this area furnishing a soft, undulating landscape which is gentle and tranquil. There are 84 acres of parkland with magnificent views, and a shop and tea room.

To the south of Derby at **Ticknall** lies Calke Abbey, known as 'the house that time forgot'. It is virtually unaltered since the death of the last Baronet in 1924 and is a fascinating place to visit. Crammed full of possessions, it portrays an English country house in decline and offers great insight into the life of an English upper class home.

Derbyshire with it's beautiful countryside has a host outdoor activities available, and many attractions which suit all the family. One of the most popular of these is Alton Towers which is travelled to from all parts of the country. The Midland Railway Centre is a great day out, or you can climb the heights in a cable car at the 'Heights of Abraham' in **Matlock Bath.**

Chesterfield is a charming market town which is famous for it's crooked spire, and which has a wonderful open air market where you can buy almost anything! Hardwick Hall, just outside, is one of the most spectacular Elizabethan homes in England and appears to have more 'glass than walls'. The inside is just as spectacular with wonderful tapestries and needlework, contemporary furniture and a striking frieze in the High Great Chamber.

Lincolnshire is a county of rich fertile lands with the gently rounded Wolds in the north and the lush farmland in the south. The great marshes of the south are a refuge for many birds and wildfowl that is unequalled anywhere in Britain. Saltfleetby-Theddlethorp dunes run over four miles along the North Lincolnshire coast and include a specially protected area for the rare natterjack toad. **Lincoln** is the main city and has over 2,000 years of history for you to enjoy. There are Roman remains, including Newport Arch, which is the oldest Roman archway still used by traffic. Lincoln was also an important centre in Viking times, and when the Norman invasion of William the Conqueror reached the city, they built a magnificent cathedral and castle. The cathedral was started in 1072 and some of the original church still exists, but some was destroyed by fire and earthquake in the 12th century, and the remainder of the existing structure is Gothic from the 13th and 14th centuries. It is a magnificent building and has many attractive features including the beautiful stained glass windows, and the splendid open nave. Lincoln Castle dates back to 1068 and is on the site of the original Roman fortress. Again, it is a glorious building with great architecture from various ages of our past - one of these being when it was used as a Victorian prison. One of the most interesting attractions for me was the Jewish quarter of the city. Jews House is thought to be one of the oldest domestic buildings in Britain, dating from around 1170, and nearby Jews Court is the site of an old synagogue. There are many black and white buildings around the city which date back to the prosperous times of the wool trade. Leisure and shopping are both catered for very well here with a multitude of shops both major and specialist, and a good cultural mixture for all tastes. Sport plays a big part with many top class sporting activities like city centre cycle rides, and of course Lincoln City Football Club, and Lincolnshire Cricket Club. The waterways offer boat trips, fishing, yachting, water skiing, while there are many excellent walks in and around the city.

Further afield there are many places to be explored, and I will mention just a few. Belton House at **Grantham** is a Restoration house built between 1685 and 1688, and has wonderful gardens and a superb orangery. The furnishings and decoration inside is breathtaking, and this house was used as the setting for 'Rosings', home of lady Catherine de Bourgh in the BBC's production of 'Pride and Prejudice'. **Tatershall** Castle was built for Ralph Cromwell, Lord Treasurer of England in 1440. Inside there are some very fine features but the views across Lincolnshire from the battlements is well worth the climb! The home of Sir Isaac Newton was Woolsthorpe Manor at**Woolsthorpe-by-Colsterworth.** This is a small 17th century farmhouse with an orchard - and perhaps having the descendant of that famous apple tree!

Gunby Hall near **Spilsby** is reputedly Tennyson's 'haunt of ancient peace' and is a red brick country house with a fine oak staircase, English furniture and pretty gardens. Nearby at **Bratoft** is Whitegates cottage which is a good example of mud and stud walling beneath a long-straw thatched roof. This has recently been restored using traditional methods proving that not all traditional crafts and arts have been lost.

At the heart of Leicestershire is a lively, cosmopolitan city - **Leicester**. This is a city at peace with the surrounding countryside and it's place in the bigger picture of things. It is environmentally conscious and offers the visitor a vibrant and entertaining stay. Historically it has been inhabited since before Roman times, and has a wealth of attractions to see. The museum and art gallery includes the famous dinosaur from Rutland, Egyptian artefacts, German expressionist painting, and a collection of important decorative arts. The massive walls built by the Romans still stand as a testament to their engineering skills, and a walk round Castle Park takes you through much of the city's rich and colourful history. Churches, buildings, ancient walls, gateways and museums are all together in this area and display a sumptuous record of the past.

Leicester is also unique in that it has the biggest proportion of residents of Indian origin in Great Britain. To sample some of this diverse culture try shopping along the Golden Mile, the busy centre of the Gujarati community. Leicester also boasts the only Jain Temple in Europe, and one of the largest saree shops outside India. Due to the diversity of the population there is a wealth of festivals and events to be celebrated, making for almost a daily carnival atmosphere, and one which all can enjoy.

The countryside is full of villages and towns waiting to be explored. Lincolnshire is cut almost equally in two by the River Soar which flows through the centre of Leicester to join the Nottinhampshire Trent, and there is a lot of history associated with the Grand Union Canal which is two hundred years old. At Foxton Locks, near **Market Harborough,** there is a canal museum, including the remains of an unusual Victorian steam powered lift designed to transport narrow boats up a set of ten canals - fascinating!

Northwards from the city lies **Melton Mowbray** (home of scrumptious pork pies) and one of the most beautiful parish churches in England. St. Mary's is quite wonderful with it's early 14th century Galilee Porch and majestic tower with it's perpendicular crown. **Loughborough** is a town famous for it's bells, and you can visit one of the world's leading bell foundries here. To the north east is **Ashby-de-la-Zouch**, a spa town in the 19th century, which has excellent shopping facilities and an indoor market. It takes it's name from the Breton la Zouch family who acquired Ashby Manor in 1160. **Coalville** is set on the edge of Charnwood Forest and takes it's name from the opening of the Colliery in the 1820s.

To the east, lovers of the countryside will delight in **Rutland Water.** This 3,300 acre man made lake has facilities for visitors of all ages, and you can enjoy the peace and tranquillity this beautiful oasis offers. There are Water Guides to help you explore, and you can sample anything from a lake cruise to visiting the exotic butterfly and aquatic centre. This is a lovely part of the country, and one which offers complete relaxation in the most serene surroundings.

GATEHAM GRANGE FARM,
Alstonefield, Ashbourne,
Derbyshire DE6 2FT.
Tel : 01335 310349

Robert and Teresa Flower are the owners of this 150 acre working farm in the delightful Peak District. Walking and cycling are the ideal hobbies with many local footpaths and 'gentle' roads around the farm. The village of Hartington is only a few miles away and here you will find a good array of shops, restaurants and an interesting cheese factory (famous for it's Stilton). This is the ideal spot for relaxing and unwinding, but within easy reach of many attractions if the need should arise!

The accommodation consists of two cottages. Gateham cottage is part of the large farmhouse that has been converted into a self contained cottage. It is charmingly decorated and furnished and can provide a perfect family holiday for up to six guests. The living room is upstairs to take advantage of the views, and is a comfortable, relaxing room. The kitchen is fully fitted, and a cot and high chair are available on request. The Coach House has been recently renovated and enjoys stunning views. Again it will comfortably accommodate six guests and has full facilities. There is ample parking space for both cottages, and guests are welcome to sit out in the garden.

USEFUL INFORMATION

OPEN : *All year*
CHILDREN : *Welcome*
PETS : *No*
SELF CATERING
DISABLED ACCESS : *No*
CREDIT CARDS : *None taken*
ACCOMMODATION : *2 cottages for up to 6 guests.*

YELDERSLEY HALL,
Yeldersley, Ashbourne,
Derbyshire, DE6 1LS.
Tel : 01335 343432

Yeldersley Hall is a charming country house with interesting and extensive grounds, in the heart of the beautiful Derbyshire countryside. It contains a fully restored Victorian green house and orangery, and guests are most welcome to wander round the estate. There are three flats, all part of the main house, which are beautifully furnished and decorated. Great care has been taken with detail, and the charm and elegance of this property shines in each apartment. Two of the flats have been created from the former laundry, and have a cosy cottage ambience. The east wing apartment has a huge amount of space, and many of the original features have been retained. All of its main rooms are south facing, with views over the garden and the surrounding countryside. Although maintaining the grace of a bygone era, the modern conveniences have been added! Genuine antiques provide a final touch of character making this a wonderful experience in comfort and luxury. The surrounding area offers many attractions, and if you should wish to venture further afield, there is a host of things to see and do. Derbyshire's National Park is ideal for walking, and there are many attractive villages and towns.

USEFUL INFORMATION

OPEN :*All year*
CHILDREN : *Over 10 yrs (Babies up to 6 mths)*
PETS : *No*
ACCOMMODATION : *3 apartments (2 sleeping 2 persons; east wing sleeeping 4)*

SLADE HOUSE FARM
Ilam, Nr Ashbourne,
Derbyshire DE6 2BB

Tel: 01663 745144

If you are after wonderful scenery, fresh air, peace and tranquillity, then look no further than Slade House Farm where Alan and Pat Philp have their superb cottages. Situated within the boundary of the Peak National Park these self-contained cottages offer quality accommodation, each with their own garden, set in 7 acres of farmland in a location that will take your breath away. There are 3 cottages, ***Slade House*** *is a listed building dating back to 1642 and was a former Yeomans House, this is a large property accommodating 8 persons comfortably. There is a charming farmhouse kitchen and a very comfortable sitting room, both rooms are large and with wood burning stoves. A shower room is also on the ground floor. On the first floor are 2 double bedrooms both ensuite, there are 2 twin bedded rooms on the second floor with exposed beams and a separate bathroom and drying room.* ***Slade Cottage*** *has outstanding views from a secluded courtyard and stone-cobbled patio. The kitchen and dining area has a quarry tiled floor and the original farmhouse range, also on this floor is a cloakroom and an ensuite double bedroom. Upstairs the former cheese room has been used to create a large sitting room with exposed beams, red brick chimney housing a wood burner, off which is a very cosy ensuite twin bedded room. And finally in this excellent setting is* ***Slade Tops*** *the most perfect accommodation for 2 people, the split level barn has been converted to provide a luxurious and spacious property. The sitting room is delightful with a pine boarded ceiling and once again a wood burner, a few steps lead down to the kitchen and dining area, there is a double bedroom and a luxury bathroom. Each cottage has been carefully and lovingly thought out, they all have central heating and logs are provided free for the first load, if you require more you may have to do some chopping! The kitchens are exceptionally furnished including fridge freezer, microwave and dishwasher. All linen, duvets and towels are provided, also electric blankets for those chilly nights. Colour televisions and pay phones. Electricity is by meter reading.*

The activities in this area are wide and varied, for the energetic there is Alton Towers and The Roaches where you can rock climb. A few miles away is Brown End Farm, here you can hire bikes plus all the equipment and cycle along The Manifold Valley, a 9 mile Tarmac, flat and safe track, where cars are banned, and drink in the beautiful countryside. There are also plenty of museums and country houses and gardens, with fishing and sailing there is something for everyone. Once you have stayed at these '4 & 5 Key Highly Commended' properties you will want to return again and again.

USEFUL INFORMATION

OPEN: *All year*
CHILDREN: *Welcome, baby sitting by arrangement, cots available*
ACCOMMODATION: *Slade House sleeps 8 Slade Cottage sleeps 4, Slade Tops sleeps 2*

GARDEN: *Yes. Garden furniture.*
CREDIT CARDS: *None taken*
PETS: *No*
Short Breaks available

All cottages are totally NON-SMOKING

THROWLEY COTTAGE &
THROWLEY MOOR FARM

c/o Throwley Hall Farm,
Ilam,
Nr. Ashbourne,
Derbyshire
DE6 2BB

Tel: 01538 308202/308243

At the gateway to the Peak District near the beautiful Manifold Valley and Dovedale are two superbly appointed self-catering properties. Throwley Cottage accommodates 7 people and Throwley Moor Farm 12. Both have dining kitchen with electric cooker, microwave oven, fridge, freezer and dishwasher.

The Cottage has storage heaters and a lounge with colour television and studio couch. Throwley Moor has central heating, sitting room with colour TV and a lounge/games room. Both houses have fitted carpets except in the kitchen, pay-phone, washer and dryer. Linen is available for hire. Cots and high chairs are supplied. Dogs are welcome at extra cost and must be kept on a lead. Throwley Moor can comfortably cater for large groups, whilst the cottage is just right for families. The English Tourist Board has given the two properties the award of '4 Keys Commended'.

The location is wonderful with breathtaking scenery, superb walks, golf, riding and fishing. Alton Towers, Gulliver's Kingdom and American Adventure are only short car journeys away. Self-catering gives you the freedom to do exactly what you want when you want, and to be able to do that here is an added bonus. You will be glad you came.

USEFUL INFORMATION

OPEN; *All year*
CHILDREN; *Welcome*
CREDIT CARDS; *None taken*
LICENSED; *Not applicable*
ACCOMMODATION; *2 self-catering properties, 1 sleeping up to 7 persons the other sleeping up to 12 persons*

DINING ROOM; *Not applicable*
VEGETARIAN; *Not applicable*
DISABLED ACCESS; *No*
GARDEN; *Yes*
PETS; *Yes at extra cost*

DOG & PARTRIDGE COUNTRY INN,
Swinscoe, Ashbourne,
Derbyshire DE6 2HS.
Tel : 01335 343183

The Dog & Partridge is a beautiful 17th century inn situated in the hamlet of Swinscoe on the Derbyshire/Staffordshire border. Here, the Stelfox family offer warm hospitality in this most welcoming of inns. The traditional bar is the ideal place to relax and unwind, and it's glowing log fires in the winter months only add to the ambience and character. Food is served all day, and there is a wide range of choices with many local specialities. Vegetarian and special diets are cheerfully catered for, and there are both outdoor and indoor play areas for children.

The self catering accommodation is of the same high standards and is purpose built. There are full facilities in each cottage and all are charmingly decorated and furnished. This is a great base from which to see the surrounding countryside, and really is a walker's paradise. The views are breathtaking with the gentle Dales and stunning sweeps of limestone cliff. There are many other attractions close by including the famous Alton Towers which provides a great day out for the children (and those adults of strong constitution). This is a beautiful area, and one to which you will find yourself returning time and time again.

USEFUL INFORMATION

OPEN : *All year* | ***RESTAURANT :*** *Food all day*
CHILDREN ; *Welcome* | ***VEGETARIAN :*** *Catered for*
PETS : *Welcome* | ***DISABLED ACCESS :*** *No*
LICENSED : *Full* | ***CREDIT CARDS :*** *All major*
ACCOMMODATION :*B&B and Self catering.*

PARKVIEW FARM,
Weston Underwood,
Ashbourne,
Derbyshire DE6 4PA.
Tel : 01335 360352

Parkview Farm is a 370 acre farm with an attractive Victorian farmhouse. Linda and Michael Adams, the owners, offer guest either bed & breakfast accommodation at the farmhouse, or self catering accommodation at one of the two cottages set in the delightful Derbyshire countryside. All are beautifully appointed with much care and attention paid to furnishings and decor. Honeysuckle Cottage is located down a peaceful leafy lane just outside the village and offers wonderful views over the surrounding countryside. It will accommodate up to 6 guests and has a beautiful four poster bed in the double room. The other cottage, Brook Cottage, is in the village of Weston Underwood and is surrounded by pleasant walks in the nearby lanes. Both cottages are comfortably furnished, with much character and charm.

There are many attractions in the area such as the Peak District National Park. Alton Towers is nearby, and there are many National Trust properties and gardens to be visited. This is a lovely spot to relax, and you will surely enjoy your stay at one of these delightful cottages.

USEFUL INFORMATION

OPEN : *All year* | ***DINING ROOM :*** *Traditional English*
CHILDREN : *Welcome* | ***DISABLED ACCESS :*** *No*
PETS : *No* | ***CREDIT CARDS :*** *None taken*
ACCOMMODATION : *B&B or self catering.*

CHAPTER 6

GLOUCESTER, OXFORD & THE COTSWOLDS

INCLUDES

GLOUCESTER, OXFORD & THE COTSWOLDS

Oxford, city of 'dreaming spires', is the oldest university city in the country, and holds a special charm in it's many colleges with their quadrangles and chapels. These are open to visitors each day and you can stroll alongside the undergraduates as they scurry to and fro on foot, or ride by, gowns flapping, on bicycles. At times like this you may feel that this city has not changed since the 12th century, (apart from the bicycles) and with the beautiful buildings on view it is a delight to wander this city. Great Tom, the bell in Wren's Tom Tower is tolled 101 times every night at 9.05pm, and is the old signal for the closing of the college gates. On May Day you will find the **Cherwell** packed with punts at 5am to hear the Choristers of Magdalen sing a Latin hymn to salute the day from Magdalen Tower.

A wonderful experience that will never be forgotten! A number of colleges have beautiful gardens including Wadham, New College, and Trinity. The Ashmolean Museum holds the lantern used by the famous Guy Fawkes and also the Alfred Jewel which is believed to have been made for King Alfred in the 9th century. Bodleian Library is one of the world's most important libraries and holds in excess of 4 million books and manuscripts. (I think I could happily spend the rest of my life here!) The Broad, the High, Cornmarket and the narrow lanes leading off them is the centre of University life, and is where you will find good shops, restaurants, public houses and the old colleges.

Radiating out from Oxford you will find many towns and villages well worth exploring. **Woodstock** is one of these, home of Blenheim Castle, built between 1705 and 1722, and presented to the 1st Duke of Marlborough by Queen Anne, after his victory over the French. This was the birthplace of Sir Winston Churchill, and includes many fine paintings, tapestries and furnishings. The gardens here are regarded as some of Capability Brown's finest works. Travelling further round we have **Witney, Abingdon,** and the pretty village of **Northmoor** which are all worth visiting. Witney has a working museum of Victorian rural life on a 20 acre site. This is a great day out with activities for all the family - Manor House, riverside walk, various breeds of animals, gardens and much more. Church Green has the beautiful church of St Mary with it's spire of 150ft soaring above the town. Again, there is a great deal of history in this town, and all just waiting to be explored!

Moving on to **Banbury** in the north takes us through Oxford Canal Country with it's pretty villages dotted adjacent to the canals, and with superb views of the gentle rolling countryside and open waterways. Banbury is in Ironstone Country with it's distinctive honey coloured stone cottages, sometimes thatched, and always pretty. It dates from medieval times and the Historic Town Trail will take you through the history of this busy market town.

Coming back down to **Bicester** we travel through Flora Thompson country, who immortalised the villages of **Fringford, Cottisford** and the hamlet of **Juniper Hill** in 'Lark Rise to Candleford.' Bicester is a busy thriving market town of Saxon origin, and is home of the purpose built Bicester Village - a New England style shopping attraction with many well known brands and shops, both designer and otherwise.

Again south of Oxford, we travel from **Wallingford** to **Henley on Thames**. Here the roads hug the riverside, but in late June and early July the area can become rather busy, as this is the time of the famous Royal Regatta.

Travelling across from Wallingford, takes you past **Didford** (the exciting home of Formula IRacing), and past **Steventon** (4 miles south of Abington), a picturesque village with a rather unique raised causeway in the village green, and on to **Swindon.** Here we are at the entry to Gloucestershire and in a town which is probably the only major one in the area. Swindon is known in it's relation to the Brunel Great Western Railway and the town that grew up around it, but in fact there has been a town here since at least the 11th century, and it is an interesting contrast of old and new. The Western Railway Museum is a must for enthusiasts, but there are plenty of other interesting spots and many leisure facilities. Swindon has been in the news lately because of its participation in the experiment of a cashless economy. This is where the pilot scheme for the 'Mondex' card is being tried; a card that can be loaded with money from your account and which can communicate with other electronic tills to lose or gain money.

Frankly I'm not sure what all the fuss is about, as we have been doing this through various cards such as Switch and Electron for some time now. I still like to have the reassuring 'wad' of *real* money in my possession - if only for a short period of time until I reach the check out and pay the shopping bill! Talking of shopping, Swindon has very good facilities - again it was a pioneer in pedestrianisation - closing its main street to traffic over 30 years ago. It has all the major shops in beautifully designed shopping centres which are modern yet tastefully reflecting the past of this town. The Brunel Shopping Centre has the feel of a Victorian railway station and is host to many of the chief names in shopping along with many individual, specialist outlets. Sports and leisure centres are plentiful, and you can enjoy swimming, ice skating, superbowl, golf and much more at any time of year.

As Swindon is where the West Country meets The Cotswolds, this leads us very nicely into the next section. The Cotswolds are one of England's most beautiful areas; the charming medieval towns and villages built in the warm mellow stone of the district, and the soft rolling countryside with it's woodlands and grasslands. Nowhere else is man seen to be so in harmony with his surroundings; the buildings are a natural part of the countryside which blend in accord with the environment. The Cotswolds are a designated area of outstanding beauty (the largest in the country) and cover an area of nearly 800 sq miles. This is an area which has been inhabited for many thousands of years, and to keep and protect this 'living landscape' income from tourism, local crafts and shops is a very important part of the local economy. Visitors are made extremely welcome, and it is delightful to spend a night's rest in some of the most charming homes in the country. I cannot mention all the market towns and villages, but a few will give you a taste of the rich history and background that assails the senses in every hamlet visited. **Bourton-on-the Water** is one of the most popular and well known villages, due to the **River Windrush** running through the centre of the village and crossed by several bridges. It is likened to Venice, and is a very appealing place to visit. One unusual exhibition is the Perfumery Exhibition. There is a 'Smelly Vision' theatre which gives an explanation through audio and vision, of plant extracts used, and a beautiful perfume garden where the fragrances are wonderful. **Chipping Campden** is often thought of as the jewel of the Cotswolds, and is an extremely attractive town. It's traditional buildings have been carefully restored in the warm honey coloured stone that is reflective of the area. St.James' Church, built around the 15th century, is interesting with it's 120 ft tower and a superb collection of monumental brasses. The 'Cotswolds Olympics' are held in this town each year, and have been so since founded by Captain Robert Dover in the 17th century. This is a great place for local arts and crafts, and a day can be spent happily browsing round the delightful shops.

The **River Thames** begins it's journey in the town of **Lechlade**, and St John's Lock is where they shipped the local stone from to build St Paul's Cathedral in London. The lock is still working today, but is more likely to carry pleasure boats than working barges. This is a peaceful, tranquil spot, and one where you can enjoy the luxury of total relaxation!

One of my favourites is the small town of **Stow-on-the-Wold.** This may be rather coloured as I have a passion for antique shops, and this (to me) is the idea of heaven. Even to window shop is a dream, and the quality and novelty of the pieces will have you exclaiming in delight (and possibly emptying the bank account!). It is the highest town on the Cotswolds Hills, and presents a rather timeless quality with the elegant 17th and 18th century buildings. Definitely not to be missed!

Minchinhampton is another of those charming ancient towns with a great history of weaving, and situated on the hilltop between the Golden and Nailsworth valleys. **Nailsworth** is a busy town which stands at the junction of the road to Tetbury and Bath, and which has a rich history as a centre of the wool industry. The lovely Georgian and Jacobean houses are attributed to the wealth brought here by the industry. Another unspoilt Cotswold town is that of **Winchcombe** near Cheltenham, and St Peter's Church with it's marvelous, irreverent gargoyles can be seen from almost any part of the town. This is where you will find Sudley Castle, where Katherine Parr, the sixth wife of Henry VIII, made her home. It was also Charles I's headquarters for some time during the civil war. The castle today is home to Lord and Lady Ashcombe, and included in the impressive collection is the prayer book of Katherine Parr and the bed of Charles I. There are some fine paintings, furniture and tapestries here, and in addition there is a children's play park and a bird garden. It is surrounded by eight charming gardens with long avenues of majestic trees, shrubs, grand old yew hedges and wide expanses of still open water. The centrepiece of these fine gardens is the Queen's Garden, named after Queen Katherine Parr, and winner of the HHA/ Chiristies Garden of the Year Award 1996.

Passing **Stroud** and **Stonehouse**, and on to **Berkeley** near the **Severn,** where stands Berkeley Castle, one of the oldest inhabited castles in England and site of the murder of Edward II in 1327.

Also here is the Jenner Museum which tells the fascinating story of Dr. Edward Jenner and his first vaccination in 1796. It is quite interesting to learn how a cow, a milkmaid and a small boy played their parts in this discovery.

Brookthorpe is a pleasant location outside **Gloucester** with good accommodation, which is an excellent base for visiting the various attractions in the surrounding area without actually staying in one of the busy towns. Gloucester is an extremely cultural city with a rich historical background and a strong tradition of welcome. The Norman Cathedral is one of the most beautiful in Britain and is a wonderful landmark for the surrounding countryside. The tomb of Edward II is here and the largest stained glass window in the country measuring 72 x 38ft depicting the Coronation of the Virgin. Step back in time and follow the monks through the fan vaulted cloisters, visit the crypt and the Cathedral Exhibition, and just enjoy this wonderful monument to Britain's history! There are lots of museums in this fine city, and the past is all around just waiting to be explored. For those interested, the Gloucester Docks is a must on the list of places to be visited. Fifteen Victorian Warehouses still stand as a reminder of the times when Gloucester was the gateway to waterbourne traffic reaching the Midlands, and you can envisage the tall ships and barges that once queued to enter this port. Nowadays it is full of museums and wonderful shops, furnishing a great 'day out' for all the family. One of the attractions is the National Waterways Museum which shows the development of the inland waterways over the last 200 years. This is a 'hands on' experience with you having the opportunity to drive a barge through a lock and see how families once lived on the barges. If you find all this just too much then there is a good variety of bars, cafes and restaurants where you can relax and enjoy a pleasant meal or snack. I cannot mention Gloucester without the dry ski slope, where I have spent many a full day at the Races. This is a fun event for the children, with parents being probably more involved than is good for their blood pressure!

Cheltenham with its impressive Regency architecture and tree lined avenues offers a rather special character and style to this spa town. Originally the spa was discovered 250 years ago, and the enterprising owner saw a future in the use of the waters. The story of this is very entertaining and although a bit incredible is ardently believed by the local people. The town became fashionable in 1788 when King George III and his family set up court here for five weeks, but was probably made more popular by the Duke of Wellington who found relief for a disordered liver and strongly recommended it to his officers and families. Along with the spa waters one of the main reasons that visitors flock to Cheltenham is for the horse racing at the Cheltenham course, one of the prettiest in the country. At times of meetings the town is full to overflowing and a wonderful atmosphere permeates the whole area.

On to **Tewkesbury** with it's old picturesque streets and interesting shops. On the edge of town, where the Severn is joined by the Avon, you will find the Benedictine monastery, Tewkesbury Abbey. This magnificent building is in wonderful condition with it's giant columns, painted and gilded ceilings and it's monuments. There are monuments to the Prince of Wales, Sir Edward Despenser, Standard Bearer to the Black Prince, and many more. Today the Abbey is a musical centre, and also has a series of tours and events which commemorates it's great history. This is where the decisive battle of the War of the Roses was fought in 1471 - a decidedly historical part of England! The Battle of Tewkesbury and the Medieval Fayre are re enacted each year, and make for a very exciting event. There are many more historic buildings such as the Old Baptist Chapel, the Little Museum and the Town Museum which are all worth a visit.

The rivers form quite a major part of Tewkesbury, and many cruises are available to take you into either Shakespeare country or down towards the Bristol Channel. A spectacular event is the Tewkesbury Water Festival with it's fireworks and displays, but at any time of year the rivers are to be enjoyed and are great for relaxing. Shopping here is a diverse activity with a variety of shops not only in Tewkesbury but in the surrounding towns and villages. Hand printed silks from **Beckford,** craft potteries at **Conderton, Bredon** and **Winchcombe** are just a couple of the interesting places that are easy to call on.

Another interesting activity in the area suitable for all ages is the Gloucestershire Warwickshire Railway. This steam railway is not only spectacular for enthusiasts, but runs a series of special events throughout the year aimed at children. Something else for the children is the Cotswold Farm Park where over 50 breeds of rare British livestock are reared. From Old Spot pigs to Shire horses, the children will be fascinated by seeing these animals in their natural habitat. For those children who may have a short attention span there is also a great adventure playground, and for the adults afflicted the same way, there is seasonal exhibitions, gift shops and a welcoming cafe.

The Forest of Dean will enchant you like no other place. King Canute in 1016 is to be thanked for this when he decreed that 27,000 acres should become a royal hunting ground. The area stretches from the River Wye on the western border to the River Severn on the eastern. It has many attractions revealing evidence of its industrial past, but the real beauty to me is in the changing landscape and wildlife which abounds in this haven of nature. At any time of year the beauty is breathtaking with autumn colours of red and golds , spring carpets of bluebells, summer tranquillity, and even the harshness of winter. Outdoor activities thrive here and you can enjoy walking, cycling, rock climbing, caving, abseiling to name just a few. Local crafts such as pottery, handmade glass and even organic foods are popular, and there are many exhibitions of local art and sculpture to entrance you. The history of the area includes coal mining and timber,and nowhere is this brought more forcibly home than at Clearwell Caves which show the dangerous and courageous lives that the miners must have lived. Eight caverns are open to the public, and although very beautiful with calcite, you can see the horrific labour involved in bringing ore to the surface. To think that small boys were used in these mines is quite unbelievable. Today one of the chambers is home to the Greater and Lesser Horseshoe Bats and the tour will take you through this - don't worry - they usually use it for hibernating through the winter months!

Nearby is Puzzle Wood, which was created out of some open cast iron workings which were left to gather moss. It was landscaped in the 19th century, creating a puzzle path with steps, bridges and seats, and is a very pleasant spot for a picnic.

There are many other places of interest in this beautiful forest; the Dean Heritage Centre, the Dean Forest Railway, the Mohair Centre, and Westbury Court Gardens are just a few of the stimulating variety of options to the visitor. To spend some time here is to find yourself eager to return and explore the many beautiful sights and sounds of this entrancing forest.

WINDMILL ANNEXE
Castle Fruit Farm,
Castle Tump,
Newent,
Gloucestershire
GL18 1LS

Tel/Fax: 01531 890428

There is seldom a more unusual sight from the windows of a self catering apartment than a windmill. That is exactly what you will find when you stay in the Windmill Annexe; an extension to a beautiful Georgian country house. The windmill is unique in design and originally used to generate electricity for the house in the 1930's.

There is much more of interest. Castle Fruit Farm, built on 13th century castle ruins, is a large working farm with orchards spreading into the distance, growing apples, pears and plums. Imagine the sight and perfume at blossom time! Situated approximately two miles between Newent and Dymock on the B4215, it is within easy access from the M50 motorway. You will find, apart from the natural beauty spots of the Malvern Hills and the Forest of Dean, popular territories for walkers. The Cathedral Cities of Gloucester, Hereford and Worcester are all within easy reach including the Regency Spa Town of Cheltenham; a veritable shopper's paradise! There are pretty villages, stately homes and many other attractions to discover as well as a good variety of pubs and restaurants. In fact, Windmill Annexe is a perfect base for a relaxed and varied holiday; so much so, that you will want to come back for more!

The Annexe has its own private entrance and safe parking for two cars. It comfortably sleeps four people in double and twin bedded rooms. The attractive lounge has large picture windows and opens on to lawns and gardens for you to wander through and seek secluded corners to relax in privacy. There is a choice of underfloor heating, central heating and the use of a log fire for really cold days if you wish. Built on one level to initially accommodate a family member using a wheelchair, it offers great benefit if you have a similar disability. There is ample room to manoeuvre and all plugs and switches are within easy reach. Support handrails are available in the bathroom and further aids can be supplied. John and Gilli Nicolson, the owners, are happy to arrange for groceries to be available upon arrival and to discuss any other requirements you may have. When in season, apples, pears, and delicious plums can be purchased from the Farm Shop.

USEFUL INFORMATION

OPEN: *All year* ***CHILDREN:*** *Welcome*
DISABLED ACCESS: *Yes, one level, special facilities* ***GARDEN:*** *Yes*
ACTIVITIES: *Walking the footpaths, fishing*

HEATH FARM HOLIDAY COTTAGES,
Heath Farm,
Swerford. Chipping Norton,
Oxon OX7 4BN.
Tel : 01608 683270/204

70 acres of farm and woodland, with fresh air and the breathtaking beauty of the Cotswolds on your doorstep. Heath Farm is a first class location to enjoy all the county has to offer, and at the same time a private, tranquil hideaway where you can enjoy the peace and serenity of the countryside.

David and Nena Barbour are your hosts at this delightful farm, and offer a standard of service that would be difficult to surpass. The apartments are converted farm buildings, and are set around a stunning central courtyard with water garden. Furniture and fittings have been built by local craftsmen, mostly from the farm's own trees, and a local blacksmith has designed and created the ironwork on many of the doors, windows and fireplaces. This is a skillfully and imaginatively thought out place, but with the warmth and ambience associated with good management and thoughtful hosts. Each apartment is fully fitted with all modern conveniences, and there are apartments for between two and four guests. Although highly recommended by the English Tourist Board, the best accolades must be from guests who return time and time again to this haven in the beautiful Cotswolds!

USEFUL INFORMATION

OPEN : *All year* ***SELF CATERING***
CHILDREN *: Welcome* ***DISABLED ACCESS :*** *Not really*
PETS : *No* ***CREDIT CARDS :*** *All major*
ACCOMMODATION : *Apartments for between 2 and 4 guests.*

VINE HOUSE
Friday Street,
Minchinhampton,
Gloucestershire GL6 9JL
Tel: 01453 884437

This attractive flat is attached to the home of the Finn family in the fine old Cotswold wool town of Minchinhampton. The sunny ground floor flat is completely self-contained. It has a twin bedroom with duvets and linen provided, a fully fitted well equipped pine kitchen with microwave. Bathroom with bath and shower (towels provided), a 20ft living/dining room with bed-settee opening into a full length 4ft 6ins double bed for extra guests. Colour TV and Video, Central heating and parking for one car. A private patio has recently been added. Vine House is within 2 minutes walking distance from the centre of the town which is fascinating in its own right with a 1698 pillared Market House, a plethora of antique shops, a good village pub, The Crown, which serves bar meals from 11am-11pm. From here the whole of the glorious Cotswolds is within reach, The Roman town of Cirencester is 9 miles away with its magnificent church and so too are Cheltenham and Bath and many more super towns and villages to explore. Slimbridge Wildfowl Trust, Westonbirt Arboretum, Berkeley Castle and The Forest of Dean are within a 30 mile radius.

USEFUL INFORMATION
OPEN; *All year except Christmas week* ***CHILDREN;*** *Over 8 years old*
CREDIT CARDS; *No* ***DISABLED ACCESS;*** *Wheelchair access*
GARDEN; *Patio With care. 2 small steps* ***PETS;*** *No*

RECTORY FARM
Northmoor,
Nr. Witney,
Oxon OX8 1SX

Tel: 01865 300207
Fax: 01865 300559

This whole area has gentle landscapes, market towns and small villages which nestle contently amongst this rural scene and none more so than Northmoor. Set in the upper Thames Valley, this attractive and friendly village can be found by taking the A415 from Witney to Kingston Bagpuize, turn off at Standlake, then follow the signs for Northmoor. In Northmoor is Rectory Farm, a working farm of over 400 acres with a superb Elizabethan Farmhouse, bearing a date-stone of 1629, but it was actually built before then, it formed part of an original endowment contained in a Charter of Sir Thomas White, the then Lord Mayor of London, dated 29th May 1555. The present owner Robert Florey, who's family has lived in this area since the 17th century and for 3 generations has farmed at Rectory Farm. The farm is situated in the Upper Thames Environmental Sensitive Conservation Area and has permanent pasture and river meadows used for grazing cattle and sheep. The farm also grows a variety of cereals, and recently established the Northmoor Herd of North Devon cattle.

The farm offers two self-catering cottages, which have been recently converted from a traditional cart shed and provide excellent accommodation, they are both warm and very comfortable. Each cottage is centrally heated and well appointed. On the ground floor is a sitting room with a wood burning stove, dining area, a shower room, a fully fitted kitchen including a dishwasher, washer/dryer, microwave, integral cooker, hob, and fridge. Upstairs there is a double and twin bedroom and bathroom. Duvets with linen and towels are provided. The cottages are in a superb position with south facing patio gardens and views over open fields towards the River Thames. There is ample parking adjacent to the cottages.

From here are some lovely walks through open and unspoilt countryside, where you can take in the wonderful fresh air and beautiful scenery. Robert can also arrange trout fishing, or he can offer fishing on the Thames path which runs through the farm. In the area there is golf, water sports, swimming and horse riding and for the more energetic squash and tennis. There are many places of interest near and far, so there will be plenty to keep you occupied during your stay at one of these superb English Tourist Board '4 Keys Highly Commended' properties. Robert and Mary Anne look forward to welcoming you to their lovely home.

USEFUL INFORMATION

OPEN; *All year*
CHILDREN; *Welcome*
CREDIT CARDS; *None taken*
ACCOMMODATION; *2 self-catering cottages sleeping up to 4 persons. Bed & Breakfast in the farmhouse*

DISABLED ACCESS; *No*
GARDEN; *Patio garden with barbecue and garden furniture*
PETS; *No*
NO SMOKING

TWINKLE TOES COTTAGE
c/o 5 Sweetmore Close,
Lower Oddington,
Moreton-in-Marsh,
Gloucestershire GL56 0XR
Tel/Fax: 01451 870932

The delightfully named Twinkle Toes Cottage is situated in the charming Cotswold village of Lower Oddington, two and a half miles from Stow-on-the-Wold where you will find antique shops and pretty art galleries. This superb beamed cottage offering peace and tranquillity is the perfect hide-away for two people. You can relax in the comfortable sitting room watch some television or read. The kitchen includes an electric cooker, microwave, cooking utensils, crockery and cutlery. Upstairs there is a cosy double bedroom with ensuite shower room. All electricity, bed linen, towels, tea towels, hair dryer and soaps are included in the tariff. Within 50 yards of the cottage is a Post Office/General Store where you may purchase your groceries. If you don't feel like cooking why not take a stroll and try one of the two Inns, they are a favourite with both visitors and locals alike and serve a good meal to boot. Other local amenities include a farm shop and garage/filling station. Twinkle Toes Cottage is ideally placed for touring the wonderful Cotswolds, renowned for its beauty spots and villages of golden stone. This captivating little cottage is owned by Mrs Knowles, who extends a very warm and friendly welcome to her guests.

USEFUL INFORMATION

OPEN: *All year; out of season short breaks*
DISABLED ACCESS: *No*
CHILDREN: *No*
GARDEN: *Stoned walled area, off road parking for one car next to cottage*
CREDIT CARDS: *None taken*
ACCOMMODATION: *Charming one bedroomed cottage - ETB '3 Keys Highly Commended'*
PETS: *One very well behaved dog at a supplement*
NON-SMOKERS ONLY PLEASE

DAMSELLS CROSS,
The Park, Painswick,
Gloucestershire GL6 6SR.
Tel : 01452 814385
Fax : 01452 814408

The country house apartments at Damsell Cross are situated in the once ancient deer park to King Henry VIII's hunting lodge. Decorated in English fine country style these apartments offer luxurious accommodation with all modern facilities, and outstanding views of the beautiful Painswick Valley. There is a heated swimming pool, tennis court, croquet lawns and extensive gardens and grounds for guests to explore, and your hosts, Linda and Alan Marshall extend a warm welcome, with home made bread, scones, local cheeses and a good bottle of French wine!

Painswick known as the 'Queen of the Cotswolds' is a beautiful village and gives easy access to Cheltenham, Gloucester, Stroud, Bath, and some wonderful villages and towns. You will be captivated by the beauty and serenity of the scenery, and by this enchanting country house in one of the most beautiful spots in the country.

USEFUL INFORMATION

OPEN : *All year*
SELF CATERING
CHILDREN : *Not really suitable*
DISABLED ACCESS : *Yes, ground floor courtyard apartment plus ramp in garden*
CREDIT CARDS : *All major*

4 GRAFTON MEWS,
Sheila Rolland,
Folly Cottage,
Paxford,
Nr. Chipping Campden,
Glos. GL55 6XG.

Tel : 01386 593315

4 Grafton Mews is a barn conversion in the charming town of Chipping Campden. Tucked away in a quiet mews, it is only minutes from the beautiful High Street, which has many buildings dating from the 14th to the 18th centuries. It accommodates four to five guests and has many interesting features, and all modern conveniences. There is a cosy beamed sitting room, luxury oak fitted kitchen with matching dining area, cloakroom, three bedrooms with sloping ceilings, bathroom and drying room. Outside is an attractive patio garden and ample parking space.

This is an ideal base for exploring the wonderful countryside, and the town of Chipping Campden is actually the start of the Cotswold Way. The surrounding countryside is stunning, and there is much to see and visit. The renowned gardens of Hidcote and Kiftsgate are nearby, while Cheltenham, Stratford-upon-Avon and Blenheim Palace are just a few of the interesting places within driving distance.

USEFUL INFORMATION

OPEN : *All year*
CHILDREN : *Welcome*
PETS : *By arrangement*
ACCOMMODATION : *For four to five guests.*

SELF CATERING
DISABLED ACCESS : *Not really*
CREDIT CARDS : *None taken*

CHAPTER 7

THE NORTH WEST COUNTIES
Including LANCASHIRE, CUMBRIA, CHESHIRE, MERSEYSIDE, GREATER MANCHESTER & THE ISLE OF MAN

INCLUDES

THE NORTHWEST COUNTIES
including **LANCASHIRE, CUMBRIA, CHESHIRE, MERSEYSIDE, GREATER MANCHESTER**

Cheshire is a county that could almost be swallowed up by Merseyside and Greater Manchester, but on the whole it is an interesting and varied county in it's own right. **Chester** is the main city, and the first thing you will notice is the steps. There are steps up to houses, to the gates in the walls,.... to everywhere. It seems to have been founded by the Romans, who took advantage of it's position at the mouth of the River Dee, and the walls still standing around the city are spectacular in their completeness. The famous walls of red sandstone are nearly 2 miles long, and make a raised walk from which to see many of the sights of the city.

The cathedral which is partly 11th century and partly restored in the 19th century, contains beautifully carved 14th century choir stalls, and the Chester Imp, a famous gargoyle, leers out from the north side of the clerestory in the cathedral nave. The 13th century castle contains an interesting military museum, and the Grosvenor Museum has a splendid collection of Roman remains and Anglo Saxon coins. The unique and world famous 'Rows' is a group of 13th century shops, and amongst the interesting buildings is the 17th century Bishop Lloyd's House. Nearby is God's Providence House, the only building untouched by the Black Death as it rampaged through the city. This is a lovely old city and one which you will find enjoyable. The racecourse attracts many people, while the magnificent zoo has 110 acres of natural enclosures, some of which can be toured by waterbus.

Nantwich is the most important town after Chester, and is a delightful place to visit. The Welsh were always trying to get their hands on the town because of the brine-pits which were the locals livelihood, but they didn't succeed! In 1604 the plague hit and killed nearly 500 people before it abated in March 1605. Nantwich has several attractive places to visit including Stapley Water Gardens, the world's largest water garden centre.

Up the A51 from Nantwich is the village of **Tarporley,** built of brick, and with a famous pub The Swan, a meeting place of the Torporley hunt. Onwards to Beeston Castle, a 12th century fortress above the Cheshire Plains which has wonderful views. Peckforton Castle, a medieval fortress, is also worth a visit if only for the views!

Congleton's prosperity was once linked with gloves, lace and ribbons. It has fine houses and from the streets, hill climbers can recognise in the distance their favourite Mow Cop. Canals are very much a part of life in

Cheshire and close to the M6 **Crewe** to **Middlewich** road is the pretty village of **Wheelock**, where the Trent and Mersey Canal runs through. The old silk town of **Macclesfield** is one that should not be missed. Even although it is a busy market town, it's full of quaint cobbled streets that add to the charm and character.

Merseyside, and you immediately think of **Liverpool**. Famous for many names such as The Beatles, Cilla Black, and many, many more, this is a city that exudes talent. It also has a colourful and interesting past - it was first settled in the 1st century, and it's position has made it a great port for all manner of trade. It was the point of massive immigration by the starving Irish in the famine of the 1840s, and Liverpool docks were known the world over. Part of them have become redundant today, but have been put to good use in telling the history of the city. It is an interesting city with a diversity of interesting people who are forthright, friendly and cheerful. **Aintree** is home of the Grand National, reputedly the best horse race in the world, and attended by thousands of spectators each year. 1996 saw them staying a little longer than anticipated, but the wonderful hospitality of the local people came to the forefront and won the day!

Albert Dock in Liverpool has lots of museums, wonderful art galleries and The Beatles Story in the Britannia Vaults. The famous Mersey Ferries are there for you to travel on and you will probably know the words to the immortal song....'So ferry, cross the Mersey'.....

Manchester has a good motorway system to hand and an international airport on it's doorstep. It is a busy cosmopolitan city, rich in life and with very good shopping facilities. There is actually quite a lot of history here with the 15th century castle, the 19th century Gothic tower which has a carillon of 23 bells, and which houses the Tourist Information Office - close to hand for all the facts! The City Art Gallery has a wonderful collection of drawings, paintings and sculptures by various artists; Stubbs, Gainsborough, Turner, Duccio and Canaletto, and also the Pre-Raphaelites. Castlefield Gallery has a changing exhibition of contemporary paintings and sculptures, and Heaton Hall is a superbly restored 18th century house. These are just a few of the attractions, and there are many more for you to discover.

Lancashire is famous for that seaside town **Blackpool** which has all the thrills and excitement of a traditional family seaside holiday. Apart from the autumn illuminations, adventure playground, aquarium and circus hall, Blackpool has a fine art gallery with a good collection of works by 19th and 20th century British artists. **Fleetwood** along the coast is just the place for bargain hunters with it's large indoor market. **Lancaster** is the capital of Lancashire and has a wonderful Norman castle on the site of a Roman fort.

Since the 18th century it has housed a prison and the countycourts. The Priory Church of St Mary is a 15th century Perpendicular on the site of a Saxon church, and has some splendid 13th century carved choir stalls; among the finest in Britain. The 18th century Customs House contains an interesting maritime history of the area.

Southport is another charming resort with large sandy beaches and a lovely wide open front. It has gained a reputation as being the floral capital of England's north west, and the Southport Flower Show is a major event in any horticulturist's diary. The formal Victorian parks and gardens in Southport are many, and you can spend a delightful day at either Heskith Park or the Botanic Gardens. There are plenty of golf courses with the most famous being the Royal Birkdale Course, and the 'Open' will be coming to Southport again in 1998. Another feature of the north west is brass bands, and during the season Southport has it's share. This is something that delights both young and old, and you will soon be clapping along in time to the music.

Moving into Cumbria and the beautiful Lake District brings us to one of the prettiest parts of the British Isles. Apart from the stunning scenery, the towns and villages are a delight to the eye with their quaint streets, curio and antique shops, and picturesque cottages of granite.

The M6 takes you to **Kendal**, home of Mint Cake, and birthplace of Katherine Parr, sixth wife of Henry VIII. The castle where she was born is 12th century, and Abbot Hall nearby is an 18th century house with a museum of local industry. Another museum here tells of the natural and human history of the Lake District and has a World Wild Life Gallery. Truly worth a visit. **Grange-over-Sands** is the next stop, and although not safe for bathing, is more than compensated by the promenade and extensive gardens.

This place became fashionable with the coming of the Furness Railway which linked it with Lancaster, and with the unusually mild climate giving rise to sub tropical plants and alpines, it has stayed one of the most perfect places in the district. Walking is wonderful here, and no more so than on the path which leads to Hampsfell Summit and The Hospice, a small stone tower with superb views of Morcambe Bay and of the rolling foothills climbing to the majestic peaks of the Lake District. The historical 'Cistercian Way' starts it's 37 mile journey here, travelling through Furness to Barrow.

Coniston is an unspoilt village nestling in the heart of the mountains, and even with the notoriety it received when Donald Campbell used the lake for his record speed attempts, it has managed to stay that way. The village is still a working one with many locals employed in the slate quarries and hill farms. It is an absolute haven for walkers and ramblers, with quiet walks through woodland, and climbing routes in Dow Crags for the more experienced climber. Brantwood House at Coniston was the home of painter John Ruskin for many years until his death in 1900, and contains much of his work. **Windermere** is always a beautiful spot whatever the time of year; the lake is 10 miles long, and the biggest in England. It is a wonderful place with the mood of each season taking you over completely and losing you in the loveliness and serenity of the setting. Winter with it's white coat takes your breath away (sometimes literarily), while a summer evening cradles you in the warmth of the setting sun shimmering over the water. You can tell that I like this place! **Grasmere** was home to Wordsworth for a period of time, and his tiny cottage is almost as he left it. You can see where his great inspiration came from - living in this sanctuary with beauty all around him. He is buried in the churchyard here, and Wordsworth Museum contains manuscripts and first editions of his works.

Travel on to the northern lakes and half a million acres of some of the most breathtaking landscapes in England, with rolling fields and sandstone villages just waiting to be discovered. **Alston**, the highest market town in England is a thousand feet above sea level, and is delightfulwith it's steep cobbled streets. Surrounded by the wonderful North Pennines, Alston and nearby villages like **Nenthead** and **Garrigill** became prosperous with the lead mining.

Penrith is the main northern gateway to the Lake District and the North Pennines. With it's good rail links and closeness to the M6, it is an ideal base for touring the area. It is a popular shopping town with it's excellent arcades and traditional markets. The town is dominated by Beacon Hill, which dates back to the Border Wars, and there are many other interesting historical places to visit. **Appleby** is another market town in the north, and one of the finest. It is justifiably proud of it's Royal Charters dating from 1174. Sitting on the River Eden it is also within easy reach of the wonderful scenery of the Pennines.

The Settle Carlisle Railway makes it's way to it's highest point below Wild Boar fell at the head of Mallestang Dale. Nearby are the villages of **Brough** with a castle built by the Normans, and **Ravenstonedale.** Here at gallows Hill in Lord Park there are traces of Ancient Britons.

Onward to **Keswick** which has some interesting historical places to visit. The Cumberland Pencil Museum is really quite fascinating (am I glad we now use computers!), and the Keswick Museum and Art Gallery contains original manuscripts by Wordsworth, Southey and Walpole.

My last stop must be **Carlisle** (this is frequently my last stop on the train journey to Scotland!). Travelling by train you do not see much of the city, and what you do see does not do it justice. The castle here was a border stronghold, and remains include a 12th century keep, a maze of vaulted chambers and passages, and Queen Mary's Tower, the enforced home of the sad Mary Queen of Scots in 1568. The tower now houses an fascinating collection of the Border Regiment. The Guildhall Museum is a 15th century town house which is now a museum of civic and local history, and a lovely silverware collection. The cathedral is 12th to 13th century, with a fine 14th century east window, and a Renaissance screen. Carlisle is a important city with good road and rail links, and it's own airport. It has some very good shopping facilities and caters well for sporting interests.

The trip through this part of England has been a lovely one, with a diversity and medley of scenery to soothe the soul and tantalise the spirit. These are the places that make me yearn to be able to paint, draw or even make some recognisable mark on paper that could capture the memory of the journey, or that special moment when the scene in front of you takes your breathe away.

BETTY FOLD,
Hawkshead hill,
Ambleside,
Cumbria
LA22 0PS.

Tel : 015394 36611

This is a large country manor, set in beautiful grounds at the heart of the delightful Lake District. Anthony Marsden is the resident owner and offers evening dinner, bed and breakfast in the Guest House, and self catering accommodation in the Garden Cottage, and Latterbarrow View and Outgate. The house has panoramic views across the Esthwaite Valley, and the garden has a variety of interesting trees and wildlife. Once owned by Henry Holiday (a friend of William Morris) who was an artist and designer of stained glass windows, his book 'Reminiscences of my life' is available for guests to read. This is the perfect spot for visiting much of the area, with many delightful walks from the house, and much more only a car journey away.

The self catering accommodation offers very comfortable living quarters with all facilities provided. The Garden Cottage caters for up to four persons, and has stunning views across the valley to Latterbarrow and Claife Heights. Latterbarrow View is a cosy ground floor apartment with views over the Esthwaite Valley, and has a double bedroom with room for a small extra single bed or cot. When required, Outgate, just off the hall is a small twin bedded room which is en suite with a dressing area. There is plenty of parking space on the grounds, and self catering guests are welcome for an evening meal at the Guest House by prior arrangement.

USEFUL INFORMATION

OPEN : *All year*
CHILDREN : *Welcome*
PETS : *Welcome (self catering)*
LICENSED : *Selection of wines*
ACCOMMODATION : *self catering cottage & apartment*
Bed & breakfast at Guest House.

EVENING MEAL : *Traditional food*
VEGETARIAN & SPECIAL : *Catered for*
DISABLED ACCESS : *Not really*
CREDIT CARDS : *All major*

GREEN VIEW LODGES
Green View,
Welton,
Nr Dalston,
Carlisle,
Cumbria
CA5 7ES

Tel: 016974 76230
Fax: 016974 76523

Green View Lodges are well named, they are surrounded by the most stunning countryside, you can see green fields and trees for miles, just the location for getting away from it all to unwind and relax. Anne and Will Ivinson have created a wonderful setting which has been recognised by many authorities including the English Tourist Board awarding 4 and 5 Keys Highly Commended, a Gold Medallion Award for saving energy, a feature in The Good Holiday Cottage Guide, and are members of the Farm Holiday Bureau and Cumbria Tourist Board. With all these accolades you would expect high quality and that is just what you get, the standard is very high indeed. The three Myhlenberg **Scandinavian Pine Lodges** *are superb, designed and built by the Danes they are comfortable and very warm. Two have three bedrooms sleeping six people and one has two bedrooms sleeping four. The kitchens are well appointed and include a microwave, electric oven and fridge freezer,* **The Chapel** *has a fridge with a freezer compartment, the furnishings are pine. As well as the lodges there are two cottages and a converted chapel,* **Well Cottage** *has been carefully converted to retain its character, this surprisingly spacious accommodation sleeps six people in three bedrooms, there is a lovely sun lounge which leads to the garden. One of the oldest houses in the village of Welton is the 17th century* **Well House**, *the sitting room oozes character with its old oak beams and wood burner, this attractive two bedroomed house sleeps 4 in total comfort.* **The Chapel** *is 155 years old and is absolutely charming, lovingly converted the interior is totally timber lined and furnished to an exacting standard, a superior holiday home for two people. The Chapel is for non-smokers only. Direct dial telephones, laundry facilities, barbecue and picnic tables are all provided*

The tiny hamlet of Welton is only nine miles south of Carlisle and within a half hours drive of Lake Ullswater, Keswick and various golf courses. Walkers and cyclists will be in their element. As Anne says 'every home comfort is provided for a relaxing country holiday, you only have to bring yourselves and your food', what could be better, you will find it very hard to leave.

USEFUL INFORMATION

OPEN: *All year*
CHILDREN: *Welcome*
CREDIT CARDS: *Some*
ACCOMMODATION: *Three pine lodges sleeping between 6 & 4, two converted cottages sleeping 6 & 4 and the Chapel sleeping 2*

DISABLED ACCESS: *3 bedroomed lodges are particularly suitable for accompanied disabled guest.*
GARDEN: *Yes with barbecue and picnic tables*
PETS: *No dogs in Lodge No3 and Chapel*
No Smoking in Chapel
Ample parking

HOLIDAY HOMES IN CONISTON

Dow Crag,
Coniston,
Cumbria
LA21 8AT

Tel: 015394 41558

Coniston is a small, friendly, quiet village with a Post Office, butcher, grocery store, several hotels, a couple of restaurants and tea shops, a children's play area, tennis courts and a bowling green all set among the hills and spectacular scenery that makes the Lake District what it is. If you are thinking of visiting this area there is nowhere better to stay than Dow Crag, this is where Mrs. Hall has her two chalet bungalows. The ***Larger Bungalow*** *sleeps 2-6, has wonderful views from the sitting room overlooking the Lake, here you can relax in comfortable surroundings watch television, read from the selection of books or play board games which are available. The kitchen is large, and is supplied with pots, pans, crockery and cutlery, and a long kitchen table. Two big windows take advantage of the surrounding fields, fells and woods. There are three bedrooms, one double, one single with the original metal bunk beds, and another single with a 4'6" divan, all have mattress covers, quilts and covers. The bathroom has the original big bath with brass taps. The three bedroomed* ***Small Bungalow*** *sleeps 2-5, it too has stunning views across the Lake taking in the surrounding fells via the large picture window in the kitchen/ living room. The bedrooms consist of one double, one single and one room with bunk beds. There is a shower room with wash basin and WC. Both bungalows are set in large gardens surrounded by the most wonderful farmland, the views will take your breath away. You are asked to bring your own sheets, pillowcases and towels, everything else is catered for.*

Walkers will be in paradise, with either mountain or lowland. Painters, sketchers and photographers are sure to capture the wonder of the moment. A superb place where the air is fresh and the scenery outstanding. You are sure to go home feeling refreshed and rested.

USEFUL INFORMATION

OPEN: *Mar-Nov*
CHILDREN: *Welcome. Cot & high chair available*
CREDIT CARDS: *None taken*
ACCOMMODATION: *2 bungalows, Large sleeping 2-6, small sleeping 2-5*

DISABLED ACCESS: *Possible on discussion*
GARDEN: *Set in extensive gardens surrounded by farmland*
PETS: *By arrangement on condition they are exercised regularly away from the premises as young children play on the grass*

FISHERGROUND FARM,
Eskdale,
Cumbria CA19 1TF.
Tel : 01946 723319

Fisherground is a wonderful mixture of old cottages and charming pine lodges set in the beautiful Cumbrian countryside. All are beautifully furnished and decorated, and offer a high standard of comfortable accommodation. This is a beautiful place in any season, and to see Beckfoot Cottage in the snowy winter sun, beside the Raft pond and with it's backdrop of hills, is just delightful. Both cottages have real fires in winter, and all accommodation is centrally heated. The pine lodges are made from 5" solid Douglas fir logs with roof of cedar shingle. These sit beautifully in their natural orchard surroundings.

There is plenty to do at Fisherground, with many facilities for children and families. There is an adventure playground, a games room, the pond with its rafts, and a wonderful miniature railway which runs through the grounds. They even have their own station! But apart from all this activity there is plenty of room for quiet walks and solitude if you desire. Getting away from it all is easy in the large grounds and you will find the time for relaxation and unwinding at this charming farm.

USEFUL INFORMATION

***OPEN :** All year*
***CHILDREN :** Welcome*
***PETS :** Welcome*
***ACCOMMODATION :** Cottages & lodges.*
SELF CATERING
***DISABLED ACCESS :** Yes, please ring*
***CREDIT CARDS :** None taken*

OLD WATERSLACK FARM,
Silverdale, Via carnforth,
Lancs, LA5 0UH.
Tel : 01524 701108

This charming farm was built in 1721, and is in a delightful woodland setting on the outskirts of Silverdale. Self catering accommodation is offered in the way of two beautifully furnished holiday cottages, and four spacious caravans. The holiday cottages are four and two bedroomed, while the caravans are four and six berth. Both cottages have full gas central heating, outside lights and plenty of parking space. Cots and high chairs are available and pets are welcome. The caravans are very well equipped, and there is a laundry room with washing machine and tumble dryer on site. There is also a pay phone and a sink with hot water.

This is an excellent base from which to explore the surrounding attractions. Lancaster is only 7 miles away with it's rich history and architecture. Kendal is only 10 miles away - gateway to the majestic Lake District. The R.S.P.B. Leighton Moss bird reserve is within walking distance, and these are just a few of the many attractions on offer. This is an area which is worth exploring and one which you will enjoy immensely.

USEFUL INFORMATION

***OPEN :** March - Oct Caravans*
Cottages : All year
***CHILDREN :** Welcome*
***PETS :** Welcome*
SELF CATERING
***DISABLED ACCESS :** No*
***CREDIT CARDS :** None taken*
***ACCOMMODATION :** 2 cottages and 4 caravans.*

HIGH MEADOW
Skiddaw Grove Hotel,
Vicarage Hill,
Keswick-On-Derwentwater,
Cumbria
CA12 5QB

Tel: 017687 73324

Skiddaw Grove Hotel is situated in Vicarage Hill, a quiet lane on the fringe of Keswick, yet only 10 minutes walk (via Fitz Park) from the town centre. Nestled in this quiet lane near the Hotel and leisure pool is High Meadow a modern three bedroomed house with superb views. It is a great place for a holiday or for a break. The Hotel and house are owned by Jonathan and Audrey Brooks, who will be more than willing to help with anything you need. High Meadow is very comfortable and well equipped. All linen and towels are provided and there are no meters to feed, it is all included in the tariff. The garden to the rear is secure and there is parking available for two cars at the front of the property. Children are very welcome but pets are strictly forbidden - not even if they sleep in the car. There are excellent boarding kennels nearby.

Keswick itself is a thriving market town and holiday centre near Derwentwater in the northern part of the Lake District. The views are stunning. It is a well loved and cared for town and has featured regularly in the finals of Britain in Bloom. One of the enchanting things about staying in the Lake District is the ability to use the regular launch service around the lakes. You will find the town interesting to explore, it has good exhibitions, excellent shops and activities for all ages, all weather and all times of the year. There is live theatre during the summer months. There are many fascinating places within easy reach. Skiddaw Grove makes an ideal base from which to enjoy all that this part of Britain has to offer.

USEFUL INFORMATION

OPEN; *Throughout the year*
CHILDREN; *Very welcome*
CREDIT CARDS; *None taken*
ACCOMMODATION; *3 bedroomed house*

DISABLED ACCESS; *Difficult, ring first*
GARDEN; *Yes, secure*
PETS; *Not permitted, boarding kennels closeby*
Private parking

CHAPTER 8

THE NORTH EAST COUNTIES
Including
YORKSHIRE, NORTHUMBERLAND, DURHAM & CLEVELAND

INCLUDES

Chapter Eight

The North East Counties

Yorkshire, Northumberland, Durham & Cleveland

They say that beauty is in the eye of the beholder, but I believe that all who 'behold' this wild, untamed land can only wonder at the loveliness and splendour of these cherished Dales, and enjoy the history and heritage preserved for our appreciation. This is an area unspoilt by time or by man's avarice (for which we can be truly thankful), and where we can enjoy nature, and all she has to offer, at her very best. For the outdoor types there are lots and lots of activities, with to my mind, the best being just walking. This way you can appreciate the ever changing colours of the landscapes, and be stimulated by the sounds and smells all around you. But don't be misled by this - for those who enjoy a more 'animate' stimulation there is plenty in the way of history, local crafts, pleasant towns and picturesque villages to be found. The tales and folklore of this great area could fill a book and more, but I will try to give you a little information - just to give you a taste!

Starting with the Northern Dales we have **Swaledale** which lies along the course of the **River Swale** in the north east, and which lends it's name to a hardy breed of sheep whose fleece are used in the local woollen industry. **Reeth**, the capital of the vale, is a delightful centre for crafts, sculpture and painting. **Richmond** is a busy market town with plenty of historical interest, including three museums and a lovely Georgian theatre. Richmond Castle has wonderful views from it's 30 metre high, 12th century keep.

To the far north east is the **River Tees**, and the rich farmland of **Lower Teesdale**. Lewis Carroll, the author, lived here, and you can understand the inspiration he must have gained from this peaceful landscape. Today, **Croft**, where he was born, is home to an exciting motor racing circuit which holds many events all year round. **Wensleydale** is a particular fine area with it's stunning fells and rich pastures. The main market towns are **Hawes, Leyburn** and **Masham**, each very individual, but with charm and presence that will delight the visitor. Masham is very proud of it's annual Sheep Fair in September, and also the Steam Engine and Fair Organ Rally in July - great for enthusiasts! Just outside Leyburn is Middleham Castle, a splendid example of an English keep and childhood home of Richard III. Between Leyburn and **Bedale** is Crakehall Watermill, which was restored in 1977, and which in 1980, ground corn for the first time in 50 years. This is a fascinating process to watch and the interesting machinery dates from the 18th and 19th centuries. Wensleydale is probably best known (apart from the cheese!)

for it's waterfalls, and fine examples of this can be seen at **Aysgarth** and **Hardraw.** Aysgarth also has an interesting Yorkshire Carriage Museum which is worth visiting. There are many varied and interesting sites on these vast moors, with charming towns and villages peeping between the hills, and all with a wealth of culture and history just waiting to be explored. To name all the Dales, towns and villages would fill the pages of this chapter, leaving nothing but facts to bore the pants off you! So, I will choose just some of the places that may be of interest, but leaving much, much more to be delightfully discovered on your travels.

The southern Dales include **Wharfedale, Airedale** and **Ingleborough.** Wharfedale is an area of breathtaking scenery such as Kilsney Craig with the Kilsney Park and Trout Farm nestling beneath it's stern rocky face. Even if you are not an angler this is a pleasant place to visit as youcan feed the fish as well as catch them - or if even that is too much effort then just buy them fresh from the local shop! **Grassington** is the main town, and with it's cobbled streets and quaint shops, you will have a delightful day out. Malharn Tarn is one of England's largest mountain lakes, and is a very popular local to visit. Artists of all abilities (including Turner) have painted this area, and it apparently was a favourite spot of Charles Kingsley the author who wrote his classic 'The Water Babies' here.

Skipton in Airedale is known as the Gateway to the Dales, and has the splendid Skipton Castle guarding the town. The Leeds-Liverpool Canal also runs through the centre of the town, and you can spend a pleasant day exploring the waterway on one of the many barges. One other place I would like to mention is **Lothersdale,** as it was here that Charlotte Bronte found inspiration for the house in that wonderful novel 'Jane Eyre'. Stone Gapp is actually a private residence, but the description of 'Gateshead Hall' in her book marries very well!

Ingleborough is part of the legendary country known as the Three Peaks, and with it's unyielding landscape of peaks, caves and rocks it is a haven for walkers and ramblers. **Settle** is the main town in the heart of the area, and is a pretty, charming place with a good market and much local history. The great Victorian railway, Settle to Carlisle, runs from here and for enthusiasts the architecture and especially the viaduct is a must.

Nidderdale is in the east and has rather a unique landscape in it's rock formations at Brimham Rocks. The unrelenting elements have formed fascinating shapes and forms over the years, and the National Trust have undertaken the preservation of this intriguing native display. Fountains Abbey and Studley Royal Water Gardens must be on your list of places to visit. This is a great day out - the Abbey dates from around 1132, and has recently gained World Heritage status, and the Water Gardens are a delight of temples, ponds and immaculate lawns. In addition the medieval park is home to Red, Fallow and Sika deer, and you can see them roam freely amongst the oak, chestnut and lime trees. The Abbey and Water Gardens unite to provide an interesting variety of activities (if wished) for all the family; from 'Flower Power' where you can discover the uses of wildflower and herbs, to 'Sleepers Awake', a 'Hunters and Gatherers Challenge' for wiggly worms! Ugh! That one wasn't for me - but those delightful little beings we call 'children' love it! A very good day's entertainment.

Moving outwards to the coastal towns we visit **Scarborough**, closely followed by **Whitby** and **Filey**. Scarborough has been a holiday destination for the British tourist from as early as 1735! Today it offers a wealth of attractions for young and old making it a platform for all types of holidays from golfing to windsurfing, with beautiful gardens and excellent walking, and with a variety of nightlife to suit all. Midsummer finds the attraction of Scarborough Fair (much notoriety gained through the canticle by Simeon & Garfunkle) when you will find a multitude of entertainment and a gay time is on every street corner. One thing of note is the beautifully restored steam railway which winds it's way to York from this pleasing town. There is a fascinating assortment of architecture down by the harbour where chapels, cafes, and curio shops sit side by side with stands selling whelks, cockles and all types of sea life. It is an interesting place, and one which should definitely be experienced. Whitby has some fine beaches and quaint streets which you will enjoy strolling around. The ruins of the Abbey here date back to the 13th century and was home of Caedmon, the first English poet. Brams Stoker was impressed by the eerie atmosphere, and set part of the blood curling novel 'Dracula' in the town. There are no vampires today (not that I met anyway), and this is a pleasant spot to spend some time. The North Yorkshire Railway passes here too, and stops at **Pickering** on it's way to York. This is a lovelymarket town with a medieval castle and church, and many fine shops to browse round. Just west of Pickering it would be remiss of me not to mention **Helmsley,** and the nearby castle. This is a spectacular 12th century fortress, and an excellent exhibition of the more modern Tudor living. A little further takes you to Rievaulx Abbey, the remains of one of the first Cistercian monasteries in northern England. The site of this abbey is one of beauty and serenity in the valley of the River Rye, and the terrace and temples are magnificent Away from York the other railway stops are at Levisham, Newton Halt and **Goathland** which you may recognise as the famous 'Aidensfield' in that engaging programme 'Heartbeat'. Filey carries on the tradition of these fine seaside towns, but with a quieter more traditional air. Six miles of safe, sandy beaches, and the quaint olde-worlde fishermens cottages make this a delightful, quiet relaxing holiday spot. The Parish Church of St Oswald (the patron saint of fishermen), is set aside from the town by a deep ravine, and dates from the time of King Stephen. It is a fine building, and at one time had a music gallery and an organ at it's west end. There is an interesting stained glass window which is dedicated to fishermen, and it is thought that St Oswald once passed through Filey on his gospel calling. It is also said that Charlotte Bronte worshipped here whilst on holiday. Filey is a great place for souvenir hunting with hand-made chocolates, shell boxes or even authentic fishermen's jumpers.

From here we jump to **Castle Howard,** rather an eccentric house with a mixture of periods from Egyptian, Roman, Tudor, and Medieval that at first confuse the eye. But this is a castle built upon the ruins of another, and as such lends a rather unique image. This house was made famous by the highly popular 'Brideshead Revisited' and you are probably familiar with the delightful interior and furnishings used in the filming. On to **Thirsk** and it's attractive setting by the river. Thirsk Church is often referred to as the Cathedral of the North and is a very handsome building. It was started in 1430 and took 70 years to complete. Thirsk is also famous for it's racing and offers some of the finest in Yorkshire, with people travelling from all over the country just to spend the day here. Thirsk Museum houses the original manuscripts of James Herriot, the real life vet who became so famous with his tales of a country vetenary practice. Having read his works you can see the warmth and fondness he had for this enticing county and it's hardy people.

On to the magnificent city of **York,** the great northern capital of Roman Britain. Clifford Tower is the place to visit to get unparalleled views over the city, and to learn the history of York's past. Not all of the history is pleasant as this is the site of the massacre of York's Jewish community in 1190. There is a good visual display of a model of the original castle and there is an additional Braille text. This city has a lot of history to offer in it's architecture and with the art galleries, museums and York Minster, which is a wonderful example of a Gothic Church with fine stained glass windows.

The Five Sisters window has 100,000 pieces containing grisaille glass; the Rose window commemorates the end of the War of the Roses; the Great Western window with it's tracery in the shape of a heart is often regarded as the heart of Yorkshire, and the Great East window in the Lady Chapel is one of the most important in the world, as it depicts the beginning and end of created things in the world. There are many churches in York; somewhere in the region of 40, and many worth visiting. One of the best ways to see York is to travel the medieval walls. This is a walk of about 2 ½ miles but a glorious way to see the city. Before leaving York I would like to mention the exciting excavation area between York's two rivers where a sunken treasure house was found preserved in the peaty soil. Travelling in electric time cars, the voice of Magnus Magnusson takes you back to a time where people conversed in Old Norse, where ships unloaded their exotic cargoes, and the people of the time went about their daily business. This is probably one of the most important insights into our past and one which all can enjoy.

Across from York is **Harrogate**, traditionally a spa town, and now one of the most important conference centres in the country. It is a very attractive town with it's Regency buildings and treelined streets. There are some good shopping facilities here, and as a 20th century town it has a lot to offer the visitor. The Royal Pump Museum offers the spa waters which once made the town famous, and the art gallery has some very fine examples of English paintings. Coming down the A64 we pass the great city of **Leeds, Bradford** and one which I shall mention **Huddersfield.** This town's reputation was built round the textile industry, and today it's fine wools are still a part of it's industry. There is splendid Victorian architecture here which in recent years has benefitted from much refurbishment and stone cleaning. Much of the town is pedestrianised, so this is a pleasant way to wander around and see for yourself all on offer. The railway station, St George's Square, is reputed to be one of the finest facades in England and has been described as a 'stately home with trains in'. The Church of St. Peter is in the Gothic Revival style and is a most imposing building. Huddersfield has plenty of parks and green spaces, and in addition you are only a fews minutes from the lovely Pennines and stunning scenery. A very good location for touring the area, with a very pleasant base to return to.

Returning back up the way takes us through **Ilkley** (the name may bring back a few scouting memories), where the walking is wonderful and the vista difficult to surpass, back over the moors and on to **Barnard Castle, Darlington** and **Cleveland**. Barnard Castle is a charming historic market town with plenty of character and a delightful array of history. It is known as one of the 51 most important historical and architectural towns in Britain, and you will not be disappointed. The ruins of the castle are 12th century with a 14th century round keep, and there are some wonderful riverside walks in what once were the hunting grounds round the castle. The Church of St. Mary is interesting, and Bowes Museum is a 19th century house created in the Fench chateau style, housing collections of European art and paintings, including some by Goya and El Greco.

Darlington is mostly associated with the 'Age of Steam' and is famous for the Stockton and Darlington railway. Darlington's Railway Centre and Museum has one of the finest collections to be found, and is a joy for enthusiasts. Today, this is a thriving market town with something for all in the way of culture, shopping, and splendid architecture. It has a wealth of leisure activities including a good golf course and an outdoor bowling green.

Taking the train from here to **Durham** is a pleasant journey, and brings you to a lovely city with a lot to give to those interested in the history of the area. Durham Castle is a magnificent Norman cathedral which was founded in 1093, and together with the adjacent castle is a World Heritage Site. The Oriental Museum is unusual in that it is the only museum in the country dedicated solely to oriental art, and covers all major cultures and periods of the East from Ancient Egypt to India, Tibet, China and Japan. **Beamish** is one of the largest tourist attractions in the area with it's turn of the century working town, where shop staff greet you costumed in the dress of the period, and guided tours are given to the underground mine in the Colliery Village. There are many more attractions in the beautiful County of Durham, and the scenery and landscape makes any type of outdoor activity a great pleasure.

BREAMISH VALLEY COTTAGES,
Branton, Powburn, Alnwick,
Northumberland NE66 4 LW.
Tel : 01665 578263

The delightful Breamish Valley Cottages were created from a range of stone farm buildings around a central sheltered courtyard. Although highly modern and fully equipped, these cottages have lost none of their rustic charm and character. Furnished in good country pine, with many features such as attractive roof timbers and original fireplaces, these cottages are thoughtfully arranged. Each is very individual and can cater for between two and six guests. Some are 'upside down' (living areas upstairs) to take advantage of the wonderful views, whilst others open on to the gravelled courtyard. This is excellent accommodation with additional facilities such as BBQ area and picnic tables, a games room, a children's play area, a grass tennis court, a small football pitch, and a top class swimming pool and gym. There is also a sauna and sunbed and guests are offered a massage and aromatherapy service. I don't think I would ever want to leave this place!

But that is not all! There is so much to do in the area that you will definitely want to return. You are close to the Scottish border country with it's wealth of towns and villages, and beautiful scenery, and Northumberland's magnificent coastline with it's wonderful sandy beaches. Add to this a host of National trust properties and great shopping, and you have the perfect location for any holiday or short break!

USEFUL INFORMATION

OPEN : *All year* — ***SELF CATERING***
CHILDREN : *Welcome* — ***DISABLED ACCESS :*** *not really*
PETS : *Well behaved welcome* — ***CREDIT CARDS :*** *No*
ACCOMMODATION : *Cottages for between 2 & 6 guests.*

VILLAGE FARM HOLIDAYS,
Town Foot farm,
Shilbottle, Alnwick,
Northumberland NE66 2HG.
Tel : 01665 575591

Village Farm is wholly committed to the self catering holiday and provides excellent facilities for any number of guests from two to twelve. Accommodation is either in beautifully converted stone cottages or in custom made Danish chalets in the grounds. Each is charmingly furnished and all necessary facilities are provided. The grounds are wonderful with riding, tennis and indoor games provided, and with a superb indoor swimming complex with sauna and sunbed. There is a large grass area with football posts and cricket net, and all properties are situated in landscaped gardens. This is a lovely location - the peace and tranquillity of the countryside - but within easy reach of many of the wonderful attractions Northumberland has to offer. Village Farm is only 3 miles from the beach, and there is a wealth of National trust properties and gardens for you to visit. There is moorland, farmland, walks and stunning vistas, and in addition the friendly Northumbrian people. This is a place you will visit time and time again.

USEFUL INFORMATION

OPEN : *All year* — ***SELF CATERING***
CHILDREN : *Welcome* — ***DISABLED ACCESS :*** *not really*
PETS : *Welcome* — ***CREDIT CARDS :*** *All major*
ACCOMMODATION : *Cottages and chalets for 2 to 12 guests.*

RIVERSBANK,
3 Front Street, Corbridge,
Northumberland NE45 5AP.
Tel : 01434 632073

Situated in the historic village of Corbridge, Riversbank is a charming stone terraced cottage, circa 1800. This self catering accommodation is of a very high standard and has recently been totally refurbished. On the south side of the cottage are stunning river views, and the other side overlooks the ancient market place and village church. This is an idyllic location, and an ideal spot for visiting the surrounding attractions.

The cottage is fully centrally heated, and has all the necessary facilities including a fully fitted kitchen with an original range, and a heated conservatory where you can relax and enjoy the scenery. The living room is upstairs to take advantage of the lovely river views, and there is access to a south facing balcony. Also upstairs is one of the double bedrooms, which has a magnificent 5ft French painted antique bed and matching furniture, while adjacent is a fitted bathroom with a corner bath. Downstairs again is a twin bedroom en suite. Pets are welcome, and parking is available.

USEFUL INFORMATION

OPEN : *All Year*
CHILDREN : *Welcome*
PETS : *Welcome by arrangement*
ACCOMMODATION : *Cottage with 2 bedrooms.*
SELF CATERING
DISABLED ACCESS : *No*
CREDIT CARDS : *None taken*

PROSPECT COTTAGE,
Reeth, Swaledale,
North Yorkshire, DL11 6SE.
Tel : 01748 884201

Peter and Elaine Brant are the proprietors of this delightful little cottage tucked behind the Post Office in the picturesque village of Reeth. Living next door ensures they are on hand if any help is required, and they guarantee a warm welcome upon arrival. The cottage has one double and one single bedroom, with a cot available if required. There is a comfortable lounge with colour TV and a coal fire for those cooler evenings, a kitchen and dining area which is fully fitted, and a bathroom with bath and electric shower. The lounge enjoys stunning views over the southern side of Reeth's village green and across Swalesdale. There is some shopping in the village, a market on Fridays, some good local craft shops and a number of eating and drinking establishments. What more could you ask for! It is an ideal spot from which to tour the surrounding area and walking boots are a must. You have the Northern Dales, the Lake District and the North York Moors all within access and it really is superb walking country. At any time of year the scenery is spectacular, whether it be in a winter white coat or the soft greens of summer, you will find a warm welcome from Peter and Elaine whenever you should visit.

USEFUL INFORMATION

OPEN : All year
CHILDREN *: Welcome*
PETS : *No*
CREDIT CARDS : *None taken*
ACCOMMODATION : *1 dbl & 1 sgl room with cot available.*
SELF CATERING
DISABLED ACCESS : *No*
PARKING : *In front of cottage*

LASKILL FARM
Hawnby, York
YO6 5NB

Tel: 01439 798268

Sometimes brochures are too fulsome in describing places but in the case of the excellent self-catering establishments offered by Sue Smith, the owner of Laskill Farm, one can honestly say that what is written there does not do these delighful houses justice. Three of the houses are numbers one, two and three St Caedda, Keldholme, the fourth is at 26 High Street Helmsley and then there is an excellent self-catering caravan situated in the garden of Laskill Farm with beautiful surroundings. It is spotless and has all the mod cons one could wish for including flush toilet, hot water, television and sleeps 4-5 people. Linen is included.Also at Laskill Farm are The Smithy and The Forge which were converted early in 1996 from an old stable block, both retaining the old beamed ceiling and both benefitting from Inglenook fireplaces. Both have large French windows opening on to a patio area, all on one level and would be suitable for partially disabled people.

All the other four houses are charmingly furnished and equippped with fully fitted kitchens and they are full of character. No 1 and 2 St Caedda are both about 300 years old. No 1 is an end of terrace cottage which has been carefully and lovingly restored retaining its olde worlde atmosphere. This one sleeeps 4+ cot in two bedrooms. There is a spacious lounge with TV and a separate dining room. The downstairs bathroom has a shower and shaver point. No 2 has three bedrooms and sleeps 5 + cot and is equally charming. No 3 has a double bedded room and a twin. Again the bathroom has both bath and shower. The cottages are warm and comfortable, have gardens and linen is included. You will find Keldholme just off the A170 and within walking distance of the market town of Kirkbymoorside. The picturesque village of Hutton-le-Hole with its Folk museum is appoximately two and a half miles from Keldholme. All three houses are ideally situated for touring the North York Moors and coastal resorts, York, Castle Howard and many historical places.

26 High Street Helmsley is a delightful terraced stone cottage. It is cosy and comfortable and has a wealth of interesting features in keeping with its age. Exposed beams, natural pine interior doors both add to the ambience. Like the other cottages it is well furnished and fully equipped. There is a small, enclosed patio at the rear with chairs to relax. Street parking. Here you are well placed for touring and walking on the North Yorkshire Moors, taking a look at the coastal resorts and enjoying the history and beauty of York.

Sue Smith also has bed and breakfast accommodation at Laskill Farm where you will be well looked after and supremely well fed.

USEFUL INFORMATION

OPEN; *All year*
CHILDREN; *Welcome*
CREDIT CARDS; *None taken*
DISABLED ACCESS; *Two suitable for partially disabled*
ACCOMMODATION; *6 cottages, 1 caravan Plus B&B at Laskill Farm*
PETS; *Permitted in 4 cottages but there is an extra charge*

STOTSFOLD HALL C OTTAGES,
Stotsfold Hall,
Street, Hexham,
Northumberland NE47 0HP.
Tel : 01434 673270

Stotsfold Hall Cottages stand in the grounds of the old manor house, surrounded by 15 acres of gardens and parklands. The manor house is situated about six miles south of Hexham, near the hamlet of Whitley Chapel. This is excellent walking country, and the surrounding peaceful scenery is the ideal haven for relaxation. There are plenty of attractions within easy distance, with many National Trust properties and gardens. There is also an abundance of castles for the explorer to visit, and for those who like to shop then the Gateshead Metrocentre (Europe's largest shopping complex) is within easy distance. The cottages are of a high standard with all necessary facilities being provided. Each cottage has one double and one twin-bedded room, a sitting room, fully fitted kitchen, and bathroom. All have double glazing and central heating, so are ideal for those winter breaks. Stotsford Hall itself has a fully licensed attractive bar for resident guests.

USEFUL INFORMATION

OPEN : *All year*
CHILDREN : *Welcome*
PETS : *No*
CREDIT CARDS : *All major*
ACCOMMODATION : *Two bedroomed cottages.*
SELF CATERING
DISABLED ACCESS : *No*
LICENSED : *Residents only*

SPITAL HILL
York Road, Thirsk,
Yorkshire YO7 3AE
Tel: 01845 522273

The cares of the world fall away on entering the peaceful and secluded gardens of Spital Hill, and once inside this elegant and genteel Victorian country house, one soaks up the atmosphere. You will be welcomed by your hosts Ann and Robin Clough who will ensure your stay is one to remember. Within the spacious grounds is a former Grooms Cottage which has been superbly and skilfully restored and is now available as a luxury self-catering holiday home. Accommodation includes 2 double bedrooms with private facilities, sitting room, dining room and kitchen. Grooms Cottage is suitable for the partially disabled having an ensuite bedroom on the ground floor. Golf, gliding and fishing are within easy reach. Thirsk was the home of the late James Herriot and if you watched the television series you will know what dramatic and stunning countryside await you. The National Trust and English Heritage own many historical houses and abbeys which are within this area, as well as museums reflecting the crafts of days gone by.

USEFUL INFORMATION

OPEN; *All year*
CHILDREN; *Over 12 years*
CREDIT CARDS; *Access/Visa/ Mastercard/Amex*
LICENSED; *Fully*
GARDEN: *Yes*
PETS: *No*
DISABLED ACCESS; *Yes for particially disabled, 2 steps up to get to front door. All doors are too narrow for a wheelchair*
ACCOMMODATION; *2 bedroomed self-catering cottage* *NO SMOKING*

24 CASTLEGATE,
Kirkbymoorside,
York,
YO6 6BJ.

Tel : 01751 431112

This 18th century, stone cottage, is one of a row situated at the northern end of this small market town, just three minutes walk from the town centre. Situated in a quiet no through road, it provides excellent accommodation for those wishing to see something of the surrounding countryside. There is a sitting room with exposed beams and a brick open fireplace (logs and coal provided for those cooler evenings), plus a colour TV. The kitchen is equipped with all the essentials including cooker, fridge, washing machine, microwave, as well as an iron and cleaning materials. There are two comfortable bedrooms; one large room suitable for two people, and one smaller with bunk beds suitable for either adults or children. The bathroom is fully rigged with bath, washbasin and lavatory. Fitted carpets are throughout the property, and there are storage heaters in every room. To the rear is a small garden overlooking a field and hills, and there is parking at the front. Allen and Elizabeth Davison, your hosts, live next door and are on hand to give you a friendly welcome and help with any queries you may have.

The town of Kirbymoorside is right on the southern edge of the North York Moors National Park. It has a good range of pubs where a choice of food is available, and a selection of shops that provide all the requirements of everyday life. It is a good base for visiting many local attractions including Rosedale, Bransdale and Farndale, and such historic sites as Rievaulx, with its temples and outstanding views, and the beautiful remains of the wonderful gothic architecture. Castle Howard, the film location of 'Brideshead Revisited', is also within easy distance and is a magnificent stately home open to the public. The Great Hall and handsome rooms are filled with beautiful furniture, exquisite paintings and family treasures. The grounds are charming with delightful rose gardens, lake and woodland, and there are licensed cafeterias for your comfort. Seven miles away is Pickering, home of North York Moors steam railway. This is a most popular venue, not only for railway enthusiasts, but for those who appreciate the scenery of this wonderful part of the country. Enjoy an 18 mile journey through the heart of the National Park with it's stunning moorland, woodlands, waterfalls and valleys. This is also walking country and there are many walks of varying degrees on your doorstep. To value the vistas that unfold before you be sure to take a camera or even a sketch pad - you will not be disappointed! Obviously there are many outdoor sports including fishing and riding, and the town has it's own 18 hole golf course. The towns of Whitby, Scarborough and York are only about 40 minutes away, so here you have the best of both worlds in a lovely rural setting with access to a host of activities and places to visit. What more could you ask?

USEFUL INFORMATION

OPEN : *All year except Xmas*
CHILDREN : *Welcome*
PETS : *By arrangement*
GARDEN : *Yes*

SELF CATERING
CREDIT CARDS : *None taken*
DISABLED ACCESS : *No*
PARKING : *Yes*

GALLOWHILL FARM,
Whalton, Morpeth,
Northumberland NE61 3TX.

Tel : 01661 881241

If your dream is to 'get away from it all' then Gallowhill Farm is the ideal location. Situated in the heart of the country it is a haven of peace and tranquillity, yet within easy access of many of the county's attractions and places of interest. Pat Coatsworth and daughter Anna are your hosts on this working farm of about 600 acres and there is a mixture of sheep, cattle and cereals farmed here. There are two self catering cottages : Orchard cottage is early 19th century semi detached, situated in the heart of the farm and overlooking green idyllic fields. Although it has very high standards of comfort, it has lost none of it's charm and character. It will sleep up to six guests and has four bedrooms; one double, one twin and two singles. There is a fully equipped bathroom on this floor, while on the ground floor is a cloakroom with basin and WC. The sitting and dining rooms are both charming, and the oak kitchen is fully equipped with all facilities.

Paddock Cottage is the other half of the semi detached, and sleeps four guests and a baby comfortably. Again it is furnished to a very high standard, and upstairs is one double room with a small side room big enough for a cot, and a twin bedded room. There is also a fully fitted bathroom. Again downstairs we have the charming sitting and dining rooms, and a fully fitted kitchen. Both cottages are centrally heated and have double glazing, and are warm and cosy properties all year round

USEFUL INFORMATION

OPEN : *All year*
CHILDREN : *Welcome*
PETS : *No*
ACCOMMODATION : *2 cottages; 4 to 6 persons.*
SELF CATERING
DISABLED ACCESS : *Not really*
CREDIT CARDS : *None taken*

PENNINE LODGE,
St.John's Chapel, Weardale,
Durham DL13 1QX.
Tel : 01388 537247

Pennine Lodge Cottage and Wear View Cottage are both self catering accommodation of very high standards. Both are delightfully furnished, mostly with antiques, and enjoy stunning views over the valleys. The River Wear flows at the back of the property, and this must be the most idyllic spot to relax. The peace and tranquillity of the countryside will leave you refreshed and recharged! This is a most excellent area for walking and touring.

Wear View Cottage sleeps two guests, and has an open plan sitting/dining room on the first floor. The atmosphere and character are captured in the open beamed ceiling and exposed stone features. The bedroom is charmingly furnished and has a double four-poster bed and en suite shower room.

Pennine Lodge cottage sleeps four guests, and again is delightfully furnished. The sitting/dining room boasts an open stone feature fireplace - heavenly for those chillier evenings- and again has a beamed ceiling. Upstairs are two bedrooms; one double with 'half tester bed' and en suite with shower washbasin and WC, and the second either the same again, or one twin with private bathroom. Outside is private parking and one pet is welcome with guests.

USEFUL INFORMATION

OPEN : *All year*
CHILDREN : *No*
PETS : *One pet welcome*
ACCOMMODATION : *2 cottages.*
SELF CATERING
DISABLED ACCESS : *No*
CREDIT CARDS : *none taken*

OLD BARN COTTAGES
Benridge Hagg, Morpeth,
Northumberland NE61 3SB

Tel: 01670 518507

These lovely cottages have been converted from a 17th century stone barn and have been designed with couples and small families in mind. Each of the four cottages, named after birds, are furnished in an attractive and simple way, they are comfortable, warm and clean. ***Magpie Cottage*** *sleeps between 3 and 5 persons and has views across fields. It has a comfortable lounge with a comfortable double sofa-bed, separate kitchen/dining room, two bedrooms, one with two single beds and one with a single bed, and a separate bathroom/WC.* ***Heron Cottage*** *is especially for families and sleeps 3/4. Downstairs it has a large open plan sitting room with comfy chairs including seating that converts into a 3ft wide bed, a fully equipped kitchen area and a large shower room/WC. Upstairs is a family bedroom with a double bed and 2 single beds, there is also room for a cot should you require one.* ***Robin Cottage*** *sleeps 2 and is very popular with couples. This charming property has an open plan sitting room and a well appointed kitchen. The double bedroom has an ensuite shower room/WC.* ***Wren Cottage*** *is very similar to Robin Cottage except it has a seat that converts to a 3ft wide bed. The ensuite bedroom has a 4ft wide bed. All the cottages are complete with duvets, bed linen, towels and tea towels, and colour televisions. The kitchens are modern and include fridge, cooker, toaster and kettle. They are insulated and double glazed throughout. A separate Laundry Room houses an automatic washer, tumble drier and ironing facilities.*

Horse riders will be in heaven here as there is an adjoining Riding Centre, where there are facilities for lessons and hacks. The area is teeming with activities and places to visit all within easy reach. Hadrian's Wall, Farne Island Bird Sanctuary, Holy Island, beaches, castles and cathedrals, not forgetting the many wonderful walks around this beautiful part of the country. Jo and Dennis Mancey, your hosts, offer a warm and friendly welcome to all their guests, you are sure to have a super holiday. Old Barn Cottages are English Tourist Board '3 Keys Commended'.

USEFUL INFORMATION

OPEN: *All year*
CHILDREN: *Welcome. Cot and high chair available on request*
CREDIT CARDS: *None taken*
ACCOMMODATION: *4 stone cottages Magpie sleeps 3/5, Heron sleeps 3/4, Robin sleeps 2, Wren sleeps 1/2*

DISABLED ACCESS: *Not really*
GARDEN: *Yes*
PETS: *By arrangement*
Plenty of parking
Electricity is metered separately
Electric heating

SPROXTON HALL FARM COTTAGES

Sproxton,
Helmsley,
York
YO6 5EQ

Tel: 01439 770225
Fax: 01439 771373

Sproxton lies half an hour from the A1, half an hour from York and one hour from the East Coast. An excellent base from which to enjoy a holiday. Sproxton Hall Cottages lend themselves to making that holiday or break quite perfect. Sproxton Hall is situated in a magnificent elevated position overlooking the Howardian Hills on the edge of the North Yorkshire Moors National Park, with truly panoramic views over open countryside, wooded valleys, crop-laden fields and grazing livestock. There can be little to match the sight of the dawn mist as it clings to the valley floors and the evening sun as it sets behind the hills. Sproxton Hall is a working farm of some 300 acres devoted to sheep, cattle, pigs and arable crops of wheat & barley, oil-seed rape, silage and hay. Within its acres the cottages stand in total peace and seclusion at the end of the cul-de-sac hamlet of Sproxton. Yet it is only one and a half miles from the bustling market town of Helmsley.

Andrew, who runs the farm with his son Mark, and Margaret Wainwright have converted 18th century stone and pantile farm buildings into five superb self-catering cottages each varying in size and character. That they were done with loving care and great attention to detail is obvious the moment you step inside anyone of them. Many of the original features have been retained, old timbered ceilings, ventilation slits, wall nest boxes, internal stone walls and at the same time there is every modern comfort. The kitchens are fully equipped with pine units, good quality fittings, attractive crockery. There is full central heating as well as open log fires, comfortable armchairs, deep sofas, matching curtains and bedcovers. The whole is totally charming and relaxing. Everything has been thought about including logs for the open fire, a welcome tray set for your arrival and at Christmas your cottage will be decorated with tree and lights. There is so much more including attractive gardens with seating, secluded patio and Barbecue area and for the business man access to a facsimile machine. There is space for children to play safely. Pets are not allowed. Named after the Dales, there is Ryedale cottage sleeping 3 and is suitable for wheelchair use, Bilsdale sleeps 4 +cot. Riccal Dale also sleeps 4 + cot. Kirkdale is larger and sleeps 6 + cot whilst the largest, Bransdale sleeps 8 + cot. There are special rates for weekends and winter breaks. You are spoilt for choice in things to do in this wondrous part of North Yorkshire.

If you would prefer to stay in luxury for bed and breakfast accommodation then Margaret and Andrew will welcome you to their 17th century grade II listed home, Sproxton Hall and look after you tremendously well. One word of warning, Sproxton Hall is a non-smoking house.

USEFUL INFORMATION

OPEN; *All year*
CREDIT CARDS; *None taken*
ACCOMMODATION; *5 cottages*
GARDEN; *Yes + Patio & BBQ*

CHILDREN; *Welcome*
DISABLED ACCESS; *Special facility in Ryedale*
PETS; *Not permitted*

EASTHILL HOUSE & GARDENS

Thornton-le-Dale,
Nr Pickering,
North Yorkshire
YO18 7QP

Tel:01751 474561

Thornton-le-Dale ranks as one of the prettiest villages in North Yorkshire, lying within the North Yorks National Park with Scarborough 15 miles away, Whitby 20, Pickering 2 ½ and York 25 miles. Thornton Beck meanders through the village with footbridges crossing to picturesque cottages; it passes by the village square which is bordered by a good selection of shops for daily provisions and souvenirs. It is an ideal spot for a holiday which combines relaxation amidst glorious scenery and activities and interests for all ages. Walking, cycling, fishing, horseriding, golf or tennis for the energetic. The more leisurely pursuits of visiting stately homes and gardens beckon many as well as the desire to explore the fascinating villages, monastic ruins all to be found nearby. The privately owned North York Moors Steam Railway operates from Pickering, and Flamingo Land Zoo and Fun Park is also nearby, both offering a great day out for all the family.

To enjoy all this there can be no better place to stay than at Easthill House standing in two and a half acres of ground. Here the beautiful family house has been sympathetically converted to provide three quiet, spacious and very attractive apartments. They accommodate from 2-8+ people and all enjoy southerly views of the gardens and beyond across the Vale of Pickering. An adjoining cottage, which sleeps 4 guests, has been converted from the coachhouse and stable of the big house and retains many of the original features, including open-beamed ceilings. All the apartments and cottage are traditionally furnished with co-ordinated soft furnishings to create a warm elegant country house atmosphere. The kitchens are well equipped and all the bedrooms, unless otherwise stated, are ensuite with bath or shower. Cots can be supplied. Laundry and drying facilities are available. Ample parking but no pets. In the midst of Easthill Gardens there are also three Scandanavian 'A' frame chalets, each in its own clearing, nestling amongst pine trees in a small wooded area. Each chalet is tastefully furnished and centrally heated with one twin and one double bedded room, shower room, and large open plan kitchen/dining/sitting area with veranda giving magnificent views over open countryside. You will also find a grass tennis court, a putting green, adventure play area, a small indoor games area, as well as quiet areas in which to sit and relax. It is a wonderful place to stay at anytime of the year.

USEFUL INFORMATION

OPEN; *All Year*
CREDIT CARDS; *None taken*
GARDEN; *Yes two & a half acres*

CHILDREN; *Welcome*
DISABLED ACCESS; *Yes*
PETS; *No*

GREENWELL FARM
Nr Wolsingham,
Tow Law,
Co. Durham
DL13 4PH

Tel: 01388 527248
Fax: 01388 526735

Greenwell Farm overlooks the hills of The North Pennines which is in an area of 'Outstanding Natural Beauty', a 300 acre traditional Dales mixed farm, where during the spring months lambs, calves and chicks can be seen and if you are really lucky a foal. With all the hard work they have to do Mike and Linda Vickers still manage to care for their guests. Situated on the farm are two self-contained properties, these once traditional farm buildings have been carefully and tastefully converted to provide excellent accommodation. **Greenwell Hill Stable** *sleeps 6 persons in total comfort, one of the bedrooms has a solid ash four poster bed. The single storey* **Byre Cottage** *sleeps 2+2, and is suitable for disabled visitors, the double room has ensuite facilities and there are twin beds on an upstairs loft balcony. Both cottages are double glazed and centrally heated making them very warm and cosy. The kitchens have all the modern conveniences including a microwave, electric oven and fridge freezer, the Stable also has a dish washer and washing machine. Each sitting room is attractively furnished with comfy sofa and chairs and wood burners. Linda also offers luxury bed and breakfast accommodation in their converted barn which sleeps up to 12 people, the barn can also be used on a self-catering basis for large family parties.*

Greenwell has it's own Nature Trails and Conservation areas where an array of birds and wildlife can be seen including owls. The farm is the ideal base for touring the region, Durham is only 12 miles away, Hexham and Newcastle-upon-Tyne are both within easy reach. Locally there is horse riding, fishing, cycling and walking to name but a few. Linda and Mike will be more than happy to give you more information. A very warm and homely welcome awaits.

USEFUL INFORMATION

OPEN: *All year*
CHILDREN: *Welcome*
CREDIT CARDS: *None taken*
ACCOMMODATION: *The Stables sleeps 6, The Byre sleeps 2+2 -*
ETB '4 Keys Highly Commended'
Linen, towels, gas & logs are included in the price

DISABLED ACCESS: *The Byre is single storey and suitable for disabled people*
GARDEN: *Yes*
PETS: *Dogs by arrangement, they must be exercised away from the cottage and never left unattended in the cottage*

CHAPTER 9

EAST ANGLIA
Including
NORFOLK, SUFFOLK & CAMBRIDGESHIRE

INCLUDES

EAST ANGLIA

Norfolk, Suffolk & Cambridgeshire

East Anglia is the epitome of that rural England we all visualise and love, with its gently rolling countryside and slow, easy pace of life. It is easily recognised as the bump on the east side of England, and although time seems to have passed this little corner by, it is easily within reach of major cities and good travelling facilities.

King's Lynn in West Norfolk is a historic port on the **River Great Ouse.** This is a beautiful town with a labyrinth of tiny streets, and history oozing out of every pore. There are medieval buildings, Georgian buildings, and many monuments to it's seafaring history. The Custom House, built by Henry Bell in 1683, is splendid and houses a special display of the maritime history of the town. 'Tales of the Old Gaol House' was opened by HRH Prince Charles in 1993, and is a delightful visionary experience of the lives and tales of some of the prisoners incarceratedwithin these cells. It is not difficult to imagine the horror and terror that some of these 'not so nice' characters installed in the local community! There are many, many more places of historical interest in this fine town, and if such is your inclination you will not be disappointed! For those who are interested in the art of shopping then you too will have plenty of opportunity - the elegant Tuesday Market Place hosts a large market on Tuesdays and Fridays where lots of interesting local produce and crafts can be found, whilst the smaller Saturday Market Place hosts another market on - yes you've guessed- Saturday. Alongside these markets is the modern, charming Vancouver Centre where all manner of shops, cafes and snack bars (where you can rest those aching feet!) can be found. King's Lynn is also excellent for antique shops, and a stroll along King's Staithe Lane, St James' Street, and Chapel Street may leave your pocket just a little lighter!

There is plenty of entertainment in the way of theatre and the arts; local and international performers can be seen at the King's Lynn Art Centre, and also in the fabulous Corn Exchange. There are any number of discos and night clubs for the more energetic, and a lot of the hotels hold dinner dances and cabaret evenings during the summer months. This is a fun place for all age groups, and with a diversity and charm that will capture each member of the family.

Inland, in the heart of Norfolk is **Swaffham.** There are many splendid Georgian buildings here, including Montpelier House and the Assembly

Rooms. The Church of St Peter and St Paul which is 15th century, is well worth visiting. There is also a good museum with a varied interesting display of artefacts.

Just along the coast is **Hunstanton**, the only west-facing resort on the east coast. The wondrous golden sands make it the ideal location for that family seaside holiday, and there is a wealth of entertainment and attractions ensuring that boredom gains no roots! Further north it becomes much quieter with curving sand dunes and clear horizons, providing the ideal habitat for much wildlife. The picturesque village of **Dersingham** is on the Hunstanton road, and has a view over the **Wash** on one side, and the lovely woods of the **Sandringham** border on the other. Here you will find one of Norfolk's many fine churches; this one from the 14th century, and with a beautifully carved wooden chest dating from the same period.

Wells next the Sea is the delightful name of a rather charming coastal port still in use, but combining rather well with a thriving tourist trade. With its Edwardian and Victorian fronted shops, a good browse is the order of the day! Before moving on, it is important to mention the Wells & Walsingham Light Railway which is just outside Wells. This runs the course of the old Great Eastern Line and is the longest 10" narrow gauge railway in the world. Even if you are not an enthusiast, the journey between Wells and **Walsingham** is a beautiful one, travelling over five bridges and through countryside renowned for its wild flowers and butterflies, with halts at **Warham St Mary** and **Wighton**. Walsingham has a great deal of history on offer, and the journey allows ample time for exploration.

Holkham Hall at Wells next the Sea, is one of Britain's most majestic stately homes, sitting in 3,000 acres on the north Norfolk coast. It is a classic 18th century Palladian style mansion, and is an absolute must on the list of places to be visited. It is full of artistic and architectural riches, and is a wonderful experience for all the family. Apart from the house, there is a museum, a history of farming exhibition, pottery, garden centre, gift shop, art gallery, tea rooms, not to mention the deer park, lake and beach. As I said; something for everyone!

Eastward, along the coast from **Sheringham** is the fishing village of **Cromer**. Although it now has a good tourist trade, the locals still depend very much on the sea for their livelihood, and a meal of fresh crab in this part of the world is a very worthwhile experience! This is great walking country, with views to stun from the clifftops, and walks of any length to suit all. The coastal road then skirts the **Broads,** which is probably what most people associate with Norfolk. This is a network of rivers and lakes, formed by flooded medieval peat diggings. There is 125 miles of lock free waterway, and is an idyllic way to spend a holiday. I can think of no better pastime than idling the day away in these peaceful waterways, and finding a nice riverside pub in which to have an evening meal and a quiet drink. Heaven! (If only I was a good sailor!)

Wroxham considers itself the unofficial capital of the Broads, and here you will find Barton House Railway, a riverside miniature railway. Also here is Hoveton Hall, 10 acres of woodland and beautiful lakeside gardens, with herbaceous borders and kitchen gardens. Wroxham is linked to **Hoveton** by means of a hump backed bridge over the **River Bure**. This is a lovely area, throbbing with vitality and active with the numerous, colourful boats busy by the river's banks. If you just fancy a day trip on the adjacent broads, then the Marina has a choice of motor launch or paddle steamer for you to enjoy. **Rackheath** is a village just outside Wroxham, and again there is one of those interesting little Norfolk churches here, this one dating from the 14th century.

Coming round the coast leads us to **Great Yarmouth**, a well known resort for all ages. This is a town with attractions from racing to fun fairs, and with marvellous long sandy beaches first discovered by the Victorians as a great holiday destination. As the local economy relied heavily at that time on the fishing industry, they quickly 'caught on' and the town has thrived ever since! But alongside the sometimes overwhelming 'attractions' there is great history in this town. The medieval stone wall is only one of a number of interesting items, along with many museums and heritage sites. The quayside is lined with fine buildings, and the maritime heritage is visible in a variety of historical buildings, including the 13th century Tollhouse which is supposedly the oldest civic building in the country. The Maritime Museum for East Anglia is at 25 Marine Parade, previously the home of a shipwrecked sailor, it now is home to Norfolk's maritime history. There are many displays from life-saving to shipwrecks, and obviously Nelson who plays a big part in the history of this area. Nelson's monument is again worth a visit - but be warned - after you have climbed the 217 steps to the viewing platform you may have to wipe the sweat from your brow to appreciate the stunning views! The monument was built 14 years after his death at Trafalgar, and shows how proud Norfolk was of their famous son, who was born at the rectory in **Burnham Thorpe.** The parish church in Great Yarmouth has a 12th century foundation and a 13th century west front. Although it was gutted during World War II, it has come some way towards it's former glory and now boasts some wonderful stained glass windows.

The more modern side of the town has many temptations of a different nature. The Living Jungle and Butterfly Farm is an indoor centre where you can walk among beautiful tropical gardens surrounded by humming birds and exotic butterflies. This is a wonderful experience for children, and you can take as many photographs as you desire to remind you of this novel event. Next door is the Sea Life Centre and further along is Wally Windmills Giant Indoor Children's Adventure Playground. (I think a shorter name may have been more memorable!) There is plenty for the family's entertainment, and a good way to spend an evening may be at the Royalty Centre which holds live family shows in the summer months. With it's long sandy beaches, unspoilt surrounding countryside and varying interests, Great Yarmouth makes for a very entertaining location for any holiday.

Norwich is the county town and regional shopping centre of the area. It is an extremely exciting place with it's modern facilities and easy access to the continent. This may account for the cosmopolitan air you find here, although the specialised shops and good quality department stores also help this image. It is an extremely cultured city with fine concert halls and theatres, and the history is all around you in every step you take. A medieval merchant's hall holds a cinema, while a charming church is used as a puppet theatre or an arts centre. This preserves the history, whilst making the money to keep it in order. The city centre is best explored on foot as some of it's network of streets are closed to traffic. It is enclosed by the old city walls, and has a substantial number of medieval buildings which tell of the wealth based on the wool and cloth trade of the Middle Ages. It was once the second largest city in England and has a grand Cathedral and Norman castle, which is a restored 12th century castle with museum and art gallery. If churches are your passion then this is the place to be - there seems to be one around every corner - the last count was 35 medieval churches - I would suggest more than one day touring these! This is a great base for exploring the Norfolk Broads, it's wildlife havens and idyllic lakes.....and still have the comfort of top quality city life and all it has to offer.

Taking the A11 out of Norfolk brings you to **Wymondham,** where the Abbey ruins have a charming story to tell. The Abbey was founded in Norman times by William D'Albini, whose desire it was that the monks and townsfolk could worship together. This was not to be, and the medieval church was almost divided in two by the factions who could not agree, and who built their own towers at each end of the church. Neither of these was ever completely finished but the size is most impressive. All was finally settled by the erection of a solid wall separating the parish at the west end from those at the east! The monastic tower is now in ruins, but a visit here is still a worthwhile experience, to see the hammerbeam roof arrayed with angels and bosses above the magnificent Norman nave. One of the Abbey's rare treasures is the 13th century Corporas Case, and along with the 16th century Renaissance monument and the superb gilt reredos, makes this a special place.

There was a great fire in the town in 1615 when at least 300 houses were destroyed. As a result there are not many houses from before this date, and today is a mixture of styles of 18th century, Victorian and more modern. One thing they all have in common is that they are all simple two storey buildings. The lovely Market cross was rebuilt almost immediately after the fire, and is octagonal and timber framed. The ground floor is open on all sides, with the building crowned by a pyramid roof and the emblems of the town, a wooden spoon and a spigot crossed, on the wood carving around the building. The Green Dragon, a 15th century pub, is one of the oldest in England.

Bungay is on the border of Suffolk, and the boundary on three sides is the **River Waveney.** Because of this it is an excellent place for walking, with delightful paths next to the river. You can see how the town developed round the 12th century castle, which is now in ruins, but the 13th century tower of St Mary's Church is definitely the centrepiece of the town.

The A143 travels through **Harleston** to the town of **Diss**. This town is an attractive mixture of Tudor, Georgian and Victorian houses, and has a weekly corn market on Fridays. Diss has been described by Betjeman as the archetypal English country town.

The last place in Norfolk I will mention is **Thetford**. South Norfolk is rural, tranquil and peaceful, dotted with pretty villages and bustling market towns. Whether you wish to cycle, walk or travel by car, the beauty and charm of the countryside will captivate and enchant you. Thetford is one of those lovely little towns, and in addition has a wonderful Forest Park of 50,000 acres of pine forest, with picnic sites, paths and trails. The town itself has some historical interest with a Norman priory and Castle Hill where earthworks, Norman motte and bailey with iron age ramparts can be found. Warren Lodge is the interesting ruin of a small two storey hunting lodge built around 1400.

Straight over the border to Suffolk, into the town of **Bury St Edmunds** and our next stop on the list. This town was named after Edmund, Anglo-Saxon King of East Anglia, who was killed by the invading Danes in 869, and who was eventually declared a saint. The town grew around the Abbey from the 11th century, which was one of the largest and influential in England. The Barons of England are reputed to have met here to swear they would force King John to sign the Magna Carta. The Abbey was mostly dismantled following its dissolution by Henry VIII, but the remainder, in the Abbey Gardens, are interestingly explained at the visitor centre. The town did well at the height of the medieval cloth making industry, but many of the buildings were later given new facades in the Georgian period which gives this town it's charm and elegance. The Theatre Royal is one building which has been beautifully restored, and there are many other places of historical interest to visit. Ickworth House and Park is an unusual 18th century stately home with fine paintings, whilst Manor House Museum has some choice paintings and clocks in an elegant Georgian town house. Moyses Hall is a 12th century house now containing an excellent display of local antiques. St Mary's Church has a magnificent roof and Mary Tudor is buried here. St Edmundsbury Cathedral was the mother Church of Suffolk and dates from around the 16th century. This is a wonderful church with a fine hammer-beam roof and a wonderful display of over 1000 embroidered kneelers. On the more modern side Bury St Edmunds has an excellent leisure centre with 3 swimming pools, giant water slides, saunaworld and good sports facilities. Activity World is an adventure playground for children under 5ft tall, and there is also a roller skating centre. As they say, 'something for all the family' in this traditional yet active country town.

Just up country from **Stowmarket** in the area of inland East Sussex is the small country town of **Eye.** This charming town's name means 'island', and although nowhere near the coast, in times gone by it was surrounded by marches and the River Dove. Again we have a ruined castle, and a great church tower with fantastic decoration. Head east from Eye and you will come to another market town with a castle; **Framlingham.** But in this case the castle is far from ruined - the views from the battlements of the town and surrounding countryside are breathtaking. Originally built in 1190, it has now been partially restored with towers, parapet walk and lower court beside an artificial lake. This is where Mary Tudor was proclaimed Queen of England in 1553 - a fascinating place.

Several miles from the open sea seems a strange place to have a port, but that is what **Woodbridge** is! The quays, boat yards, and tide mill and the tang of the salt air that comes along the **River Deben,** all add to the feeling that you are by the sea. The narrow streets and medieval buildings are worth exploring, and there are many interesting shops in the town. There is an interesting museum here; the Suffolk Horse Museum, which tells the history of the Suffolk Punch, the oldest breed of heavy working horse in the world. This is housed in a beautiful Elizabethan building and has displays of how the horse was worked, the blacksmiths, harnessmen and horseriders, and also the story of how the breed was rescued in the 1960s.

Felixtowe, on the coast is probably known as being a container port, but it is also an excellent family holiday resort. With it's south-facing beaches, charming gardens, and entertainment it has a lot to offer the tourist. Onward to **Ipswich**, again a port, but one which was founded in the6th/7th century by the Anglo-Saxons for trading with continental Europe. This is still it's role today but combined with being an important regional centre and country town. It is well equipped with good quality hotels and facilities, and is excellent for touring the surrounding area. There is a variety of good architecture both old and new including the internationally acclaimed Willis Corroon insurance building. I must admit to preferring Christchurch Mansion, a 16th century house in a historic park. The rooms are furnished in various styles from Tudor to Victorian, and there is the best collection of Constable and Gainsborough paintings outside London.

The **Stour Valley** is birthplace of two of Britain's finest painters - a few miles and half a century apart. Thomas Gainsborough was famous for his paintings of the rich and famous in Ipswich, London and Bath, although some of his writings indicate that his first love may have been landscape painting, and many of his portraits contain recognisable local scenes. John Constable was supposedly influenced by some of Gainsborough's early landscapes, and his most famous and inspired paintings were of where he grew up and spent his youth. **Flatford**, where Constable's father was the miller, has changed little in the passing of time, and even today you can understand the inspiration that Constable could have received in the sparkling river and the rustling trees.

At this stage I should just like to pop over the border into Essex and visit **Colchester.** This is Britain's oldest recorded town, and has a wealth of history and fascinating stories within it's walls. It was the first capital of Roman Britain, and William the Conqueror's 11th century castle which was built here, is the largest surviving Norman keep ever built. It was recently discovered that the keep was built on the remains of a Roman temple, and today you can visit the 'murky deeps' below the Castle Museum. The town has over a dozen museums and galleries, and there is a fascinating profusion of architecture throughout. Stop in at Hollytrees, an elegant Georgian house which has a wonderful collection of costume, pottery, toys and dolls. The Minories Art Gallery holds a wide variety of 20th century art exhibitions, with a delightful garden where sculpture exhibitions are held in the summer months. Apart from the many historical interests that this town holds, it is also a great cultural centre, with it's lively network of music, cabaret and theatre. Shopping is a delight in the narrow alleyways and lanes, while the larger shopping centres hold all the large company names. There are lots of traditional delicatessens and English tea-rooms where you can 'break' from the spending to watch the world go by. Antiques and bric-a-brac are obviously very popular here (after all, Lovejoy has picked up a few bargains here), and in addition there are excellent shopping facilities for people with disabilities. A lovely town, and one which should not be missed!

Back over the border South Suffolk is probably what we epitomise rural England to be, with its medieval towns, villages and pretty countryside. **Lavenham** is one of the best of these with its timbered, white-washed buildings crowding the hilly narrow streets, and its perfect market place (it could almost be from a film set). The Guildhall, Priory and Little Hall are good examples of medieval buildings, and all have interesting displays within.

Going towards **Haverhill** we reach the town of **Clare**. This town gets it's name from one of our most ancient families; the Earls of Clare. This is a well known name in Cambridge as Elizabeth, fathered by the ninth Earl of Clare, became the founder of the second oldest college in the university. It is a beautiful town of handsome houses with wonderfully patterned plasterwork, one of which, The Ancient House, now serves as a museum of Clare's history. The Country Park, just off the High Street, has as an attractive feature the **River Stour,** and a stroll along theriverside path is a pleasant way to spend a couple of hours. Kingfishers, swans and many other birds can be seen here, and birdwatchers will most certainly enjoy it. The path leads you to the remains of the Austin Friars priory which was originally founded in 1248, and after a lapse of many years is now once again in use by the Augustinian order. In the town is the Church of St Peter and St Paul, with it's fine 13th century tower. This is a lovely church with it's rood-stair turrets with crocketed spirelets, Jacobean gallery pew, and the chancel that was practically rebuilt in the 16th century.

Travelling through **Stumer** brings you to Haverhill which is well situated on the A604 between Cambridge and Colchester. It is an excellent stopping place being about mid way between the two. It has a fine shopping centre which is mostly pedestrianised and there are many interesting shops to browse through. In addition there is a fine old church which is well worth a visit.

On up to **Newmarket** and you will find that you are seeing sleek thoroughbreds grazing in paddocks, or going through the streets to the clatter of hooves. This is nothing unusual as since the 17th century Newmarket has been a centre for horse racing in Britain. Everywhere you go, you will either see horses or hear people speaking about them, and it is nothing unusual to see strings of horses in the High Street. Many of the finest race horses have been born, bred and trained in this fine town. The National Horse Racing Museum will give you an insight into the history, and the paintings of famous racehorses by local artist Alfred Munnings will show you the beauty and elegance of these wonderful animals. Many of the stables provide tours, and watching the horses in their exercise areas you cannot help but become involved and interested in what is going on around you.

Cambridgeshire is a beautiful county with **Cambridge** (probably the best known city in Britain), as it's pride and joy. It was established as a teaching centre for the nearby monasteries, and by the 13th century the University was established. Peterhouse, the oldest college was founded in 1284, with many others such as Trinity, Magdalene, and King's to follow. The representation of architectural styles is magnificent, and to see some of the students scurrying along, robes billowing, almost takes you on a medieval journey through some of these wonderful buildings. King's College Chapel is the city's 'Crowning Glory' with it's smooth lawns, formal gardens and large open spaces, and Henry VIII's Trinity, and can best be viewed from the 'Backs'(a punt along the river). These punts are normally 'chauffeured' by students who can give you a lively insight into the background and sights, and also a bit about life as a student! It is a lovely way to see Cambridge, and very relaxing too! Because of the history and architecture in this great city there are many tours organised by the Tourist Information Centre. These are worthwhile as you may otherwise miss some of the more interesting places that you may find difficulty in accessing. During the school year it swarms with academics, and it may be advisable to plan your trip well in terms of accommodation and access, as various parts may only be open during the academic terms.

Apart from the very obvious historical interest, Cambridge is a very lively city, from classical recitals to jazz concerts and various theatrical performances. In July there are festivals of classical music, art, theatre and film, the Cambridge Folk Festival and a huge carnival and fireworks. The city has many excellent shops, especially it's book shops, and I suppose some thanks may be given to the University for this. It is a city to be enjoyed at any time of the year, and one to which many visitors return as they often find that one visit is not enough!

Cambridge is surrounded by the rural countryside of South Cambridgeshire with many attractive villages and historical buildings. One such is Wimpole Hall, an 18th century country house with a colourful history of owners! This is a charming house with interiors by celebrated architects, an interesting collection of furniture and pictures, and lovely formal gardens in the landscaped park grounds. The Imperial War Museum at **Duxford** contains the finest collection of civil and military aircraft in Britain.

Huntingdonshire is centred around the **River Great Ouse,** and is the land of Oliver Cromwell, and Queen Catherine of Aragon. It is charming, gentle countryside with fascinating market towns and small villages nestling in the vales. Oliver Cromwell was born and lived in this area. The Falcon Inn at **Huntingdon** was at one time his headquarters, and you can see his statue in St Ives Market Square and visit the Cromwell museum. Queen

Catherine of Aragon was sent to Buckden Castle near Huntingdon before her death. **Godmanchester** was, in Roman times, a major settlement and is still separated from Georgian Huntingdon by water meadows which are criss-crossed with footpaths, and rivulets from the River Great Ouse. A beautiful 13th Century road bridge still links the two towns over the river. **St Ives** boasts only one of four surviving medieval bridge chapels, while **St Neots'** history dates back to the 10th century. It's 15th century church has a splendid roof with carvings of animals, birds and angels. Visit **Ramsey** and the Abbey Gatehouse and St Thomas A Becket church which was originally used as a hospital for the Abbey.

There are some wonderful places to visit and it is a gentle, quiet area with over 600 miles of public footpaths and bridleways to explore. The Ouse Valley Way is a 26 mile distance footpath that takes you through several of the old attractive villages, offering you a rich tapestry of the history and culture of the area.

Moving on to **The Fens** we can see a unique landscape - vast areas of artificially drained land that was reclaimed from it's marsh like state. The Romans, to their credit, made the first attempt at drainage, but it was Cornelius Vermuyden in 1630 who successfully completed the job! The landscape gives us wide open views, exposed skyscapes and breathtaking sunsets. Examples of fen drainage include Stretham beam Engine, built in 1831 and preserved today.

Ely was where the family home of Cromwell was located, and today you can visit this Cromwellian style house which has a visual presentation about the man's life. The house sits in the shadow of Ely Cathedral, a wonderful architectural achievement of the Middle Ages. Wonder at the Octagonal Tower; over 400 tons suspended in space without visible support! The Cathedral is located in a close containing the largest collection of medieval domestic architecture in England. The Cathedral can be seen for miles around Ely; a beacon of beauty in the rich dark landmass of the Fens.

To the north is the Georgian market town of **Wisbech.** This is probably one of the finest examples of Georgian architecture in the country, and you cannot leave without visiting The North Brink, the Crescent and Museum Square. Peckover House is of particular interest with its fine Georgian plaster and wood rococo. The Victorian gardens are notable for their unusual trees, orangery, stables, thatched barn, and summer house. Incidentally, this is where Barclay's bank first came into being in 1896, and at one time 'Peckover' notes were looked upon with greater favour than the Bank of England notes! Elgoods historic brewery is another must, but tours are by appointment only.

March and **Whittlesley** are two other places to be visited. March has St Wendrera's Church, with it's splendid double hammer beam roof, and Whittlesley has a variety of very well preserved architecture including some unusual mud walls. Both towns are tranquil, peaceful havens, with the old course of the River Nene flowing through both, making it a fisherman's heaven, or the perfect place for a stroll along the riverbank with lunch at a riverside inn.

Peterborough is classed as a 'new city' but really has history dating back thousands of years. The Norman Cathedral has been there for over 750 years and is the burial place of Queen Catherine of Aragon (Henry VIII's first wife), and was for a short time, that of Mary Queen of Scots. The architecture is magnificent, the West Front with it's three soaring Gothic arches is said to be one of the finest in Europe, and the medieval painted ceiling is not to be missed! The city museum has a fine collection of mainly local material, showing how life has changed since the time of the dinosaurs, and there are also two excellent paintings by Turner. One of the most exciting attractions to me was Flag Fen, a fairly recent archaeological discovery of artefacts from the Bronze Age. Visitors can actually watch the uncovering of a large 3,000 year old bronze age timber platform.

The Nene Valley Steam Railway travels from **Wansford** through Nene Park; a 2,000 acre park of lakes, woodland and watermeadows, to Peterborough. This is great for steam enthusiasts, but for anyone it is a very pleasant way to see the countryside. Historic buildings include Longthorpe Tower, with a superb collection of medieval wall paintings, Burghley House, a grand example of an Elizabethan stately home, and Elton Hall, home of the Proby family since 1660. There is plenty to see and do in this fine city, and the new is combined very tastefully with the old, taking nothing away from the rich cultural history this city has to offer. Many of the old streets are now pedestrianised so you can enjoy shopping and admiring the architecture at the same time, while the newer shopping centres are attractive with household names at your fingertips!

This is a very short trip round an exquisite county, but I hope you may find it useful and add to the extensive memorable places yourself!

POPPYLAND HOLIDAY COTTAGES,
Walnut Cottage,
The Street,
Aylmerton,
Norfolk
NR11 8AA

Tel : 01263 837672 (Mrs Bacon)
01263 577473 (Mrs Riches)
www.broadland.com/poppyland

Poppyland Holiday Cottages are a range of family run holiday accommodation, in the beautiful county of Norfolk. Offering both coastal and countryside habitats, these cottages are furnished and equipped to a very high standard. Four of the properties are in the centre of the pretty fishing village of Overstrand, where there is a long sandy beach, shops and places to eat. Two of the cottages are at Wickmere, a small rural village in a beautiful conservation area. This is an ideal spot from which to tour the area, and visit the many attractions on offer.

The properties cater for anything from two adults plus two children (plus cot), to four adults plus two children (plus cot). They are full of charm and character, and each is very individual in it's decor and furnishings. All amenities are provided such as central heating, colour TV, and a fully fitted kitchen. The gardens have BBQs and garden furniture, and there is parking at all properties. Whether it is a fun seaside holiday or a relaxing break in the peaceful countryside you are after, then these cottages give you the choice.

USEFUL INFORMATION

OPEN : *All year*
CHILDREN : *Welcome*
PETS : *No*
SELF CATERING
DISABLED ACCESS : *No*
CREDIT CARDS : *None taken*
ACCOMMODATION : *5 cottages + 1 house*
Accolades include ETB '3 Key Commended' - '5 Key Highly Commended'
Excellence in Tourism in North Norfolk Self-Catering Award - Winner in1995 & 1996, Runner-Up in 1994

THE GRANARY AND STABLE COTTAGES
Chattisham,
Nr Ipswich,
Suffolk
IP8 3QD

Tel/Fax: 01473 652210

In the small quiet village of Chattisham set in the heart of Constable Country and the Suffolk river valleys, Margaret and Hugo Langton have their arable farm surrounded by wonderful countryside. On the farm the Langtons have created three attractive cottages, **The Granary, Coachmans** *and* **Stable Cottage**. *These once farm buildings have been carefully converted, retaining many original beams, to provide top class accommodation. Positioned around a sunny courtyard where one may sit and relax on the garden furniture provided. The standard of furnishings and facilities is very high, the kitchens are fully fitted with electric cooker, microwave, fridge freezer and plenty of crockery and cutlery, some bedrooms are ensuite, central heating and colour television add to the comfort. Outside you can enjoy the heated swimming pool, a hard tennis court which you may use by arrangement. A Games Room provides snooker and table tennis. For those of you who are interested in art a Studio/Craft Room offers decorative china painting, jewellery making, modelling and painting for both adults and children. All bed linen, towels and heating is included in the tariff. Margaret is an excellent cook and makes her own delicious bread, jam and cakes which she sells.*

This unspoilt area is just waiting to be explored, there are Waymarked paths and circular walks through beautiful countryside with the help of maps and brochures provided by the Langtons. Picturesque towns and beaches along the heritage coast offer something for everyone. Other activities include golf, sailing, cycling and horse riding. So come and stay at Margaret and Hugo's lovely farm and experience the slower pace of life.

USEFUL INFORMATION

OPEN: *All year*
CHILDREN: *Welcome. Secure play area, cot & high chair available*
CREDIT CARDS: *None taken*
ACCOMMODATION: *3 cottages, Granary sleeps 6-8, Coachman sleeps 4-6 8 with bunk beds, Stable Cottage sleeps 2-4 6 with bunk beds*

DISABLED ACCESS: *Stable & Coachman are fully wheelchair accessible, adapted bathrooms, Games & Craft Rooms accessible*
GARDEN: *Heated swimming pool, tennis court Games & Craft Rooms, patio area & barbecue*
PETS: *Dogs by arrangement*

All NON-SMOKING in 1998

THE GROVE GUEST HOUSE

Overstrand Road,
Cromer,
Norfolk
NR27 0DJ

Tel: 01263 512412
Fax: 01263 513416

The area in and around Cromer is delightful. Cromer itself is a peaceful seaside town with lovely long, safe sandy beaches where the children can play quite happily. The cliffs and the golf course are not far away and just beyond is the village of Overstrand. The village of Aylsham with its charming Monday morning market selling all sorts of intriguing items, and the lovely town of Holt where one can wander round the many small shops selling paintings and antiques.

The Grove stands in 3 acres of fields, gardens and trees. It was built by Joseph Gurney in 1797 for his family as a holiday home, today it is owned by Mr and Mrs Graveling, who have created a superb nine bedroomed Guest House. In the grounds are six self-catering cottages each with its own character sleeping between two and six persons. They have been converted, with the help of the East Anglian Tourist Board, from former barns and an old coachman's cottage, a bungalow at the back of The Grove, also provides accommodation. All the cottages are extremely well furnished, spacious and fully heated. Washing machines, fridge freezers, colour televisions, bed linen and towel are all provided. These comfortable cottages have been awarded '4 Keys Commended', the bungalow is '3 Keys Commended', and it is not difficult to see why, once you have stayed here you will want to return to this wonderfully idyllic setting.

USEFUL INFORMATION

OPEN: *All year*
CHILDREN: *Welcome*
CREDIT CARDS: *None taken*
DISABLED ACCESS: *Not really*
GARDEN: *Yes with furniture*
PETS: *In some cottages*
ACCOMMODATION: *B & B and evening meal available in 9 bedroomed Guest House, 6 cottages which sleep between 2 and 6*

MIDDLEGATE BARN
Dunwich,
Suffolk
IP17 3DW

Tel: 01728 648741

If you wish for a peaceful holiday in tranquil surroundings then Middlegate Barn is the place for you. Situated in an area of Outstanding Natural Beauty in the small unspoilt coastal village of Dunwich, these lovely self-catering holiday cottages are everything one could wish for. There are three altogether, ***The Close, Maypole*** *and* ***Bowmans Cottage,*** *each are exceptionally well furnished with the emphasis on cleanliness and comfort. The Close and Maypole sleep 5 persons, each having a double room, a twin and a single room, the Bowmans Cottage sleeps 2 persons in one double bedroom, there is also a bed settee in the sitting room. The facilities in include fridge, electric cooker, microwave and dish washer (The Close and Maypole only). In the sitting rooms you will find a colour television along with plenty of books and board games to keep you amused incase it rains. Garden furniture is provided for those lovely sunny days. A washing machine and spin dryer are available and the cost of this is included in the tariff along with electricity, hot water and central heating. Also for your convenience all bed linen and towels are provided.*

David and Elizabeth Cole, your hosts, live close by and are on hand to assist you in any necessary, they are a warm and friendly couple who will make you extremely welcome at Middlegate, it will be very hard to leave.

USEFUL INFORMATION

OPEN: *All year*
CHILDREN: *Welcome. Cots and high chair available on request*
CREDIT CARDS: *None taken*
ACCOMMODATION: *3 very comfortable cottages sleeping 5 or 2 + 2 persons*

DISABLED ACCESS: *Not really*
GARDEN: *Yes, secluded sunny gardens with garden furniture provided*
PETS: *Welcome provided they are well behaved*
Ample parking space

CHURCH FARM COTTAGES,
Brisley,
East Dereham,
Norfolk
NR20 5LL.

Tel : 01362 668332

Brisley is a small rural village just between East Dereham and Fakenham, and is ideally situated for visiting such attractions as Norwich and kings Lynn. There are many walks in the area, with some interesting and varied scenery, and although very quiet and tranquil, it is not an isolated area. There is plenty of room for children to play, and the Bell public house/restaurant is just 300 yards across the village green.

Swallow Cottage stands beside the village green and backs on to open farmland belonging to the owners. It is a fine cottage constructed of brick and flint, and was part of the original 400 year old farmhouse. It is private, with enclosed garden and ample parking space. It is delightfully furnished in cottage style, and can comfortably suit four adult guests. In addition there is a cot, high chair and stair gate for any additional baby. There are two bedrooms; one double and one twinbedded room. The kitchen is fully equipped with all necessities, and the dining room has a charming log fire for those cosy evening meals. The lounge is bright and comfortable, and garden furniture and sun loungers are provided for outside. A portable barbecue is available on request. If less than four guests are staying then there is a discount available, and there is another cottage to the same high standards if this one is already booked.

USEFUL INFORMATION

***OPEN :** All year*
***CHILDREN :** Welcome*
***PETS :** Welcome*
***ACCOMMODATION :** 2 cottages suitable for 4 guests.*

SELF CATERING
***DISABLED ACCESS :** No*
***CREDIT CARDS :** none taken*

WOOD FARM COTTAGES

Plumstead Road,
Edgefield,
Melton Constable,
Norfolk
NR24 2AQ

Tel/Fax: 01263 587347

The countryside around North Norfolk is an ideal holiday location, being surrounded by wonderful scenery and within reach of the coast. It is in this lovely rural setting Doug and Diana Elsby have their superior self-catering farm cottages. Traditional Norfolk flint barns and stables have recently been converted to provide seven extremely comfortable cottages, retaining many of the original features, with the addition of modern facilities including central heating. All the cottages have attained the English Tourist Board '4 Keys Commended' award and it not hard to see why, fully carpeted and furnished in a similar way, yet each one is individual. The comfy sofas and chairs make the sitting rooms very easy to relax in, added to this colour television which receives free satellite channels and a choice of books. The kitchens are very well equipped with all you will need including microwave ovens, fridge freezer and a coffee maker. The bedrooms are furnished with pine suites and cosy duvets enhancing the warm atmosphere. In some of the cottages the bathrooms have showers. All bed linen and towels are provided. Electricity is through meters taking £1 coins. The outside is delightful with lots of open space and grassed areas for the children to run around including a large enclosed paddock which houses a children's play ground with swings, slide, climbing frame, see-saw, sand pit and an old tractor. Barbecues and garden furniture are supplied for your use. Laundry facilities are available.

The area here is teeming with activities and places of interest, Diana will be more than happy to help with information and ideas. You are assured a warm and friendly welcome at these charming cottages.

USEFUL INFORMATION

OPEN: *All year*
CHILDREN: *Welcome. Cots & highchairs on request*
GARDEN: *Yes.*
CREDIT CARDS: *None taken*
ACCOMMODATION: *7 cottages sleeping between 2 and 6 persons*

DISABLED ACCESS: *2 cottages are accessible for wheelchairs, but not adapted - please ask for details*
Children's play ground, covered area for ball games, indoor games room, bicycle hire, garden furniture and barbecues
PETS: *Well behaved pets welcome*

JOCKEY COTTAGE
Dalham, Newmarket,
Suffolk

Contact: *Richard Williams*
Scorrier House, Scorrier,
Redruth, Cornwall TR16 5AU

Tel: 01209 820264

Standing well back from the road at the end of a row of cottages and reached via a small bridge is Jockey Cottage, a charming thatched property surrounded by trees, shrubs and flowers . It is delightfully furnished with a mixture of antique and comfortable modern furniture which blend well together, giving a warm and cosy feeling. On the ground floor is a sitting room with exposed beams and colour television, fully equipped kitchen, dining room and a bathroom. Upstairs is a double bedroom with fitted wardrobes. A camp bed or sofa bed is available for a child or an extra visitor. This cottage is extremely well thought out and provides you with all the essentials including electricity, all bed linen, towels and garden furniture. As a special touch a welcome pack is offered filled with cereal, orange juice, bread, butter, milk and marmalade.

The village of Dalham is set amidst beautiful countryside and well known as one of the prettiest villages in Suffolk, it is very peaceful and just the place for a relaxing holiday or short break. It is ideally placed for Newmarket, only five miles away, ten miles from Bury St Edmunds and a twenty minute drive from Cambridge. Horse lovers will be in their element with race meetings together with various racing tours and the National Stud to see, not forgetting the gallops, it is a great experience to see the horses training. This is a lovely part of the country to visit, and staying at Jockey Cottage is the icing on the cake.

USEFUL INFORMATION

OPEN: *End Mar-End Nov. After Nov by arrangement*
CHILDREN: *Welcome*
CREDIT CARDS: *None taken*
ACCOMMODATION: *Charming thatched one bedroomed cottage*

DISABLED ACCESS: *No*
GARDEN: *Yes with furniture*
PETS: *No*
Mini Breaks or Long Weekends available for a minimum of two nights

HALL COTTAGE
Gresham,
Sheringham,
North Norfolk

Contact:- *Mrs W Heal*
Burgh Parva Hall, Melton Constable,
Norfolk NR24 2PU

Tel: 01263 860797

The delightful rural village of Gresham is tucked away amidst beautiful farmland, which is the character of Norfolk. It is here at the end of a long private drive you will find Hall Cottage, surrounded by wooded parkland. This lovely red brick spacious five bedroomed house sleeps eight people in total comfort. On the ground floor is a large sitting room with a wood burner, for which logs are supplied free of charge, and colour television, just off this room is a small playroom for the children. The kitchen is well equipped including an electric cooker, a microwave and with enough cutlery and crockery for all your needs. The dining room is large enough to accommodate ten people. The utility room houses a sink, washing machine, ironing board and cleaning equipment. There is also a toilet with basin by the back door which leads to the garden. The bedrooms, one double, two twin and two single, are very pleasant. There are two bathrooms with shower attachments, and two of the bedrooms have their own wash hand basins. A pay phone is available in the front hall. Outside is a partially walled, lawned garden where you can sit and eat at the table and chairs provided. Electricity is metered using £1 coins. You may bring your own bed linen or it can be supplied at £5.00 per person per week. Towels and tea towels are not provided.

Two miles from Gresham is the traditional seaside town of Sheringham, with its long safe, sandy beaches just what you need for those important tools - the bucket and spade. There are plenty of good shops, restaurants and pubs to choose from. On a Saturday you will find a bustling market where you can leisurely amble taking in the atmosphere.

USEFUL INFORMATION

OPEN: *All year*
CHILDREN: *Welcome*
CREDIT CARDS: *None taken*
ACCOMMODATION: *Spacious 5 bedroomed house*

DISABLED ACCESS: *No*
GARDEN: *Yes with table and chairs*
PETS: *No*

SPIXWORTH HALL COTTAGES,
Grange Farm,
Spixworth,
Norwich,
Norfolk
NR10 3PR

Tel: 01603 898190/898272

Three attractive cottages are available throughout the year on a 700 acre working farm for those who enjoy a peaceful self-catering holiday or break in the glorious Norfolk countryside, the Broads and the coast. The situation is wonderful with the freedom to roam on the farms private footpaths and bridleways through bluebell woods, across the open farm and along the water meadows. One can never be bored whilst staying here. You are only 5 miles from Norwich, a fascinating city with a superb cathedral and a great history.

Spixworth Hall was demolished after the war but fortunately the Coachman's Cottage, Jacobean stable block and surrounding farm buildings were saved and they are now listed and retain much of the 17th and 18th Century character. Gaffer's Cottage was originally the coachman's cottage and has been fully modernised and furnished to a high standard with exposed beams throughout. It has full central heating and a wood burning stove in the Lounge. French windows lead onto the patio and garden. There is a well equipped kitchen with breakfast area, Dining Room, Utility area, downstairs WC and shower. Upstairs there are 4 bedrooms and a Bathroom. There is a large garden. Waterside and Granary Cottages have been created by the skilful conversion of the front of the beautiful Jacobean stable block Great care has been taken to retain as many features as possible including the clock, sundial and weather vane, flooring and beams. The resulting cottages are delightfully furnished and decorated. The arched entrance under the clock gable gives access to the cottages on either side and also to a large enclosed courtyard garden at the rear. They are both equipped with everything you could wish for. Waterside sleeps 5-6 with 1 single, 1 twin, 1 double + single. Granary Cottage sleeps 6-7 with 2 twin bedrooms, 1 double + single bed if required. The stable block is set in open grounds grassed at the front and sides. There is a barbecue and garden furniture in the courtyard.

The nearest shops are 1 mile away. During the summer months it may be possible to use the owners heated pool and lawn tennis court. There are 2 Golf courses within 3 miles and Snooker and Table Tennis can be played in the barn. The Cooks, the owners also run a livery stables and they may occasionally be able to arrange stabling for a visiting horse or pony. Fishing - a small lake has recently been stocked with coarse fish for holiday makers' use.

USEFUL INFORMATION

OPEN; *All year*
CREDIT CARDS; *None taken*
ACCOMMODATION; *3 cottages Excellent standard*

CHILDREN; *Welcome*
DISABLED ACCESS; *No special facilities*
GARDEN; *Yes with Bbq & furniture*

MRS JANE GOOD LTD.
HOLIDAY COTTAGES,
Blandings,
Hasketon,
Woodbridge,
Suffolk
IP13 6JA.

Tel : 01394 382770
Fax : 01394 380914

The property management specialists of Mrs Jane Good Ltd. Holiday Cottages offer an unique service in this part of the world. With cottages of all sizes, smoking and non smoking, with pets and without pets, you are sure to find that one of these delightful properties, which are carefully maintained by individual owners, will suit your every need. Foxvale Cottage is just one example. A single storey dwelling suitable for up to four guests, with a charming living room leading to a newly built conservatory. The views are rural and you are told to watch for the fox and family who visit at dusk! There is a fully fitted kitchen, one double bedroom and one twin bedded room, and a comfortable bathroom. Pets are regrettably not allowed as the owner has an assortment of dogs, cats, horses and chickens! There is a garden area and ample parking available.

This, as I said, is just one of many, and if perhaps you prefer a seaside location then this too is available. You can be confident that Mrs Jane Good Ltd. Holiday Cottages can suit your requirements, and make your stay in this charming part of the country a memorable and enjoyable one!

USEFUL INFORMATION

OPEN : *Some properties available all year*
CHILDREN : *Welcome*
PETS : *Some*
ACCOMMODATION : *Various.*
SELF CATERING
DISABLED ACCESS : *Some*
CREDIT CARDS : *None taken*

ST PETER'S VIEW
The Lodge,
Monk Soham Hall,
Monk Soham,
Nr Framlingham,
Woodbridge,
Suffolk
IP13 7EN

Tel/Fax: 01728 685358

The delightful sounding hamlet of Monk Soham in the heart of the Suffolk countryside is where you will find Geoffrey and Gay Clarke's spacious and excellently maintained properties. St Peter's View is situated just 5 miles from the traditional market town of Framlingham and within easy reach of Suffolk's Heritage Coastline, where the lovely sandy beaches are perfect for the children with their bucket and spades. The 4 bungalows are very well designed with the main living areas open plan, giving a light and airy atmosphere, they also enjoy uninterrupted views of the surrounding area. The bedrooms are either double or twin, with large ensuite shower rooms, No1 also has a separate shower room/WC. The patio doors lead out to the garden where you can relax and unwind. To make life easier for you the bungalows are exceptionally well equipped with microwave, electric cooker, fridge, colour television, shaver point, pillows, duvets or if you prefer sheets and blankets, towels and bed linen. Disabled access is very good with all properties fully wheelchair accessible, and No2 has low-level kitchen units. A Laundry Room with washing machine, tumble dryer and iron is available. There is a Games Room and for the golfers - a practice area. The grounds are extensive, there are trees, shrubs, flowers and plenty of lawn for the children.

Your days will certainly be filled to overflowing, the area has so much to offer everyone, the bird reserve at Minsmere, the seaside town of Aldeburgh, Snape Maltings where you can visit the craft centre or take a river trip along the picturesque River Alde. There are castles, country houses and gardens. St Peter's View is the perfect holiday location.

USEFUL INFORMATION

OPEN: *All year*
CHILDREN: *Welcome*
CREDIT CARDS: *None taken*
ACCOMMODATION: *4 superb bungalow style properties either double or twin*
PETS: *No*

DISABLED ACCESS: *Very good, all wheelchair accessible and equipped to an excellent standard. No2 has low-level kitchen units*
GARDEN: *Extensive with garden furniture and barbecue area*
NO SMOKING indoors

CHAPTER 10

WALES

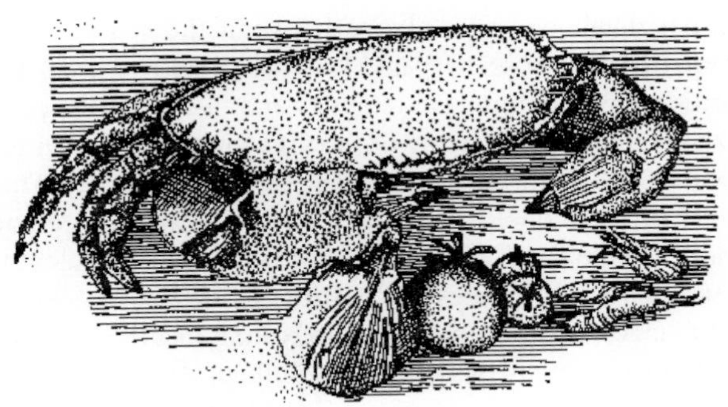

INCLUDES

WALES

To attempt to describe Wales in a chapter, albeit a lengthy one, is ludicrous. To do it justice in a large volume would still be difficult but as this option is not open to me I hope you will find the tales of my journeying an appetiser encouraging you to delve into, and enjoy the beauty, the splendour, the warmth and the people of this wonderful Principality.

I decided to start by embracing Anglesey, Snowdonia and the Lleyn Peninsula which allows me a choice between the sea and land, with a breathtaking diversity of scenery and activities. Firstly, I used **Bangor** as a base. Here is a city of impressive religious and historic heritage. A place in which to enjoy the natural beauty of the area and to be drawn to the many old buildings which have been carefully maintained or restored. **The cathedral** was founded by St Deiniol in 575Ad - 70 years before Canterbury - and is built on one of the oldest Christian sites in Britain. Its turbulent history has included sacking by the Vikings and destruction by King John's forces when they burnt Bangor in 1210, and it is the resting place of Prince Owain of Gwynedd. Work was begun on the present Cathedral in the mid 13th Century, and was finished with the completion of the Central Tower in 1967.

The City of Bangor is dominated by the academic towers of the **University of Wales** - the 'college on the hill' - which celebrated its centenary in 1984. Apart from good shopping in pedestrianised streets I wandered down to the waterfront intent on visiting the Pier. It stretches a full 1500feet into the Menai Straits, and has recently been restored to its Victorian splendour.

As I moved away from the coast and drove into the mountains the scenery became truly spectacular. Dyffryn Ogwen - the Ogwen Valley - delights artists and photographers. My route took me through **Bethesda**, a village with a Hebrew name which means 'a house of mercy', and along the shores of Llyn Ogwen. The landscaped was dominated by the mountain ranges of Carnedd Llywelyn, Carnedd Dafydd, Tryfan, Glyder Fach and Glyder Fawr. Salmon and sea-trout ascend the River Ogwen as far as the falls below Llyn Ogwen, and many of the lakes in the area - Ogwen, Bochlwyd, Ffynnon Lloer - provide excellent sea-trout fishing, for which permits are available locally.

And so to **Llanberis**. With a history going back to the Iron Age, the town is one of the oldest settlements in Wales and a bastion of the Welsh language and tradition. Old Roman forts lie to the east and west, and the uplands behind Llanberis are reputed to be linked to the legends of King

Arthur. Although perhaps best known as the lower terminus of the **Snowdon Mountain railway**, Llanberis is also renowned as a centre for climbers.

The views across the twin lakes to the mountains are stunning, and from here their grandeur contrasts sharply with the softness of lush green meadows and the beauty of the lower wooded slopes. You may well opt for the Mountain Railway, as I did, as the favoured way of reaching Snowdon's summit - climbing up tracks is no longer for me! The Mountain Railway is Britain's only public rack and pinion railway. It was opened in 1896 and climbs more than 3,000 feet, the journey lasting approximately an hour. Views on the way up are spectacular, and from the summit, on clear days, you can see the Isle of Anglesey, the Wicklow mountains in Ireland, and the Isle of Man. First train of the day is usually at 9am from Llanberis - much depends on the weather.

Two places to visit in Llanberis - **The Piggery Pottery** and **The Snowdon Honey Farm** which are right in the centre of town. **The National Museum of Wales** has its Northern branch in Llanberis, and the Power of Wales Exhibition is particularly well-presented.

To most people, at least since 1969, **Caernarfon** means ' castle'. It was then that the Investiture of HRH Prince Charles as Prince of Wales took place, although what is not quite such common knowledge is that Caernarfon was also the scene for the Investiture of Prince Edward in 1911 - later to be Edward VIII and then Duke of Windsor, after his abdication. The setting of the castle is superb. The King's Gate is said to be the mightiest in the land; the Eagle Tower houses an exhibition and audio visual programme; the Royal Welch Fusiliers have their museum in the Queen's Tower; the Prince of Wales' exhibition is in the North-East Tower; and in the Chamberlain Tower there is an exhibition of the Castles of Edward I.

But Caernarfon is much more than a magnificent castle. In the past the landscape artist, Turner, came here, and marvelled at the quality of the light and sunsets. At the turn of the century so many famous newspaper men had connections with the town that it was known as the Fleet Street of Wales. The River Seiont flows past the castle walls into the Menai Strait. There can surely be no finer way of viewing both town and castle than from a boat on one of the regular trips run from the quayside.

The lovely, quiet part of Britain that is the Lleyn Peninsula is full of rare, natural treasures, whether it is the Peninsula's own breed of sheep, the abundant wild flowers, the hedgerows abounding in honeysuckle, rosehips and blackberries, or the overwhelming sense of history. It is a very Welsh heartland.

The journey down the Peninsula is dominated by the two peaks of Yr Eifl (The Rivals) mountains, proof surely that nowhere in North Wales can you ever be far from high ground! Going along the B4417 one comes to **Nefyn**, a coastal resort which was once a halt for pilgrims on their way to **Bardsey Island** (Ynys Enlli - the island of tides, where 20,000 saints are said to be buried.) Now, the village's church of St Mary houses a maritime museum, and if you have time to pause take a look at the fine, sweeping bay formed by Nefyn, Morfa Nefyn and Porth Dinllaen. The 'Whistling Sands' at **Porthoer** is one of the area's outstanding beaches, an ideal spot to take the folding chairs out of the car boot and relax for a while. It is fact that the golden sands whistle mysteriously as one picks one's way across the picturesque bay.

Churches in the Lleyn Peninsula are among the most attractive in Wales. There is a stunningly simple example at **Llangwnnadl**, which lies to the north-east of Porthoer, and a mile or so inland at **Bryncroes** is St Marys on the site of St Mary's Well, an important watering place on the Pilgrim's Route. By taking a minor road across country I came to **Llangian** where, in the churchyard of St Gian's, one of the earliest known doctors from the 16th century is buried.

The final point of interest on the southernmost tip of the Lleyn Peninsula is **Aberdaron**, which was always the last port of call for pilgrims on their way to Bardsey. The place is steeped in history. At least one Prince of Wales has sheltered in the 6th-century church of St Hywyn which nestles on the seashore, as have Cromwell's soldiers. It is said that the marks still visible on the door pillars were made by those same soldiers as they sharpened their swords.

Next to **Abersoch**. This is best done by taking the A499, which together with the A497, is a most attractive road following the southern coastline of the Peninsula as far as Porthmadog. Thissection of the coast is stunningly beautiful and has the weather to match. It is a mecca for sailing enthusiasts and sometimes referred to as ' Cowes of the North'. Ideal conditions mean that Abersoch and nearby Pwllheli are frequent locations for major British, European and World sailing championships, and for the casual sailor the waters offer some of the very best sheltered sailing facilities in Britain.

Until the earlier part of this century **Porthmadog** was a bustling shipping port. It served the international Welsh slate trade which was brought down from **Blaenau Ffestiniog** by the Ffestiniog Railway, now a major tourist attraction. The full round trip takes about 2 hours, and is well worth taking because of the wonderful scenery. Much of the town is flat - it is recognised as a model of 18th century town planning.

Whatever you do, do not leave this beautiful coast without visiting **Portmeirion**. This unique village was created by Sir Clough Williams-Ellis between 1925 and 1972 in what he calls his 'light opera approach'. It is located on a secluded peninsula which juts out into Traeth Bach. It consists of fifty buildings arranged around a central Piazza, all predominantly Italianate in style, and is surrounded by the sub-tropical woodlands of Y Gwyllt. I love the place for its beauty, its escapism and the totally peaceful atmosphere. To stay here either in self-catering accommodation in one of the villas or houses or to enjoy the superb hotel is a never to be forgotten experience. It is equally pleasureable for day visitors to wander round the village, have a meal in one of the restaurants, sit a while on the Piazza and dream dreams. Portmeirion Pottery is available in the shop - seconds in the Portmeirion shop and others in one of the delightful little shops.

Leaving the Lleyn Peninsula I took the A498 which led me to the A4085 and a spectacular, if slightly tortuous journey through the Snowdon mountain range to **Beddgelert**. There is a tradition here, and romantic legend, which suggests that the village's name (Geldert's Grave) comes from Prince Llywelyn's heroic dog Gelert, slain by the Prince who mistakenly thought the dog had killed his son. Later the prince realised a dead wolf was to blame, and the blood-spattered dog had been killed defending the boy. The village which won the Queen Mother's Birthday Award 1992 - Keep Wales Tidy Campaign, is vastly different from those I visited on the Lleyn Peninsula. There the sea was always evident, the small hamlets bright and airy, a feeling of space all around. In the Aberglaslyn Valley lushness prevails. Paths close by lead to Snowdon, Moel Hebog, Moelwyn and the Cnicht, and the Rivers Glaswyn and Colwyn merge to flow through the glorious beauty of the Aberglaslyn Pass. Other beauty spots not to be missed include the Nant Gwynant Pass, and Cwm Pennant, where the River Dwyfor flows through one of Britain's most lyrical valleys.

Conwy is, literally, a fortress city by the sea. As you swoop down from the Sychnant Pass you will see that it is dominated by the castle built by Edward I as part of his master plan to subdue the Welsh. That was between 1283 and 1289 and today the castle is perhaps the most picturesque in Wales, the town walls with 22 towers and 3 original gateways the most complete of any in Europe. To make room for his castle, Edward moved Cistercian monks from their Abbey to Maenan in the Conwy Valley. Of the Abbey all that remains is the Abbey church which is still in use after seven centuries - a haven of peace in the very centre of the busy town.

Thomas Telford's graceful suspension bridge is one of three crossing the river Conwy. It was opened in 1826 and in use until the modern road bridge was completed in 1958. As you drive east out of Conwy you will see alongside both bridges the tubular railway bridge, built by Robert Stephenson in 1846. A superb technical achievment, it is still a vital link on the railway line between Chester and Holyhead. Odd, how even in those days, care was taken in building themock-medieval towers so that they harmonised with the castle. We are surely wrong to believe that our generation is the first to care about the environment!

From **Llandudno Junction** the A470 goes through another area famed for its scenery. The Vale of Conwy is more usually referred to locally as the **Conwy Valley**, and the road winds up the eastern bank of the river. This really is a lovely area to explore, and I suggest a drive as far as **Betws-y-Coed** where you can cross the river by bridge and so return to Conwy.

Llanrwst is an old market town and famed for its bridge built by Inigo Jones in 1636. Pont Fawr is narrow and humped, and until traffic lights were installed it was frequently the scene of heated arguments as drivers claimed right of way! If you walk to the centre of the bridge you will see a group of standing stones on the far bank. These are the Gorsedd Stones, and they are closely connected with the ceremonies associated with the bards who attend the National Eisteddfodau. At Llanrwst the stones are frequently marooned when the River Conwy breaks its banks during the winter months.

Betws-y-Coed is four miles further on. It is just 50 feet above sea level and entirely surrounded by hills of an average height of 1,000 feet. 'Y Coed' is the Welsh for 'the wood', and as you drive in over Telford's cast-iron Waterloo Bridge you must be captivated by the surrounding woodlands - native hardwoods, and many species of conifer. This famous little village has four churches, of which St Michael's is the most venerable. The old part of the building dates back to the 14th century, while the large transept at the northern end and the vestry at the south-east were added in 1843.

Three rivers - the Conwy, the Lledr and the Llugwy - pass through or very close to Betws-y-Coed. This means there are several old bridges in the area. The Waterloo bridge I have mentioned already, and the other one that attracts tourists is Pont-y-Pair - the Bridge of the Cauldron. The River Llugwy passes beneath it, cascading out of the foaming waters of the upstream 'cauldron' formed by masses of black rock.

That water has already had a tumultous passage before it reaches Pont-y-Pair. The Swallow Falls are the most famous of several in the area, and these are found but a short drive up the A5. Steps lead down to the water's edge, and during the rainy season they are a truly spectacular sight as the waters of the Llugwy thunder down the rocky gorge, drenching the unwary.

High up in the hills there are the most beautiful lakes you could imagine, at altitudes ranging from 600 feet to almost 1500 feet. Lead pollution from old mines means that there are no fish in Llyn Gerionwydd, but it is a superb sailing and water-skiing venue. Llyn-y-Parc is shallow and also dead, but it is reachable from Pont-y-Pair and can be exceedingly beautiful, particularly when bracken and larches change colour in the autumn. There are gentle river walks along the banks of the Llugwy from Pont-y-Pair.

You will probably know of **Harlech** for its castle, again the work of Edward I, and from hearing those magnificent Welsh male voice choirs singing the rousing 'Men of Harlech'. The Castle does dominate the town. It was the stronghold of Owain Glyndwr, and was the last castle to fall in the Wars of the Roses.The town is charming with narrow streets and a wonderful golf course at Royal St Davids with International Class facilities. If you are a walker you will delight in the Rhinog range of mountains which form a grand backdrop to all these coastal towns and villages. You can reach them through the valleys of Cwm Bychan and Cwm Nantcol.

Barmouth is famed for its two miles of golden sands and is hard to beat for a family seaside holiday in Wales. You simply cannot get away from the sight of sleek sailing boats in this part of the world, and at Barmouth they look a picture. Moving inland from Barmouth on the A496 which hugs the wooded banks of the Afon Mawddach is no hardship. The route is one followed by the art critic Ruskin and the poet Manley Hopkins. Wordsworth too loved this magnificent walking country.

At **Bontddu** is **The Clogau Gold Mine** - the Old Clogau - situated in a fold eight hundred feet up in the hills alongside the Hirgwm stream which tumbles downhill to Mawddach. It sounds extraordinary to those who do not know the story, but it is one of many in the area - so many that a ring round the Rhinog mountains has been called 'the Dolgellau Gold Belt'. Princess Margaret, the Princess Royal and the Princess of Wales all wear wedding rings fashioned from Clogau's Welsh gold.

15th-century **Dolgellau** was the Welsh Parliament capital of Owain Glyndwr. It is built of Welsh granite and roofed with grey-blue Welsh slate, yet what might be an unremittingly bleak scene is overwhelmed by the majesty of Cader Idris range of mountains, and further relieved by the softer beauty of the Mawddach Estuary.

Penmaenpool is on the south bank of the river at the point where the Mawddach estuary opens out. An ideal place to watch a wide variety of birds in their natural habitat from the RSPB Observatory and afterwards to call at **Penmaenuchaf Hall** for one of their famous afternoon teas. The Hall was built as a summer house for the Leigh-Taylor family in 1860, a Lancashire family with cotton connections, and has since housed two High Sheriffs of Meirionnydd. A delightful spot.

Bala, a pleasantly flat, market town makes a wonderful base for a holiday. Here there is a lake which when the water is low may allow you to see the remains of Pentre Celeyn, the tiny village which was flooded to create what is now a reservoir supplying water for Liverpool. It seems always that progress has its down side, doesn't it? Yet filled with crystal-clear water from the mountains, stocked with lake trout and perch, this man-made lake is beautiful, hides its secrets well, and serves many useful purposes.

The town is best known as an international centre for watersports, with the five mile long Llyn Tegid judged by many to be the finest sailing lake in Britain. So you will head here if you are a yachtsman, and turn to the River Tryweryn if you are keen to hone your canoe slalom skills or try the wild white waters that make the river one of Europe's finest venues for canoeists. Llyn Tegid will also attract you if you intend to pit your wits against the perch, pike and roach. The deep water gwyniad fish has been unique to the lake since the Ice Ages.

Bala is famous too for its Sheepdog Trials. They began here and the town has been associated with television's 'One Man and his Dog'.

Finally in this section, **Anglesey**. You cross one of the two bridges over the Menai Strait. The Menai Suspension Bridge was built by Telford in 1826, with graceful arches of Pemmon limestone and a central span suspended high above the water by massive chains. The nearby Britannia Bridge was once a tubular structure built by Stephenson, but while his similarly constructed bridge at Conwy is still in use in its original state, this one was destroyed by fire in 1970. It has since been remodelled, and is now a twin road and rail link with its new road deckcarrying the A5. You cannot fail to notice that each bridge carries a large sign which reads 'Mon Man Cymru'. It is the Welsh for 'Anglesey, Mother of Wales'. For centuries this island's mild climate and rich farmland has made it the provider of grain for the harsher highlands of the Welsh interior. So you will find windmills here too, Llynnon Mill at **Llanddeusant** near Holyhead was built in 1775 and has recently been restored.

Anglesey is wonderful. It has a tremendous sense of freedom. Gone are the immensity of the mountain ranges, so much a part of this journey and instead there are gently rolling hills, low white cottages, and skies which seem endless. The whole of the island is criss-crossed with enticing small roads although there are two or three excellent A roads. I made for **Menai Bridge** with the intention of making my way up the east coast.

You will reach **Beaumaris** along a delightful wooded section of the A545 which follows the coast past the landscaped gardens of elegant Victorian mansions. The town was Edward I's 13th-century English garrison borough, which later became a busy seaport and fashionable Victorian resort. There is a castle, of course, and the one at Beaumaris was the last and largest of those Edward built to contain the Welsh.

Llansadwrn off the B5109 has a gem of a Victorian church which is home for the oldest memorial stone in Wales. It is dedicated to St Saturnius and his wife, and you will find it set into the wall of the chancel.

Anglesey is famed for its sheltered beaches. **Red Wharf Bay** is a snug cove that reveals fifteen square miles of sand at low tide. Bathing only advisable on the incoming tide - the soft sands can be a trap for the unwary. Charles Dickens came here to report on the wreck and called in at **The Panton Arms** at **Pentraeth** for refreshment.

At **Moelfre** you will be able to take a headland walk to the site of the 'Royal Charter' shipwreck in 1859.

There are so many ancient sites on Anglesey, it is impossible to mention them all. At **Din Lligwy** between Moelfre and Amlwch, for example, there are the remains of six foot thick hut walls that were once part of an iron age village.

Llaneilian has a 15th-century church with Norman tower - passageways link the church to an old chapel with well-preserved carvings and decorative features. To the east of **Llangadrig** lies the site of an oratory or chapel established by a female recluse in the 7th century. At **Valley** I rejoined the A5. This wonderful old London to Holyhead road has been with us since the time of Elizabeth I - England's link with Ireland. A causeway carries it across from the mainland of Anglesey to Holy Island, and after a mile or so it reaches **Holyhead** and swings sharply right towards the inner harbour.

Holyhead was founded in the 3rd century AD, when the Romans built a fortress. St Cybi's Church is named after a Celtic saint who settled here in the 6th century, and dates from the 13th century to the 17th century. Holyhead mountain is a modest 220 metres high, but Celtic warriors once stood watch on the ramparts of the Iron Age hillfort, and Roman soldiers lit beacons from a watchtower.

From these heights if you look down and a little way to the west you will see South Stack, a lump of rock joined to Holy Island by a precarious suspension bridge. Unfortunately the bridge is closed to the public. Nevertheless there is a fine view of the lighthouse, built in 1909 and nowautomatic. This is where wildlife really flourishes. The RSPB confidently expect about 3,000 guillemots, 400 razorbills and 100 puffins each year. The best time to come is during the breeding season in late May or June.

If the weather is fine and sunny there is no finer spot to spend an hour or so than **Trearddur Bay**. Slip down to one of the rocky coves and inlets for a quiet picnic, or if you want to stay, there is plenty of excellent holiday accommodation ranging from simple caravans to the finest hotels. The journey back across the island along the A5 will take you through **Gwalchmai** where the Anglesey Agricultural Show is held each August. Electricity there now comes from the national grid, which is no doubt an improvement on the supply - the first on Anglesey - which was once generated by a watermill.

No one should miss **Plas Newydd**. This elegant 18th-century house by James Wyatt, is the home of the Marquess of Anglesey, and is set in a landscaped garden on the banks of the Menai Strait. It contains an exhibition devoted to the work of Rex Whistler, and a military museum with relics of the Battle of Waterloo. You will find it open from April to late September, and it will be one of the fond memories you take with you as you retrace your route across the Britannia Bridge.

My next adventure took me to the north-east coast and to **Llandudno**. This elegant 19th-century purpose built holiday resort retains its character and the local council lays down strict guidelines which ensure that the many hotels on the sea front perpetuate the old world charm. The curved promenade stretches for two miles between Great Orme to the west and the slightly less impressive bulk of the Little Orme to the east. A visit to Llandudno must always include a trip to the summit of the Great Orme, and there are two excellent ways of getting there. The Great Orme Tramway was opened in 1902, and is the longest cable-hauled tramway in Britain. From Victoria Station in Church Walks the climb is at first steep, the views spectacular. Yet, even that experience is surpassed by the breathtaking exhilaration afforded by the alternative route - The Cable Car. This, too, is reputed to be the longest in Britain.

The Great Orme has a history dating back some 300 million years. The newest tourist attraction in this designated Country Park, the Great Ore Copper Mine, is also of a great age, and is opening the eyes of visitors and experts alike.

Over recent years the discovery of rib and thigh bones which once served as scrapers and picks suggest that mining was carried out here more than 4000 years ago. Now it is possible to go on a short guided tour through candlelit Bronze Age tunnels, and one can only marvel at the work that was done by native Britons in a mining complex that went out of business 2000 years ago!

From **Llandudno Junction** it is easy to pay a visit to **Glanwydden** where **The Queen's Head** in the capable hands of Robert Cureton has won many awards for its imaginative food. The A55 will take you to **Rhos-on-Sea**. Here lie the dried-up beds of three long-dead creeks that once carried small timber ships inland from the coast. But for many years now Rhos-on-Sea has been a delightful backwater where holidays proceed at a leisurely pace.

Colwyn Bay next. The Welsh mountains form an impressive backdrop to the wonderful crescent of golden sands. The whole stretch of coastline is a combination of its Victorian ancestry and modern times. The town's Victorian architecture delights the historian, while Theatr Colwyn will provide for the lover of music and drama, a programme of productions that has included a visitby the Welsh National Opera.

The arrow straight road into **Abergele** will take you past Gwyrch Castle, a romantic 19th-century folly which was built to a medieval design by Lloyd Bamford Hesketh. Nestling against wooded hills the castle looks in excellent condition, yet closer examination will reveal broken windows and other signs of neglect. Many ambitious plans for its use have been mooted, sadly, none so far has reached fruition.

Abergele is an historic market town, with some splendid walking country in the hills behind the excellent golf course. Nearby **Pensarn** is its seafront suburb. As well as fine sandy beaches there are long walks here too, along grassy dunes which afford an alternative view of Gwrych Castle.

There is a landmark familiar to all regular visitors to this area; the graceful spire of St Margaret's Church, **Bodelwyddan**. You can reach this wonderful building - popularly known as the Marble Church - by taking the A55 out of Abergele until you reach the first exit. The foundation stone was laid in 1856, and the church was built of native limestone to a design by John Gibson. There is a marvellous hammer-beam roof with arched principals and collars and cusped spandrils together with beautiful stained glass windows by Burne-Jones, T.F. Curtis and Michael O'Connor. Four traceried windows, portraits on the four finials, and finely worked flying buttresses, all combine to make the 202 foot spire unique.

The tiny city of **St Asaph** has a beautiful and superbly appointed cathedral. The site at the top of the narrow, gently sloping High Street has a history dating back to a monastic community founded by St Kentigern, Bishop of Strathclyde, in 560AD. Associated with him are the Kentigern Window in the North Aisle, and the emblem of Salmon and the Ring on the carving in the Choir ceiling. His successor was Asaph who gave his name to the City and Diocese in 570AD.

In passing it is worth mentioning that archaeological treasures abound in this part of the world. There are hundreds of prehistoric burial grounds and a site in a cave close to St Asaph dates back some 250,000 years.

My journey towards Rhyl brought me within sight of **Rhuddlan Castle**, which dates back to 1277 - again courtesy of Edward I - but it is built on the site once occupied by other castles dating back to the 10th century. **Rhuddland** itself is a deceptively sleepy little town hugging the banks of the River Clwyd. If you take a diversion of two miles or so along the A5151 you will reach **Dyserth**, where you must see the spectacular 60 foot waterfalls located in a delightful wooded glen.

Rhyl is a totally different kettle of fish from the resorts I have seen. It is brash, vibrant, unashamedly a traditional seaside playground where life is lived to the full. Undoubtedly the liveliest resort in North Wales.

The A548 runs straight into **Prestatyn**. A very popular resort but without the overt brashness that characterises its close neighbour. Here the attractions are less blatant, yet once sought out they are immensely varied, and again a blend of the modern and traditional. Offa's Dyke was, or is, the defensive earthwork along the Welsh Border and it stretches from Prestatyn to Chepstow. A great walk but not for me, however there are many intrepid walkers who tackle its beautiful length.

The attractions to be reached from the A55 as it makes its way to the English border are of a very different nature from what I have just seen. There is always a new discovery like Pont Dafydd -David's Bridge - at the village of **Waen**. This very old bridge spans the River Clywd, in 1630 it replaced an even older bridge. **Pantasaph** is quite close to the larger market town of **Holywell**, and is the home of an ancient Franciscan Friary.

It came into being in 1852 when Rudolph Viscount Fielding and his wife Louisa invited Capuchin friars to accept a missionary opportunity. As a result, Italian and Flemish friars created an oasis of prayer, and today it offers residence to retreatants of both sexes.

Naid Y March, between Pantasaph and **Brynford**, is the name given to a pair of Bronze Age standing stones. The name - The Horse Leap - recalls a legend which tells how Thomas ap Harri jumped the stones on his horse. **Llanasa** lies to the south of the A55, and is well worth a visit because of the delightful stone cottages which in colour are similar to those found in the Cotswolds.

Compared to some major roads the A55 is relatively calm. Nonetheless I was quite pleased to leave it for a while to take a look at **Holywell**, a town with an absorbing history. St Winifred's Well has been a place of pilgrimage for 1300 years and the legend behind this Holy well tells of the fair maid, Winefride. She was the daughter of a local prince, and became a martyr in 660AD. Apparently she was pursued by a young nobleman called Caradoc, whose intentions were far from honourable. He caught her, and in his anger, cut off her head. Where her head came to rest, a spring flowed from the earth. Later, she was brought to life by St Beuno, while Caradoc sank to the ground never to be seen again. The Chapel and Well buildings - erected circa 1500 - are open to visitors. The Cistercian monks of Basingwerk were in possession of the Well from 1240 to 1537, so a drive down the steep hill to Basingwek Abbey makes a neat historical link.

You may remember the name of Master James of St George from Beaumaris Castle on Anglesey. At **Flint** you will come across one of the most unusual fortresses built under his direction. **Flint Castle** was one of four to be built by Edward I after his first campaign against Llywelyn ap Gruffydd. Construction work on the castle and town began in 1277, and quickly involved some 2,300 diggers. Historically the castle is remembered for the imprisonment of King Richard II in 1399 who was then transported to London where he abdicated. A unique feature is the Great Tower of Donjon, which is outside the main structure and from which you can get a wonderful view of the Dee Estuary.

Driving into **Mold** down a steep hill brought me past a modern complex which many feel is the cultural heart of the town, if not the whole of North Wales. Within neatly-lawned landscaped grounds overlooking the town is the Civic Centre - Mold is the county town of Clywd - the studios of HTV, and Theatr Clwyd. This is a marvellous venue which stages the very best in theatre, dance, film and music, plus a variety of exhibitions. Entertainment here is of a standard rarely found outside London - indeed, Theatr Clywd is the only regional theatre to have transferred ten shows to the West End in three years.

The parish church is 500 years old. Stanley, Lord of the Manor of Mold, and his second wife, Margaret Beaufort, were learned, and devout, and they also had considerable wealth. They undertook the rebuilding of the 'Stanley churches' of which Mold is a fine example. There is a stunning window portraying the Patron Saints of Britain. It commemorates the landscape painter, Richard Wilson, whose tomb is outside the window. The town is delightful and has lively street markets on Wednesday and Saturdays. There are many features of historical interest within a few miles, all of them in glorious unspoilt countryside.

The quickest way to learn about Wrexham is in The Heritage Centre in King Street, where a permanent exhibition traces the story of the town since the Bronze Age. Wrexham is often described as the 'Capital of North Wales', and has grown from a small market town into a major shopping centre. There have been many changes in recent years, including pedestrianisation of part of the town centre, and the opening of The People's Market.

The Parish Church of St Giles was built in the late 15th and early 16th centuries, and is one of the 'Seven Wonders of Wales'. Incidentally all seven are mentioned in the 19th century rhyme which goes:

Pistyll Rhaeadr and Wrexham Steeple,
Snowdon;s Mountain without its people,
Overton Yew Trees, St Winefride's Well,
Llangollen Bridge and Gresford Bells.

You reach the church by strolling through Church Walks, a gentle little backwater with quaint half-timbered buildings. The church is at least the third to be built on the site - there was one already standing in 1220. It is a church full ofinterest and one or two surprises.

Before I set off to explore the border country starting at Chirk, I went to **Holt** taking the A534 out of Wrexham. Apart from its beautiful Norman church,Holt is so closely linked with **Farndon** that you proceed from one to the other without noticing the difference. There is the ancient, narrow bridge crossing the River Dee, a brief wait if the traffic lights are against you, but no matter which direction you are taking, if the prominent signs are ignored then, logically, there should be nothing at all to say that one town has been left behind and another entered. Yet, each town has its own, distinctive character and charm. Each has developed quite differently - and the reason is that Holt and Farndon, not only straddle the beautiful River Dee, but also the border between England and Wales.

I love **Bangor-on-Dee** (Bangor-is-y-Coed) with its superb medieval bridge spanning the River. Racegoers will already know of the racecourse which provides an excellent mix of steeplechasing, hurdle races, and the occasional National Hunt Flat Race. South east of Bangor lies the village of **Hanmer** - you can reach it by taking the A525 and the A539 - where in the 15th century the legendary Welsh leader Owain Glydwr married Margaret Hanmer. Close by is **Penley**, which is believed to be the only thatched school in Britain. **Overton** is a mile or so further on. In St Mary's Churchyard you will find the glorious yew trees mentioned as one of the 'Seven Wonders of Wales.'

Chirk from the south is the Gateway to Wales and for many years it was a bottleneck on Thomas Telford's London to Holyhead A5 road. Thankfully, the heavy traffic now bypasses the town, and conditions are much improved for residents and visitors.

Chirk Castle has been continuously occupied since it was built by a Marcher Lord, Roger Mortimer, in the early 14th-century, and the elegant staterooms with Adam-style furniture, tapestries and portraits bear testimony to the loving care bestowed on it over the years. On a more sombre note, there is also a nightmare dungeon which reminds us all of the violence and cruelty that once ravaged the Welsh Marches. Now looked after by the National Trust, the castle is located one and a half miles west of the town, set in beautiful gardens amid fine parkland. Offa's Dyke traverses the grounds. In the 12th century St Mary's Church you will see monuments to theMyddleton family occupiers of Chirk Castle for almost 400 years.

Two immense structures are famous landmarks hereabouts: a wonderful viaduct constructed in 1848 to carry the former Great Western Railway, and running alongside and below it Telfords Shropshire Union Canal aqueduct, built in 1801. Both of these are best viewed on foot - and you will be able to see a quarter mile long canal tunnel, which lies immediately to the north. Along the A5 and within a few miles you will pass close to yet another spectacular aqueduct, this one an iron trough, 1006 feet long which soars 121 feet above the River Dee between Froncasyllte and Trevor. It is the Pontcysyllte Aqueduct, again the work of Thomas Telford.

If you remain on the A5 you can easily pass through Llangollen and feel that you have not missed a great deal. That would be a pity. You must turn right at the traffic lights and proceed down Castle Street, and at once you will see that this is a little town of great character. There is a large car park, and you will find that many of the attractions here are within easy walking distance. Trevor Bridge is one of the ' seven wonders' dating back to the 14th century. Beneath it the waters of the River Dee tumble wildly over black rocks. Here, white water canoeing championships have been held, on a testing and hazardous course.

A handsomely converted Baptist Chapel in Castle Street is now the European Centre for traditional and Regional Cultures, and reflects Llangollen's stature as the home of the International Music Eisteddfod.

The Llangollen Steam Railway is of standard gauge and was restored by volunteers. It will enthrall steam buffs, while others will simply sit back and enjoy the five and a half mile trip through beautiful countryside. Along the route there are stations, halts and restored workshops, all open to visitors throughout the year. The trips start from Trevor Bridge, and continue up the Dee Valley as far as **Glyndyfrydwy**.

Plas Newydd must be seen although it is a bit of a climb up Hill Street. This is a wonderful half-timbered building with ornate woodwork and a lovely interior filled with rare medieval oak carvings. Inside and out it is beautiful. It was the home of Lady Eleanor Ponsonby and Miss Sarah Butler, two Irishwomen who eloped from Waterford in 1778 and became known as the 'Ladies of Llangollen. In Sarah's words, the area is 'the beautifullest countie in the world.'

You can view Llangollen Canal by taking a more gentle climb up Wharf Hill. There is an information museum for canal enthusiasts, and wonderfully relaxing trips on horse-drawn barges. Many of the local walks are very strenuous but keen walkers will delight in the views from the Panorama Walk - another section of the Offa's Dyke National Trail - Llantysilio Mountain, and Geraint's Hill.

From Llangollen you will have a drive of no more than fifteen or sixteen miles to **Ruthin** which has been a seat of administrative and commercial importance for more than 700 years, and recent discoveries suggest a Roman connection. It has St Peter's Square in a lovely elevated position with splendid old buildings put to excellent modern use. The half-timbered old Courthouse of 1401 is now the National Westminster Bank. Exmewe Hall is now in the hands of Barclays. Outside its doors is the Maen Huail Stone, said to be where King Arthur had a rival beheaded.

As you wander across the Square your eyes will be drawn to the Myddleton Arms, which is at it should be. For gazing back at you will be the 'Eyes of Ruthin', an extraordinary multi-dormer roof in the Dutch style whose seven windows flash in the bright sun. It was built in the 16th century. In CastleStreet is Nantclwyd House, a fine Elizabethan town house built around an earlier medieval structure. A little further along is the pillared entrance to a long, shaded drive which will bring you to Ruthin Castle. Now a gracious hotel, it was built between 1277 and 1282 by Edward I.

During the Civil War the garrison at Ruthin capitulated to Cromwell's forces after a severe bombardment, and in 1646 the castle was demolished. The ruins and land were owned by the Myddleton family from 1677, and remained in a sorry state until 1826, when a castellated, two storey, double block of limestone was built on the south-east corner of the ruined site. Then, in 1849, part of that building too was demolished, and the present building designed by Henry Clutton, was erected on the same site.

Eight miles north-west of Ruthin along the A525 is **Denbigh**, also set on a hill, with a castle that dominates the town. Denbigh has ample free parking, most of it close to the town centre. This is important, because although High Street itself is well elevated, there is a stiff walk to the castle - and it is best approached on foot.

You will reach it through the impressive Burgess Gate, or by passing Leicester's Church (intended to supplant St Asaph Cathedral) and St Hilary's Church tower, which will bring you to the green where the medieval Denbigh once stood. This is another of the strongholds Edward I built as part of his plans for subjugating Wales.

Construction under the direction of Henry de Lacy was begun in 1282 - and there is a strong gatehouse with a trio of towers. The town walls are almost complete. The castle is sited on a limestone bluff, and there are splendid views. The town is delightful with an exceptionally wide High street flanked by colonnades. If you are here on any Wednesday you will be able to wander among the stalls in the small but lively street market. If perchance your visit includes Boxing Day you will see a strange happening - a barrel race that takes place on a straw-lined course up and down the High Street.

Having travelled through Anglesey, Denbighshire and Caernarvonshire, and touched on Merioneth. Now for Montgomeryshire and a final tour of the southern part of Merioneth.

There is a wonderful scenic route out of Dolgellau, up a steep, winding road past Cader Idris, which at almost 3,000 feet is an attraction to both walkers and climbers. Charles Darwin once said that 'Old Cader is a grand fellow' but my own recent memories of that road are of descending it and experiencing some shock as an RAF jet came screaming up towards me from somewhere far below!

Eventually the road begins to tumble down towards less giddy heights, and before taking the B4405 towards **Trwyn** it's worth going on the couple of miles into **Corris**. You will first pass through **Corris Uchaf**, along a stretch of road lined with pine, beach and oak, and picturesque cottages once used by quarry workers. The craft centre at Corris is open all year. In summer you will appreciate the splendid picnic area, while in winter the warmth of the restaurant will beckon after you have watched various craftspeople at work.

Almost as soon as you turn onto the B4405 you are on the shores of Lake Tal-y-Llyn. For a mile or so the southern bank of a stretch of water is breathtakingly beautiful, and especially popular with fishermen in season.

At **Abergynolwyn** there is a small slate museum and here too is the inland terminus of the Tallyn railway. This 'Great Little train of Wales' - there are eight of them altogether - was bought and rescued in 1951, and now travels the six miles or so from Tywyn through wild hills and thickwoodland around **Nant Gwernol** and Abergynolwyn. On the way it passes close to the rushing waters of Dolgoch Falls.

Tywyn is a popular seaside resort which has six miles of firm sands. At the right time of the year the conditions are perfect for swimming, sailing and windsurfing.

Before you drive into **Aberdovey** on the A493 you will see on the right the lush greens of Aberdovey's championship golf course, whose two mile long links occupy an enviable position twixt hills and sea. Aberdovey is almost Mediterranean in character, with the proximity of the Gulf Stream ensuring that temperatures are always higher than further inland. Its pleasures are unashamedly of the sea, with fishing, windsurfing and waterskiing favoured sports, and private yachts of all sizes making splashes of bright colour in the waters of the pretty harbour. Many of its fine hotels and guesthouses were built during the Edwardian era when it was at the height of its popularity.

The drive inland towards **Machynlleth** is along an exceptionally pretty stretch of the A493 that hugs the cliffs as it takes one through an area of the Dovey Estuary rich in rhododendrons. The town has an impressive broad main street and a wonderful old clock tower with needle sharp spire and arched openings.

In 1991 Machynlleth celebrated the 700th anniversary of its market charter. It was granted in 1291 by Edward I to Owen de la Pole, Prince of Powys, and enabled two fairs in Spring and Autumn and a weekly street market ' to be held in perpetuity'. The midweek market has been held ever since, and has grown to become one of the largest and liveliest street markets in Wales.

It would be strange to visit any part of Wales without hearing mention of Owain Glyndwr, and Machynlleth does not disappoint. The great man held a Welsh parliament here in 1404. An old stone building in Maengwyn Street is now the Owain Glyndwr Centre, and home to an absorbing heritage exhibition that displays his campaigns and charts his contribution to Welsh history.

Newtown is the commercial capital of Montgomeryshire, and like Machynlleth it has a well-known street market held on Tuesdays with one in the Market Hall on the same day. The town has a delightful situation in a loop of the River Severn, and as the home of the Welsh flannel industry it was at one time known as the 'Busy Leeds of Wales'. One of the original hand-loom weaving factories

is now the Newtown Textile Museum on Commercial Road. You will find in Newtown a bewildering mixture of architecture with Tudor, Gothic, Jacobean, Georgian, Victorian and modern buildings standing cheek by jowl so that scarcely two blocks are alike. The Royal Welsh Warehouse is the tallest building in the town. It was built in 1861 by Sir Pryce-Pryce Jones. His mail order company was the world's first - so now you know where all those catalogues originated! Queen Victoria was one of the company's customers, and the warehouse is still open to the public to this day.

Montgomery, a delightful border town is a wonderland of Georgian architecture, perhaps the finest example of which is the imposing Town Hall with its white clock tower. The ruins of the old Montgomery Castle stand on a rocky promontory overlooking the town, a position which made it virtually impregnable until the Civil War. For once Edward I had no hand in it; it was built at the command of Henry III in 1223.

The garrison Parish Church of St Nicholas contains the chapel of the poet, George Herbert, andin the graveyard you will find an odd grave. John Davies was convicted of murder in 1821. Before he died he swore his innocence, and declared that as proof nothing would grown on his grave for one hundred years. When you visit the Robber's Grave you can judge for yourself whether he was innocent or not!

Not many people know that **Welshpool** was originally called Poole. It is built on the banks of the River Severn, and long ago the flatlands were criss-crossed by a network of creeks known as 'pills'. These were frequently devastated by flash floods from the river, hence the town's original name. But they have long since been drained, and the name of the town was eventually changed to Welshpool to distinguish it from the English town of Poole.

You will see a wide diversity of attractive buildings and as well as having the river close by, Welshpool is also a canal town. The Montgomery Canal passes through the town. It was part of a grand scheme to link the rivers Mersey and Severn. Work finished in 1821, and it was a busy inland waterway until long decline led to its closure in 1944. Volunteers are valiantly bringing it back to life, and at the Powysland Museum situated in a restored canal warehouse you can see some important local collections covering the archaeology and social history of Montgomeryshire **Powys Castle** stands on a dramatic, rocky outcrop one mile south of Welshpool. It was built by the medieval Princes of Upper Powys in the 13th century, and has been occupied continuously for 700 years. In 1587 it was bought by Sir Edward Herbert, and has been the family's ancestral home ever since. That family, and later the Clives - descendants of Clive of India - continually laboured to create a jewel of a building set in the most beautiful gardens. These are thought to have been planted by William Wilde. Dating from the 17th-century, they are laid out in four formal terraces influenced by French and Italian styles. Those hanging, terraces are the most famous in the world. Each is 200 yards long, falling away towards the Severn Valley. In the 18th-century an informal wilderness was added. The extensive parklands were landscaped by Capability Brown in the 19th-century. The castle is full of atmosphere and crammed with treasures. In particular are those brought from India by Clive and his son, and on display in the Clive Museum since 1987: relics of Tipu, Sultan of Mysore, Moghul jades, textiles and ivories, and a wonderful array of Chinese and Indian bronzes.

Amongst the many wonderful sights to be seen there is one just eight miles or so from **Llangedwyn**. It is well off the beaten track but take the B4396 towards **Llanrhaedr-ym-Mochnant** onto a minor road into stunning countryside. Cadair Berwyn lies ahead of you as you approach the Berwyn Mountains beyond which lies Corwen and the Dee Valley. It is **Pistyll Rhaeadr** I wanted to see, one of the highest waterfalls in Britain, cascading over a narrow ledge with delicate trees on all sides. George Burrows found this an enchanting place, and said of Pistyll Rhaeadr 'I never saw water falling so gracefully, so much like thin beautiful threads, as here'. There is a legend which relates how giants were disturbed while building a bridge and dropped the huge rocks which now lie scattered at its base.

Driving south-west along the A487 from Machynlleth will immediately transport you into an area with an astonishingly rich history. I was not aware that the lands belonging to the Welsh once stretched as far north as Strathclyde in Scotland. They did and in 451 AD the chieftain Cunedda and his sons marched an army south to the area we know as Wales, where they succeeded in freeing those lands from seaborne invaders. A district known as Tyno Goch was awarded to Cunedda's son, Ceredig. Today Ceredigion -

the land of Cerig - stretches from the Dovey Estuary to Cardigan in the south, with its inland boundary following a semi-circular path.

My route took me along the south side of the Dovey Estuary where I visited the Ynis-Hir Reserverun by the RSPB. The easiest way to find it is to follow the signposts from the village of **Eglwysfach**. The reserve attracts some 67 species of bird to its salt and fresh water marshes, reed beds, peat bogs, woodland and open hillside.If you are a keen bird-watcher you will be reaching for your field-glasses at the mere mention of the pied fly-catcher, wood warbler, blacktrap and treecreeper.

Borth has three miles of virtually unbroken sands. It also has an interesting legend. Stumps in the sand, which you will see if the tide is right, are said to be the vestigial remains of an ancient forest - the last reminder of the drowned Welsh lowlands of Cantre'r Gwaelod.

The last village before Aberystwyth is **Clarach**, where the fine beach is sheltered by steep shale cliffs along which there are magnificent coastal walks. This was my first visit to **Aberystwyth**. It is one of Wales' favourite seaside towns, and for the academic it provides unrivalled facilities with the University of Wales and the National Library of Wales on the one site off Penglais Road. There are three good beaches. Tanybwlch Beach to the south of the harbour, while North and South beaches are separated by the wind driven headland which is the site of Aberystwyth Castle. Its history has a familiar pattern. Built by Edward I in 1277, damaged and rebuilt in 1282, captured by Prince Owain Glyndwr in 1404. Uniquely coins from the local silver mine were minted here between 1637 and 1646. The castle was doomed to fall to the enemy soon after: Cromwell's army overcame its defences, and it was blown up in 1649.

An interesting and unusual attraction can be found on the 450 foot summit of Constitution Hill which stands at the north end of North Beach. Equally unusual is the manner in which you can reach the apex. **The Aberystwyth Electric Cliff railway** is the longest in Great Britain. It dates back to Victorian times and once again demonstrates how much we owe to the people who lived and worked in that imaginative age.

The ride to the summit is nothing short of spectacular, and once there you will find, in a fascinating octagonal tower, the **Great Aberystwyth Camera Obscura.** The very name spells out that it was a popular Victorian amusement, and it consists of a massive 14 inch lens which focusses detailed views onto a screen in a darkened viewing gallery. The outside viewing balconies will reward you with a beautiful panorama.

The Vale of Rheidol Railway runs from Aberystwyth to **Devil's Bridge**. It is a narrow gauge steam railway and there are conflicting theories about why it came into being. One suggests that it was opened in 1902 to serve the lead traffic of the valley. Another says that it is the only one of the 'little trains' to have been built to satisfy the tourist trade. At any rate, now it is British Railway's last operational link with the 'age of steam' and is an exciting ride. the line clings to the hillside as it climbs towards Devil's Bridge, affording views of the broad river valley, thickly wooded hillsides, and the wonderful open moorland of Plynlimon. The train is pulled by the engines 'Owain Glyndwr', 'Llewlyn' or 'Prince of Wales' on a journey through a natural wonderland.

Devil's Bridge (Pontarfynach)is a village set amid scenery which needs to be explored at length on foot. There are three bridges over the River Mynach, built one on top of the other. The first dates back to the 11th century, probably built by Cistercian monks. The second bridge was built in 1708, the third in 1901. You can take an easy path to visit the bridges but it is an area of such charm that you will almost certainly opt to do some energetic scrambling. There are 94 steps of Jacob's Ladder to be descended, the 300 foot cascade where the Mynach tumbles through spectacular chasms carved in the rock to join the River Rheidol, and nature trails and footpaths. Not suitable for the disabled or the infirm and please do wear sensible shoes.

You will get a different view of Devil's Bridge after turning right onto the A4120, but you must then turn smartly onto the B4343 which will take you south along a lovely, winding route to the village of **Pontrhydfendigaid**. The Cistercian Abbey of Strata Florida was founded in 1164 and by 1184 had acquired thye patronage of Rhys ap Gruffydd, the last independent native prince of South Wales. Here at Ystrad Fflur, in 1238, Llywelyn the Great called together the Welsh Princes to swear allegiance to his son, Dafydd. Later, hard on the trail of Owain Glyndwr (the last native prince of a fully-independent Wales), Henry IV expelled the monks, and took the abbey as his headquarters. The building fell into disrepair after the Dissolution, but you can still see the magnificent Norman arch. In the abbey grounds are buried some of the princes and princesses of old Ceredigion, while Dafydd ap Gwilyn, the amorous medieval Welsh poet - still popular to this day - is buried under the spreading yew tree in the adjacent churchyard. Once the Westminster of Wales, the Abbey's name means 'Vale of Flowers'.

Tregaron lies at the junction of several roads, in countryside which is now a Natural Nature Reserve and famous for the variety and numbers of wild birds. George Borrow was reminded of 'an Andalusian village overhung by its sierra', and the mile upon mile of heathered upland to the east was once the haunt of Twm Sion Cati, the Robin Hood of Wales.

Before leaving this stunningly beautiful area and making my way towards the coast, I continued along the B4343 as far as **Llanddewi Brefi**. Ceredigion was the birthplace of St David, Patron Saint of Wales, and the church at this tiny village is dedicated to his name.

In **Llandiloes** we are back in Montgomeryshire, and this bonny little town is the first the River Severn encounters as it flows down from its source in the high moorlands of Plimlumon. History here in full measure with a Market Charter granted in 1280 and a 16th-century Market Hall of black and white timber which is the only one in Wales to survive on its original site. The town owes much of its prosperity to the lead mining which took place in the surrounding hills. Relics of the woollen trade can still be seen in the neat row of weaver's cottages, and there is a fine, half-timbered merchant's house on Llangurug Road.

Natural and man made lakes abound in the Montgomeryshire countryside, and Llyn Clywedog, between Llandiloes and Machynlleth is one of the more recent of the latter. The dam was built in the 1960s, and is the tallest in Britain. From Llandiloes you can reach the lake by taking the B4518; it is a short and very pleasant drive. LLyn Clywedog is used to control flooding on the River Severn, but wherever there is an expanse of water you will find sailors of one kind or another. This is also ideal walking country in the green pastureland and sweeping open hills that surround it. The three mile route of the Llyn Clywedog Scenic Trail has been carefully designed to reveal the best features of the reservoir and the wooded slopes flanking the deep valley. An alternative walk pays more attention to the engineering feats involved in the dam's construction. The Clywedog Gorge Trail is self-guided, and also takes in the abandoned lead mine.

There are two rivers of note as you travl south along the A470. One is the River Wye, and the other is the River Elan whose course follows another wonderful valley.

The gateway to the Elan Valley is **Rhayder**, a town dating back to the fifth century and the setting for one of the most important markets of the area. For a small town it also has an extraordinarily violent past: in Tudor times the assize judge was murdered and the town razed, the castle was destroyed during the Civil War, and more recently it was the scene of the Rebecca Riots which were protests against toll gates. Like Machynelleth, the town centre features a fine clock tower, and in Rhayader the main streets radiate from this focal point.

There are five reservoirs quite close by and no shortage of Information Centres for those wishing to explore this wonderland of lakes and hills. The main one to note is the Elan Valley Visitor Centre which is located on the B5418 south-west of Rhayader. Interesting to note that it was these dams Barnes Wallace used when trying out the famous bouncing bomb.

Although **Llandrindod Wells** is not an old town, the chalybeate springs there have been used from time immemorial. The first reference to the Saline Spring was in 1694. The town was built to fulfil the Victorian's increasing demand for healing waters. They came for sulphur for their complexions, magnesium to aid their digestion, chalybeate for the blood and saline for 'inner cleanliness' - all were available and still are at the restored Pump Room in Rock Park. There is a good leaflet available from the Memorial Gardens in Temple Street which proves to be an excellent guide around the town.

Hundred House Village has a splendid inn of the same name and it is possible that when the Shire was divided into 'hundreds' and courts were held, they might well have used the Inn as well as the Vicarage. The Hundred House Inn was used by cattle drovers, who, because of the distance between West Wales and London, would provide their cattle with shoes - and ducks and geese had their feet dipped in tar!

Builth Wells is another example of a town that grew up around a spa, although the saline and sulphur springs are no longer used. Ask a farming Welshman - there for the Monday sheep and cattle markets - about the town and he will immediately lift his head and tell you with pride of the Royal Welsh Agricultural Show which is held here each year. It is the biggest agricultural show in the country, and is held on a permanent site alongside the River Wye.

Llandovery is quite charming with Town Hall and Market Square and a feeling of history which comes from being a former cattle collection point for drovers about to make the long walk to the English cities. Stock markets are still held two or three times weekly, and market stalls make a splash of colour under the Town Hall each Friday.

I found the task of exploring the peninsula to the south of Cardigan Bay - the area now known as Dyfed - quite daunting. It takes in most of the coast in a great sweep from Aberaeron right round to Carmarthen plus a whole lot of inland areas of special interest.

Aberaeron does not immediately spring to mind as a place likely to attract lovers of history but how wrong can one be. I soon discovered that in this corner of Wales one house in every four in Aberaeron is designated of special architectural interest and it is one of Wales' first planned towns. August

1807 seems to be the recognised starting point of any study of the town's history. On that date Royal Assent was given to an 'Act to enable the Reverend Alban Thomas Jones-Gwynne, his Heirs and Assigns, to repair and enlarge the Harbour and Port of Aberaeron...and to regulate the mooring of Ships and Vessels there'. The good Reverend carried out his task well providing money for design and construction which involved the eminent engineer John Rennie, and takingthe advice of John Nash on the layout and design of the fledgling town.

The town is now a gracious, picturesque place, with well laid out streets and squares, and a charming, stone-walled harbour. It is very worthwhile spending some time here.

From Aberaeron to **Newquay** is just a short distance even on the minor roads. Establishing New Quay's origins is difficult, though an admiralty survey undertaken in 1748 does mention the name, albeit with a different spelling (New Key). It is a lovely little town, thoroughly deserving its reputation as the 'jewel of the Welsh Coast'. It is built on terraced slopes which fall steeply to a crescent of sand and a sheltered harbour, and is thought to be the town Dylan Thomas used as a model for Llareggrub in'Under Milk Wood'. He spent some time in new Quay between 1944 and 1945.

Aberporth is another wonderful seaside gem with a snug little bay and a wedge of clean sand that will delight all children and many adults. Moderately high cliffs on either side make fine natural boundaries, a comforting situation. It is a place well known for its cliff-top walks and one in particular is very popular. It links Aberporth with the neighbouring village of **Tresaith** - no more than a mile to the east - and at low tide you can then go on to reach the golden beach at **Penbryn**. If you take that path you are moving back towards New Quay. Penbryn beach, once beloved by smugglers, can also be reached by road from **Sarnau** on the A487. The name Tresaith is said to derive from the landing of seven banished Irish princesses, who settled in the area and married local Welshmen. If you have no romance in you then you are more likely to believe that the name comes from the local river - the Saith!!

Llangrannog is a little further on in the same direction, another village bounded by rocky headlands. One of them, which I believe is known as Ynys-Lochtyn, is worth exploring more fully for it has the remains of a prehistoric fort.

The correct name for **Cardigan** is Aberteifi - the mouth of the Teifi - and the word Cardigan is a derivation from a word already familiar to us: Ceredigion, for which Aberteifi was once the county town. Today the town is of strategic importance to visitors, not invaders, for its position makes it an ideal base for those wishing to explore the spectacular Pembrokeshire countryside. Cardigan is famous for staging the very first competitive National Eisteddfod, which was held in the castle under the patronage of Rhys ap Gruffudd in 1176. That event was commemorated in 1976 when the Eisteddfod came back to the town to celebrate the eight hundredth anniversary of Rhy's original event.

Cilgeran an be found by driving a little way south of Cardigan, and on a crag overlooking a deep gorge of the River Teifi the two powerful towers of Cilgerran Castle dominate a romantic scene. The castle was begun in 1220 and was the subject of a well knwon painting by Richard Wilson. No finer setting could have been chosen for any fortress - both beautiful and unassailable - and in August each year it is all enhanced with the staging of the annual coracle races.

A glance at any good map will show you that Cardigan is the start of the Pembrokeshire Coast Path which wriggles its tortuous way around the jagged coastline and is almost unbroken until it reaches distant Milford Haven. Heading south from Cardigan you will find the village of **St Dogmaels** by taking the B4546 especially taking a look at the ruins of the Benedictine Abbey. The story is interesting. TheBenedictine Abbey was founded by monks of the French order of Tiron in 1113. The Sagranus Stone now in the parish church dates from the 6th century, and the Latin inscriptions on its face provided the key to the interpretation of the ogham alphabet of the ancient Giodelic language.

The church at **Nevern** - quite hard to find, best off the A487 and B4582 - was founded by St Brynach. A dark avenue of yews leads to the church door and one of them exudes a blood-red stain from a sawn branch. This is the bleeding Yew. The ogham alphabet is again encountered on the Vitalianus Stone which stands beside the church porch: it commemorates a prominent man who died around 500 AD. This one I found absolutely charming: there is a carved cross some 13feet high standing in the churchyard, and from it, each year on April 7th (St Brynach's Day), the first cuckoo sings.

Another interesting church can be found at Eglwyswrw which lies on the A487. This one is an early foundation that may have been built within a pre-Christian earthwork. Roughly between Nevern and Eglwyswrw you will find Pentre Ifan, which was one of the finest burial chambers in the country. A massive capstone is supported by three tall pillars, and George Owen once described it as 'one of the wonders of Pembrokeshire'.

Newport is an Ancient Borough with its own Mayor, Burgesses and Court Leet. It lies on the slope of a hill beneath a Norman castle, and below the town the River Nevern meanders across a wide estuary to enter the sea in Newport Bay, the Welsh name for Newport is Tredraeth Edrywy, and it is said not only that the original settlement stood near the shore, but that it was 'swallowed by the sands, like another Peranzabuloe'.

Not far from the old trading quays there is a beautiful sandy beach, with the shallow surf of **Newport Sands** offering safe bathing for all. If you intend staying here for any length of time, you will find plenty to do, with sailing, pony-trekking and golf - on a pleasant, nine hole course adjoining Newport Sands. Fishermen of all temperaments will find sport here. Salmon, sea trout and brown trout are found in the Nevern, and surf fishing from Newport Sands will often bring good catches of bass. During the season there is also salmon fishing from those same sands, using seine-nets.

In 1191 the Lord of Cemais, William Martin, was driven out of Nevern, and he established his stronghold at Newport where he built a castle. The castle was captured by Llywelyn the Great in 1215, and by Llywelyn the Last in 1257; during the revolt of Owain Glyndwr it suffered heavily, and was reckoned to be worth no more than £33!. By 1583 the castle had been in ruins for many years, and it was not until 1859 that the gatehouse was converted into a residence by Sir Thomas Lloyd, and the ruins substantially restored. You can still see what remains of the Hunter's Tower, the Kitchen Tower and the Great Tower, and the site on a spur standing over the estuary is most impressive.

Cwym-yr-Eglwys is tucked away at the eastern curve of Newport Bay, and this 'valley of the church' is one of the loveliest little bays in Wales. Most road atlases will show you Dinas Head, but only the larger Ordnance Survey maps will show the tiny peninsula bearing the name **Dinas Island**. In fact this small promontory was once cut off from the mainland by the Pwllgwaelod - Cwmyreglwys depression, and was once known as Ynys Fach Lyffan Gawr - ' the little island of Lyffan the Giant'. The Pembrokeshire Coastal Path leads around it, and there are two interesting books by R.M. Lockley -Island Farmers and The Golden Year - which tell of the author's life on Dinas Island Farm.

I was eager to visit **Fishguard**. With its wonderful harbour and fascinating town, it demands attention, but beyond that it also holds a unique place in the history of our islands; it was the scene of the last invasion of Britain. In 1797, French troops led by Colonel William Tate, an American, landed in a rocky bay beneath Carresgwastad Point, with the intention of rousing the population against George III. Popular legend tells us that the attack ended when the troops mistook Welsh women wearing traditional red cloaks for British soldiers. They advanced no further than Goodwick Sands, where they laid down their arms. Today a stone marks their landing place at Carregwastad.

The eastern coast of Dyfed has several fair-sized islands of the kind which are always formed as exposed coastlines are gradually eroded by the hungry seas. Ramsey Island and Skomer Island are the two largest, and from Fishguard I took the A487, this time towards **St Davids**. I knew that it is quite easy to get from the town to the coastal path, from which Ramsey is clearly visible - but my main intention was to spend some time at St David's Bishop's Palace, which I had briefly visited once before. It was built largely by Henry de Gower (1328-47). The richly decorative building stands within the Cathedral Close, among a group of buildings unique in Wales. The arcaded parapets of Bishop Henry extend along both main wings of the palace, and are decorated with some of the finest medieval sculptured heads and animal figures in Wales. The entrance to the Great Hall is also impressive, and the other great joy is the piscina in the Palace Chapel - a stone basin which carries away water used in rinsing chalices. Supposedly the presence of the Cathedral makes St David's the smallest city in Britain. The people of St Asaph will tell you differently!

Skomer Island can be rached by taking the A487 for six or seven miles in a south-westerly direction, then switching to a delightful minor road that hugs the coastal path. Skomer is included in the Marine Nature Reserve which takes in the island and the coastline around the Marlowe Peninsula - the only one of its kind in Wales, and only the second in the UK. Over 150 seals are born regularly making it the second largest pupping site in South West Britain. In addition, it is home to the largest concentration of sea birds such as puffins, guillemots and 5 razor bills in England and Wales, and over half the world population of the Manx Shearwater.

To get to Pembroke I meandered, quite intentionally, and found the easiest way, having got quite lost en route, was to take the B4327 and follow that to **Haverfordwest**. This market town of narrow streets which overlooks the River Cleddau is attractive, and like many others all over Wales is overlooked by an ancient castle. Built in 1100 it was part of a chain of fortifications erected across Pembrokeshire by English invaders to pen in the Welsh to the north. Later modifications strengthened the walls which are between six and twelve feet thick, and although Cromwell ordered the castle's destruction during the Civil War, much of it was left intact. It is now an appropriate site for the area's Information Centre, and it also houses a museum.

The road into Pembroke passes conveniently close to **Carew** with its castle built between 1280 and 1310, and considerably enlarged in the 15th century. It is particularly interesting because it has a long window and large galleries which illustrate the transition from the original stronghold to a charming Elizabethan country residence. Also in Carew there is a tidal mill -**Carew French Mill** - which is one of only three restored tidal mills in Britain, and the only one remaining intact in Wales. This grand, four-storey building dates back to 1558, and almost all its original machinery has been retained. Restoration of the huge south wheel has taken place in recent years.

Whilst there is no apparent direct route from Carew to **Upton**, although the distance is no morethan a mile, it is somewhere worth seeking out. Upton Castle grounds offer hours of enjoyment. The 35 acres contain almost 200 different species of trees and shrubs. Woodland and formal gardens are thoughtfully provided with all weather footpaths. There is also an interesting 11th-century family chapel.

Pembroke did not begin its development until the late 11th century although there is ample evidence, with standing stones and burial mounds, of an earlier, prehistoric occupation. Not surprisingly the development was around the splendid castle, the oldest in West Wales. It is certainly one of the best preserved Norman castles in Britain. It was founded by the Montgomerys in 1093, and around the year 1200 work was started on the Great Tower. This enormous structure is 75ft high and has walls at the base up to 19ft thick. Its circular shape is unusual, and it is also roofed, which was not common practice. Other claims to fame include the birth within the castle walls of the founder of the House of Tudor - Henry VII. It was held by both Royalists and Parliamentarians during the Civil War, and the siege that led to its final surrender was led by Cromwell himself. You may visit the castle on any day of the year except Christmas Day, Boxing Day and New Year's Day. From the end of May to the end of August guided tours are available.

The town experienced a period of decline until about 1814, when the Royal Naval Dockyard was moved from Milford Haven to Pembroke Dock, and brought prosperity with it. Since that date over 250 warships have been built at Pembroke Dock, as well as three Royal yachts for Queen Victoria. If nautical history interests you there are boat trips which will take you to see Warrior, the first iron-clad warship, which was launched in 1860 and is now at Pembroke Ferry. From there they continue the short distance to Milford Haven.

Milford Haven is both the name of the town and the stretch of water it overlooks, which was fittingly described by Nelson as ' one of the finest natural harbours in the world'. In fact the town was founded in 1793 - by Sir William Hamilton, husband of Nelson's mistress, Emma - and was a whaling port before becoming a dockyard. Milford Haven was used by Henry II to launch his invasion of Ireland in 1172, and Henry Tudor, Earl of Richmond landed there in 1485 on his was to defeating Richard III at the Battle of Bosworth Field. Since 1960 Milford Haven has gradually expanded to become a major oil port, its huge refineries fed by supertankers from all over the world.

Daniel Defoe described **Tenby** as ' the most agreeable town on all the south coast of Wales, except Pembroke', and since then thousands of visitors have echoed those words in one way or another. It is sheer delight, a compact little town with shops and houses almost touching across the narrow streets packed inside the town walls. Appropriately, the remains of a 13th-century Norman castle overlook the old fishing harbour, standing on the site occupied by a Welsh fort called Dinbych-y-Pysgod - Little Fort of the Fish. The town is also the birthplace of the portrait painter Augustus John, and of Robert Recorde, the mathematician who invented the = sign.

In Tenby you cannot escape the wonderful beaches, four of which encircle the headland. But they can be boisterous or placid as the fancy takes you, with quiet picnic spots always available to those who will venture away from the crowds.

Carmarthen shares with **Caerleon** the title of the oldest town in Wales, and settlement in the area can be traced back almost 2,000 years. There are remains of a large hill fort at Abergwili, three miles to the east, and a local bastion of Roman rule that was built near the centre of the present town survives in the modern name: Moridunum (mor dinas, or sea fort) became Caer-mori-dunum, and then Carmarthen! A Roman ampitheatre that once seated 5,000 people was identifiedin the 1930s on a site at the east end of Priory Street, and saved for posterity by the quick thinking of a former Borough Engineer, George Ovens. The arena wall has been reconstructed, and adjacent gardens cover still more remains.

Life is nothing without legend to intrigue and inspire, and here Welsh folklore tells how King Arthur's wizard, Merlin, was born near the town in 480AD. The story is given further credence by the decayed stump of an oak that stood at the end of Priory Street and apparently carried his spell: 'When Merlin's oak shall tumble down, then shall fall Carmarthen town'. But a more likely story is that it was planted at Priory Street's junction with Oak Street to commemorate the accession of Charles II to the throne - and what is absolutely certain is that it was removed in the interests of road safety in 1978. Carmarthen is fascinating to explore and demands attention.

South West Wales has its own charm. I proceeded along the A40 in the direction of **Llandeilo** with the intention of branching off to view two nearby attractions. The first, **Dinefwr Castle**. This is not one of the country's better known ruins, yet for all that it has an air about it, a certain brooding presence that on gloomy days can set the imagination racing. It was built on the site of an older castle, and its position has a lot to do with its undoubted attraction, for it is poised on the edge of a precipice. Its moats were carved from the rock and, like the keep and parts of the curtain wall which are all that remain, were designed to keep out the enemy in the long struggles with the Anglo-Normans. From 877 AD it was the principal residence of the princes of South Wales. I'm told the castle can be reached by walking through Castle Woods, where there are fine nature trails and superb parkland landscaped by Capability Brown. The paths are waymarked, and easily followed, though if you are going to be brave enough to walk from Llandeilo, you have a long walk ahead of you. En route you will come across the church of Llandyfeisant, which is within the park and is reputed to be built on the site of a Roman temple. The second is **Paxton's Tower**, a mile or so south of Dinefwr Castle, and surely one of the finest follies ever. Designed by Samuel Pepys Cockerel, it is triangular and crenellated, and was apparently erected in honour of Lord Nelson. It dates from the 19th century, and affords magnificent views of the Tywi valley. National Trust owned, it is open all the year round, whereas Dinefwr Castle is open only on appointed days.

There is yet another castle a few miles further west. **Dryslwyn** is again in a magnificent position, and was the scene of a three week siege in 1287 at the beginning of a revolt led by Rhys ap Meredudd. Some among you may know that Sappers are soldiers in the Royal Engineers and that their name comes from work they once did which involved the 'digging of saps for the purpose of moving towards the enemy, being under cover at all times'. The reason I bring that up is because Dryslwyn Castle had its defences quite literally undermined when what must have been the distant forerunners of those Sappers dug tunnels under the walls, which led to their collapse. There is a car park and a picnic site at Dryslwyn.

Llandeilo is a pleasant market town, built on a hill, and you will notice that most of the buildings in the main part of the town are early Victorian. the bridge over the river was built in 1848 - a splendid structure. The restored Church is mainly Victorian but has an interesting 13th-century tower. If you turn from the A40 onto the B4302, after a few miles you will reach the skeletal ruins of **Talley Abbey**. It dates back to the late 12th century when Rhys ap Gruffydd founded a House of Premonstratension Canons, which was severely handled in uprisings and revolts during the Middle Ages. Although once protected by Edward I it was again much abused, and after the rebellion of Owain Glyndwr there was little left of it. Nevertheless the site in the Carmarthenshire hills is a pretty one, and what is left is impressive - part of the central tower ofthe church has survived and there are two, high-pointed arches and several lancet windows.

If by now you have a nodding acquaintance with the Welsh language you will know that **Pumsaint** means 'five saints'. The name of this pleasant little village comes from the quintuplets born to Cynnyr Farfdrwch ap Gwron ap Cunedda. However my real reason for driving up the A482 was to visit the Roman gold mines at **Dolcaucothi**, which were actually worked as recently as 1938 - though not by the Romans! They were exploiting it almost 2000 years ago, and although you will now have difficulty interpreting the site on your own, there are self-guided trails which you can follow using the explanatory leaflets. As proof of the advanced techniques used so long ago, there is a fragment of a timber waterwheel - used to drain the galleries - in the National Museum at Cardiff.

Back tracking a bit along the A482 and then the A40 my intention was to seek out the village of **Bethlehem**. Not surpisingly this is a popular posting place for Christmas mail. Near it lie the ancient earthwork remains known as Carn Goch. This is well known as the largest Iron Age hill fort in Wales. It is enormous with its two forts spread over 800 metres. The views from here were breathtaking. Stay on the minor roads and you will see **Carreg Cennen**. This one outdoes most castles you will ever see! Its limestone eyrie must be seen to be believed - and if you intend taking a closer look you must be prepared for a stiff climb from the farmyard beneath its walls. The remote, timeless air which pervades appealed to artists during the Romantic Revivial, and it is not hard to understand why. The building dates back to the 13th and 14th centuries, but there was a castle on the site long before then. There is an inner ward with a fine gatehouse, and this is the earliest part of the castle. The arrow slits in the gatehouse walls are of the cross-slit variety, which apparently gave cross-bows more freedom of movement, and thus a greater arc of fire. The castle fell to Edward I in 1277 and seems to have remained in English hands from that date. Edward I gave it to John Gifford and another owner was John of Gaunt. Lancastrian supporters during the Wars of the Roses overcame the defence and the castle was demolished in 1462 to prevent its use as a robbers' refuge. That work was accomplished by 500 men armed with picks and crow bars - a task of monumental proportions!

You will certainly head towards **Trapp** when you leave Carreg Cennen. The latter is isolated and it is really hard to imagine why the village ever came about. There is a good Arts and Crafts Centre here with a charming tea-room. There is also a splendid working Welsh hill farm with a 17th century longhouse and a number of rare and unusual farm animals. Here too you can eat in the converted 18th-century barn. On the menu good home-made farmhouse cooking. Either before or after your meal you can enjoy walking along riverside or hill footpaths. and there is every chance that you will see many of Britain's rarest birds of prey.

Whilst I am aware that from here **Swansea** is close by, I want to leave it for now and tell you about the Gower Peninsula. Gower has long been an Area of Outstanding Natural Beauty, and most of it is protected by the National Trust and the Gower Society. It is a peninsula but its extreme isolation brought about by the flanking estuaries and the sandstone scarp at its eastern or inland border has enabled it to escape the industry that has mushroomed close by. There is just one major road (the A4118), a sparse network of byways - and that is it. The rest is sheer beauty, an area to explore until intoxicated.

The A4067 comes to an abrupt end just before Mumbles Head which marks the eastern end of the Gower. The name Mumbles actually refers to the two rounded rocks at the entrance to the bay, but has gradually come to cover the whole area from the pier to the shopping centre.

Mumbles is just five miles along the shore from Swansea, but it has established a unique reputation for itself while managing to retain a delightful village atmosphere. I knew Mumbles from details of the lifeboat tragedy, when the entire crew of the Mumbles lifeboat perished during rescues from the merchant ship Tampana. So the images I bore with me were of stormy seas and jagged rocks, and while those conditions do exist, Mumbles boasts wonderful sandy beaches, quaint coves just around the headland, and waters that are ideal for the staging of international yachting events.

Oystermouth is of interest for several reasons, not least the restored church which has a low tower often seen in this corner of Wales. The three bells came to the Mumbles from the burned cathedral of Santiago, Chile, and part of the aisle consists of fragments of Roman paving stones which were found nearby. Oystermouth Castle stands above the A4067; it was constructed in the late 13th century by the infamous Norman lord, de Breos, a member of a family noted for their villainous deeds. The drum towers that once flanked the main gateway leading to the single courtyard have long since disappeared, but there is doubt about Cromwell being instrumental in their destruction for the castle was not involved in the Civil Wars. Oystermouth Castle is full of interest. the keep has fine domestic apartments with beautiful windows, and there is a romantically named room - the White Lady's Chamber. The chapel adjoins the banqueting hall on the second floor, and here you can see a piscina, and more elaborate windows.

I like **Bishopston**. Such a tranquil place with a small church containing an interesting font, and earthwork remains on nearby Pwlldu Head. There are also delightful little coves nearby with firm, sandy beaches.

Oxwich National Nature Reserve and Centre is an area of dunes, marshes and woodlands above the sweeping curve of Oxwich Bay, and you will find here a wonderful concentration of wildlife. Information is readily available at the Centre, though opening times vary. But much of the Reserve is there for you to explore, and it is always open.

You will find **Oxwich** church on a rocky ledge near the sea. The Tudor Mansion known as Oxwich Castle is on a hill above the village. In the 16th century the Mansel family abandoned Penrice Castle to move into their new home, and there is still an impressive crested gateway leading into the courtyard. From Oxwich Bay you can see the medieval castle at **Penrice** that was abandoned in favour of Oxwich; as you would expect, it was built round about the 12th century, and is now in ruins.

Port Einon is just beyond Oxwich and is a fishing hamlet overlooking its own small bay. Tales of smuggling and piracy abound, and at the base of a reef known as Skysea you will come across the ruins of the Salthouse, which once had contrband wine stored in its cavernous vaults. The bay is often stormy, and evidence of this can be found in the churchyard where there is a statue commemorating a lifeboat hero. From Port Einon there is a wonderful cliff-top walk as far as **Rhossli**, but even keen and experienced walkers will need to take care on the rocky paths. It is well worth the effort, for the caves here are large enough to be marked on maps; both Culver Hole and Paviland Cave can be reached, but it is difficult. Of the two it is Paviland (actually a number of caves) that has a tale to tell. The 'Red Lady of Paviland' was a red-stained, human skeleton - minus skull - that was discovered in the Goat's Hole in 1823. A hundred years later, research resulted in a change of sex, for the remains turned out to be those of a youth who had been buried some 18,000 years ago. The gory stains were red ochre.

If you are still full of energy you can continue walking beyond Rhossli, Rhossisli Downs are quite desolate but they have more than their fair share of secret places, and budding archaeologists will pick their way quite happily through the rough grass around two Neolithic chambered tombs. These are Sweyne's Houses (or Swine Houses'), and date from around 2500BC. Beneath the Downs there is probably the finest beach on the Gower, with sands stretching for three miles in a graceful curve between Worm's Head and Burry Holms, a tiny island with the remains of a ruined church and a teeming bird population.

Llandewi is where you will find the **Gower Farm Museum** in a cluster of old farm buildings in which the owners have recreated rural life as it was at the turn of the century. The farm courtyard is stocked with many animals - chickens and ducks, goats, even rare breeds such as Gloucester Old Spot pigs - and there is a pets corner where children can gently handle guinea pigs and rabbits. The Gower Farm Museum is open May to September.

Another minor road off the A4118 would bring you to **Reynoldston**, which is considered to be the central point of the Gower. It is a pretty village with a green, and if you make the stiff walk to the summit of nearby Cefyn Bryn, a clear day will allow you to see across the Channel to South West England. It is worthwhile continuing your walk from there, for you will soon come across Arthur's Stone, a prominent landmark backed by interesting legends. It is actually four stones supporting a mighty capstone, and this is rumoured to have been split by Arthur.

There are conflicting historical details about **Weobley Castle** which you will find near **Cheriton**. It seems that all or part of this late medieval fortified house was built towards the end of the 13th century, probably by Henry Beaumont, Earl of Warwick. Later, it was occupied by the de la Bere family. Other sections were added in later centuries, and of the substantial remains perhaps the biggest difference you will notice between Weobley and other castles is the sheer variety of towers. Some have six or eight sides, some are square, yet all come together to form a complete square. If you visit on any day of the year you will be able to see the hall, kitchens and cellar, and an interesting exhibition on the history of the castle and of the Gower through the ages.

Llanrhidian is worth an hour of your time. Among the sights to be seen is St Rhidian's church, which has a curiously carved stone in the porch for which no-one can offer an explanation. As you stroll through the village you will see two standing stones on the green, and the old village stocks. Nearby Cil Ifor Top is the site of an Iron Age fort of considerable size, with terraces which can still be clearly seen.

Once upon a time you would have seen the cockle-women of **Penclawdd** in their bonnets and flannel dresses crossing the sand at low tide, their donkey carts ready to be loaded with the fresh harvest of shellfish. Things have changed but the sprawling village is still the centre of the cockle industry.

I left The Gower with reluctance but the history of **Kidwelly** beckoned me. It is a fine example of a town that has grown around a Norman castle. The estuary location at the mouth of the river Gwendraeth again demonstrates how the rulers and military commanders of the day recognised the importance of access from the sea. The earthwork defences of Kidwelly date back to the reign of Henry I, when they were raised by Roger, Bishop of Salisbury. The semi-circular moat is early 12th century, the inner ward was constructed by Payn de Chaworth late in the 13th century, and the cliffside chapel - it juts out over a scarp which formed a natural defence to the east - was added around 1300. In fact most of the existing building is the work of castle builders who were active in the 13th and 14th centuries.

Even before that period was reached, the castle had changed hands several times. One notable battle involved Maurice de Londres, Lord of Kidwelly, who in 1136 was faced by an army led by a woman - Gwenllian, the wife of Gruffydd ap Rhys. The Normans won the day in a fierce, bloody fight, and both Gwenllian and her son, Morgan, were beheaded.

Centuries later, Kidwelly Castle suffered severe damage in the Glyndwr rebellions. Concentric castles, of which Kidwelly is a fine example, had two rings of defences. The inner bailey or ward would have high walls with their own gateway. This would be encircled by the outer bailey protected by exterior walls with towers and - in Kidwelly's case - a massive gatehouse. You can see that three-storey structure to this day, and several of the towers are complete to their turrets. The old town of Kidwelly would have been completely walled; now, although it has lost its medieval buildings, the roads almost certainly follow their original lines and you can still see the early 14th-century town gate, which lies to the south.

If you continue on the A484 out of Kidwelly you will come to Ferryside, a little village with wonderful views and super sands with the sheltered waters of the estuary making it a lovely spot to spend a lazy afternoon.

Swansea makes a wonderful starting point from which to set out on the next stage of my travels, a remarkable journey which includes the two largest cities in Wales - one of which is the capital - and the astonishing contrast between vast urban industrial complexes and the breathtaking beauty of the Brecon Beacons. Cardiff may be the capital, but Swansea is justifiably proud to be the second largest city in Wales. Its name has buccaneering undertones, too, for it reached its present form from the original Sweyn's Ea (the island of Sweyn). Sweyn was a Viking pirate who used the site on the River Tawe as a base from which he could plunder the south coast. The docks at Swansea were established in 1306 for the purpose of ship building, but by the 18th century a change was underway as the exporting of Welsh coal, copper and iron ore became big business. The city is full of interest with an excellent market on Oxford Street, an exciting Maritime Quarter which has a marina with berths for 600 craft, a waterfront village, restaurant, art gallery, theatre, sailing and sea angling schools, and an unusual floating restaurant. The centrepiece of the Maritime Quarter is the Maritime and Industrial Museum with Wales' largest collection of historic vessels; the lightship Helwick and steam tug Canning can be boarded.

The Glynn Vivian Art Gallery on Alexander Road should not be missed. Among its static displays is one of the largest collections of Swansea porcelain and an outstanding collection of European ceramic and glass. These and many other displays which are constantly changing bring to the people of Swansea and visitors, the best in art from around the world.

The Brangwyn Hall is a mile from the city centre and just off the A4067 as you head back towards Mumbles. It could actually be called two buildings in one, for it was built in 1934 as the Guildhall and now comprises Swansea's civic offices, and the Brangwyn Concert Hall. The latter was named after Sir Frank Brangwyn, who designed the murals of the British Empire which were intended for the House of Lords but now adorn the walls of this splendid building. They did not get there without some difficulty - the 18 panels are so big that in order to accommodate them adjustments had to be made to the building! Brangwyn Hall is the focal point for the Swansea Festival of Music which is held each Autumn. International orchestras and soloists perform there, while opera is staged at the Grand Theatre.

The Vale of Neath is renowned for its own natural beauty and a number of major attractions that draw visitors in their thousands. **Neath** town centre is fully-pedestrianised, and as in Swansea,there is a thriving Victorian covered market. The Neath Borough Museum is housed in a beautifully refurbished Grade II listed building. Neath has a castle too, which was built in 1284 on a promontory guarding the approach to the town. It is currently being restored. Neath Abbey was founded in 1130 by the Norman Baron Richard de Granville.

Today it can be found on the edge of the Tennant Canal in an industrial area just off the A465. It does not sound like the ideal position for an Abbey that became Cistercian in 1147, and was considered by the Tudor historian, John Leland to be, 'The fairest Abbey in all Wales.' In fact the site is still tranquil and haunting and now in the care of CADW: Welsh Historic Monuments. The substantial ruins are open all year.

Aberdulais Falls and Ironworks will interest people with disparate tastes. I was intrigued to learn the natural waterfalls are not just beautiful to behold: a new water wheel will soon harness the natural energy source to produce electricity in a wooded gorge that contains the remains of 400 years of industrial activity. There is an interesting exhibition which deals with history and displays works of art by famous painters, and guided tours are available at this important National Trust site.

On the A4109 you will find the Cefyn Coed CollieryMuseum. So much of this part of the world is inextricably linked to the production of coal that a brush with the reality of the industry, however brief, is a must. The museum is located a little way south of **Crynant**, and is next to an operational mine. Most of the surface buildings remain from the former active colliery, and in the museum there are simulated underground workings, a huge steam winding engine, and massive boilers that once powered the pithead winding gear. There is also a good display of photographs which vividly trace the history of the workings, and round about there are lovely forest walks and picnic sites. An unusual and fascinating attraction.

On the same subject, it is worth going to Afon Argoed Country Park where there is the Welsh Miners Museum. Best reached by returning to Neath and taking the B4287 and then the A4107. You can look at this as confirmation that here the countryside and industry have always been uncomfortable bedfellows, or as an example of how two different natural resources complement each other - the one never complete without the other.

Afon Argoed Country Park has wonderful facilities on a beautiful steep sided valley that can be explore in several ways. Cycle tracks run along both banks of the River Afan (bikes can be hired), there are waymarked walks fanning out from the Countryside Centre, which is situated to the west of Cynonville, and landrover tours operate from the main car park during the summer season. My own reason for taking a look was to add to the coalmining information I had picked up at Cefyn Coed. Here, the story is by miners, from their point of view: there is a traditional miner's cottage scene, historic photographs, the story of children underground and a lot of mining equipment in realistic settings. Quite absorbing and always there is the knowledge that it can be tempered with the beauty of the Country Park waiting to embrace you when you tire of your research.

The Neath Canal deserves a mention. Some sections of it have recently been restored and now offer delightful diversions. Head for **Resolven** on the A465 where there is a tea room and gift shop in an 18th century cottage, and the 'Thomas Dadford' waiting to transport you along the placid waterways through idyllic scenery. Good towpath walks, too.

Porthcawl is regarded as the leading resort in South Wales - no doubt some would argue that it is not but what is certain is that it grew up as a coal port in the 19th century, and with the declineof that industry turned naturally to the holiday trade. Brochures will tell you of the seven beaches and coves of the district, in particular Sandy Bay which is overlooked by the massive Cony beach entertainment complex. However, at the risk of being dubbed an old stick in the mud, I'd like to draw your attention to the dunes to the north west where the lost city of Kenfig lies buried by the sand. It was apparently engulfed in the Middle Ages, and today you may still see the ruins of Kenfig Castle poking through the sands. Kenfig Pool is also something of an oddity. Scarcely a mile from the sea, it is locked in by the dunes and is the county's largest freshwater lake.

Porthcawl is famous for golf. The Royal Porthcawl Club will be known to most people, if only by name, for it has hosted many international events including in recent years the Coral Classic. But there is also Pyle and Kenfig Club, the Southerndown Club and the Maesteg Club, the last two having wonderful views which could possibly result in ruined handicaps (or better handicaps, depending on how you view these things!) A word of warning - letters of introduction from your own club are usually required before you can tee off.

This is an outstanding stretch of coast for castles. The three main castles of Ogwr - all clustered around **Bridgend** - bear testimony to the ruthlessness of Prince Llywelyn, who partially destroyed them to prevent their being used by invaders. Ogmore Castle guarded a river crossing on the River Ewenny. It was constructed of undressed boulders, and probably dates back to the 12th century. Stepping stones lead across the river to the tiny village of **Merthyr-Mawr**, perhaps the most attractive in Ogwr. **New Castle**, paradoxically, controlled a ford on the River Ogmore.

The third castle is Coity, and this one can be traced back to the days of the Norman Lordships. Those of you who have read Thomas Hardy will recognise the name when I tell you that Coity Castle was held by the Turbevilles. Legend has it that the family acquired the castle through marriage, but certainly their descendants were one of Glamorgan's most powerful families. The castle was rebuilt in the 14th century, and added to in Tudor times.

Bridgend straddles the River Ogmore where three valleys meet - the Ogmore, Garw and Llynfi, and as well as being the traditional market town of the area it is now an industrial centre. The A48 from Bridgend will take you to **Cowbridge** whose origins lie in the first century AD and its location is on the important Roman road between Carmarthen and Caerleon. Modern thought also suggests that it is the sight of a missing Roman fort - Bomium - though nothing has been found to support the theory. It is now largely Georgian in character with many of the buildings listed. Charming place to be and full of interest.

The Vale of Glamorgan next with its plethora of places to see. **Llantwit Major** was once known as Llanilltud Fawr - 'Great Church of Illtud' - and as such was the first Christian College in Britain. It is also mentioned in the Guiness Book of Records as the site of the oldest school in Britain, and in legend St David, St Gilda and St Patrick are said to have been educated in this little town.

Barry or the old Port of Barry was first mentioned in 1276, and went on to flourish in the 16th and early 17th centuries. The larger, more modern town of Barry grew up as a port in the 1880s, like Porthcawl there to serve the needs of the South Wales coal industry. Now this bustling town is an excellent shopping centre, with good leisure facilities and a varied night life. It is also the location of Glamorgan Borough Council's head office, a fact worth noting as they can supply a wealth of information on accommodation, and places to see in the Vale of Glamorgan. Barry Island is linked by road and rail, and is a flourishing holiday resort. Its situation is ideal, for as apeninsula it has sea on three sides and all road and rail communications in the centre. There are two very large sandy beaches, plenty of rock pools to explore, and promenades and landscaped gardens ideal for strolling or lazing in the sun.

The B4267 is the road you need to take you towards Cardiff, and there are several interesting places to visit en route. Cosmeston Lakes Country Park has all the attractions you would expect, and in addition a Medieval Village which is not a reconstruction. Archaeologists are excavating and restoring, and a personal guide is there to introduce you to the history of Comeston Village.

Like Llandudno on the north coast, **Penarth** has a fine Victorian esplanade that provides a touch of old world charm. It is a pleasant resort on high ground to the west of Cardiff, which has been in turn fishing village and coal-exporting port. This is probably not the place for those who like sea swimming, for there are strong currents running off the shingle beach that is backed up by cliffs up to 100 feet high. There are, however, several swimming pools which make ideal alternatives. From Penarth pier you can embark on The Waverley, the world's last, sea-going paddle steamer. Five miles offshore - almost midway between Penarth and Weston-Super-Mare - Flat Holm island is reputed to be the burial place of the knights who murdered Thomas Becket.

We must go back to 75AD to learn of the first settlements where **Cardiff** stands today, for it was then the Romans built a fort by the River Taff to control Welsh tribesmen. It was extended in 300 AD, this time as a defence against pirates from across the Irish Sea. The town grew up around a fort built by Robert FitzHamon - which can still be seen in the grounds of Cardiff Castle -and it was given its first Royal Charter by Elizabeth I in 1581. Coal played a big part in the town's prosperity, leading to the construction of docks which in 1794 were linked by canal to Merthyr Tydfil.

Shirley Bassey fans will know of **Tiger Bay**, a region of sprawling quays to the east of the Taff where seamen frequented taverns with names such as The Bucket of Blood and the House of Blazes. A once tough area, now developed into a modern city suburb with up to date docks.

It is almost impossible to know where to start exploring Cardiff, and you will be guided by preferences. Sports fans are certain to head for Cardiff Arms park, others will go first to the waterfront, while the Castle will for many be the magnet that first attracts. **The National Museum of Wales** is located at Cathays Park. Permanent exhibitions here cover an enormous range of subjects such as geology, botany, zoology, archaeology - surely enough 'ologies' to keep Maureen Lipman happy for months! Other sections feature industry and art, and there are temporary exhibitions, holiday activities for children, lunchtime and evening concerts and regular lectures and readings.

The Welsh Industrial and Maritime Museum is on Bute Street and, appropriately, the site is adjacent to the Bute West Dock Basin. It was opened in 1977 so is comparatively new, but its comprehensive coverage of industrial and maritime matters in Wales over the past two centuries is staggering. This is very much an open air site too; the steam tug 'Sea Alarm', a pilot cutter and a canal boat, a number of cranes and industrial locomotives as well as a railway footbridge and a lifeboat, will have people from all walks of life enthralled.

The Welsh Folk Museum is some distance away at St Fagans - about five miles west of the city centre. This is a museum packed with fascinating exhibits, and I found it wonderful because it reflects everyday life in Wales, which of course is of interest to absolutely everybody. The settingis super - an Elizabethan mansion standing within the walls of a medieval castle.

Cardiff Castle is different in several respects from others we have seen. It is for a start, in the very centre of this capital city, and it is also the creation of a Victorian Architect. The castle was considerably extended in the 13th century, but the ornate 150 foot clock tower, the Guest Tower, the guest rooms and Octagonal Tower are all the work of William Burges, who rebuilt the castle in the 1870s to fulfil the dreams of John Patrick Crichton-Stuart, the third Marquess of Bute.

There are mixed opinions about this castle, some love it, some think it to be so lavishly decorated that it is vulgar in parts and yet the design and construction of other parts approaches perfection. The Entrance Hall has elegant stained glass windows showing the monarchs who have owned the castle. The Library also has lovely stained glass windows - this time with a Biblical theme.

St David's Hall is the National Concert and Conference Hall of Wales and was completed in 1982. I always associate it with that wonderful television programme 'Cardiff - Singer of the World' - which appears every two years and allows me to listen to truly wonderful voices every night for a week. It is centrally located alongside the St David's Shopping Centre, and as well as an auditorium seating 2000 there are numerous meeting rooms and dressing rooms. Excellent bar facilities and an in-house catering department.

What can one say of **Cardiff Arms Park**? An ideal situation alongside the River Taff, minutes away from the town centre and Cardiff Central railway station, and of course known to millions of Rugby Union fans all over the world. If you are there on the day of an international - perhaps Wales versus England -the singing may well move you to tears.

Singing of a different kind can be heard at the New Theatre, which opened in 1906 and is Cardiff's sole surviving traditional theatre. The Royal Shakespeare Company, London Contemporary Dance Theatre and Sadlers Wells Royal Ballet have all appeared here, plus West End Musicals, and, of course, the Welsh National Opera for which the new Theatre provides a fitting home.

Probably one of my favourite locations in Wales is **The Brecon Beacons.** The scenery is stunning and varied as are the villages. Along the A470 for just five miles and you come to Castell Coch. This is the first fairy-tale castle

I have seen in Wales. A marvellous jumble of round towers and conical turrets. Yet, like Cardiff, it is the physical representation of a Victorian dream - and the same two people are responsible: William Burges, and John Patrick Crichton-Stuart. The work on Castell Coch ran in parallel with the work five miles down the road, and if anything Burges gave even freer rein to his imagination. All is lavishly decorated with murals, carvings, paintings and figures taken from Aesop's Fables and Greey mythology - yet there is a sombre note, too, for a flight of stone steps lead down to a gloomy dungeon.

I suggest the simplest way of tackling the Brecon Beacons National Park is to drive slowly through to **Brecon** and then pause to catch your breath and take stock. You are in exhilirating mountain country all the way and some six miles from Garwnant you will come abreast of the three peaks of the beacons: Pen-y-Fan (2907 ft), which is flanked by Cribyn (2608 ft) and Corn Du (2863 ft). They are the highest mountains in South Wales, and it is very easy to see why this daunting terrain is ideal training ground for elite army units, and the haunt of mountaineers.

Brecon is situated at the junction of the rivers Usk and Honddu, and is one of the oldest Welsh towns. It was granted its first charter in 1246 and a second granted in 1366 gave it the right to hold a fair. That right is never taken lightly in Wales, and pleasure fairs are still held in the Brecon streets for three days each May and November. The town has a bewildering mixture of architectural styles - Medieval, Georgian, Jacobean and Tudor, as well as excellent modern buildings. There was a castle, but all that remains now are a tower and battlemented wall.

If you are tired of driving yet determined to see more of this beautiful part of Wales, all is not lost. Brecon and Beyond is the name of a firm running luxury landrover tours, and they offer the ideal way to get off the beaten track without ruining the family car's suspension. Drovers' tracks criss-cross a 12,000 acre private estate, and there are super views, rugged mountains, waterfalls and limestone gorges.

It was a great disappointment to me to discover that **Caerphilly** cheese is mainly made in Somerset today and not in this small town where until 1910 there used to be a bustling cheese market. Caerphilly has experienced enormous changes, as have most towns and villages in this land with an unusually turbulent history. In the hills around the town the Welsh held out against the Norman invaders for 200 years after 1066. Later, around 1268, Gilbert de Clare, the Red Earl of Gloucester, began the construction of Caerphilly Castle, which is the largest in Wales and the second largest in Britain. It was destroyed just two years later by Llywelyn ap Gruffydd, Prince of Wales, when it was still only partially built. A second attempt at construction was begun - again by the Earl - in 1271, and this time it was successful. The site is right in the middle of the town and very impressive. The concentric ground plan and huge encircling moat rendered normal siege methods ineffective, and even in mopdern times it's easy to visualise the attackers' abortive attempts to break through. A magnificent sight!

One of the first things a visitor notices is a tower that leans almost 12 feet off the perpendicular, and not for the first time I came across conflicting stories when I tried to root out an explanation. The first suggests that during the Civil War - in 1646 - the Royalists attempted to blow up the castle to prevent the Roundheads from using it, and in so doing badly damaged the tower. The other theory is that the lean is caused by subsidence. The first appeals to me infinitely more than the second!

Caerphilly Castle has a ghost. Known as the Ghost of the Green Lady, it is said to be Alice of Angouleme, bride of Gilbert de Clare, who fell for a Welsh Prince called Griffith the Fair and was immediately banished to her home in France. Since then her spirit has looked out from the grey ramparts, waiting for the return of her prince....

The ruins of Newport Castle stand close to the bridge over the River Usk. It was built in the 15th century and has a wonderful Gothic arch on which can still be seen the grooves of the original portcullis. By the 16th-century Newport was already known for its excellent harbour; three hundred years later that came to good use when the Industrial Revolution brought coal pouring down from the Monmouthshire valleys. **Newport** is now the foremost shopping and commercial centre in Gwent, with a heritage dating back three thousand years and a character moulded by Celts, Romans, Saxons, Normans, Plantagenets and Tudors.

You will need to take the B4236 to reach old **Caerleon,** which today is an attractive village, of interest in its own right. Visitors flock to see Caerleon Isca, a fortress laid out beside the River Usk in about 74AD which became one of the three principal military bases in Roman Britain,headquarters of the 2nd Augustan Legion. The aerial photographs I had seen clearly show the shape of these wonderful remains, but actually walking through them left me with the uncanny sensation of having stepped a long way back in the past - obviously true, yet I felt it here stronger than anywhere else (except perhaps canterbury cathedral).

The Barracks at Caerleon are the only Roman legionary barracks on view anywhere in Europe. It is an extraordinary feeling to see the buildings that once housed 80 men, and realise you are walking down a Roman street. Broadway is the course of the Via Principalis, and a sign on a farm wall to the left marks the site of the sout-west gateway - Port Dextra. The Fortress Baths are if anything more impressive. They served as the main leisure centre for the soldiers, and the building once stood 60 feet high. There is an open air swimming pool - now displayed under cover - that was discovered as recently as 1964.

The Ampitheatre stands outside the fortress walls. It once seated 5,000 spectators - the whole garrison. Today it is still a superb setting for open-air theatrical events and festivals. All the separate parts of this wonderful site are brought together and thoroughly explained in the spacious Legionary Museum.

From Caerleon I had intended to go straight to Caldicot. But there is no M4 junction there so instead I took the A48, which allowed me to call at Penhow and Caerwent.

Penhow Castle is the home of the Seymour family, and the oldest lived-in castle in Wales. It was restored in 1973 by the owner, who still lives there. An interesting way of touring the building is provided: audio cassettes in handy 'walkman' players act as guides, providing an acommpaniment of authentic period music.

Caerwent is just a few miles further on, a peaceful village that is built on the site of the Roman walled town of Venta Silarum. Excavations here have revealed houses, shops and a temple, and in places the well-preserved walls stand 15 feet high. All of this interests me tremendously, because it is not something I have delved deeply into yet in the space of a few short miles I have come across a Roman fortress, a Roman town, and a little further on is **Portskewett,** a tiny village close to the River Severn, which centuries ago was an important landing stage for the Romans when they first came to Wales. The landing point at Black Rock is now a delightful picnic site.

From Caerwent it is a short drive down a minor road to **Caldicot,** a lovely town which was mentioned in the Domesday Book in the 11th century. Rich in history - in particular that relating to the Roman occupation. At nearby Mount Ballan, Crick - home of showjumper David Broome - the Wales and the West Showjumping events are held.

Caldicot Castle was built in stages during the 12th and 14th centuries, but unlike others that were left to decay it was restored by a wealthy Victorian and converted into a family home. The castle is the focal point of a delightful country park and also renowned for its medieval banquets. Large parties must be booked but quite often there are tables available for smaller numbers.

Chepstow marks the western edge of my tour through Wales. It is delightfully situated in a loop of the River Wye and has streets that slope down to the river. There are many tea-houses, antique shops, galleries and craft shops on the way down to the riverbank which is the spectacular setting for, among other things, the fine new bandstand.

The castle dominates the town and is the earliest Norman stone castle in Wales. William Fitzosbern, Earl of Hereford, built it on limestone cliffs at the water's edge, and it was greatly enlarged in the 12th and 13th centuries. It is one of the few sites where it is possible to follow the many phases of castle building in Britain. It was considered impregnable until the walls were breached by Cromwell's guns during the Civil War.

Several grand walks are waymarked from Chepstow. one of them beginning on the Welsh side of the river, is the Wye Valley walk, which starts at the castle and passes through glorious countryside. For the other you will need to cross to the English side; it is Offa's Dyke.

You must look out for the signs to the village of **Tintern**. This is an attractive hamlet with a south-facing hill overlooking the Abbey where Welsh table wines are produced from a fine vineyard. But it is Tintern Abbey that folk come to see and it really is a wonderful sight.

The original abbey was a Cistercian house founded by Henry I in 1131, but the existing remains are much larger, and date from the late 13th century. The setting is superb, with the river flowing through grassy banks dotted with white cottages, and all around thickly wooded hills. Wordsworth was impressed while on a walking tour, and indeed the abbey ruins are among the most beautiful and best preserved in Britain.

Monmouth is a splendid town. It stands at the confluence of the Wye, Monmnow and Trothy rivers, and this former county town of Monmouthshire boasts many well-preserved Tudor and Georgian buildings. Agincourt Square is elegant, bordered by a cluster of fine inns and the Shire Hall and library, and a statue there is itself a tribute to a man who helped bring elegance to the motor industry: Charles Stewart Rolls, co-founder of Rolls-Royce, who was born at nearby Rockfield.

I am sure you will be smitten by Usk. It is a wonderfully picturesque town that has sveral times been voted 'Best Kept Small Town in Wales'. It has also won the small town category in the 'Britain in Bloom' competition, and in the summer months you will find it ablaze with masses of flowers in beds, window boxes and hanging baskets. July and September are good months to visit Usk. The Usk Festival is held in midsummer, and in recent years jousting tournaments have been added to the traditional music and drama. The Usk Agricultural Show takes place at summers end, and is held in Trostrey on the outskirts of the town.

Abergavenny was my last port of call on this tour of Wales. If I were asked to name my favourite spot in this old market town then I would certainly plump for Castle Meadows alongside the River Usk. On a summer's day there can be no more idyllis place to be and a picnic beneath tall trees on the gently sloping banks is certainly my idea of heaven.

This has been a wonderful journey for me, and I hope you have found something along the way to inspire you and room in your heart to forgive my ommissions. Some have been deliberate, giving me the excuse to return.

SARNFAEN FARM
Talybont, Barmouth,
Gwynedd,
Wales LL43 2AQ
Tel: 01341 247604

Cardigan Bay extends to visitors, golden sandy beaches, boating, surfing and many more leisure pursuits, as well as lovely coastal walks and stunning scenery. The adjacent resort of Talybont is where Tom and Jean Jones own a very pretty and totally private chalet, positioned on their farmland, but enclosed within its own boundary of neat lawns, with a shallow stream percolating on the fringe. Sleeping up to 4/5 persons, there are 2 bedrooms, bathroom, dining room/lounge with coal effect fire and colour television. The attractive and modern kitchen is very well equipped with electric cooker, refrigerator and microwave oven. A cot and high chair are available. The Wales Tourist Board has awarded this delightful, well presented chalet '4 Dragons' making it an ideal holiday home. A choice of shops are within walking distance.

USEFUL INFORMATION

OPEN; *All year*
CHILDREN; *Yes*
CREDIT CARDS; *None taken*
ACCOMMODATION; *2 bedroomed self-contained chalet. Electricity by meter reading*

DISABLED ACCESS; *No*
GARDEN; *Yes, private*
PARKING; *For 2 cars*
PETS; *By arrangement*

CROSSWAYS HOUSE
Cowbridge,
Vale of Glamorgan CF71 7LJ
Tel: 01446 773171

The Ballroom Flat in this beautiful country mansion is self-contained with double bedded room and large living room with double sofa-bed and kitchen. Separate bathroom and hall. It sleeps 4 people and is available to rent by the week or month. The house built in 1921 is impressive and set in open countryside in 6 acres of grounds with a tennis court . Situated just one mile outside the historic and picturesque town of Cowbridge with its smart shops, pubs and restaurants, Crossways is splendidly placed for anyone wanting to explore the Heritage Coast and the Vale of Glamorgan. Crossways House also offers bed and breakfast accommodation in three attractively appointed ensuite rooms. The proprietor, Anne Paterson, is a charming lady who strives to ensure all her guests enjoy their stay.

USEFUL INFORMATION

OPEN; *All year*
CREDIT CARDS; *None taken*
ACCOMMODATION; *Self-contained flat Sleeps 4. 2 ensuite rooms & 1 with private bathroom*

CHILDREN; *Welcome*
DISABLED ACCESS; *No special facilities*
GARDEN; *6 acres*
PETS; *By arrangement*

MELIN LLECHEIDDIOR
Garndolbenmaen,
Gwynedd LL51 9EZ
Tel/Fax: 01766 530635

Steep valleys, craggy mountains and stunning clear lakes all go to make up the Snowdonia National Park, with Snowdon being the main attraction. This wild landscape is criss-crossed by roads and narrow-gauge railways, and in between small villages can be found nestling in the peace and tranquillity of this wonderful scenery. One such village is Garndolbenmaen near which is located 'Melin Llecheiddior' a delightful 2 bedroomed self-contained cottage clothed in ivy. It is the ideal place to explore the mountains, and the sea is also within easy reach. The cottage is well appointed with a full equipped kitchen including a microwave, lounge with colour television, one double room and one twin bedded room. A sun lounge where you can relax after a hard days activities. A cot and high chair are available, pets are welcome by arrangement. This lovely area has so much to offer including fishing, golf, cycling, riding and of course extensive walks. If you are artistic then this really is the place for you, with all that superb scenery you are sure to paint a masterpiece.

USEFUL INFORMATION

OPEN; *All year*
CHILDREN; *Welcome*
CREDIT CARDS; *None taken*
LICENSED; *Not applicable*
ACCOMMODATION; *2 Bedroomed self-contained cottage*
DINING ROOM; *Not applicable*
DISABLED ACCESS; *No*
GARDEN; *No fields down to the river*
PETS; *Yes by arrangement*

RIVERSIDE HOLIDAY BUNGALOWS
Llanbedr, Gwynedd,
North Wales
LL45 2NW,
Tel/Fax:: 01341 241223

Riverside Holiday Bungalows are situated about 200 metres from the village of Llanbedr alongside the beautiful River Artro. This small peaceful site of eight brick built bungalows offers modern conveniences including; tiled bathroom, shower, bath and heated towel rail, fitted kitchen, conventional and microwave cooker, refrigerator, colour TV and central heating. The larger bungalows have sleeping accommodation for six, whilst the two bedroom version offers four persons the same level of amenities. There is ample parking, cots are available, as is linen hire.

The village is only two minutes walk and here there are some excellent shops to supply your needs. If you feel disinclined to cook, the vicinity offers a variety of excellent places to eat inexpensively. You will never be at a loss for something to do. There are many places of interest and sporting activities right on the doorstep. The site's Riverside Fitness Centre with its well equipped gymnasium is available to Riverside clientele during their stay. The centre caters for all levels of fitness having single station machines. Olympic weights and fitness classes. Expert tuition from a qualified instructor is also on hand for the beginner.

USEFUL INFORMATION

OPEN; *All year*
CREDIT CARDS; *None taken*
ACCOMMODATION; *8 bungalows*
CHILDREN; *Welcome*
DISABLED ACCESS; *Limited*

BWLCH FARMHOUSE
Llananno,
Llandrindod Wells,
Powys,
Wales LD1 6TT

Tel: 01597 840366
Fax: 01597 840366

Bwlch is a beautiful old cruck farmhouse, a 'cruck' being a pointed timber arch forming the framework of a house from ground to gable. Bwlch is a wonderful example. Attached to the house is Swallow Cottage with its thick stone walls and beamed ceiling, and its own front and back doors. The cotttage is very warm and comfortable, the sitting room has a colour television and fitted kitchen area complete with washing machine, fridge, microwave oven and integral oven and hob. Upstairs there is a double and single bedroom, and a shower with basin and toilet. Attached to the otherside of Swallow Cottage is Honeysuckle Cottage, a delightful property all on one level. There is one double bedded room, one twin bedded room, a bathroom and a large hall.

The sitting room has a colour television while the kitchen/dining has the same standard of equipment as Swallow Cottage, with the added luxury of a Rayburn, which heats the radiators and hot water. Both cottages have ample parking space. Set amidst the hills of mid-Wales and overlooking the Ithon Valley, these cottages are ideal for walking holidays, especially along the 'Glyndwr's Way' and the breathtaking Elan Dams. There is fishing, golf and riding nearby and Bwlch can offer basic stabling for 2 horses, by arrangement. A short drive away is Knighton where you can visit Powys County Observatory and Offa's Dyke Heritage Centre. The elegant Victorian spa town of Llandrindod Wells is only 12 miles away. If you require peace and tranquility then Bwlch Farmhouse Cottages are just the place.

USEFUL INFORMATION

OPEN; *Easter-October*
CHILDREN; *Welcome*
CREDIT CARDS; *None taken*
LICENSED; *Not applicable*
ACCOMMODATION; *2 self-catering cottages, all linen provided, except towels or tea towels. Meter read at end of week*

DINING ROOM; *Not applicable*
VEGETARIAN; *Not applicable*
DISABLED ACCESS; *No*
GARDEN; *Yes*
PETS; *Yes must be kept under control*

THE OLD STABLES
Trefeinin Farm,
Llangorse,
Brecon,
Powys
LD3 0PS

Tel: 01874 658607

Trefeinon Farm is a pleasure to visit in its own right but if you take the opportunity of staying here in one of the attractively converted flats or the cottage which have all been created out of an old barn you will be superbly situated in magnificent countryside and within easy reach of so much that is beautiful and interesting about Wales. Judith Chalmers and the team from ITV's 'Wish You Were Here' visited not so very long ago. The farm has 200 acres with spectacular views of the Black Mountains to the North with Llangorse Lake, the largest natural lake in South Wales 2 miles to the South with the Brecon Beacons beyond. The farm provides wonderful walks, there is canoeing, indoor rock climbing, horse riding, mountain biking, golf and fresh water fishing nearby.

The accommodation which is spotless and well equipped has either one or two bedrooms each with its own character to sleep 2 or 4-5 people. They all have kitchens with all you could possibly require including a full size cooker and fridge. There is either a bath or shower, colour TV and a woodburning stove for Winter use. Off peak heating is also installed. All the flats run on a 50p electric meter. Duvets and pillows are provided but not linen, i.e. pair sheets or sheets/duvet cover and pillow cases, but these can be hired if required. Cots and high chairs are also available.

Breakfast can be taken in the Farmhouse if required and Pete and Liz Shepherd will point you in the right direction for the variety of restaurants within easy reach, to suit all pockets.

USEFUL INFORMATION

OPEN; *All year*
CHILDREN; *Very welcome*
CREDIT CARDS; *None taken*
PETS; *Yes by arrangement*

DINING ROOM; *Breakfast available in farmhouse if required*
DISABLED ACCESS; *No*
GARDEN; *Yes. 200 farm acres open to non-residents*

LLORAN GANOL FARM GUEST HOUSE

Llansilin,
Oswerstry,
Clwyd,
Wales
SY10 7QX

Tel: 016917 91287

Lloran Ganol Farm Guest House is situated in the most glorious countryside set in it's own valley surrounded by fields and woodland. You can be guaranteed a very warm and friendly welcome on arrival at this 300 acre working farm. Mrs. Jones and her family work this busy dairy, sheep and cattle farm, yet they still have time to share their lovely home with visitors. In the grounds of the farm is a three bedroomed detached luxury bungalow. The bungalow is exceptionally well appointed and comfortable. The bedrooms, one double, one twin and a single, all have bed linen provided. The fully equipped kitchen has the convenience of microwave oven, fridge, washing machine, tumble dryer and a dishwasher, so you won't have to spend time at the kitchen sink! The dining room is combined with the kitchen. The large sitting room is comfy just right for relaxing or watching television after a hard days sightseeing. Attached to the bungalow is a glass conservatory. Outside there is a lovely secluded garden with a lawned area, trees and shrubs, delightful to sit in on balmy summer evenings listening to the sound of the cows lowing. This is a attractive area the scenery is outstanding, painters, photographers and sketchers will be captivated by its beauty. Walkers will be in their element. There are other activities such as bird watching, horse riding, shooting and private trout fishing. Mrs. Jones also opens her farmhouse to guests for Bed and Breakfast and is a member of the Wales Tourist Board.

USEFUL INFORMATION

***OPEN:** All year*
***CHILDREN:** Welcome*
***CREDIT CARDS:** None taken*
***DISABLED ACCESS:** Not really*
***GARDEN:** Yes with garden furniture*
***PETS:** No*
***ACCOMMODATION:** Three bedroomed bungalow. B&B available*

RHIW FFRANC FARM HOLIDAY APARTMENTS
& RIDING CENTRE

Pentwyn,
Abersychan,
Nr Pontypool,
Gwent
NP4 7TJ

Tel: 01495 775069/772886
Tel & Fax: 01633 250660

This interesting place set in 90 acres of quiet, unspoilt Mountainside with breathtaking panoramic views stretching 30 miles, is within 5 minutes walk of the village post office and bus service. You are invited to relax and enjoy the comfort and peace of the three self-catering holiday apartments which were once Iron Workers' cottages - within the history of Rhiw Ffranc one can see that it is mentioned in the early 1840's with 'The Pentwyn Iron Company' attempting to find accommodation for their workers from 1827 onwards. The three traditionally stone-built converted cottages with 3ft thick walls sleep up to 4 people in the two downstairs apartments and up to 6 upstairs. Each apartment has its own stone-built porch entrance leading to the lounge with colour TV and bed settees, kitchen/dining room with electric cooker, fridge and microwave, one bedroom with double bed (leading onto patio on the downstairs apartments) plus extra bedroom with bunk beds in the upstairs apartment. The bathrooms have showers and there is electric central heating. They are all tastefully decorated and comfortably furnished. One of the downstairs apartments is adapted for any handicapped guests.

Rhiw Ffranc Riding Centre is ideally suited for treks through forestry and over mountains with breathtaking views. The horses and ponies are safe but willing and all have a gentle disposition. There are qualified instructors. Accommodation for those on courses is full board and caters for vegetarians. You can bring your own horse or pony. Rhiw Ffranc also offers riding for adults and children who are staying in the magnificent self-catering apartments. A super way to spend a holiday.

USEFUL INFORMATION

OPEN; *All year*
CREDIT CARDS; *None taken*
CHILDREN; *Welcome*
DISABLED ACCESS; *Yes, ground floor apartment*
ACCOMMODATION; *3 self-catering cottages*

BRYNDERI
2 High Street,
Saundersfoot,
Pembrokeshire,
Wales
SA69 9EJ

Tel: 01834 813496

Brynderi has a well equipped self-contained flat available for people wanting to stay in Saundersfoot at anytime of the year. Almost on top of the beach and the harbour it could not be better situated. You will find it spotlessly clean and well equipped with everything you need to make you comfortable and relaxed.It is very spacious with large kitchen/diner, comfortable lounge, large bedroom with twin beds and smaller bedroom with double bed.

The bathroom has a shower over the bath and an airing cupboard. The large garden has beautiful views over Carmarthen Bay. It is owned by Hazel Wadey and John James who own the next door, Harbour Light, an excellent guest house with a great reputation for food and hospitality. Saundersfoot is a pleasant holiday resort, with a pretty 17th century harbour and safe sandy beaches. The scenery is wonderful and the village charming. Winter short breaks are very attractively priced.

USEFUL INFORMATION

OPEN;*All year*
CREDIT CARDS;*Visa/Access/Master/Diners*
PETS;*Yes, by arrangement*

CHILDREN;*Welcome*
DISABLED ACCESS;*No*
PARKING; *Yes*

MAERDY COTTAGES
Taliaris,
Nr. Llandeilo,
Carmarthenshire
SA19 7DA

Tel: 01550 77448
Fax:01550 777067

The Maerdy nestles in a protected corner of the particularly pretty Talley Valley on the norther edge of the Brecon Beacons National Park. The farmhouse is probably 300 years old and steeped in history and around it are grouped some of the most attractive and superbly equipped self-catering cottages all with their own mature gardens and streams. The cottages all have generous log fires - wonderful for the winter evenings especially at Christmas time. It is idyllic and no one would ever be at a loss for something to do or see in this romantic part of Wales. Such is the care and thought with which these old stone buildings have been converted and furnished that details such as 'allergy bedding' are catered for. Talking of catering, if you do not wish to cook for yourselves you can order meals from a menu supplied prior to your arrival. The food is delicious and especially welcome if you have a special occasion to celebrate during your stay. Mrs Jones the owner is renowned for her catering service. Each cottage uniquely different. The Maerdy Farmhouse with its typical farmhouse kitchen, big enough for 8 to sit comfortably round the table is the largest. People used to larger houses will particularly enjoy the unique atmosphere of the Farmhouse. Beautiful old furniture, impressive beams and panelling with modern comforts and a splendid feeling of relaxation makes this house enjoyed by young and old alike. The Granary Cottage is upside down! To capture the view of the valley the living room and kitchen are upstairs; this will sleep 5 comfortably. The smallest Maerdy Cottage is ideal for a couple or a young family. The comfortable living room has a door that leads onto the patio. The cottages face south and catch the sun from 7am-7pm.The Stable Cottage, a C17th stable block, is uniquely different with its original beams and impressive arches. Set slightly above the other cottages, it nestles against the hill overlooking the valley and alongside the stream. Being on one level this is ideal for the elderly, parents with toddlers, the infirm and the disabled. The interior has been planned for wheelchair users.Barn Cottage is recently converted from the old farm barn. All the original features have been retained creating a genuine cottage feel plus its own little private garden. Dan y Cefn set on the other side of the River Dulais, is just a few minutes drive from The Maerdy. It commands fabulous views up the valley towards Talley, an idyllic location. Starter hampers of food, shopping for the disabled or for anyone else is all part of the excellent service The Maerdy has to offer. It would be true to say that here you will find the services of a first class hotel with the comforts of a country cottage.

USEFUL INFORMATION

OPEN;*All year*
CREDIT CARDS;*Yes*
DISABLED ACCESS;*Yes. One cottage Wheelchair accessible. 2 suitable for the less able.*
ACCOMMODATION; *6 cottages, very high standard*

CHILDREN;*Welcome. Cots, high chairs, stair gates*
CATERING;*Daily catering service for lunches and dinners by arrangement*
PETS; *By arrangement*

RED HOUSE FARM,
Trefeglwys,
Caersws,
Powys
SY17 5PN

Tel: 01686 430285

Red House Farm is a self contained part of a 300 acre working family farm with beef, sheep, pigs and poultry. A wonderful place to stay for people of any age but perhaps especially good for children who can learn what farming is all about. You will find Red House Farm just two miles from three villages, Trefeglwys, Caersws and Llandinam where there are shops and a good inn. The situation is superb with stunning panoramic views over the Trannon Valley, and perfectly placed for anyone who wants to enjoy the freedom of a self-catering holiday based in a house which is ideally situated for touring Mid-North or South Wales. Within a radius of 7 miles you can find; Pony trekking, Sailing, Angling in a variety of waters, Nature Trails and woodland walks. There are two leisure/sports centres, a Quad motor cycling centre, Golf practice range and course as well as Clay Pigeon Shooting.Bird watchers will think they are in paradise with 150 recorded species to look for including the red kite. Many seasonal events offer great days out and slightly further field are several narrow gauge railways, the National Centre for Alternative Technology, historical sites from Roman times onwards, Powys Castle, Theatr Hafren, Acton Scott working farm museum, and the coast is only 35 minutes by car. Because Red House Farm is a working farm dogs are not permitted.

The accommodation is self-contained and will sleep up to 5 people with 2 double bedrooms and 1 twin bedroom with a cot. The whole house has an air of relaxed comfort about it. The cosy carpeted lounge has a supply of logs for chilly days although the efficient central heating does keep the house beautifully warm even on the worst of winter days. Kitchens sometimes let one down in self-catering establshments but not so here. Everything is spotlessly clean and equipped with all you could wish for including laundry facilities. It is an ideal family holiday house. The finishing touch to a holiday at Red House Farm is the warmth of welcome on arrival when you will always find someone to meet you and provide you with a welcome cup of tea.

USEFUL INFORMATION

OPEN; *All year*
PETS; *Not permitted*
GARDEN; *Yes*
W.T.B Grade 4 - ***Welcome Host***

CHILDREN; *Welcome*
DISABLED ACCESS; *No*
ACCOMMODATION; *Sleep up to 5 + cot*

PANTGWYN FARM,
Whitemill,
Carmarthen,
Carmarthenshire
SA32 7ES

Tel: 01267 290247
Fax: 01267 290880

Nestling in the hills above the beautiful Towy Valley, just 10 minutes from the end of the M4 and 4 miles from Carmarthen, lies the 18th century Farmhouse, Pantgwyn. Owned and run by Tim and Sue Giles, it is a quiet haven where guests are welcome to roam the farm and explore the local byways. In the spring you will see the sheep with their lambs. The pet goat will be found munching in some quiet corner, Chloe the dog will be happy to take you for a walk while Thomas the donkey, and Bobby the Shetland Pony will oblige with rides by prior arrangement, and along the farm lane to the house you will undoubtedly encounter the farm's free range chickens. It is a very happy place to stay and with so much to occupy one that you could almost have a holiday without leaving the farm! Wildlife abounds, foxes can be seen crossing the newly mown meadows where rabbits play. At dusk bats flit across the farmyard in search of insects or watch for the Barn Owl on the old cowshed. It is a truly delightful place.

In the Farmhouse there is very comfortable bed and breakfast accommodation and in the converted barn there are family suites and self-catering accommodation. The ground floor suite has been specially designed for the disabled or the less mobile visitor. There are no steps and all doors are wide enough for wheel chairs. The Farmhouse has been renovated to a very high standard whilst not losing its original features. You have the opportunity to join residents in the attractive dining room for meals if you wish. Non-residents may also dine here on Friday and Saturday nights but must book in advance. The Restaurant is a friendly meeting place after the day's exploration which might have taken you bird watching, pony trekking or perhaps sketching or painting the glorious countryside. Sea and Freshwater fishing is available and there is both an 18 and a 9 hole golf course.

USEFUL INFORMATION

OPEN; *All year except Christmas.* ***RESTAURANT;*** *Super food. Welsh produce*
CHILDREN; *Welcome* ***VEGETARIAN;*** *Catered for*
CREDIT CARDS; *All major cards* ***DISABLED ACCESS;*** *Special suite*
LICENSED; *Yes* ***GARDEN;*** *Yes + farm*
ACCOMMODATION; *2 self-catering units each sleeping 4 people* ***PETS;*** *By arrangement*

DYTHEL HOLIDAY FLATS
Trimsaran Road,
Llanelli,
Carmarthenshire,
Wales

Tel: 01554 810849

Panoramic views of the fascinating Gower Peninsula and Black Mountain can be seen from the rural setting of Dythel Holiday Flats. Original farm buildings have been converted to modern well furnished and equipped holiday homes. The kitchens are well provided with microwave, fridge, automatic washer, iron and ironing board. Fresh linen is provided but not towels. The flats have night storage heaters and colour television. Cot with linen and duvet and high chair can be pre-booked. You can be assured of a personal and friendly welcome where nothing is too much trouble. Local amenities are many and varied and include fishing both sea and river, rambling and pony trekking. The country park at Pembrey offers lovely woodland nature trails and a superb beach.

USEFUL INFORMATION

OPEN; *March 18th-January 6th*
CHILDREN; *Welcome*
CREDIT CARDS; *None taken*
ACCOMMODATION; *3 self-catering flats sleeps up to 7, 2 are*

DISABLED ACCESS; *No*
GARDEN; *Play area/reception area*
PETS; *Yes by arrangement*

NON SMOKING

WHERE TO EAT

AVON

BATH

LE BEAUJOLAIS, 5 Chapel Row, Queens Square.
Tel: 01228 423417. A charming, informal French restaurant with red checked table cloths and fresh flowers on the tables. Food is a mixture of classic French styles prepared by French chefs. An excellent range of wines and liqueurs. Garden area has seating. Open: lunch Mon-Sat 12-
2.30pm. Dinner Mon-Sat 7-11pm. Children welcome. All major cards. Vegetarians catered for. Disabled access.

CORNWALL

BODMIN

WAFFLES COFFEE HOUSE, 14 Market House Arcade.
Tel: 01208 75500. A self-catering coffee shop and licensed restaurant, popular with locals and visitors alike. Superb range of food which is all home-made and prepared daily. Cordial staff and efficient service. Open 6 days from 8am-5pm. Children welcome. No credit cards. Take away service.

THE OLD INN, St Breward, Bodmin Moor.
Tel: 01208 850711. The classic Cornish Moorland pub is a great find for any visitor. Warm friendly atmosphere with stone walls, flagged floors, beamed ceilings and even a bar built from solid granite. An amazing selection of 80 Malt Whiskies. The food is excellent and extremely reasonable and served in an intimate restaurant. A wide range of Bar meals. Open: 12-3pm & 6.30-late. Children welcome. No credit cards. At least 5 vegetarian dishes. Pets welcome.

BUDE

THE BRASSERIE RESTAURANT, Lower Wharf Centre.
Tel: 01288 355275. A fascinating conversion of a 19th century warehouse, beautifully decorated with paintings and works by local artists. The areas inside the restaurant are totally 'non- smoking'. A very comprehensive menu, serving lunch and evening meals, and always a 'Dish of the Day' for vegetarians. Open: Mar-Oct 10-8.30pm 7 days a week. Children welcome. All major cards not Amex. Alcohol is served as a supplement to meals.

FALMOUTH

THE GEM FISH BAR & RESTAURANT, 6 Quarry Hill.

Tel: 01326 313640. This is a pleasant no nonsense eating establishment with attractively laid up tables and bench seating. The emphasis is on delicious food at reasonable prices and you can have anything from a cup of tea to a full blown 3 course meal with wine. The fish is especially good. Open daily 11.30-2pm & 4-7.30 Mon-Wed. 4-9pm Thurs-Sat. Children welcome. Good choice os vegetarian dishes. No credit cards.

THE PEAR TREE, 2 Bank Place.

Tel: 01326 312566. This fine, unassuming, brick built Georgian house is home to a restaurant of outstanding choice and service. There are 2 rooms available, one is non-smoking. The menu is mouthwatering and offers a choice of superb food, catering for vegetarians and special diets, with some notice. Comprehensive wine list. Open summer 7 till late. Winter 7-9pm Mon- Thurs, 7pm till late Fri & Sat. Open sun in July and August. All major cards. Children welcome.

HELSTON

THE COFFEE BEAN, 32 Coinagehall Street.

Tel: 01326 572970. This very nice family restaurant is not only warm and welcoming, it is quaint, small and has a wonderful atmosphere. Every month there is a 'Specials List'. You can drop in for a cup of coffee or a specialist pot of tea and indulge in a jam doughnut, oozing with home-made preserve, split and filled with cream!. Gourmet food at inexpensive prices. Open Mon-Sat 9-5pm Fri-Sat evening from Easter-Autumn. Children welcome, own menu. No credit cards. Vegetarians catered for.

THE YARD BISTRO, Trelowarren, Mawgan.

Tel: 01326 221595. Situated in the converted carriage house of Trelowarren, a 1000 acre estate on the banks of the Helston River. Trevor Bayfield is your host and chief chef, and ensures a delectable range of dishes for all palettes. The choice is anything from delicious local fresh fish to lamb or guineafowl. You will not be disappointed in either the food or the standard of service. Open through quiet periods; weekends only by booking. Closed Sun & Tues evenings, all day on Mon. Vegetarians very well catered for. Visa/ Master.

LOSTWITHIEL

TREWITHEN RESTAURANT, Fore Street.

Tel: 01208 872373. If you like to eat in a relaxed unhurried cottagey atmosphere then this is the place for you. Nestled in the Fowey River Valley.

Excellent food, specialises in Steak, Duckling, lobster and local fish. The menu is supplemented by a 'Specials Blackboard'. Open all year. Closed Sun & Mon in winter and Sun in summer. Visa/Master/Diners/Switch/Delta. Children welcome. At least 2 dishes for vegetarians.

MOUSEHOLE

CORNISH RANGE, 6 Chapel Street.

Tel: 01736 731488. 18th century licensed restaurant situated in a wonderful setting in the picturesque harbour village of Mousehole. Excellent food, specialising in the finest seafood, with chargrilled steaks and vegetarian dishes. Choice of wines. Served in attractive surroundings. Open all year. All major cards. Children welcome.

ST AGNES

SCHOONERS BISTRO, Trevaunance Cove.

Tel: 01872 553149. The murmur of the waves lapping the beach, the smell of the tangy salty air, the cries of the seagulls, fishing the shallows, - all this and superb food too! The Bistro is situated **on** the beach, in the cove, and is unique both in its position, and its quality and service. Wide and varied menu from traditional to more continental dishes. Open: Easter-Sept, daily 10.30-4pm. Evenings 7pm till late. All major cards. Children welcome. Vegetarians and special diets catered for. Excellent wine list.

ST CLEER

THE STAG INN

Tel: 01579 342305. Believed to be 250 years old and complete with ghost, this friendly pub has stories of lights falling, glasses chinking and bar stools moving! Stone walls and simple furnishings go well with the local produce and real ales. Good value pub food, intimate diningroom for the evening. Extensive menu catering for every taste. Open 12-11pm. Children welcome in dining room, own menu. No credit cards. Vegetarians catered for.

ST IVES

THE GARRACK HOTEL, Burtallan Lane.

Tel: 01736 796199 Fax: 01736 798955. For those wanting a special meal in delightful surroundings, The Garrack Hotel has everything. Wonderful, locally produced food whenever possible, nearby Newlyn supplies fresh fish and fine seafood. The Garrack has its own storage tank for live lobsters The unique pricing policy on wines offers exceptional value for more expensive wines. Open All year except January 1st. Children welcome. Coffee Shop. Vegetarians catered for. Disabled access.

ST MAWES
BROOMERS, 14 Marine Parade.
Tel: 01326 270440. The views from this charming restaurant are perfect, added to this the quality service and superb food offered, and you have the makings of a meal to remember. The extensive menu offers breakfast, morning coffee, lunch, afternoon tea, evening meal and even a take-away service. Booking for an evening meal is advised as the restaurant is usually rather busy and is a popular venue. Good wine list. Open daily mid Mar-end Jun Tues to Sun, Jun-Sept 7 days, Oct & Nov Tues to Sun, Dec-Mar evenings only. Times 10am-5pm & 7-10pm. Special children's menu. Visa & Mastercard. Vegetarians catered for. Special diets - please phone.

THE LIZARD
MOUNTS BAY INN, Churchtown, Mullion.
Tel: 01326 240221 Fax: 01326 240249. This 100 year old pub is home ot Barrie and Crystina Petterson, who extend their hand of hopsitality to all their customers. Having the charm and atmosphere of a good country inn, you can enjoy a pleasant drink in good company, and sample the menu of classic English pub food. The menu is stimulating and enticing with a varied choice and price range for all. Open: summer-pub hours plus all day Sat & Sun. Winter-normal pub hours. Children in restaurant and childrens room. All major cards. Bar snacks. Accommodation. Pets welcome.

TRURO
FODDERS, Pannier Market, Back Quay.
Tel: 01872 71384. Fodders is quite unique and has a steady following of local people which always bodes well for any restaurant. Situated in an 18th century hayloft featuring much of the original stonework and beams. It is a friendly, informal establishment. Restaurant serving delicious wholefood menu. Tea room serving a wonderful 'teatime' spread. Open 10-5pm Mon-Sat inc. Not Bank Holidays. Children welcome. Wines and beers only. Vegetarian and special diets catered for.

KINGS ARMS, Tregony.
Tel: 01872 530202. A 16th century Inn with a welcoming, friendly atmosphere where you can relax and enjoy a drink and the good home-cooked fare from the wide ranging menu which caters for all tastes. Specials Blackboard. Bar food. Open all year. All major cards. Children welcome, own section on menu. At least 2 vegetarian dishes.

CLEVELAND

SALTBURN-BY-SEA

THE ELLERBY HOTEL, Ellerby, Hinderwell.

Tel: 01947 840342. Offers a wide range of meals both at lunchtime and in the evening every day of the week plus traditional Sunday lunch. Comprehensive menu. For the really hearty appetite the 'Farmhouse Supper' is a winner, and they also have an extensive 'Specials Board'. Rest: Sun-Thurs 12-2pm 7-9pm. Fri-Sat: 7.15-9.30pm. Children welcome. Games provided. All major cards. Always dishes for vegetaians.

Price Band: B

GRINKLE PARK HOTEL, Easington.

Tel: 01287 641278. Emphasis on quality and presentation in Restaurant. Good value bar food. Open all year. All major credit cards. Children welcome. Vegetarians catered for.

Price Band: B

DEVON

BLACKAWTON

THE SPORTSMAN'S ARMS, Henborough Post.

Tel: 01803 712231. This interesting pub is rapidly making a name for itself for its food and especially for the speciality of the house - fish. The steaks are also excellent along with lamb, duck, chicken and delicious local ham. This pub has a happy atmosphere and is well worth a visit. Open all year. Children welcome to eat. All major cards. Vegetarians catered for.

BOVEY TRACEY

INDIA COTTAGE, 38 Fore Street.

Tel: 01626 833111. An excellent Indian restaurant and take-away. This high quality establishment serves traditional Indian cuisine in pleasant and comfortable surroundings. Comprehensive menu, well stocked bar. Open summer 6-11.30pm 7 days a week. Winter 6-
11.30pm (closed Mon) 6 days a week. Excl. Bank Holidays. Children welcome. All major cards except Amex/Diners. Vegetarians catered for.

BUDLEIGH SALTERTON

MARIO AND FRANCO, Italian Restaurant, 1A High Street.

Tel: 01395 443330. The reputation of Mario and Franco's has grown rapidly and spread far and wide people come from quite long distances to take part in the gastronomic experience. The menu is full of delicious dishes , everything is prepared and cooked on the premises including the bread.

Superb Italian food Mario and Franco's is a great find. Open all year. Children welcome. All major cards. Vegetarians catered for. Award winning wine list.

CHAGFORD

WHIDDONS COFFEE HOUSE & ANTIQUE SHOP, High Street.

Tel: 01647 433406. The timeless town of Chagford is home of the delightful establishment named Whiddons. This thatched 16th century cottage in the heart of the town specialises in good old fashioned courtesty and service. Sandwiches, home-made cakes, strawberry jam, freshly baked scones and lashings of clotted cream! Wonderful. Open all year except Christmas Day. Children welcome. No credit cards.

EXETER

THE COWICK BARTON, Cowick Lane, St Thomas.

Tel: 01392 274011. Built in the late 16th century you enter Cowick Barton through a four-foot wide door and walk straight into an amazing interior. The Great Hall has a remarkable Tudor fireplace modernised by the Victorians by a facing of coloured tiles. It is gracious and welcoming and here you may dine extremely well, looked after by a well-trained courteous staff. Well presented good value menu, wide choice. Open every day. Last orders Lunch 2pm. Evening 9.30pm. Children welcome. All major cards. Always a vegetarian choice.

HOLSWORTHY

THE WHITE HART HOTEL

TEL: 01409 253475. This 400 year old inn is very special, especially to the people of Holsworthy and those who stream into the busy town on market days. You will always feel comfortable here, the locals are friendly and cheerful chatter makes a happy atmosphere on its own. Food is all important and there is great emphasis on local produce. Good, wholesome and imaginative menu. Wide ranging bar food meals. Separate menu for vegetarians. Open all year 11-3pm & 6-11pm. Children welcome. Visa/ Mastercard. Accommodation.

ILFRACOMBE

THE HELE BAY HOTEL, Hele.

Tel: 01271 867795. The Hele bay is a comfortable establishment, run along the lines of a friendly 'local pub'. It offers good service in a warm, imformal atmosphere. There is a childrens games room, a skittles rooms and a large car park. The restaurant covers between 35 and 40 persons, and there are special meals for children, all are at very reasonable prices. Open all year. Children welcome. Visa. Vegetarians catered for. Bar snacks. Accommodation.

KINGSBRIDGE

CYDER PRESS RESAURANT, Stancombe Farm, Sherford.

Tel: 01548 531151. If you thought it was impossible to find total peace, quiet and tranquillity then you have not visited Stancombe Farm in the glorious South Hams of Devon. At the beautiful 17th century thatched Cyder Press Restaurant you will receive the warmest of welcomes, offering the best of West Country fare and traditional Sunday lunches (booking advisable). Open evenings all year. Daily Apr-Oct (light lunches, cream Teas etc). Children welcome. All major cards. Licensed. Vegetarians catered for.

JOURNEY'S END INN, Ringmore.

Tel: 01548 810205. Nestling very comfortably in the beautiful and unspoilt, thatched village in the heart of the South Hams countryside, Journey's End is one of the oldest pubs in Devon. There are open log fires in all the bars and in the intimate dining rooms which seats 30. The menu at the Inn is interesting and varied and there are regular 'Food Feature' weekends. Fresh local produce used whenever possible. Open weekdays: 11.30-3.30pm & 6.30-11pm. Open all day Sunday. Children welcome, games room and garden, own menu. Mastercard/Visa. Vegetarians catered for. Accommodation.

LYDFORD

LYDFORD HOUSE HOTEL

Tel: 01822 820347. This award winning hotel is 'One of Britain's Great Little Hotels', situated just outside the historic village Lydford on the edge of Dartmoor. You are invited to enjoy leisurely meals served by an efficient and unobtrusive staff, the table d'Hote dinner is a three course meal of generous proportions with a wide choice at each course. Afternoon tea served in the Tea Room during the season. Traditional Sunday lunch. Open all year. Children over 5years. Visa/Mastercard. Licensed. Accommodation.

OKEHAMPTON

PLYMOUTH INN, 26 West Street.

TEL: 01837 53633. 16th century coaching inn in the small market town close to Dartmoor. Excellent home-cooking using local produce, Mexican, English and French. Lovely family room has been attractively furnished, children may eat in the restaurant where they have their own menu. Full bar menu. Take-away pizza service. Open all year. Children welcome. All major cards except Amex & Switch. Vegetarians catered for.

THE BARTON, Belstone.

Tel: 01837 840371. This is the quintessential Dartmoor village tea shop, situated in an idyllic position in the heart of Belstone Village. Renowned for it's cream teas and delicious home-made cakes. It is recommended by the 'Ramblers Association' and featured in the 'Teapot trail'. Sunday lunches available but must be booked in advance. Open all year summer 2-6pm, winter 2-5pm. Children welcome. Licensed for Sunday lunch. Accommodation.

OTTERY ST MARY

OSWALDS, 25 Silver street.
Tel: 01404 812262. Oswalds is an old stone building, lying adjacent to the magnificence of St Mary's, the parish church. A congenial French restaurant offering a wide ranging menu enhanced by an interesting use of sauces, many flavoured with fruit and other original ingredients. The result is memorable eating. Open Mon-Sat 7pm Lunch by appointment. Children welcome. Visa/Master/Diners/Amex. Vegetarian on request.

PLYMOUTH

THE BABA INDIAN RESTAURANT, 134 Vauxhall Street, The Barbican.
Tel: 01752 250677/256488. This is an excellent restaurant, the owner is 'Baba' Laskar has everything under control, his friendly and efficient staff will tend to your every need. The restaurant is situated in one of Plymouth's oldest buildings on the delightful Barbican and has just the right atmosphere in which to enjoy a meal. The menu is wide ranging to suit your taste and temperature! On the first Tuesday of every month a 9 Course Banquet is held, with two sittings 6pm and 9pm, these are very popular so booking is essential. A Take Away Service is available delivered free of charge within four miles for orders over ten pounds. Open Sun-Thurs 5pm-midnight, Fri-Sat 5.30-1am, every Sunday Family Buffet 12 noon-6pm, every first Tuesday of the month 9 Course Banquet - first sitting 6pm second sitting 9pm booking only. English dishes. Children welcome. All major cards. Several vegetarian dishes.

PIERMASTERS RESTAURANT, The Barbican.
Tel: 01752 229345. Just 10 minutes from the city centre, on the historic Barbican, is this charming restaurant and bistro. Excellent cuisine, you will not be disappointed either in the service provided, or the food consumed. Open all year, lunch and evening meal. Children welcome. All major cards. Vegetarians catered for.

TRATTORIA PESCATORE, 36 Admiralty Street, Stonehouse.
Tel: 01725 600201. This highly recommended restaurant serves the most delicious gourmet food in very pleasant surroundings. The regularly changing menu has meat and poultry dishes with an emphasis on fish. Super starters and delectable desserts. There is a good wine list to compliment the food. The owner is a talanted chef who goes out of his way to make sure yourmeal is just right. An excellent choice you will want to return again and again.

Open Mon-Fri for lunch, Mon-Sat for dinner. Children welcome. All major cards except Amex and Diners. Always several vegetarian dishes.

ROCKBEARE

ORIENTAL PROMISE, Old London Road.

Tel: 01404 823323/823328 Fax: 01404 823203. Wonderful oriental restaurant serving the most delicious food, Peking, Szechaun, Cantonese and Far East. You can have a set meal which can be varied to suite individual taste, or simply choose from the extensive menu. Superb. Open for lunch & evening meal except Tuesday. Children welcome. All major cards. Vegetarians catered for. Good take-away service.

SEATON

THE KETTLE RESTAURANT & BED AND BREAKFAST, 15 Fore Street.

Tel: 01297 20428. This very homely restaurant was built around 1800 and is situated on the main street. Traditional English fare and Continental dishes. Open all year. Children welcome. No credit cards. Several dishes for vegetarians. Licensed. Accommodation.

SIDMOUTH

DI PAOLO'S RESTAURANT, Radway Place, Vicarage Road.

Tel: 01395 578314. The finest Italian restaurant in East Devon is housed in a late 1800 Victorian building. The food is just superb, with a Tuscan influence. Being so close to the sea the seafood dishes are wonderful. Local produce is used as much as possible including fresh fish, meat and vegetables. Open lunch 12noon-2pm. Evenings 6.30-10pm(last order), Fri-Sat 6.30-10.30pm. Closed Mon. Children welcome. All major cards except Amex/ Diners. Vegetarians catered for.

TAVISTOCK

THE HARVEST HOME, Gulworthy.

Tel: 01822 611022. This is such a welcoming pub in a delightful setting near Tavistock. A glassroofed, non-smoking family rooms with exposed beams. Best described as high quality, traditioan West Country Pub Fare. The menu changes daily and there are always very tasty Daily Specials. Open summer 11-11pm Sun 12-10.30pm. Oct-Apr 12-3pm & 6-11pm Sun 7-10.30pm no food Sun/Mon evenings in winter. Children welcome. All major cards. Bar food. Wide range of vegetarian dishes.

THE PETER TAVY INN, Peter Tavy.

Tel: 01822 810348. A 15th century inn set on the Western fringe of Dartmoor just two miles north of the delightful market town of Tavistock. The food served is rapidly acquiring a fine reputation. Everything from fish to venison and cheese is local and the vegetables are grown in the South Hams. The menu is mouthwatering and delicious. Open all year summer Mon-Thurs 11.30-2.30pm, Fri & Sat 11.30-3pm, Sun 12-3pm. Eve Mon-Sat 6.30-11pm Sun 7-10.30pm. Winter Mon-Thurs 12-2.30pm, Fri-Sun 12-3pm. Children accompanied by adults. All major cards except Diners/Amex. Vegetarian and other diets catered for. Accommodation.

THE ROYAL STANDARD, Mary Tavy.
Tel: 01822 810289. The Royal Standard has stood since the 16th century and at one time had a miners' cottage attached to it. It is a comfortable, popular pub with chunky pine tables, a roaring log fire and an attractive bar. The reputation for taditional pub fare grows steadily, thereis an extensive vegetarian selection and everyday the Specials Board announces one or another of ones favourite dishes. Open 11-2.30pm & 6.30-11pm. Children welcome. No credit cards. Garden. Disabled access.

TOTNES

ANNE OF CLEVES LICENSED TEA ROOMS & RESTAURANT, 56 Fore Street.
Tel: 01803 863186. Originally an ex-sea captains house built about 400 years ago it still retains the exposed beams and timber joists. When you walk in you are welcomed by the restful ambiance created by the antique furniture and fresh flowers. Wide selection of delicious dishes catering for all tastes. Home-made cakes and scones for cream teas. Traditional Sunday Roasts. Open Mon-Sat 9.15-5.30pm Sun 10.30-5.30pm. Children welcome, own section in menu. No credit cards. At least 5 vegetarian dishes. Licensed.

COPPA DOLLA INN & RESTAURANT, Bradhempston, Nr Totnes.
Tel: 01803 812455. The charm of this delightful inn is undoubted but it is enhanced by the blissful absence of any form of machine or pool table. The bars are alsways busy and welcoming. It is a perfect atmosphere in which to enjoy the top of the range cuisine, including an A La Carte menu, varied home-cooked bar meals, snacks and a choice of six excellent vegetarian dishes. Open 11.30-2.30pm & 6.30-11pm. Children in dining areas only. Visa/Master. Lovely garden. 2 luxury apartments.

THE RED SLIPPER, Stoke Gabriel.
Tel: 01803 782315. The Red Slipper is situated in the heart of the charming, unspoilt village of Stoke Gabriel, and is pleasing guest house and restaurant. Serving traditional English fayre and is open for morning coffee, lunch, afternoon teas, evening meals and Sunday Lunches, (booking is essential for evening meals and Sunday lunch). Open all year. Children welcome. No credit cards. Vegetarians catered for. Garden. Accommodation.

DORSET

BLANDFORD FORUM

TANNERS RESTAURANT, 13/15 West Street.

Tel: 01258 453233. Situated in West Street close to the English Tourist Board stands Tanners Restaurant, where fodd has been served since 1906. Margaret and David Bunch offer a pleasant and friendly atmosphere, where the service is attentive. All dishes are traditionally British, and offer a set luncheon, all day breakfasts, a wide and tasty choice of grills and vegetarian dishes. Home-made cakes and a Dorset Cream Tea. Open 9.30-6.30. Closed Mondays. Sun 10.30-
6.30pm. Children welcome. No creadit cards. Licensed.

DURHAM

BARNARD CASTLE

THE MORRITT ARMS HOTEL, Greta Bridge, Rokeby.

Tel: 01833 627232. Charles Dickens stayed here when he was researching 'Nicholas Nickleby'. Reomantic and unspoilt, the food is imaginative both in the restaurant and the bar. Open 24 hours. Children welcome. All major cards. Always several choices for vegetarians.

Price Band B

DARLINGTON

THE COACHMAN HOTEL & LAS CAROZZA RESTAURANT, Victoria Road. Tel: 01325 286116. Charming hotel with a restaurant that is renowned in the area. Open all year. Children welcome. All major cards. Vegetarians catered for.

Price Band B

WALWORTH CASTLE HOTEL

Tel: 01325 485470. Unique hotel in 12th century castle. Excellent food, bars, entertainment. Open all year. Children welcome. All major cards. Vegetarians catered for.

Price Band: B

DURHAM

CENTURION INN, Firs Terrace, Langley Park.

Tel: 0191 373 1323. 3 miles from Durham, this is an interesting inn which is very different. Converted from a large house, it is welcoming and friendly and has two talented chefs who produce delicious and imaginative food both in the restaurant and bar. Open 12-3pm & 6-11pm. Mastercard/Visa/ Barclaycard. Vegetarian dishes. Children welcome - half portions.

Price Band: A

MIDDLETON-IN-TEESDALE

THE TEESDALE HOTEL, Market Square.

Tel: 01833 640264. Located in the heart of the majestic and colourful High Pennines, possessing the highest and perhaps most dramatic peaks of the whole Pennine range. Family run hotel that once was a coaching inn. Delicious food, tasty Bar Meals, Daily Specials, Morning Coffee, Afternoon Tea. Open all hours. Children welcome. All major cards. Several dishes for vegetarian.

Price Band A

STRATHMORE

ARMS INN, Holwick.

Tel: 01833 640362. Attractive inn in an old lead mining hamlet. Wonderfully remote but easily accessible in an area of the North Pennines of outstanding beauty. Home-prepared food, local ingredients. A little different to normal. Open 12 noon-11pm. Children welcome in room at side of bar. No credit cards. 2-3 vegetarian dishes daily. 2 bedrooms not ensuite. Ideal for families.

Price Band: A

GLOUCESTERSHIRE

BIBURY'

THE SWAN

Tel: 01285 740695. 17th century Cotswold stone coaching inn. Attractive gardens by the river. Fishing. Beautifully cooked and presented food both at lunch and dinner. Children welcome. All major credit cards. Open all year. Vegetarians catered for.

Price Band: B/C

BOURTON-ON-THE-WATER

THE MOUSETRAP INN, Lansdowne.

Tel: 01451 20579. This old fashioned pub has a major plus - a car park, something that is like gold dust in Bourton. Good, well kept beer and home-cooked food including the specialities'Desperate Dans Cow Pie' and Rabbit Pie. Friendly, unpretentious and sensible prices. Bed and Breakfast available. Children welcome. No credit cards. Open: 12-3pm & 6.30-11pm. Vegetarians dishes.

Price Band: A

THE OLDE CHARM, 1, The Chestnuts.

Tel: 01451 20244. Charming 300 year old restaurant with unobtrusive, friendly service. Food is available all day, the hours depending on the time of the year. Excellent home-made soups, fresh salads, succulent roast meats and a

selection of desserts. Cotswold Cream Tea very popular. The bedrooms are beautifully appointed and en suite. Access/Visa/Amex/Diners. Children welcome but no under 5 facilities. Open: approx 10.30am-9.30pm.
Price Band: A/B

CHEDWORTH
THE SEVEN TUNS, Queen Street.
Tel: 01285 720242. Small 17th century pub - the small lounge bar only seats 16-18. Charming walled water garden. Simple, good pub fare with the emphasis on steaks at night. Great value for money. Open: 12-2.30pm 6.30-11pm. Closed Monday lunch in winter. No credit cards. Well behaved children welcome. Usually 2 dishes for vegetarians.
Price Band: A/B

CHELTENHAM
THE KINGS HEAD, Church Road, Bishops Cleeve, Cheltenham
Tel: 01242 673260. 3 miles from Cheltenham on the A435 Evesham road, this wonderful old thatched 16th century inn is a listed building standing next tot a tithe barn and believed to be the oldest inhabited building in the village. No restaurant but delicious 'Daily Specials' and snacks served in the busy bar. Open: 11-2.30pm & 6-11pm. Children not allowed in bar area. Beer garden. No credit cards. 2 dishes for vegetarians.
Price Band: A

CHIPPING CAMDEN
THE SEYMOUR HOUSE HOTEL, High Street.
Tel: 01386 840429. Lovely mellow building, with all sorts of interesting shapes in the beautifully appointed rooms. Delicious food at all times, morning coffee and afternoon tea. Open all year. Children welcome. All major credit cards. Vegetarians catered for.
Price Band: B

FRAMPTON MANSELL
THE CROWN HOTEL, Frampton Mansell, Nr Stroud.
Tel: 01285 760601 Fax: 01285 760681. Parts of this fascinating building date back to 1595. It is tucked away in the corner of the village looking out over a magnificent valley. You would be difficult to please if you did not enjoy the traditional home-made food which includes Pan Fried Liver and Onions, Gloucester Sausage served with Bubble and Squeak and Poached Fillet of Salmon with Hollandaise Sauce. Bread and Butter Pudding is another favourite with diners. Children welcome. All major cards except AMEX.
Price Band: A/B

GLOUCESTER

FLEECE HOTEL, 19 Westgate Street.

Tel: 01452 522762. Modernised Tudor coaching inn with 12th century vaulted crypt. Good food, sensible prices. Access/Visa/AMEX. Children welcome. Vegetarians catered for.

Price Band: A

MORETON-IN-MARSH

THE MARSHMALLOW RESTAURANT, High Street.

Tel: 01608 651536. This charming restaurant has many accolades one such being the Good Food Guide and another being voted tea shop of the year 1993/4. It is open for morning coffee, lunches, afternoon teas, candlit suppers and traditional Sunday lunch. The food is superb quality and meticulously prepared. Open 7 days & 5 nights. Children welcome. No credit cards. Vegetarian and special diets catered for. Licensed.

NEWLAND

THE OSTRICH, Nr Coleford.

Tel: 01594 33260. Charming village pub, no juke boxes, no one armed bandits but superior quality food with normally a choice of ten dishes including local specialities Venison Pie and Game Casserole. Wide choice of bar snacks. Attractive walled garden. Open: Mon-Sat 11.30-

3pm &6-11pm. Sun 12-3pm & 7-10.30pm. Children welcome in the restaurant and garden. No credit cards. Vegetarian dishes.

Price Band: A/B

NORTH NIBLEY

THE BLACK HORSE INN

Tel: 01453 546841 Fax: 01453 547474. 16th century true village inn which opens its welcoming doors with the same friendliness to strangers as it does to those who come in regularly for a pint and a chat, a good meal or a game of dominoes. You will find it on the B4060 midway between the old market towns of Dursley and Wotton-under-Edge. Full of old world charm the pub offers an extensive lunchtime and evening menu from good home-cooked dishes to light bar snacks. Try their home-made mushroom soup - it will be hard to find its equal. Children permitted if eating. All major cards.

Price Band: A/B

STOW-ON-WOLD

OLD STOCKS HOTEL, The Square.

Tel: 01451 830666 Fax: 01451 870014. A Grade II Listed 16th-17th century building enhanced by the mellow Cotswold stone of the period. The restaurant offers a wide variety of dishes including those for vegetarians which will tempt even the most jaded palate. The chef is always happy to

produce something special for a child. Good range of bar food. Children welcome. Visa/MasterCard.
Price Band: A/B

THE ROYALIST, Digbeth Street.
Tel: 01457 830470. The oldest building in Stow and features in the Guinness Book of Records as the oldest inn in England dating from 947AD. It is a Grade II Listed building of both architectural and historical interest. The 'Coffee Shop' is open from 10am-5.30pm serving tasty home-made bar food. Children welcome. Visa/MasterCard.
Price Band: A/B

GRAPEVINE HOTEL, Sheep Street.
Tel: 01451 830344 Fax: 01451 832278. Delightful award winning hotel where nothing is too much trouble. Dinner 7pm-9.30pm, Bar Meals 12-2pm & 7-9pm. Closed Christmas Eve - January 12th. English and French haute cuisine. Daily changing menu. The bar serves a delicious selection of unusual dishes. Children welcome. No dogs. Afternoon teas. No smoking restaurant. All major credit cards. Vegetarian dishes.
Price Band: C

TETBURY
THE TROUBLE HOUSE INN, Cirencester Road.
Tel: 01666 502206. 17th century inn with fascinating history plus a friendly ghost. Traditional and friendly. Serves good casserole and Indian curries at night. No cooked meals on Sundays. Open: 11-2.30pm &6-11pm. Children welcome. Large garden and field to play in. No credit cards. 4 dishes for vegetarians.
Price Band: A/B

TEWKESBURY
THE ABBEY MILL, Mill Street.
Tel: 01684 292287. Originally built in the 8th century, The Abbey Mill belongs to the past but today it still has the same charm even though the interior has given way to a modern comfortable restaurant. The food is wonderful with many themed nights including Medieval Banquets!. It is beautifully run and will never disappoint. Open all year for banquets & restaurants, Tea Shop & Patio Easter-September. No credit cards. Children welcome. Vegetarians catered for. Disabled access in summer only via Tea Shop.

UPPER ODDINGTON
THE HORSE AND GROOM, Upper Oddington, Nr Stow-on-the-Wold.
This 16th century inn is as charming inside as it is out. Very much the focal centre of the village - you will find regulars at the bar every day. Everyone is

made to feel welcome. Good traditional food comes out of the immaculate kitchen which offers everything from fresh fish to game in season. The bar menu suggests home-cooked daily. Specials as well as the simpler freshly cut sandwich. Children welcome. All major cards except AMEX and Diners. Price Band: A/B

HAMPSHIRE

BARTON-ON-SEA
THE VENTANA, Marine Drive.
Tel: 01425 610309. This friendly pub run by the Blanksby family stands literally on the edge of a cliff giving it one of the best pub views in England. To the east is Hurst Castle, to the south east the Isle of Wight and the Needles, on the west is Hengesbury Head and Swanage. The emphasis is on a warm welcome and quality products and value for money. Home-cooked traditional but slightly adventurous food is on the menu. There are always vegetarian dishes and small meals for children. There is a Play Area and a Barbecue which seats 40. Visa/Mastercard only.
Price Band A

BROCKENHURST
THE THATCHED COTTAGE HOTEL & RESTAURANT, 16 Brookley Road. Tel: 01590 623090 Fax: 01590 623479. This very pretty hotel has a charming Tea Garden wherein summer the tables have lace tablecloths and napkins and are protected by umbrellas. The hotel specialises in a complete English Breakfast and their famous afternoon teas, complete with a three tier cake stand. It has the accolade of being voted by the English Tourist Board, one of the best cream teas in the south of England. In the evening exquisite culinary delights are freshly prepared by 'Chefs on Show' in thier open kitchen. A gourmet table d'hote menu complimented by a selection of fine wines and beverages, is set in a unique and casual atmosphere by romantic cnadlelight. Children welcome. Visa/Mastercard.
Price Band: A/B

THE SNAKE CATCHER, Lyndhurst Road.
Tel: 01590 622348. Interesting pub with strange tale about the name. Wide range, exciting dishes, value for money. Open all year. Visa/Mastercard. Children welcome. Vegetarians catered for.
Price Band A

CHERITON
THE JOLLY FARMER, Petersfield Road.
Tel: 01962 771252. Next to National Trust property, Hinto Ampner on the A272 Winchester to Petersfield Road, 6 miles outside Winchester.

Hospitalbe, small tasty menu which includes a Beef stew and a Hot Pot that would be hard to equal for miles around. Accommodation available. No credit cards. Children to eat only. Vegetarian dishes on request.
Price Band: A

DAMERHAM

THE COMPASSES INN, Nr Fordingbridge.
Tel: 017253 231. Friendly 16th century coaching inn on the village green. Damerham is a Conservation Area on the edge of the New Forest. An extensive, beautifully cooked and presented menu makes food a must here. Real fires in winter, large garden for summer. Accommodation. Open 11-2.30pm & 6-11pm. Sat 11-11pm. Visa/Mastercard. Well behaved children welcome. Vegetarian choice.
Price Band: A/B

EAST MEON

YE OLDE GEORGE INN, Church Street.
Tel: 01730 87481. Freehouse with origins dating back to the 13th century. From May-September open all day and in addition to the bars and restaurant, both serving fresh and imaginative food, you can call in for a Cream Tea. Mastercard/Visa. Children in play area. 6 plus dishes for vegetarians. Ensuite accommodation.
Price Band: A/B

EMSWORTH

THE BLUE BELL INN, 29 South Street.
Tel: 01243 373394. This delightful inn is within 100 yards of Emsworth Harbour and Mill Pond and is a Mecca for many people who live in the area and who have discovered the warm, genuine welcome offered by Tom Babb and his partner Jackie. Fish is the main dish in various forms however, there are plenty of good tried and trusted favourites included in the menu. Daily Specials Blackboard. Open all year. Well behaved children welcome. No credit cards. Limited wine list. Vegetarians catered for.

THE CROWN HOTEL, High Street.
Tel: 01243 372806 Fax: 01243 370082. Jester's Restaurant, with it's comfortable and pleasant surroundings, offers an exciting International menu and comprehensive wine list. For a more informal meal or snack the buffet bar has outstanding reputation for serving home-made quality fayre at inexpensive prices. The hotel is situated in the idyllic harbourside village of Emsworth whcih encompasses a wealth of fishing, boat building, sailmaking and leisure pastimes and experiences. Children welcome. Major credit cards.
Price Band: A/B

36 ON THE QUAY, South Street.
Tel: 01243 375592. This is probably the best restaurant between Brighton and Southampton. The dining room of this yachting village cottage is full of surprises. What appears to be a bookcase opens to reveal a door to the wine cellar - with over 200 excellent wines from eleven pounds to one hundred and fifty pounds. The very grand cooking is executed with an ease that speaks of the true professional. There are courses of amuse-bouches and friandises and between them lightly fried scallops and bacon with herb noodles, salmon with olive oil dressing, and potato souffle with superb smoke salmon. If you enjoy sauces there are no better in the county especially with meat dishes. You really should try the Grand Marnier souffle afterwards. The service is perfection though a trifle pretentious - but who can fault this standard of excellence.
Price Band C

FACCOMBE
THE JACK RUSSELL INN, Faccombe, Nr Andover.
Tel: 01264 737315. Friendly pub 1,000ft above sea level on a privately owned estate. Opposite the manor house overlooking the village pond. Attractive food at affordable prices. Freehouse. Open all year. Children welcome to eat in conservatory. BBQs & Pig Roasts in summer. All major cards. Vegetarians catered for.
Price Band: A

FORDINGBRIDGE
LIONS COURT RESTAURANT & HOTEL, 29-31 High Street.
Tel: 01425 652006. Fine food and accommodation in a classic. 17th century English setting with gardens extending down to the River Avon. The area around Lions Court is rich in interest and activities. Delightful place. Children welcome. Visa/Amex/Diners/Mastercard.
Price Band: B

GREATHAM
THE SILVER BIRCH INN, Petersfield Road, Nr Liss.
Tel: 01420 538262. The food is plentiful, tasty and true good pub food. Friendly, welcoming landlords. For Golfers there are three courses nearby. Open 11-2.30pm & 5.30-11pm. No credit cards. Children to eat and in garden. Vegetarian dishes on request.
Price Band: A

HAMBLE
THE VILLAGE TEA ROOMS, High Street.
Tel: 01703 455583. The present owner, Christina Pullen, is a skilled and enthusiastic cook who virtually cooks or bakes everything she serves. Her

pastry is melt in the mouth and her cakes are irresistible and the scones are freshly baked served either with jam and cream or jam and butter or just butter. Delicious. It is AA recommended and also by the 1993 'Lets Stop for Tea' andthe 1995 'That Tea Room'. Open all year. Children welcome. No credit cards.

HIGHCLERE

THE YEW TREE, Hollington Cross, Andover Road, Nr Newbury.
Tel: 01635 253360. Highclere Castle is a mile away. For over 350 years travellers have been beating a path to this good inn. It is full of character and the food is superb. In the Restaurant the menu is fresh, cosmopolitan and traditional fare. In the Bar there are sandwiches and a range of Platters etc. It is a place that delights all who visit it. Open: 11-3pm &5.30-11pm. Children welcome. Visa/Euro/Mastercard. Vegetarian dishes.
Price Band:A/B

HORDLE

ORDLETON MILL HOTEL & PROVENCE RESTAURANT, Silver St, Nr Lymington.
Tel: 01590 682219. This privately owned hotel is a 17th century water mill house which has been sympathetically restored, extended and refurbished. The riverside location is spectacular with grounds that extend to five and a half acres on the banks of the River Avon Water. The nationally acclaimed Provence style dining room serves superb meals. During the summer months, breakfast and luncheon are served from the terrace, whcih also makes the perfect spot in which to take evening aperitifs whilst watching the fish jump. Children over 10 years. All major credit cards.
Price Band: B

LYNDHURST

THE NEW FOREST INN, Emery Down.
Tel: 01703 282329. Delightfully situated in the heart of the New Forest, the Inn has an unusual history, in the early 1700s, before a licence to sell beer was necessary, the story goes that a caravan stood on this site having claimed squatter's rights. The caravan now forms all of the front lounge porchway and the inn has been extended on either side. Open all year for Bed and Breakfast and has excellent food at sensible prices.
Price band: A

THE CROWN STIRRUP, Clay Hill.
Tel: 01703 282272. Mark & Kim Pycroft welcome you to this historic 15th century inn. The name relates to the King's law regarding the size of dogs. During Tudor times only the King and his entourage went into the forest to hunt. The Commoners were allowed only if their dogs were small enough

to fit through the 'Verderers Stirrup'. Very popular pub, good fun and excellent food. Regular theme evenings are well attended and you should make sure you book in good time. Tuesday Music evenings are also a great hit. Please ask for a programme of events. Children welcome. This is essentially a value for money pub.
Price Band: A

FOX AND HOUNDS INN, 22 High Street.
Tel: 01703 282098. 15th century coaching inn. Black and white building full of charm. Open all year. Children welcome. Visa/Mastcard. Vegetarians catered for.
Price Band: A

LYMINGTON
THE RED LION INN, Boldre.
Tel: 01590 673177. This pretty black and white, flower bedecked inn is as welcoming insideas it appears on approach. Attractively furnished it is a good place to make for if you want a meal in the New Forest. Children welcome.
Price Band: A/B

THE TOLLHOUSE INN, 167 Southampton Road.
Tel: 01590 672142. Charming 17th century country pub serving some of the best pub food in Hampshire. Freshly cooked, reasonable. Open 11-3pm & 6-11pm. Visa/Mastercard. 4 dishes for vegetarians. Children welcome.
Price Band: A/B

MINSTEAD
HONEYSUCKLE COTTAGE, Minstead, Nr Lyndhurst.
Tel: 01703 813122. A thatched cottage in the heart of the New Forest conjures up a delightful picture and the reality is greater than the anticipation! Honeysuckle Cottage restaurant stands in one and a half acres of lovely grounds which also house the Honeypot Tea Rooms with seating for 40 inside and 40+ in the garden. The delicious varied menu which changes every ten weeks to allow for seasonal food, incororates all that is good in English cooking. The cakes and scones are wonderful. The Honeysuckle Cottage Restaurant has a set price for the three and four course menu, both of which are extremely good value for money. Children are welcome. Visa/Master.
Price Band: B

NETLEY MARSH
THE WHITE HORSE, Ringwood Road, Woodlands, Southampton.
Tel: 01703 862166. Traditional village pub about 200 years old. Good atmosphere and serves freshly prepared home-cooked food at reasonable

prices. Sunday lunch is recommended. Vegetarian dishes. Children welcome. Visa/Master.
Price Band: A

RINGWOOD
THE LAMB INN, 2 Hightown Road.
Tel: 01425 473721. 250 year old inn where the landlords are quite prepared to rise early to give fishermen a substantial breakfast before they make for the first rise. Golf and horse racing vie with fishing in this friendly establishment. Bar food is available at all times; it is true pub grub, plentiful and inexpensive. Open: 11-3pm & 6-11pm. Children welcome. No credit cards. Vegetarian dishes on request.
Price Band: A

ROMSEY
THE ABBEY HOTEL, Church Street.
Tel: 01794 513360 Fax: 01794 524318. Bar meals daily except Sunday evenings. Sold by Henry VIII to the townspeople for one hundred pounds, Romsey Abbey was of some importance. Naturally there was an inn to service the many visitors, and the one you see today was built in 1880 on the site of its medieval predecessor. The original cellars and an underground passage to the Abbey are still there; it seems this may still be used by a spectral nun who likes to turn off the gas! The atmosphere upstairs is, however warm and convivial. After a good meal of home-
cooking from a varied menu, relax by an open fire or in the colourful garden, watching the dragonflies over the stream. Children welcome. Car park. Visa/Master.
Price Band: A

STROUD
THE SEVEN STARS INN, Winchester Road, Stroud, Nr Petersfield.
Tel: 01730 264122. Owned by two welcoming and experienced publicans, Jake and Barbie Cable, this delightful inn has much to offer. Wonderful views, a designated area of 'Outstanding Natural Beauty', it is close to a number of tourist and leisure activities. Golfers will think they are in paradise! There are 15 golf courses within a 20 mile radius of the pub. Ther A La Carte menu and bar meals both offer a wide choice and everything is freshly cooked on the premises. Your choice extends from steak and grouse to moussaka and fish pie. Real ales come straight from the cask. Children welcome within the law. Mastercard/Visa/Switch.
Price Band: A/B

WEST LISS

THE SPREAD EAGLE, Farnham Road.

Tel: 01730 892088. Set in 3 acres it has a superb view of the 13th century church. The Grade II listed building dates partly from the 15th century. Even if the food here was not as good as it is and very reasonable the pub would still be a must for people visiting the area. Open: 11-
3pm & 5-11pm. No credit cards. Children welcome. Always dishes for vegetarians. Price Band: A

WEST WELLOW

THE RED ROVER, Salisbury Road, Nr Romsey.

Tel: 01794 22266. 400 year old coaching inn. Full of character and impedimenta. Simple bar food, no restaurant. Master/Visa. Children allowed in the garden. 6 dishes for vegetarians. Open: 10.30-3pm & 6.30-11pm. Price Band: A

WHITSBURY

THE CARTWHEEL INN, Nr Fordingbridge.

Tel: 017253 362. Cosy pub with beams and open fires. Horseracing and training is the basic conversation in the bar - Whitsbury was the home of Desert Orchid. Extensive menu in restaurant and bar. Daily Specials. Crab, lobster and fish. Summer barbecues. Open: 11-2.30pm & 6-11pm. No food Tuesday evenings. Children in restaurant and garden only. Visa/Mastercard/Amex. 10 dishes for vegetarians. Price Band: A/B

WINCHESTER

THE ELIZABETHAN RESTAURANT, 18 Jewry Street.

Tel: 01962 853566. Table d'hote, A La Carte, fixed price menu. Exciting food. Children welcome. All credit cards. Vegetarians catered for.
Price Band: A/B

WOODLANDS

BUSKETTS LAWN HOTEL

Tel: 01703 292272. Delightful family run country house hotel is near the village of Lyndhurst, eight miles west of Southampton. You eat either in The Crystal Room with its beautiful Italian chandeliers or in The Francis Room with its delightful garden aspect. An excellent table is offered, with fine homely cuisine served by cheerful and helpful staff. You are invited to take tea on the Terrace and snacks, teas and drinks are always available around the heated swimming pool, while poolside lunches, buffets and barbecues are held during summer. Children welcome. Al major credit cards. Price Band: Restaurant B Teas etc A

HEREFORDSHIRE

BISHOPS FROME

THE GREEN DRAGON.

Tel: 01885 490607. If you are a traditionalist when it comes to pubs, this one you will enjoy. In the heart of hop farming country it has an oddly cosmopolitan air which blends in well with the past traditions of the area. Oak beams, flagstone floors and large fireplaces with roaring fires in winter. Real Ale and home-cooked food, especially pies. Open: 12-3pm & 5-11pm. Children welcome. Access/Visa. Several dishes for vegetarians.

Price Band: A/B

GLEWSTONE

GLEWSTONE COURT HOTEL, Nr Ross-on-Wye.

Tel: 01989 770367 Fax: 01989 770282. Spacious, elegant, Listed Country House in 3 acres. Half a mile off the A40 and 3 miles from the centre of Ross-on-Wye. Georgian Restaurant offers food of a very high standard. Bar meals would outshine most restaurants. All major credit cards.

Price Band: B

HEREFORD

GILBIES BISTRO, 4, St Peters Close, Commercial Street.

Tel: 01432 277863. Modelled in many ways on the kind of Bistro you might find in any of the lager French of Spanish cities, the hours are flexible. Somewhere you can go early for breakfast if it is pre-arranged - have coffee, maybe a snack or a full meal throughout the day. The proprietor describes his food modestly as 'good but not great, at reasonable prices, eaten in a completely relaxed atmosphere'. The menu changes hour by hour and covers all styles of cuisine from steaks to kebabs - from fish to sea-food or simple snacks like bacon sandwiches through to New Zealand mussels. Open: 10am-11pm every day. Good children welcome. Visa/Access. At least 3 vegetarian dishes.

Price Band: A/B

KENTCHURCH

THE BRIDGE INN

TEL: 01981 230408. Wonderful 400 year old building lying on the banks of Monnow River with a delightful riverside restaurant and a large geer garden. Nothing pretentious about the menu in the restaurant or the bar, just good, imaginative, home-made fare. Open: 11-2.30pm & 6-11pm. No credit cards. Always 4 dishes for vegetarians. Children welcome.

Price Band: A/B

LEOMINSTER

THE BLACK HORSE COACH HOUSE, 74, South Street

Tel: 01568 611946. This Listed building has its own brewery attached producing very good Real Ale. Excellent choice of home-made food at very reasonable prices. Open: 11-2.30pm & 6-
11pm, sat 11-11pm. No credit cards. Several dishes for vegetarians. Children welcome.

Price Band: A

MICHAELCHURCH ESCLEY

THE BRIDGE INN

Tel: 01981 23646. One of those story book places, situated at the foot of the Black Mountains between Hereford and Hay-on-Wye right by Escley Brook, surrounded by fields. In summer, customers can drink and dine outside watching the trout in the river. Some parts date back to 14th century. Tremendous atmosphere. Home-cooked fare by the Jean Draper, who is a talented chef using many of her own recipes, vegetarian ones in particular. Her Leek Croustade is a mega favourite. Open: 12-2.30pm & 7-11pm. Closed Mon lunch. Well behaved children welcome. No credit cards.

Price Band: A

PEMBRIDGE

THE NEW INN, Pembridge, Nr Leominster

13th century, all black and white painted brick on a massive stone base. Enchanting place with uneven stone floors, low beamed ceilings, roaring fires plus two ghosts!. Traditional home-made fare using local produce and as much game as possible in season. Bar food offers a wide range with Daily Specials including vegetarian dishes. No credit cards. Food available lunch and evening everyday.

Price Band: A/B

THE CIDER HOUSE RESTAURANT AT DUNKERTONS, Luntley

Tel: 01544 388161. Described as 'the best restaurant between Chester and the Channel Islands'. Warm, friendly and beautiful with the emphasis on revival British Cooking. Lunch: everyday except Sunday. Open for coffee, tea, home-made cakes and biscuits, local ice cream and...Dunkertons delicious cider and perry on draught. 10am-6pm. Dinner: from 7.30pm Friday and Saturday evenings. Booking for dinner is essential.

Price Band: B

WEOBLEY

YE OLDE SALUTATION INN, Market Pitch

Tel: 01544 318443. On the outside it is a black and white timber-framed building which dates back over 500 years. Inside it is delightful with a large

inglenook fireplace, a comfortable lounge bar leading into 40 seater Oak Room restaurant. The food is of a very high standard and you can stay here in great comfort. Open: 11-3pm & 7-11pm. Children in eating area, lounge conservatory. MasterCard/Visa. 3/4 dishes daily for vegetarians.
Price Band: B

ROSS-ON-WYE
THE CHASE HOTEL, Gloucester Road
Tel: 01989 763161 Fax: 01989 768330. Handsome Regency Country House standing in own grounds, a few minutes walk from town centre. The chef favours a modern British approach with a continental influence and takes full advantage of the fine local produce. Bar snacks, cold buffet, vegetarian dishes. All major cards.
Price Band: B

PHEASANTS RESTAURANT, 52, Edde Cross Street
Tel: 01989 65751. Once a tiny pub building this has now become an acclaimed testaurant with a Victorian style dining room with no more than a dozen tables, fronted by a dispense bar and a fireside lounge. Intimate dining both at lunch and in the evening on old English recipes makesthis special. You can stay here, there are two rooms. A 10% discount on evening meals is offered to those staying. Open: Tues-Sat 12.30-2pm & 7-1-pm. Well behaved children welcome. AMEX/Access/Visa. Vegetarians catered for. Walled courtyard garden with pond in summer.
Price Band: B

CLOISTERS WINE BAR, 24, High Street
Tel: 01989 67717. This 18th century building stands out in the High Street because of the golry of its stained glass windows. The wealth of exposed beams and nooks and crannies make it a truly secluded and intimate restaurant full of olde worlde charm. The menu is full of gastronomic delights including some unusual fish, such as Parrot Fish, Sweet Lips, Monkfish and Groupa, if you are not adventurous there are steaks of all kinds with or without sauces. Wide selection of wines & beers. Open: Mon-Sun 6-11pm, Sat/Sun lunchtimes. No credit cards. 6 dishes for vegetarians. Difficult for the disabled.
Price Band: A/B

THE CROSS KEYS INN, Goodrich
Tel: 01600 890650/890203. Traditional village pub complete with a resident ghost. Two friendly bars offering good simple Pub Fare. The pub has 5 double and 2 single rooms, not en suite.
Price Band: A

NORFOLK

BRANCASTER STAITHE
THE LOBSTER POT, Main Road.
Tel: 01485 210262. Charming fishing village with this very nice pub from which there ar stunning views. The restaurant overlooks the harbour, the salt marshes and Scuit Island. Specialise in sea food and fish but there are many other dishes always using fresh produce. Open: Summer 11-3pm & 6.30-11pm, Winter 11-2.30pm & 7-11pm. Children welcome. No credit cards. Several dishes for vegetarians.
Price Band: B

BURNHAM MARKET
FISHES RESTAURANT, Market Place
Tel: 01328 738588. Standing on the village green this 18th century building is a restaurant of great charm and character. Two simply furnished dining rooms have a vast open fire and bookcases full of the sort of books one might have at home. Specialising in fish, Gillian Cape, the owner, makes one of the best crab soups you will ever taste. It is a very special place. Children welcome. No credits cards. Several dishes for vegetarians.
Price Band: B

THE LORD NELSON
Tel: 01328 738321. Friendly pub run by two talented people - Peter Jordan is a keen fungus hunter which provides the pub with some exciting offerings in the autumn when his findings become part to the menu. Valerie Jordan is a skilled artist and regular art exhibitions are held in the stables. Children welcome. Open: Mon-Sat 11.30-3pm & 7-11pm, Sun 12-3pm & 10.30pm. No credit cards.
Price Band: A/B

COLKIRK
THE CROWN, Crown Road,Colkirk, Fakenham
Tel: 01328 862172. A pub for over 300 years but rebuilt after a fire. Friendly, comfortable and with a reputation for good food. The portions are generous and it is value for money. Open: 11-
2.30pm & 6-11pm, Sun 12-2.30pm& 7-10.30pm. Access/Visa. Children welcome. Vegetarian dishes.
Price Band: A

DICKLEBURGH
THE KINGS HEAD, Norwich Road, Nr Diss
Tel: 01379 741481. Welcoming, unpretentious pub with a ghost!. Three letting rooms. Probably the best Steak and Kidney Pie in the country.

Surrounded by open ground which is available for 5 caravans and 10 tents. Open: 12-2pm & 7-10pm. Children welcome. No credit cards. Vegetarian dishes on request.
Price Band: A

GORLESTON
THE CLIFF HOTEL, Cliff Hill
Tel: 01493 662179 Fax: 01493 653617. Attractive 3 star hotel is open to non-residents and offers good quality traditional dishes. Children welcome. All major cards.
Price Band: B

THE PIER HOTEL, Harbourmouth
Tel:01493 662631 Fax: 01493 440263. Overlooking sandy beach, open to non-residents. A la carte and table d'hote. Fish a speciality. Wide range of bar meals and for vegetarians. Children welcome, high chairs and childrens menu. All major cards.
Price Band: B

GT RYBURGH
THE BOAR INN, Gt Ryburgh, Fakenham
Tel:01328 829212. Sitting on the suntrapped patio of the delighful inn looking out on the garden, enjoying a good lunch on a summer's day, is one of life's great pleasures. Inside the 300 year old pub is full of warmth and character. Food of an International flavour is served at lunch and in the evening 7 days a week. Well known locally it has a deserved repution. Childrens meals. Access/Master/Visa/Barclaycard/Euro. Always five dishes plus salads for vegetarians.
Price Band: A/B

GT YARMOUTH
THE GALLON POT, 1-2 Market Place
Tel: 01493 842230. Amusing pub offering good food at sensible prices plus afternoon tea which far exceeds most. Children welcome. No credit cards. Limited dishes for vegetarians.
Price Band: A/B

THE IMPERIAL HOTEL, North Drive
Quite seafront location. The intimate Rambouille Restaurant offers table d'hote and a la carte menus with wide range of dishes to appeal to the gourmet and the more traditional diner. Bar food available for those who want quick service and tasty dishes. All major cards. Children welcome. Dishes for vegetarians.
Price Band: B

HAPPISBURGH

THE HILL HOUSE

Tel: 01692 650004. Friendly old coaching inn dating back to the 16th century. It was a favourite retreat of Sir Arthur Conan Coyal. Full of character, oak beams, large fireplaces. Here you can relish Real Ales at their best, good home-cooked meals which are substantial and reasonably priced with a sea view thrown in. Children welcome. Visa/Access/AMEX. 2 dishes for vegetarians.
Price Band: A/B

HEVINGHAM

THE MARSHAM ARMS HOTEL

Has a newsletter of its own edited by the inn's proprietor, Nigel Bradley. Anyone unfamiliar with this excellent hostelry cannot fail to pick up some of the enthusiasm as you read its humourous message. The food in the bar or in Bradley's Restaurant is excellent with a wide choice and sensibly priced. There are 8 self-contained study bedrooms, all en suite and beautifully furnished. Open: 11-3pm &6-11pm. Children allowed in certain areas. Visa/Access. Many varied vegetarian dishes.
Price Band: B

HORNING

PETERSFIELD HOUSE HOTEL

Tel: 01692 630741 Fax: 01692 630745. Elegant, comfortable, family run 18 bedroomed hotel, open to non-residents. Impressive restaurant overlooking the garden. High standard of cuisine both a la carte and table d'hote. Saturday night Dinner Dances a major attraction. Children welcome. All major cards. Several dishes for vegetarians.
Price Band: B

KINGS LYNN

THE PARK VIEW HOTEL, Blackfriars street

Tel: 01553 775146 Fax: 01553 766957. Unfussy 47 bedroom hotel. The bar is welcoming and serves both traditional ale and good, inexpensive bar snacks and meals. The 52 seater Edwardian restaurant offers a wide range of dishes, beautifully presented and at sensible prices. Children welcome. All major cards. Several dishes for vegetarians.
Price Band: A/B

THE ROCOCO RESTAURANT, 11 Saturday Market Place

Tel: 01553 771483. Situated next to the Guildhall, the building is 300 years old and has panache. The food is of the highest quality as are the wines. Comfortable lounge for morning coffee, light lunches and afternoon teas. Dinner is a gastronomic delight. It is not cheap but it is money well spent.

Open: Mon Dinner 7pm, Tues-Sat 10-3pm Dinner 7pm, Sun 12-3pm. Booking advisable. Afternoon teas May-September.
Price Band: B

LODDON
THE LODDON SWAN INN, Church Plain
Tel: 01508 20239. Fascinating history here. Good home-made food. Unpretentious. Book for Sunday lunch - one of the best in Norfolk. Open: 11-3pm & 6.30-11pm, Sun 12-3pm &7-
10.30pm. Children welcome. Visa/Access/JCB. 2 dishes for vegetarians.
Price Band: A/B

NEATISHEAD
BARTON ANGLER COUNTRY INN, Irestead Road
Tel: 01693 630740. 500 years old and once a rectory, this is a welcoming, informal establishment. Menu best described as 'English Country House Cuisine with a slight French influence'. It is certainly delicious food. Children welcome. AMEX/Visa/Master. 2 dishes + salads for vegetarians.
Price Band: B

NORTH WALSHAM
SCARBOROUGH HILL HOUSE HOTEL, Old Yarmouth Road
Tel:01692 402151 Fax: 01692 402151. Open to non-residents and set in a 4 acres of gardens this is a charming spot and within easy reach of The Broads and sandy beaches. The menu is varied and encompasses a range of dishes, mainly English at its best but with a touch of French and the East. Everything is freshly cooked. Bar meals are prepared daily. Vegetarians will find at 2 dishes. Children welcome. Access/Visa/Diners/AMEX.
Price Band: A/B

NORWICH
BEECHES HOTEL & VICTORIAN GARDENS, 4-6 Earlham Road
Tel: 01603 621167 Fax: 01603 620151. Restaurant offers an interesting menu with an Italian bias but using mostly fresh local produce and cooked to order at modest prices. Children welcome. High Chairs. All major cards. 2 dishes for vegetarians.
Price Band: B

BRASTEDS RESTAURANT, St Andrews Hill
Tel: 01603 625949 Fax: 01603 766445. Here John Brasted will invite you to enjoy what can only be described as a culinary experience. Customers will tell you that part of the pleasure of eating here is to experience the peculiarly welcoming and friendly atmosphere that emits from the ghost who has haunted 8-10 St. Andrews Hill since the 17th century. Children welcome.

Visa/Access/AMEX/Diners. Good selection for vegetarians. No lunch Saturdays. Closed Sundays.
Price Band: B/C

ST BENEDICTS RESTAURANT, 9 St Benedicts Street
Tel: 01603 765337. Busy city centre restaurant in a bustlin street full of atmosphere. You sit on church pews, choose your food from a blackboard, changed daily which temps the most jaded palate. Well chosen wine list. All at affordable prices. Closed Sunday & Monday. Children welcome. All major cards. Vegetarian choice.
Price Band: B

REEDHAM
REEDHAM FERRY INN
Tel: 01493 700429. Well maintained late 16th century inn alongside working car ferry. The pub is full of fascinating memorabilia. Varied menu including game in season, prime meats, fresh produce and home grown herbs. Open: Summer 11-3pm & 6.30-11pm, Sun 12-3pm, Winter 11-
2.30pm & 7-10.30pm. Access/Visa. Children in Sun Lounge or restaurant until 9pm. 3 dishes for vegetarians. Wide doorways for the disabled.
Price Band: A/B

WELLS-NEXT-THE-SEA
THE GLOBE INN, The Butlands
Tel: 01328 710206. Busy, much sought after pub run with efficiency and charm. Steaks are the speciality of the house but there is a good choice. Full bar menu and snacks. Open: 10.30-11pm. No credit cards. Several dishes for vegetarians. Children welcome in Pool room. 4 letting rooms.
Price Band: A

WROXHAM
THE BROADS HOTEL, Station Road
Tel: 01603 782869 Fax: 01603 784066. Much used by local people, the bars are fun and the a la carte and carvery restaurant is of a very high standard. Children welcome. All major cards. 5 vegetarian dishes daily.
Price Band: A/B

OXFORDSHIRE

BLEDINGTON

THE KINGS HEAD INN, The Green.

Tel: 01608 568365 Fax: 01608 658365. This is one of the most picturesque village in The Cotswolds on the Oxford/Gloucester border 4 miles from Stow-in-the-Wold. It is everything that a 15th century inn should be facing the village green, complete with brook and friendly ducks. It has a high reputation for its excellent cuisine. Game of all kinds features largely on the menu. The starters are imaginative, delicious fish simply cooked is very popular and for those who want a simple meal in the bar there is a wide choice at sensible prices. A cosmopolitan selection of good quality wines, competetively priced is the icing on the cake. A marvellous base for a meal, a holiday or a short break. Children welcome. Mastercard/Switch/Visa.

Price Band: B/A

BURFORD

THE ANGEL INN, Witney Road.

Tel: 01993 822438. In just a few inspired years Jean Thaxter has become recognised as the owner of one of the most atractive and exciting small inns in the Cotswolds. Its charm lies in the atmospheric interior which will not have changed much in the 400 years it has been in existence. Low ceilings, a roaring log fire, beams, nooks and crannies make it a delightful meeting place for those who want to enjoy good wine in old world surroundings or to cross the stone flagged floor to eat in the small, intimate restaurant which is run rather like a good bistro than a stuffy dining room. Fish and Game are the specialities of The Angel. Children over 7 years. Mastercard/Visa.

Price Band: B

CHARLBURY

THE BULL, Sheep Street.

Tel: 01608 810689. 16th century coaching inn tastefull restored. Traditional home-made English food comes to the table in a whole range of dishes, sometimes the expected and sometimes innovative. Children welcome. Visa/ Mastercard.

Price Band: B/A

CHIPPING NORTON

THE WHITE HART HOTEL, High Street.

Tel: 01608 642572 Fax: 01608 644143. Behind the 18th century facade lies an inn with 13th century origins. The whole atmosphere is one of friendliness and a desire to please. The bar and restaurant are popular with people who live locally. Good food which you choose from colourfully chalked blackboards, offering a range of dishes and well chosen wines from around

the world, make eating a pleasure. It is the perfect place for morning coffee or afternoon tea. Children welcome. All major cards.
Price Band: B/A

CLIFTON

THE DUKE OF CUMBERLAND'S HEAD, Clifton, Nr Deddington.
Tel: 01869 338534. Over 300 years old this atmospheric establishment is wonderful. Walk through the main entrance and the smell of logs burning in the big fireplace plus the air of well being that pervades the inn, and you will recognise that you have found somewhere that will remain in your memory as one of the good things of life. The food is very French with international overtones. Beautifully cooked and presented at sensible prices, you may eat in the candlelit restaurant or in the low, beamed bar. Lunchtime Blackboard Specials and a traditional Sunday lunch. No food Sunday evenings and the restaurant is closed on Monday evenings. Well subscribed Themed evenings attract people from as far away as Wales and the Fens to enjoy the fun and the feast. Children welcome. Visa/Master.
Price Band: B/C

DUNSTEW

THE WHITE HORSE INN
Tel: 01869 40272 Fax: 01869 47732. 17th century quiet inn off the beaten track. Excellent, sensibly priced and freshly prepared food. Ideal venue for a weekend away or an evening out; a business lunch or a simple drink with friends. Children welcome. Master/Visa.
Price Band: B

KINGSTON LISLE

THE BLOWING STONE INN
Tel: 01367 820288. Friendly, charming establishment with the most welcoming of landlords, David and Ann Fearn. Pretty conservatory restaurant, two attractive lounges and lively public bar. The food in the restaurant is very special with imaginative dishes on offer according to the season and availablity. Peace and fun just fifteen minutes off the M4. You take the B4507 between Ashbury and Wantage where a left turn will take you into the village. Children welcome in restaurant. All major cards except Diners.
Price Band: B/A

LOWER BRAILLES

THE GEORGE HOTEL
Tel: 01608 685223. Much has happened at The George throughout 7 centuries and as one dines on good food and drinks fine wines it is wonderful to dwell on the past whilst savouring the food of the present. Fresh home-cooked

food is served all the year round. Fresh fish is prominent on the menu. Children welcome. No credit cards.
Price Band: B

SHROPSHIRE

BISHOP'S CASTLE
TROTTERS RESTAURANT, At the Boars Head Hotel, Church Street.
Tel: 01588 638521. This elegant, beautifully appointed restaurant was opened at Whitsun 1995 within the doors of the historic Boars Head Hotel. Delicious food is served in the Dining Room or if you wish to eat less formally there is a dining area in the main bar. Open 12.00-2pm & 6.30-9.30pm, Sun 12.00-2pm & 6.30-9.30pm. Children welcome. Vegetarians catered for.

SOMERSET

CREWKERNE
GEORGE HOTEL, Market Square.
Tel: 01460 73650. A much loved hostelry in the town that has been here for centuries, full of local people frequenting both its bars and restaurant. Whilst there is an excellent restaurant you may choose to eat wherever you like from the same wide ranging menu. Open all year. Restaurant: lunch 12-2.30pm Dinner 6.30-9.30pm. Children welcome. All major cards. Bar food. Vegetarian choice. Accommodation.

FROME
LA BISALTA, 6 Vicarage Street.
Tel: 01373 464238. Everything an Italian restaurant should be, from the moment you step through the door, the itimacy and ambience will make you feel as if you've gone to a good friend's for dinner. The food is delicious with lovely cheeses, vegetables and a variety of sauces to tantalise. Open 6 days-closed Sun 12-2pm & 7pm till late. Children welcome. All major cards. Vegetarians catered for. Licensed.

GLASTONBURY
ABBEY TEA ROOMS & RESTAURANT, 16 Magdalene Street.
Tel: 01458 832852. Probably best known for the excellence of its home-made cakes which make afternoon tea so special, a delightful place to rest awhile after exploring Glastonbury. Lunch, Sunday roasts and on Friday and Saturday evening meals are served. You will be extremely well fed at

extremely reasonable prices. Open 7 days a week and Fri & Sat evenings from 7pm. Children specially well catered for. Vegetarian & vegan menus. Visa/Master/Amex. Disabled access. Licensed.

PORLOCK
CAMELLIA TEA & COFFEE HOUSE, High Street.
Tel: 01643 862266. Excellent home-made fare. Light lunches, savouries, afternoon teas are all available. Open Dec-Jan: weekends 1-4pm, Feb-Apr: Thurs-Sun 1-5pm, summer: 7 days 12-5pm. Children welcome. No cards. Pets welcome. Vegetarians catered for. Licensed with full meals. Accommodation.

SUFFOLK

ALDEBURGH
NEW AUSTINS HOTEL, 243 High Street
Tel: 01728 453932 Fax: 01728 453668. Close to the sea, good food both in restaurant and the bar. All major cards except AMEX. Children welcome. Vegetarains catered for. Open all year.
Price Band: B

BATTISFORD
THE PUNCH BOWL, Bildeston Road
Tel: 01449 612302. Pretty village with thatched cottages. Pub has oak beams, open fires, plenty of gelaming brass and a wonderful welcome. Simple home-cooked fare. Garden for children. Traditional Sunday lunch. Open: 11-3pm & 7-11pm. No credit cards. 2-3 vegetarian dishes. Children welcome in the restaurant and garden.
Price Band: A

BECCLES
WAVENEY HOUSE HOTEL, Puddingmoor, Beccles
Tel: 01502 712270 Fax: 01502 712660. Friendly, beautifully run small hotel with excellent restaurant. Riverside frontage & moorings. Lively bar serves good bar food. Children welcome. Access/Visa/AMEX/Diners. 6 dishes for vegetarians. Open all year. Dogs not permitted in bar or restaurant.
Price Band: A/B

BENTLEY
THE CASE IS ALTERED, Caple Road, Nr Ipswich
Tel: 01473 310282. Nothing pretentious about this oddly named pub but it does offer good home-cooking. The spicy curry and the cauliflower cheese

are particularly good. Inexpensive and value for money. Open: 11.30-3pm & 6-11pm, Sat 11-11pm. No credit cards. Dishes for vegetarians. Children welcome.
Price Band: A

BLAXHALL
THE SHIP INN, Nr Woodbridge
Tel: 01728 88316. If you are a lover of bird life, a rambler or a devotee of music then Blaxhall and this inn are just the place for you. The village is well known to the people who come to the concert hall at Snape, a mile away. 17th century inn much used in BBC productions. Simple pub food at sensible prices. 4 well equipped twin chalets converted from the old stables. Open: 11-3pm & 7-11pm. Not open Monday lunchtime. No credit cards. Children welcome if eating. One or two dishes for vegetarians.
Price Band: A

BRANDESTON
THE QUEENS HEAD, The Street, Nr Woodbridge
Tel: 01728 685307. Set in picturesque countryside near the Deben. Over 400 years old but has been modernised. Letting rooms. Good home-cooked traditional fare is available every day lunch and evenings, except Sunday evenings. Traditional Sunday lunch. Warm and friendly. Certified as camping and Caravan Club accommodaion for 5 touring vans and 15 tents. Open: Mon-Sat 11.30-2.30pm & 5.30-11pm, Sun 12-3pm & 7-10.30pm. Children welcome in restaurant and Family Room. No credit cards. Vegetarian dishes.
Price Band: A

BURY ST EDMUNDS
GRILLS AND GILLS, 34, Abbeygate Street
Tel: 01284 706004. You will find this restaurant as unique in name as it is in its food and Mediterrannean style interior. The food is exciting and beautifully cooked, whether meat or fish. A daily changing Fish Board which also features an extension to the lunch menu with Pies,Cromer Crab, Mussels, Liver and Bacon and a host of other dishes. It is a sister restaurant to 'Somewhere Else' at 1 Langton Place, Hatter Street which is equally good. Open daily. Children welcome. Visa/Access/Master. 10 vegetarian dishes.
Price Band: A

CLAYDON
CLAYDON COUNTRY HOUSE HOTEL, 16-18, Ipswich Road
Tel: 01473 830382. Small enough to ensure that every guest receives individual attention. Traditional English and French menu. Children welcome. Garden. Visa/Access/AMEX. 5/6 choices for vegetarians.
Price Band: B

EAST BERGHOLT

THE RED LION, The Street, Nr Colchester

Tel: 01206 298332. 15th century inn in historic village. Ideal place from which to explore Constable country. First class interesting food. Try Pidgeon in Elderberry Wine or Chicken, Cheese and Mustard Pie. Wide variety of dishes. Bar meals. Children welcome in dining room and garden. 4 letting rooms. No credit cards. Vegetarian choice. Open: 12-3pm & 7-11pm.
Price Band: A/B

FELIXSTOWE

THE FERRY BOAT INN, Felixstowe Ferry

Tel: 01394 284203. Pub dates from 1450. Recently renovated - we have not seen it since. The hospitality is renowned and the food is good home-cooked fare with a blackboard menu that changes regularly. Open: 11-2.30pm & 6-11pm. No food Sunday evening. Access/Visa. Children in dining area only.
Price Band: A/B

GILLINGHAM

THE SWAN MOTEL, Loddon Road

Tel: 01502 712055 Fax: 01502 711786. 78 cover restaurant serving freshly prepared English home-made fare. Blackboard specials and snacks. Children welcome. All major credit cards. Vegetarians catered for.
Price Band: A/B

HARKSTEAD

THE BAKERS ARMS, The Street, Nr Ipswich

Tel: 01473 328595. You will find this friendly pub on the Shotley Peninsula, 6 miles from Ipswich and five minutes walk through fields from the charming tidal River Stour. Amazing value home-cooked food. Just the thing after a walk and no one minds muddy boots, wellies or dogs. Open: 11.30-3pm & 7-11pm. Children welcome in games room. 3-4 dishes for vegetarians. No credit cards.
Price Band: A

IPSWICH

THE SINGING CHEF, 200, St Helens Street

Tel: 01473 255236. Not to be missed, this very different and refreshing establishment provides a touch of France. Ken and Cynthia Toye are les patronnes, the food is regional French and quite wonderful. Very much a family restaurant, they close when the customers go. Ken lives up tohis name, the 'Singing Chef' and at the end of the evening he sings like an angel. Most customers stay for the whole evening. This is a gastronomic and personal experience to be enjoyed.
Price Band: B

KERSEY

THE BELL INN, The Street, Nr Hadleigh

Tel: 01473 823229. This 1,000 year old village is almost like a stage set and has been used by film makers time and again. The bell is a Grade II Listed building, the second oldest in Kersey. You can now stay as well as eat and drink here. Wonderful food produced by an imaginative chef. The bar food is definitely above average. Kersey will put a spell on you and so too will The Bell. Open: Mon-sat 10.30-2.30pm & 6.30-11pm, Sun 10.30-3pm & 7-10.30pm. Children if well behaved to eat. Visa/Access/Diners/AMEX. Vegetarian choice in bar and restaurant.

Price Band: A/B

KETTLEBURGH

THE CHEQUERS INN, Nr Woodbridge

Tel: 01728 723760. Super site with a garden that runs down to the banks of the Deben. Good choice of food at realistic prices. Try the Kettleburgh Ploughman with a choice of cheese, ham Mackerel or pate. Childrens menu. Access/Visa. Vegetarian dishes. Open: Mon-Sat 11-2.30pm & 5.30-11pm, Sun 12-3pm & 7-10.30pm.

Price Band: A

LEISTON

THE WHITE HORSE, Station Road

Tel: 01728 830694. The village dates back before the Norman Conquest. Purpose built in 1770 by the family Gildersleeves, a well known inn-keeping family who supplemented their regular income by a heavy involvement in the smuggling trade. Comfortable hotel provideng first class French/English fare in the restaurant and a wide range of food in the bar. Childrens menu. Sunday lunch. Access/Visa. Vegetarian dishes. Open all day weekdays, Sun 12-3pm & 10.30pm.

Price Band: A/B

PIN MILL

THE BUTT AND OYSTER INN, Pin Mill, Chelmondiston

Tel: 01473 780764. A very special, traditional inn right on the river's edge, with old Thames barges tied up alongside. The ale is superb, the food traditional and interesting, and the company unbeatable. Dick Mainwaring is the jovial landlord whose warmth of character spills over onto all the people he welcomes into this, one of Suffolk's nicest pubs. Children allowed in to eat and in smoke room. No credit cards. Dishes for vegetarians.

Price Band: A/B

SAXMUNDHAM

THE BELL HOTEL, High Street

Tel: 01728 602331. Renovated carefully since 1991, this early 17th century building is comfortable and charming. Good food, good hospitality and well equipped bedrooms. Strong emphasis on Italian cooking and wines. Open: Mon-Sat 11-11pm. Normal Sunday hours. Children welcome. Choice for vegetarians. Access/Visa/Diners.

Price Band: B

THE WHITE HORSE, Darsham Road, Westleton

Tel: 01728 73222. This is a pretty and well kept village with a thatched church just outside Saxmundham. The partially 16th century inn is on the green. It is cosy with lots of brass and paintings on the walls. Excellent home-cooking using local produce and locally caught fish. Probably the largest Mixed Grill you will ever see. Sunday lunch, Daily Specials, cream teas in the summer plus what is best described as a Scottish High Tea served from 6-7pm, in which for an all inclusive price, you can feast on a main meal, bread and butter, scones, cakes, jam, cream

and a pot of tea. Comfortable bedrooms and you will certainly be well fed. Open: winter 12-

3pm & 7-11pm, summer 11-3pm & 5.30-11pm. Children welcome. No credit cards. Vegetarian choice.

Price Band: A/B

SOUTHWOLD

THE RED LION INN & RESTAURANT, 2 Southe Green

Tel: 01502 722385. Good, sensibly priced food in a pleasant atmosphere. Open all year.

Price Band: A

STOKE-BY-NAYLAND

THE ANGEL INN

Tel: 01206 263245. All fresh international cuisine. Welcoming, beamed bars, nice atmosphere. All major cards. No children. Open all year. Vegetarians catered for.

Price Band: A/B

WOODBRIDGE

THE CAPTAIN'S TABLE, 3Quay Street

Tel: 01394 383145. For 25 years Tony and Jo Prentice have owned and run this excellent restaurant in what was once a farmhouse with land going down to the Deben. The Tudor buildings are painted Suffolk pink, and in summer the small patio in front of the restaurant is a suntrap protected from the

world by the outer brick wall. The extensive menu specialises in fish and sea food. 'Starters from the Net' include Moules Mariniere, hald a dozen oysters from Bentley Creek or a Mousse of Avocado with a fresh tomato and herb dressing. Main courses maybe local Dover soles, or Scallops tossed in butter with bacon and garlic. There is an alternative selection for those not keen on seafood. A fixed price menu which is value for money. 'All dishes are offered subject to wind and tide, fisherman's fancy, farmer's whim and gardener's back'!. If you only desire a bar snack you will still be very welcome.
Price Band: B

SUSSEX

BOGNOR REGIS
THE CAMELOT HOTEL & RESTAURANT, 3 Flansham Lane, Felpham. Tel: 01243 585875 Fax: 01243 587500. Situated on eht A259 Bognor Regis to Littlehampton main coastal road in the village of Felpham, ten minutes walk to the sea. 70 seater restaurant and King Arthur's Room with unique round table for twelve people. Good food catering for the trencherman as well as more delicate eaters. Sensible prices.
Price Band: B

BRAMBER
THE OLD TOLLGATE RESTAURANT & HOTEL, The street, Bramber Steyning.
Tel: 01903 879494 Fax: 01903 813399. This has been a renowned and popular 'eating spot' for over twenty years. The 'visual A La Carte' menu features The Tollgate's famous cold table as the first course, with some 30 different starters. The carvery is laden with at least four different roasts plus pies, casseroles, curries and vegetarian dishes. Sumptuous sweets and a cheeseboard will delight if you are still hungry! Children welcome. Visa/ Diners/Master/Amex.
Price Band: B

CHICHESTER
THE WHITE HORSE INN, Chilgrove.
Tel: 01243 535333. This award winning inn offers some of the finest food in the county and boasts a superb wine cellar. Alongside it Forge Cottage which opened in the spring of 1995 offers first class accommodation. Visa/ Diners. Children welcome to eat.
Price Band: B

SUFFOLD HOUSE HOTEL & RESTAURANT, No 3 East Row.
Tel: 01243 778899 Fax: 01243 787282. Stylish Georgian building, privately owned and run quite beautifully. Excellent bar and restaurant open to non-residents. Dine on Cordon Bleu Cuisine with imaginative and innovative dishes. Children welcome. Vegetarian dishes to order. All major cards. Pets are permitted.
Price Band: B

COWDEN
THE COWDEN CROWN, Market Square.
Tel: 01342 850477. Everything about this pub is charmingly different. The Inglenook fireplace is a major attraction on which pheasant and other game, steaks and fish are cooked, all over apple logs. Wide menu with additional Daily Specials. The restaurant features French cuisine and is renowned for its sauces. You can stay overnight if you wish in authentically decorated bedrooms. Open: 11-3pm & 6-11pm. Closed Monday evening. Visa/ Mastercard. Children welcome in restaurant and garden. Notice required for vegetarian dishes.
Price Band: B

CUCKFIELD
THE KINGS HEAD, South Street, Nr Haywards Heath.
Tel: 01444 454006. A personal favourite of the Prince of Wales, later, George IV, it is beautifully appointed and offers everything expected from a coaching inn of the modern era. A popular intimate restaurant serves great value home-cooked food at lunchtime plus Tues-Fri evenings. Bar food is always available. 9 ensuite rooms. Open: normal pub hours. Children welcome. Garden and games room. Vegetarian dishes daily. Mastercard/Visa/Amex.
Price Band: B

EASTBOURNE
BROWNINGS HOTEL, 28 Upperton Road.
Tel: 01323 724358 Fax: 01323 731288. Dignified Victorian mansion on the main A22 from London. Wonderful homely atmosphere. Small intimate dining room open to non-residents. Good food at realistic prices. Children welcome. One vegetarian dish daily. No pets allowed. All major credit cards.
Price Band: B

LANDOWNE HOTEL, King Edward Parade.
Tel: 01323 725174 Fax: 01323 739721. High standard, delicious food in gracious surroundings. There are 125 ensuite rooms. Open all year except New Year and the first two weeks in January. All major cards. Children's

menu. Vegetarians catered for.
Price Band: B

FISHBOURNE
THE WOOLPACK, Fishbourne Road.
Tel/Fax: 01234 782792. Known for its culinary delights. The steaks melt in your mouth. Simple bar fare also available. Children are welcome - adults tolerated! Large garden. No pets. Visa/Master/Switch.
Price Band: A/B

LITTLEWORTH
THE WINDMILL, Partridge Green, Nr Horsham.
Tel: 01403 710308. Attractive pub that was once three cottages. 'Rural Memorabilia' adorns the walls and every corner that can be found for it. Whilst good, traditional food is served, the landlords, John and Gill Booth, are determined that it remains a pub that serves food rather than a restaurant serving ale! Open: 11-3pm & 5.30-11pm. No credit cards. Children welcome. One dish always available for vegetarians.
Price Band: A/B

MIDHURST
THE CROWN, Edinburgh Square.
Tel: 01730 813462. 16th century inn behind and below the church, in the old part of the town. Opposite the famous 14th century Spread Eagle Hotel. Good value, home-made food, imaginative and chip free. Open: Mon-Sat 11-11pm. Sun: 12-3pm & 7-11pm. Children welcome in a limited area. No credit cards. 3-4 vegetarian dishes.
Price Band: A/B

SLINDON
THE SPUR INN
Tel: 0124365 216/635. Charming 17th century coaching inn. Roaring fires and mulled wine in winter. The food is memorable covering every possible tastes both in the restaurant and the bar. Open: 11-3pm & 6-11pm. Sun 12-3pm & 7-10.30pm. Children welcome. Visa/Mastercard. 7+ dishes for vegetarian.
Price Band: A/B

SOUTH HARTING
THE SHIP INN
Tel: 01730 825302. 17th century traditional village pub in picturesque South Harting. Recommended in The Good Beer Guide and renowned for high quality food all home-prepared at sensible pub prices. Well worth seeking

out. Children over 14. Dogs permitted. All major cards.
Price Band: A

TANGMERE
THE BADER ARMS, Malcolm Road, Nr Chichester.
Tel: 01243 779422. Built at the end of the runway at this once famous airfield, and named after Sir Douglas Bader, this friendly pub is a fitting tribute to the 'The Few'. Food at luchtime andevenings both in the bar and restaurant. Restaurant closed Monday and Sunday evenings. Traditional Sunday Lunch. Theme evenings are very popular. Good value. Open all year, pub hours. Children welcome. Master/Visa. Always at least 4 dishes for vegetarians.
Price Band: A

RYE
THE FLACKLEY ASH HOTEL, Peasmarsh.
Tel: 01797 230651 Fax: 01797 230510. This hotel has everything including a Health and Leisure complex. Wonderful gardens and a charming restaurant with an English/French menu specialising in Rye Bay fish. Special menu for vegetarians. Children permitted. All major cards.
Price Band: B

WEST WITTERING
THE LAMB INN, Chichester Road.
Tel: 01243 511105. This Freehouse is a traditional pub and a friendly place. No background music or amusement machines. Fifteen wines, including champagne are available by the glass. The emphasis is on home-made food whether a toasted sandwich or a full meal. Fish is the speciality of the house. Open 11-2.30pm & 6-11pm. Children welcome if eating. Mastercard/Visa. Usually 2 dishes for vegetarians. No accommodation.
Price Band: A/B

TYNE AND WEAR

NEWCASTLE
THE PLOUGH INN, Mountsett, Nr Burnopfield.
Tel: 01207 570346. The Plough stands 800ft above sea level with magnificent views up the Derwent Valley and on a clear day you can see the glory of the Cheviot Hills. Traditional country inn with a great deal of charm. Fresh food, high quality, home-cooked served daily in the bar. Open Mon-Sat 11.30-11pm. Sun 12-3pm & 7-10.30pm. Children's menu. Master/Visa. 3 dishes always for vegetarians.
Price Band: A

WARWICKSHIRE

KENILWORTH

CLARENDON HOUSE, Old High Street

Tel: 01926 57668. Old building in the heart of Kenilworth. Full of atmosphere. Cromwells bistro restaurant, partially housed in the original kitchen of the Elizabethan Castle Tavern, offers an extensive menu of fine foods and wines in a relaxed and informal setting. Royalist Retreat Bar has an extensive range of bar snacks available at lunchtime. Open all year. Children allowed. Visa/Access/Switch. Vegetarian dishes.
Price Band: A/B

SHIPTON-ON-STOUR

GEORGE HOTEL, High Street

Tel: 01608 661453. In historic small town, this delightful inn dates back to the 15th century. Has an unbelievable air of the past. Delicious food in the restaurant and a varied and exciting bar menu. Open all year 10.30-11pm. Children welcome, special space. Visa/AMEX. Vegetarians catered for.
Price Band: A/B

STRATFORD-UPON-AVON

THE FALCON, Chapel Street

Tel: 01789 205777 Fax: 01789 414260. 16th century inn beautifully extended. Restaurant renowned for its friendly service and the culinary skills of the chef and his team. Good food in the lounge and Oak Bars. Coffee or afternoon tea in the 'covered walkway' overlooking the garden. Open all day, all year. Children welcome. All major credit cards. Vegetarians catered for. Price Band: A/B/C

ETTINGTON PARK, Aldminster

Tel: 10789 450123 Fax: 01789 450472. There can be few hotels in this country more grand or beautiful that Ettington Park. Dine here in the spectacular Oak Room on the very finest of English and French cuisine and it will be never forgotten. Everything about the hotel is superb.
Price Band: C

WORCESTERSHIRE

ARLEY

THE NEW INN, Pound Green

Arley is three and a half miles from the historic riverside town of Bewdley. A pub in which Acoustic Musicians are especially welcome - the landlord Malcolm Gee publishes the international magazine 'The Accordion News'

and runs high profile accordion concerts. The pub is essentially a 'conventional' one and caters for families although children are not allowed to roam the lounges. The 40 cover restaurant is provided over by a Head Chef who has an excellent reputation for good traditional food,generous portions and modest prices. Godd bar food is available. Several vegetarian dishes. No credit cards.
Price Band: A

ECKINGTON
THE ANCHOR INN & RESTAURANT, Cotheridge Lane
Tel/Fax: 01386 750356. On the edge of the Cotswolds, Eckington, close to Pershore, is a quiet village dating back to Saxon times. The 18th century Anchor Inn, full of character is famous for the excellence of its restaurant. Fish and Steaks are the speciality but there is an excellent, varied menu which includes dishes for vegetarians as well as Daily Specials. The bar food is exciting and home-made. Cheildren welcome. All major cards within Cardnet.
Price Band: A

LITTLE MALVERN
HOLDFAST COTTAGE HOTEL
Tel: 01684 310288 Fax: 01684 311117. This is a charming 17th century hotel set in its own grounds surrounded by orchards and open farmland; far removed from traffic noise although it is less than 15 minutes drive from the M5 and M50 and only 4 miles from Malvern and Upton-Upon-Severn, offers dinner to non-residents. The delicious food is cooked by the owners Stephen and Jane Knowles whose love of food is reflected in the varied choice and the delicate use of herbs from the hotel's Victorian Herb Garden. Visa/Access/Master/Euro. Licensed.
Price Band: B

MALVERN WELLS
THE COTTAGE IN THE WOOD HOTEL, Holywell Road
Tel: 01684 575859 Fax: 01684 560662. Excellent hotel with stunning views perched high on the Malvern Hills. The Daily Mail calls it 'The best view in England'. Delightful restaurant open to non-residents. At lunchtime choose from the Light Bite menu which reflects the modern trend for healthy eating. Dinner is a gastronomic dream, essentially English at heart, but influenced by styles and flavours of the world. Children and vegetarians welcome. Access/Visa/Amex/Switch.
Price Band: B

FLYFORD FLAVELL

THE RED HART INN, Kington, Flyford Flavell

Tel: 01386 792221. Over 400 years old and much of the original black and white building remains. You will find it on the A422 halfway between Worcester and Stratford-upon-Avon. Over the years it has become known as the 'Sportsmans Pub' because of its great cricketing connections. A la carte restaurant serving traditional food. Sunday carvery lunch. Good bar meals. From Easter to September breakfast and a super afternoon tea are available. Open: Sat 11-2.30pm & 6-11pm, Sun 12-3pm & 7-10.30pm, longer Easter-Sept.

Price Band: A/B

PERSHORE

THE OLD CHESTNUT TREE, Manor Road, Lower Moor

Tel: 01386 860380. This Grade II Listed building has a gently flowing river behind it, along whose banks is a delightful walk. Black and white with ancient leaded windows, it was built in 1547 as a Granary for the Manor House. Heavy beams, open fireplaces, ghosts!. Good, traditional food at reasonable prices. 2 letting rooms not en suite. Open: Mon-Fri 11-2.30pm & 6-11pm, Sat 11-11pm, Sun 12-3pm & 7-10.30pm. Children welcome. No credit cards. Vegetarians catered for.

Price Band: A

THE ANGEL INN & POSTING HOUSE, High Street

Tel: 01386 552046. In the heart of the town, welcoming, family run. Extensive bar food. Imaginative meals.

Price Band: A

ST MICHAELS

CADMORE LODGE

Tel/Fax: 01584 810044. Situated 2 miles west of the market town Tenbury Wells, and lying in its own secluded valley with 60 acres of woodland with a nine hole golf course and 2 shimmering lakes. The skilled chefs offer a tempting menu whether it is the set price dinner, dishes taken from the a la carte selection or the good value bar food. Vegetarians catered for. Children welcome. Access/Visa/Master.

Price Band: B

SEVERN STOKES

THE OLD SCHOOL HOUSE HOTEL & RESTAURANT

is only 35 miles from the centre of Birmingham and is a popular venue for diners who come to enjoy 'School Dinners' - gastronomic feasts that bear no resemblance to those we remember!. The only similarity is the superb

range of old fashioned steamed puddings with custard. Themenu is imaginative, beautifully presented and the price is reasonable. Snacks and Daily Specials are available served in the Study. During the summer one can enjoy drinks and meals on the terrace overlooking the garden with its swimming pool and marvellous views of the Severn Vale. Vegetarians & children welcome. All major cards.
Price Band: B

UPTON-ON-SEVERN
THE WHITE LION HOTEL, High Street
Tel/Fax: 01684 592551. Famous old inn on banks of the River Severn, in the centre of this historic Tudor town. Surrounded by a wonderful pastoral landscape leading to the majestic Malvern Hills. Charming restaurant serving interesting English fare with a French influence. Busy bar offering good meals with an emphasis on fresh fish. Open all year. Access/Visa/Amex/ Diners. Vegetarians catered for.
Price Band: B

YORKSHIRE

AINTHORPE
THE FOX AND HOUNDS INN, Ainthorpe, Danby.
Tel: 01287 660218. Nice village pub in a wonderful setting. Good, home-cooked food. Open normal pub hours. Children welcome. Vegetarians catered for.
Price Band: A

DONCASTER
THE DUKE WILLIAM, Church Street, Haxey.
Tel: 01427 752210. Close to the Lincolnshire Wolds and historic Lincoln. Pretty and very ancient village, the old capital of the Isle of Axholme. Popular village pub with great food using local produce, restaurant and bar food. Children welcome. Open 11-11pm. Mastercard/Visa. 6 dishes for vegetarians.
Price Band: A/B

EGTON BRIDGE
THE POSTGATE, Egton Bridge, Whitby.
Tel: 01947 895241. Pretty creeper covered inn on the North Yorkshire Moors close to the sea. Popular with television companies. High quality traditional fare in restaurant and bar with Blackboard Specials. Open normal pub hours.

No credit cards. Children welcome. Vegetarians catered for.
Price Band: A/B

GOATHLAND

THE MALLYAN SPOUT HOTEL, The Common.
Tel: 01947 896486. Yorkshire Television filmed the successful series 'Heartbeat' in Goathland. On the village green is The Mallyan Spout Hotel which is open all day from 8am-12 midnight. Good wholesome Englsih food in the restaurant and freshly cooked fare in the bar every day. Children welcome in lounge only. Master/Diners/Visa. Several dishes for vegetarians.
Price Band: A/B

HARROGATE

THE RUSKIN PRIVATE HOTEL & GALLERY RESTAURANT
Tel: 01423 502045 Fax: 01423 506131. Charming private hotel. French/English cuisine. Table d'hote and A La Carte. Children over 3 years. Master/Visa. Always 4+ dishes for vegetarians. No disabled access.
Price Band: A/B

HEMINGBROUGH

HEMINGBROUGH HALL HOTEL, School Road.
Tel: 01757 630393. Close to York and Selby and set in 7 acres of rural countryside. Peaceful and undisturbed by the outside world. Delicious food prepared by Classical French chef. Bar food between 12-2pm daily. Open every day. Children welcome. Visa/Amex. Vegetarian dishes on request.
Price Band: A/B

HUTTON-LE-HOLE

THE FORGE TEA SHOP.
Tel: 01751 417444. Once and old smithy it is now a very attractive tea room serving delicious home-cooked food. Simple or sophisticated snack or a meal, delectable home-made cakes, scones with lashings of butter, jam and cream. Nothing could be better. Open Mar-Oct 10-5pm 7 days in summer, Nov-Feb: weekends only 10-4pm. Children welcome. No cards.

KNARESBOROUGH

THE YORKSHIRE LASS, High Bridge, Harrogate Road.
Tel: 01423 862962 Fax: 01423 869091. Filming of 'Emmerdale' goes on around here. The pub sits on the banks of the River Nidd opposite Mother Shipton's Cave. Quite often see TV and Film stars plus their film crews here lunching on the home-cooked food. Open 11-3pm & 5.30-11pm. Children to eat only. Visa/Master/Amex. Always 5 dishes for vegetarians.
Price Band: A/B

LEYBURN

KINGS ARMS HOTEL, Market Place, Askrigg in Wensleydale.

Tel: 01969 650635. Totally delightful - known throughout the world as The Drovers at Daroby in the television series 'All Creatures Great and Small'. Wonderful food both in the bar and restaurant. Open all year. Children welcome. All major cards. Vegetarians catered for.

Price Band: A/B/C

MIDDLEHAM

THE RICHARD III HOTEL, Market Place.

Tel: 01969 232240. Set in the heart of 'Herriot Country' in the smallest town in the country. This double fronted building backs onto the original boundary wall of Middleham Castle. Intimate 'olde worlde' restaurant with a home-cooked menu. Bar food served daily with a variety of 'Daily Specials' 4 choices for vegetarians. Open 11-3pm & 6-11pm and Fri-Sat 11-11pm. Sunday normal pub hours. Visa/Master. Children welcome in rear bar area.

Price Band: A

OTLEY

CHEVIN PARK COUNTRY LODGE HOTEL, Yorkshire.

Tel: 01943 467818. Unique hotel with a difference set in glorious grounds. The lakeside restaurant forms the centrepeice of what is the largest log building in Britain and has a cosy and intimate atmosphere. The cuisine is recognised and commended by all the major guides. Openall year. Children welcome. All major cards. Vegetarians catered for.

Price Band: B

PETELEY BRIDGE

HAREFIEDL HALL HOTEL, Ripon Road.

Tel: 01423 711429. Superb hotel and leisure complex nestling deep within its own grounds in the Nidderdale Hills. Full A La Carte and Table d'hote served every evening from 7pm. Bar meals on scenic patio with views over Pateley Bridge or in lounge bar both lunchtime and evenings. Open all year. All major cards. Children welcome. Vegetarians catered for.

Price Band: A/B

SCARBOROUGH

KAM SANG CHINESE RESTAURANT, 3-3A North Marine Road.

Tel: 01723 501718. A superb Chinese restaurant. All food is cooked to order, and where possible good local produce is used. Excellent choice. Open lunch: Mon-Sat 12-2.30pm, dinner Mon-Sat 6pm to midnight. Children welcome. Vegetarians catered for. All major cards. Disabled access.

SKIPTON

BIZZIE LIZZIES FISH & CHIP RESTAURANT, 36 Swadford Street.

Tel: 01756 703189. It would seem that there is no doubt the North Country produces the best fish and chips in the whole of England. This is confirned by the excellence of Bizzie Lizzies. Seats up to 76 people in comfort with special non-smoking and smoking areas. Open all year Mon-Sat 11.30am (last orders 10pm), Sun Noon-last orders 10pm from 1st Oct until Easter last orders will be 9pm. Children welcome. Licensed. Vegetarian upon request. No credit cards.

SINNINGTON

THE FOX AND HOUNDS COUNTRY HOTEL, Main Street.

Tel: 01751 431577 Fax: 01751 432791. Sinnington demonstrates what a true Englsih village should look like. The Fox and Hounds offers good food both in the restaurant and at the bar. Daily Specials. Open 12-2.30pm & 6.30-11pm. Children welcome. Master/Visa/Euro. Dishes for vegetarians.

Price Band: B

WHITBY

THE MAGPIE CAFE, 14 Pier Road.

Tel: 01947 602058/821723. The accolades of this fine licensed restaruant immidiately tell you that there is something special about the establishment. Excellent fayre fresh fish is a great speciality here with 12 to 15 varieties being available at any time. Children are most welcome here with high chairs, toy boxes and a special menu. Open Feb to Dec, Easter-Oct 11.30-9pm daily, Feb-Easter & Nov-Dec 11.30-6.30pm Sun-Thurs, 11.30-9pm Fri & Sat. All major cards. Vegetarians catered for.

YORK

LASTINGHAM GRANGE, Lastingham.

Tel: 01751 417345/402. If you leave the A170 at Kirby Moorside and follow the road north to Hutton-le-Hole, you will find the historic village of Lastingham, five miles away. Relaxed friendly atmosphere in a house that has a justifiable reputation for good food and personal, courteous service. Open to non-residents. Open all year. Children welcome. No credit cards. Vegetarians catered for on request.

Price Band: B

WALES

BRECON

SELAND NEWYDD, Pwllgloyw, Brecon, Powys.

Tel: 01874 690282. One of Wales's most exciting eating experiences is to be found on the 'old road' from Brecon to Builth Wells. The restaurant is sufficiently small with 35 covers to be intimate and ideal for a special evening out. Wonderful food at affordable prices. Not to be missed. Open 11-3pm & 6-11pm Mon-Sun. Children - yes cooked to order! All cards except Amex. Bar food Mon-Fri lunch and evenings meals Fri & Sat lunchtimes, and Sun Lunch. Accessible disabled access.

CARDIFF

BENEDICTO'S, 4 Windsor Place, Cardiff.

Tel: 01222 371130. This attractive Continental style restaurant has a great atmosphere, delightful furnishings and a welcoming host, Ben Lado. The food is superb you will certainly have a problem deciding what you would like form this imaginative and beautifully compiled menu. Open 12-2.30 & 7-11.30pm all year except Christmas Day and Boxing Day. All major cards. Children welcome. Good wine list. Daily vegetarian choice.

GOYCHURCH

THE WHITE HORSE INN, Goychurch, Mid-Glamorgan.

Tel: 01656 652583. This attractive inn which was once an hotel has something for all ages. The food is delicious with home-made pies being the speciality of the house. The pastry melts in your mouth and there are a whole variety of different, tasty fillings. Excellent A La Carte menu. Open Mon-Thurs 11-4pm & 5.30-11pm Fri/Sat 11am-11pm Sun 12-3.30pm & 7-10.30pm. Children welcome. All cards except Amex/Diners. Wide range of Bar Food with Daily Specials. Always a vegetarian choice. Award winning Beer Garden.

SWANSEA

WINDSOR LODGE HOTEL & RESTAURANT, Mount Pleasant, Swansea.

Tel: 01792 642158/652744 Fax: 01792 648996. Within the confines of the elegant, comfortable Windsor Lodge Hotel, right in the heart of Swansea's city centre, is a restaurant which has become one of the best known and most popular in South Wales. The dishes have a British and French influence using fresh ingredients allowing the menu to change with the seasons. Award winning food. Open all year 24 hours except Christmas and Boxing Day. All major cards. Children welcome. Good vegetarian choice. Good wine list. Accommodation

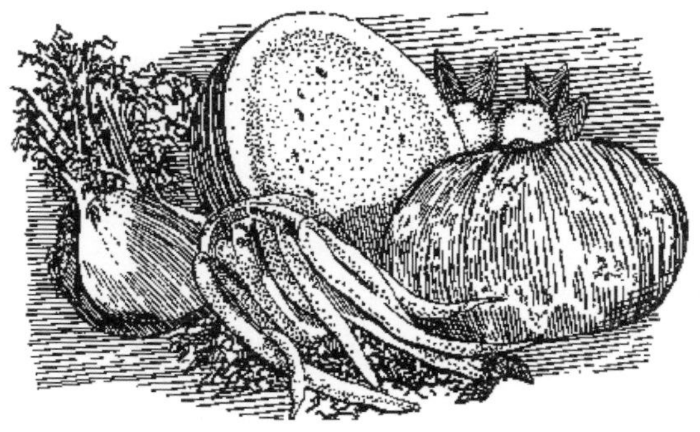

PLACES TO VISIT

BEDFORDSHIRE

BEDFORD DISCOVER THE BEDFORDSHIRE COUNTRYSIDE

Tel: 01234 228671
Discover the wonderful landscape and varied heritage by taking a family day out to visit one of the many country parks and cyclewalks that Bedfordshire has to offer. Throughout the year there is plenty to do. Visitor Centres and Country Parks are open all the year round.

BEDFORD MUSEUM

Tel: 01234 353323
This lively museum is set in attractive surroundings close to the River Great Ouse. Excellent displays interpret the human and natural history of the region. Open Tues-Sat 11-5pm Sun & Bank Holidays 2-5pm. Closed Mondays. Admission free.

PRIORY COUNTRY PARK

Tel: 01234 211182.
This Country Park is a tranquil countryside area just a stone's throw from Bedford town centre. The park, with lakes surrounded by trees and grassland, is a great place to see wildlife. Prioiry Water Sports offer sailing, sail boarding and canoeing. Open all year round.

CECIL HIGGINS ART GALLERY & MUSEUM

Tel: 01234 211222.
A Victorian mansion, original home of the Higgins family, is furnished in authentic style, with an adjoining modern gallery displaying fine collections of watercolours, prints, drawings, ceramics, glass and lace. Open all year Tues-Sat 11-5pm Sun & Bank Hols 2-5pm. Admission free.

THE BUNYAN MEETING FREE CHURDH & MUSEUM

Tel: 01234 358870.
Scenes from The Pilgrim's Progress are depicted on the bronze entrance doors, presented to the church in 1876 by the 10th Duke of Bedford, and on the five stained glass windows. The museum contains most of the known possessions of Johm Bunyan, many editions of his 60 recognised works, including The Pilgrim's Progress in 168 foreign languages. Open Apr-Oct Tues-Sat 2-4pm & Jul-Sept 10.30-12.30pm.

BROMHAM MILL

Tel: 01234 824330.

Built in 1695, Bromham Mill is an attracive stone building set by the River Great Ouse. Now restored to its former working glory, the enormous revolving water wheel is the focal point. Open April 12-4pm, Sundays & Bank Holidays 10.30-5pm. Closed Mondays & Tuesdays.

DUNSTABLE WHIPSNADE ANIMAL PARK

Tel: 01582 872171

Location: 20 miles from the M25 junction 21 following elephant signs from Dunstable. Europe's largest conservation centres offering 2,500 rare and endangered species in 600 acres of beautiful parkland, including all the family favourites - elephants, tigers, penguins, bears, rhinos and many more. Free daily demonstrations of Elephant Encounters, Californian Sea Lions and free flying Birds of the World will keep all the family entertained. Opendaily 10-6pm.

HARROLD-ODELL COUNTRY PARK

Tel: 01234 720016.

Tufted duck, great crested grebe, Canada and greylag geese, coots, moorhens, swans, mallards and kingfishers are just some of the birds that visit the landscaped lake of Harrold-Odells' 144 acre country park. Open Apr-Sept Tues-Sat 1-4.30pm Sun & Bank Holidays 1-6pm. Oct-
Mar Sat-Sun & Bank Hols 1-4pm.

LEIGHTON BUZZARD RAILWAY

Page's Park Station, Billington Road (A4146)

Tel: 01525 373888

This is one of England's foremost narrow gauge preservation sites; home to over fifty engines. It provides a great day out. Page's Park Station is situated alongside a large public recreational area offering grassy open space, children's play equipment and sports facilities. The station has a souvenir shop and buffet serving hot and cold snacks and refreshments at most times when trains are running. There is a picnic area, free car parking and space for coaches. The five and a half mile return journey by historic steam train takes just over an hour. A museum project display is open to visitors and much of the railway's historic locomotive and wagon fleet is based here. Steam locomotive viewing, a working quarry display and the demonstration sand trains are planned throughout the year. Industry Train Displays are live demonstrations of authentic locomotives and wagons which represent the major industries served by narrow gauge railways. Another form of heritage transport can be enjoyed on your day out to the railway. Cruises on the 19th century Grand Union Canal can be combined with your historic steam train ride. Ring or write for details. Although the trains mainly operate on Sundays from mid March-mid October, there are Festive Specials in December complete with Father Christmas, mince pies etc.

LEIGHTON BUZZARD GREBE CANAL CRUISES

Pitstone Wharf, Pitstone, Nr Leighton Buzzard LU79AD

Tel: 01296 661920.

Rod and Margaret Saunders founded this business some 20 years ago and operate passenger vessels on the Grand Union Canal on a most beautiful length of the Canal where it climbs up the Chiltern escarpment from the Vale of Aylesbury into the Chilterns themselves. Built 200 years ago, the passage of time has seen the canal mellow into the beautiful countryside, it's quaint hump-back bridges and locks complimenting the scene. The fleet of passenger vessels operate from the purpose built base, Pitstone wharf, near to the village of Cheddington (of 'great train robbery fame') and there is a regular service of one and a half hour trips run during the peak summer months via the Chiltern Summit level of the canal at Tring, the highest point of the waterway, 396 feet above sea level. Passengers have the opportunity to leave the boat in the lock flight and view Marsworth reservoirs and nature reserve and to picnic ashore if they wish. The boats are mainly wide-beam, offer all weather protection, and provide considerable comfort for the passengers. There are bars on all the boats and for pre-booked parties meals can be served while cruising - try the very popular afternoon cream teas. At Pitstone Wharf the Saunders have developed a boat yard which is open to everyone, where the non-boat owner can come and enjoy the canal and if so wished, can hire a self-steer boat, from a single day hire to a week or fortnight's holiday. Tuition is available for the beginner. Superbly run, with efficient professional crews, you can relax aboard and enjoy Grebe Canal Cruises.

LUTON WOODSIDE FARM & WILD FOWL PARK

Tel: 01582 841044.

At Woodside Farm Shop and Wild Fowl Park, there are over 160 different breeds of animals and birds to see and feed with special feed from the Farm Shop. Large picnic areas, pony rides, tarzan trails, birds of prey displays and daily tractor and trailer rides are available. Open all year round Mon-Sat 8-5.30pm. Closed Sunday.

THE WERNHER COLLECTION

Tel: 01582 22955

The works of the Russian Court Jeweller,Carl Faberge are part of the finest private art collection in Great Britain. There are many paintings, costumes and other personal possessions of the Russian Imperial Family Romanov. Treasures include old master paintings, magnificent tapestries, English and

French porcelain, sculpture, bronzes and renaissance jewellery. Open to the public 29th Mar-16th October Fri-Sun 1.30-5pm.

RSPB NATURE RESERVE & GARDENS

Tel: 01767 680551.

Enjoy a day out and discover a wealth of wildlife when you visit The Lodge nature reserve set in the beautiful Bedfordshire countryside. A great day out will include woodland walks and nature trails, observation hides and wildlife garden and picnic area. Open all year round 9-9pm.

SILSOE WREST PARK HOUSE AND GARDENS

Tel: 01525 860152

The history of English gardening from 1700-1850 is set out in acres of stunning delights at Wrest Park. In the Great Garden, water catches the eye in every direction, while intersecting alleys provide splendid vistas of the many garden buildings and ornaments. West Park House was inspired by an 18th century French chateaux. the delightful intricate French Garden, with statues and fountains, enhances any view of the house from The Great Garden. Open 1st April-30th Sept weekends & Bank Holidays only 10-6pm.

THE SWISS GARDEN

Tel: 01767 627666.

Regarded as one of the top ten gardens in the country, though still under restoration, the secret of The Swiss Garden's romantic charm lies in its unique landscape design of the early 19th century. Shubberies and ponds, intricate ironwork bridges, an award-winning fernery and grotto, in a variety of follies and tiny Thatched Swiss Cottages are all contained within just ten acres. Open Mar-Jul & Sept, Sat, Sun & Bank Hols 10-6pm. Oct-Jan & Feb Sun 11-4pm.

WOBURN ABBEY

Tel: 01525 290666

Home of the Dukes of Bedford for over 350 years, Woburn Abbey is now lived in by the Duke's heir, the Marquess of Tavistock and his family. The house contains one of the most important collections and works of art in the world and is surrounded by a 3,000 acre deer park with nine species of deer. Open 1st Jan-26 Mar weekends only 27th Mar-30th October everyday.

WOBURN SAFARI PARK

Tel: 01525 290407.

Britain's largest drive through safari park with lions, tigers, rhinos, wolves, bears, hippos, monkeys and many more are all part of the attractions which make the safari park a great family attraction. New attractions include: The Adventure Ark, Penguin World and Great Woburn Railway. Open 5 Mar-30 October everyday.

BUCKINGHAMSHIRE

AYLESBURY AYLESBURY BREWERY COMPANY

Tel: 01296 395000

The company has been part of Buckinghamshire since 1895. It has some 200 Public houses most of them in the county, but you can see the ABC sign in parts of neighbouring Bedfordshire and Oxfordshire too. In addition to its own wide range of beers and lagers, you'll find a number of outstanding products from several other breweries. Visit Aylesbury and sample for yourself.

THE CHILTERN BREWERY

Tel: 01296 613647

Location: A413 Aylesbury. The ancient and revered art of the English Brewer can still be discovered flourishing in the beautiful countryside of Buckinghamshire. Completely independent and family run since its inception in 1980, this unique small brewery specialises in the production of high quality, traditionally brewed English beers with a real local flavour. Included in the large selection of home brewed ales is a 300 year old ale available in imperial pint bottles. Open Mon-Sat 9-5pm.

BUCKS RAILWAY CENTRE

Tel 01296 75440

Home to the private collection of steam locomotives. The centre boasts vintage carriages, signal box, station and gift shop. Throughout the year the centre holds special events and steaming days including regular visits by Thomas the Tank Engine, steam train rides and the extremely popular Victorian afternoon cream teas.

BUCKINGHAMSHIRE RAILWAY CENTRE

Tel 01296 655450.

The centre's 25 acre site is at Quainton Road station and exchange sidings, the last remaining Metropolitan Railway county station. On display is one of the country's largest collection of historic steam and diesel locomotives as well as a comprehensive collection of coaching and freight rolling stock. Open 11-6pm daily.

BEACONSFIELD BEKONSCOT MODEL VILLAGE

Tel: 01494 672919

The oldest model village in the world is a charming minature covering over one and a half acres. Included in the many things to see are beautifully landscaped gardens, miniature houses, castles,churches, shops and railway stations, through which runs the finest outdoor model railway (Gauge One) open to the public in the United Kingdom. The 'country' of Bekonscot is planted with 8,000 conifers, 2,000 minature shrubs, and 200 tonnes of stone used for the rockeries alone.There are no less than one hundred and sixty buildings icluding churches, hotels, shops and private houses constituting Bekonscot and the outlying villages. Souvenir Shop. Refreshment Kiosks, 2 Picnic Areas, Childrens Playground, Miniature Tramway and many other scenes. It is a paradise for photographers, a fascination for model-makers, an admiration for gardeners, 'Heaven' for small children. In fact a must for the whole family. OPEN; Every day from 10am-5pm from 16th February to 1st November.

BUCKINGHAM SILVERSTONE MOTOR RACING CIRCUIT

Tel: 01327 857271.

Home of the internationally famous British Grand Prix, Silverstone is the centre of the British motor racing industry. Throughout the year there are regular national and international race meetings featuring all shapes and forms of motor vehicles.

STOWE LANDSCAPE GARDENS

Tel: 01280 822850.

These beautiful gardens are placed in an impressive 18th century mansion set in over 500 acres of landscaped gardens inspired by William Kent and Capability Brown. The gardens feature a multitude of follies, ornate lakes, temples and monuments. Once home of the Dukes of Buckingham it is now home to one of the nation's premier independent schools, whose old boys include jazz singer George Melly and entrepreneur Richard Branson. During the summer months a series of musical events are regularly organised including music and firework concerts and the famous Stowe Opera.

CLAYDON HOUSE

Tel: 01296 730349.

Famnous as the home of the Verney Family and a house which Florence Nightingale often visited, Clayon House has impressive rococo state rooms, and a Chinese tea-room. Florence Nightingale's bedroom and a museum of her nursing work from the Crimean Wars are also open to the public.

HADDENHAM OAK FARM RARE BREEDS PARK

Tel: 01296 415709.

Aylesbury is perhaps best known for its association with ducks. In the 18th and 19th century many people in the town kept the distinctive pure white ducks considered to be a delicacy by the rich and famous in London. The ducks became known as the Aylesbury. By the 20th century tastes changed and duck breeding died out in Aylesbury. Nowadays, one of the few remaining breeds can be seen at Oak Farm Rare Breeds Park at Broughton. The park which opened in 1993 is a traditional livestock farm featuring a variety of farm animals including sheep, goats, cattle, pigs and poultry, many of which are rare breeds.

BUCKS GOAT CENTRE

Tel: 01296 612983.

One of the most comprehensive collections of goats in Britain as well as a fine selection of other livestock. The centre can also boast a farmand gift shop, plant nursery and Naughty Nanny Tea Rooms making it ideal for a family or educational visit. Open daily.

GRAND UNION CANAL

Tel: 01296 661920.

A branch of the Grand Union Canal connects into Aylesbury offering a variety of waterside walks and excellent course fishing. Picnic sites can be found beside the canal at Pitstone Wharf and at the three Locks of Soulbury. Grebe Canal Cruises run regular scheduled services into the Chiltern Hills from Pitstone Wharf.

CAMBRIDGESHIRE

CAMBRIDGE OLIVER CROMWELL HOUSE

Tel: 01353 662062.

Standing almost in the shadows of Ely Cathedral this was the home of Oliver Cromwell and his family for some ten years. Several rooms have been refurbished in Cromwellian style to show features of the house which Cromwell would have known in his time. Displays tell the story of the house's history, for although Cromwell was still the most famous occupant, the house itself has medieval origins and a fascinating past. Built in the early 14th century for the collection of tithes, it was used as a brewery and inn during the 19th century. Open 1st Apr-30th Sept 10-6pm daily including Sat, Sun and Bank Holidays 1st October-31st March 10-5.15pm.

DUXFORD AEROPLANE MUSEUM

Tel: 01223 835000

Location: Duxford is next to junction 10 off the M11 motorway, 48 miles from London. A day at Duxford is a day you'll never forget. You'll find Europe's biggest collection of historic aircraft, over 130, displayed in the giant exhibition hangers. Flimsy biplanes that fought over the trenches of the First World War through to Gulf Jets are on show at this preserved wartime airfield. See the legendary Spitfire, Lancaster and B-17 Flying

Fortress. Marvel at the U-2 Spyplane that flew on the edge of space and climb aboard Concorde. Look at the only F-111 supersonic swing-wing bomber on show in Europe and be amazed by the Harrier jump-jet. Open everyday except 24,25 & 26 December. Summer 26-Mar-16 October 10-6pm. Winter 10-4pm.

ELY CATHEDRAL

Tel: 01353 667735.

Location: A10 from Cambridge. In 673 St Ethelreda, Queen of Northumbria, founded a monastery in the centre of the Fens on the Isle of Ely where she was Abbess until her death in 679. Some 400 years later in 1081, work on the present building was begun, under the guidance of Abbot Simeon. It was completed in 1189 and the cathedral now stands as a remarkable example of Romanesque architecture. Undoubtedly, the most outstanding feature of the cathedral is the octagon, built to replace the Norman tower which collapsed in 1322. The regular free guided tours will help you appreciate all that is special about the cathedral. The Cathedral Shop in the High street offers an imaginative selection of beautiful greetings cards, pottery, glassware, and jewellery. Open daily all year round. Summer 7-7pm and in the winter 7.30-6.30pm. Sun 5pm.

LINTON ZOO

Tel 01223 891308

Location: Ten miles east of Cambridge on the B1052 just off the A460. All set in 16 acres of beautifully landscaped gardens. Find time to visit the zoo and you will find lots to interest the whole family from Sumatran Tigers,African Lions, Snow Leopards, Lynx, Wallabies and Toucans and many exciting and unusual wildlife to be found at Cambridgeshire's Wildlife Breeding Centre. The zoo is continually expanding as more of the world's threatened species are taken on board. Open all year round every day including Bank Holidays.

CORBY KIRKBY HALL

Tel: 01536 203230

Location: Off A43, four miles North East of Corby. Begun in 1570 and completed by Sir Christopher Hatton, an Elizabethan courtier who built on a scale matching his ambition to entertain the Queen. The ruins of this marvellous country house show the dawning influence of the renaissance on more traditional Tudor forms. Impressive in its sheer grandeur, the house is still partially roofed and glazed with many rooms to explore, and a wealth of richly carved stonework to discover. Kirby's Great Garden is the scene possibly of the most important formal garden restoration project in England. Open daily 10-6pm 1st April-31st October 10-4pm.

LYDDINGTON BEDE HOUSE

Tel: 01572 822438

Location: 6 miles north of Corby. Amidst the picturesque golden stone of the Leicestershire village of Lyddington, next to the handsome medieval parish church, stands Bede House. For more than 300 years, since 1602, the building was used as an almshouse, but its beginnings were less humble. It was once part of the rural palace of the Bishop's of Lincoln. Many fine details from beautiful 16th century wooden ceilings, 15th century painted glass and a grand fireplace remain to remind us of the original purpose. Open daily 10-6pm 1st April-30th Septenber.

HUNTINGDON HAMERTON WILDLIFE CENTRE

Tel: 01832 293362.

Location: 20 minutes away on the A1 from Peterborough. Set in lovely rolling countryside, Hamerton's fifteen acres are home to a fascinating array of beautiful creatures from around the world. Opened in June 1990, the centre was established as a Wildlife Conservation Sanctuary. The families and colonies of animals, some virtually extinct, can be found at the wildlife sanctuary. Over 120 species including owls, parrots, wallabies, kookaburras, meerkats and small cats can be seen here. The centre is open every day all year from 10.30-6pm in the summer and 10.30-4pm in the winter.

HINCHINGBROOKE COUNTRY PARK

Tel: 01480 451568.

At Hinchingbrooke Country Park you can wander freely through beautiful, unspoilt Cambridgeshire countryside, through woodland glades and meadows or along river banks and lakesides. Set in 156 acres of woodland, there is a natural habitat home to a suprising variety of wildlife. Here you can see herons, woodpeckers, snipe, foxes and even deer, especially on a peaceful early morning walk. Terns and dragonflies hunt over the lakes in the summer and butterfliesdrift effortlessly over the meadows. As dusk falls bats emerge and you may even hear a nightingale sing. Open all the year round.

THE OLD HUNTINGDON CAR TRAIL

Tel 01480 425831

This wonderful car trail has been designed to allow motorists or cyclists to join at any point, journeying around until you return to your starting point. Travelling through all parts of Cambridgeshire taking in all the major sights and attractions, the trail is a great way to travel. Open throughout the year Mon-Fri 9.30-5.30pm Sat 9-5pm. Closed Bank Holiday Mondays.

BUCKDEN TOWERS

Tel: 01480 811868.

Former Palace of the Bishops of Lincoln. Splendid 15th century gatehouse and tower, catherine of Aragon was imprisoned here. Open Wed 1.30-5.30pm Thurs-Sat 9-5pm Sun 9-12.30pm. Admission free.

RUTLAND WATER RUTLAND NATURE RESERVE & BIRDWATCHING CENTRE

Tel: 01572 770651.

Within easy reach of Peterborough. The Nature Reserve lies at the western end of Rutland Water, and consists of a narrow strip of land stretching for seven miles around the perimeter of the reservoir and covering an area of 350 acres between Lyndon and Egleton. Anglian Water's new Birdwatching Centre at Egleton offers superb views across the lagoons where huge flocks of waterfowl can be seen at close range. More than 200 different species of birds have been recorded at Rutland Water including ospreys and Great Northern Divers. Open all year round.

CORNWALL

BODMIN AND WENFORD RAILWAY.

Bodmin Station just south of town centre on B3268 to Lostwithiel.

Tel: 01208 73666.

Bodmin General Station is a typical Great Western Railway terminus connected by three and a half miles of line to Bodmin Parkway. (British Rail main-line) The railway passes through lovely Cornish countryside and gives access to walks and other attractions. Most trains are steam hauled. For timetables ring or write. Open April-1st week in November plus Christmas and New Year.

LANHYDROCK, National Trust.

Two and a half miles south east of Bodmin-Liskeard or B3268 Bodmin-Lostwithiel roads. Tel: 01208 74281. The finest house in Cornwall, superbly set in wooded parkland of 450 acres and encircled by a garden of rare shrubs and trees, lovely in all seasons. Allow time ot view the 42 rooms. Through the crenellated gatehouse (1641) an idyllic walk on to the River Fowey and back through the woods should not be missed. Open 30th March-31st October daily except Monday when the house only is closed, garden, shop and restaurant remain open. Open Bank Holiday Mondays 11-5.30pm, 5pm in October.

PENCARROW HOUSE AND GARDENS

Pencarrow, Washaway, Bodmin. Tel: 01208 84369.

Georgian House belonging to the Molesworth-St AubynFamily. 4 miles north-west of Bodmin, signed off the A389 and B3266 at Washaway. Mile long drive through an Ancient British Encampment, flanked by huge rhododendrons, blue hydrangeas, and specimen conifers. Historic Georgian house and Grade II listed garden; still owned and lived in by the family. Superb collection of pictures, furniture, china and some antique dolls. Marked walks through beautiful woodland gardens. Imaginatibve children's play area. Dogs welcome in grounds. Craft centre, picnic area, plant shop, self-pick soft fruits, facilities for the disabled. Open: house, tea rooms & craft centre open daily except Friday and Saturday. Easter to 15th October 1.30-5pm (1st Jun to 10th Sept and Bank Holiday Mondays open 11am) gardens open daily during season.

COLLIFORD LAKE PARK

Bolventor, Bodmin Moor. Tel: 01208 82469.

3 miles south of Bolventor. On the north-shore of Colliford Lake, a man-made reservoir completed in 1988. The 50 acre moorland park is dedicated to pleasure, education and conservation to suit all age groups and contains rare breeds of birds, cattle, poultry and sheep; many unusual and endangered species as well as more common domestic and household animals. Covered walkways. Indoor and outdoor play areas. Wide range of activities. Undercover assault course and museum. Sheltered nature walks. Open Easter until end of October 10.30am daily

JAMAICA INN

... just off A30 at Bolventor. Made famous by Daphne du Mauriers novel of the same name. For 400 years it has stood high on Bodmin Moor welcoming smugglers, highwaymen and travellers of all descriptions. It is an experience and in addition to the bars, restaurant and accommodation there is MR POTTERS MUSEUM OF CURIOSITY - showing the remarkable work of Walter Potter the famous Victorian Taxidermist who created the most imaginative animal scenes with loving care. Jamaica Inn is open all year and so too is Mr Potter's Museum except January. Tel: 01566 86250.

CAMBORNE SCHOOL OF MINES GEOLOGICAL MUSEUM & GALLERY.

Pool on the A3047 between Camborne and Redruth Tel: 01209 714866.

Display of rocks and minerals from all over the world - colourful and interesting as well as educational. Added to this a backdrop of pictures by artist living in Cornwall. Coffee corner.Shop. Open Mon-Fri 9-5pm except Bank Holidays. Admission free.

NORTH CORNWALL MUSEUM

The Clease.

Tel: 01840 212954. Opened in 1974. Privately owned and covers many aspects of life in North Cornwall from fifty to a hundred years ago. Changing exhibitions throughout the season of crafts and paintings. Open 1st Apr-30th Sept 10-5pm daily except Sundays. Free Council car park opposite.

MUSEUM OF HISTORIC CYCLING

The Old Station. Tel: 01840 212811.

One mile north of Camelford on the Boscastle road. Over 250 examples of Cycles. Old cycle repair workshop. A history of cycling from 1818. Fascinating. Open Sundays to Thursday 10-5pm all year.

DOBWALLS FAMILY ADVENTURE PARK

Tel: 01579 320325/321129.

Look for signs at Dobwalls on the A38. Wonderful day out for the whole family with one admission fee allowing you to travel ont eh Rio Grand Miniature Railroad and The Union Pacific Miniature Railroad. Access to Locomotive sheds with their 6 steam and 4 diesel locomotives including the famous 'Big Boy'. Unlimited use of Adventureland. Mr Thorburn's Edwardian Countryside. Beautiful picnic areas and Woodland Walks. Open 30th March-30th September 10-6pm. October weekends only but daily durning Devon and Cornwall Half Term holidays.

CORNWALL MARITIME MUSEUM

Bell's Court, up alley opposite Marks and Spencers in Market Street.

Tel: 01841 520413.

Cornwall's Maritime History, new 'Cornwall and the Sea' exhibition. Marine paintings, ship models, navigation and marine instruments etc. Open Easter-31st October. Opening hours are flexible.

TREBAH GARDEN, Mawnwn Smith, Nr Falmouth

Tel: 01326 250448.

This magical old Cornish garden is listed by the Good Gardens Guide as being one of the eighty finest gardens in the world. The twenty five acre, steeply wooded ravine garden falls 200 feet from the 18th century house down to a private beach on the Helford River. It is truly wonderful. The garden is undergoing a major replanting and the beach which is open to visitors to the gardens, is a secluded haven with superb views. Visitors are welcome to use the beach for swimming and picnics. Open every day of the year 10.30-5pm.

GLENDURGAN GARDENS adjoining Trebah on the Helford River, the steep, sheltered valley garden harbours a gloriously lush display of trees and flowers. The famous cherry laurel maze of 1833 reopened in July 1994 after three years of restoration. Open 1st Mar-31st Oct Tues-sat (closed Good Friday) open Bank Holiday Monday 10.30-5.30pm.

TRELISSICK
National Trust. 4 miles south of Truro on both sides of the B3289 above King Harry Ferry. A garden which offers both peace and tranquillity and splendid panoramic views across the River Fal to the Carrick Roads and Falmouth harbour. Trelissick has been planted with an abundance of those tender shrubs so characteristic of Cornish gardens. Fine woodlands encircle the gardens through which a varied circular walk can be enjoyed all year round. The house is not open. Open 1st Mar-31st Oct wed, Thrus, Fri, Sat & Bank Holiday Mondays 10.30-5.30pm (5pm in Mar and Oct).

THE TAMAR VALLEY DONKEY PARK, St Ann's Chapel, Gunnislake.
Tel: 01822 834072.
14 acres for children to explore. The donkeys enjoy it as much as the visitors and so do the loved and well cared for tame cuddly animals. Donkey rides, cart rides, rabbit warren, goat mountain, adventure play ground and much more. Picnic area, cafe, disabled facilities. Good fun for everyone and not expensive. Open every day Easter to end October 10-5.30pm.Weekends from Nov-Mar. Closed January.

THE CORNISH SEAL SANCTUARY, Gweek.
Tel: 01637 872822.
Located on the upper reaches of the Helford River by the creekside village of Gweek, approximately 6 miles from Helston. Europe's largest rescue centre for seals and occasionally even rarer sea creatures including dolphins and turtles - specially equipped hospital. Feeding time is the highlight of any visit, when the resident seals and sea lions each have their own amusing techniques and tactics for trying to steal more than their fair share. It is a different adventure every time you come here. Open all year except Christmas Day from 9am. Feeding times twice daily.

LAND'S END where the land meets the mighty Atlantic.
It is still spectacular, standing majestically, dramatic and defiant. A powerful Celtic mixture of heritage, mystery, legend and sheer natural beauty. A day out for the whole family with every concievable attraction from Moghar's Lair to the Lobster Pot Maze and The Land of Greeb and Little Cornwall bo Blackbeard's Drop. Restaurants, cafes, an hotel make this unique. 9 miles from Penzance. Open every day except Christmas Day from 10am. Tel: 01736 871501.

LANREATH FOLK AND FARM MUSEUM
Nr Looe. Village Tithe Barn - home of hundreds of vintage exhibits, craft workshops, local crafts and bric-a-brac shop. Farmhouse Kitchen, Pets corner, play area. Open daily except Saturdays Easter-June 11-5pm June to September 30th 10-6pm October 11-5pm.

LAUNCESTON STEAM RAILWAY
Station car park on Launceston's Newport Industrial Estate.
Tel: 01566 775665.
Runs through the beautiful Kensey valley from Launceston to the hamlet of New Mills. Locomotives built in Victorian times are among the oldest in regular use. The teminus also provides a buffet, book and gift shop and a transport museum. Trains run at frequent intervals from 11-4.30pm. Open Easter to end of October (closed Saturdays) Santa Specials in December.

LAWRENCE HOUSE MUSEUM
9 Castle Street.
Tel: 01566 773277.
1993 Gulbenkian Award Winner. The house built in 1753 was scheduled as a building of special historical and architectural interest in April 1950. Wide diversity of exhibits about Launceston and its history. Run by voluntary helpers, you receive a warm welcome and willing answers to any of your questions. Open 1st Apr-30th Sept including Bank Holidays 10.30-4.30pm Mon-Fri inclusive.

LAUNCESTON CASTLE English Heritage.
Tel: 01566 772365.
Launceston is crowned by the ruins of its castle, set high on a grassy mound above the town with commanding views of this beautiful corner of England. Built in the years after the Norman Conquest, it became a symbol of the power of the Earls of Cornwall. The remains of a mighty keep, high tower and surrounding walls testify to their authority and status. Parts of the castle are currentlyinaccessible due to essential conservation work. Access for visitors in wheelchairs to outer bailey; picnics welcome. Open 1st Apr-31st Oct daily 10-6pm. English Heritage members free admission.

TAMAR GLASS
Units 2C North Petherwin Workshops, North Petherwin.
Tel: 01566 785527.
Easy access from the B3254 six miles north of Launceston. Take Week St Mary turning at North Petherwin village cross roads, then 200 yards past church. Watch the Glassmakers blowing beautiful, original 'Tamar Glass' designs. Mon-Fri 10-1pm, 2-5pm. Showroom also open Sundays 2-5pm. Closed saturdays. Open Apr to end Sept, including Bank Holidays. Free

entry. Ample Free parking. Tableware and gifts for all. Quality 'Seconds' available. Commissions welcomed.

COLD NORTHCOTT WIND FARM on the A395 between Launceston and Camelford. Come and see modern technology working to produce electricity enough to supply 5,500 homes. Set amid farmland with scenic views of North Cornwall countryside. The Windmill Tea Room serves delicious homemake cakes, pasties and light refreshments. Open daily 10-6pm 7 days a week.

TREDIDON TRAILS
Tredidon Barton, St Thomas, Nr Launceston.
Tel: 01566 86288.
Signposted one mile off the A395 approximately one mile from the A30 Kennard's House junction, down a country lane. Tredidon Trails welcomes you to a new exciting countryside experience. Here are a series of different trails designed to challenge all ages and provide both fun and education, set in a beautifully landscaped area of natural beauty, with woodland, lakes and wildlife. Open Mon-Sat 9.30-5pm Easter until the end of October. Special opening in December.

PAUL CORIN'S MAGNIFICENT MUSIC MACHINES just off the B3254 at St Keyne Station, near Liskeard.
Tel: 01579 343108.
Come to the Old Mill in the lovely Looe valley, for an unforgettable nostalgic Musical entertainment - Fair Organs, Orchestrions, Player Pianos, and the Might Wurlitzer Theatre Pipe Organ. A great experience. Free car park, picnic area by the river, light refreshments, books and recordings, photography welcome, also dogs on leads. Open 10.30-5pm Easter: Good Friday for 10 days inclusive. Daily May 1st until last Sunday in October. Spring: Sundays and Thursday in April.

THE CHEESE FARM, between Upton Cross and Rilla Mill.
Tel: 01579 62244.
Discover the secrets of Yarg nettle Cheese. Visit the working Cheese Farm, Wild Boar Paddock. Entertaining Guided Tours. Barn Shop and restaurant. Drop in between 10-4pm Mon-Sat Easter to October.

THE MONKEY SANCTUARY is signposted on the B3253 at No Man's Land between East Looe and Hessenford. From Liskeard or Plymouth take the A38 to the Trerulefoot roundabout then follow the signs for Looe. Tel: 01503 262532. Beautiful woodland setting overlookingLooe Bay. For 25 years the Victorian house and gardens have been the home of a natural colony of woolly monkeys. Extensive grassed enclosures, heated indoor rooms and access to trees provide an environment in which these monkeys can thrive.

Three generations of these beautiful monkeys, all born in Cornwall, may now be seen at the Sanctuary. The special relationship between monkeys and Sanctuary staff can be observed both inside and outside their territory talks are given throughout the day explaining monkey life at the sanctuary as well as how to behave if you meet a woolly monkey in the gardens. Open Easter: Sunday before till Thursday after inclusive. Summer: Beginning of May to end of September, Sunday to Thursday 10.30-5pm (closed Friday and Saturday). Allow at least 2 hours for your visit.

MARAZION ST MICHAEL'S MOUNT, Marazion, Penzance. National Trust. Tel: 01736 710265.

This magical island is the jewel in Cornwall's crown, a national treasure which is a must for every visitor to the far west. The great granite crag which rises from the waters of Mount's Bay is surmounted by an embattled 14th century castle, home of the St Aubyn family for over 300 years. On the water's edge there is a harbourside community, an ancient trading place for tin and other Cornish goods which today features shops and restaurants. Open: 30th March-31st October Mon-Fri (shop and restaurant open daily) 10.30-5.30pm November - 29th March. Guided tours as tide, weather and circumstances permit.

NEWLYN ART GALLERY.

Approaching Newlyn, the gallery is the first building on the sea-side of the coast road from Penzance.

Tel: 01736 63715.

Presents an exciting and varied programme of contemporary art and related events throughout the year. The Gallery is a dynamic artistic activity. One of the most important visual arts resources in the South West. Open: Mon-Sat 10-5pm Admission free.

NEWQUAY TRERICE National Trust.

Tel: 01637 875404.

An architectural gem - a small Elizabethan manor house, built before the Armada in 1571. The summer-flowering garden is unusual in content and layout and there is an orchard planted with old varieties of fruit trees. A small museum traces the history of the lawn mower. Open: 30th Mar-31st October daily except Tuesday 11-5.30pm Closes 5pm in October.

SPRINGFIELDS PONY CENTRE AND FUN PARK

St Columb Major. Well signposted from the St Columb Major roundabout. Tel: 01637 881224.

All wather attraction. Friendly Shetland ponies, pony rides. Pets Corner. Enjoy feeding lambs, calves and goats and hand feed the ducks fish and Sika deer. Springfields is a paradise for children. Burger Bar. Lake View restaurant. Dogs not allowed. Open: 31st March-30th October, 7 days a week 9.30-5.30pm October 10-4.30pm.

NEWQUAY SEA LIFE CENTRE

Towan Promenade.

Tel:01637 872822.

Experience the thrill of a deep sea dive without getting wet asyou journey through a wondrous watery world with a surprise around every corner. Fascinating and extraordinary experience. Open: All year except Christmas Day 10am.

PRIDEAUX PLACE

Tel: 01841 532411/532945.

Follow brown tourist signs from A389 Padstow Ring Road. Free parking in grounds. Dogs welcome in grounds on leads. For 400 years, Prideaux Place has been the home of the Prideaux family, an ancient Cornish clan who can be traced to Prideaux Castle, Luxulyan at the time of the Conquest in 1066. Completed in 1592 the Grade I Listed building has been embellished and extended by successive generations. Filled with treasures, including royal and family portraits, porcelain and fine furniture, this beautiful Cornish mansion is still very much a family home with the majority of rooms still in regular use. Open: Easter-Sept 30th 1.30-5pm Sundays to Thursday inclusive. Easter, Whit and late summer Bank Holidays from 11am.

GEEVOR TIN MINE

Beside the B3306 coast road from St Ives to Land's End, at Pendeen, St Just. Tel/Fax: 01736 788662. The last tin mine in Penwith, in spectacular coastal setting. A unique Cornish Mining Museum, with a video showing surface and underground working. Personal guided tour of surface plant, the most complete historic mining/processing plant in Britain. Open: Easter to October daily 10.30-5.30pm,not Saturdays except Bank Holiday Weekends. November-Easter Sun-Fri 10.30-5pm.

PENZANCE AND DISTRICT MUSEUM AND ART GALLERY.

Off Morrah Rd.

Tel: 01736 363625.

New Interactive Multimedia computer technology which has been istalled in the new Archaeoloty gallery. Discover the shops of the 1890s and 1030s and use the new computer image data- bank to discover what the area looked like in times past. The Art Galleries contain the largest collection of Newlyn School paintings in public ownership. Open: Mon-Fri 10.30-4.30pm Sat: 10.30-12.30pm.

TRINITY HOUSE NATIONAL LIGHTHOUSE CENTRE
The Old Buoy Store, Wharf Road. Tel: 01736 360077.
One of the few national museums outside London, it houses the finest collection of lighthouse equipment in the world. Audio-visual. Open: Daily April-October.

TRENGWAINTON GARDENS
Nr. Penzance. In the far west, the uncommonly mild climate encourages the most tender and exotic shrubs and trees to flourish. A unique feature is the complex of walled gardens with west-facing raised beds, built c1820 for the gorwing of early vegetables. Open: 1st March-31st October, Wed, Thurs, Fri, Sat and Bank Holiday Mondays 10.30-5.30pm (5pm in March and October) National Trust.

THE EGYPTIAN HOUSE c.1835.
Built to contain a Geological Museum. After years of neglect was artistically restored by the Landmark Trust in 1973. The Royal Arms are of the period George III,IV and William IV.

PERRANPORTH NANSMELLYN MARSH RESERVE is to be found where the stream flows into the outskirts of Perranporth - here there is the remnant of a large reed bed which used to occupy the valley floor. The reeds provide shelter and food for Sedge Warblers and Reed Buntings, whose songs can be heard all night in May. Several species of the very local Wainscott moths are also well established in the reserve. A hide on the east side of the reserve provides a good vantage point from which to observe the birds. Keys from Perranporth Information Centre.

PORTHCURNO THE MINACK THEATRE
Tel:01736 810181.
The theatre is on the south coast ablut 3 miles from Land's End and 9 miles from Penzance. At the seaward end of the Porthcurno valley go up the winding hill. The Theatre is on your left. Wonderful open air theatre. Audience are admitted one and a half hours before 'curtain up'. The earlier you arrive the closer you will be to the stage. The sun can be very hot at matinees and it is advisable to wear warm clothes in the evening. The seats are very hard but they do hire cushions! If you are disabled, please bring at least one able bodied person with you and try to let the management know in advance. Parking is free. Sandwiches and confectionery, hot and cold drinks are available pre-show and during the interval. There is an Exhibition Centre. Hours 10-5.30pm daily from 1st April-31st October (closing at 4.30pm in Oct). On days when there is a matinee, the Centre will be closed from 12-2.30pm, and viewing of the Theatre will be restricted durning the performance. A fabulour experience and unlike any other theatre in the world.

REDRUTH CORNISH ENGINES, National Trust, Pool, Redruth. Tel: 01209 216657. In the heart of Cornwall's richest mining district there is a rare opportunity to see two fine Cornish beam engines preserved in their imposing houses. One can be seen in action. Open: March-October daily 11-5pm (or sunset if earlier) 11-6pm July and August.

SALTASH COTEHELE. National Trust.
On the west bank of the Tamar 1 mile west of Calstock by footpath, 8 miles south west of Tavistock, 14 miles from Plymouth visa Saltash Bridge. Tel: 01579 51222. Recorded Information 01579 51222. Enchantingly remote, perched high above the wooded banks of the Tamar. For nearly six centuries the home of the Edgcumbe family. The manor house gives the impression of having been woven through time. It retains a medieval atmosphere. Cotehele today is a romantically unique estate - the terraced garden with its pools and dovecote, a working watermill and adjoining ciderpress, the Quay with its evocation of Victorian bustle. Now the home berth of the Shamrock, one of the last surviving Tamar sailing barges. Worth spending a day here. Open: 30th Mar-31st Oct. House, restaurant and mill daily except Friday (open Good Friday) House 12-5.30pm. Tearoom on Quay, shop and garden daily 11-5pm. Quay gallery daily 12-5pm.

ST AUSTELL WHEAL MARTYN CHINA CLAY HERITAGE CENTRE.
Follow the signs to Carthew on the B3274, 2 miles north of St Austell.
Tel/Fax: 01726 850362.
Historic trail - discover the history of this important Cornish industry. Open air historic clay workings, indoor exhibitions, displays and audio-visual show, 1899 locomotive working water wheels and 1916 Peerless lorry. Nature Trail - mile long walk through the beautiful wooded site and spectacular views of a moder day working clay pit. Childrens Adventure Trail - picnic area, mineral displays, gift and pottery shop. Open: daily April to October 10-6pm.

LOST GARDENS OF HELIGAN, Pentewan, St Austell.
Tel: 01726 844157/843566.
Award winning gardens, asleep for more than seventy years, are the scene of the largest garden restoration project in Europe. Most exciting, must be seen. Open: every day of the year 10-4.30pm.

KIDS KINGDOM Albert Road, St Austell.
Tel: 01726 77377.
Indoor Adventure Play Centre for the under 12's who must be accompanied by a responsible adult. Great fun, plenty to do. Open: 7 days a week Easter-end September 10-9pm. October-Easter 10-6pm.

ST IVES SOCIETY OF ARTISTS, Old Mariners Church, Norway Square adjacent to Sloop car park. Exhibits representational work. Gallery overlooks harbour that was the inspiration for so much of their work. Open: March-early November Mon-Sat. 10-12.30 & 2-4.30pm Mid-December-Mid January sam hours. Closed Christmas Day and Boxing Day.
Tel: 01736 795582.

BARBARA HEPWORTH MUSEUM Barnoon Hill,.
Tel: 01736 796226.
Sculptures in wood, stone and bronze can be sen in the late Barbara Hepworth's house, studio and sub-tropical garden where she lived and worked form 1949-75.

TATE GALLERY, Porthmeor Beach.
Tel: 01736 796226.
Presents changing displays of 20th century modern art in the context of Cornwall. Displays are drawn from the Tate Gallery collection. Open: all year. Closed 24,25,26 Dec and 1st Jan.

ST KEW THE CORNWALL DONKEY & PONY SANCTUARY.
Lower Maidenland.
Tel: 01208 841710.
Plenty to do. Help groom the donkeys and ponies. Play area. Adventure Swamp. Cart rides for children. Picnic by the stream. Under cover: The Eeyore Club for younger children. Bouncy Castle. Meet the baby animals. Coffee Shop and Tea Garden. Just off the A39 Wadebridge to Camelford road, 3 miles form Wadebridge. Open: daily one week before Easter-October 10-5pm. Telephone for winter opening hours.

TINTAGEL OLD POST OFFICE
Tel: 01840 770024.
National Trust. One of the most characterful buildings in Cornwall, and a house of great antiquity, this small 14th century manor is full of charm and interest. Tumble-roofed and weathered by the centuries, it is restored in the fashion of the Post Office it was for nearly50 years. Open: 1st Apr-31st Oct daily 11-5.30pm. Closes 5pm Oct.

TINTAGEL CASTLE
Tel: 01840 770328.
Off Tintagel Head, half a mile along a track from Tintagel (no vehicles). Throughout the ages Tintagel has exerted a profound fascination for writers, artists and travellers. Even today this wild and windswept corner of the Cornish coast preserves its mystery. Associated in legend with Merlin and King Arthur it remains an enigma. Clearly it was occupied long before the

medieval castle, whose ruins you can see, was laid out in the 13th century. Whatever the truth, Tintagle Castle, clinging to its lonely island, with the surf thundering against the cliffs below and the waves breaking over the threshold of Merlin's Cave, remains one of the most spectacular and romantic spots in the British Isles. Toilets on site. Land Rover service from village to castle. Open: 1st Apr-31st Oct open daily 10-4pm. English Heritage members free admission.

TORPOINT ANTHONY, National Trust.
Torpoint 01752 812191.
A superb example of an early 18th century mansion. The main block is faced in silver grey stone, with red brick wings. Set in parkland and fine gardens overlooking the Lynher River, home of the great Cornish family of Carew. Anthony contains a wealth of paintings, tapestries, furniture and embroideries. An unusual Bath House in the grounds can be viewed by arrangement. Open: 30th Mar-31st Oct Tues, Wed, Thurs and Bank Holiday Mondays plus Sundays in June, July and August 1.30-5.30pm. Tea room opens 12.30pm.

TRESCO ABBEY GARDENS, Isles of Scilly.
Tel: 01720 422849.
The garden flourishes on this small island only two miles long. Nowhere else in the British Isles does such an exotic and exciting collection of plants grow in the open. Within its 14 acres, palms shoot skywards; stately echiums resemble burning rockets. Quite wonderful to see. From its early days Tresco has welcomed visitors; the effect is so stunning that even the non-gardener cannot fail to be impressed. Open: everyday of the year. 10-4pm.

TRURO ROYAL CORNWALL MUSEUM, River Street.
Tel: 01872 272205.
Superb collections of Cornish history and archaeology, paintings, ceramics, silver and gold. Examine a genuine Egyptian mummy of the world famous collection of Cornish minerals. Shop and cafe. Open: Mon-Sat 10-5pm except Bank Holidays.

TREWITHEN GARDENS, Grampound Rd, Nr Truro.
Tel: 01726 882763/4.
Adjoining Probus Gardens on A390. Covering some 30 acres and created in the early years of this century, the gardens are outstanding and internationally famous. Renowned for the magnificent collection of camellias, rhododendrons, magnolias and many rare trees and shrubs. Extensive woodland gardens surrounded by traditional landscaped parkland. Teas and light refreshments. Plants and shrubs for sale. The house goes back to the 17thcentury and has been cared for and lived in by the same family since

1715. Open: Gardens: 1st Mar-30th Sept Mon-Sat 10-4.30pm Nursery: All year Mon-Fri 9-4.3-pm House: Apr-Jul Mon and Tues only and August Bank Holiday Monday 2-4pm.

PROBUS GARDENS,
Probus.
Tel: 01726 882597.
A garden with a difference; a true centre of excellence. Here you can enjoy literally thousands of specimen plants and shrubs growing in superb settings - and find new ways to get more out of your garden. Whether you live in Cornwall or are visiting, a real enthusiast or an enthusiastic amateur you'll find something here to inspire you. Open: every day 1st April-30th Sept 10-5pm and Mon-Fri in the winter from 10-4pm

THE ORIGINAL CORNISH SCRUMPY CALLESTOCK CIDER FARM,
Penhallow.
Tel: 01872 573356.
Traditional Cider farm with a Jam Kitchen. Shire Horses and other friendly farm animals. Free samples of all their products. Signposted off the A3075 Newquay road at Penhallow. Designated as being of outstanding natural beauty and listed as being of special historical interest. Open:Feb-Dec Mon-Fri 9-6pm and Saturdays from Easter-Oct. July/August Mon-Fri 9am- 8pm. Sundays:10-6pm.

WADEBRIDGE SHIRE HORSE ADVENTURE PARK,
Tredinnick, Wadebridge.
Tel: 01841 540276.
8 miles from Newquay, 6 miles Wadebridge. Take A39. Bigger every year this provides a fantastic day out. 6 major attractions in one. Magnificent Shire Horses, unique owl sanctuary, the thrilling world of Adventure, amazing Playhouse for younger children, Old McDonald's Barn, full of baby animals to pet and feed. Jungle Fantasy, 9,000ft of ropes, balls, nets and slides. The whole family will be entertained for hours on end - regardless of weather and all for one all-inclusive entry price. Dogs welcome on a lead. Opem daily 1st Apr-28th Oct 10-5pm. Closed Saturdays in October.

MELLINGEY MILL WILLOW CRAFT CENTRE, St Issey.
Tel: 01841 540604.
Basket Workshop, Willow Beds, Nature Walks, Willow Walks with play houses. Illustrated history and nature displays. Photographic Exhibitions. Basket Showroom. Picnic and play area, tearoom and terrace, waterwheel, gift shop. Ample parking. Open: Easter-30th Sept 10-5pm.

ZENNOR THE WAYSIDE MUSEUM

B3306 St Ives to St Just coast road.

Tel: 01736 796945.

A unique private museum, founded in 1935, covering every aspect of life in Zennor from 3,000 BC to 1930s. Waterwheels, Millhouse, Wheelwrights, Blacksmiths, a Miller's cottage with kitchen and parlour etc. nearby is the famous Mermaid Chair in the village church. Open: Easter to October 31st daily from 10am plus evenings in high season.

DEVON

ASHBURTON THE RIVER DART COUNTRY PARK,

Holne Park.

Tel: 01364652511.

Country fun for everyone. Adventure Playgrounds, Bathing, Picnics, Woodland Walks, Pony Riding, Ananconda Run and more. Suitable for any age. Open: Easter to September.

ASHBURTON MUSEUM,

1 West Street.

Tel: 01364 63278.

Attractive small town museum displaying local artifacts and items of local history, geology and social customs. The home of the Paul Endacott North America Indian Collection. Open: Tues, Thurs, Fri & Sat. 2.30-5pm, mid-May to end of September.

AXMINSTER THE MINSTER CHURCH OF ST MARY.

Tel: 01297 32264.

There has been a church in Axminster for over 1200 years. Open all day.

BABBACOMBE THE MODEL VILLAGE

Tel: 01803 328669.

Unique reproduction of the English countryside often featured on TV. A Masterpiece of miniature landscaping. Press Button information in English and French. Illuminated every evening from dusk (Easter to October). Buses direct from Brixham, Paignton, Torquay, Teignmouth, Dawlish and Exeter. Open: every day except Christmas Day. Easter to September 9am-10pm. October 9am-9pm. November 9am to dusk.

BARNSTAPLE ARLINGTON COURT. N.T.
Tel: 01271 850296.
Houses one of the country's finest collection of carriages in the stables. Walk through peaceful woods, a haven for birdlife. See Shetland ponies and Jacob sheep in the park. The Regency House has fascinating Victorian collections of model ships, animals, exotic shells, pewter and snuff boxes, and the history of a 600 year old Devon family. Open: Mar 30th-Oct 30th daily except Sat 11-5.30pm. Dogs in park only on short leads. Refreshments and Shop.

MARWOOD HILL GARDENS
4 miles north of Barnstaple, signed from the A361 (Barnstaple-Braunton road). Beautiful gardens with many RHS Awards for plants.

GREEN LANES SHOPPING CENTRE
- at the heart of the town. Excellent shopping centre. Every Wednesday afternoon there is the sound of live music. Thrpughout the week, the Centre plays host to a wealth of displays and exhibitions. So whether shopping, dining, or just enjoying the experience - make a day of it in Green Lane.

BICKINGTON GORSE BLOSSOM MINIATURE RAILWAY PARK
Tel: 01626 82361.
Off old A38 near Bickington, 3 miles north-west of Newton Abbot. The 7 1/4 inch guage trains, carring all the family, run for nearly 3/4 mile, twisting and turning through acres of gardens and natural woodland, in cuttings on high banks, recapturing the great days of steam in miniature. Unlimited train rides for an all inclusive admission price. Large car park. Adventure play ground. Picnic area, restaurant and shop. A great family attraction. Open Easter daily to first Sunday in October 10am-4.30pm.

BICKLEIGH BICKLEIGH MILL
Tel: 01884 855419.
Mid-Devon's largest and most popular award winning centre. Craft Centres, Farm & Fishing Centres, Picnic, Leisure and Bird Garden. Special events. Don't come without a camera or with less than an hour to spare. Open: Easter to Christmas 10-6pm (5pm in Nov & Dec).

BICKLEIGH CASTLE
Tel: 01884 855363.
Ancient Royalist stronghold spanning 900 years of history and architecture - and still lived in! The 11th century detached Chapel with pre-tudor furnishings, the Armoury including Cromwellian arms and armour, the Guard Room, The Great Hall, 'Tudor' Bedroom, and the 17th century farmhouse - are all shown. Excellent Museum. Picturesque moated garden. A great tome for the whole family - and educational too! Open: Easter week

and then Wednesdays, Sundays and Bank Holidays to late May Bank Holiday; then to 2nd October daily. (Except Saturdays) 2-5.30pm. Refreshments and Shops.

BIDEFORD THE BIG SHEEP

Tel: 01237 477916.

2 miles west of Bideford on the A39 North Devon link road. Look for the big flag! A working farm turned wacky tourist attraction. Combining traditional rural crafts, such as cheesmaking and shearing, with hilarious novelties such as sheep racing and duck trialling. An amusing programme of events throughout the day. Hours of entertainment for all ages whatever the weather. The main programmes start at 10.30am and 1.15pm. Phone for details. Shop and restaurant. Open: daily 10-6pm all year.

BLACKAWTON WOODLANDS LEISURE PARK

Tel: 01803 712598.

60 acres of indoor and outdoor fun for a full day of variety for the whole family. Experience 12 challenging Play-Zones for every age and ability plus great Entertainment Days. Go walk-about round the seven acre Animal park then linger by the exotic Waterfowl Collection. Take time to relax by a woodland pool; enjoy that cream tea on the Rose Terrace or a delicious meal in the cafe. Browse round the Gift Shop for that souvenir of a fantastic day out. Discount Ticket for 2 adults and 2 children. Open daily March until the beginning of November 9.30am until dusk.

BOVEY TRACEY THE DEVON GUILD OF CRAFTSMEN

Riverside Mill.

Tel: 01626 832223.

Constantly changing series of exhibitions of the finest craftsmanship in Britain today. There is a shop where members of the Guild sell a wide range of top quality goods, and an attractive Granery Coffee Shop serving light meals including imaginative vegetarian dishes throughout the day. Open 10am-5.30pm seven days a week all year.

PARKE RARE BREEDS FARM.

N.T.

Haytor Rd.

Tel: 01626 832093.

Over 200 acres of parkland in the wooded valley of the River Bovey, forming a beautiful approach to Dartmoor. Lovely walks through woodlands, beside the river and along the route of the old railway track. National Trust and Dartmoor Park information centre and National Park headquarters. A private collection of rare farm animals. An interpretation centre and farm trail helpspeople to discover yesterday's farm and bring it to life. National Trust

members must pary the admission charge. Open: parkland all year. Rare Breeds Farm, April to October daily 10-
5pm.

HOUSE OF MARBLES,
The Old Pottery, Pottery Rd.
Tel: 01626 835358.
At the House of Marbles they have been manufacturing their unusual range of games, toys, marbles and glassware for many years. Visitors are welcome to view the old pottery buildings with their listed kilns. Watch the glass blowing work in progress and browse in the factory showroom/seconds shop. Coffee Shop/Restaurant. Museum area. Open: Shop. Mon-Sat 9-5pm. Sundays (easter-September). Glassmaking can be viewed Mon-Fri 9-5pm. Sundays and Bank Holidays 10-3pm (Easter-Sept).

BRENTOR ROWDEN GARDENS,
Nr Tavistock.
Tel: 01822 810275.
Rare, unsual and aquatic plant specialists. Open: 1st Apr-30th Sept. Sat, Sun and Bank Holidays 10-5pm.

BRIXHAM BRIXHAM MUSEUM,
New Road.
Tel: 01803 856267.
Brixham is Torbay's oldest town, and the museum has been created by the local community to portray its own unique history. A history close to the sea and rich in fishing, trawling, shipbuilding, the dangers of life at sea, and reliance on the lifeboat. Enjoy a charming historical insight into the lives of Brixham people, from early times to the present day. Open: April-October Mon-Sat 10am-5pm.

BUCKFAST ABBEY
Tel: 01364 43723.
The Abbey is a living Benedictine monastery and the only fully restored medieval monastery in Britain. The church contains many internationally known works of art. Shops, refreshments, ample car park and caravan park. An audio-visual and exhibition tells you about the Abbey from its foundation in AD 1018 to the present day. Church open daily. Exhibition: Easter to end October.

BUCKFAST BUTTERFLY FARM,
Buckfastleigh Steam & Leisure Park.
Tel: 01364 42916.
Wander through the tropical landscape gardenwith its ponds, waterfalls and

bridges and see exotic butterflies and moths from many parts of the world - live - flying around you. An all weather educational attraction for all the family. Free parking for cars and coaches. Gift Shop. Picnic area. Open: daily Apr-1st Nov from 10-6pm.

SOUTH DEVON RAILWAY

Tel: 01364 642338.

Buckfastleigh Steam and Leisure Park takes you right back into the steam age with a seven mile Great Western branch line alongside the beautiful River Dart to Totnes, a museum, other attractions and extensive riverside picnic grounds, putting, maze, pets corner and much more. Trains run at Easter and daily during the summer season. For other days, exact dates and train times see timetable or telephone.

PENNYWELL DEVON'S FARM & WILDLIFE CENTRE

Tel: 01364 642023.

Take your most direct route to the A38 between Exeter and Plymouth. Follow the brown signs for Pennywell near the town of Buckfastleigh. Traditional farming mixes easily with modern tourism here. Christopher and Nicola Murray, with their team of helpers, show tremendous skill at introducing even the youngest child to all the animals. Great value for the whole family. A wonderful day out. Excellent meals, snacks and drinks at realistic prices. Family ticket for 2 adults and 2 children. Open daily 10am-5.50pm from the end of March until the end of October. 10am-5.30pm. Discount for group bookings.

BUCKLAND MONACHORUM THE GARDEN HOUSE, Nr Yelverton.

Run by the Fortescue Garden Trust, the walled garden has been discribed as the 'most beautiful 1 ½ acres in England'. It is certainly a very beautiful garden from March to October, with an enormous range of plants and colour. Teas and light lunches are served in the main rooms of the elegant house. There is also a well-stocked plant centre, which has an enviable reputation as a source of well-grown unusual plants. Open every day March-October 10.30am-5pm.

CHUDLEIGH THE WHEEL CRAFT WORKSHOPS & RESTAURANT

Tel: 01626 853255(Rest) 01626 852698(Workshops).

Workshops producing high quality craft/designer goods in and around restored mill. Items always for sale. Large working backshot wheel with extensive interior machinery. Licensed restaurant. Home-made food. Open in the evenings. Open 1-am-5.30pm 7 days a week all year. Admission free.

SILVERLANDS,
Stokelake.
The exciting new all-weather family attraction set in the heart of the beautiful Teign Valley. Delightful model displays, fascinating exhibitions, craft workshops, animal meadow, special events. Cafe, gift shop, free parking. Direct access from A38 Exeter/Plymouth road, take Teign Valley exit on to B3193. Open daily 1-am-6pm Easter to late October.

CANONTIEGN FALLS,
Nr Chudleigh.
Tel: 01647 52434.
Set in the heart of a private 100 acres estate, it is a joy to visit in any season, with its waterfalls, lakes and abundant wildlife. Lady Exmouth Falls has a sheer drop of 220ft, making it the highest fall in England. Clampitt Falls and Secret Garden Falls must also be seen. Canontiegn Nature Trails about one mile in length take in the woods, waterfalls and lakes. Licensed restaurant and cafe plus all weather barbecue offers a wide range of meals and snacks including delicious cream teas. Turn off the A38 at Teign Valley Cudleigh junction. Follow the brown tourist signs for 3 miles on the B3193. Open 10-5.30pm mid March-mid November. Winter: Sundays only and school holidays. One overall charge.

CLOVELLY THE MILKY WAY,
Downland Farm, Nr Clovelly.
Tel: 01237 431255.
Offers one of th largest undercover attractions in the South West. It is a family run countryside experience, featuringshows, demonstrations, train rides, play areas, history and much more. The North Devon Bird of Prey Centre is part of the Milky Way. Wonderful day out. Inside and outside picnic areas. Tea garden. Free parking. Dogs allowed on leads. No need for wellies. Open Mar 31st-31st Oct 10.30-6pm. On the main A39 Bideford-Bude road, 2 miles from Clovelly.

COMBE MARTIN WATERMOUTH CASTLE
Tel: 01272 867474.
Between Ilfracombe and Combe Martin. One price covers all attractions except coin operated machines, catering and shop goods. One of the UK's most exciting and unique all weather attractions. Enter the castle and experience nostalgic displays, brilliant sights and sounds, breathtaking beautiful coloured waterfalls, haunted dungeons, magical fairy tales that come to life before your very eyes. And that's not all. Ring to confirm dates and times.

DALWOOD BURROW FARM GARDENS,
Nr Axminster.
Tel: 01404 831258.
Beautifully landscaped gardens extending to over 5 acres. Superb views. The fascinating woodland garden, created in an ancient Roman clay pit, features wild flowers and an array of moisture loving plants including candelabra primulas. These provide a wonderful compliment to the rhododendrons and azaleas. This area is particularly beautiful early in the season. Gardens open daily 1 Apr-30th Sept 2pm-7pm. Home-made Cream Teas Sundays, Wednesdays and Bank Holidays. Ample parking with picnic area.

DARTINGTON THE DARTINGTON CIDER PRESS CENTRE,
Skinners Bridge.
Tel: 01803 864171.
The Cider Press Centre just 2 miles from Totnes on the A384 Buckfastleigh road offers a complete day out for all the family. Well known for its exhibitions, the centre also house some unusual shops including Tridas Toys and Dartington Glass. There are two restaurants and lots of special events throughout the summer. Plenty of free parking. Open 9.30-5.30pm Mon-Sat and on Sundays during school summer holidays.

DARTMOUTH DARTMOUTH CASTLE,
Tel: 01803 833588.
Guarding the narrow entrance to the Dart estuary - one of the loveliest in England - the Castle was one of the first to be built for artillery. Dates from 15th century. It says much for the foresight of the burgesses of Dartmouth that the site of the fortress has not been bettered. Guns were mounted there in the Second World War. Open: all year round except for Dec 24/25/26 and Jan 1st. Car park. Toilets. Refreshment facilities nearby.

WOODLANDS LEISURE PARK
Blackawton.
Tel: 01803 712598.
An all action day out, set in over 60 acres of glorious Devonshire countryside. This awarding winning park offers excellence, service, quality and value. The new Cyclone Twin Watercoaster the ultimate watercoaster, The Tornado a 500 metre twisting and turning toboggan run. Toddlers Village, Paddling Pool, Circus Drome Indoor Play & Equipment Centre, Animal Farm, Falconry Centre with displays throughout the day, the list is endless. Great fun for all whatever the weather. Open daily Mar 15th-Nov30th 9.30-dusk.

DAWLISH DAWLISH MUSEUM

... is open to and for the benefit of the public for the display of exhibits relating to the history of the Town of Dawlish, and of the South West of England in general. Open daily May-Sept 10-12.30pm, 2-5pm. Sunday 2-5pm.

THE CRAWSHAW GALLERY

Priory Road.

Tel: 01626 862032.

Talented artist family led by Alwyn Crawshaw. The gallery houses his paintings, fine art prints, his many books on learing to paint and also general artisic memorabilia. The work on show for sale varies greatly from small sketches through to large paintings in all mediums. Car park. Open Wed-Sat 9.30-1pm & 2-5.30pm.

DREWSTEIGNTON CASTLE DROGO

Tel: 01647 433306.

Perched on a crag overlooking the Teign Valley, the castle is a marvel of the ingenuity of the architect Sir Edwin Lutyens. The house was built during the early part of this century and not fully completed before the Second World War. It is full of fascination; magnificent craftsmanship combines with the grim splendour of a medieval castle. There are magnificent views from the castle standing above the wooded gorge of the Teign to Dartmoor. Beautiful secluded garden containing a circular croquet lawn. Equipment may be hired from the Administrator. Open daily, except Friday, 30 Mar-30 Oct 11-5.30pm. Tearoom in car park.

EXETER CREALY COUNTRY PARK

Sidmouth Road, Clyst St Mary.

Tel: 01395 233200.

Fun for everyone. Buzzard's Swoop Freefall Slide. Archery, Animal Farmand Barnyarn. Bug Club Corner, Games Meadow, Discovery Trails, Milk-a-Cow and many more attractions. Open every day 10-6pm closed 25th & 26th Dec. Dogs welcome in most of the park.

MARITIME MUSEUM

Tel: 01392 58075.

The World's biggest and best collection of World's Boats. This is a 'Please Touch' Museum where you go where you like, when you like. There are boats of every kind from Canoes to Coracles, Row Boats to Steamers. Super place. Free parking. Tea room. Summer Boat Hire. Open daily all year except Christmas and Boxing Day 10-5pm (6pm in summer).

TOPSHAM MUSEUM
25 The Strand, Topsham.
Tel: 01392 873244.
Late 17th century merchants house with period rooms and sail loft. The Exe Estuary story of shipbuilding and maritime trade of Topsham. 1900 model of Topsham. Honiton lace and lace making. Open 2-5pm Mar-Oct Mon, Wed, & Sat. Sundays in July, Aug & Sept. Tearoom Shop and garden.

ROYAL ALBERT MEMORIAL MUSEUM
Queen Street.
Tel: 01392 265858.
One of the finest Victorian buildings in Exeter holds outstanding collections of local and national importance. Fine Art includes Devon artists of the 18th and 19th centuries. Open East-October. Mon-Sat. Nov-Easter Tues-Sat 10-5.30pm Coffee Shop & Gift Shop. Admission Free.

GUILDHALL,
High Street.
Tel: 01392 265500.
Earliest reference contained in a deed of 1160. One of the oldest municipal buildings in the United Kingdom still regularly used for council meetings and civic functions. The City Silver and Regalia, and an interesting portrait of Princess Henrietta, sister to Charles II is on display. Open Tues-Sat subject to Civic requirements. Ring first.

ST NICHOLAS PRIORY
The Mint, off Fore Street.
Tel: 01392 265858.
Originally the guest wing of a Benedictine Priory, St Nicholas Priory is now displayed as it later became, the house of a rich, Elizabethan merchant. Splendid 15th century guest hall with period furniture and fine plaster ceilings. Very limited opening. Ring for opening times.

UNDERGROUND PASSAGES off High Street.
Tel: 01392 265887.
Unique medieval water supply of the city and an amazing experience. The passages are very narrow and are not suitable for anyone prone to claustrophobia.

THE CATHEDRAL
Open daily. Cathedral shop. Licensed refectory. Somewhere that deserves your time.

KILLERTON
Broadclyst.
Tel: 01392 881345.
A National Trust property. Wonderful house the home of the Acland family. There are 15 acres of beautiful hillside gardens which sweep down to wide lawns and formal herbaceous borders. The garden and park offer delightful walks through rare trees and shrubs. Ice house and bear hut. The Pauline de Bush collection of costume is displayed in the house in a series of rooms furnished in different periods, ranging from the second half of the 18th century to the present day. Licensed restraurant. Light refreshments in the Coach House. Shop including plant sales. Fresh home-baked bread and cake sales. Open April-end of October, daily 11-6pm. You will find Killerton 2 miles north of Broadclyst on the west side of the B3181 Exeter to Cullompton road. The entrance is off the B3185.

POWDERHAM CASTLE
Kenton.
Tel: 01626 890243.
In a tranquil and beautiful setting beside the picturesque estuary of the River Exe lies the medieval Castle of Powderham. Visit a succession of magnificent Halls and State Rooms filled with lavish furnishings, tapestries and historic portraits of the fascinating Courtenay family. The castle has been their home for over 600 yeas and the present Earl of Devon is a direct descendant of Sir Philip Courtenay who built the Castle between 1390 and 1420. It was extensively damaged during the Civil War and considerable restoration and alterations followed during the 18th and 19th centuries. Open every day except Saturday from 10-5.30pm (last guided tour 5pm) April to September inclusive. Cream teas, light lunches available in the Courtyard Tea Rooms. Gift Shop.

GREAT TORRINGTON DARTINGTON CRYSTAL
Tel: 01805 624233.
A uniqueworking factory where you can watch skilled craftsmen at work blowing and shaping beautiful crystal. A superb exhibition 'Glass the Incrdible Liquid' reveals glass in a new light - its history fashion, colour and science from Egyptians to spacecraft - with 'hands-on' exhibits for the young. Open all year. Visitor Centre including Factory Visit Mon-Fri 9.30am-3.30pm except Bank Holidays. Visitor Centre only - Glass the Incredible Liquid Mon-Sat 9.30am-4.30pm (open Sundays during July & August). Factory Shop and Pavilion Restaurant Mon-Fri 9.30am-5pm (Sundays from June-Dec 10.30am-4.30pm).

ROSEMOOR GARDEN,
one mile south-east of Great Torrington on the B3220 Exeter Road.
Tel: 01805 624067. Visit this famous garden, beautiful in all seasons and now

being expanded by the Royal Horticultural Society to 40 acres. The year round display from Lady Anne's internationally renowned 8 acres garden is now complemented by a variety of exciting plantings in the new garden. Herb garden. Ornamental vegetable garden. Cottage garden and foliage garden. New in 1994 a fruit and vegetable garden. Open: Garden all year, April to September 10-6pm. March and October 10-5pm. November-February 10-4pm. Closed Christmas Day. Visitors Centre March 1st to 4th December. Licensed Restaurant. Shop and Plant Centre.

KINGSBRIDGE MINIATURE RAILWAY gives a half-mile return ride for the length of the quay alongside the estuary. The track guage is only 1 1/4 inches, yet the train is robust enough to take the whole family. The miniature railway is right by the quay car park, ideally placed for rides to keep the children amused while shopping in Kingsbridge or on the way to and from the beaches. Trains run at Easter, then daily mid-May to mid-Sept. 11-5pm weather permitting.

KINGSBRIDGE TO SALCOMBE RIVER CRUISES.
Tel: 01548 853607.
Weekday scheduled Kingsbridge to Salcombe Ferry service, evening cruises, Sunday estuary and coastal cruises. The ferry operates from its boatyard and the quay, Kingsbridge and from Ferry pier, Salcombe. It takes about half an hour each way. The scenic beauty and maritime activity provide estuary and land views of unrivalled magnificence. Boats run daily from May to end of Sept. For details ring.

COOKWORTHY MUSEUM OF RURAL LIFE
108 Fore Street.
Tel: 01548 853235.
A lively, local museum housed in a beautiful 17th century school building. Children particularly love the miniature world of the dolls house and toys while parents enjoy costumes, porcelain, craft tools, old local photographs, Victorian kitchen, dairy and the farm machinery gallery, plus a complete Victorian pharmacy. Open 1st Apr to 30th Sept 10-5pm Mon-Sat. Oct 10-4.30pm Mon-Fri.

LODDISWELL VINEYARD & WINERY,
Lilwell, Loddeswell, Nr Kingsbridge.
Tel: 01548 550221.
Six-acre vineyard growing traditional and newvarieties for commercial wine production, including the use of polthene tunnels. Wines prodiced have received the coveted Gold Seal of Quality. An opportunity to taste the wines and buy a bottle to take home. Video films of planting, harvesting and wine-mak8ing. Large picnic area and tea room. Open 2pm-6pm Mon to Thurs 1st

Apr to 30th Oct and Sundays during July and August. Guided tours start 2.30pm and 4pm. May to September.

LYDFORD LYDFORD GORGE NT

At Lydford village half-way between Okehampton and Tavistock, 1 mile west of A386.

Tel: 01822 82441 or 320.

This famous gorge is one and a half miles long, providing enchanting riverside walks leading to the spectacular 90ft White Lady Waterfall. The walk then enters a steep sided, oak-wooded ravine scooped out by the River Lyd as it plunges into a series of whirlpools including the thrilling Devil's Cauldron. A home to a wide variety of animals, birds and plants. Visitors must wear stout footwear and take care at all times. There may be delays at the Devil's Cauldron during busy periods. Open: 30th Mar-30th Oct daily 10-5.30pm. Nov-Mar 10.30am-3pm. Dogs on leads only. Light refreshments daily in July and August. Sundays and Bank Holidays during the remainder of the season.

LYNMOUTH EXMOOR BRASS RUBBING AND GOBBYCRAFT CENTRE,

Woodside Craft Centre, Watersmeet Road.

Tel: 01598 52529.

Well established family attraction with an exciting collection of over one hundred facsimiles of Monumental Brasses and special Rubbing Plates for small children. Choose from Knights dating from 1277, Ladies and Clergy, the Nobility, animal footrests and even a skeleton. The aim is to help visitors discover an easy and rewarding craft. Open: Easter Holidays, Spring, Half-term, Summer Holidays (from 3rd weekend in July to end of August) and Autumn Half-term. 10.30-5pm. At all other times from Monday to Friday 11-4.30pm. The Public are asked to note that due to school visits they are sometimes closed during term time. Visitors are advised to check first by telephone.

MANATON BECKY FALLS

On the B3344 Bovey Tracey to Manaton Road. Nature Trails, 70ft Waterfall in a private estate of 50 acres, set in a beautiful deep wooded valley. Safe attended car park. Restaurant and Tea Rooms. Gift Shop, Picnic areas. Super family day out at a reasonable inclusive price - car including all occupants. Open 10-6pm Easter to October.

MORETONHAMPSTEAD THE MINIATURE PONY CENTRE

Tel: 01647 432400.

Acres of fun in this beautiful country park. Tiny cuddly ponies, rare miniature donkeys and many other animals. Pony rides. Action packed adventure playground - indoors and out. Lakes, birds and giant trout. Licensed restaurant. Gift shop. Open end of March to 31st October 10.30-5pm. Closed Fridays except Easter.

NEWTON ABBOT TUCKERS MALTINGS,
Teign Road, Osborne Park.
Tel: 01626 334734.
England's only working Malthouse open to the public. This spectacular unique Victorian building is one ofDevon's most fascinating family days out. Become a maltster and help produce malt for over twenty five West Country breweries. There is a 19th century street, with audio and video effects. Open: Easter to 30th October. (Closed Saturdays) 10-4pm (July & August 10-5pm). Follow the brown and white signs from Newton Abbot railway station. Allow at least three hours for your visit.

OKEHAMPTON FINCH FOUNDRY, NT.
Sticklepath.
Tel: 01837 840046.
Fascinating early 19th century forge, powered by three water wheels, which produced sickles, scythes and shovels for both agriculture and mining. The forge is situated in the centre of this picturesque village with attractive countryside and river walks adjoining. Picnic area, refreshments available. Open: Apr to Oct, daily except Tuesdays 11-5pm.

MUSEUM OF DARTMOOR LIFE.
Tel: 01837 52295.
The galleries tell the story of the people who have lived and worked on Dartmoor from pre-historic times to the present day. Displays also examine issues such as the environment and the effects of social change. Open Easter to October 10-5pm Monday to Saturday plus Sundays from June to September. Weekdays only through winter.

OKEHAMPTON CASTLE half a mile south west of Okehampton signed from the old A30.
Tel: 01837 52844.
Established by the Normans as the seat of the first Sheriff of Devon. It was largely rebuilt in the 14th century as a lavish country home for the Courtenays, Earls of Devon. Beautiful woodland setting. Inclusive Soundalive personal stereo tours. Picnic area. Free car park. Open: 1st April-30th September, 10-6pm daily.

OTTERY ST MARY CHADHAY,
1 mile northwest of Ottery St Mary.
Tel: 01404 812432.
Mentioned in the reign of Edward I. The main part of the present house was

built about 1550. An Elizabethan Long Gallery was added at the end of the 16th century, thereby forming a unique and lovely courtyard. Some alterations in the 18th century. The house is occupied by the present owners. It is viewed by conducted tours. Open: Spring Bank Holiday, Sunday and Monday and then each Tuesday, Wednesday and Thursday during July and August. Also Late Summer Holiday Sunday and Monday.

PAIGNTON ZOO

Tel: 01803 527936.

Tucked away in a lush green valley Paignton Zoo has 75 acres of botanical gardens and one of England's largest zoos with over 1,300 animals. Excellently laid out and informative. Children love the hands-on activity centre. Meet zoo keepers and hear how they care for the animals. Allow 3-5 hours. Open: Every day except Christmas Day from 10am. Close 6pm summer and 5pm in winter. Restaurant. Picnic lawns and indoor picnic area. Shops.

PAIGNTON & DARTMOUTH STEAM RAILWAY.

Queen's Park Station, Paignton.

Tel: 01803 555872.

Steam trains run for seven miles in Great Western tradition along the spectacular Torbay coast to Churston and through the wooded slopes bordering the Dart estuaryto Kingswear. The Boat Train circular journey from Paignton to Kingswear by steam train, by ferry to Dartmouth, then a river cruise or the Round Robin tour which includes the river trip to Totnes and return by bus to Torbay. Services run from April to October with Santa Special trains in December. Ring for times.

OLDWAY MANSION.

Tel: 01803 296244/386880.

Guided tours round this imposing mansion, set in 17 acres of beautiful, landscaped gardens, which was built as the home of Isaac Merritt Singer of sewing machine fame, and made even more impressive by his son, Paris. Open: Daily from 8am-6pm during the week and from 9-5pm Sundays. Refreshments are available

PLYMOUTH DOME.

On Hoe overlooking Plymouth Sound.

Tel: 01752 600608.

Since the days of Drake, Cook and Darwin, Plymouth has been associated with adventure and discovery. Today, visitors can embark on their own adventures and discover the rich heritage and fascinating history of this great seafaring City in the award-winning Plymouth Dome. Atmospheric reconstructions and high-tech equipment take you on an extraordinary journey through time, through the sights and smell of Elizabethan Plymouth;

on dramatic voyages across the world; and through the tragic devastation wrought by the Blitz on Plymouth. Full access and facilities for people with disabilities. Its a great adventure for all the family come rain or shine. Open: daily at 9am. Closed Christmas Day. Cafe. Shop.

SALTRAM HOUSE,

Plympton.

Tel: 01752 336546.

A magnificent George II mansion complete with its original contents, set in a lovely landscaped park overlooking the estuary. There is superb plasterwork and decoration including two important rooms designed by Robert Adam. The house contains fine period furniture and pictures, including many portraits by Sir Joshua Reynolds. There is an Orangery and the woodlands run down to the river. Beautiful stables. Restaurant. Shop. Saltram is three and a half miles from Plymouth City Centre and 2 miles west of Plympton, between the A38 and A379. Open: House - April to end of October Sundays to Thursday, but open Good Friday from 12.30-6pm. Garden: daily from 2.30-5.30pm.

SOUTH MOLTON QUINCE HONEY FARM,

North Road.

Tel: 01769 572401.

Signposted from A361. Free parking and picnic area. Home to a million honey bees, this unique world famous exhibition is acknowledged by experts to be the best in the world. Fascinating place. Open: end of March-end of September 9am-6pm daily. October 9am-5pm daily. Cafeteria serving breakfast, lunch, afternoon tea and light refreshments. Shop: open all year. Sells Devon Honey in jars, combs and pottery, beeswax candles, honey and beeswax cosmetics.

SPARKWELL DARTMOOR WILD LIFE PARK.

Nr Plymouth.

Tel: 01752 837209.

The park is situated on the South Western edge of Dartmoor in thirty acres of beautiful Devon countryside, threemiles from Plymouth and one and half miles from the A38. It has one of the most comprehensive Big Cat collections in the South West, a Falconry Centre second to none and a very successful animal breeding programme. Daily Events: Flying Displays 12 noon-4pm. Animal Encounters 2pm-3.30pm. Big Cat Feeding Time 3.30pm. Seal Feeding Time 4.30pm. Open every day of the year.

TAVISTOCK MORWELLHAM QUAY
off A390 between Tavistock and Gunnislake.
Tel: 01822 832766.
Award winning 'Leading West Country Day Out'. 150 acres of family fascination and fun with The Copper Mine, Wagonette Rides - shire drawn carriages. Try on Costumes from the 1860's wardrobe (bring your camera). Guided tours of port and ships, village school, workshops, farm. Open 10am-5.30pm daily. Winter: 1st November-Easter, Copper Mine and grounds only 10am-4.30pm (closed Christmas week). Licensed restaurant. Pasty House. In winter light refreshments only. Shop.

COUNTRYMAN CIDER,
Felldownhead, Milton Abbot.
Tel: 01822 870226.
Located in the 15th century stables of a former coaching inn, on the Devon side of the lovely Tamar Valley. You are welcome to visit all the year round to see how their traditional Farmhouse Ciders are made. Countryman Cider is available on Draft. Opening hours: Mon-Sat 9am-6pm all year round. Closed Sundays.

TIVERTON GRAND WESTERN HORSEBOAT
7 miles from M5 J27. On approaching Tiverton follow brown signs for 'Grand Western Canal'.
Tel: 01884 253345.
From Tiverton's historic Lime Kiln Wharf, traditionally painted barges are gently pulled along by heavy horses wearing colourful harness and brasses, as you travel the same journey as their predecessors 100 years ago. At the Wharf there is a permanently moored Restaurant Barge, picnic area and car park. Enjoy a quiet stroll along the towpath or hire an electric or rowing boat. Open: Easter-end Sept. Many trips, please phone to confirm.

TORQUAY KENTS CAVERN SHOWCAVES.
Off Babbacombe Road.
Tel: 01803 215136.
A masterpiece of nature which cannot be copied. Spectacular formations. Stalagmites, stalactites and limestone naturally sculptured and coloured over 2,000,000 years. A natural underground world. Accompany a member of the team who will help you discover the mystery of prehistory on a 40 minute stroll. Open: all year. July and August 10am-8.15pm (Sat 5.15pm). April, May June and September 10am-5.15pm. October 10am-4.15pm, November to March - winter timetable applies, please enquire. Refreshments Easter to October. Well stocked shop.

TORQUAY MUSEUM,
529 Babbacombe Road. Tel: 01803 293975.
Here you will find exhibits that are unimaginably ancient. Discoveries from Kents Cavern which helped unravel the antiquity of man and how he lived. The evidence of animals that lived 400 million years ago. As well as these early exhibits you can see the quaint bygones and pictures which trace the history of Torquay from the Victorian Age to Agatha Christie in our own century. Open: allyear round. Mon-Fri 10am-4,45pm Sunday afternoons 1.30pm-4.45pm. Easter to October Mon-Sat 10am-4.45pm Closed Christmas Week and Good Friday.

TORRE ABBEY,
The King's Drive.
Tel: 01803 293593.
History comes alive at Torbay's most historic building. Built in 1196 you can trace the 900 years of development from monastery, imposing home of wealthy families to Mayor's official residence of modern day. Eight galleries house stunning collections of pictures and works of art, twelve historic rooms, the Agatha Christie Memorial Room, and refreshments in the Victorian Kitchen. Outside the colourful gardens, gatehouse and the magnificent 'Spanish Barn' of Armada fame. Open: easter to October daily 9.30am-6pm. November-March parties only by appointment.

BYGONES,
Fore Street, St Marychurch.
Tel: 01803 326108.
Wander back in time, explore an olde worlde street with over 20 life size shops and period rooms including a forge and pub with authentic smells and sounds. Allow at least one hour for your visit. Summer opening June to end of August. Sunday to Friday 10am-10pm Winter opening March, April, May, September, October. Daily 10am-6pm January, February, November, December, Monday to Friday 10am-2pm. Saturday & Sunday 10am-5pm.

TOTNES BOWDEN HOUSE,
1 mile west of Totnes off A381.
Tel: 01803 863664.
Photographic Museum. Fascinating. Guided tours - allow one hour. Family in Georgian Costume - welcomed by the footman in the courtyard. Tudor and Queen Anne architecture. Movie memorabilia coffee bar. Licensed cafe, cream teas - served by wenches. Picnic area - enjoy the grounds with farm views. Open: Tuesdays, Wednesday and Thursday plus Bank Holiday Sundays and Mondays. From first Tuesday in April to last Thursday in October. Grounds and Museum 11am. House 2pm. Open all year for coaches by appointment.

WIDECOMBE-IN-THE-MOOR THE CHURCH HOUSE,
NT.
Tel: 0136 41321.
Originally a brewhouse dating back to 1537, this former village school is now leased as a village hall and occasionally open to the public. The adjacent Sexton's Cottage is a National Trust and Dartmoor National Park information centre and gift shop. Open: Information Centre and shop, mid-February to Christmas daily 10am-5pm.

YEALMPTON NATIONAL SHIRE HORSE CENTRE.
Tel: 01752 621321.
A big day come rain or shine. Get close to the gentle Giants, watch the unique Parade of the Shires. See thrilling Birds of Prey flying displays. Try the excitement of the Adventure Playground. Restaurants. Open every day 10am-5pm. Stables and Restaurant 10am-4pm. Closed 24th-26th December. Please phone to confirm winter opening times.

KITLEY CAVES.
Tel: 01752 880202.
The cave research team based here is continually extending the known limits of the caves andadding to the information on their formation. Visitors are free to wander through the illuminated cave passages where information panels are set amongst the strange and spectacular rock formations. Surrounded by pretty countryside and close to the River Yealm, this makes a very pleasant outing. The caves, gift shop, museum and children's play area are open for Easter weekend and daily from the Spring Bank Holiday until the end of September 10am-5.30pm.

YELVERTON BUCKLAND ABBEY
Tel: 01822 853607.
N.T. 11 miles north of Plymouth and 6 miles south of Tavistock to the west of A386 at Yelverton. Buckland's peaceful atmosphere belies its fascinating past. Once inside, the story of this 13th century monastery, which later became home to Sir Francis Drake, and his descendants, unfolds through exhibitions on monastic life, the Battle of the Armada and Drake memorabilia including his famous drum. The Tudor Great Hall features beautiful plasterwork and the Kitchen has a range of cooking utensils, open hearth and 'hams' hanging form the ceiling. Wonderful grounds. Open: 30th Mar-10th Oct daily except Thrus 10.30-5.30pm. Nov, Mar, Sat and Sun 2pm-5pm. Dogs in car park only, on leads. Licensed restaurant. Light refreshments in tea room at peak times. Shop.

YELVERTON PAPERWEIGHT CENTRE.

Tel: 01822 854250.

Houses the famous 'Broughton Collection' of antique and modern glass paperweights. Both the casual visitor and the serious collector are fascinated by the beautifully handcrafted milleriori and abstract designs. Open: 2 weeks before Easter to end of October Mon-Sat. 10am-5pm. Sundays end of May-mid September Sun 10am-5pm. All winter Wed 1pm-5pm. Sat 10am-5pm. December 1st-24th Mon-Sat 10am-5pm. At Leg O'Mutton Corner, large car park, toilets, restaurant, pub, post office, corner shop, moorland for picnics.

DORSET

ABBOTSBURY TITHE BARN COUNTRY MUSEUM

Tel: 01305 871817.

This fascinating collection of farm tools, machinery and rural bygones is housed in one of the largest thatched barns in the country. Exhibits include, a farm workers kitchen, game keeping, 17th century working Dovecote, Monastic Remains, and rare poultry. Open daily in the summer Apr-Oct 10-6pm. Winter Sun only Children free entry.

SUB TROPICAL GARDENS

Tel: 01305 871387.

These magnificent gardens are famed for their stunning magnolias, ancient camellias and rhododendrons. Set in over 20 acres of woodland valley with 18th century walled garden, peacocks, ponds and streams, the gardens are home to many rare and record breaking plants from all over the world, thriving in its own unique micro-climate. The Sub Tropical Gardens include a woodland trail, Victorian Garden, children's play area and guided tours. Open daily in the summer mid Mar-Nov 10-5pm and in the winter Nov-mid Mar 10am-dusk. Free admission for children.

SWANNERY & THE FLEET

Tel: 01305 871684.

Famous as the home for the only managed colony of mute swans in the world that can be visited during nesting time. Situated on the shore of the fleet, separated from the sea by the Chesil Bank, it is a place of great beauty, teeming with wildlife, where you can watch the family life of swans at close quaters. Little changes since 1400AD. Attractions include children's Ugly Duckling activity trail, gift shop and Ancient Duck Decoy. Open daily from Apr-Oct 10-5pm.

BEAMINSTER PARNHAM HOUSE

Tel: 01308 863130.

Location: Exit 25 from M5 in Taunton. Parnham House is a restored manor house and gardens that are the focal point for a renaissance in English furniture design. A whole day can be enjoyed exploring the extensive gardens, playing croquet, picnicking and paddling. See the spacious interiors where the leading artists and craftsmen show their work and then discover the innovations in a working woodland. The magnificent Great Hall with heraldic stained glass is the heart of the house, the major staircase is embellished with anotable trompe l'oeil, the delight of many visitors. Open 10-5pm Wed, Suns & Bank Holidays from Apr-Oct.

BOURNEMOUTH THE BOURNEMOUTH BEARS.

Tel: 01202 293544.

Explore the cuddly world of the teddy bear. Old bears, new bears, famous bears and designer bears. A fluffy wonderland for the young, a nostalgic journey for the not so young. Open daily all year round 9.30-5.30pm.

MUMMIES & MAGIC

Tel: 01202 293544.

An amazing exhibition featuring Royal Mummies and Ancient Egypt from the earliest sand-dried bodies to the majestic mummy of Rameses the Great. Discover the secrets of mummification and the magic that protected them. Open daily all year round9.30am-5.30pm.

DINOSAUR SAFARI

Tel: 01202 293544.

Bournemouth's great hands-on indoor adventure of discovery. See life-size dinosaurs, bones, fossils and computers that let you experiment with dinosaurs. A great day out for all the family. Open daily 9.30-5.30pm.

BOVINGTON THE TANK MUSEUM.

Tel: 01929 403463.

Six large exhibition halls include fascinating displays including World War I, Inter War Years, World War II, Post War, Experimental Tanks and carriers. They all make for an exciting and enjoyable day out for the whole family. Many of the 270 plus armoured fighting vehicles are permanently on show, but there is always something new and exciting to be seen. There are permanent attractions including video theatres, Costume Collection, Challenger Tank Ride, Simulator and much more. Open daily.

CHARD FORDE ABBEY & GARDENS

Tel: 01460 20231.

Location: four miles south of Chard on the B3167. Founded by Cistercian Monks over 800 years ago, the monastery still stands transformed by the architecture of the 16th and 17th centuries into a splendid Country House. The gardens extend to 30 acres with origins in theearly 18th century. They are landscaped around this great building. There are lakes, magnificent trees and shrubs and in the kitchen garden there is an extensive nursery specialising in rare and unusual plants. Open daily throughout the year 10-4pm. The Abbey is open from 1st April-end of October Wed, Sun and Bank Holidays 1-4.30pm.

DORCHESTER ATHELHAMPTON HOUSE & GARDENS

Tel: 01305 848363.

A visit to Athelhampton will attract you to one of the fines examples of 15th century donestic architecture in the kingdom. Enjoy the lived in family house with its Great Hall, Great Chamber, Wine Cellar and King's Room all exquisitely furnished. Wander through 20 acres of beautiful grounds including eight walled gardens, fountains, pavillions and topiary pyramid all encircled by the River Piddle. Home-made cream teas, gift shop and free car park. Open daily 27th Mar-30th Oct, Wed, Thurs, Sun and Bank Holidays.

TUTANKHAMON - THE EXHIBITION

Tel: 01305 269571.

An unforgettable experience can be had by all at Tutankhamon's Tomb and Treasures exhibition. Walk into the past to recapture the mystery and magnificence of ancient Egypt. Open daily all year round 9.30-5.30pm.

POOLE COMPTON ACRES

Tel: 01202 700778.

Location: Three miles to the south of Bournemouth. Compton Acres is a wonderful set of international gardens. There is a delightful Herbaceous Border, Italian Garden, Palm Court, Woodland Walk and Glen, Rock and Water Garden all of which are separate and distinct gardens. The Japanese Garden opened in 1986 and is reputed to be the only completely genuine Japanese Garden in Europe. Open daily from 1st Mar-end of October from 10.30am-6.30pm.

NATURAL WORLD

Tel: 01202 686712.

The Natural World is one of Poole's biggest attractions, housing the widest collection of fish, insects, amphibians and reptiles in the area providing all year-round indoor entertainment. Watch the reptiles being fed on Saturdays and for a big thrill see the sharks being fed on Wednesdays, Fridays and

Sundays. Open daily ghroughout the year. Summer 9.30-9pm and Winter 10-5pm.

WAREHAM MONKEY WORLD

Tel: 0800 456600.

Monkey World was opened in 1987 to rescue chimpanzees and rehabilitate them into natural surroundings. See the baby chimps playing in their nursery or visit some of the other monkeys having fun in the natural habitat. Apart from visiting the monkeys test your skill on the new 15 stage obstacle course and enjoy the three outdoor play areas, including mini motor bikes, swings and slides. Open every day from Apr-end of October 10-5pm.

CORFE CASTLE

Tel: 01929 481294.

Location: on 351 Wareham to Swanage Road. Corfe Castle is one of the most impressive ruins in England. An important medieval Royal fortification commandinga cleft in Purbeck hills. Bought in 1635 by Sir John Bankes, Attorney General to Charles I; in 1646 his wife Lady Bankes withstood two long sieges in the Civil War, only surrendering the Castle to the Parliamentary Forces after treachery. The Castle was then systematically demolished. Today it stands ruined on a hill and the only natural route is through the Purbeck hills. Open from Feb-end of Oct daily. 10-5.30pm and Nov-Feb Sat & Sun only 12-3.30pm.

WEYMOUTH SEALIFE PARK

Tel: 01305 788255.

Location: short walk from Weymouth town centre on A353 towards Wareham. Don't miss the chance to voyage to the bottom of the sea, take a wildlife trek through a tropical rain forest and brave the jaws of a giant shark in Captain Kid's World......all on the same day! In Neno's Discovery you'll experience the spine-tingling sensation of peering through the windows of a sunken wreck whilst special outdoor rock-pools provide 'hands on' encounters with a host of sturdy rockpool creatures like hermit crabs and starfish. With regular talks and feeding displays adding to the entertainment, along with a challenging quiz trail to test the fishy knowledge of young and old alike, the day is sure to be a fun-filled memorable adventure for everyone. Open from 10am seven days a week.

BREWERS QUAY

Tel: 01305 777622.

Brewers Quay is an amazing complex of so many interesting and exciting attractions it is difficult to know where to begin. From the Famous Timewalk with its Brewers Tale, free entry to the shopping village, craft centre and

'Grannys Attic' antiques loft, through to the hands on Discovery experience, magnificent Shire Horse Centre and Boat Trips, not to mention the town museum, exhibitions and regular festivals, to the wonderful cafes, bars and restaurants. Brewers Quay is a treasure just wating to be discovered. Open seven days a week 9.30-5.30pm except Christmas Day and Boxing Day.

THE DEEP SEA ADVENTURE

Tel: 01305 760690.

Come and explore for yourself the undersea world and experience the story of underwater exploration and maritime exploits through the ages. As you enter the scene is set. You pass through a creaking, rusty shipwreck, and travel back to the 17th century discovering the ancient means used to explore the oceans. Follow the diver signs around this 9,000 square foot maritime adventure story and you will descend through three floors of exciting displays. As you pass through the sights, sounds and smells of the deep, the story is one of underwater discovery, shipwreaks and survival exploits brought to life by the use of animation and interactive displays covering over 300 years. Open 9.30-8pm July and August and 9.30-7pm Winter.

WIMBORNE MERLEY BIRD GARDENS

Tel: 01202 883790.

Location: 15 minute drive from Bounremouth along A35. Visit this fascinating combination of exotic birds, formal gardens, shrubberies and water gardens all set in one of the largest and most beautifulhistoric walled gardens in the country. Walk through aviaries and see an extraordinary variety of birds or visit the herb gardens or children's pets corner. Open daily throughout the year.

KINGSTON LACY

Tel: 01202 883402.

Location: on B3082 Wimborne to Blandford Road. 17th century house designed for Sir Ralph Bankes by Sir Roger Pratt. It was altered by Sir Charles Barry in the 19th century. Houses one of the finest picture collections in the country with paintings by Titian, Rubens and Velasquez. Fine collection of Egyptian artefacts collected by William John Bankes in the 19th century. The house is set in 13 acres of formal gardens and woodland walks surrounded by a park of 254 acres with a fine herd of Red Devon cattle. Open 26th Mar-30th Oct daily except Thurs and Fri, 12-5.30pm.

ESSEX

BRAINTREE THE WORKING SILK MUSEUM

Tel: 01376 553393.

Visitors to this wonderful museum will get a unique insight into silk production and find that the preparation of fibres in the silk trade provides a fascinating living spectacle. You'll be able to see the brilliantly coloured silks stored on hundreds of bobbins. Come along to The Working Silk Museum and just enjoy watching skilled craftsmen at work, in an age when that is a rare sight indeed. Open Mon-Sat 10-12.30pm & 1.30-5pm. Closed Sundays & Bank Holidays.

DISTRICT MUSEUM

Tel: 01376 325266.

'Threads of Time' tells the story of Braintree District and its important place in our island's history. By creativity and skill, the people of the area developed ideas which shaped 20th century life. Gallery heritage, the production of fabrics for state occasions during the past 200 years and innovations in metal window design and man-made textiles in which this District is the best in the world. The Museum has a retail outlet with a wide range of crafts, original artwork and publications for sale. Open Tues-Sat 10-5pm.

COGGLESHALL THE SECRET GARDEN OF ESSEX

Tel: 01376 563796.

Visit the estate of Marks Hall and stroll around the beautiful parkland and unspoilt countryside, little changed in 100 years. See the ornamental lakes, cascades and wall garden or have a longer walk through the ancient woodlands and enjoy the peace and tranquillity of this historic estate. Open Easter-31st October 10.30-4.30pm weekdays. 10.30-6pm weekends and Bank Holidays. Closed every Monday except Bank Holidays.

COLCHESTER ZOO

Tel: 01206 330253.

Award winning Colchester Zoo, set in 40 acres of beautiful grounds is home to 150 species of animals from around the world including Snow Leopards, Siberian Tigers, Orangutans, Elephants and breeding Chimpanzees. Children will enjoy the chance to stroke the animals in the centre's Children's Paddock and can also play amoung a menageries ofrescued animals and birds, open: daily from 9.30.

COLCHESTER LEISURE WORLD

Tel: 01206 766500.

A fun-filled exercise day out for the whole family can be enjoyed. Get wet in the split level leisure pool with two stunning flume rides, outside river rapids and water cannons or relax in the Agna Springs with saunas, thermal hydro massage pool, spa pools, steam rooms, solaria and plunge pools. Open daily every day of the year.

COLCHESTER CASTLE MUSEUM

A day which will allow you to be a Roman and take a step back into their way of life. Visit the vaults of a Roman Temple, try on a toga, touch genuine Roman pottery or dress up as a Roman Soldier. Discover the secrets of the Castle Prisons and learn the story of the Colchester martyrs and find out about the prisoners themselves and the prison conditions over the centuries. Open daily 10-5pm Mon-Sat all year round and 2-5pm on Sundays from Mar-Nov.

STANSTEAD HOUSE ON THE HILL TOY MUSEUM.

Tel: 01279 813237.

This interesting place is one of the largest toy museums in the world covering 7,000 square feet and housing a vast collection of toys, games and books from the late Victorian era, right up to the 1970s. The Museum offers a nostalgic trip back to childhood with a wealth of displays, some of them animated, there is apuppet theatre, moving Meccano fairground, military displays, space toys, books, comics, games and much, much more. Open: daily Mar-Nov 10-4pm.

MOUNTFICHET CASTLE & NORMAN VILLAGE

Tel: 01279 813237.

Why not wander through the mists of time and visit this historic castle, the only Norman motte and baily Castle in the world, re-constructed on its original site, steeped in 900 years of history. From 1215, the castle lay forgotten and overgrown for over 750 years until its re-creation today and the site now offers the visitor an opportunity to be transported back through the centuries. Open daily March-November 10-5pm.

SAFFRON WALDEN AUDLEY END HOUSE & PARK

Tel: 01799 522399.

Location: one mile west of Saffron Walden on B1383. The facade of Audley End, glimpsed across the superb landscaped parkland that surrounds it, is one of the great sights of East Anglia. From the columns of the elaborate twin porches to the distinctive turquoise copper caps of the turrets, the whole beautiful sight of the building speaks of the ambitions of the Jacobean Lord, the Earl of Suffolk. The richly decorated interiors of the house are arranged to show how they would have appeared in particular periods in history. Amongst the highlights of a tour of the house - with 30 rooms - are the Great Hall with its massive wooden Jacobean screen, the decorative little Drawing Room designed by Robert Adam. Visits to the house can be taken daily. Open 1st April-30th September Wed, Sun and Bank Holidays.

THE FRY ART GALLERY

Location: 15 miles north of Cambridge.

Thisart gallery which could be called 'The Gallery in the Garden' houses a unique collection of works brought together during the lidetime of many of the artists who were part of the artistic community which flourished in and around the nearby village of Great Barfield before and after World War II. The Fry Gallery exhibits examples of work by George Chapman, Sheila Robinson, Marianne Straub and Kenneth Rowntree to name but a few, and demonstrates the continuing artistic tradition of north-west Essex by including a number of works of other artists who have local connections. Open on Sat and Sun afternoons 2.45-5.30pm from Easter Sunday to the last Sun in October. Free admission.

SAFFRON WALDEN MUSEUM

Tel: 01799 510333.

From moccasins to mummy cases and woolly mammoths to Wallace the Lion, there is something to please everyone. The Museum is close to the parish church of this lovely medieval market town and the ruins of Walden's 12th century castle stand in the grounds. Displays include fine ceramics, glass, furniture and woodwork, costume, needlework, dolls and toys. The Museum also hosts The Worlds of Man Gallery showing objects of international importance from the peoples of Africa, Australia and the Pacific, mainly collected in the 19th century. Open Mon-Sat 10-5pm Mar-Oct. Mon-Sat 11-4pm Nov-Feb.

SOUTHEND ON SEA SEALIFE CENTRE

Tel: 01702 462400.

Visitors to this new underwater attraction can journey beneath the ocean waves and discover thousands of amazing sea creatures. A dramatic walk-through tunnel creates the illusion of a walk on the sea bed with sharks, rays and many others gliding silently by, inches above your head. Open daily from 10am all year round.

THE LYNN TAIT GALLERY

Tel: 01702 471737.

This wonderful gallery can be found in the heart of the historic old town of Leigh. In this lovely atmosphere of times gone by you can discover unusual gifts, local paintings and early local photographs from the turn of the century, all displayed on delightful arefacts from yester-year, including a magnificently restored Southend Pier Train. Open from 11am till dusk.

GLOUCESTERSHIRE

BERKELEY BERKELEY CASTLE

off A38

Tel: 01453 810332

Perfectly preserved 800 year old castle. Keep, dungeons, staterooms, Great Hall kitchen, tapestries, furniture, silver. Ornamental gardens and Butterfly house. Open Apr-Sept Tues-Sun. October Sundays only.

BIBURY BIBURY TROUT FARM

Tel: 01285 740215.

A working farm which breeds Rainbow Trout. Visitors can see developing trout in 20 ponds and may feed the fish. Gift shop, picnic area, fishing. Open March-September.

BOURTON ON THE WATER COTSWOLD MOTOR MUSEUM

Tel: 01451 21255.

30 motor vehicles and the largest collection of vintageadvertising signs in Britain. Also Village Life exhibition. Open daily Feb-Nov.

BIRDLAND

Rissington Road.

Tel: 01451 20689

Bird garden on the banks of the River Windrush. Penguins, waterfowl, tropical and sub tropical birds, many at liberty. Open daily all year.

BOURTON-ON-THE-WATER THE MODEL VILLAGE

Situated behind the Old New Inn, this is an incredible piece of work which delights and intrigues people of all ages from childhood upwards. The idea of building came from the late Mr C.A.Morris, landlord of the inn who in 1935 decided to turn his vegetable garden into something more decorative. It was not his intention to build a miniature model village but gradually the idea evolved and the model village was born. Every building and every feature of the landscape was built carefully to a scale of one ninth of the original and everything was erected exactly in position with the sole exception of the Church of St Lawrence, which stands at the far end of the model from the inn. One of the most fascinating aspects of the village is the miniature River Windrush, which is an artifical stream about three feet wide flowing from the working model of the mill through the whole length of the village. It is spanned by five little stone bridges, all of which are precise replicas of the famous bridges of Bourton. Now that the Model Village has been standing for some years the Cotswold stone of which all the buildings are constructed has begun to mellow. Each year it looks more and more like the original. OPEN; Summer 9-6pm. Winter 10-dusk. Not Christmas Day. Pets on leads. No access for disabled.

FOLLY FARM WATERFOWL
Off A436 near Bourton-on-the-Water.
Tel: 01451 20285.
Collection of rare poultry breeds and waterfowl including endangered species, in natural Cotswold farm surroundings. Open daily all year.

BROADWAY SNOWSHILL MANOR
NT.
Tel: 01386 852410.
Location: 3 miles south west of Broadway, off A44, the Cotswold manor house is full to the brim with Charles Wade's collection of craftmanship from all over the world. Each room has a theme from Samurai armour to navigation, from musical instruments to carts and bicycles. The cottage garden is charming. Open Easter Sat, Sun and Mon 1-6pm. Closed Good Friday. April-October: Sat and Sun 1-5pm. May to end September: daily except Tues 1-6pm.

CHELTENHAM CHEDWORTH ROMAN VILLA
Yarnworth.
Tel: 01242 890256
Location: 10 miles south east of Cheltenham. One of the best exposed Romano-British villas in Britain. Open March-end October Tues-Sun and Bank Holiday Monday 10-5.30pm Closed Good Friday. 2nd November -4th December: Wed-Sun 11-4pm. National Trust.

CHELTENHAM ART GALLERY & MUSEUM
Clarence Street.
Tel: 01242 237431.
Important arts and crafts collection, including furniture, pottery and silver inspired by William Morris. Alsolocal history and archaeology, rare Oriental porcelain and Dutch and British paintings. Admission free. Open all year. Mon-Sat plus Sunday afternoons in summer.

HOLST BIRTHPLACE MUSEUM
4 Clarence Road.
Tel: 01242 524846.
Regency house where the composer of 'The Planets' was born, showing the

'upstairs-downstairs' way of life in Victorian and Edwardian times. Admission free. Open Tues-Sat. Closed Bank Holidays. Open all year.

PITTVILLE PUMP ROOM MUSEUM
Pittville Park.
Tel: 01242 512470.
Housed in the magnificent Pump Room overlooking its own beautiful lake and gardens, the Museum imaginatively uses original costumes to bring to life the history of Cheltenham from its Regency heyday to the Swinging Sixties. Jewellery showing changing taste and fashion from Regency to Art Nouveau, and a spectacular collection of tiaras are also included. Open end of May-September Tues-Sat 10-4.20pm. Sunday 11-4.20pm. Bank Holiday Mondays 11-4.20pm.

CHIPPING CAMDEN HIDCOTE MANOR GARDENS
Hidcote Bartrim
Tel: 01386 438333
Location: 4 miles east of Chipping Camden off B4632, Internationally renowned, this memorable garden is, in reality, a series of smaller gardens. Each has its own special atmosphere and leads on to the next surprise. Open: April to end of Oct daily except Tues and Fri. 11-7pm. Closed Good Friday. Shop. Restaurant. Plant Sales Centre. National Trust.

WOOLSTAPLERS HALL MUSEUM
High Street. Tel: 01386 840289.
Constructed in 1340 for merchants to buy the staples of Cotswold fleece; the Hall, with its superb roof carving, is now a museum. It houses an interesting collection of town and country bygones. Open: daily 1st April-31st October 11-6pm.

KIFTSGATE COURT GARDENS
Tel: 01386 438777.
A magnificently situated house with fine views and trees. The garden, created over three generations, has many unusual shrubs and a good collection of old fashioned and specie roses including RosaFilipes Kiftsgate, the largest rose in England. Open: Wed, Thurs and Sun 2-6pm. Also Bank Holiday Mondays and Saturdays in June and July 2-6pm. 1st April-30th Sept.

CINDERFORD DEAN HERITAGE CENTRE
Camp Mill, Soudley on B4227.
Tel: 01594 822170.
The museum of the Royal Forest of Dean interpreting the natural and man-made environment. Nature trails, shop, picnic/barbecue sites, art and craft exhibitions. Open daily all year.

CIRENCESTER CORINIUM MUSEUM

Park Street.

Tel: 01285 655611.

One of the finest collections of antiquities from Roman Britain. Full scale reconstructions of kitchen, dining room and mosaic craftsman's workshop bring Corinium (Roman Cirencester) to life. New Cotswold pre-historic gallery. Special exhibitions of localhistory and archaeology. Award winning museum and one of the Good Museums Guide 'Top Twenty'. Open daily all year, Sunday afternoons and all Bank Holidays. Closed Mondays from November to March and Christmas. Facilities for the disabled.

BREWERY COURT

Tel: 01285 657181.

The Cirencester Workshops and the Niccol Centre are housed in a converted Victorian Brewery and comprise a specialist craft centre where 20 professional craftworkers run their businesses, a shop selling the best of British craft work, a theatre, studios where courses are held in a wide range of disciplines, a gallery showing exhibitions in applied and fine art and a Wholefood Coffee House. Open: Cirencester Workshops - Mon-Sat 10-5pm. Niccol Centre - Mon-Fri 9.30-5.30pm and Sat 9.30-1pm. Admission free. Open all year.

COTSWOLD WATER PARK

Tel: 01285 861459.

It lies to the south of Cirencester and offers exciting and varied activities based on a network of lakes formed as a result of 60 years gravel extraction. In addition to the variety of water-based activities including angling, windsurfing, sailing, water, skiing and power boat racing, there are lakeside walks and picnic sites provided at two country Parks. The area is recognised as being nationally important for nature conservation. A number of public and private nature reserves provide an opportunity to study the enormous variety of its wetland flora and fauna. Open all the year. Facilities for the disabled.

BARNSLEY HOUSE GARDEN

The Close

Tel: 01285 740281 Spring bulbs, autumn colours. Mixed borders, climbing and wall shrubs. Knot garden, herb garden, laburnum walk (early June). Decorative vegetable potage. 18th century summer houses. House (not open) 1697. Interesting plants for sale. Carpark. Pub lunches available in Barnsley at the village pub.

COLEFORD CLEARWELL CAVES

Royal Forest of Dean.

Tel: 01594 32535. Superb caverns and tunnels stretching far under the Forest of Dean. Worked for iron ore over 2,000 years until 1945. Open daily Mar-Oct.

PUZZLEWOOD

Lower Perrygrove Farm on B4228.

Tel: 01594 33187.

Open Roman iron mines in 14 acre woodland setting. Paths arranged in apuzzle, landscaped in 1800s. Open Easter-October Tues-Sun and Bank Holidays.

GLOUCESTER GLOUCESTER CITY MUSEUM

Brunswick Road

Tel: 01452 524131

Famous Iron Age mirror, Roman sculptures and mosaics. Also Georgian silver, barometers, furniture and exhibitions. Admission free. Open Mon-Sat & Bank Holiday Mondays all year.

GLOUCESTER FOLK MUSEUM

Westgate Street.

Tel: 01452 526467.

Social history folklore, crafts and industries of Gloucester, housed in Tudor timber framed buildings. Special exhibitions. Admission free. Open Mon-Sat & Bank Holiday Mondays all year.

HOUSE OF THE TAILOR OF GLOUCESTER

9 College Court.

Tel: 01452 422856.

The building chosen by Beatrix Potter to illustrate her famous story. Now a gift shop and exhibition. Admission free. Open Mon-Sat all year.

NATURE IN ART

On A38 2 miles north of Gloucester.

Tel: 01452 713422.

Unique collection of wildlife art from all parts of the world and all periods. Specially commended in National Heritage Museum of the year awards. Nature gardens and outdoor sculptures. Full programme of artists in residence. Open Tues-Sun and Bank Holidays all year.

REGIMENTS OF GLOUCESTERSHIRE MUSEUM
The Docks,
Tel: 01452 522682 Museum of the Year Award for the Best Small Museum 1991. New displays tell the story of Gloucestershire's soldiers in peace and war. Gift shop. Open Tues-Sun & Bank Holidays all year.

ROBERT OPIE COLLECTION
MUSEUM OF ADVERTISING AND PACKAGING
Albert Warehouse, Gloucester Docks.
Tel: 01452 302309.
Memories of childhood brought to life. Goods which since Victorian times have crowded the shelves of Britain's grocers, confectioners, chemists, tobacconists, pubs and corner shops. Vinage TV Commercials. Open all year but closed winter Mondays.

GLOUCESTER SKI CENTRE
Robinswood Hill.
Tel: 01452 414300.
240m, 200m nursery slopes. Full length ski lifts. Beginners to experts. Full tuitions and equipment. Ski shop. Open daily all year.

GLOUCESTER ANTIQUES CENTRE
Severn Road, Gloucester Docks
Tel: 01452 529716
Collections of all kinds of antiques taking up four floors of a magnificent restored warehouse. Admission free. Open daily all year.

CRICKLEY HILL COUNTRY PARK
6 miles east of Gloucester on B4070.
Tel: 01452 863170.
145 acres of grassland, woodland and parkland with panoramic views. Site of archaeological interest. Visitor centre and 5 self-guided trails. Admission free. Open daily all year.

ROBINSWOOD HILL COUNTRY PARK
2 miles south of Gloucester.
Tel: 01452 412029.
250 acres of countryside with walks and views. Waymarked trails. Visitor centre. Gloucester Trust for Nature Conservation centre. Admission free. Open daily all year.

GUITING POWER COTSWOLD FARM PARK RARE BREEDS CENTRE
off B4077.
Tel: 01451 850307.
The country's most comprehensive collection of rare breeds of farm animals. Adventure playground, farm trails, pets corner. Open daily Easter-September.

MORETON-IN-THE-MARSH BATSFORD ARBORETUM
Batsford. Tel: 01608 50722.
Fifty acres of garden containing over 1200 different species of trees, many rare with superb views over the vale of Evenlode. Springtime carpets of bulbs, magnificent magnolias,flowering cherries and a spectacular 'Handkerchief' tree. Later in the year the large collection of maples and sorbus provide wonderful autumn colour. Refreshments. Open 1 Mar-early Nov 10am-5pm daily.

COTSWOLD FALCONRY CENTRE
Batsford Park.
Tel: 01386 701043.
Located adjacent to Batsford Arboretum, eagles, hawks, owls and falcons are flown throughout the day giving you a chance to see their grace, speed and agility and the close relationship with the falconer. The emphasis here is on the breeding and conservation of these magnificent birds. Open: Mar-Nov daily 10.30 to last admission at 5pm. Facilities for the disabled.

LECHLADE COTSWOLD WOOLLEN WEAVERS
Filkins.
Tel: 01367 860491.
Working woollen mill showing traditional skills in 18th century buildings. Permanent exhibition areas. Large mill shop. Admission free. Open Mon-Fri and Sat am. Restricted opening Christmas, Easter, Bank Holidays.

NEWENT THE NATIONAL BIRDS OF PREY CENTRE
Tel: 01531 820286.
A full day out for the family is offered plus the chance to experience Birds of Prey at close quarters. The Daily Flying Demonstrations are undoubtedly the highlight of the day but there is so much more to see and do. Coffee-shop. Book and Gift Shop. Children's Play Area and Picnic sites. No pets. Free parking. Open: 7 days a week 10.30-5.30pm Closed December-January. Facilities for the disabled.

THE SHAMBLES 16-20 Church Street.
Tel: 01531 822144.
A staggeringly large collection laid out as a complete Victorian town of shops, cobbled streets, gas lamps and alleyways, rural and town trades and crafts. All approached through a fully furnished four storey house, in an unexpectedly spacious location behind the main streets of this attractive market town. Open: 10-6pm mid March-December Tues-Sun and Bank Holiday Mondays. Facilities for the disabled.

THREE CHOIRS VINEYARD
Welsh House Lane.
Tel: 01531 890555
Production of English Wine reviving the ancient tradition of Gloucestershire wine making. Admission free (Charge for tours) Open daily all year.

NEWENT BUTTERFLY & NATURAL WORLD CENTRE,
Birches Lane off B4215
Tel: 01531 821800
Tropical Butterfly house, Nature Exhibition, Menagerie and Water Life. Spiders, snakes, rabbits, guinea pigs, rare breed fowl, waterfowl, pheasants, peacocks, parakeets and other small birds. Open daily Easter-October.

LYDNEY DEAN FOREST RAILWAY
Norchard Steam Centre B4234 Nr. Lydney.
Tel: 01594 843423.
Full size railway engines, coaches and wagons. Admission free to site. Open daily all year. Admission charge for steam rides (certain days throughout the year).

NORTHLEACH COTSWOLD COUNTRYSIDE COLLECTION
Tel: 01451 60715.
Fine collection of agricultural history, set in former 'House of Correction'. Restored cells and courtroom. Special exhibitions. Open daily Apr-Oct.

KEITH HARDING'S WORLD OF MECHANICAL MUSIC
Oak House. T
el: 01451 60181.
A museum of antique clocks, musical boxes, automata and mechanical musical instruments in an old wool merchant's house. Restorers of clocks and musical boxes. Gift shop. Open daily all year.

PAINSWICK PAINSWICK ROCOCO GARDEN,
The Stables, Painswick House.
Tel: 01452 813204
18th century, 6 acre Rococo garden with garden buildings. Vistas and woodland paths. Open Feb-mid Dec. Wed- Sun.

PRINKNASH ABBEY
Nr. Painswick. On A46.
Tel: 01452 812455.
Benedictine Abbey with world famous pottery worked by local craftsmen. Adjoined by Bird Park. Open daily all year.

SLIMBRIDGE THE WILDFOWL AND WETLANDS TRUST.
Off A38
Tel: 01453 890065.
World's largest collection of wildfowl in 73 acres of grounds. Tropical house. Permanent exhibition. Open all year. Closed Dec 24th & 25th.

STANWAY STANWAY HOUSE,
Near Cheltenham.
Tel: 01386 73469
The jewel of Cotswold manor houses is very much a home rather than a museum. The mellow Jacobean architecture, the typical squire's family portraits, the exquisite Gate House, the old Brewery and medieval Tithe Barn, the extensive pleasure grounds and formal landscape contribute to the timeless charm of what Arthur Negus considered one of the most beautiful and romantic manor houses in England. Open: June, July, August Tuesdays and Thursdays 2-5pm.

TETBURY CHAVENAGE
Tel: 01666 502329. Elizabethan Manor House (1576). Tapestry rooms, furniture and relics of Cromwellian period. Chapel and Edwardian Wing. Personal tours by the owner. Spacious gardens for visitors to the house to enjoy. See where Agatha Christie's 'Hercule Poirot' was filmed. Open: May-Sept, Thurs, Sun, Bank Holidays 2-5pm. Also Easter Sunday and Monday.

WESTONBIRT ARBORETUM
on the A433 nr Tetbury. Tel: 01666 880220. 600 acres containing one of the finest collections of temperate trees and shrubs in the world. Open all year. Visitor Centre open daily Easter-mid November.

WESTBURY COURT GARDEN
Tel: 01452 760461 Location: 9 miles south west of Gloucester on A48. Laid out between 1696 and 1705, this formal Dutch water garden is a rare survival

of its type in England. Historical varieties of apple, pear, plum, along with many other species of plants introduced to England before 1700, make this a fascinating study for any gardener. Open: April-endOctober: Wed to Sun and Bank Holiday Monday 11-6pm. Closed Good Friday. National Trust.

WINCHCOMBE HAILES ABBEY

Tel: 01242 602398

Location: 10 miles north east of Cheltenham off B4632. Picturesque ruins of great Cistercian Abbey and centre of pilgrimage. English Heritage. Open: April 1st- end September daily 10-6pm. Oct-March Tues-Sun 10am-4pm. Closed 24-26 December and New Year Bank Holiday. Museum may be closed on certain days from October-end of March for staffing reasons. Ring first.

SUDELEY CASTLE AND GARDENS

Tel: 01242 602308.

Once the residence of Queen Katherine Parr, Sudeley is now the charming home of Lord and Lady Ashcombe. Sudeley houses many fine antiques, civil war relics and old-master paintings. The gardens with the Queen's garden as their centrepiece, are quite magnificent and are complemented by 'Sudeley Castle Roses' a specialist plant centre. Also available: craft workshops, adventure playground, castle shop, licensed restaurant. Calendar of special events throughout the year. OPEN: Apr 1st-31st October. Grounds 11am-5.30pm. Castle apartments 12 noon - 5pm. Sudeley Castle Roses; 10am-5.30pm. Free parking for cars and coaches.

GLOUCESTERSHIRE - WARWICKSHIRE RAILWAY,

Toddington, at intersection of B4632/A438.

Tel: 01242 621405.

Restored GWR Station. Mainline steam rides. 8 miles round trip. Large rail complex, rolling stock under restoration. Admission free to site. Open daily. Admission charge for steam rides (Easter-October Sat, Sun & Bank Holidays) Open all year.

HAMPSHIRE

ALDERSHOT MUSEUM OF AIRBORNE FORCES

Browning Barracks.

Tel: 01252 349619.

Briefing models of World War II (Normandy, Arnhem and Rhine Crossing) post war operations including Suez and the Falklands campaigns. Open all year. Mon-Fri 9-12.30pm & 2-4.30pm. Sat/Sun 10-12.30pm & 2-4.30pm.

ROYAL ARMY MEDICAL CORPS HISTORICAL MUSEUM

Tel:01252 314598.

Items of medical interest from 1660. Over 2500 items on display including Falkland Islands War. Horse drawn and motor ambulance. Open 9-4pm.

AMPFIELD SIR HAROLD HILLIER GARDENS AND ARBORETUM

Jermuns Lane, Nr Romsey.

Tel: 01794 368787.

See the trees of the world in a glorious setting. In the grounds of 160 acres grow some 40,000 plants originating from every Continent. This unique collection is attractive throughout the year to both the plantsman and novice gardener, and those who just like to be amongst lovely things. Light meals and teas available in Jermyns House Testaurant. Open all year 10.30-6pm April-31st October. 10.30-5pm or dusk 1st November-31st March. Closed Christmas Day, Boxing Day and New Year's Day.

ANDOVER CHOLDERTON RARE BREEDS FARM PARK.

Just off A303/338 9 miles west of Andover.

Tel: 01980 629438.

Superb collection of rare and young alike. Many under cover attractions. Water gardens, Toddler's and adventure playgrounds. Picinc areas, restaurant and shop. Open daily mid-March-30th October 10-6pm.

THE HAWK CONSERVANCY.

4 miles west of Andover just off the A303

Tel: 01264 772252.

This is the largest and most comprehensive collection of Birds of Prey in Southern Englsnd. You can see and photograph Birds of Prey from all over the world, these include Hawks, Falcons, Eagles, Owls Vultures and Kites. The Flying Demonstrations could be the highlight of your visit. These take place at 12 noon and 2-3pm. (Weather permitting, as flying is not possible on wet days). Open: 1st March to last Sunday in October. 10.30-5pm spring and autumn. 10.30-5pm summer. Refreshments available. Children are not permitted unless accompanied by an adult. No dogs or pets allowed.

FINKLEY DOWN FARM PARK

situated 1 ½ miles north of the A303, 2 miles east of Andover.

Tel: 01264 352195.

The farm has a comprehensive selection of rare and not so rare breeds of all farm animals including ponies, shire horses, cattle, sheep, pigs, goats and poultry. Always many baby animals. Barn of 'Bygones'. Romany encampment. Adventure playground. Picnic under spreading chestnut trees of enjoy the Barn Cafe. Open mid-Mar to end Oct 10-6pm. Large free car park.

ALRESFORD THE WATERCRESS LINE,

Mid-Hants Railway PLC. The Railway Station.

Tel: 01962 733810/734200.

Talking timetable 01962 734866. This historic steam railway runs over ten miles through Hampshire's rolling countryside between Ropley, where a variety of steam locomotives can be seen at various stages of restoration. Open Sundays in February Weekends and Bank Holidays March-October. Mid-week running beginning of June-mid July. Daily running during school holidays (check for details).

ASHURST

A must for animal lovers young and old. A modern working farm, it combines the hustle and bustle of a busy dairy unit with all the fun of children's farm. You can watch the herd being milked and find out how a modern farm is managed, get to know lots of friendly animals and even test your knowledge on the farm's computer. Video room, picnic area, playground and farm shop. Free car parking. Open 7 days a week. Easter to 30th October 11-5pm. Just off the A35 between Lyndhurst and Southampton.

NEW FOREST BUTTERFLY FARM,

Longdown.

Tel: 01703 292166

Just beyond the outskirts of Southampton you will find one of Hampshire's most popular attractions. The main attraction is a huge indoor jungle where butterflies and moths from all over the world live and breed in temperatures of up to 80 degrees. It is very much a wildlife attraction with its woodland walk, aquarium tanks and aviaries. Picnic area. Adventure playground. Restaurant and shops. Open: 7 days a week 10-5pm from end of March until 31st October.

BASINGSTOKE STRATFIELD SAYE HOUSE

AND WELLINGTON COUNTRY PARK signposted off A33 between Basingstoke and Reading. The House is still the home of the present Duke and Duchess and retains, with many of his personal belongings, much of the atmosphere created by the Great Duke. The Wellington Exhibition shows the life and times of this famous soldier and statesman, also a special display of his magnificent funeral carriage. In the grounds are gardens and the grave of Wellington's horse Copenhagen. Three miles away the Wellington Country Park has something for everyone. Tel: House 01256 882882. Country Park: 01734 326444. House open: daily (except Fridays) from May 1st to last Sunday in September 11.30-4pm. Country Park daily from 1st March to 31st October and at winter weekends 10-5.30pm.

THE VYNE

Sherborne St John, 4 miles north of Basingstoke.

Tel: 01256 881337.

National Trust. A splendid Tudor Mansion with fine stained glass in the Chapel. The first English country house to acquire a portico (1654). Peaceful garden with lawns sloping to lake. Open 30th March-30th September. Daily except Monday and Friday (open Good Friday and Bank Holiday Monday but closed Tuesday following). Garden 12.30-5.30pm House 1.30-5.30pm Garden only: weekends in March and October 12.30-4pm. Light refreshments and home-made teas.

BEULIEU THE NATIONAL MOTOR MUSEUM.

Tel: 01590 612123.

One of the world's most famous attractions. Inclusive admission covers The National Motor Museum, a superb exhibition of over 250 historic vehicles dating from 1895 to the present day and including Donald Campbell's 'Bluebird'. 'Wheels' an amazing journey throughout the history of motoring. Palace House, the ancestral home of the Montagu family since 1538 and former Gatehouse to Beaulieu Abbey, founded in 1204 by Cistercian monks, it lies mainly in ruins today. It is a fantastic and thrilling outing. Open: Every day except Christmas Day. Easter to September 10-6pm. October- Easter 10-5pm.

BRAMDEAN HINTON AMPNER

... on the A272 west of Bramdean, 8 miles east of Winchester.

Tel: 01962 771305.

A Georgian style Hampshire Manor. Fine Regency furniture, pictures and porcelain. The gardens are a tribute to their former owner who conceived the delightful walks with many prospects and unexpected vistas. Open: April-end September. Gardens: Sat, Sun, Tues & Wed only, also Sat & Sun in August 1.30-5.30pm Tearooms sam days as gardens 1.30-5pm. National Trust.

BREAMORE BREAMORE HOUSE

.. on the A338 between Salisbury and Ringwood.

Tel: 01725 512468.

Breamore is a beautiful and unspoilt village on the edge of the New Forest. The Countryside Museum is designed to explain the development of village life from a self-contained unit to the post-war period. At the house,the stables which were built about 1700, have been used to show the vehicles of the orse era. A fine collection includes the Red Rover, which was the London to Southampton Stagecoach. The house in 1538 has a splendid collection of pictures and furniture contributed by ten generations. The trees in the park must be admired and a visit to the Saxon church should be included. Open Easter, Bank Holidays and 1st Apr-end of Sept 2-5.30pm (Countryside 1pm) April: Tues/Wed/Sun. May, June, July, Sept : Tues/Wed/Thurs/Sat/Sun and all Bank Holidays. August: every day.

BUCKLERS HARD

Historic 18th century village, maritime museum, display cottages, river cruise and riverside walks. Tel: 01590 616203. Open every day except Christmas Day.

FARNBOROUGH ST MICHAELS ABBEY,

.. the Empress Eugenie built the abbey, adjacent to Farnborough Hill in 1886 in memory of her busband and son. A year later she also had built an impressively flamboyant and colourful mausoleum for herself, Emperor Napoleon and their son. Below the dome and reached by an imposing staircase is the vaulted crypt. Both crypt and mausoleum can be visited by prior arrangement. Treasures in the Abbey include several personal relics of the Imperial family. With the status of a Priory, St Michaels Abbey is now a community of Benedictine Monks. For further information and details of guided tours ring: 01252 372822.

FORDINGBRIDGE ROCKBOURNE ROMAN VILLA,

Rockbourne.

Tel: 01725 518541.

The villa nestles in the bottom of a wide chalkland valley about 3 miles north of Fordingbridge. It was discovered in 1943 and excavations revealed it to have been one of the largest Roman villas in the country. Open Easter to 1st October. April-June and September: weekdays from 12 noon until 6pm. Saturday/Sunday 10.30am until 6pm.

KEYHAVEN HURST CASTLE,
South of Keyhaven on pebble spit, best approached
by ferry from Keyhaven.
Tel: 01590 642344.
Built by Henry VIII to counter the threat of invasion from Europe and then added to in Victorian times. See the immense and formidable fire power it possessed from its battlements using 38 ton guns. A site exhibition explains the running and history of the fort and spectacular views over the Solent, Isle of Wight and South Coast must be seen. Open 1st April-31st October daily 10-6pm 1st November-31 March weekends 10-4pm.

LYNDHURST NEW FOREST MUSEUM & VISITOR CENTRE.
Tel: 01703 283914.
There's so much more to the story of the New Forest than ponies and deer and you can discover it all at the New Forest Museum and Visitor Centre. Open daily from 10am.

MIDDLE WALLOP MUSEUM OF ARMY FLYING,
Nr Stockbridge.
Tel: 01264 781086.
It houses a unique and award winning collection of aircraft World War II gliders and helicopters depicting the role of Army Flying since the late 19th century. Next to the Army AirCorps active airfield visitors can experience 100 years of history and watch the pilots of tomorrow training on Lynx and Gazelle helicopters. On A343 between Andover and Salisbury. Open 10-4pm daily. Restaurant. Coffee shop. Pcinic area. Free parking.

MILFORD ON SEA LYMORE VALLEY HERB GARDEN,
Braxton Courtyard, Lymore Lane.
1 mile from Milford.
Tel: 01590 642008.
These beautiful gardens set around attractive Victorian farm buildings have now become well established. A tranquil courtyard leads into a walled garden overflowing with aromatic herbs. The nursery produces a comprehensive selection of plants. Good shop. Open daily 9-5pm. Closed December 25th to end February.

MINSTEAD FURZEY GARDENS,
Nr Lyndhurst.
Tel: 01703 812464.
Set in the heart of the New Forest, Furzey Gardens can offer you a peaceful time away from the rush and hurry of our world. It has eight acres of delightful, informal landscape. Visit the ancient cottage, believed to have been built in the 16th century. The gallery displays and sells the work of local

crafts people. Gardens open daily throughout the year 10-5pm (earlier in the winter). Cottage and Gallery open daily in the summer and on weekends in the winter.

NEWBURY HIGHCLERE CASTLE,
4 miles south of Newbury,
off the A34 road to Winchester.
Tel: 01635 253210.
Home of the Earl and Countess of Carnarvon, Victorian splendour at its very best. Stunning interiors, grounds of Capability Brown. The 5th Earl discovered the tomb of Tutankhamun. An exhibition of his Egyptian antiquities is on display. The present Earl is the Queen's Racing Manager and recently opened his own racing exhibition. Location of many TV and Film productions. Open: May-Sept, Tues-Fri and Sun 11-5pm (last admission 4pm). Sat 11-3.30pm (last admission 2.30pm). Bank Holiday Mondays during May & Aug.

PORCHESTER CASTLE
off A27, south of Porchester.
Surprisingly perhaps, the impressive outer walls of the castle, unbroken and standing to their full height were built as a fortress in Roman times. Within these walls you will find plenty of evidence of the use of Porchester as a prisoner of war camp in the 18th and 19th centuries. Many of the walls of the castle keep are scratched with the names of the inmates. The exhibition of the history of the castle will provide a fascinating conclusion to your tour of 2,000 years of history. Open: daily 10-6pm 1st Apr-31st Oct. 10-4pm 1st Nov-31st Mar. Closed 24-26 Dec and 1st Jan. Tel: 01705 378291 for further details. English Heritage.

ROMSEY MOTTISFONT ABBEY,
4 ½ miles north west of Romsey 3/4 mile west of A3057.
Tel: 01794 340757.
This tranquil garden beside the River Test contains magnificent rees, walled gardens and the Trust's National collection of old fashioned roses. The Abbey contains a drawing room decorated by Rex Whistler and thecellarium of the old priory. Open: Garden; Apr to end Nov Sat-Wed 12 noon-6pm. Jun Sat-Wed 12 noon-8.30pm House (Whistler Room only) Apr to end Nov Tues, Wed, Sun 1-5pm.

WELLOW WINE CENTRE AND VINEYARD,
Tanners Lane, East Wellow.
Tel: 01794 830880.
A taste of the Test Valley awaits you at Hampshire's largest vineyard. A refreshingly new experience in an outstandingly beautiful setting. Wine

centre and licensed bar. Meals, free parking for cars and coaches. Unguided vineyard and woodland walks. Open daily from 11-10.30pm. Mon-Sat 12-3pm & 7-10.30pm Sundays. Winter opening times may vary.

BROADLANDS
located on the A31 at Romsey.
Tel: 01794 516878.
Famous as the home of Lord Mountbatten. Braodlands is an elegant Palladian mansion in a beautiful landscaped setting on the banks of the River Test. Visitors may view the house with its art treasures and mementoes of the famous, enjoy the superb views from the Riverside lawns or relive Lord Mountbatten's life and times in the Mountbatten Exhibition and spectacular Mountbatten A-V Presentation. Open: Easter to last Sunday in September, 12 noon-5.30pm. Closed Fridays except Good Friday and in August. Self service tearoom. Gift shop. Free parking.

PAULTONS PARK,
Ower, between Romsey and Cadnam.
Just off Exit 2 M27 junction A36/A31.
Hotline 01703 814455.
A great day out for all ages. Over 40 attractions included in admission price. Thrilling rides on Runaway train, Bumper Boats and Astroglide. Kids Kingdom is a paradise of play activities. Visit land of Dinosaurs, Pets Corner and Magic Forest where nursery rhymes come to life. See Romany and Village Life Museums and take a ride on the Rio Grande Railway. See over 1,000 exotic birds, wildfowl and animals in beautiful gardens, parkland and Japanese garden. Restaurant, Tearooms, Picnic areas. Speciality shops. Open daily 10-6.30pm mid-Mar to the end of Oct. Earlier closing spring/autumn. No dogs allowed.

SELBOURNE GILBERT WHITE'S HOUSE & GARDEN AND THE OATES MUSEUM,
The Wakes, High Street, Selbourne.
Tel: 01420 511275.
Historic house and glorious tranquil five acre garden, home of famous 18th century naturalist Gilbert White, author of 'The Natural History of Selborne'. Furnished rooms, original manuscript and beautifully embroidered bed hangings. Charming garden with many fascinating old plants, a ha-ha rose and herb gardens, topiary and laburnum arch. The Oates Museum celebrates the lives of Frank Oates, a Victorian explorer in Africa and Captain Lawrence Oates, hero of Scott's Antarctic Expedition. Picnic area. Open: daily from Easter to end of October then weekends during November and December 11-5pm.

SHEDFIELD WICKHAM VINEYARD,
Botley Road, on the A334 halfway between Botley and Wickham. Take J7 or J10 off M27. Find out all about grape growing and the amking of the award winning wines of Wickham. Highly acclaimed self-guided tour. Picnic garden. Nature Trail through ancient woodland and conservation area. Wine tasting. Open all year 10.30-6pm Mon-Sat. Sun 11.30-5.30pm. Tel: 01329 834042.

SOUTHHAMPTON EXBURY GARDENS (Beaulieu 3 miles).
Tel: 01703 891203.
These 200 acres landscaped woodland gardens include an outstanding collection of Rhododendrons, Azaleas, Camellias and Magnolias. In addition to many other notable trees and shrubs they feature a Rock Garden, Heather Gardens, Daffoldil Meadow, Iris Garden, Ponds, cascades and unlimited walks. Lunches and cream teas. Free parking. Plant Centre. Gift shop. Open: March to October 10-5.30pm.

HISTORIC SOUTHAMPTON
Why not spend the day in medieval town Southampton. Walk the walls around the Old Town, and visit historic sites including three museums. This is a self-guided walk with signposts, panels and historic characters to help you find your way around the medieval town.

TUDOR HOUSE MUSEUM,
Bugle Street. A fascinating 16th century house with unique Tudor Garden and exhibitions of domestic and social life in Southampton from the Tudors to today.

MARITIME MUSEUM,
Bugle Street/Town Quay. The story of the port of Southampton from the age of steam to the modern docks, with popular exhibits including the Titanic story.

MUSEUM OF ARCHAEOLOGY,
Winkle Street. Visit Roman, Saxon and medieval Southampton with a rich display of finds from archaeological excavations.

SOUTHAMPTON HALL OF AVIATION,
Albert Road South. Tel: 01703 635830. The official and the Supermarine Company. The museum dipicts the story of some 26 aircraft companies, the legendary Spitfire and the history of the biggest flying boat operation in the world. Fascinating. Open: 10-5pm Tues-Sat. 12 noon-5pm Sundays. Open 10-5pm Mondays during School Holidays.

WINCHESTER CITY MILL,
.. foot of High Street beside City Bridge. Tel: 01962 870057. Positioned over River Itchen the mill was rebuilt in 1744 using materials dating back to the 15th century. There is a delightful island garden and an impressive millrace. Open: 1st April to end Sept daily 11-4.45pm. Open Sat and Sun in October 12 noon-4pm. Shop open April-31 Dec daily 10-5pm.

MARWELL ZOOLOGICAL PARK,
Colden Common.
Tel: 01426 943163. Marwell is world famous for its dedication to the conservation of Endangered Species. There are nearly 1000 animals and some are the rarest on earth. Its 100 acres of beautiful parkland are ideal for a relaxing day out with all the family. Open: every day except Christmas Day. 6 miles south east of Winchester.

HEREFORD AND WORCESTERSHIRE

DROITWICH HANBURY HALL

Tel: 01527 821214

Location: Off M5 Junction 5 to Droitwich, 4 miles east of Droitwich off B4090. William and Mary style brick house, notable for the famous Thornhill staircase. Fine collection of porcelain. Re-creation of formal 18th century garden. Open: Easter to end October; Sat, Sun and Mon 2-6pm. Closed Good Friday. Aug: also open Tues and Wed 2-6pm. Shop, Tearoom, National Trust.

HEREFORD CITY MUSEUM & ART GALLERY,

Broad Street. Full of interest. Open: Tues, Wed, Fri 10am-6pm. Thurs & Sat 10-5pm 10-4pm in winter.Sunday May-September 10-4pm.Open Bank Holiday Mondays.

THE OLD HOUSE

17th century museum open Monday 10-1pm Tues-Sat 10-1pm & 2-5.30pm Sat (winter) 10-1pm. Sunday May-December 10-4pm open Bank Holiday Mondays

CHURCHILL GARDENS MUSUEM & THE HATTON GALLERY,

Venns Lane. Furniture and costume. Open Tues-Sat 2-5pm Sunday(summer) 2-5pm. Open Bank Holiday Mondays. Visit the Fragrant Garden open daily throughout the year until dusk. Admission free. Suitable for visits by blind persons and the disabled.

DINMORE MANOR AND THE COMMANDERY
OF THE KNIGHTS HOSPITALLER OF ST JOHN OF JERUSALEM.

6 miles north of Hereford on A49. Tel: 01432 830322. Spectacular hillside location. A range of impressive architecture dating from the 12-20th century. Chapel, Cloisters, Great Hall(Music Room) and extensive roof walk giving panoramic views of the countryside and beautiful gardens below. Large collection of stained glass. Open 9.30-5.30pm daily all year. Refreshments available most afternoons during summer.

LEDBURY EASTNOR CASTLE

Tel: 01531 633160.

Splendid Georgian Castle in fairytale setting with Deer Park, lake and arboretum. Inside this family home tapestries, fine art, armour and furniture from the Italianate and Gothic in richly decorated interiors, many recently restored to critical acclaim. Home-made cream teas and ice cream. Open Sundays Easter to end September, Bank Holiday Mondays. Sunday to Friday during August 12 noon-5pm.

LEOMINSTER BERRINGTON HALL

Nr. Leominster.

Tel: 01586 780246

Location: 3 miles north of Leominster. Signposted off A49. A classical elegant 18th century mansion by Henry Holland, set in a gracefully landscaped park by 'Capability' Brown. Park walk open July to end October only. Open Easter to end September; Wed-Sun (open Bank Holiday Mon. closed Good Friday) 1.30-5.30pm. October Wed-Sun 1.30-4.30. Grounds open from 12.30pm. Shop. Licensed restaurant. Dogs on leads in car park only. National Trust.

CROFT CASTLE

Tel: 01586 780246

Location : 5 miles north west ofLeominster. Signposted off A49 and A4110. Just 5 miles from Berrington Hall, this Marcher Castle has been the home of the Croft family since Domesday (with a short break of 170 years). Ancient walls and castellated turrets house an interior shown as it was in the 18th century with fine ceilings and Gothic staircase. The surrounding parkland is open all year. Open: Easter Sat, Sun & Mon 2-6pm. Closed Good Friday. April and October Sat & Sun 2-5pm. May to end Sept: Wed-Sun and Bank Holiday Monday 2-6pm. National Trust.

LYDE KENCHESTER WATER GARDENS

Church Road.

Tel: 01432 270981.

Largest and perhaps best stocked aquatic centre in the South Midlands. More than two hundred tropical fish tanks, fresh and saltwater, are filled with some of the most fascinating, colourful and eye-catching sea and fresh water creatures. The best view of these beautiful gardens is from the Tea Rooms. On the A49 Hereford to Leominster Road - two miles north of Hereford. Free admission. Carpark. Disabled access. Open every day of the week.

BRINGSTY LOWER BROCKHAMPTON

Tel: 01885 488099

Location: 2 miles east of Bromyard on A44. A 14th century half timbered moated farmhouse with a very unusual gatehouse. Only the medieval hall and parlour are shown. Open: House; April-end September; Wed-Sun and Bank Holiday Monday. 10-5pm. Closed Good Friday. Oct: Wed-Sun 10am-4pm. Estate open all year.

ROSS-ON-WYE THE BUTTON MUSEUM

Kyrle Street.

Tel: 01989 566089

Unique award winnng Museum of Dress and Uniform Buttons, worn by ladies and gentlemen over the last two hundred years. Museum shop. Open 7 days a week 1st April-31st October 10-5pm.

SWAINSHILL THE WEIR

Location: 5 miles west of Hereford on A438. Fine views of the River Wye and the Welsh Hills from a steep bank studded with trees, shrubs and plants. Beautiful, particularly in springtime, with drifts of flowering bulbs. Open: Mid-February to end October; Wed to Sun (including Good Friday) and Bank Holiday Monday 11am-6pm. National Trust.

TENBURY WELLS -BURFORD HOUSE GARDENS

Tel: 01584 810777 Fax: 01584 810673.

Burford House is an early Georgian House built on the ancient site of Scrob's Castle, at the confluence of the River Teme and Ledwych Brook. It was acquired by the late John Treasure in 1954 as the ideal setting for his new garden. Since then and until his death in 1993 John Treasure transformed the grounds of this austere Georgian red brick house from a scattering of a few good trees and an elegant summerhouse into an eloquently defined twentieth century garden. Contrasting its spare symmetry on the north front with curving vistas and beds on its south side, he elegantly described the setting of the house in the fertile alluvial loam of the River Teme which weaves around the garden. As an architect by training he brought that all too rare combination of the positive discipline of design to a passion forplants and the result is a garden of quiet serenity and fascination. John Treasure's high standards of discipline are revealed in the crisply edged and well groomed beds. This is a plantsman's garden, laid out to display myriads of forms and species in ordered frameworks. There are special combinations and ideas which gardeners of all kinds will be inspired to study and copy. Harmonising combinations of colour have been brilliantly achieved throughout the garden, and especial use made of clematis, a favourite of John Treasure. The garden now boasts over 150 varieties and is home to the National Collection. There are so many kinds of plants to be seen especially those that grow on neutral to limey soils, and many marginal plants that grow along the stream gardens. Of the genera that are well represented there are, Hosta, Hydrangea, Philadelphus, grasses, hellebores, shrub roses, penstemons, birches, irises, astilbes, agapanthus, daylilies and hosts of bulbs and rarities, all grouped beautifully and new ideas and plants are finding homes here in this dynamic and graceful garden. Many of the unusual plants in the garden can be found in Treasures Plant Centre adjacent, who specialise in clematis, herbaceous, shrubs, trees and climbers. There is a Gallery open in the House and a new Craft Shop in the grounds. The Burford Buttery serves hot and cold meals together with home-made cakes, tea and continental coffee throughout the day. Coach parties are welcome and The Buttery is happy to cater for special occasions. OPEN: Monday-Sunday 10am-6pm (Dusk if earlier).

WELLINGTON QUEENSWOOD GARDEN CENTRE

Wellington HR4 8BB

Tel: 01432 830880. Fax: 01432 830833.

The Milne Family - Tony, Frank,Kathleen, Eric and Alexi own and operate this attractive garden centre which is far more than somewhere one comes just to buy plants. It is an outing that is thoroughly enjoyable and one from which you can gain gardening advice from an expert and helpful staff. The plants are second to none. The company offers all its customers a unique plant and gardening equipment ' finder service'. If they do not have a product in stock they will make every attempt to source it for their customers to collect or have sent to them by post. To help gardeners and those interested in horticulture a joint venture with Pershore College of Horticulture has been set up resulting in Pershore setting up a lecture hall at Queenswood and offering courses/qualifications to local people. All of this demonstrates how dedicated the Milne family and their staff are to the centre. A large pet shop on the site offering small domestic pets such as rabbits and guinea pigs and a huge selection of tropical and cold water fish attracts many people. Here too advice is top notch from PTIA trained staff. The Tea House is a favourite place for customers. Not only does it serve excellent tea but lunches and evening meals are available including cakes and specialities made on the premises.OPEN; Mon-Sat 1st April-30th June & 1st Dec-23rd Dec. 9am-8pm. 27th Dec-31st March & 1st July -30th Nov 9am-6pm. Sundays. Teahouse & Outdoor Plant Area 9am-5pm. Main Building and Pet Shop 11am-5pm. Easy parking - 500 spaces. Coaches welcome.

WHITNEY ON WYE CWMMAU FARMHOUSE

Brilley.

Tel: 01497 831251.

Location: 4 miles south west of Kingston between A4111 and A438. Attractive early 17th century timber-framed and stone-tiled farmhouse. Open: Easter, May, Spring and Summer Bank Holiday weekends only and Weds in August 2-6pm. National Trust.

WORCESTER THE GREYFRIARS,

Friar Street.

Tel: 01905 23571

Still surviving in the heart of Worcester, this medieval timber-framed house has been carefully restored. Delightful walled garden. Open: April-end October. Wed, Thurs and Bank Holiday Monday 2-
5.30pm. National Trust.

HERTFORDSHIRE

BARNET RIDING CENTRE

Tel: 0181 449 3531.

Location: Situated only 25 miles from Central London ideally situated off the A1 and on the border of Hertfordshire junction 23 off the M25. Away from the hustle and bustle of inner-city life children and adults alike can take time off to spend some time amongst nature and take horse riding lessons. Amateurs and professionals can spend one hour or more learning how to ride and hack through the Hertfordshire countryside. Open Tues-Sat all year including Bank Holidays.

BROXBOURNE PARADISE WILDLIFE PARK

White Stubbs Lane, Broxbourne EN10 7QA

Tel: 01992 468001.

Paradise Wildlife Park is unique! As Britain's most interactive Wildlife Park it is an ideal place to touch, feed and meet many animals - both domestic and exotic. You can learn a great deal during the 'meet the animals' session where experienced keepers impart information about the wonderful creatures and answer visitors questions. The 'Meet the Animals' experience includes: foxes, birds of prey, reptiles, chinchilla, camels, llamas and zebras. There are many other daily events including Dr Do and Dr Little amazing animal facts show, the Sweetie man, the feeding of the lions and tigers and lion and tiger cub talks. The friendly family run Park is very compact and is set in the wonderful backdrop of Broxbourne woods. Other attractions on the site comprise a Woodland Railway, Crazy Golf, Children's rides and Tractor Trailer rides for which there is a fee of 50p per ride. FREE facilities include 3 superb adventure playgrounds, Fantasy Land, Adventureland and Fun Land plus a woodland walk. There is a wide range of catering from Mannings Snack Cabin, The Pembridge Cafeteria to a Barbecue and Bar area and The Pembridge Restaurant. There are also ample picnic areas spread across the park. Paradise Wildlife Park also offers the public the chance to meet their lion or tiger cubs. This is literally the opportunity ofa lifetime and is available outside the normal opening hours of the park. The money raised goes to Project Life Lion, a registered charity which helpe to save African lions in the Serengeti from Canine Distemper. The sessions last up to 30 minutes and are for a group of up to 4 people. Priced at forty pounds a session - numbers are strictly limited. For further details or to book ring 01992 470490. The Park is located 6 miles from Junction 25 off the M25. Brown and White tourist signs direct you to the Park from the A10 at the Broxbourne/Turnford Junction. Admission prices are as at January 1996 £4.50adults, £4.00 senior citizens and £3.50 children (3-15yrs.) Opening times are 10am-6pm (Summer) and 10am-dusk (Winter). Paradise Wildlife opens every day of the year. Information line 01992 468001. Paradise Wildlife Park is a truly wonderful place with something for everyone - whatever your age!

HATFIELD MILL GREEN MUSEUM

Tel: 01707 271362.

This local museum is housed in what was for centuries the home of the millers who worked in the adjoining water mill. Mill Green Museum has two permanent galleries where local items from Roman times to the present day are on show - everything from pottery and craft tools to underwear and school certificates. Open throughout the year Tues-Fri 10-5pm and Sat,Sun and Bank Holidays 2-5pm Admission free.

MILL GREEN MILL

Tel: 01707 271362.

Adjoining the museum is the water mill which has been restored to its full working order, as it would have been during the 18th and 19th century. Visitors can take a look at how a mill used to work, with the reconstruction of a new water wheel. Mill Green Flour freshly ground from organically grown wheat is on sale. Open throughout the year Tues-Fri 10-5pm and Sat, Sun and Bank Holidays 2-5pm. Admission free.

WELWYN ROMAN BATHS

Tel: 01707 271362.

Preserved under the A1(M) in a steel vault, Welwyn Roman Baths are the remains of a bathing suite which was originally part of a country villa. The site was evacuated during the 1960s and early 70s by the Welwyn Archaeological Society and the vault installed to save the bathing suite from deconstruction when the motorway was built. The layout of cold room, warm room, hot room, cold and hot baths and furnace room can be clearly seen together with the remains of the hypocaust. Also on show are related archaeological finds from the Welwyn area and an explanatory exhibition on Roman baths and the history of the site. The site is open on Thurs-Sun and Bank Holidays from 2-5pm.

HATFIELD HOUSE;

Tel: 01707 262823.

Location: 21 miles north of London on the Great North Road (A1), seven miles from M25. This celebrated Jacobean house, which stands in its own great park, was built between 1607 and 1611 by Robert Cecil, the first Earl of Salisbury and Chief Minister to King James I. It has been thefamily home of the Cecils ever since. The State Rooms are rich in world famous paintings, fine furniture, rare tapestries and historic armour. The beautiful stained glass in the chapel is original. Within the delightful gardens stands the surviving wing of the Royal Palace of Hatfield (1497) where Elizabeth I spent much of her childhood. Open 25th Mar-9th October weekdays from 12-4pm, Sun 1.30-5pm.

HATFIELD GARDEN

Tel: 01707 262823

Connected to Hatfield House, the West Gardens date back to the late 15th century when the Palace of Hatfield was built. Keeping in line with the manner of the garden of the 17th century, the garden has been planted with a great variety of sweet smelling flowers, bulbs, trees and shrubs for every season of the year. Although the West Garden is planted with mainly herbaceous plants, roses, irises and peonies, with a considerable number of rare and unusual plants. The West Gardens are open daily except Good Friday 11-6pm.

THE OLD PALACE, HATFIELD PARK

Tel: 01707 262055

Location: 31 miles north of London AI (M) junction 4. Take an exciting trip back to Elizabethan times by visiting The Old Palace for an authentic Banquet. Set in the Great Hall people enjoy a magnificent five course meal of royal proportions including red or white wine and mead. From the moment you take your seat you are under the spell of a troop of costumed minstrels and players. Singing songs from the period, performing some of the picturesque ceremonies and customs of the Elizabethan era, they move from table to table serenading you as you dine. The authentic setting, the cuisine, the atmosphere and spectacle combine to make this not just a feast of entertainment but an unforgettable experience too. The Banquets are held every Tues, Thurs, Fri and Sat evenings.

KNEBWORTH KNEBWORTH HOUSE & GARDENS

Tel: 01438 812661

Location: entrance direct from Junction 7 of the AI (M) at Stevenage. Hours of fun can be had by all the family at the historic home of the Lytton family since 1490. The house contains many beautiful rooms, and magnificent paintings, fine furniture and objects d'art. As well as a visit to the historic house children can enjoy hours of fun at the giant Adventure Playground which includes a fort, suspension slide, bouncy castle and miniature railway, or a trip around the 250 acres of Parkland to see the herds of Red and Sika deer. Open daily 26th March-17th April and 28thy May-4th September. 11-5.30pm.

ROYSTON WILLERS MILL WILD ANIMAL SANCTUARY

Tel: 01763 262226

Moulded out of a wilderness of nettles, rubbish, and an old deserted cottage, between the railway line and the village cricket pitch of Shepreth, Terry and Gill Willers have created a wonderful setting for their animal sanctuary. Here between a duck pond and in a totally enclosed environment, young children are able to come into direct contact with a variety of animals, often for the first time, and are able to touch and handle allspecies, much to their obvious enjoyment. It is a place for unwanted or injured animals to live in safety and to be well cared for, just as homes exist for unwanted cats and dogs. The animals come from a variety of sources, such as road, gun and gassing casualties, unwanted pets, research centres, zoos, safari parks and meat markets. Some even arrive by themselves! The majority of the animals have the run of the sanctuary and can indeed leave at any time if they wish to. However, some have to be kept in enclosures for their own protection as their injuries prevent them from leading a normal life. The more exotic species require special diets and a heated environment to keep them healthy. Willers Wildlife Park receives no form of government grant or other help. Entrance fees are its sole source of revenue so please do go and visit. OPEN; Summer 10am-6pm every day. Winter: 1st Nov-28th Feb 10-5pm every day. Closed Christmas Day.

ST ALBANS BOWMANS OPEN FARM

Tel: 01462 424055.

Bowmans Farm is open daily throughout the year and provides both an entertaining and educational day out for the whole family. It will allow you to see both the livestock and arable enterprises, see the herd of pedigree Freisian cows being milked every afternoon, see the new born piglets and calves, visit the pets corner and take a stroll around the lake to observe the nature and wildlife. Or why not visit the farm shop and restaurant and sample a wide selection of fresh vegetables, home-made yoghurt and award winning ice-cream. Open throughout the year 9-5.30pm.

STEVENAGE STEVENAGE MUSEUM

Tel: 01438 354292.

When you step inside you enter another world. Fascinating collections of everyday objects tell the story of Stevenage from pre-history to the present. There are hundreds of objects for you to see including a 1950s living room, a perfect 1930s dolls house, gas masks, old farm tools and a Roman silver coin hoard. Open Mon-Sat 10-5pm. Free admission.

ROGER HARVEY GARDEN WORLD

Tel: 01438 814687.

A 400 year old complex of farm buildings has been converted into a Garden Centre. Seasonal displays of plants, bulbs and Christmas Wonderland decorations means that there is something special for everyone including tropical fish, children's adventure playground, pets corner, gift hall and houseplant conservatory. Open daily 9.30-5.30pm. Admission free.

WELWYN GARDEN CITY PANSHANGER GOLF COMPLEX

Tel: 01707 333350.

Set in some of Hertfordshire's most delightful countryside this offers one of the most popular 'Pay as you Play' courses in the country. The Herts Golf Academy offers men, women and children of all ages the opportunity to learn to play golf or improve their skills. The golf course offers a scenic and challenging eighteen hole par 72 golf course, nine hole pitch and putt, putting green and cafe open from 9am providing excellent refreshments. Open daily.

WHITEWELL WATERHALL FARM & CRAFT CENTRE

Tel: 01438 871256.

Open all year round this farm and craft centre offers adults and children the opportunity to take a step back to nature to see how many farm animals live today. A wide range of quality gifts and souvenirs is always available from the craft shop including antiques, bric-a-brac and pine furniture. A visit can also be made to the tea-room which serves a selection of light lunches, delicious cream teas and home-made cakes. Open Wed-Sun 10-5pm March-October and all Bank Holidays.

HUMBERSIDE

SCUNTHORPE ELSHAM HALL COUNTRY PARK Tel: 01652 688698. Elsham Country Park was opened in 1970 by Captain and Mrs Elwes because they wanted visitors to enjoy the Park and appreciate wildlife, Rural Crafts and Arts. The award-winning facilities now include the Granary Restaurant and Tea-Rooms, the 'Haybarn Centre', the new Garden Centre; Monk's Wood Arboretun; Children's Animal Farm and Pets Corner. There are also many special events and Arts Exhibitions throughout the year. Why not take a look for yourself. Open Easter Sat- mid Sept 11-5pm and mid-Sept-Easter Sun 11-4pm. Closed Good Friday and Winter Bank Holidays.

LEICESTERSHIRE

ASHBY THE FERRERS CENTRE FOR ARTS & CRAFTS.

Tel: 01332 863337.

Fourteen craft workshops around a magnificent Georgian courtyard. Skills include pottery, woodworking, handweaving, quilt making, automata making, china restoration and sign designs. The tea-room serves morning coffee, a variety of home-cooked lunches and cream teas. Open daily throughout the year 10.30-5pm in summer and 10.30-4.30pm in winter. Admission free.

CASTLE DONNINGTON AEROPARK AND VISITOR CENTRE

Tel: 01332 810621

See the action from this 12 acre park next to the taxiway at the eastern end of the airport. Aircraft exhibitions in the Aeropark include a Lightning jet fighter, Vulcan bomber, Canberra bomber, Argosy freighter and Whirlwind helicopter. There is also a viewing mound, themed children's play area and picnic tables. Open Easter-October Mon-Fri 10-5pm Sat 11-4pm Sun 11-6pm.

COALVILLE SNIBSTON DISCOVERY PARK

Tel: 01530 510851

Built on the 100 acre site of a former colliery, Snibston Discovery Park is Leicestershire's largest attraction where finding out is a great day out for everyone. The Exhibition Hall contains five galleries exploring the Industrial Heritage of Leicestershire including transport, engineering, extractive industries, textiles and fashion. Follow fashion through the ages, travel through time from 1600 until the present day or see what it was like for a miner in the mid 19th century. Open daily all year round from 10-6pm.

HINCKLEY ASHBY CANAL

Tel: 01455 232789

The Ashby-de-la-ZouchCanal was a relative latecomer being completed in 1804 but had many of the attributes of the earliest navigations. It follows the contours of surrounding countryside and has no locks throughout its lengths. The Canal is home to a wonderful variety of creatures and plants, including ducks, fish, dragonflies, waterlilies, kingfisher and many more. Open daily it is a great escape from the hustle and bustle of everyday life.

LEICESTER THE JEWRY WALL & MUSEUM.

Tel: 01533 473021.

The Jewry Wall is the largest Roman Civil building to survive in Britain. It forms part of the Roman public baths, the foundations of which are also visible. The Museum houses a range of prehistoric, Roman, Anglo-Saxon and Medieval exhibits. Open Mon-Sat 10-5.30pm, Sun 2-5pm.

THE GUILDHALL

Tel: 01533 532569

The Guildhall is within five minutes walk of the City Centre. From the Clock Tower, turn into East Gate, and turn left onto Silver St. The Guildhall is on Guildhall Lane, the continuation of Silver St. It is a unique Grade I listed building and has been the scene of many significant events in Leicester's history. The Building comprises the following rooms: THE GREAT HALL: The timber framed Great Hall is the original Guildhall of the Gild of Corpus Christi dating back to c1390 and evokes a wonderful sense of space and time. As well as direct promotions, the Hall, outside museum hours, is available for public hire. THE MAYOR'S PARLOUR; The ground floor of the West Wing c1490 contains the Mayor's Parlour, a smaller civic room, remodelled in 1563. The room is oak panelled with a beautifully carved and painted overmantle above the fireplace. THE JURY ROOM; The west wing also contains The Jury Room, above the Mayor's Parlour and was originally the retiring room for the Jury after Quarter Sessions. It now houses the Library of the Leicestershire Archeological and Historical Society founded in 1855. The room is available as a study and meeting room and seats 30 people. THE LIBRARY; The upper floor of the East Wing houses the Town Library. The Library is the third oldest public library in the country and was established in 1632. THE POLICE STATION; Leicester's first police force was established in 1836 and is the third oldest in Great Britain. The Borough Police Force was based at the Guildhall, and originally had 3 cells. The Cells have 2 replica criminals based on real criminals of the Victorian period. THE RECORDER'S BEDROOM; The office of Recorder was established in 1464 and the Recorder was required to visit the borough at least 4 times a year to preside over the Quarter Sessions. A bedroom was granted to the Recorder and it's fitting out is recorded in the Chamberlain's records for 1581-82. THE CONSTABLE'S HOUSE: The brick built house off the side of the courtyard was built in 1836 for Leicester's first Chief Constable and is now the administrative base of the Guildhall and will shortly be converted into a new exhibition hall. GUIDED TOURS; Available on request. PUBLIC HIRE; Available for both community and commercial hire. PERFORMANCES AND CONCERTS; Magical atmosphere with its audience capacity of 100 people. SPECIALEVENTS;Throughout the year. OPEN; Mon-Sat: 10am-5.30pm Sundays:2-5.30pm. Admission Free.

THE CATHEDRAL

Tel: 01533 625294

The Church of St Martin's was one of six parish churches recorded in Leicester in 1086. Extended in the 14th and 15th centuries and restored in the 19th century it was hallowed as the Cathedral of Leicester in 1927. Visitors are invited to tour the building and see its impressive roof, stained glass windows and stone and wood carvings. Inside the chancel is a memorial to

King Richard III. Outside the graveyard has been laid out as a garden containing many interesting slate headstones. Open every day.

THE JAIN CENTRE.

Tel: 01533 543091.

A 19th century Congregational chapel was converted in the 1980's into a magnificent Jain Centre; the only one of its kind in the western world. The centre boasts a white marble frontage, 52 hand carved marble and stone pillars, hand carved ceilings and domes, mirror mosaic walls and stained glass windows. Visitors can view by appointment.

NEWARKE HOUSE MUSEUM.

Tel: 01533 473222.

The Museum of the Social History of Leicestershire is contained within two 16th century houses; the Chantry House of 1511 and Skeffington House 1570. The Museum contains displays and artefacts dating from 1500 to the present day and includes a 17th century panelled room with period furniture, a 19th century street scene and collections of toys and games. Open Mon-Sat 10-5.30pm.

CASTLE GARDENS & CASTLE MOTTE

This used to be a low-flying marshy area of reeds and willows. At the end of the 19th century the land was drained and used for allotments before being opened as public gardens in 1926. The Motte is a man-made mound built by Leicester's first Norman Lord in about 1070. It may originally have been several metres higher and would have had timber fortification on the top. The Motte is open to the public and in the gardens is the statue of Richard III which commemorates his links with Leicestershire. Garden open daily during daylight hours.

ST MARY DE CASTRO.

Tel: 01533 628727.

St Mary's was founded in 1107 and is still in regular use. It has excellent examples of Norman work, especially the chancel, stained glass, stone and wood carving and interesting tombstones. Geoffrey Chaucer was probably married here and King Henry VI was knighted in the church in 1426. Open with guides on Sat & Bank Holiday afternoons from Easter to end of October.

RIVERSIDE PARK

This eight mile stretch of footpaths along the banks of the River Soar and Grand Union Canal passes through Castle Park and allows an insight into Leicester's early industrial history. The dominant Pex Building was originally a worsted spinning factory providing yarn for the knitting trade. Goods were brought to and from the City by the major waterwaynetwork. Flood alleviation work to the river in the late 19th century formed the 'Mile straight' on which rowing regattas are held annually. The line of the Great Central Railway has now been developed as a pedestrian walk and cycleway.

LOUGHBOROUGH STONEHURST FAMILY FARM & MUSEUM.
Tel: 01509 413216.
All the family will enjoy visiting Priscilla Pig, Dink the Donkey and their friends on a walk around the farm. Small animals can be held and stroked in 'Cuddle Corner'. On the farm there is an old blacksmiths forge, also a Motor Museum with vintage cars, motorbikes and memorabilia. Open 10-5pm daily except Wed.

MARKET BOSWORTH TWYCROSS ZOO
Tel: 01827 880250
This is an ideal day out. There is a wide variety of animals including gorillas, chimps, orangutans, gibbons, elephants, lions and giraffes. There is also an adventure playground, pets corner and penguin pool. Open daily from 10-6pm all the year round.

OADBY FARMWORLD,
Stoughton Farm Park, Gartree Road, Leicester LE22FB.
Tel:01162 710355
This is an exciting day out for every age group. You will find it 3 miles SE of Leicester City Centre and 6 miles off the M1/M69 Junction 21. Follow the southerly ring road. Signposted 'Farm Park' from A6 and A47. It is a real working Dairy Farm with acres of Parkland for pleasure and play. There are Shire horses and cart rides, rare farm animals, lakeside and woodland walks, a picnic area, Toy Tractor park and indoor sandpit. A special Children's Farmyard and Playground. You are invited to the Milking Parlour to watch the herd being milked and to try your hand at operating a milking machine. The Craft workshops are fascinating and quite frequently there are demonstrations. Add to this lots of lovable pets, an Edwardian Ale House, Audio Visual Theatre and Exhibitions and displays featuring the countryside at work and it becomes very clear why Farmworld is so popular. In keeping with Leicester's innovative and go ahead thinking, Farmworld also offers a unique Conference venue. It is housed in beautifully restored and converted 18th century farm buildings and equipped with a wide range of modern facilities to provide for every business requirement. For further details please ring 01162 710355 or Fax: 01162 713211 FARMWORLD IS OPEN; Daily 10am-5.30pm (Winter 5pm) except December 25th &26th and January 1st. Dogs cannot be admitted. (Except Guide dogs) Disabled access. Gift Shop. Wheatsheaf Cafe.

OAKHAM RUTLAND FARM PARK

Tel: 01572 756789

In 18 acres of beautiful parkland Rutland Park Farm has a wonderful selection of farm animals, goats, poultry and wildfowl for the whole family to see. Apart from visiting the animals and old farm vehicles why not stroll through the countryside and look at the fern, bamboo and wildflower meadow. Open 3rd April-18th Sept 10-5pm.

RUTLAND WATER ANGLIAN WATER BIRD WATCHING CENTRE AND RUTLAND WATER NATURE RESERVE.

Egleton, Oakham, Rutland, Leicestershire LE15 8BT

Tel: 01572 770651

Rutland Water has become one of the most importnt wildfowl sanctuaries in Great Britain, regularly holding in excess of 10,000 waterfowl of up to 28 species. It is a Site of Special Scientific Interest and has received recognition of its international importance by the European Community and has been designated as a globally important wetland. It covers an area of 450 acres and the wide variety of habitats ensures that many species of birds are present throughout the year, but the reserve is best known for the thousands of wildfowl which flock to spend the winter on the lagoons and open water. Gadwall shoveler, teal, tufted duck, pochard and shelduck are present all year round; in winter they are joined by pintail, goldeneye, goosander, wigeon and other, rarer ducks, such as smew, red-breasted merganser and long-tailed duck. Rare grebes and divers are frequent visitors. In summer common terns and cormorants breed communally on the lagoons. During spring passage, little gulls, Arctic terns and black terns pass through, often in their hundreds, while rare Caspian and white-winged black terns have been recorded. Wader passage may bring up to 19 species in a single day. Birds of prey include breeding kestrel and sparrowhawk; osprey and harriers during migration; regular sightings of peregrine and merlin in winter; and spectaculr views of hobbies in summer as they feed on insects over the lagoons. Three lagoons and 9 miles of shore and open water are overlooked by a total of 17 hides. Other attractive wildlife habitats contain species rare elsewhere; wildflowers, butterflies and dragon flies. Old hay meadows, rough grassland, hedges, plantations and woodland invite wildlife and visitor alike. On both reserves, trails lead to the hides through all these habitats. Car parking is provided free to reserve visitors at Egleton and Lyndon. There are toilets in both reserves. Disabled facilities at Egleton. Dogs not allowed at Egleton. At Lyndon they must be on a lead. Disabled visitors access is available at Egleton at the Anglian Birdwatching Centre and Shoveler hide and at Lyndon Centre using Teal and Swan hides.

LINCOLNSHIRE

GRANTHAM BELVOIR CASTLE
Tel: 01476 870262
Location: Near Grantham signposted off A607. Home of the Duke and Duchess of Rutland, Belvoir Castle is superbly situated overlooking the Vale of Belvoir. The house has magnificent staterooms, containing notable pictures, tapestries and fine furniture. The Queen's Royal Lancers Museum is also situated within the Castle. Open April 1st -29th Sept. Tue, Thurs, Sat, Sun & Bank Holidays 11-
5pm.

LINCOLN LINCOLN CATHEDRAL is one of the largest in England and has many attractive features including the magnificent open nave, St Hugh's Choir, the Angel Choir and beautiful stained glass windows including the 14th century 'Bishop's Eye'. The Chapter House Cloisters, Wren Library and Treasury are other interesting features and all visitors are invited to seek out the Lincolnimportance... Services are held daily and there are generally guided tours and tower tours.

LINCOLN CASTLE is on the site of the original Roman fortress and the present castle dates back to 1068. Interesting architectural features include the keep known as the Lucy Tower, Cobb Hall which was the site of the public gallows, and the Observastory tower which offers tremendous views of the cathedral and city as a whole. The Victorian prison includes a unique prison chapel with separate pews like upright coffins. This building also houses an original version of the famous Magna Carta from 1215, and an exhibition interpreting the history of this document and its importance to modern freedoms and democracy. Guided tours and wall walks are available.

MIDDLESEX

EPPING LEE VALLEY PARK. Tel: 01992 700766. Location: along M25 from Potters Bar. The Lee Valley is Britain's first regional park devoted entirely for the enjoyment of leisure and recreation and the conservation of countryside and natural environment. Only a walk or boat trip away is splendid countryside, a Wildlife Oasis and Sporting Paradise along with the fascinating history and secrets of the Lee Valley industrial heritage. Admission free. Open throughout the year.

NORFOLK

AYLSHAM BLICKLING HALL & GARDEN

One and a half miles west of Aylsham on the B1354, signposted off the A140 Cromer Road.

Tel: 01263 733084.

One of the most spectacular Country Houses in East Anglia. 17th century red brick house, extensive colourful garden, surrounded by wonderful parkland and woodland. National Trust. Open: Easter to end October Tues/Wed/Fri/Sat/Sun & Bank Holiday Mondays 1-5pm. Closed Good Friday. Garden same as Hall and also open daily in July and August.

BURE VALLEY RAILWAY

Tel: 01263 733858.

Travel in style through 9 miles of beautiful Norfolk countryside as the Bure Valley Railway takes you from the historic market town of Aylsham to Wroxham. Regular services run most days from Easter to October. There is a unique Boat-train service that combines a trip on the train and a cruise on the Broads.

BANHAM BANHAM ZOO

Tel: 01953 887771.

A great day out in a zoo which has just celebrated its 25th year. Open daily from 10am except Charistmas and Boxing Day.

BRANCASTER

The National Trust's property at Brancaster includes four and a half miles of tidal foreshore comprising just under 2200 acres of beach, sand dunes, marsh and saltings, including Brancaster Staithe Harbour and the site of the Roman shore fort of Branodunum. Most of the area is designated a Grade I Site ofSpecial Scientific Interest. The North Norfolk Coast footpath runs through the Trust property. Guided walks from Apr-Oct. Meet at the NT Information Centre, The Harbour, Brancaster Staithe. Toilets and car parking. Walks 4 hours with 3 stops. Bring a picnic and wear Wellingtons (or remove footwear to cross shallow creeks at end of walk). Short walk of 2 hours with 2 stops. Wellingtons not essential.

CROMER CARTING ACTION SPORTS,

The Avenue, Northrepps, Nr Cromer.

Off A 149 opposite Aldis Service Station.

Tel: 01931 111819.

If you are aged 12 and over and have ever wanted to be a Formula One or Rally Driver, Grass Carting can satisfy your ambitions. Its fast, fun and above all affordable. Whether you are a novice or an accomplished driver you are bound to gain both experience and pleasure from this sport. Wise to book in advance.

THE NORFOLK SHIRE HORSE CENTRE
& COUNTRYSIDE COLLECTION

West Runton Stables, West Runton.

Tel: 01263 837339.

See Heavy Horses bred, preserved and protected. Show Itinerary every day. Indoor Area for wet weather demonstrations. Museum of farm equipment and bygones. Picnic area, cafe. Open 10-5pm. Easter to end October. Closed Saturdays unless Bank Holiday weekends.

FELBRIGG HALL

2 miles south east of Cromer off B1436.

Signposted off A148 and A140 at Roughton.

Tel: 01263 837444.

17th century house built on site of an existing medieval Hall. Bequeathed to National Trust in 1969. 27 rooms to visit. Superb collection 18th century furniture, pictures and an outstanding Library. Walled garden, Dovehouse, Woodlands, Park and Lake. Turret Tea Room, Park Restaurant and Shop.

BRESSINGHAM

2.5 miles west of Diss on A1066. Tel: 01379 88382.

See Alan Bloom's world famous Dell Garden, Adrian Bloom's 'Foggy Bottom' Garden. Bressingham Plant Centre. Historic locomotives. Three train rides. Victorian steam Gallopers. Historic fire engines. Steam traction engines and wagons. Restaurant, shop, picnic and play areas. Open Apr 1st-30th Sept Tues-Sun and Bank Holiday Mondays. Sundays only in Oct apart from school half term. Phone for details of 'Gardeners Days'.

EARSHAM THE OTTER TRUST

A unique wonderland of waterfowl, Otters, Night Herons and Muntjac Deer, on the banks of the River Waveney. The worlds largest collection of otters in natural enclosures where the British Otter is bred for re-introduction to the wild. Open daily 1st April-31st October 10 One mile south-east of Fakenham, clearly signposted off the A1067 Norwich road. Tel: 01328 851465. In two hundred acres of beautiful reserve, Pensthorpe brings visitors and wildlife close together. Outside the visitor centre explore waterside walks and nature trails. There are excellent access facilities for the elderly and disabled, quiet picnic areas and plentiful seating. Courtyard Restaurant. Children's Adventure Playground, wildlife, brass rubbing centre and discovery areas. Open 7 days a week (exceptChristmas Day) from mid-March to beginning of January. Weekends only January, February to mid-March. Dogs not allowed (Guide dogs excepted).

FAKENHAM PENSTHORPE WATERFOWL PARK & NATURE RESERVE
one mile south east of Fakenham,
clearly signposted off the A1067 Norwich Road.
Tel: 01328 851465.
In two hundred acres of beautiful reserve, Pensthorpe brings visitors and wildlife close together. Outside the visitor centre explore waterside walks and nature trails. There are excellent access facilities for the elderly and disabled, quiet picnic areas and plentiful seating. Courtyard Restaurant. Children's adventure playground, wildlife brass rubbing centre, and discovery areas. Open 7 days a week (except Christmas Day) from mid-Mar to beginning of Jan. Weekends only Jan, Feb to mid-Mar. Dogs not allowed (Guide dogs excepted).

MILL FARM RARE BREEDS,
Hindringham.
Tel: 01328 878560.
Over 50 breeds of rare and minority farm animals on display. Pets Corner. Nature Trail. Adventure playground. Tea rooms. Open Tues-Sun 10-5pm Easter-September 30th.

THE THURSFORD COLLECTION
Thursford Green, Thursford.
Tel: 01328 878477.
Wonderful, exciting collection and constant live musical shows. Christmas is especially magical. Open daily April-May-Sept-Oct 1pm-5pm. June-July-August 11am-5pm. Off the A148 Fakenham to Holt Road.

GREAT YARMOUTH THRIGBY HALL WILDLIFE GARDENS,
Filby. Tel: 01493 369477.
6 miles from Norwich. A family outing with acres of marvellous grounds and many animals from Asia. Open every day of the year from 10am.

BYGONE HERITAGE VILLAGE,
Burgh St Margaret, Fleggburgh. On A1064 between Acle and Caister.
Tel: 01493 369770.
Replica 19th century village, classic vehicle collection. Traditional arts and crafts. Over 40 acres of fun. Open throughout the year Easter-October daily from 10am. Nov-Easter Sun-Thurs from 10am.

THE LIVING JUNGLE,
Central Sea Front, Marine Parade.
Tel: 01493 842202.
The Genesis Experience takes you back to the beginning before mankind, to give you an insight into what heaven must be like. You will see a lush tropical

jungle garden, butterflies, birds and fish. You will hear the sound of the garden's creatures and the gentle trickle of warm waters. Open daily March to end October 10am.

NORFOLK RARE BREED CENTRE & FARM MUSEUM,
Decoy Farm House, Ormesby St Michael.
Tel: 01493 732990.
14 rare breeds of sheep. 9 rare breeds of cattle and all 9 rare breeds of pigs plus 70 varieties of poultry, Shire horses and Clydesdales, Shetlands, donkeys and goats. Picnic on the 17 acre site. Parking is free. Open daily 11-5pm Good Friday until end of Sept and Sundays all year. Closed Saturdays.

STRUMPSHAW OLD HALL
STEAM MUSEUM & FARM MACHINERY COLLECTION.
Follow brown tourist signs, off A47 between Gt Yarmouth and Norwich.
Tel: Norwich 712339.
Beam Engines, Mechanical Organs, Narrow Gauge Railway, Steam Rally. Working Toy Train layout for children. 10,000 sq ft filled with Steam Engines and working Beam Engines. Picnic in park. Free parking. Open: Easter, Spring Bank Holiday weekend, 14th Jul-2nd Oct 11-4pm everyday except Saturday.

GRESSENHALL NORFOLK RURAL LIFE MUSEUM AND UNION FARM.
Union Farm is a working 1920s farm with rare breeds of horses, sheep, cattle, pigs and poultry. There is a nature trail. The Museum is housed in an imposing 18th century workhouse, has thousands of exhibits. Tea room. Gressenahll is 2 miles from East Dereham on the B1146. Open Easter-30th Oct Tues-Sat 10-5pm. Sun 12-5.30pm Bank Holidays 10-5pm.

HEACHAM NORFOLK LAVENDER,
Caley Mill.
Tel: 01485 70384.
England's working Lavender Farm and the home of the National Collection of Lavenders. Excellent cream teas and home-made cakes. Shops selling lavender products + plants and herbs, gifts. Free Admission and Car Parking. Open daily 10-5pm (Closed for 2 weeks at Christmas). On A149 3 miles south of Hunstanton. Guided tours from end of May to end of September.

KENNINGHALL. THE PARTICULAR POTTERY
Church Street, Kenninghall Nr16 2EN
Tel: 01953 888476.
Kenninghall is a delightful conservation village with a lovely old market place. The Pottery is in quaint Church Street. Built in 1807, it was formerly the Particular Baptist Chapel which accounts for the name of the Pottery. It is

both the workshop and the home of potter, David Walters and his family. In addition it provides a superb gallery environment for the work of many of East Anglia's finest crafts people. In creating a home, some changes were inevitable but the result is exciting. David works exclusively in Porcelain, creating hand-thrown bowls of all sizes, as well as large platters, vases and urns. **OPEN;** Tuesday to Saturday 9AM-5PM. Also Bank Holiday Weekends. If the family are there on Sundays, they are usually open. Please ring first to be sure or take pot luck! Off street parking. Disabled access. Affordable workshop prices. Visa/Access/American Express welcome. Children should be accompanied by an adult.

KING'S LYNN THE OLD GAOL HOUSE,
Saturday Market Place.
Tel: 01553 763044.
Let your imagination run riot as your personal stereo guide takes you through King's Lynn 1930's Police Station and into the cells beyond. Open daily Easter and Spring Bank Holiday until the end of September 10-5pm. Closed Wednesdays and Thursdays October-Easter.

BIRCHAM WINDMILL
6 miles from Sandringham.
Tel: 01485 23393
Bakery, Tea Rooms, Cycle Hire, Free Parking. Open daily Easter-30th September 10-6pm (Tea Rooms and Bakery closed Saturdays).

CAITHNESS CRYSTAL VISITORS CENTRE,
Oldmeadow Road, Hardwick Industrial Estate.
Tel: 01553 765111.
Marvel at the skills of the glassmakers. Watch the centuries old craft at close quarters. Factory shop. Tea room. Free parking. Glass making: Mon-Fri 9.15-4.15pm. Also Saturday (Easter-Dec) 9.30-3.30pm. (Jun to mid-Sept) 11-4pm. Open Bank Holidays. On south side of the town - watch for the road signs.

ENGLISH HERITAGE IN NORFOLK.
Tel: 01604 730320.
Climb the steep flights of stone stairs inside the Keep of the aptly named Castle Rising Castle. Look down into the shell of the Great Hall and imagine Medieval festivites when the castle played host to a succession of English Kings. Castle Rising lies north east of King's Lynn from where it is a short journey to the tranquil setting of Castle Acre Priory. Open: 1st Apr-31st Oct daily 10-6pm. Sept 1st-31st Mar Wed-Sun 10-4pm. Closed 24-26 Dec and Jan1st. Small admission charge.

LANGHAM LANGHAM HAND-MADE CRYSTAL,
The Long Barn, North Street, Nr Holt
Tel: 01328 830511.
Glassmaking Mon-Fri Nov-March. Sun-Friday April-October 10-5pm. Free parking. Live Glass Making Museum. Adventure Playground. Restaurant/ Cafe.

LETHERINGSETT WATERMILL
(signposted on A148)
Tel: 01263 713153.
Step back in time and visit a water powered mill producing 100% wholewheat flour from locally grown wheat. Demonstrations Tues-Thurs and Sun Plus Bank Holiday Sundays and Mondays 2-4.30pm Open Tues-Sat 9-1pm & 2-5pm. Closed Saturday afternoon. Whitsun to first week Sept Sun 2-5pm.

LONG SUTTON BUTTERFLY AND FALCONRY PARK
signposted off A17 Kings Lynn-Seaford road.
Tel: 01406 363833
Stroll through one of the largest tropical Butterfly Houses in Britain. A wealth of tropical, Mediterranean and temperate flowers and foliage set around ponds, streams and waterfalls adds to the enjoyment. A small insectarium contains scorpions, tarantulas and giant stick insects all safely housed behind glass. In the Falconry Centre watch the stunning flying displays. Tea Room and Tea Garden. Adventure playground. Animal Centre & Nature trail. Mouse house. Picnic area. Open mid-March-October 31st daily 10-6pm Sept & Oct 10-5pm.

NORWICH THE MUSTARD SHOP
3 Bridewell Alley
Tel: 01603 627889
Trace the history of Colman's Mustard over 150 years. Buy a sample of the extensive range of mustards or browse through the kitchen ware and other items in the shop. Open: Mon-Sat 9.30-5pm. Closed all day Sunday and Bank Holidays.

REDWINGS HORSE SANCTUARY,
Hill Top Farm, Hall Lane, Frettenham.
Tel: 01603 737432.
6 miles out of Norwich on the North Walsham Road (B1150). Founded in 1984 to provide a caring and permanent home for horses, ponies, donkeys and mules, rescued from neglect and slaughter. Visitors are welcome every Sunday and Bank HolidayMondays from 1-5pm from Easter-midDecember. Also open every Monday afternoon from 1-5pm during July and August.

THE FAIRHAVEN GARDEN TRUST,
Woodland and Water Garden, South Walsham.
Tel: 01603 270449.
9 miles north east of Norwich on B1140. Delightful natural woodland and water gardens set in the heart of Broadland. Enjoy the Rhododendrons, Primulas, Azaleas, Giant Lilies, Rare Shrubs and plants. Native Wild Flowers and the 900 year old King Oak. 'The Lady Beatrice' a vintage style river boat runs trips every half-hour from within the gardens on all open days. Open: 11-6pm weekdays and Sundays. 2-6pm Saturdays. Easter week daily. Wed-Sun and Bank Holidays form May to Sept.

NORFOLK WILDLIFE CENTRE & COUNTRY PARK
Gt Witchingham. On A1067 Europe's mammals and waterfowl in 40 acres beautiful parkland. Rare and unusual trees and flowering shrubs. Command and Adventure Play area. Woodland Steam Railway. No dogs. Open daily April 1st-31st October.

CASTLE MUSEUM houses one of the country's finest regional collections of natural history, archaeology and art. Busy programme of temporary exhibitions and free talks, tours and activities for all the family. Open: Mon-Sat 10-5pm Sun 2-5pm.

NORWICH & BROADS CRUISES
Southern River Steamers from Elm Hill Quay and Foundry Bridge Quay. Tel: 01603 624051. Enjoy a cruise to Surlingham Broad through historic Norwich. Either cruise to Surlingham Broad via Brundall or take a trip under Norwich bridges, daily throughout the season. Ring for times.

OXBOROUGH HALL,
7 miles soth west of Swaffham on the Stoke Ferry Road. Signposted from Swaffham and A134. A moated house, built in 1482 by the Bedingfeld family. Its rooms show the development from medieval austerity to Victorian comfort. Massive Tudor Gatehouse. The chapel in the grounds is open to the public and contains a magnificent altarpiece. Beautiful and colourful garden, an orchard, a Victorian wilderness garden and a charming woodland walk. Shop and Restaurant. Open: Easter-Oct Sat-Wed 1-5pm, Bank Holiday Mon 11-5pm. Garden Easter-30th Oct Sat-Wed 12-5.30pm. Dogs only in car park.

SANDRINGHAM SANDRINGHAM HOUSE, GARDENS & MUSEUM
Tel: 01553 772675
The private country retreat of Her Majesty the Queen is at the heart of the beautiful estate which has been owned by four generations of Monarchs. All the main rooms used by the Royal Family are open to the public. The Museum

contains fascinating displays of Royal memorabilia ranging from photographs to vintage Daimlers and an exhibition of the Sandringham Fire Brigade. Sandringham Country Park is open daily all year 10.30-5pm. House, Grounds and Museum open daily from Good Friday until the beginning of October with certain exceptions. Grounds 10.30-5pm House and Museum 11-4.45pm. Dogs except Guide Dogs not permitted in Grounds. Sandringham Visitor Centre open daily Easter to endof October.

SHERINGHAM NORTH NORFOLK RAILWAY

The Station.

Tel: 01263 822045.

Runs regularly from Sheringham to Holt. Climb aboard for an historical ride back in time and relive the memories of a bygone age. Ring for details.

SNETTISHAM PARK FARM

Nr King's Lynn off A149 in Snettisham.

Tel: 01485 542425.

Deer safari. Sheep Centre. Giant Adventure Playground. Horse and pony rides. Childrens Farmyard. Tea room. Theatre and Information room. Free parking.

WELLS-NEXT-THE-SEA NORTH NORFOLK RAILWAY

Tel: 01328 710227.

One of Britain's most majestic stately homes, situated in a deer park. This classic 18th century Palladian style mansion is a living treasure house of artistic and architectural history. Apart from a tour of this stunning house with its superb alabaster entrance hall, there are Bygones Museum, Pottery, 18th century Walled Garden. Deer Park & Lake and a sandy beach. Open daily (except Fridays and Saturdays) from the beginning of June to end of September 1.30-5pm, also Easter, May, Spring and Summer Bank Holiday Sundays and Mondays 11.30-5pm.

WELLS & WALSINGHAM LIGHT RAILWAY

Tel: 01328 856506.

Visit the longest 10 1/4 inch narrow gauge steam railway in the world. See the unique Garratt Locomotive 'Norfolk Hero' which was specially built for the four mile journey between the seaside town of Wells and the pilgrimage town of Walsingham. Open daily from Easter - 30th September. Free parking. Follow the Brown Tourist signs on the A149 coast road.

WEYBOURNE THE MUCKLEBURGH COLLECTION,

Weybourne Military Camp.

Tel: 0126 370210.

On the coast road A149 between Sheringham and Blakeney. Exciting collection. Britain's largest private Military Collection 1759-1991. Whatever the weather it is a great day out. All the exhibitions are under cover. Open: Easter to end Oct 10-5pm.

WROXHAM NORFOLK DRIED FLOWER CENTRE

Willow Farm, Cangate, Neatishead.

Tel: 01603 783588

A dazzling display of dozens of varieties and colours. Flower arranging classes and demonstrations. Free admission and parking. Two miles east of Wroxham just off the A1151 and follow the Brown Tourist signs on the A149 coast road.

WROXHAM BARNS

Tunstead Road, off B1354.

Tel: 01603 783962.

Discover the finest rural centre of craftmanship in East Anglia. See resident craftsmen at work producing original and exclusive gifts. Enjoy browsing in the Gallery Craft Shop, offering unusual gifts and stylish clothing. Junior Farm is a farmyard full of friendly animals sure to delight children and adults alike. Open: 7 days a week all year round. Parking and admission is free except to the Junior Farm.

BROADS TOURS

The Bridge

Tel: 01603 782207

Enjoy a relaxing trip on the Norfolk Broads on luxurious passenger boats. Ring for details.

NORTHAMPTON FLAMINGO GARDENS & ZOOLOGICAL PARK

Tel: 01234 711451

This has been built over the last three decades by its owner, Mr Christopher Marler, into one of the finest bird collections in the country. In lovely natural surroundings the gardens are situated in the peaceful stone village of Weston Underwood, one mile from the market town of Olney. The flowers and blossom in the spring and autumn make the gardens an attractive alternative to the avian beauty; but the breathtaking colour of the Flamingos must surely make a lasting impression on the visitor. Open: Good Friday & Bank Holiday Mondays, Sat,Sun,Wed & Thurs until end of June. Every day except Mondays in July & August. Opening hours 2-7pm.

ST GILES CHILTERN OPEN AR MUSEUM

Tel: 01494 871117

Many wonderful aircraft to be seen which would otherwise have been destroyed. These have been re-erected in 45 acres of countryside. The buildings illustrate everyday life and work of planes in the Chiltern region. Open 2-6pm 1st April-31st October.

NORTHUMBERLAND

BAGPIPE MUSEUM
Tel: 01670 519466.
Location: Morpeth Chantry.
This unusual museum specialises in the history and development of Northumbrian small pipes and their music from India to Inverness. Small admission charge. Open Mon-sat 9.30-5.30pm Mar-Dec, Mon-Sat 9.30-5.30pm Jan-Feb. Closed between Christmas and New Year.

BATTLEFIELDS CASTLE.
Tel: 01670 514343.
English Heritage battlefields and castles which display the roots of history in Northumberland from the Battle of Heavenfield in 635 and the Battle of Carham in 1018. Many of the Castles are owned by Englsih Heritage and are open daily from 10-6pm Apr-30th Sept and 10-4pm 1st Oct-31st Mar.

BELSAY AHLL & GARDENS.
Tel: 01661 881636.
Location: 14 miles NW of Newcastle on A696.
Belsay Hall, Castle and Gardens is one of the most remarkable estates in the border country. Set admist beautiful gardens and occupied continuously by the same family for nearly 600 years the medieval hall and castle encapsulate much of the history of this often turbulent region. Open daily 10-6pm 1 Apr-30Sept Tues-Sat 10-4pm 1 Oct-31 Mar.

KIELDER WATER CRUISES.
Tel: 01434 240398.
Enjoy a 10 mile cruise in comfort on Europe's largest man-made lake in a covered ferry with commentary, licensed bar and light refreshments on board. Take a round trip calling at places of interest or use the ferry as access to self-guided walks on the north side of the lake. Open throughout mid-Mar to 31st Oct, weather permitting.

NORTHUMBRIA CRAFT CENTRE.
Tel: 01670 511217.
Location: Just off the A1 15 miles north of Newcastle.
Take a day out to browse around a selection of high quality, reasonably priced crafts including pottery, jewellery, knitwear and stained glass. Choose

from a variety of goods produced by over 40 Northumbrian craftsmen. Open Mon-Sat 9.30-5.30pm Mar-Dec. Mon-Sat 10-4pm Jan-Feb.

CHANTRY SILVER.
Tel: 01670 511323.
Location: Just off the A1 15 miles north of Newcastle.
Housed within the Chantry Court Yard one can purchase hand-made jewellery and silver from Chantry Silver. Also on view and for sale are original paintings, tapestries and glass engravings by many local artists. Admission free. Open Mon-Sat 9.30-5.30pm.

THE NORTHUMBERLAND WILDLIFE SHOP.
Tel: 01670 519001.
Location: Just off the A1 15 miles north of Newcastle.
The friendly atmosphere of the Trust shop staffed by Trust members is the ideal place for the unusual gift or souvenir or for information about Northumberland Wildlife. Admission free. Open Mon-Sat 10-4pm.

THE NORTHUMBERLAND COASTAL ROUTE.
Tel: 01670 511323.
A 35 mile signed Coastal Route from Druridge Bay to the village of Belford, on the A1, 5 miles south of Holy Island. Attractions along the route include a Country Park at Druridge Bay, a marina at Auble, castles at Warkworthy, Dunstanburgh and Bainburgh, fishing harbours at Auble, Craster and Seahouses, and delightful sandy beaches all along the coast.

NORTHUMBERLAND NATIONAL PARK.
Tel: 01434 605555.
The Northumberland National Park stretches for over 40 miles from Hadrian's Wall in the south and round the Cheviot Hills which form the border of Scotland. Its 398 square miles also contain delightful wooded valleys and some of the finest stretches of moorland in the country.

ENGLAND'S LAST WILDERNESS.
Tel: 01434 605225.
South of Hexham is the North Pennines, the most recent part of the country to be officially declared an 'Area of Outstanding Natural Beauty'. It spans 3 counties: Northumberland, Durham and Cumbria and comprises magnificent moorlands, wooded valleys and small unspoilt villages.

WALLINGTON HOUSE.
Tel: 01670 74283.
Location: 12 miles west of Morpeth (B6343). Built in 1688 and altered in the 1740s, the house features exceptional plasterwork; fine collections of porcelain

and dolls houses and the Museum of Curiosities. The house is set in 100 acres of lakes, lawns and woodland with a beautiful Walled Garden. Admission to House, Walled Garden and Grounds £4.00. Open daily 1st Apr-31st Oct, except Tues 1-
5.30pm. Last admission 5pm.

OXFORDSHIRE

BURFORD COTSWOLD WILD LIFE PARK

Tel: 01993 823006

Situated in 180 acres of gardens and woodland around an old English manor house, a large and varied collection of animals from all over the world can be seen in spacious grassed enclosures. There is also a reptile house, aquarium, tropical house, exhibition of fruit bats, picnicking areas, narrow gauge railway (Apr-Oct), adventure playground, bar, restaurant, children's farmyard, insect house and gift shops. Special events during summer months. Open; Daily (except Christmas day) from 10-6pm or dusk (whichever is the earlier).

OXFORD THE OXFORD STORY

6 Broad Street

Tel: 01865 790055

Created by Oxford University and the people behind York's 'Jorvik' Viking Centre, this is an extraordinary exhibition about Oxford's 800 years past. Now recognised as the best short introduction to Oxford. The Oxford Story uses a ride through the streets from the past, from medieval Oxford to Inspector Morse Magnus Magnusson or Timothy Mallett (for children) provide the commentary. Open: April-October 9.30-5pm. July-August 9.30-7pm. Nov-March 10-4pm. Closed Christmas Day.

WITNEY COGGES MANOR FARM MUSEUM

Church Lane.

Tel: o1993 772602

A working museum of Victorian rural Life on a 20 acre site, close to Witney town centre. The historic site includes the manor house with room displays, walled garden, orchard, riverside walks, farm buildings housing traditional breeds of animals, exhibitions in the barns, daily demonstrations of cooking on the kitchen range and special weekends and activities. Buttery serving light lunches and teas, gift shop and car park. Open: April-end October, Tues-Friday abd Bank Holiday Mondays 10.30-5.30pm. Saturday and Sunday 12 njoon- 5.30pm.

WOODSTOCK BLENHEIM PALACE

Tel: 01993 811091

Home of the 11th Duke of Marlborough, birthplace of Sir Winston Churchill. A visit to Blenheim is a wonderful way to spend a day. An inclusive ticket covers the Palace tour, and Gardens, Butterfly House, Motor Launch, Train, Adventure Play Area and Nature trail. Optional are the Marlborough Maze and Rowing Boat hire on Queen Pool. Car parking is free for Palace visitors. Shops, Cafeterias and Restaurant. Special events include the Blenheim Audi International Horse Trials. Mid- March- 31st October daily 10.30-5.30pm.

SUFFOLK

ALDEBURGH MOOT HALL,

Sea Front. Town history and maritime affairs including prints, paintings, relics of Snape Anglo-Saxon ship burial. In 16th century timbered town hall. Open: April, May Sat & Sun 2.30-5pm. Jun-Sept daily 2.30-5pm. Jul, Aug daily 10-12.30pm & 2.30-5.30pm.

BURY ST EDMUNDS MANOR HOUSE MUSEUM,

Honey Hill.

Tel: 01284 757072.

A new museum of art and horology in refurbished Georgian Mansion. Colliection of clocks, watches, paintings, furniture, costumes and ceramics. 'Hands On' Gallery. Cafe & shop. Open all year Mon-Sat 10-5pm Sun 2-5pm. Closed Good Friday, Christmas Day and Boxing Day.

SUFFOLK REGIMENTAL MUSEUM,

The Keep, Gibraltar Barracks, Out Risbygate.

Tel: 01284 752394 ext 6.

Military uniforms, weapons, medals, photographs, drums etc, illustrating history of the Suffolk and Cambridgeshire regiments from 17th century. Open all year. Mon-Fri 10-12, 2-4pm. Closed Bank Holidays. Admission free.

ST EDMONDSBURY CATHEDRAL

Angel Hill 11th century Mother church of Suffolk with fine hammer beam roof and a display of 1,00 embroidered kneelers. Open Jun-Aug 8.30-8pm Sept-May 8.30-6pm. Exhibitions in the Cloisters.

BURY ST EDNUNDS ABBEY.
Ruins of St Edmunds Abbey church. 12th century Norman Tower and magnificently restored Abbey Gate. Set in attractive gardens. Guide from TIC. Open daily. Admission free.

EUSTON HALL.
Tel: 01842 766366.
18th century house, set in Evelyn and Kent landscaped park. Paintings by Lely, Van Dyck and Stubbs. 17th century church with Wren style interior. Jun-Sept Thurs 2.30-5pm. Tea room.

CHARSFIELD ARKENDIELD,
1 Park Lane. Half an acre cottage garden in village made famous by Ronald Blythe's book. Orchard/picnic area. Mid Apr-Oct 1st daily 10.30-dusk.

CHEDBURGH REDE HALL FARM PARK
off A143 near Chedburgh.
Tel: 01284 850695.
Working farm based on agricultural life of the 1930s-1950s. Suffolk Punch horses working with agricultural implements and wagons. Rare breeds of cattle, sheep and pigs. Working displays of seasonal farm activities. Children's pet area. Tearoom. Gift shop. Open Apr-Sept inc daily 10-5.30pm

CLARE CLARE PRIORY.
Ruins of 13th century Monastery and Monastic Church. Open: daily.

COTTON COTTON MECHANICAL MUSIC MUSEUM
off B1113 south of Diss.
Tel: 01449 613876.
Extensive collection, includes organs, street pianos, polyphones, gramophones, music boxes, musical dolls, fruit bowls and even a musical chair. Also the mighty Wurlitzer Theatre pipe organ in specially reconstructed cinema. Open: Jun-Sept 2.30-5.30pm.

DUNWICH DUNWICH MUSEUM,
St James' Street.
Tel: 0172 873796.
History of the town of Dunwich from Roman times, chronicling itsdisappearance into the sea over the centuries. Open: Mar Sat& Sun 2-4.30pm. Good Friday-Sept 30th daily 11.30-4.30pm. Oct daily 12-4pm. Admission free.

EAST BERGHOLT BRIDGE COTTAGE,
Flatford.
Tel: 01206 298260.
16th century cottage in Dedham Vale close to Flatford Mill (Mill not open to public). Easter, Apr, May Oct: Wed-Sun. Jun-Sept daily 11-5.30pm. Free, but fee for car park. National Trust.

EAST BERGHOLT CHURCH.
Impressive perpendicular exterior. Tower never completed. Unique 16th century timber framed bell cage. Open in daylight.

FLIXTON NORFOLK AND SUFFOLK AVIATION MUSEUM.
On B1060 Homersfield Road. 17 historic aircraft; toher aviation material. 446th Bomb Group Museum. Royal Observer Corps Museum. Open: Apr-Oct Sundays and Bank Holidays 10-5pm. Also summer school holidays, Tues, Wed & Thurs 10-5pm. Free.

FREMLINGHAM FREMLINGHAM CASTLE.
Tel: 01728 724189.
Built in 12th century by the Bigod family. One of the finest examples of a curtain walled castle. Open Apr-30th Sept daily 10-6pm. Oct1st-Mar 31st daily but closed Mon, Dec 24-26 and Jan 1st. 10-4pm. English Heritage.

FREMLINGHAM CHURCH.
Outstanding hammer-beam roof/monuments. Open in daytime.

HARTEST GIFFORD'S HALL.
Tel: 01284 830464.
'A small country living', 33 acres with vineyard/winery (free tastings), wild flower meadows, organic vegetables, rare breeds sheep/chickens. Flowers Rose Garden. Shop and Tea room. Children's pet and play areas. Open: Easter-Sept 30th daily 12-6pm.

HEMINGHAM OTLEY HALL
Tel: 01473 891264.
Outstanding late medieval moated hall. Historical associations. Open: Easter, Spring & August Bank Holidays. Guided tours by arrangement all year.

ILKETSHALL ST LAWRENCE THE CIDER PLACE,
Cherry Tree Farm on A144.
Tel: 01986 781353.
Traditional farm-brewed ciders, apple juices, country wines, mead and preserves. Tastings. All year: 9-1pm & 2-6pm. No admission charge.

IPSWICH TOLLY COBBOLD BREWERY & BREWERY TAP,
Cliff Road.
Tel: 01473 281508.
Taste the malt, smell the hops and enjoy a complimentary glass of beer at one of the country's oldest breweries. A must for those interested in beer, heritage and history. Artefacts from 1723. Guided tours. Open: Easter & May-Sept daily 12 noon. (Extra tours weekends). Oct-Apr: Fri, Sat, Sun 12 noon. Min age 14. Public bar/food.

KEDDINGTON KEDDINGTON CHURCH.
Fine roof, delightful interiorwith superb wood carvings, monuments, screen, pulpit, box pews. Saxon crucifix. Easter-end September: weekends and Bank Holidays 2-4pm

KETTLEBURGH EASTON FARM PARK.
Tel: 01728 746475.
Victorian model farm with many breeds of farm animals including rare breeds. Modern milking unit with viewing area. Unique Victorian Laundry and Dairy. Early farm machinery, rural bygones. Green Trail. Food and Farming Exhibition. Tea room. Gift shop. Open Easter-beginning of October 10.30-6pm.

LAVENHAM THE GUILDHALL OF CORPUS CHRISTI.
Tel: 01787 247646. History of the wool, cloth and horsehair industries, historic Lavenham and its timber-framed guildhall. Open Easter-31 Oct daily 10-5pm. Closed Good Friday.

LITTLE HALL.
15th century 'hall' house with crown post roof. Rooms furnished with gayer-Anderson collection of furniture, pictures, sculptures and ceramics. Walled garden. April-October Wed, Thurs, Sat, Sun, Bank Holidays 2.30-5.30pm.

THE PRIORY.
Tel: 01787 247003.
14th-16th century timber-framed house. Paintings. Herb garden. Gift shop. Restaurant. Easter-October daily 10.30-5.30pm.

LAVENHAM CHURCH.
Outstanding 'Cloth' church. Richly carved screens. Fine tower. 10-5.30pm in summer. 10-3.30pm in winter.

LAXFIELD BIRDS OF PREY CONSERVATION CENTRE,
St Jacobs Hall.
Tel: 01986 798844.
On B1117 from the A140 Stowmarket-Norwich road. The Centre is in the heart of rural Suffolk, just one and a half miles from the delightful village of Laxfield. You can spend time studying a wide variety of Birds of Prey in their large aviaries, or walking amongst the newly planted woodland trees covering around 4 acres of the 12 acre site. There are 3 flying displays every day, at 11.30, 2pm and 4pm. Open all year 10.30am-5.30pm every day.

LEISTON THE LONG SHOP MUSEUM,
Main Street.
Tel: 01728 832189.
Award winning steam and industrial museum. History of Richard Garrett engineering works and Leiston town featuring original machinery and memorabilia. In restored 1853 Grade II listed factory, one of the earliest examples of assembly line production of steam engines. Open April 1st-31st July 10-5pm except Sun 11-5pm.

LITTLE BLAKENHAM BLAKENHAM WOODLAND GARDEN
March 1st-June 30: daily, except Sat, 1-5pm.

LONG MELFORD MELFORD HALL.
Tel: 01787 880286.
Turreted brick Tudor mansion. Rooms in various styles. Chinese procelain collection. Gardens. Apr: Sat, Sun & Bank Holidays. May-Sept 30th Wed, Thurs, Sat, Sun & Bank Holidays. Oct: Sat, Sun 2-5.30pm. NT.

KENTWELL HALL
Elizabethan manor house with moat and gardens. Unique mosaic Tudor rose Maze. Rare breeds farm animals in park. Home-made teas. House, moat house, gardens and farm open 12-5pm (except for Re-creations) Late Mar to mid Jun and Oct: Sun only and Bank Hiliday weekends. Mid-Jul-end Sept daily. Ring for details of re-creations and other times. Tel: 01787 310207.

LONG MELFORD CHURCH.
Outstanding 'Cloth' church in fine setting of parkland and historical buildings. Fine medieval glass. Good brass rubbings. Open in daytime.

LOWESTOFT EAST ANGLIA TRANSPORT MUSEUM,
Chapel Road, Carlton Colville. On B1384. Working trams, trolley buses in reconstructed 1930s street scene. Also narrow gauge railway, battery powered vehicles, commercial vehicles, steam rollers etc. Open Easter Sun & Mon,

other Bank Holidays and Sundays from May to the end of Sept 11-5pm. Sats first week in Jun to end of Sept. Weekdays mid-Jul-beginning of Sept 2-4pm.

SOMERLEYTON HALL.

Tel: 01502 730224.

Rebuilt in Anglo-Indian style in 1840s. Fine state rooms, period furnishings and paintings. Superb gardens with famous maze. Deer Park. Tea Room. Picnic area. Hall open: Easter-Sept, Thurs, Sun and Bank Holidays. Also July & August: Tues, Wed 2-5pm. Gardens and tea room open from 12.30pm. Miniature railway Sun, Thurs, Bank Holidays from 3pm Guided tours of house, gardens, Luncheons, suppers, by prior arrangement. Lord and Lady Somerleyton hope that you will enjoy your day here and also that you will pay a visit to Fritton Lake Countryworld, part of the Somerleyton Estate, which is only a 10 minute drive and is open from 10am every day during the season.

SUFFOLK WILDLIFE PARK, KESSINGLAND.

Tel: 01502 740291.

The African Wildlife experience set in over 100 acres. Take the Safara Road-train or enjoy a leisurely walk to discover the many rare and endangered animals. Gnus and visitors shelters with interesting animal facts. Children's play area, cafeteria, shop. Open daily 10am except Dec 25/26. Telephone for admission charges.

NEWMARKET NATIONAL HORSE RACING MUSEUM,

High Street.

Tel: 01638 667333.

Story of the development of horse racing over 300 years, house in Regency subscription rooms. Arts, bronzes, development of the rules, institutions and the great men of the sport. Also British Sporting Art Trust Vestey Gallery. April-end of November Tues-Sat 10-5pm Sun 2-5pm except July, Aug 12-5pm. Also Bank Holiday Mondays and July, August Mondays 10-5pm. Various guided tours of the gallops, training grounds. National Stud, Jockey club, musuem and historic town by prior arrangement.

ORFORD CASTLE.

Tel: 01394 450472.

Built in 12th century forcoastal defence by Henry II. Near perfect example of Norman Keep with panoramic views. Opening times as Framlingham Castle.

SNAPE MALTINGS.

Converted Maltings beside River Alde. Home of world famous Aldeburgh Festival in June and other concerts/master classes during year. Tel: 01728 452935. Riverside centre includes six unusual shops and galleries, tea shop, pub and restaurant. Open all year daily 10-6pm (5pm in winter). River trips in summer. Tel: 01728 688303/5.

STOKE-BY-NAYLAND.
Tower brasses, tombs. Open in daytime, but closed on wet days.

STOWMARKET MUSEUM OF EAST ANGLIAN LIFE,
Iliffe Way.
Tel: 01449 612229.
Fine collectikons of East Anglia's rural past on attractive 70 acre site. Displays on gypsy caravans, domestic life, farming etc. Working watermill and wind pump. Craft workshops smithy, tithe barn etc. Suffolk Punch horses. An exciting outing. Refreshments, picnic area. Open April, May, October Tues-Sun and Bank Holiday Mondays June-Sept daily 10-5pm.

HAUGHLEY PARK.
Tel: 01359 240205.
Jacobean manor house, gardens and woods. May-Sept Tues 3-6pm.

SUDBURY GAINSBOROUGH'S HOUSE
Gainsborough Street.
Tel: 01787 372958.
Birthplace of Thomas Gainsborough RA 1717-88. Georgian fronted town house, with attractive walled garden, displays more of the artist's work than any other British Gallery. 18th century furniture and memorabilia. Open: Easter-Oct Tues-Sat 10-5pm Sun & Bank Holiday Monday 2-5pm Nov-Easter Tues-Sat 10-4pm Sun 2-4pm. Closed between Christmas and New Year, Good Friday.

SUTTON HOO SUTTON HOO
Archeological site, burial ground of Anglo Saxon Kings of East Anglia. Access by foot from B1083 at Hollesley turn. Open: Easter, Sat, Sun, Mon. May-early Sept Sat, Sun & Bank Holidays. Guided Tours at 2 & 3pm.

WEST STOW WEST STOW ANGLO SAXON VILLAGE.
6 buildings reconstructed on original sites. Open daily 10-4.15pm. Access via Visitor Centre in West Stow Country Park.

SHROPSHIRE

BRIDGNORTH RAYS COUNTRY MATTERS.

Tel: 01299 841255.

Enjoy a warm welcome at this farm set in the heart of unspoilt Shropshire countryside and spend a relaxing day delighting in the many varieties of animals at this traditional English farm. A great selection of unusual animals include Martha, the famous pot-bellied pig and sevastian the Llama, along with Rufus the Red Deer Stag, or why not take a stroll around the farm and look at the many attractions, or take a woodland walk strolling along the well marked paths past many different varieties of trees, shrubsand wild flowers. Open every day 10-6pm.

CHURCH STRETTON ACTON SCOTT WORKING FARM

Tel: 01694 781306.

A visit to Acton Scott will enable visitors to experience life on an upland farm at the turn of the century. The waggoner and his team of shire horses work the land with vintage farm machines. Daily demonstrations of rural crafts complete the picture of estate life 100 years ago. There are weekly visits from the wheelwright, farrier and blacksmith and children will love the cows, pigs, poultry and sheep in the farmyard and fields. Open 29th Mar-3oth Oct Tues-Sat 10-5pm Sun and Bank Holidays 10-6pm.

IRONBRIDGE JACKFIELD THE MUSEUM

Tel: 01952 433522

One of the several museum sites within the famous Ironbridge Gorge which no one should miss. . Within the Gorge you will find hours of pleasure and fascinating features to absorb. Jackfield the Museum was a world centre of the decorative tile industry. The museum houses an impressive collection of wall and floor tiles ranging from the Victorian era, through the art deco periods, to a range of attractive silk-screened designs from the 1950s. Open daily all year round.

IRONBRIDGE TOY MUSEUM

Tel: 01952 433926

Overflowing with toys, games and childhood memorabilia from magic lanterns to Bayko building sets, clockwork trains to Rupert Bear can all be seen at this wonderful museum. See how toys reflect our lifestyle from houses, cars, fashion and TV culture. Also visit the well-stocked shop selling high quality traditional toys, collectors' models, dolls and teddies, children's books and greeting cards. Open daily from 10am.

IRONBRIDGE GORGE MUSEUM

Tel: 01952 433522

This is one of Britain's 11 World Heritage Sites, where the modern world began over 250 years ago. This was the birthplace of the Industrial Revolution, and here were made the first iron railing the first iron wheels and even the first high pressure steam locomotive. Today the Ironbridge Gorge Museum shows 20th century visitors how and why these events took place and how people lived during those momentous years. Open daily through the year 10-5pm.

KIDDERMINSTER WYRE FOREST NATURE RESERVE.

Tel: 01562 827800.

The Wyre Forest Area offers many excellent examples of nature and man-made habitats for everyone to enjoy. Whether you want to picnic with the family, take a gentle stroll or enjoy a nature ramble, there are plenty of lacations to visit including the Springfield Nature Reserve which is an important habitat for many species of plants and wildlife. Or why not visit Burlish Top Heathland Nature Reserve which gives you an excellent opportunity to enjoy a habitat which is now scarce both nationally and internationally. Open daily throughout the year.

MUCH WENLOCK MUCH WENLOCK MUSEUM

Tel: 01952 727773

Interestinglocal museum, housed in former market hall. It contains new displays on the geology and natural history of Wenlock Edge, local history, exhibits including the Wenlock Olympics and information about Wenlock Priory. Open Apr-Sept Mon-Sat.

WENLOCK PRIORY

Tel: 01952 727466

Much Wenlock is a picturesque market town lying between Wenlock Edge and the Ironbridge Gorge in some of the most attractive countryside in Shropshire. Set amongst smooth lawns and ornamental topiary, are the magnificent remains of Wenlock Priory. A prosperous and powerful monastery in its time and a place of pilgrimage, Wenlock is an inspiring place to visit. There is plenty to explore and the Priory church still dominates the scene. The Norman Chapter House has some superb decorative arcading and you can also see the remains of the Cloister, once the bustling hub of daily life. Open daily 1st April-31st October 10-6pm 1st November-31st March Sun & Wed 10-4pm.

BENTHALL HALL.
Tel: 01952 882159.
An attractive mullion-windowed stone house with an impressive carved oak staircase and elaborate plaster ceiling. Family collections of furniture, ceramics and paintings are on display with a carefully restored plantsman's garden to visit at the rear of the house. Open Apr-Sept Wed, Sun and Bank Holidays 1.30-5.30pm.

THE AEROSPACE MUSEUM
Tel: 01902 374112
Locaton: On A41 just one mile from junction 3 on the M54.
One of the largest aviation collections in the UK with over 70 aircraft on display, including many unique examples, together with missiles, engines, uniforms and aviation memorabilia. Open all year round.

SEVERN VALLEY COUNTRY PARK.
Tel: 01746 781192.
The Severn Valley Country Park which covers both banks of the Severn near Highley and Alveley, about six miles south of Bridgnorth, contains some of the finest scenery in the Severn Valley. There is a visitors centre with education, display and information facilities as well as a car park. Open daily throughout the year.

WYRE FOREST
Tel: 01299 266302
This magnificent 6000 acre forest nature reserve is home to a variety of wildlife, including deer, butterflies and wild flowers. A visitor centre includes forest information, exhibitions and a shop and cafe. Explore the forest on a range of way-marked paths, including a special wheelchair route. Open daily all year round. Visitor Centre open 11-4pm.

MARKET DRAYTON HODNET HALL GARDENS
Tel: 01630 685202
Over 60 acres of brilliantly coloured flowers, magnificent forest trees, sweeping lawns and a chain of ornamental pools which run tranquilly along the cultivated garden valley to provide a natural habitat for waterfowl and other wildlife are just some of the many attractions on offer. No matter what the season, visitors will always find something fresh and interesting to ensure a full and enjoyable days outing. Open from 1st April-endSeptember Mon-Sat 2-5pm. Sun & Bank Holidays 12-5.30pm.

SHREWSBURY ATTINGHAM PARK

Tel: 01743 709203.

Attingham Park is one of the finest houses in the country, set in its own grounds of 250 acres, and offers the whole family a wealth of things to see and do. Explore the landscaped park, take a gentle stroll by the river or through the woods, discover the estate history at the Bothy exhibition, enjoy the elegant house and its beautiful furnishings, learn about the Berwick family and end your visit with home-made refreshments in the tea-room or purchasing a gift or souvenir from the shop. The Park and House are open throughout the year from the end of March until the end of September. 1.30-5pm, last admission 4.30pm.

HAUGHMOND ABBEY

Tel: 01743 709661.

Just three miles north east of Shrewsbury stand the evocative ruins of this 12th cnetury abbey. A flourishing religious community in the reign of Henry II, the abbey was dissolved under Henry VIII. The church was demolished and the abbots lodging, Great Hall and kitchens were converted into a private house. Indeed, the first impression given by the grey stone tiles, with there large and airy bay windows is of a gracious country house. A peaceful place, it is amongst pleasant wooded countryside. Open 1st Apr-30th Sept Wed & Sun 10-6pm.

BUILDWAS ABBEY

Tel:01952 433274

Founded in the 12th century Buildwas Abbey was largely untouched by the great events of history though periodically attacked by raiders from across the Welsh border. Its simple, sturdy buildings give a powerful impression of both grandeur and the austerity of monastic life, with its fine vaulted roof and unusual medieval floor tiles, depicting birds and animals. Open 1st April-30th September 10-6pm daily.

WROXETER ROMAN CITY

Tel: 01743 761330

To visit Wroxeter today is to step back in time to the heyday of Roman Britain. The centrepiece is the remains of the extensive bath complex, one of the best preserved in England. The enormous hill which divided the baths from the exercise area still stands, and whilst walking around you can recreate the everyday activities of the thriving Roman City. Open; April 1st - 31st October 10-6pm.

TELFORD BOSCOBEL HOUSE

Tel: 01902 850244.

A visit to Boscobel House will take you to the scene of one of the most romantic stories in English history. King Charles II sought refuge in an oak tree at Boscobel House when he was chased by Cromwell's soldiers after the Battle of Worcester in 1651. The Royal Oak can be seen to this day painted on signs outside countless pubs all over the country, and you can still see a direct descendant of the famous oak itself now nearly 300 years old, in fields surrounding the house. A visit to the house will show that it has retained its romantic character. There are panelled rooms andhiding places, including the 'sacred hole' in the attic where Charles is said to have stayed at night. Open daily from 1st April-31st October 10-6pm. 1st Nov- 31st Dec & 1st Feb - 31st March Wed 7 Sun 10-4pm.

WEST MIDLANDS

BINLEY COOMBE ABBEY PARK COUNTRY FAIR.

Tel: 01336 411285.

Location: Brinklow Road, Binley, Nr Coventry. Coombe Abbey Park is a major new outdoor events and entertainment centre for the Midlands. Already famous for its beautiful parkland and teeming wildlife, Coombe Abbey Park is the ideal place for a Country Fair which brings the past to life and explores the way forward. Open all year round 10-6pm.

COOMBE ABBEY PARK FOLK FESTIVAL.

Tel: 01336 411285.

A non-stop weekend of first class folk music in an idyllic setting takes place in September each year. Two performance marquees plus tents for dancers, singers and musicians will ensure non-stop music and entertainment from Friday evening to Saturday afternoon.

COOMBE ABBEY COUNTRY PARK.

Tel: 01203 453720.

Come and explore the splendid beauty of Coombe Abbey Country Park with its beautiful gardens, woodland and lakeside walks and drink in the historic surroundings. There are plants, animals and birds in abundance and everyone has the chance to get close to nature. Most of the parkland is classified as a Site of Special Scientific Interest in recognition of its importance to wildlife. Country Park open every day 7.30am-dusk.

COVENTRY GODIVA CITY.

Tel: 01203 832630.

Location: The Herbert Art Gallery and Museum.

Godiva City is an exciting new exhibition of over one thousand years of history. The exhibition looks at Lady Godiva as a real person, who had a huge influence in the Midlands through her wealth and estates. The exhibition discovers the 'real' Lady Godiva, but gives people the opportunity to also find out how she was marketed as a tourist attraction over 300 years ago! Admission free. Open Mon-Sat 10-5.30pm. Sun 2-5pm.

KENILWORTH CASTLE.

Tel: 01926 52078.

Location: Off the M40 near Warwick.

Great and gaunt against the Warwickshire sky, Kenilworth Castle rises up to doninate the surrounding town and peaceful countryside. Kenilworth is the finest and most extensive castle ruin in Britain. As you survey the soaring walls of the Great Hall and the elegance of the Earl of Leicester's additions to the castle for the visit of Queen Elizabeth I in 1575, you can almost re-creat the pomp and pageantry of life here in the past. Open: 1st April-October 10-6pm, 1 Nov-31 Mar 10-4pm.

MUSIC HALL ABBEY GATE.

Tel: 01203 452406.

The Abbeygate Empireproudly present its own evening of contentment and conviviality. Come and listen to the songs and humour of an apocalyptic era, join lustily in the chorus and refrains and partake in a mouth-watering three course supper.

LUNT ROMAN FORT.

Tel: 01203 832381.

In AD 60, seventeen years after the Roman invasion, the Britains rebelled against foreign rule. It took more than a year for the Roman Army to put down the revolt by the East Anglian Iceni tribe. As a result forts were rebuilt, and the army moved to new strategic locations. The lunt is the only reconstructed Roman Fort of this type in Britain and provides valuable evidence about life in a Roman Cavalry fortification. Situated on a spur of high ground overlooking the River Sowe, the lunt was in an ideal location, typical of rural Roman forts. Museum shop, free parking, picnic area and toilets. Open 2 Apr-30 Oct 10-5pm and everyday from 16th Jul-31st Aug inclusive.

RYTON ORGANIC GARDENS.

Tel: 01203 303517.

Location: Off the A45, five miles south of Coventry.

There's something for all the family at Ryton Organic Gardens. Ten acres of beautiful grounds with formal rose gardens, ornamentals, alpine banks, colourful flower beds, not to mention the wonderful array of vegetables - many of them rare or unusual - and a top and soft fruit collection. Open everyday except during Christmas week 10-5.30pm last admission to the garden is at 5pm.

CATHEDRAL LANES SHOPPING CENTRE.

Tel: 01203 632532.

Cathedral Lane provides an ideal setting for shopping, meeting and eating in the heart of Coventry. Browse in a wide range of shops selling books, fashion, beauty, sportswear, gifts and much much more. Relax over a drink or meal in the light, airy brasserie, or just sit and watch the regular, fun entertainment.

SHOPMOBILITY.

Tel: 01203 832020.

Location: The Shopmobility Unit, Upper Precinct, Coventry.

Shopmobility is a service which provides powered and unpowered wheelchairs and scooters for people who have either permanent or temporary limited mobility. It will allow them greater independence to use the pedestrianised shopping areas in the City Centre. The opening hours ar Mon-Sat 9-5pm.

THE GUILDHALL OF ST MARY.

Tel: 01203 832381.

Location: High Street, Coventry.

The Guildhall of St Mary has a long and glorious history reflecting the changes in Coventry's fortunes as well as changes in our society. It has been a feasting hall for Kings and Queens, a soup kitchen for unemployed weavers during the slump period of 1858 to 1865, a fish market in the 16th century, damaged by 18th century rioting, and 20th century bombing, but lovingly restored to its former glory. However, the Guildhall's main purpose has been to act as a centre of civic life in Coventry. Open to the public May-Sept, closed over the winter period.

MUSEUM OF BRITISH ROAD TRANSPORT.

Tel: 01203 832425.

At the Museum of British Road Transport you'll delight in the largest display of Bitish made road transport in the world. All under one roof. With more than 150 cars, 75 motorcycles and 200 cycles, the Museum tells the fascinating story of Coventry's contribution to Britain's road transport history, as seen through the famous Marques of Alvis, Daimler, Hillman, Jaguar, Riley, Rover, Standard, Triumph and many more. Open: daily all year round from 10-5pm.

WARWICK ARTS CENTRE.

Tel: 01203 524524.

Warwick Arts Centre - a resource provided by the University of Warwick - attracts over 250,000 visitors a year to the artistic programme and provides a vital link between the local and regional community. Entertainment facilities include the arts, dance, exhibitions and a selection of International Celebrity Concerts. Open daily throughout the year.

THE HERBERT ART GALLERY & MUSEUM.

Tel: 01203 832381.

Introduction to Weaving is a Crafts Council exhibition which takes an intriguing and delightful look at woven textiles from the Crafts Council Collection, with weaving by local maker Susan Wright. Admission free Mon-Sat 10-5.30pm, Sun 2-5pm.

WALES

BEDDGELERT SYGUN COPPER MINE,

Beddgelert, LL55 4NE

Tel: 01766 890595 24 hour info/line: 01766 890564.

Sygun is one mile from the village of Beddgelert on the A498 road to Capel Curig. Sygun Copper Mine is one of the wonders of Wales - a remarkable and impressive example of how part of our precious industrial heritage can be reclaimed, restored and transformed into an outstanding family attraction. The mine provides an excellent and informative experience of the underground world of the Victorian miner.The mine, a unique modern day reminder of 19th century methods of ore extraction and processing is situated in the glorious Gwynant Valley - the heart of the stunning Snowdonia National Park - and on probably the most popular tourist route in Wales. The incomparable scenery captured the imagination of movie-makers, who turned the mountainside surrounding Sygun into a Chinese village in 1958 for the filming of 'The Inn of the Sixth Happiness' which starred the late Ingrid Bergman. Sygun offers a rare opportunity for those with a sense of adventure and curiosity, from the young to the elderly, to discover for themselves the wonders it still shelters after being abandoned in 1903. Audiovisual tours allow you to explore the old workings on foot in complete safety. there are winding tunnels and large chambers, magnificent stalactite and stalagmite formations and copper ore veins which contain traces of gold, silver and other precious metals. It usually takes about 40 minutes to complete the quarter mile route which rises 140feet via stairways to emerge at the Victoria level for a breathtaking view of the Gwynant Valley and surrounding Snowdonia mountain range. A shorter, less demanding tour can be arranged. Refreshments and a wide range of souvenirs are available in the visitors centre. **OPEN;** All year. Oct, Nov, Feb, March 10.30am-4pm. (11am Sunday) Dec, Jan 11-3.30pm. Main season: Easter or late March - Sept inc. 10am-5pm (11am Sun. & 4pm Sat.) Visa/ Access/Switch. Flat soled shoes advisable. Dogs not permitted underground.

BLAENAU FFESTINIOG LLECHWEDD SLATE CAVERNS,
Blaenau Ffestiniog, LL41 3NB
Tel: 01766 830306 Fax:01766 831260.
This is a day out to remember. Winner of all Britain's top tourism awards, Llechwedd Slate Caverns have been visited by five million people, including Edward VIII when he was Prince of Wales, the Princess Margaret, the Duchess of Gloucester and the Crown Prince of Japan. The spectacular underground lake has been used for a Walt Disney film set. Other sites have endeavoured, unsuccessfully, to copy the magic of Llechwedd - where the tourist operation has the benefit of historic authenticity while also remaining part of the biggest working slate mine in Wales. Here you can take two quite different rides, one exploring the complexities of old slate mining skills, the other the triumph, humour, religious fervour, and the pathos of the Victorian miner. Visitors are at liberty to take either or both. Add to that an exploration of the Victorian Village, and some refreshment at one of the wide selection of catering facilities, and there is no reluctance to spend at least a day at Llechwedd. A very interesting and informative little book about Llechwedd written by Ivor Wynne Jones, a Director, is well worth acquiring. Not only does it tell you about the mine but also about the history of slate, and relates Llechwedd Slate Caverns' unexpected contribution to the conservation of Wales' endangered wild life. Choughs' Cavern which visitors see while the Miners' Tramway, was named after the shy crow-like birds which nested there for many years,returning in 1969, disappearing in the 1970s but rediscovering the same unlikely spot in 1991, since when annual nesting has been re-established. On the surface hovering kestrels are a common sight and buzzards nest on the northern rock face. One of nature's most beautiful contributions is rhododendron ponticum which bursts into flower each spring. An interesting highlight of a visit to Llechwedd is the facility for spending Victorian coins, at Victorian prices, in the village shops and the ever popular Miners Arms. This journey back in time begins at the Old Bank of Greenway & Greaves. This is a banking museum, preserving the appearance of a small country branch early in the last century. The Llechwedd 'bank' has a shop counter where five pre-decimal coins may be purchased. They show correct designs on the reverse, but with modern dating. All prices

in the Victorian Village -Pentre Llechwedd - are shown in old and new currencies, enabling such experiences as buying a 'pennorth' of sweets or a 3d pint at the Miners' Arms. In 1972 when a half-mile level section of the Miners' Tramway was opened to the world revealing the vast workings, it was immediately given the top awards of both the British Tourist Authority and the Wales Tourist Board.Boarding a train in a corner of the original slate slabbing mill of 1852, visitors now ride into an 1846 tunnel, hauled by battery-electric locomotives. Entering through the side of the mountain, this journey into the early Victorian past remains on the level, and traverses some spectacular caverns. Passengers alight at various points to learn something of the strange skills needed to extract slate. There is a sound and light tableaux deep underground and guides describe the other chambers. OPEN: Daily 10am including Sundays. (Closed on Christmas Day, Boxing Day and New Year's Day) Last tours into mines: 5.15pm March to September 4.15pm October to February. Access, Visa, Switch. Special terms for parties of 20 or more. Free car parking, free surface exhibitions. Dogs not allowed on either ride. Separate cafe. Victorian Pub and Licensed restaurant.

CAERNARFON CAERNARFON AIR WORLD,
Museum and Pleasure Flights
Caernarfon Airport, Dinas Dinlle, Nr Caernarfon, Gwynedd LL545TP
Tel: 01286 830800.

In the great hangar here you can see planes and helicopters in landscaped settings, aircraft engines, ejector seats and over two hundred model aircraft. If you enjoy the history and nostalgia associated with planesand flying,this is the place for you and it is 'Hands On'. You can sit in cockpits, take the controls in the Varsity Trainer and wander round full size planes. There are also exhibitions featuring Local Aviation History, the story of the Dambusters, Welsh Flying V.C's, the first RAF Mountain Rescue Service, fascinating wartime newspapers and historic First Day Covers. There is a cinema where you can watch aviation shorts and full length films. The well stocked museum shop has been extended, and for small children there is a themed adventure playground, built around a Dragonfly helicopter. Pleasure Flights will provide you with a unique experience in North Wales. Take a bird's eye view of mountains, castles and coastline in a Cessna or the Vintage de Havilland Dragon Rapide. There are three standard flights, but you can always plan your own. The first is a ten minute flight over the Menai Strait around the 13th century Caernarfon Castle and back over the 18th century Fort Belan. The second flight is a breathtaking 25 minute experience flying over the mountains of Snowdonia, over the summit of Snowdon, the highest peak in England and Wales, over Crib Coch and the Llanberis Pass, then back to the airport taking in Caernarfon Castle and Fort Belan. The third is another 25 minute flight that is offered if weather conditions do not favour a mountain trip. This one flies over the Menai Strait and the lovely island of Anglesey, taking in the foothills of Snowdonia and Caernarfon Castle on the return journey. OPEN; MUSEUM Daily 1st March -31st October 9am-5.30pm. PLEASURE FLIGHTS Daily, weather permitting throughout the year. Check by phone prior to visit. RESTAURANT Open daily all year. Coffee Shop open from Easter to 31st October.

COLWYN BAY EIRIAS PARK,
Colwyn Leisure Centre, Colwyn Bay LL29 8HG
Tel: 01492 533223
Here you will find something for all the family. With over half a million visitors annually to Eirias Park its popularity as a tourist and recreational attraction cannot be questioned. Set in 50 acres of beautiful parkland, the facilities on offer provide a unique recreational experience and offer an outstanding day out for all ages. Facilities available all year round include: Leisure Pool/Waterchute, Sports Halls, Squash Courts, Sauna/Solarium Suite, Function Room, Fitness Room, Lounge Bar/Cafe, Athletics Stadium, Indoor/ Outdoor Tennis Courts and Synthetic Pitch. Facilities available throughout the summer season include: Crown Green Bowling Greens, Boating Lake with small and large pedaloes, Model Yacht Pond, Mini Golf Par Putting, Children' Play Area, Picnic Areas and Dinosaur World. From a promotional point of view, the facilities within Eirias Park, serve as an ideal location for the hosting of a corporate day and last year such days were organised on behalf of the Inland Revenue for Wales and the Post Office, North West. Simply choose from the available facilities or allow the competent, friendly staff to arrange a programme of activities to suit your company's personal needs. To complement the days activities, the Catering Manageress will be delighted to arrange a buffet with a wide selection of menus to choose from. From its commanding position overlooking the promenade and beach, the park is easily accessible by road via the A55 Expressway which links North Wales with the UK Motorway network and by rail with regular inter-city services from all parts of Britain. Easy access for the disabled. Free Car Parking.

CWMBRAN GREENMEADOW COMMUNITY FARM,
Green Force Way, Cwmbran NP44 5AJ
Tel: 01633 862202
In the early 1980's a group of local people formed an action committee in a bid to protect one of the last green spaces in Cwmbran from further development. The group came up with the exciting prospect of establishing a Community Farm. Today, the original, fully refurbished c17th farmstead with 150 acres of land throughout Cwmbran, offers a magnificent rural retreat in an urban setting. It is a place full of excitement where you will see traditional farm animals and Rare Breeds, a well-stocked aviary, an Exhibition Barn with ever changing exhibits. On the woodland trails you will see a surprising

variety of wildlife and the Pets Corner is a place in which children have a chance to make friends with the smaller animals. All visitors are encouraged to feed and handle selected farm animals. The Farm House Tea Room offers traditional home-made fare. The Sheep Dip Bar is open every evening and the 16th century Cordell's Restaurant is ideal for an intimate meal. It opens every evening 7-10pm and for Sunday lunch. Special events are organised throughout the year. OPEN; All year except Christmas Day Summer 10-6pm Winter 10-4.30pm. Disabled people welcome. Pets allowed. Licensed. Conference facilities.

DOLGELLAU GWYNBFYNYDD GOLD MINE,
The Marian, Dolgellau, Gwynedd LL40 1UU
Tel: 01341 423332 Fax: 01341 423737
To get to the mine take the courtesy bus from Welsh Gold in Dolgellau and enjoy the short guided journey through some of the most beautiful countryside in Wales. Here you will see the place where a hugebonanza of gold was found a century ago: worth £5 million if found today. As far as one can tell Gwynfynydd Gold mine is the only working gold mine open to the public. Gold ore is mined daily but actual gold is very rare ; the mine yields about 25g per month on the whole but most times it can be less. 8 full time miners work here with additional staff to guide people through the mine during the summer season. Once you arrive at the mine you are presented with protective clothing which include a hard hat, waterproof jacket and boots. (It is advisable to take a sweater with you as it can be quite cold underground.) On the tour itself you can experience the roar and thunder of modern machinery, the blast of explosions, and take away your own free sample of a Welsh Goldmine ore. You will also see how they mined in the olden days, by candle light. After being underground for around one hour you will see the Gold Smelting room, where gold is melted down to a small gold bullion. At the end of your tour you may pan for gold, should you find any, which is normally found in small pieces of rocks, you may take it home!! The retail shop sells Welsh Gold Jewellery which is displayed amongst other crafts from Wales. It is advisable to book in advance for tours throughout the year. The gold centre is open throughout the year 9.30am until 5.00pm, later on some occasions in the summer. It is open 7 days from Easter to September and closed on Sundays during the winter.

HOLYWELL HOLYWELL LEISURE CENTRE
Fron Park, Holywell CH8 7UZ
An exciting Leisure Centre offering something for every age. The 6 lane swimming pool incorporates broad shallow steps for easy access. Contained within the pool hall is a small shallow water area where toddlers can play in safety and a splash pool which provides a safe landing area to the 42 metre corkscrew water slide. The swimmng pool is open from 10am each day but

closes each weekday between 3.45pm and 5.15pm for junior swimming classes. Indeed there is a whole range of classes for swimmers of all ages and all stages. The Silhouette Fitness Centre and the Silhouettes Health Suite are both excellent for anyone and supervised by an experienced and caring staff. Both open from 10am-10pm seven days a week. The Sports Hall has five a side football, basketball, volleyball and four badminton courts, bookable from 10am-10pm each day. The Dance Studio has a comprehensive range of dance classes and some popular aerobic and step aerobic sessions. This multi use area is excellent for small theatrical productions, drama workshops, film shows, seminars and training courses. The Hall is also used for Karate, Thai Boxing, Kung Fu, 50+ Exercise classes and children's birthday parties. Open from 10am-10pm seven days a week. The Snooker Room has 6 tables. For Bowling, two crown greens, one of which is floodlit are available for casual use from the beginning of April to the end of October. There is an Outdoor Area, two floodlit tennis courts, and a Synthetic Pitch for soccer. The Cafeteria is open from 9.30am-9.30pm each day and there is a comfortable lounge bar which opens from 7.30pm each evening. For further details please ring 01352 712027.

LLANDRINDOD WELLS THE RADNORSHIRE MUSEUM,
Temple Street, Llandrindod Wells, LD1 5LD
Tel: 01597 824 513
Situated in the centre of Llandrindod Wells, the museum houses exhibits relating to the history of the old mid-Wales county of Radnorshire. Displays illustrate the largely rural farming lifestyle of the area as well as the development of Llandrindod Wells as a country Spa Resort during the Victorian and Edwardian Era. The museum also displays material relating to Fine Art, costume and the Prehistoric,Roman and Medieval history of the area: including the Roman Fort of Castell Collen. New for 1995 was the Red Kite Centre: set on the museums first floor, this exhibition highlights the lifestyle and successful fight back from the edge of extinction of Britons most beautiful bird of prey. The exhibition also includes a thirty minute video on the Red Kite and computer information station on the birds of Europe. **OPEN;** 10-12.30 and 2-4.30. Closed Wednesday (all year) and Saturday afternoon and Sunday (winter only).

TEIFI VALLEY RAILWAY,
Henllan Station, Henllan, Nr Newcastle Emlyn SA44 5TD
Tel/Fax: 01559 371077
The only Famous Little Trains of Wales in West Wales gives hours of pleasure to people of all ages. A 40 minute train ride experience for which you pay once and ride all day (if seats available). Facilities include Woodland Theatre (Phone for details), Woodland Trails, Cafe. Shop, Pictorial Museum, Crazy Golf/Quoits/Skittles, Childrens'Play Areas, Picnic and Barbeque Areas. W.C's,

large Car Park, Coaches Welcome. Usual Coach Driver Facilities. OPEN; Easter-Oct inc 10.30am-6pm. Closed: Saturdays. Apr 13/20/27 May 4/11/18 Oct 5/12/19. TRAINS: Apr. May. June Oct. 10.30,11.30, 12.30, 2pm, 3pm, 4pm. July, Aug-Sept Last train 5pm + Bank Holidays. SPECIAL EVENTS: April 6th, Aug 17th, 25th and 26th, Oct 26th, December - SANTA SPECIALS Entrance/Parking 50p (Adults) £3.50 (Children) £1.50(OAP) £3 Dogs 50p. Opending hours: daily Easter -26th October.

LLANGOLLEN MODEL RAILWAY WORLD & DR WHO EXHIBITION,

Lower Dee Mill Llangollen LL20 8SE

Tel: 01978 860584.

These two exciting attractions opened in the summer of 1995 and rapidly drew attention from visitors to the area as well as curious locals! The Model Railway World Museum is based around the original Hornby Dublo Factory from Binns Road, Liverpool. You will see 24 large superb layouts with 1000s of models on display. You can try shunting in the hands-on section and watch and talk to experts about building these models. Fascinating and educational. Dapol Ltd design and manufacture precision model railways and a wide range of toys including Dr Who models. The move to Lower Mill not only enabled Dapol to improve its manufacturing but also to realise the life-long dream of its Managing Director, David Boyle - to establish a National Model Railway Museum. Over the years David has amassed a huge collection of model railway artefactsand memorabilia including the original design drawings, art work, photographs, lathes, jigs, etc from Hornby, Dublo, Mainline,Wrenn. Airfix. All these are displayed together with the working layouts resulting in a unique exhibition relating to the history of model railways from the very beginning to the present day. The DR WHO exhibition adds yet another fascinating dimension at Lower Dee Mill. It was opened by former Dr Who actor, Colin Baker on the 17th June 1995 and has been mounted in association with the BBC who have provided the original costumes, Daleks, Cybermen monsters, visual effects (many of which are priceless).In consultation with BBC Dr Who producer, John Nathan-Turner the exhibition, covering three huge rooms, has been designed more as an experience than an exhibition with a full size working TARDIS and original sound effects give a fascinating insight into how the longest running science fiction series in the world was made for television. Please ring 01978 860584 for opening times.

LLANGOLLEN LLANGOLLEN HORSE DRAWN BOAT TRIPS

Llangollen Wharf, Llangollen

Tel: 01978 860702 for general enquiries.

0169 175322 for Group bookings, Day Boats and Holiday Hire.

To take a trip on one of these boats eases you back to the days of leisure as you glide noislessly through the spectacular scenery of the Vale of Llangollen. You may find yourself being pulled along by one of five horses who are all friendly and have names. Spot is the old boy who only works occasionally and then there is Fred, Sam, Stan and Arthur. They seem to enjoy their work as they go slowly along the towpath. In this timeless setting, the horse-drawn canal trips are as relaxing today as they were when the first pleasure boats slipped away from the Wharf in 1884. On the Wharf, you will find the Canal Exhibition Centre, telling the Canal Story with words, pictures and models. It is good to wander among the gaily painted canal ware in the gift shop and delightful to take tea on the terrace overlooking the town. Llangollen Wharf is a fascinating place for a day out. The popular cruise on the luxury narrowbat Thomas Telfrod includes a crossing of the Pontcysllte Aqueduct. OPEN; Daily for 45 minute horse-drawn boat trips and exhibition visits from Easter to September with limited opening in October.

LLANGOLLEN LLANGOLLEN RAILWAY,
Abbey road, Llangollen LL208SN
Tel:01978 860979
Llangollen is at the junction of the A5 and A539. The railway station is by the bridge over the River Dee. The nearest car parks are in Market Street in the town and at Lower Dee Mill on the A539 approaching from Ruabon. The nearst British Rail station is 5 miles away at Ruabon. Bryn Melyn buses operate hourly to Llangollen from Wrexham and Ruabon, two hourly on Sundays. The Llangollen Railway Society rescued this delightful line and have spent years bringing the track, the station and the trains back to their original beauty and splendour. The Railway you see at Llangollen today is a directresult of the dreams and aspirations of the former Flint and Deeside Railway. The work has been done mainly by volunteer enthusiasts who removed masses of undergrowth and rubble from the trackbed and vandalised buildings without water or supplies to be restored. The journey in the restored carriages through the countryside with the River Dee appearing constantly, is both beautiful, exciting and relaxing. Thrilling for youngsters and an outstanding experience for steam railway enthusiasts. There are opportunities for people to spend two hours on the footplate on 14 miles of firing and driving. Full hot meals for the trainee and light refreshments for up to six guests. Try the Llangollen Steam Driving Course - something you will never forget or regret. There are special dining opportunities and Sunday Lunches aboard the Berwyn Belle. Friends of Thomas Events, Santa Specials and much more. Ring for further information 01978 860979.

COWBRIDGE TASKFORCE PAINTBALL GAMES

(147 Ynysddu, Pontyclun CF7 9UB office)

Tel:01443 227715 Fax:01443 225803

Situated just off the A48 west of Cowbridge, part of a large three and a half thousand acre estate at Penllyn. With easy access from the M4, just 10 minutes away, it can be reached with ease from most of the south west's major towns via the motorway network. Task Force is set in 30 acres of woodland within a deep undulating valley. It has been a venue for Paintball games since 1989 and during this period has had many special features added to it to create an exciting and varied site to play. Amongst its many varied features and scenarios are numerous bunkers, dugouts, a helicopter, bridges and a HUGE 'woodland village'. Your day will begin with a comprehensive briefing, followed by the issuing of all the equipment you will need for the day. Then once you are all kitted up and have had a practice on the firing range, you are ready for battle to commence. During the day you will play approximately 12 games. You do not need a special amount of players to book. There is an excellent Junior Paintball Game exclusively for 11-16 year olds. Open; Saturday and Sunday or during the week if you have a group of 15 or more people. Credit Cards: Visa/Delta/Access/Master .

LLANDYSUL TY HEN FARM

Llwyndafydd, Nr New Quay, Llandysul SA44 6BZ West Wales.

Tel: 01545 560346

Approached by a bumpy lane and set on a sheep farm in peaceful countryside close to the Cardigan coast, near Cwmtudu, this attractive Guest House which also offers delightful, converted self-catering cottages is wonderful for people who want to relax, be well cared for and within easy reach of a whole host of exciting places. The main house has well appointed en suite bedrooms, the self-catering cottages and apartments are around the farmyard and so too is The Pits Centre which houses the restaurant and leisure facilities which comprise an indoor heated pool, well equipped gymnasium, sunbed, sauna, changing rooms, toilets, bowls/skittle alley, coin operated washing machine and drier. Good food is part of the reason this excellent place was awarded 3 Crowns and the farm-house award. **OPEN;** Mid-Feb - Mid-Nov. Residential & Table Licence. Pets by prior arrangement. Disabled Access. Visa/Mastercard. Children welcome

MACHYNLLETH KING ARTHUR'S LABYRINTH

Corris, Machynlleth, SY20 9RF

Tel: 01654 761584 Fax: 01654 761575

King Arthur's Labyrinth is a fairly recent visitor attraction which has delighted people since it opened in 1994. An underground boat takes visitors deep into the spectacular caverns under the Braichgoch mountain at Corris. As visitors walk through the caverns, Welsh tales of King Arthur are told with tableaux and stunning sound and light effects. The journey ends with a return trip along the beautiful subterranean river into the grounds of the Corris Craft Centre. This exciting centre is the starting point for King Arthur's Labyrinth and home to six craft workshops at which visitors are invited to see at first hand the skills of the craft workers and, if they wish, to buy from the displays of woodcraft, toy making, jewellery, leather work and hand-made candles, while the Labyrinth shop provides a range of souvenirs, books and gifts on the Celtic Arthurian theme. The Crwbyr Restaurant provides full meals, teas and refreshments throughout the day. There is also a picnic area in the gardens and an extensive children's play area. Visitors to the Labryinth are advised to wear warm clothing as the underground caverns are cool. The 45 minute tour of the caverns involves a walk of about half a mile along level gravel paths unsuitable only for the very frail. However the variety of craft shops, gardens and refreshments within the Corris Craft Centre and the stunning scenery of the Corris valley provide ample enjoyment for everyone. Group bookings are welcome. OPEN; 10-5pm daily from April to October.

MACHYNLLETH MEIRION MILL,
Dinas Mawddwy, Nr Machynlleth SY20 9LS
Tel: 01650 531311

In a wonderful setting in the mountains of the Snowdonia National Park, shopping becomes a sheer delight when you see what wonderful goods, clothing, crafts and gifts are on offer.There is a tremendous range of wool products all under one roof: traditionally woven tweeds and rugs, skirt lengths, wool jackets, knitwear from black sheep, warm jumpers, subtle blended colours in ties and hats, sheepskin slippers, hats and gloves and of course, sheepskin rugs. The shelves are full of locally produced honey and jams, slate gifts, Celtic jewellery, lovespoons, jumping sheep and small items for children tocollect. They also stock Portmeirion Pottery. Meirion Mill has everything going for it; parking couldn't be simpler nor the access easier. The Old Station Coffee Shop has a restaurant licence and serves delicious home-cooked fare. There is a level entrance to the shop and all areas are accessible by wheelchair. You will find Meirion Mill situated on the Powys/Gwynedd border at the southern end of the National Park. The Mill site was originally the terminus for the old Mawddwy railway which ran for six miles down the valley to join the main railway at Cemmaes Road. The double arched Pack Horse Bridge spans the River Dyfi next to the entrance gate. Heavily laden donkeys were led across this narrow bridge transporting bolts of flannel to be sold over the border. OPEN: Daily early March to late November. Mon-Sat 10am-5pm. Sun: 10.30am-5pm. Times do vary in the early and late season. Current times can be obtained by phoning 01650 531311. Normally closed during winter months. Amex/Visa/Access/Mastercard/Delta/Switch. Childrens Play Area. Picnic area. Dogs not allowed in play area, shop or coffee shop.

CENARTH THE NATIONAL CORACLE CENTRE,
Cenarth Falls, Newcastle Emlyn

NEWCASTLE

EMLYN
SA389JL
Tel: 01239 710980
Rescued from decay by Mr and Mrs Martin Fowler in 1983, Cenarth Mill was re-roofed in 1991 and the National Coracle Centre stands in the grounds of the 17th century flour mill where the mill pig stys and workshops once were. The mill is included in your visit here. An organised tour of the Centre takes you back to one of the earliest forms of transport, and presents a unique display of Coracles from many parts of the world. As well as nine varieties of Welsh Coracle and those from other British rivers, you can see examples from Iraq, Vietnam, India and North America. The workshop is an important part of the Centre and the ancient craft of Coracle making is displayed here. Coracles can be seen on the river during the summer holidays, and trips in one can sometimes be arranged. Viewing areas and pathways allow easy access for disabled people and provide wonderful views of the falls, salmon leap and 200 year old bridge. **OPEN;** Easter-October Sunday to Friday 10.30am-5.30pm and other times by appointment. Gift Shop. Tea rooms.

PORT DINORWIC
Y FELINHELI THE GREENWOOD CENTRE
Tel: 01248 671493 Fax: 01248 670069
Indoors and outdoors the Award Winning Greenwood Centre is all about discovering the fascinating World of Trees. It is an enjoyable and educational experience for all ages. You can find out how trees work, how they clean the air, visit the Rainforest and hear its sounds, see a banana plant and find stick insects. Try out your sense of smell at the scent boxes and see if you can identify the fragrances. Find out about the history of forestry in Wales. Explore the rhododendron maze, treenursery, root circle. See the wildlife pond and make friends with the rabbits in pets corner, and in the main holiday season, watch forest craft demonstrations and try out a Welsh Longbow from May to September.Enjoy a picnic outdoors or sample some of the tasty snacks and light lunches in the Tea Room. OPEN; Daily 10am-5.30pm March to October inclusive. Winter visits by arrangement. Dogs on leads welcome. Free car & coach park. Disabled and baby changing facilities.

PORTMEIRION,
Gwynedd LL48 6ET
Tel: 01766 770228
One single word, Portmeirion, conjures up a magical place, somewhere that everyone should visit at least once in a lifetime. It is the realisation of a dream by its creator Sir Clough Williams-Ellis who had long nurtured the idea of one day building his own ideal village on some romantic coast. Eventually he was offered the Aber la peninsula, only five miles from his ancestral home- a perfect place to prove that the development of a naturally beautiful site need not necessarily lead to its defilement. Work began when he ws 42 in 1925 and when Sir Clough died in 1978 at the age of 95 he was content in the knowledge that his dream had become a reality. For people like myself the sheer beauty, colour and charm of Portmeirion is enough to make me want to just stand and stare. There are different vistas at every turn and each one you think cannot be more beautiful than the last, but it always is. Portmeirion is a world apart and you may come here as a day visitor - not the best way because you cannot see and absorb all it has to offer. Portmeirion has six different shops including the Seconds Warehouse, which is the only place in Wales selling second quality Portmeirion Pottery, designed by Susan Williams-Ellis. The Ship Shop sells best quality Portmeirion Pottery plus a wide range of design led gifts for all ages. There is also a Papur a Phensal for cards, the Golden Dragon bookshop, and Pot Jam selling Portmeirion preserves and confectionery. The Six of One shop specialises in The Prisoner TV series. The village has a licensed self-service restaurant with a pleasant terrace for meals outside. There is an ice-cream parlour and several ice-cream kiosks. The Hotel restaurant on the quayside welcomes non-residents and provides reasonably priced two and three course lunches.

RHAYADER WELSH ROYAL CRYSTAL,
5 Brynberth, Rhayader LD6 5EN
Tel: 01597 811005
Winner of Wales Tourism Awards 1995 'Highly Commended' Welsh Royal Crystal is the Principality's own complete manufacturer of hand-crafted lead crystal products in tableware,stemware, presentation trophies and gift items. All production processes are undertaken on the one manufacturing site situated in Rhayader in the heartlands of Wales. Welsh RoyalCrystal melts glass containing a lead content in excess of 30% (known as Full Lead Crystal) which is considered to be the best quality glass from which fine quality crystal glass products are made - weight and feel, definition of cutting and polishing brilliance are very much enhanced. Welsh Royal Crystal's range of products is traditional and the decoration combines classic florals (intaglio) with straight diamond cuts. A unique range of Celtic themes reflecting the design

images of the Welsh Celtic heritage has been successfully introduced. The design and supply of presentation trophies and gifts is an expanding area of the Company's business. Welsh Royal Crystal can number within its customer portfolio important corporate customers in Wales and is pleased to be associated with the Cardiff Singer of the World Competition sponsored by British Petroleum, the Young Welsh Singer Competition sponsored by the Midland Bank and more recently, the Welsh Women of the Year sponsored by the Western Mail and HTV. In addition to supplying our fine Welsh crystal to over 100 retail accounts in Wales, sales are increasing across the borders of the Principality into England, Scotland, Saudi Arabia, North America, Australia and Canada. Time spent in the Welsh Royal Crystal Visitor Centre provides an opportunity to see the WELSH MASTERS OF FIRE AND GLASS handcraft full lead crystal products to the finest quality. A visit to the Welsh Crystal Shop presents an enviable opportunity to purchase quality crystal manufactured in Wales, whether it be a valuable centre piece or small gift item. **OPEN;** All year round 9am-12.30pm and 1.30-4.30pm. Glass blowing demonstrations may not be available on some weekdays, Saturdays and Sundays.

MUMBLES THE LOVESPOON GALLERY
492 Mumbles Road, Mumbles, Swansea SA348X
Tel: 01792 360132.
You will find this unique gallery located on the right opposite the 1st Car Park just before the mini-roundabout in Mumbles. Do not miss the opportunity of visiting The Lovespoon Gallery. It is the world's first gallery devoted entirely to Welsh Lovespoons. Until you have seen the astonishing range you will have no idea that there are literally hundreds of designs made by some of the very best carvers in Wales. The Lovespoon has a well earned reputation for having only genuine carved Lovespoons and is known world wide. A Lovespoon makes a wonderful gift for special occasions like weddings, anniversaries christenings, birthdays and any important event. For 400 years this has been a Welsh tradition which is another good reason for buying one. When you examine the spoons you will see what wonderful artistry is employed when they are carved. They are certainly collectors' items. **OPEN:** 10am-6pm Sunday opening in August. Children welcome. Credit cards: Visa.Mastercard. Suitable for the disabled, just one small step. Assistance given. Amex and Diners.

Notes

Notes

Notes

Notes

JOY DAVID'S CHOICE

If you would like to have any of the other titles currently available in this series, please complete the coupon and send to:

JOY DAVID'S CHOICE
4, St. Andrews Street, Plymouth,
Tel: 01752 220774

I would like to receive the following (please tick as appropriate):

❒ An Invitation to Plymouth £12.00 inc p&p

❒ *Joy David's Choice - England Second Edition £15.95 inc p&p

❒ Joy David's Choice - Wales, Central England & East Anglia £12.00 inc p&p

❒ Joy David's Choice - Great Britain £15.95 inc p&p

❒ Joy David's Choice - Eat Out, Eat Well in Britain £16.25 inc p&p

❒ *Joy David's Choice - Classic Choice in Britain £15.95 inc p&p

❒ *Joy David's Choice - Ireland £15.95 inc p&p

❒ **Joy David's Choice - Castles, Cathedrals & Country Houses £12.95 inc p&p

*Due out in late 1997
**Due out in 1998

Please tick to receive more information about future titles

NAME..

ADDRESS..

....

....

Tel. No. (Daytime)..

Please make cheques payable to 'Joy David's Choice'

ADVANTAGE CARD - JOINING FORM

TITLE.....................INITIALS...

SURNAME...

SEX M........... F..................

NATIONALITY...

AGE GROUP 18-30................... 31-49.................... 50+.....................

ADDRESS...

TOWN................................ COUNTY..

POSTCODE..

HOW MANY HOLIDAYS DO YOU TAKE A YEAR?..........................

HOW MANY OF THESE IN THE UK?............. EUROPE...............

OTHER..

HOW MANY OF THESE ARE SHORT BREAKS?............................

W/ENDS............................

PLEASE STATE YOUR INTERESTS

i.e. Fishing, Golf, antiques etc...

DO YOU NORMALLY BOOK IN ADVANCE?....................Y..........N

WHICH OF THESE DO YOU NORMALLY STAY IN?

HOTEL.................... INNS................ COUNTRY HOUSE..................

HOW DO YOU SETTLE YOUR ACCOUNT?

CREDIT CARD ....CHEQUE ....CASH ....

HOW OFTEN FO YOU EAT OUT?..

WHERE DID YOU BUY THIS BOOK?

....

SIGNATURE..

DATE...

Please note that this is not a credit card and is provided for the use of the applicant only at the venues included in the quarterly list which will be sent to you. The publishers cannot be held responsible for any changes in the offers made by establishments. Information is sent out in good faith and is believed to be correct at the time issued to Advantage Club members.

Please return your application form to: JOY DAVID'S ADVANTAGE CARD, FREEPOST, 4 St. Andrews Street, Plymouth, and allow 28 days for delivery.

JOY DAVID'S CHOICE

4, St Andrews Street, Plymouth
Tel: (01752) 220774

Dear Reader,

I hope you have enjoyed my choice of places of all kinds - I have certainly enjoyed researching them in order to write this book.

It would make the next edition much easier if you would help by suggesting places that could be included and your comments on any establishment or attraction you have visited, would be much appreciated.

I enjoy corresponding with my readers and look forward to hearing from you.

Yours sincerely,

Joy David

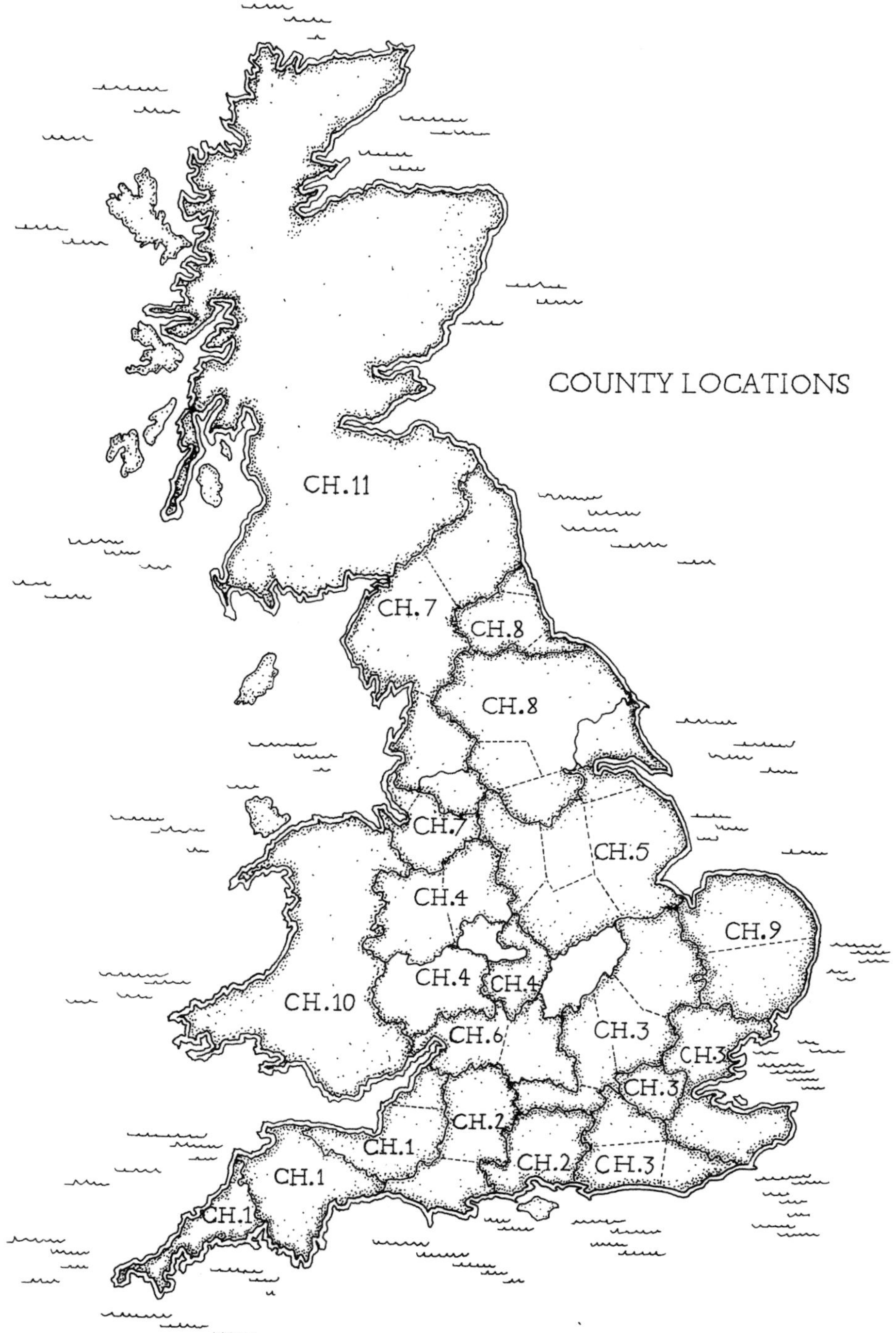
COUNTY LOCATIONS
CH.11
CH.7
CH.8
CH.8
CH.7
CH.5
CH.4
CH.9
CH.4
CH.4
CH.10
CH.6
CH.3
CH.3
CH.3
CH.2
CH.1
CH.2
CH.3
CH.1
CH.1